HELLENISTIC CULTURE AND SOCIETY

General Editors: Anthony W. Bulloch, Erich S. Gruen, A. A. Long, and Andrew Stewart

I. *Alexander to Actium: The Historical Evolution of the Hellenistic Age,* by Peter Green

II. *Hellenism in the East: The Interaction of Greek and Non-Greek Civilizations from Syria to Central Asia after Alexander,* edited by Amélie Kuhrt and Susan Sherwin-White

III. *The Question of "Eclecticism": Studies in Later Greek Philosophy,* edited by J. M. Dillon and A. A. Long

IV. *Antigonos the One-Eyed and the Creation of the Hellenistic State,* by Richard A. Billows

V. *A History of Macedonia,* by R. Malcolm Errington, translated by Catherine Errington

VI. *Attic Letter-Cutters of 229 to 86 B.C.,* by Stephen V. Tracy

VII. *The Vanished Library: A Wonder of the Ancient World,* by Luciano Canfora

VIII. *Hellenistic Philosophy of Mind,* by Julia Annas

IX. *Hellenistic History and Culture,* by Peter Green et al.

X. *The Best of the Argonauts: The Redefinition of the Epic Hero in Book One of Apollonius' Argonautica,* by James J. Clauss

XI. *Faces of Power: Alexander's Image and Hellenistic Politics,* by Andrew Stewart

XII. *Images and Ideologies: Self-definition in the Hellenistic World,* by A. W. Bulloch et al.

XIII. *From Samarkhand to Sardis: A New Approach to the Seleucid Empire,* by Susan Sherwin-White and Amélie Kuhrt

XIV. *Regionalism and Change in the Economy of Independent Delos,* by Gary Reger

XV. *Hegemony to Empire: The Development of the Roman Imperium in the East from 148 to 62 B.C.,* by Robert Kallet-Marx

XVI. *Moral Vision in the Histories of Polybius,* by Arthur M. Eckstein

XVII. *The Hellenistic Settlements in Europe, The Islands, and Asia Minor,* by Getzel M. Cohen

Regionalism and Change in the Economy of Independent Delos

Regionalism and Change in the Economy of Independent Delos, 314–167 B.C.

GARY REGER

University of California Press
BERKELEY LOS ANGELES OXFORD

University of California Press
Berkeley and Los Angeles, California

University of California Press, Ltd.
Oxford, England

Library of Congress Cataloging-in-Publication Data
Reger, Gary.
Regionalism and change in the economy of independent Delos, 314–167 B.C.
p. cm. — (Hellenistic culture and society ; 14)
Includes bibliographical references and index.
ISBN 0-520-08460-8
1. Delos Island (Greece)—Economic conditions. I. Title.
II. Series.
HC297.D45R44 1994
330.9495′85—dc20 93-22738
CIP

Printed in the United States of America
9 8 7 6 5 4 3 2 1

The paper used in this publication meets the minimum requirements of American National Standard for Information Sciences—Permanence of Paper for Printed Library Materials, ANSI Z39.48-1984.

Contents

	List of Figures and Tables	vii
	Acknowledgments	xi
	Special Abbreviations	xiii
	Note on Transliteration and Translation	xvii
CHAPTER 1:	INTRODUCTION	1
CHAPTER 2:	THE POLITICAL POSITION OF INDEPENDENT DELOS	15
CHAPTER 3:	DELOS AND THE KYKLADES: A REGIONAL ECONOMY	49
CHAPTER 4:	THE GRAIN SUPPLY OF DELOS AND THE DELIAN GRAIN TRADE	83
CHAPTER 5:	THE PRICES OF OLIVE OIL, PIGS, AND FIREWOOD	127
CHAPTER 6:	THE RENT HISTORIES OF ESTATES AND HOUSES	189
CHAPTER 7:	TOWARD A DELIAN ECONOMIC HISTORY	249
APPENDIX I:	ADDITIONAL NOTES	277
APPENDIX II:	SOME REMARKS ON STATISTICAL ANALYSIS	287
APPENDIX III:	PRICES OF FIREWOOD, OLIVE OIL, PIGS, AND GRAINS (BARLEY AND WHEAT) ON DELOS, 314–169 B.C.	289

APPENDIX IV: RENTS OF ESTATES AND HOUSES ON DELOS, 314–169 B.C. 309

Ancient and Premodern Weights and Measures, with Modern Equivalents 351

Works Cited 353

General Index 381

Index of Sources 389

List of Figures and Tables

Figure 5.1.	Indexed Olive Oil Prices, Delos, 304–169 B.C.	*156*
Figure 5.2.	Indexed Firewood Prices, Delos, 304–169 B.C.	*172*
Figure 5.3.	Indexed Pig Prices, Delos, 302–169 B.C.	*176*
Figure 5.4.	Indexed Firewood and Pig Prices, Delos, 274–169 B.C.	*179*
Figure 6.1.	Average Aggregated Indexed Rents of Apollo's Estates, by Group, 314–179 B.C.	*196*
Figure 6.2.	Movement of Group I Estate Rents in Relation to *alphita* Prices, 279–179 B.C.	*198*
Figure 6.3.	Movement of Group II Estate Rents in Relation to *alphita* Prices, 279–179 B.C.	*199*
Figure 6.4.	Correlation of Olive Oil Prices with Group I Estate Rents, 304–179 B.C.	*202*
Figure 6.5.	Correlation of Olive Oil Prices with Group II Estate Rents, 304–179 B.C.	*203*
Figure 6.6.	Correlation of Pig Prices with Group I Estate Rents, 301–179 B.C.	*207*
Figure 6.7.	Olive Oil Prices and Rents for Phytalia, 290–179 B.C.	*208*
Figure 6.8.	Aggregated Indexed Rents of Apollo's Houses, 287–182 B.C.	*243*
Table 1.1.	Selected Olive Oil Prices	*11*
Table 1.2.	Prices and Suppliers: Barley for Geese, *IG* XI 2.287	*11*
Table 1.3.	Names of the Delian Months, with Attic and Modern Equivalents	*13*
Table 4.1.	Annual Grain Consumption on Delos	*88*

Table 4.2.	Annual Grain Consumption on Delos Allowing for a Surplus of 50 Percent	*94*
Table 4.3.	Delian Productivity Estimated from Modern Yield Data from the Kyklades (1), Krete (2), and All Greece (3)	*99*
Table 4.4.	Rainfall on Naxos, December–May, 1967–1982	*103*
Table 4.5.	Rainfall on Thera, December–May, 1901–1905	*103*
Table 4.6.	Estimated Yields for the Kyklades, with 10–60 Percent of Surface Cropped Kyklades (1), Krete (2), All Greece (3)	*106–7*
Table 4.7.	Wheat and Barley Prices on Delos, Second Century B.C.	*125*
Table 5.1.	Indexed Olive Oil Prices on Delos, 304–174 B.C.	*133*
Table 5.2.	Olive Oil Price Changes in Years with Fewer than Three Prices or Lacking Months of Purchase	*139*
Table 5.3.	Indexed Firewood Prices on Delos, 272 or 271–70 B.C.	*142*
Table 5.4.	Indexed Pig Prices on Delos, 269–169 B.C.	*145–46*
Table 5.5.	Mean Annual Indexed Prices on Delos for Olive Oil, Firewood, and Pigs, 307–169 B.C.	*154*
Table 5.6.	Olive Oil Prices, Sorted before and after 279 B.C.	*156*
Table 5.7.	Firewood Prices, Sorted for 250 B.C. and before and after 218 B.C.	*172*
Table 5.8.	Pig Prices, Sorted for 302–301 B.C. and before and after 200 B.C.	*177*
Table 5.9.	Pig and Firewood Prices, Lagged One Period	*179*
Table 5.10.	Mean, Mode, and Range of Indexed Prices for Olive Oil, Firewood, and Pigs on Delos, 307–169 B.C.	*183*
Table 6.1.	Indexed Estate Rents by Rental Period, 314–179 B.C.	*191*
Table 6.2.	Aggregated Average Indexed Estate Rents, by Group and Rental Period, 314–170 B.C.	*195*
Table 6.3.	Mean *alphita* Prices on Delos, 282–169 B.C.	*198*
Table 6.4.	Group I Estate Rents and *alphita* Prices	*199*
Table 6.5.	Group II Estate Rents and *alphita* Prices	*200*

Table 6.6.	Group I Estate Rents and Olive Oil Prices	*202*
Table 6.7.	Group II Estate Rents and Olive Oil Prices	*204*
Table 6.8.	Rents for Phytalia and Olive Oil Prices, 272–169 B.C.	*209*
Table 6.9.	Group I Estate Rents, Sorted before and after 290 B.C.	*210*
Table 6.10.	Group IIA Estate Rents, Sorted before and after 290 B.C. and by Kent's Wine Price Factor	*211*
Table 6.11.	Group IIB Estate Rents, Sorted before and after 290 B.C. and by Kent's Wine Price Factor	*211*
Table 6.12.	Group IIC Estate Rents, Sorted before and after 290 B.C. and by Kent's Wine Price Factor	*212*
Table 6.13.	Planting Ratios and Personnel for Delian Vineyards	*233*
Table 6.14.	Delian Wine Prices, Early Second Century B.C.	*235*
Table 6.15.	Aggregated Indexed Rents for Apollo's Houses, 287–182 B.C.	*242*
Table 6.16.	House Rents, Sorted by Change over Time and for 247 and 197 B.C.	*244*

Acknowledgments

Μέγα βιβλίον, μέγα κακόν, wrote Kallimakhos; he might have added, μεγάλα ὀφειλήματα. In the many years that have passed since I began research on this book, which started as a dissertation but evolved well beyond my original intentions, I have incurred many debts. My Ph.D. supervisor, F. M. Clover, deserves first place; I cannot express how much I owe him. Of my many outstanding teachers at the University of Wisconsin, I would like to express special thanks to Kenneth Sacks, Paul Plass, Paul MacKendrick, and John Scarborough. A session at the American School of Classical Studies at Athens as a regular member in 1984–85 piqued my interest in epigraphy; it was during my year there that this topic was first conceived. During the summer of 1986 I studied Kykladic coinages at the American Numismatic Society under the direction of the late Nancy Waggonner and of Tony Hackens. I was lucky to spend the 1986–87 academic year at the Institut für Alte Geschichte at the Universität München, where I benefited from discussions with Hatto Schmitt, Jakob Seibert, and Hartmut Beister. Miguel Ramirez, my colleague at Trinity College, gave generously of his expertise to help me through the intricacies of statistical analysis; he and Helen Lang read large portions of an early draft and offered useful criticism. I want to thank Roger Bagnall, Christian Habicht, and the Press's anonymous reader, whose careful, detailed criticism substantially improved this book. Finally, I am especially grateful to Erich Gruen, without whose constant support and incisive but encouraging criticism this book would not exist.

For assistance in Greece I remain indebted to William Coulson, director of the American School; to Dina Peppa-Delmouzou, former director of the Epigraphical Museum in Athens, for permission to study inscriptions in her care and for every assistance in Athens; to Fotini Zafiropoulou, ephor of the Kyklades, and Olivier Picard, then director of the Ecole française d'Athènes, for permission to study the Delian inscriptions; to Jean-Yves Empereur, then secretary-general of the Ecole française, for arranging my stay on Delos in the summer of 1991, and to Panayotes Chatzidakes, director of the Museum on Delos, for every assistance with my work on Delos. I owe a great debt to Tom Palaima and Jean-Pierre Olivier, who rendered indispensable aid at a crucial moment.

I am very grateful to Michèle Brunet for permission to cite her unpublished thesis.

For financial support at various stages in the composition of this book I am indebted to the University of Wisconsin; to the American School for a fellowship in 1984–85; to the Fulbright Foundation for the fellowship that took me to Munich; to Trinity College for several summer grants for research in Greece; to Jan Cohn, dean of faculty at Trinity College; and finally to the National Endowment for the Humanities.

The staff of the reference department at Trinity College Library, Pat Bunker, Linda McKinney, and Peter Knapp, not only provided fast, efficient help, but also showed a genuine and gratifying interest in my research.

For the production of the book, I am indebted to Mary Lamprech, Classics editor at the Press, and Peter Dreyer, whose close attention to a complex text uncovered many errors and inconsistencies.

A different kind of debt is owed to my many friends, both inside and outside academia, who have provided me with a happy and supportive network within which to work: Elise Garrison, Michael Arnush, and Martha Risser at the American School; Kai Brodersen, Elka Bernlocher-Rettstatt, and Thomas Rettstatt at Munich; and Cheryl Greenberg and Julia Smith at Trinity College. I have also benefited from interactions with a number of excellent students at Trinity, including Jennifer Chi, Melissa Moss, Beka Jennette, and Robert Sickinger.

Finally, through the many years of research and composition that this book required, I have enjoyed the support and intellectual companionship of Edie Folta. Her level head and critical acumen helped me sharpen my arguments, make them more accessible to the nonspecialist, and saved me from many errors. This book is dedicated to the memories of Joseph Reger and William Folta.

Special Abbreviations

In addition to the standard abbreviations used in English scholarly literature for journals and reference works, I employ the following special abbreviations.

Agriculture in Ancient Greece = *Agriculture in Ancient Greece: Proceedings of the Seventh International Symposium at the Swedish Institute at Athens, 16–17 May, 1990*, ed. Berit Wells.

Bad Year Economics = *Bad Year Economics: Cultural Responses to Risk and Uncertainty*, ed. Paul Halstead and John O'Shea.

Bagnall = Roger S. Bagnall, *The Administration of Ptolemaic Possessions outside Egypt.*

BE = J. and L. Robert, "Bulletin épigraphique," *REG.*

BEFAR = Bibliothèque des Ecoles françaises d'Athènes et de Rome.

Berthold = Richard M. Berthold, *Rhodes in the Hellenistic Age.*

Bogaert = Raymond Bogaert, *Banques et banquiers dans les cités grecques.*

Brulé = Pierre Brulé, *La Piraterie crétoise hellénistique.*

Bruneau = Philippe Bruneau, *Recherches sur les cultes de Délos à l'époque hellénistique et à l'époque impériale.*

Brunet = Michèle Brunet, "Chôrai grecques antiques," pt. 2, "Le Territoire délien."

Buraselis = Kostas Buraselis, *Das hellenistische Makedonien und die Ägäis.*

Casson, "Grain Trade" = Lionel Casson, "The Grain Trade of the Hellenistic World."

Casson, *Ships* = Lionel Casson, *Ships and Seamanship in the Ancient World.*

Choix = Felix Durrbach, *Choix d'inscriptions de Délos avec traduction et commentaire.*

CIGC = *Comptes et inventoires dans les cités grecques: Actes du colloque de Neuchâtel en l'honneur de Jacques Tréheux,* ed. Denis Knoepfler.

Les Cyclades = *Les Cyclades: Matériaux pour une étude de géographie historique. Table ronde réunie à l'Université de Dijon les 11, 12 et 13 mars 1982.*

EAD = Exploration archéologique de Délos.

Etienne = Roland Etienne, *Ténos II.*

FAO = FAO/WHO, *Energy and Protein Requirements: Report of a Joint FAO/WHO* Ad Hoc *Expert Committee.*

FGr Hist. = F. Jacoby, *Die Fragmente der griechischen Historiker.*

Foxhall-Forbes = L. Foxhall and H. A. Forbes, "Σιτομετρεία."

GD[3] = Philippe Bruneau and Jean Ducat, *Guide de Délos.*[3]

Gallant = Thomas W. Gallant, *Risk and Survival in Ancient Greece.*

Garnsey = Peter Garnsey, *Famine and Food Supply in the Graeco-Roman World.*

Gonnoi II = Bruno Helly, *Gonnoi,* vol. 2, *Les Inscriptions.*

Greek City = Oswyn Murray and Simon Price, eds., *The Greek City from Homer to Alexander.*

Hammond-Walbank = N. G. L. Hammond and F. W. Walbank, *A History of Macedonia,* vol. 3, *336–167 B.C.*

Heichelheim, "Sitos" = Fritz Heichelheim, "Sitos."

Heichelheim, *Wirt. Schw.* = Fritz Heichelheim, *Wirtschaftliche Schwankungen der Zeit von Alexander bis Augustus.*

Heichelheim, *Wirtschaftsgeschichte* = Fritz Heichelheim, *Wirtschaftsgeschichte des Altertums vom Paläolithikum bis zur Völkerwanderung der Germanen, Slaven und Araber.*

Heinen = Heinz Heinen, *Untersuchungen zur hellenistischen Geschichte des 3. Jahrhunderts v. Chr.*

Holleaux = Maurice Holleaux, *Etudes d'épigraphie et d'histoire grecques.*

Huss = Werner Huss, *Untersuchungen zur Aussenpolitik Ptolemaios' IV.*

IC = *Inscriptiones creticae.*

ID = *Inscriptions de Délos.*

ID Index = Jacques Tréheux, *Inscriptions de Délos: Index,* vol. 1, *Les Etrangers, à l'exclusion des Athéniens de la clérouchie et des Romains.*

IG = *Inscriptiones graecae.*

IK = *Inschriften griechischer Städte Kleinasiens.*

IOSPE = *Inscriptiones antiquae orae septentrionalis Ponti Euxini graecae et latinae.*

Isager-Hansen = Signe Isager and Mogens Herman Hansen, *Aspects of Athenian Society in the Fourth Century.*

Isager-Skydsgaard = Signe Isager and Jens Erik Skydsgaard, *Ancient Greek Agriculture.*

Island Polity = Colin Renfrew and Malcolm Wagstaff, eds., *An Island Polity.*

IvMag = *Die Inschriften von Magnesia.*

IvPerg = *Die Inschriften von Pergamon.*

IvPriene = *Die Inschriften von Priene.*

Jardé = Auguste Jardé, *Les Céréales dans l'antiquité grecque.*

Kent = John Harvey Kent, "The Temple Estates of Delos, Rheneia, and Mykonos."

Labraunda III.1 = Jonas Crampa, *Labraunda: Swedish Excavations and Researches,* vol. 3, pt. 1, *The Greek Inscriptions.*

Landscape Archaeology = John F. Cherry, Jack L. Davis, and E. Mantzoutani, eds., *Landscape Archaeology as Long-term History.*

Larsen = J.A.O. Larsen, "Roman Greece."

Launey = Marcel Launey, *Recherches sur les armées hellénistiques.*

LGPN I = *A Lexicon of Greek Personal Names,* vol. 1, *The Aegean Islands, Cyprus, Cyrenaica.*

Lindos = Chr. Blinkenberg, *Lindos: Fouilles de l'Acropole, 1902–1914,* vol. 2, *Inscriptions.*

Marasco = Gabriele Marasco, *Economia, commerci e politica nel Mediterraneo fra il III e il II secolo a.c.*

Marek = Christian Marek, *Die Proxenie.*

Meiggs = Russell Meiggs, *Trees and Timber in the Ancient Mediterranean World.*

Meiggs-Lewis = Russell Meiggs and David Lewis, eds., *A Selection of Greek Historical Inscriptions.*

Migeotte = Léopold Migeotte, *L'Emprunt public dans les cités grecques.*

Milet III = *Milet: Ergebnisse der Ausgrabungen und Untersuchungen seit dem Jahre 1899,* vol. 3, *Das Delphinion in Milet.*

MME = *The Minnesota Messenia Expedition,* ed. W. A. McDonald and G.R. Rapp.

Moretti, *ISE* = Luigi Moretti, *Iscrizioni storiche ellenistici.*

OGIS = *Orientis Graeci inscriptiones selectae.*

Op. min. sel. = *Opera minora selecta.*

Paton-Hicks = W. R. Paton and E. L. Hicks, *The Inscriptions of Cos.*

Petropoulou = Angeliki Petropoulou, *Beiträge zur Wirtschafts- und Gesellschaftsgeschichte Kretas in hellenistischer Zeit.*

Rathbone = Dominic Rathbone, "The Grain Trade and Grain Shortages in the Hellenistic World."

Rostovtzeff = Michael Rostovtzeff, *The Social and Economic History of the Hellenistic World.*

Sallares = Robert Sallares, *The Ecology of the Ancient Greek World.*

Schmitt, *Staatsverträge* = Hatto H. Schmitt, *Die Verträge der griechisch-römischen Welt von 338 bis 200 v. Chr.*

ΣΕΕ = Στατιστικὴ ἐπέτηρις τῆς Ἑλλάδος.

Shear = T. Leslie Shear, Jr., *Kallias of Sphettos and the Revolt of Athens in 286 B.C.*

Stemmata = *Stemmata: Mélanges de philologie, d'histoire et d'archéologie grecques offerts à Jules Labarbe,* ed. Jean Servais, Tony Hackens, and Brigitte Servais-Soyez.

Tod II = M. I. Tod, *Greek Historical Inscriptions,* vol. 2.

Tréheux, "Dernières Années" = Jacques Tréheux, "Les Dernières années de Délos sous le protectorat des Amphictions."

Vallois = René Vallois, *L'Architecture hellénique et hellénistique à Délos.*

Vial = Claude Vial, *Délos indépendante (314–167 avant J.-C.).*

Welles = C. B. Welles, *Royal Correspondence in the Hellenistic Period.*

Will I^2, II^2 = Edouard Will, *Histoire politique du monde hellénistique (323–30 av. J.-C.),* vols. 1 and 2.

Note on Transliteration and Translation

I have not striven for full consistency in the transliteration of Greek proper names. Generally, I have preferred a direct transliteration (using kh for χ, k for κ, and y for υ [except in diphthongs]) even when a romanized form is fairly common in English: thus for Ἀντίοχος, Antiokhos, not Antiochus, and for Πτολεμαῖος, Ptolemaios, not Ptolemy. But in some cases (guided purely by personal taste) I have preferred the familiar English form: thus Philip, not Philippos, Athens, not Athenai, and Egypt, not Aigyptos. I hope the resultant inconsistencies will not cause the reader difficulties.

All translations, except where noted, are my own.

Chapter 1
Introduction

The island of Delos is a very small place. Despite its location more or less in the center of the Kyklades, it would probably have figured even less in history than neighboring Gyaros, that "worthless" island incapable of paying even 150 drachmas tribute in the days of Augustus (Strabo 10.5.3 = C485), but for one extraordinary circumstance: it had been the birthplace of Apollo and Artemis. The presence of a sanctuary and its centrality in the Aegean attracted the attention of outsiders from the Ionians and Naxians in the Archaic age to the Athenians, who controlled the island as a whole or just the sanctuary for much of the fifth and fourth centuries. When the Delians controlled their own sanctuary between 314 and 167 B.C. (the years of independence), they imposed an administration that recorded the business of the temple in scrupulous detail in a series of inscriptions that came to light in excavations of the late nineteenth and early twentieth centuries.

These inscriptions provided a wealth of economic data, which was quickly subjected to analysis. Over fifty years have now passed since the last systematic treatment.[1] In the meantime, much has changed. New readings and joins have added further data to those available in 1938 and rendered some obsolete. Systematic study of Delian society has greatly expanded our understanding of the world that created these documents. New excavation has brought to light some evidence for the independent city. Exploration of the Delian countryside has revealed private farms in a landscape long thought to have been composed exclusively of estates owned by Apollo. These advances have created a new context in which to place the economic data Delos provides; the time is long past for a reconsideration.

1. That of Larsen.

Perhaps even more important, the theoretical framework within which the Delian data were interpreted has changed radically. In 1938, when J. A. O. Larsen published his synoptic study of the Delian economy, our understanding of the Hellenistic economy generally, and of the information Delos offered, was structured by the views of scholars like Gustave Glotz, Fritz Heichelheim, Johannes Hasebroeck, and Michael Rostovtzeff.[2] Broadly speaking, and ignoring very real and very significant differences of detail and emphasis, they saw the economy of the Hellenistic world as a unity in which a universal price-setting market determined prices for staples like grain and oil all over the Greek world from Sicily to Afghanistan. This was a world where "demand for Greek goods of special types was large, the buying capacity of the market was continually increasing," and "the successful efforts of the Hellenistic kings to intensify production . . . [led to] a steady fall of prices in the Aegean Sea."[3] A vast network of traders tied this world together, enabling the price-setting market, while cities concentrated on the production of "industrial" goods for a long-distance export market and a kind of quasi-capitalism flourished. This view perhaps reached its apex with the interpretation of Aristotle Karl Polanyi advanced in his posthumous *The Livelihood of Man.*[4]

Needless to say, this view has come under serious criticism in recent years. Probably the most important sustained attack flowed from the pen of M. I. Finley, who argued eloquently in *The Ancient Economy* for a "primitivist" view that emphasized nonmarket exchange, the predominance of subsistence farming, and the universal economic goal of self-sufficiency (whether in an οἶκος or a πόλις) among the many factors that made the ancient economy qualitatively different from the "modernizing" economy his predecessors had seen. Finley's views too have come under increasing criticism from scholars who either reject his "consumer city" or are willing to see rather more sophistication in ancient production and exchange than he allowed. Reaction against both Finley's "primitivism" and the older "modernism" is beginning to develop new views about the char-

2. Gustav Glotz, *Journal des Savants* 11 (1913): 16–29, and ibid., 206–15, 251–60; id., *REG* 29 (1916): 281–325; id., *REG* 45 (1932): 241–49; Heichelheim, *Wirt. Schw.*, passim. Johannes Hasebroek, *Trade and Politics in Ancient Greece,* tr. L. M. Fraser and D. C. MacGregor (London, 1933), vi, although see the curiously contradictory remark at viii. Rostovtzeff, passim.

3. Michael Rostovtzeff, *AHR* 41 (1935–36) 235, 239–40, which summarizes the views subsequently elaborated in Rostovtzeff, 1026–1312.

4. Karl Polanyi, *The Livelihood of Man,* ed. Harry W. Pearson (New York, 1977), 238–51.

acter and significance of ancient economic activity, but no new orthodoxy has yet emerged.[5]

The time seems ripe for a reexamination of the data from Delos. This book is thus intended as a contribution to the continuing debate about the character of the ancient economy and a corrective to some of the problems I see in that debate.

General Considerations

Let me begin with the theoretical and methodological assumptions that underlie this project. I do not pretend to be "objective" in the debate about the ancient economy. In my view, it is a mistake to regard "the ancient economy" as a unity, as have scholars like Finley. The ancient world supported a variety of economies, which changed over time. Regional differences, which have only begun to be explored, were extremely important. Explanations for ancient economic phenomena must, I believe, be sought first in their local context. Local political and social circumstances must be canvassed to account for an economic phenomenon before the historian looks outside the immediate region. Not surprisingly, Delos was in its own way both unique and typical. It must be seen in the Kykladic context within which it was embedded, and in that context it and its immediate neighbors formed a relatively closed world (see chapters 2–3). Delos was unique in being a very small island (only about 6 km^2) with pan-Hellenic importance because of its temple; its "insularity" also had an important impact on the character of its economy (chapter 5). Delos's long history of domination by outsiders distorted the typical relations between the wealthy and their exploitation of the island's economic resources (chapter 6) and in part prevented the development of a full local set of suppliers for some essential goods (chapter 5). The economic changes of the years of Delian independence can thus not be understood independently of their local political and social context.

Peasant farmers constituted the vast majority of the ancient population. For most of their needs—food, clothing, shelter—they depended on their own labor and that of their closest relatives and neighbors. While they certainly needed local markets to buy goods they could not produce them-

5. Lutz Neesen, *MBAH* 4.1 (1985): 49–66; H. W. Pleket, *MBAH* 3.1 (1984): 3–36; see also the essays in *Opus* 5 (1986). L. de Ligt, *MBAH* 9.2 (1990): 24–56, 10.1 (1991): 33–77; Edmund Burke, *TAPA* 122 (1992): 199–226; Isager-Skydsgaard, 199–202; Dominic Rathbone, *Economic Rationalism and Rural Society in Third-Century* A.D. *Egypt: The Heroninos Archive and the Appianus Estate* (Cambridge, 1991).

selves, like iron plows and large fired pottery, to sell excess produce, and to buy necessities during shortages, they lived largely independent of any large- or even small-scale trade networks. Like institutional peasants, cities too strove to live off the production of their own agricultural hinterlands, their χώραι. The debate over whether cities were only consuming centers or actually "gave something back" to their rural citizens is irrelevant to this issue; in practice, cities sought an economic independence predicated on local production of as many goods as possible. Of course, like the peasant, the city could not make everything it needed, had to dispose of excess goods, and, most important, sometimes was forced to import necessities because of transient local shortages or crop failures. A trade network served these purposes, and Greek cities saw to it that they were plugged into that network to the extent necessary. But the typical Greek city, if there was such a thing, was not Athens, extraordinarily dependent on the regular import of grain to feed a population much too large for its hinterland to support. To the extent possible, Delos sought to satisfy its needs from its own *khora* or, where that was impossible, from the *khorai* of its immediate Kykladic neighbors. These sources certainly covered typical requirements in typical years (chapter 4). In turn, Delos served its neighbors as a regional center of exchange, a function that grew out of Delos's own needs. For in times of shortage, Delos was dependent like any other city on imports. But these imports were not its main source of food, and models of the Delian economy that assume so distort our picture of the island.

In principle, then, and as a model of the economy of Delos and its Kykladic neighbors, I have preferred local explanations for local phenomena. They do not require appeal to a great unified Greek or Mediterranean market. They are sensitive to local variation in geography, climate, and social and political attitudes. Only when local explanations for economic phenomena cannot be found should one search outside the immediate vicinity. For my purposes, the immediate neighborhood of Delos is the Kyklades, which include southern Euboia, whose cities (and especially Karystos, understandably given its location) had long-standing ties with Apollo's birthplace. The next step outward reaches the wider Aegean basin, and here we shall deal especially with the three poles of travel through the Kyklades: Athens, the coast of Asia Minor (including islands like Khios), and Rhodos. Beyond lay Egypt, the northern Aegean, Byzantion, the Black Sea, and the Levant. It is in that order that I seek explanations for the economic phenomena I examine here.

My exploration of Delian economic phenomena depends in part on a statistical approach (see chapters 5 and 6). I am reluctant to call it "cliometrics," although certainly this work falls, in some sense, into the body of cliometric studies of antiquity that have been popular in recent years. Finley has warned in no uncertain terms against the "current number fetishism," by which ancient historians "are beginning to claim quantitative proof where the evidence does not warrant it, or to misjudge the implications that may legitimately be drawn from their figures."[6] Finley's emphasis on the absence of "ancient statistics," by which he meant "a series . . . available [as] a check on the impression of directionless variations (or of stability),"[7] has issued in such bald statements as "to have produced statistics, properly so called, ancient authors would have had to assemble, classify, and tabulate numerical data in a systematic fashion. . . . Such material does not appear in antiquity."[8] This of course ignores a whole body of epigraphical evidence, as Finley himself recognized. He recommended "a shift in the still predominant concentration of research from individual, usually isolated documents to those that can be subjected to analysis collectively, and where possible over time; an emancipation from the magnetism of the words in an individual text in favour of a quasi- (or even pseudo-) statistical study," and pointed to two examples of bodies of documents that could receive "cliometric" analysis, the Athenian *horoi* he himself had studied, and the accounts of L. Caecilius Iucundus of Pompeii. He added, tellingly: "Of course groups of documents that also have genuine contents can be more productive, but they are few in number and surprisingly neglected as groups. . . . The neglect has become nothing short of a scandal in the case of the documentation from the two great temple-centres, Delos and Delphi; one need only contrast the dismal scholarly record of the past half-century with the enormously promising previous half-century in both cases."[9]

And indeed the Delian documents provide the kind of time-series for which Finley urged "quasi- (or even pseudo-) statistical study," and that pursuit forms the heart of my work. The statistics I have used, mostly straight-line regression analysis,[10] are not especially complicated or sophisticated, but they seem best suited to the relatively simple, straightforward, and lacunose data we have. I have limited statistical treatment to data that

6. M. I. Finley, *The Ancient Economy*² (Berkeley, 1985), 25, and generally 17–34.

7. M. I. Finley, *Ancient History: Evidence and Models* (New York, 1985), 27–46, quotation at 45.

8. Edward E. Cohen, *Athenian Economy and Society: A Banking Perspective* (Princeton, 1992), 27.

9. Finley, *Ancient History*, 44, 45. The nuances of Finley's views are largely ignored in the negative assessment of "cliometrics" in C. R. Whittaker, "La Cliometria e lo storico," *Opus* 5 (1986): 127–32.

10. See Appendix II.

are substantial enough to support it; thus there is no general statistical analysis of grain prices in chapter 4 because the data points are few and scattered. Nor have I subjected the monthly prices of individual years for pigs, olive oil, and firewood to statistical investigation. On the other hand, I have sometimes presented very thin data in statistical form when the results are especially interesting from the point of view of economic activity and of modeling: the relation between prices for olive oil and barley and rents for sacred estates offers a good example.

The virtue of the statistical analyses lies exactly in their ability to grasp the data as a whole and permit a check on "directionless variations." It then becomes possible to answer, however tentatively, questions about change in economic activity over time: Did prices and rents rise, fall, or remain stable? Did the prices of different goods move in tandem or independently? Were there connections between commodity prices and land rents? From the answers to these and similar questions, we can move on to treat the development and change of the Delian economy over time, and to try—however hesitantly—to offer explanations for change over time, and to test theories that earlier scholars had propounded. This eminently historical enquiry would be impossible without the statistical analysis that lies behind it.

At the same time, we must be fully conscious of the limitations of such a pursuit. As noted more fully in chapter 5, vast realms of Delian economic activity must be left aside because the inscriptions do not provide suitable data. Most disappointing is the practically complete absence of any real data for wages, despite literally thousands of payments to workers. Because the inscriptions rarely treated the city, we are generally ignorant about non-temple finances, occupations, and private trade. On the other hand, nonstatistical analysis has produced some striking results, particularly Claude Vial's evocation of the place and status of landowners and renters and her important claim, on the basis of careful prosopographical study, that a good many loans on Delos were intended for productive ends: the very opposite of Finley's own conclusion about the Athenian *horoi.*[11] In part because of its method, my work has a limited purpose—the exploration of certain aspects of the economic history of independent Delos—and is envisioned as a contribution to ongoing study, argument, and revision. I hope I have shown that the data, limited and recalcitrant as they may be, can yield considerably more than they have yet been asked to, and that the economic

11. Vial, 317–38, 375–83. M. I. Finley, *Studies in Land and Credit in Ancient Athens, 500–200 B.C.* (New Brunswick, N.J., 1951).

history of the sacred island was more complicated, but more limited in its implications, than has been thought.

Matters of Detail

In the rest of this introductory chapter, I briefly discuss, first, the character of the epigraphic evidence, the duties of the *hieropoioi* who administered the temple, and the publication of the data. There follow treatments of some important preliminary economic questions: the currencies in circulation on independent Delos and the relation of the prices recorded in the inscriptions to market prices. I end with a brief note on the Delian calendar.

THE CHARACTER OF THE EVIDENCE

Although some Delian inscriptions had been discovered before 1872, the real wealth of finds began only with the onset of French excavations. Many of the temple accounts—as well as decrees, treaties, and other documents—first saw print in a series of articles in the *Bulletin de Correspondance Hellénique* or in monographs by Théophile Homolle, Felix Durrbach, and others.[12] A corpus of the Delian inscriptions was planned as volume 11 of *Inscriptiones Graecae*, but World War I intervened and postwar tensions prevented further cooperation.[13] The accounts are thus divided between two series, both edited by Felix Durrbach:

> *Inscriptiones Graecae* XI 2 (Berlin, 1912), which contains nos. 135–289; and
>
> *Inscriptions de Délos: Comptes des Hiéropes (nos. 290–371)* (Paris, 1926); and *Inscriptions de Délos: Comptes des Hiéropes (nos. 372–498), Lois ou règlements, contrats d'entreprises et devis (nos. 499–509)* (Paris, 1929),

to which must be added important new readings and restorations offered over the years by Gustave Glotz, Maurice Lacroix, J. H. Kent, Jacques Tréheux, and others.[14]

The accounts were the responsibility of the *hieropoioi*, the chief administrators of the Temple of Apollo during the years of independence. The magistracy was annual; a full panel consisted of four members, but the Delians often had to do with only two, and sometimes just one. Their duties touched on every aspect of the administration of the temple's business.

12. For full details, see the lemmata in *IG* XI 2 and *ID*.
13. See the rather cryptic remarks of Felix Durrbach in *ID* (1929), p. vii.
14. See Appendices III and IV.

They oversaw the rental of sacred estates and houses and the collection of rent; hired and paid laborers; granted loans to individuals from the temple funds; disbursed payments to contractors (whose work, however, was supervised by special boards of ἐπιμεληταί and the architect, who approved their work and payments); compiled inventories of the vast body of dedications Apollo collected; bought items necessary for ritual and the running of the temple (including occasionally slaves); and last, but not least, recorded their activities on inscriptions published annually. For my purposes their most important function was the procurement of ritual needs, which included the regular purchase of pigs, firewood, lamps, olive oil, and other commodities.[15]

The accounts give, in a fairly straightforward fashion, income and outgo of the temple during the *hieropoioi*'s year in office. For the most part the information is simply listed in categories, which include the total amount of cash received from their predecessors; collections in the form of loans and rents; outlays by month for ritual and other purposes; outlays for the maintenance, repair, and construction of temple buildings; and the total amount of money passed on to their successors. The reverse sides of the stones generally carry inventories, ordered by the treasury in which the goods were stored. Additional (late) payments are often recorded on the narrow sides.[16]

The annual publication of prices was not intended as economic data; like most ancient accounting, it kept officials honest and provided records that anyone who wanted to challenge the officials could review.[17] This is perfectly clear from the layout of the data on the *stelai* themselves. The order-

15. Vial, 111–12, 151–54, 156–58, 216–32. Slaves purchased at *ID* 290.113–15.

16. Good examples include *IG* XI 2.199 and 287 and *ID* 442.

17. On the probable absence of a power of *euthynai* in the Delian *logistai*, see Vial, 161. *IG* XI 2.203A62 records pay for a heliastic court that heard a case brought against Euboulos, *hieropoios* in 273 B.C. (see *IG* XI 2.199B98). The case brought against the contractor Simon for unknown delinquencies may have rested on specifics of his contract; a number of these documents have been preserved (for the case, see *IG* XI 2.163Bg18, cf. 165.37; contracts at *ID* 500–502, 504–8). Cf. Finley, *Ancient History*, 32, on the purpose of documents. On ancient accounting in general, see G. E. M. de Ste. Croix, "Greek and Roman Accounting," in *Studies in the History of Accounting*, ed. A. C. Littleton and B. S. Yamey (London, 1956), 14–74, who, however, has nothing specific to say about Delos (31 n. 10). Richard H. Macve, "Some Glosses on Ste. Croix's 'Greek and Roman Accounting,'" in *Crux: Essays in Greek History Presented to G. E. M. de Ste. Croix*, ed. P. A. Cartledge and F. D. Harvey (London, 1985), 233–64, adds nothing of substance. For a good overview, see now Rathbone, *Economic Rationalism and Rural Society in Third-Century A.D. Egypt*, 331–35, 369–87.

ing follows category of income or outlay: rents from estates, rents from houses, payments from the farmers of concessions (like the ferry to Mykonos or Rheneia), interest payments, defaults, expenditures by month, expenditures ordered by the *boule* (such as for special purification sacrifices), payments to contractors, and so on. It is easy to check whether the *hieropoioi* collected someone's loan payment, or whether the payment to the contractors building the theater was made with approval of the architect and board of overseers; but to check, say, pig prices over the year required a laborious search through an undifferentiated mass of monthly data, as well as review of other sections (like that for payments ordered by the *boule*, or the accounts of festivals like the Posideia) where payments for pigs might be recorded. The *hieropoioi* clearly had no intent to facilitate collection and comparison of time-series of data, and the fact that this is possible is only an accidental consequence of the real reasons so much detail was committed to stone.[18]

As a result many of the data from Delos, as abundant as they may be, are useless for economic analysis. There are hundreds of instances of payments to unskilled laborers for cleaning, carrying roof tiles, hauling building stone, or transporting wood, but only very rarely do the *hieropoioi* tell us enough to compare any two such payments. Generalizations about the "level of wages" or attempts to reconstruct a budget or cost of living from such data are very hazardous.[19] Likewise, the lack of figures for quantity bought for some goods (such as charcoal and rope) and the absence of any descriptive information (weight, length, cost of manufacture) for other items (such as rakes) render the abundant recorded prices useless.[20]

These inherent limitations have determined the kinds of data I have been able to work with. In every case, prices must be accompanied by enough information to be sure we are dealing with the same good or object

18. That the Athenian administrators abandoned the Delians' practice after 167 and published only summary accounts proves the point.

19. Because the data are almost never comparable—that is, we have no idea how long a job took, exactly what work was involved, and sometimes not even how many workers divided the pay—studies of Delian wages offer far less than they appear to: cf. Glotz, *Journal des Savants* 11 (1913): 206–215, 251–60; Larsen, 408–14. W. W. Tarn, in *The Hellenistic Age* (Cambridge, 1923), 115–27, founders in a mass of circular argument (p. 121: skilled workers at Delos "practically always get two drachmae" per day; p. 124: "a lump sum of 140 drachmae, which at the usual two drachmae a day means 70 days' work") and unsubstantiated assumptions (such as that workers received their *entire* annual income from temple employment). Budgets at Larsen, 408–14.

20. Gustave Glotz, *REG* 45 (1932): 241–49, is too sanguine about the usefulness of some of these data.

over time. In practice, these requirements have meant confining my investigation to wheat and barley, olive oil, firewood, and pigs; the agricultural estates owned by Apollo, identified by name, and inventoried every ten years; and the buildings also owned by the god and identified by name.

PRICES AS MARKET PRICES

The nature of the accounts leads directly to an important question: are the prices recorded in the accounts market prices—that is to say, prices any purchaser would have to pay? If the temple could command special discounts, or make special contractual arrangements with sellers, then the prices it paid would have correspondingly limited value in a reconstruction of price history; indeed, they might be grossly misleading. An example of the kind of distorting effect the temple might have on market prices appears in its relations with two smiths.

In 281 the temple paid the smiths Dexios and Herakleides an obol per piece to sharpen tools for a total of 47 dr 5 ob. For the year 279 B.C., the temple contracted with Dexios alone to sharpen tools for a flat price of 40 dr. The temple therefore secured a 17 percent discount, assuming that Dexios sharpened the same number of tools in 279 as in 281 B.C. A few years later the temple returned to a piece-rate arrangement. This time Dexios accepted half an obol per piece, which suggests that a decline in the market rate for sharpening had triggered a resumption of the older, and now cheaper, arrangement.[21]

Fortunately, for the three commodities we shall deal with, there is clear evidence against discounts. Pigs were not bought "on contract." Three pigs acquired in three different months in 301 B.C. were supplied by three different men, although the price was always the same. In 269 B.C. no fewer than seven suppliers vied to sell pigs; none appears more than twice.[22] The temple was also unable to command discounts for bulk purchases of olive oil. Enormous quantities were bought for athletic games in tandem with the regular small purchases of a few *khoes* for the use of the *hieropoioi*. The purchases show no indication of a discount for quantity; instead, the price paid per *khous* seems to follow the prevailing pattern in prices for that year. The prices for 250 B.C. are especially revealing, since the *hieropoioi* paid more per *khous* for the 81 *khoes* of oil for the games than for forty times less oil bought for themselves (table 1.1). Here it is clear that the temple could not—or would not—command quantity discounts.

21. *IG* XI 2.159A58, 161A107–8, and 199A87 with Glotz, *Journal des Savants* 11 (1913): 255–56. Glotz thinks the temple cleverly forced down prices through the expedient of a temporary contract.

22. See under the appropriate years in Appendix III, s.v. "Pigs."

Table 1.1. Selected Olive Oil Prices

Source	Date	Cost/kh	Amount (khoes)	Purpose
IG XI 2.161A108	279	2.000	12	athletics?
IG XI 2.161A92	279	2.333	1.5	*hieropoioi*
IG XI 2.287A131–32	250	1.500	81	athletics
IG XI 2.287A133	250	1.333	—	athletics
IG XI 2.287A43	250	1.333	2	*hieropoioi*

Table 1.2. Prices and Suppliers
Barley for Geese, *IG* XI 2.287 (250 B.C.)

Line	Month	Price	Supplier
A45	1	3.333	Kaibon son of Sotion
A59–60	5	3.223	Peisikrates
A64	6	3.000	Antigonos
A66	7	2.667	Leostratides
A67–68	8	2.333	Leostratides
A71	9	2.000	Antigonos

Finally, wood bought by the temple after sometime between 250 and 220 B.C. must have been offered at the same price as to any other customer. A law passed by 220 B.C. to regulate the trade in wood and wood products forbade sellers to offer their wares for a higher or lower price than they had declared on import to the Delian harbor officials known as the πεντηκοστολόγοι.[23]

The accounts may preserve one clear instance of keen and open competition among suppliers. In 250 B.C. suppliers of raw barley the temple bought as feed for the holy geese jockeyed rapidly and vigorously with one another for Apollo's trade, apparently under conditions of continuously declining prices (table 1.2).

The evidence favors the hypothesis that the *hieropoioi* bought commodities for temple use on the open market at fair market prices.

23. *ID* 509.9–10 (= *SIG*³ 975; *Epigraphica,* vol. 1, *Texts on the Economic History of the Greek World,* Textes Minores 31, ed. H. W. Pleket [Leiden 1964], I.10.9–10). I use Pleket's date. Cf. chapter 5, pp. 173–5, below, for more detailed discussion of this law, where I argue that the law did distort the market for wood products.

CURRENCIES

Like many Hellenistic cities, Delos issued its own coinage. Finds have been sparse, and until Tony Hackens's promised full study appears, we must rely on a few brief synopses.[24] Like the other Kyklades, Delos coined on the Rhodian standard, which was considerably lighter than the Athenian standard that Alexander the Great and his successors—except Ptolemaios I and the Attalids—adopted. Despite domination by the Ptolemies in the first half of the third century, the islanders never struck on the Ptolemaic standard.[25] Coins of the island for the third century are very rare, and silver practically unknown; the collection of the Staatliche Münzsammlung in Munich, for instance, contains only three rather poor bronze specimens.

The other Kyklades coined as well. From Tenos, Paros, Andros, Naxos, Keos, and Syros come silver tetra-, di-, or single drachmas. Many date to the 230s or 220s B.C., although the fine Syrian coins are second century. The islands also issued bronzes, and from Keos are known a series of federal bronzes associated with the third-century federation of Ioulis, Karthaia, and Koresia.[26]

These coins and others circulated on Delos, sometimes ending up immobilized and unspendable in the coffers of the temple.[27] Indeed, the existence of these issues sometimes posed problems. In the 190s, when a delegation from the newly reformed Island League was sent to Delos to buy grain, the Tenian currency they carried was not acceptable to the grain dealers, and only the unexpected intervention of a Rhodian banker who was willing to exchange the money without charging an *agio* (a fee for changing currencies) saved the day.[28] The *hieropoioi* solved the accounting problem that this swirl of currencies posed by converting all payments into

24. Tony Hackens in Philippe Bruneau et al., *L'Ilot de la maison des comédiens* (Paris, 1970), 387–419, and his remarks in *GD*³, 105–11. For Delian moneyers, see *ID* 461Aa76, with Vial, 186 n. 139, 245 with n. 295. Cf. also Jacques Tréheux, *BCH* 109 (1985): 489 n. 15, contra Adalberto Giovannini, *Rome et la circulation monétaire en Grèce au II*ᵉ *siècle avant J.-C.*, (Basel, 1978), 52, with n. 96 there.

25. Introduction in Will I², 175–79, with citation of recent discussions.

26. See provisionally G. Reger, *AJA* 91 (1987): 272; Etienne, 197–200, 225–38.

27. See Tony Hackens's studies cited in n. 24 above; Louis Robert, *Etudes de numismatique grecque* (Paris, 1951), 143–78; J. R. Jones, *ANS Museum Notes* 17 (1971): 127–36, and John R. Melville-Jones, *University of London Institute of Classical Studies Bulletin* 21 (1974): 55–74.

28. *IG* XII 5.817. See Bogaert, 49, 176–78.

Table 1.3. Names of the Delian Months, with Attic and Modern Equivalents

Delian	*Attic*	*Modern*
Ληναιών	Γαμηλιών	Dec./Jan.
Ἱερός	Ἀθεστηριών	Jan./Feb.
Γαλαξιών	Ἐλαφηβολιών	Feb./Mar.
Ἀρτεμισιών	Μουνιχιών	Mar./Apr.
Θαργηλιών	Θαργηλιών	Apr./May
Πάνημος	Σκιροφοριών	May/Jun.
Ἑκατομβαιών	Ἑκατομβαιών	Jun./Jul.
Μεταγειτνιών	Μεταγειτνιών	Jul./Aug.
Βουφονιών	Βοηδρομιών	Aug./Sept.
Ἀπατουριών	Πυανοψιών	Sept./Oct.
Αρησιών	Μαιμακτηριών	Oct./Nov.
Ποσιδεών	Ποσιδεών	Nov./Dec.

Athenian standard equivalents.[29] Their administrative decision eliminates for us any concern about varying values of individual currencies one against the other, which would have affected prices of imported goods, but it does leave unanswered nagging doubts that price variations, even in standard currency, may hide variations in the value of the currencies in which sale and purchase were taking place. However, as long as any such variation was not unidirectional—that is to say, inflationary—it may be assumed to have reflected real economic changes in the relative values of goods. I shall show below in chapter 7 that there was no general inflation on Delos between 314 and 167 B.C.

A NOTE ON THE DELIAN CALENDAR

There is nothing very unusual about the Delian calendar (table 1.3) and the order of the months is assured (see, for example, *IG* XI 2.287A41–81).[30] Like all ancient calendars, the Delian required occasional adjustment to

29. See Hackens in *GD*[3], 107–11. Athenian equivalent at, e.g., *IG* XI 2.161A4–5.

30. Brief accounts of the Delian calendar in Alan E. Samuel, *Greek and Roman Chronology: Calendars and Years in Classical Antiquity* (Munich, 1972), 99–101, and E. J. Bickerman, *Chronology of the Ancient World*,[2] (Ithaca, N.Y., 1980), 20.

bring it into line with the seasons. The new year began on the first new moon after the winter solstice. Special sacrifices were made then to Apollo, Artemis, and other deities.[31] To keep the beginning of Lenaion, as reckoned by their calendar, in coordination with the appearance of the first new moon, the Delians had from time to time to insert an intercalary month that followed Panemos and was called "intercalary Panemos."[32] The procedure was probably required about every four years, as in *IG* XI 2.162A47 of 278 B.C. and 199A, 274 B.C.[33] As a result, in any given year, a Delian month might correspond roughly to either of two of our months: Lenaion, for example, might fall in December or January. I give these equivalences in table 1.3 and use them throughout, but it should be kept in mind that they are approximate, and that the exact equivalence of any given month in any given year is impossible to determine from the data in the inscriptions.

31. *IG* XI 2.154A11, with Bruneau, 92; 269.15; 287A42. Imprecisely in Jacques Tréheux, *Etudes d'archéologie classique* 5 (1976): 88 n. 20: "l'année délienne commençait aux alentours du solstice d'hiver."

32. E.g., *ID* 290.79, Πανήμου ἐμβολ[ί]μου.

33. But not exactly every four years: *ID* 290 (cf. l. 79) of 246 B.C. was intercalary, but 250 B.C. was not (*IG* XI 2.287A61, 65). Bruneau, 11, gives equivalences a month later than those in table 1.3, but they cannot be right; he has evidently not considered the way in which the Delian calendar would tend to shift dates. His various studies of the calendar of festivals (Bruneau, 86–93, 523–25, 559–64) do not help answer questions about the calendar itself. I want to acknowledge my debt here to Hartmut Beister, who helped me through the complexities of ancient calendars, and Ken Sacks, who first drew my attention to the problems inherent in Greek calendar systems.

Chapter 2
The Political Position of Independent Delos

For most of their history, Delos and the other Kyklades lived under the control of an outside power. In the Archaic period, Miletos and the cities of Asia Minor exercised hegemony over some of the islands through the Ionic League. Later, Naxos wielded considerable influence over Delos, while the Naxian tyrant Lygdamis himself had ties of dependence with the Peisistratids of Athens. The Ionian revolt against Persia in the early fifth century spilled over into the islands, which came under Persian control. After the Persian wars, the Athenians (with their Samian, Khian, and Mytilenian collaborators) reduced the islands they had "liberated" from the Persians to subordination, exacting tribute and assuming control of the sanctuary on Delos. Despite brief periods of independence in the fourth century (first under Spartan sponsorship directly after the Peloponnesian War), the Kyklades remained under Athenian authority until the Social War of the 350s, and Delos itself was administered by an *amphiktyonia* run by Athens first alone and later with Andrian cooperation. The coming of the Romans in the second century brought the subjection of Andros to the Attalids of Pergamon, the return of Delos to Athenian control after 167 B.C., and ultimately the attachment of the entire archipelago to the Roman province of Asia.

The situation from 314 to 167 B.C. was only partly different. Delos was "independent" in those years only in the sense that the Delian demos enjoyed full authority over its own sanctuary and that it acted like any other free and autonomous polis of the Hellenistic age. At the same time, the island was usually subordinate to, or at least recognized the authority of, some greater, non-Aegean power. The position of the remaining Kyklades was the same. These ties of subordination connected the islands to a larger outside world, and certainly had some impact locally. The details of these relations, however, remain murky; most important for our purposes, it is very unclear whether the mechanisms that outside powers used to control the islands also forced the islanders to participate regularly in a world larger than the Aegean; whether, in fact, the terms of Kykladic politics and economy were set outside the archipelago.

This chapter and the next explore these issues. I shall postpone treatment of economic matters to the next chapter. In what follows, I first briefly review the political fate of the Kyklades from 314 to 167 B.C. I have made no effort to discuss the issues in detail or to review all the many divergent views scholars have offered on the numerous problems the period presents; like Hellenistic history generally, the history of the Kyklades in these years is plagued with obscurities and uncertainties. I have done nothing more than cite the most important primary evidence and a few secondary studies that can lead the interested reader to the details.

The balance of the chapter is devoted to more detailed analysis of the impact of outside hegemony on the islands. In particular, I hope to illuminate the interplay between the interests of the *hegemon* and those of the locals to see where loyalties and concerns lay. As we shall see, non-Aegean *hegemones* were rarely interested in the islands for their own sake. Rulers therefore generally administered the Kyklades through intermediaries rather than directly. This conditioned the response of the islanders to outside control: they exploited the opportunities their *hegemones* provided to bolster their own positions in their cities, but rarely had any impact on the policies of the rulers or events outside the archipelago. The character of hegemonic interest meant that the islanders were often left alone until political or military exigencies redirected the rulers' attention to the central Kyklades, and even then, it was almost always events outside the islands themselves, rather than in the Kyklades, that provided the impetus. That is to say, as a political unit, the Kyklades remained a regional phenomenon, focused primarily on themselves.

The Political History of the Kyklades, 314–167 B.C.

In September 314 B.C., as a result of the operations in the Aegean of a fleet representing Dioskourides, general of Antigonos Monophthalmos and his son Demetrios Poliorketes, Delos was freed from Athenian control. The following summer Antigonos's general Dioskourides swept through the Aegean again, "providing security to the allies and bringing over islands not yet in the alliance" (συμμαχία, Diod. 19.62.9). This alliance—dubbed by modern historians the Nesiotic, or Island, League—became the mechanism through which Antigonos and his son controlled the Kyklades.[1]

The seas around the Kyklades were not entirely smooth for the Antigonids, however. Antigonos's nephew Polemaios, whom he had dispatched to the Aegean to rule in his interests, revolted in 311 B.C. and went over to Kassandros. But Polemaios did not get along well with Kassandros either, and went over to Ptolemaios I, who soon forced him to take poison. Ptolemaios himself made a brief attempt on part of the Kyklades in 308 B.C., but soon abandoned his activities. The loss of the islands that Polemaios's revolt entailed had to be made up in 307 by an expedition under Demetrios, who also liberated Athens.[2] Despite the ups and downs of the Antigonid house in the years following, the Kyklades remained firmly under Antigonid control until Demetrios's flight from Athens in 287 B.C.

It was the Ptolemies who benefited from Demetrios's discomfiture in 287, but not without competition. Probably starting in the previous year, Ptolemaios's forces had begun to seize control of the islands; the activities of the Ptolemaic admiral Zenon fit here. However, Lysimakhos was also interested in the Kyklades. The foundation of Lysimakheia near the straits advertised his intent to create a Greco-Aegean empire, "a realm centered on the Aegean Sea, all of whose coasts would be held by the same sovereign." The importance of the Kyklades in such a plan is obvious, and Lysimakhos tried to pave the way for his plans by dispatching to Delos an ambassador of Spartan descent, who assured the Delians of Lysimakhos and his wife Arsinoë II's εὔνοια toward them and dilated on the role the Lakedaimonians generally and his own ancestors in particular had played in the liberation of Delos at the end of the Peloponnesian War. But despite the clever propaganda, it was Ptolemaios I who ultimately brought the Kyklades under his control, certainly by no later than 285 B.C.[3]

The Ptolemies retained undisputed control of the Kyklades from ca. 285

1. See Buraselis, 41–44, 60–67 for details; cf. also Richard A. Billows, *Antigonos the One-Eyed and the Creation of the Hellenistic State* (Berkeley, 1990), 220–25. Islands not incorporated in 314 were brought in the following year by Dioskourides; see Diod. 19.62.9, with R. M. Errington, *Hermes* 105 (1977): 496–97.

2. Polemaios: Diod. 19.77.3, generally, Billows, *Antigonos*, 426–30; Schmitt, *Staatsverträge*, III.426; Berthold, 61; Diod. 20.27.3, *IG* II² 469.3–5; Buraselis, 45–46. Ptolemaios: Holleaux, I.32, 34–35, ll. 21, 24, 26. Diod. 20.37; cf. also Th. Homolle, *Les Archives de l'intendance sacrée à Délos* (Paris, 1887), 39–40, Buraselis, 66. Demetrios: Diod. 20.45–46, Plut. *Dem.* 8–15.

3. Buraselis, 93–94 n. 230; cf., however, Will I², 94. Zenon: *IG* II² 650, *IG* XII 5.1004. Lysimakhos: Will I², 98 (quotation), *IG* XI 4.542, cf. Marek 251–52, Philippe Gauthier, *Symbola* (Nancy, 1972), 380–81 (on *ID* 87).

to ca. 260 B.C. They administered the islands through the Nesiotic League, which they kept largely unchanged, and through certain new officials like Philokles, king of the Sidonians, and an οἰκονόμος. Some islands received garrisons, and several played an important role in the Khremonidean War. The end of that war, which was marked by a signal Ptolemaic naval defeat by Antigonos Gonatas at the battle of Kos, spelled the end of Ptolemaic predominance in the Aegean. Ptolemaic officials vanished, the league broke up, dedications on Delos dropped off, and although the Ptolemies continued to maintain their garrison at Thera, they turned their attention instead to their possessions in Asia and the Levant.[4]

The vacuum in the islands after 260 again attracted outsiders, this time the Rhodians. For reasons that remain obscure, the Rhodians chose to abandon their long-standing relations with the Ptolemies to fight on the Seleukid side in the Second Syrian War. Their contribution to the defeat of the Ptolemies at the battle of Ephesos, now generally dated ca. 258 B.C., opened up the seas to the west to them, and their forces quickly appeared on Delos, and very probably in the other Kyklades as well.[5]

This period of Rhodian control was brief; within a few years the Ptolemies had returned. Unfortunately, the precise sequence of events and the motivations of the actors have remained entirely unrecoverable. It is possible that Rhodian-Ptolemaic reconciliation after the end of the Second Syrian War led to a reintroduction of Ptolemaic forces into the Kyklades, now under "friendly" Rhodian hegemony; it seems less likely to me that the peace of 255 B.C., which was almost certainly a Rhodian-Ptolemaic accord, returned the Kyklades to Egyptian authority. In any case, by the start of the Third Syrian War, the Ptolemies were holding the islands.[6]

4. League decrees: *IG* XI 4.1037–48. Philokles: Hans Hauben in *Studia Phoenicia V* (Leuven, 1987), 413–28; other officials: Irwin L. Merker, *Historia* 19 (1970): 141–60. Garrison on Thera: *IG* XII 3.320 = *OGIS* 44, with Heinen, 148–50, Bagnall, 123–34. Garrison on Keos: Louis Robert, *Hellenica* 11–12 (1960): 146–60, Bagnall, 141–45, Heinen, 149–50, John F. Cherry and Jack L. Davis, *BSA* 86 (1991): 9–28. Khremonidean War: Heinen, 95–213, Janice J. Gabbert, *CJ* 82 (1986/87): 230–35. Kos: G. Reger, *AJAH* 10 (1985 [1993]): 168–69. Dedications: Bruneau, 515–45.

5. Ephesos: Polyain. 5.18, *Lindos*, 2C, XXXVII, ll. 97–99, Berthold, 89–91. Delos: *IG* XI 4.1128, 1135 (= *Choix*, 38, 40), cf. *Lindos*, 88a1, Bagnall, 138–39, Huss, 215–16 n. 288. Ios: *IG* XII 5.1009 + XII suppl. p. 96. On the date, see *IG* XII 5, p. 303; F. Hiller von Gaertringen, *RE* suppl. 5 (1931), s.v. Rhodos, col. 785, gives a range of 257–220 B.C., but ca. 220 B.C., suggested by Etienne, 114 n. 51, is excluded in my view on the basis of the letter forms, see G. Reger, *Historia* 43 (1994): 35–38. On *IG* XII 5.1010, see Alain Bresson, *Index* 9 (1980): 144–49.

6. The evidence for a Ptolemaic recovery: *OGIS* 54.5–8; Bruneau, 523; P. M. Fraser and C. H. Roberts, *Chronique d'Egypte* 47 (1949): 289–94; *IG* XI 2.287A82, ἀνήχθη ὁ στόλος; *IG* XI 4.677. Very problematic is Ps.-Aristeas 180.

Another naval defeat, again at the hands of Gonatas, at the battle of Andros in late 246 or early 245 B.C. probably contributed to the final departure of the Ptolemies from the central Aegean (again excepting Thera), although, as we shall see, other considerations may have made an even more important contribution. For the period after 245 B.C., however, the defining feature is not the identity of the *hegemon* but the lack of one. Various scholars have from time to time championed a Makedonian, a Rhodian, or even a Ptolemaic suzerainty, but in fact the evidence supports none of these. Instead, the forty-five years from the battle of Andros to the beginning of the Second Makedonian War provide a rare glimpse into the politics of a genuinely free Kyklades. As we shall see, the islands looked not outward but inward in these years.[7]

The last two decades of the third century saw a number of incursions by outsiders into the Kyklades. In 219 B.C., Demetrios of Pharos raided the islands, exacting money from some and plundering others; the Rhodians chased him out of the Aegean, perhaps using a detachment of the fleet operating around the Hellespontos in the opening moves of the war against Byzantion (Polyb. 4.16.6–8). The First Kretan War, now dated 206–205 B.C., embroiled the Rhodians again in the Aegean, this time against Kretan piracy. Philip V of Makedon secretly encouraged the Kretans. When the war ended favorably to the Rhodians, who were able to extract treaties with some Kretans forbidding piracy, Philip V secretly dispatched the pirate Dikaiarkhos against the islands in 205 or 204 (Polyb. 18.54.8, Diod. 28.1.1).[8]

These Rhodian ventures in the late third century—along with their "trade war" against Byzantion—justified Polybios's description of the Rhodians' προστασία of the sea in these years (4.47.1, 5.90.5). Polybios's language most certainly does not imply Rhodian control of the islands. But Rhodian activity in the Aegean surely familiarized them with conditions there. The successful piracy of Demetrios and Dikaiarkhos was emblematic of the prosperity the Kyklades enjoyed in the years when they were left to themselves, and this must have interested the Rhodians. Their chance came with the Second Makedonian War. The Rhodians and Eumenes of Pergamon allied with the Romans against Philip; both reaped benefits in the

7. Andros: Buraselis, 119–51. For the rest, see Reger, *Historia* 43 (1994): 46–48.

8. B. Niese, *Geschichte der griechischen und makedonischen Staaten seit der Schlacht bei Chaeronea* (Gotha, 1893–1903), 2: 385–86 n. 6; Berthold, 95. On the First Kretan War, see Brulé, 35–56; the treaties: *IC* III Hieraptyna 3A51–58 (= *SIG*³ 581; Schmitt, *Staatsverträge,* III.551), whose date is disputed (I follow Brulé, 51–54), Schmitt, *Staatsverträge,* III.552 (Olos). Dikaiarkhos: Holleaux, IV.124–45, which makes the case and is still generally accepted (cf., e.g., Berthold, 109, Etienne, 99, with n. 68).

Aegean. Eumenes was given the island of Andros, which Philip had garrisoned and which was captured from him in a joint Attalid-Rhodian operation (Livy 31.45.2–8). The Rhodians did even better. They swept through the Aegean, "taking into alliance all the islands except Andros, Paros, and Kythnos, which were held by garrisons" (Livy 31.15). These alliances formed the basis for a new Nesiotic League, by means of which the Rhodians assembled their authority in the central Aegean.[9] They continued to exercise that authority until political missteps in the war with Perseus roused Rome's anger, which discharged in the removal in 167 B.C. of Delos from Rhodian control and the gift of the island to the Athenians, who expelled the Delians and created a new *kleroukhia.* The Nesiotic League fell apart soon thereafter.

The Strategic Interest of the Kyklades to Outside hegemones

The Kyklades had little to offer a conqueror. Some of the islands had been wealthy in the Archaic period, like Siphnos, which boasted productive gold and silver mines (Herod. 3.57.2). Under the Athenian Empire in the fifth century, a number had paid fairly high tribute.[10] But by the fourth century the mines on Siphnos and Keos were largely tapped out, and whatever had sustained the wealth of Naxos and Paros seemed in decline. Some islands did continue to produce some goods of importance to the greater world; Keos had its *miltos,* or red ocher, vital for vase-painting and architecture, and Paros and Naxos exported marble. But generally the islands were poor in natural resources: dry, windswept, producing enough to feed small local populations (as we shall see in chapter 4), and surely unable to offer conquerors much in the way of income.[11]

THE ISLANDS AS STEPPING-STONES

For outsiders the real importance of the islands lay in their role as stations on routes elsewhere. The most important route ran west to east, from Athens, the Saronic Gulf, and Euboia to Asia Minor. The Delphic *theorodokoi* lists name in order, under the rubric τᾶς ἐπ' ['Ι]ωνίαν, the *theorodokoi* of

9. Very probably evidence of the stopover on Keos is preserved in Chr. Dunant and J. Thomopoulos, *BCH* 78 (1954): 338–44, no. 14 (= *SEG* 14.544), cf. BE (1955): 180. Cf. also Berthold, 128–29. On the new Nesiotic League, see Etienne, 101–124.

10. E.g., Paros, 16 talents 1,200 dr; Naxos, 6 talents 4,000 dr; Andros, 6 talents; Keos, 4 talents. Conveniently summarized in Russell Meiggs, *The Athenian Empire* (Oxford, 1972), 558–59.

11. For classical gold and silver mines of Siphnos, see *BCH* 113 (1989): 670; for Keian mines, L. Mendoni, *Arkhaiognosia* 4 (1985–86): 181. Keian *miltos:* John F. Cherry et al. in *Landscape Archaeology,* 299–303.

Khalkis, Eretria (both on Euboia), Athens, Karystos (on Euboia), Andros, and, after a mutilated passage, Koresia, Ioulis (both on Keos), and Kos. The Parian decree accepting *asylia* for Magnesia lists at the end sixteen Kykladic states, all surely visited by the same Magnesian embassy. A Rhodian ambassador traveling to Akhaia in the second century stopped off on Tenos; Tenos itself maintained frequent relations with the cities of Asia. A letter of [Aiskhines] reports an unintended stopover on Keos owing to a storm during a trip to Rhodos. The Rhodian entourage escorting Laodike, daughter of Seleukos IV, to Makedon for her marriage to Perseus naturally sojourned on Delos. Cicero stopped on Keos, Gyaros, Syros, and Delos on his way from Athens to take up his gubernatorial duties in Ephesos. Herodas Antipas visited Kos and Delos (*OGIS* 416; *ID* 1586 = *Choix*, 176 = *OGIS* 417). Strabo reports that Delos "is well situated for people sailing from Italy and Greece into Asia." Coin finds illustrate the axis Rhodos-Histiaia-Makedon.[12]

In contrast, there is less evidence for an important north-south route, although it is of course not entirely absent; three Roman envoys traveling from Khalkis to Egypt paused on Delos in 168 B.C. (Livy 44.29.1, see 45.10.2). But for Egypt, Krete was surely the crucial island, as Ptolemaic control of Itanos illustrates. Krete was an important stopover on one of the main routes from Egypt to Rhodos and Asia Minor (the others led directly to Rhodos or to Kypros), anchored by Itanos on the eastern end of the island. North of Tenos and Mykonos lies mostly open sea; ships coming out of the Black Sea sailed either south along the coast of Asia Minor or west past Samothrake, Thasos, and the Khalkidike, depending on where they were bound. Amphora finds support this view; amphorae from Black Sea and northern Greek states are rare on Delos and Tenos, whereas Rhodian, and later Knidian, finds are common.[13] The link between the north-

12. André Plassart, *BCH* 45 (1921): 5–6, I.27–40 (on the date, see now M. Hatzopoulos, *BCH* 115 [1991]: 345–47); and see generally, J. M. Cook, *BSA* 83 (1988): 7–19, with further references. *IvMag*, 50.77–85. Louis Robert, *Op. min. sel.*, I.328, Georges Rougement in *Les Cyclades*, 131–34; *IG* XII 5.829, Etienne, 185–87; [Aiskhines] *Ep.* 1.1; *IG* XI 4.1074, 1112–13 = *Choix*, 70–71, cf. *ID* 443Ab 29, 44, Bb71–74, with *Choix*, pp. 95–96, Polyb. 25.4.8–10; Livy 42.12.3–4; App. *Mak.* 11.2, Berthold, 174–78; Cic. *Att.* 105.1; Strabo 10.5.4 (486C). Coins: Etienne, 182–83; Louis Robert, *Etudes de numismatique grecque* (Paris, 1951), 179–216. Cf. also Plut. *Per.* 17.2–3, Holleaux, II.164–65, J. B. Bury, *A History of Greece to the Death of Alexander the Great*[3] (London, 1951), 3.

13. M. Zimmermann, *ZPE* 92 (1992): 207–8 (Krete); contra M.-F. Baslez, *L'Etranger dans la Grèce antique* (Paris, 1984), 230, Kypros is not a suitable jumping-off point for expeditions into the Aegean. Etienne, 217–19; J.-Y. Empereur, in *GD*[3], 97–98.

west, particularly Makedon, and the Aegean was, of course, Histiaia at the northern end of Euboia.[14]

The role of the Kyklades as stepping-stones from Athens to Asia conditioned the interest of outsiders in them. As a general rule, outside *hegemones* who sought control of the Kyklades did so as a prelude to conquests elsewhere, either on mainland Greece or in Asia. Antigonos Monophthalmos planned to reassemble Alexander's empire; since he operated from a base in Asia, the natural first step in his plans to unseat Kassandros from Makedon was to send troops to secure the islands. It was his expedition of 314 B.C. that freed Delos from Athenian domination—Athens, it should be remembered, was then under Kassandros's control—and established the Nesiotic League. His son Demetrios used the Kyklades as a base for launching attacks on Athens in 307 B.C. And Antigonid troops under Demetrios's command frequently passed through the islands on their way to or from Athens or Asia: 250 ships with siege engines in 307 (Plut. *Dem.* 8.4, Diod. 20.45.1); perhaps similar numbers the next year (Plut. *Dem.* 15.1, Diod. 20.46.6); before Ipsos in 301, 1,500 cavalry, 8,000 Makedonians, 15,000 mercenaries, 25,000 allied troops from the Greek cities, 8,000 lightly armed troops, and an unspecified number of "pirates" (Diod. 20.110.4, 111.3); after Antigonos's defeat, 5,000 infantry and 4,000 cavalry. On the way, Demetrios stopped over in the Kyklades, where he resided in the temple of Apollo on Delos and received ambassadors from Athens, who announced the city's new policy of nonalignment. After his final defeat in Athens in 287 B.C., he again fled to Asia with his fleet and 11,000 soldiers (Plut. *Dem.* 46.4).[15]

The powers that took advantage of interludes in Antigonid control had similar interests. When Polemaios rebelled against his uncle Antigonos in 311 B.C. and went over to Kassandros (Diod. 20.19.2), the inconvenience of his headquarters in the Hellespontos became immediately apparent, and he moved to Khalkis on Euboia, where he had operated in 312 B.C. in Antigonos's interest (Diod. 19.77.3, 20.27.3). His activities clearly illustrate the

14. J. A. O. Larsen, *Phoenix* 19 (1965): 117–19; Robert, *Etudes de numismatique grecque,* 179–216. Some doubts about Robert's identification of the taurophoric coins: C. Boehringer, *Zur Chronologie mittelhellenistischer Münzserien, 220–160 v. Chr.* (Berlin, 1972), 32–37, followed by M. J. Price in *Kraay-Mørkholm Essays: Numismatic Studies in Memory of C. M. Kraay and O. Mørkholm* (Louvain-la-Neuve, 1989), 237–38.

15. On the freedom of Delos, cf. J. Tréheux, *Rev. Arch.* 31/32 (1948): 1008–32. On Demetrios's last expedition, see Gabriele Marasco, *Res publica litterarum* 8 (1985): 148–63.

connection between the islands and central Greece. Likewise, the prelude to Ptolemaios's expedition of 308 B.C. against the Peloponnesos was the establishment of forces on Melos, Aigina, Eretria, and Andros; the king himself stopped on Delos on his way to Greece. Tenos may have issued coinage to commemorate this expedition.[16]

Perhaps the nicest illustration of the role of the islands comes from the periods of Ptolemaic control. Throughout the 280s, 270s, and 260s the Ptolemies pursued a vigorous policy on the mainland, which entailed a heightened presence in the Aegean. On Delos they seem to have established a cache of grain, undoubtedly for military use. They located garrisons at Itanos on Krete and on Thera, which guarded the routes from Egypt to Greece.[17] At the beginning of the Khremonidean War,[18] the Ptolemaic admiral Patroklos sailed from Itanos in Krete to Keos, where he established a base at Koresia (renamed Arsinoë) facing the Attic coast. At Thera either the passage of an important official or the establishment of a new naval station prompted locals to put their grievances to Patroklos, who dispatched a board of dikasts from Ioulis. The war ended with a battle at Kos, which implies the movement of the Antigonid fleet through the islands to challenge the Ptolemies off the coast of one of their most important possessions in Asia.[19] Again in the late 250s and early 240s, the Ptolemies reappeared in the central Aegean, and once again it was interests in Greece that conditioned their appearance. In 253/2 B.C., Alexandros, son of Antigonos Gonatas's loyal general Krateros, revolted. His rebellion denied Antigonos Korinthos and the chief cities of Euboia, which proclaimed Alexandros king and petitioned for the removal of garrisons Gonatas had installed. Alexan-

16. Polemaios: Buraselis, 45–46. Ptolemaios's expedition: Holleaux, I.32, 34–35, ll. 21, 24, 26, Diod. 20.37, cf. also Homolle, *Archives*, 39–40, Buraselis, 66; stopover on Delos, *IG* XI 2.161B20–27 with Bruneau, 516; Etienne, 227.

17. Delos: *IG* XI 2.159A54–55 with chapter 4, pp. 116–17. Itanos on Krete: *IC* III Itanos 3, with Hermann Bengtson, *Die Strategie in der hellenistichen Zeit* (Munich, 1964–67), III.184–88; Heinen, 143–44; Bagnall, 120–21. Thera: *IG* XII 3.320 = *OGIS* 44, with Heinen, 148–50, Bagnall, 123–34.

18. Janice J. Gabbert, *CJ* 82 (1986/87): 230–35, dates the war to 265/4–263/2 B.C., but this view considers only activities at Athens and ignores other evidence for the war.

19. Robert, *Hellenica* 11–12 (1960): 146–60, Bagnall, 141–45, Heinen, 149–50, Cherry and Davis, *BSA* 86 (1991): 9–28. See Reger, *AJAH* 10 (1985 [1993]): 155–77, arguing for the traditional date against Buraselis's proposal of 255/4 B.C. On the Ptolemies at Kos, see Susan Sherwin-White, *Ancient Cos* (Göttingen 1978), 90–131.

dros's attack on Athens failed only because of the resistance of Antigonid troops there. Ptolemaios II supported the revolt.[20] In addition, Aratos of Sikyon abandoned his long-standing friendship with Gonatas to bring his hometown into the Akhaian League. In 250 B.C., he traveled secretly to Egypt to beg successfully for financial support. The activities of Glaukon son of Eteokles on behalf of Ptolemaios II in central Greece may also belong in this context.[21]

The collapse of Egyptian interests in Greece entailed the collapse of their interests in the Aegean. This happened twice, from 260 B.C. after their defeat in the Khremonidean War, and again after 245 B.C., with their loss of the battle of Andros. But the latter defeat was compensated by signal success in Asia and Thrake; for the balance of the period, those regions attracted Ptolemaic attention, and the islands were left on their own.

As an example of the use of the Kyklades as stepping-stones in the other direction—from Greece to Asia—we can consider the behavior of Philip V of Makedon in the last years of the third century. Philip hoped to revitalize his house's traditional claim to Karia, and in preparation for operations there, he worked hard to gain control of the Kyklades. Appian (*Mak.* 4) alleges that he struck a secret treaty with Antiokhos III to divvy up Ptolemaic possessions, in which Philip claimed the Kyklades. Whether the treaty is historical or not,[22] Philip certainly stirred up trouble first by supporting the Kretans in their war against Rhodos and then by secretly sending Dikaiarkhos to raid the islands. In 201 B.C., he garrisoned Andros, Kythnos, and Paros (Livy 31.15, cf. Polyb. 16.26) and seized Ptolemaic bases on Samos and Khios. On Paros he cleverly (and ironically) advertised his opposition to pirates—policing the sea was a traditional duty of the

20. Trog. *Prol.* 26. *IG* XII 9.212.4 (king), 10–12 (garrisons); *IG* II² 774 and 1225 (attack on Athens); Plut. *Aratos* 17.2, 18.1–2. B. D. Meritt, *Hesperia* 30 (1960): 214, no. 9.3, associates this decree with the war with Alexandros: rejected by Heinen, 138 n. 188; accepted as "am wahrscheinlichsten" by Christian Habicht, *Studien zur Geschichte Athens in hellenistischer Zeit* (Göttingen, 1982), 24 n. 56. On Alexandros's career, see Olivier Picard, *Chalcis et la confédération eubéenne* (Paris, 1979), 272–74; Will I², 316–24. Contra: Ralf Urban, *Wachstum und Krise des achäischen Bundes* (Wiesbaden, 1979), 31–32.

21. Plut. *Aratos* 12. Cf. Hammond-Walbank, 301–2, Will I², 321, and, still, F. W. Walbank, *Aratos of Sicyon* (Cambridge, 1933), 36–40. Roland Etienne and Marcel Piérart, *BCH* 99 (1975): 51–75. There is a long and growing bibliography on this decree; see Kostas Buraselis, *AE* (1982) [1984]: 136–60; Roland Etienne in *La Béotie antique* (Paris, 1985), 259–63; G. A. Lehmann, *ZPE* 73 (1988): 144–47.

22 Will II², 114–18; more recently, Etienne, 100, R. E. Allen, *The Attalid Kingdom* (Oxford, 1983), 73 n. 151, cf. 60 n. 108. Patrick Baker, *Cos et Calymna* (Québec, 1991), 7 n. 21.

Aegean *hegemon*—in an inscription recounting his capture of the Aitolian capital of Thermon (*IG* XII 5.125). His next move was to invade first Pergamon and then Karia, but without much success.[23]

There is no need to review the other instances of the Kyklades as strategic stepping-stones. It is clear that from Antigonos Monophthalmos to Philip V, the real appeal of the Kyklades lay in their location between Asia and Greece, as an easy and reliable route for armies and a necessary possession for any power that hoped to assert itself on both sides of the Aegean. In this context, however, the interests of the Rhodians are less clear. They obtained the Kyklades as a result of the Second Makedonian War, when it was crucial for Rome and her allies both to deny Philip easy passage between Makedon and the East and to assure communications between Rome's mainland allies and Pergamon and Rhodos. The Rhodians' original interest in the islands thus resulted from familiar strategic considerations. But over the following third of a century, when they controlled the islands, they did not use them as stepping-stones to the west. The Rhodians, of course, had vitally important interests in Asia in their Peraia, but the islanders were irrelevant to that. It may be that commercial interests played some role; we shall return to this question in chapter 7.[24]

Individual islands also had their own strategic roles. It was crucial for anyone who hoped to take or control Athens to hold the islands that ring the Saronic Gulf. In 308, Ptolemaios I seized Andros and expelled an Antigonid garrison there (Diod. 20.37). The following year, Demetrios may have launched his expedition against Athens from the island of Tenos. Andros was again the staging ground for Ptolemaios's troops' attack on Athens in 287. Patroklos, Ptolemaios II's commander in the Khremonidean War, based his fleet at Keos and seized a small island off Sounion as a subsidiary base.[25] Antigonos Gonatas learned the lesson well; he prob-

23. Polyb. 16.1–12 (esp. 2.1, 2.9), 14.5–15, 24; 18.2.2–4, 44.4; Diod. 28.5; App. *Mak.* 4.1; Graham Shipley, *A History of Samos* (Oxford, 1987), 191–94. Polyb. 16.24.4–9; cf. Berthold, 117 n. 32, for Philip's operations in Pergamon and his abortive attempt to get aid from Zeuxis. On Philip's Asian expedition, see still Holleaux, IV.211–335.

24. It is worth noting that routes of travel were not entirely predetermined by geography: the changing interests of hegemonic powers and social and economic factors played a role too; see the views of Zimmermann, *ZPE* 92 (1992): 216, on the changes in routes between Lykia and Egypt in response to the demands of the Roman imperial army.

25. G. Reger, *CQ* 42 (1992): 366–68. Shear, ll. 20–21. Robert, *Hellenica* 11–12 (1960): 146–60, Bagnall, 141–45, Heinen, 149–50, Cherry and Davis, *BSA* 86 (1991): 9–28; Paus. 1.1.1. For a possible Ptolemaic base at Hydria (*IG* II^2 1024.10–11), see Christian Habicht, *Classical Antiquity* 11 (1992): 88–90.

ably held Andros, as well as Kimolos, Geraistos on Euboia, and possibly Kythnos.[26]

Thera played a similar role for the Ptolemies. It served as an outpost guarding the routes to Krete and from there to Egypt. This strategic role, separate from that of the rest of the Kyklades, explains why the Ptolemies did not abandon Thera when they retreated from the rest of the islands. Minoa on Amorgos played an analogous role for Antigonos Doson. Doson and his predecessor Demetrios struck alliances with a number of Kretan cities that permitted them to call up soldiers for combined operations; some of these Kretan troops showed up at Sellasia. The Makedonians needed to keep open their access to Krete, which, however, the powerful Ptolemaic garrison at Thera threatened. Minoa, with its fine protected harbor facing south, offered a perfect counterweight to the Egyptian forces.This helps to account for Doson's interest in the city.[27]

THE EFFECTS OF WAR

As a result of the character of outside rulers' interests in the islands, the islanders often felt the impact of their *hegemones* only in time of war. The Kyklades saw much troop movement and a good deal of fighting that spilled over from wars whose strategic goals lay elsewhere. From 314 to 288, Demetrios Poliorketes often passed through the islands with troops, sometimes in large numbers; when he chose to stop over on the islands, as at Delos in 301, after the defeat at Ipsos, the presence of his soldiers might have considerable economic impact.

Unfortunately, we are very poorly informed about military activities in the third century. No fighting in the Kyklades is recorded for the Khremonidean War, although the Ptolemaic base at Koresia and the battle of Kos both imply frequent troop movements between 267 and 261 B.C. The decision of the *hieropoioi* of Apollo on Delos to record the peace of 261 that ended the war (*IG* XI 2.114.1–2), one of only three such references out of almost thirty inscriptions (*IG* XI 2.105–33), suggests the intensity of the impact of the Khremonidean War. A few years later, the Nesiotic League honored the Rhodian admiral Agathostratos, who defeated the Egyptian fleet commanded by Khremonides at the battle of Ephesos in 258 B.C. (Polyain. 5.18; *IG* XI 4.596 = *Choix,* 39). Rhodian forces dedicated booty to Apollo on Delos (*IG* XI 4.1135 = *Choix,* 40); their commander Peisistratos had probably been the Rhodian *theoros* who visited Delos in or before 257

26. Reger, *Historia* 43 (1994): 53.
27. Ibid.

(*IG* XI 2.226B5, 287B85). The Delians also honored a Rhodian *nauarkhos* elected "for guarding of the islands and for the safety of the Greeks" (*IG* XI 4.596.3–6 = *Choix*, 39). The Delians again gratefully recorded the peace that ended this spate of fighting in 255 (*IG* XI 2.116.2). In 219, Demetrios of Pharos raided the Kyklades; and, as we have seen, at the end of the century, the pirate Dikaiarkhos, supported by Philip V, carried out depredations (Polyb. 4.16.6–8, 19.8; Polyb. 18.54.8, Diod. 28.1.1).

The Second Makedonian War brought more fighting to the Kyklades. I have already discussed the Pergamene-Rhodian expedition of 199 B.C. through the islands. This fleet also "collected supplies" from Skyros, Ikos, and Skiathos, which Philip was said to have recently plundered (Livy 31.45.2–13); we may wonder whether the locals regarded the Rhodians and Pergamenes much differently from Philip. In 197 B.C., the Akhaian general Theoxenos with 1,000 infantry and 100 cavalry passed through Delos on his way to or from assisting the Rhodians in Asia Minor, and stayed long enough to dedicate a silver *phiale* (*ID* 425.11, 442B67–68; Livy 33.18.5).

The war with Antiokhos III (191–189 B.C.) had particularly grueling effects on the islands. They escaped the initial phases of the war because Antiokhos mustered his forces at Ilion in Asia Minor and crossed the sea by the northern route, by way of Imbros and Skiathos (Livy 35.43.3–4, 6).[28] His retreat in 191 B.C. after Thermopylai, however, brought him directly through the islands: "Antiochus sub adventum consulis a Chalcide profectus Tenum primo tenuit, inde Ephesum transmisit" (Livy 36.21.1).[29] During his retreat, Antiokhos was attacked by the Roman naval commander A. Atilius, headquartered in the Peiraieus, who caught Antiokhos in the channel by Andros, where he sank some of his ships and captured others (Livy 36.20.7). Antiokhos put in at Tenos, the next island eastward, where the locals and probably Rhodian forces stationed there resisted. The defenders suffered casualties, and this first direct conflict between Antio-

28. There is a tantalizing honorary decree from Delos, *IG* XI 4.750, which shows the stay on Delos (cf. ll. 6–8) of one Ἀλέξανδρος Φιλίππου, ἀπόγονος ὢν βασιλέως Ἀλεξάνδρου (ll. 3–4), who has been identified with the ruler of Megalopolis. This Alexandros's son Philippos intrigued with Antiokhos III after the king had landed on Euboia and struck an alliance with him in return for a promise of ruling Makedon (App. *Syr.* 13, cf. also Livy 35.47.5–6). Could the father's stay on Delos attest to active participation by the family in the war on Antiokhos's side?

29. For the necessary textual correction to "Tenum" (Tenedum: MSS), see John Briscoe, *A Commentary on Livy Books XXXIV–XXXVII* (Oxford, 1981), 251. No mention of Tenos in App. *Syr.* 20.

khos and Rhodians or Rhodian allies persuaded the Rhodians to join the war against Antiokhos.[30] In the summer of 191 B.C., the new Roman fleet commander, C. Livius, arrived in the Peiraieus with more than fifty ships, bringing the fleet total to over one hundred. He sailed immediately for Delos, where heavy winds trapped him for a few days before he proceeded to Khios.[31]

The participation of the Rhodians necessarily augmented operations in the Kyklades. The Nesiotic fleet stationed on Tenos, probably under Rhodian command, sailed with the Roman ships. The four ships dispatched from Samos to deal with piracy at Kephallonia—they never made it, having met up at the Peiraieus with the new Roman commander, L. Aemilius Regulus, who sent them back to the East—were under the command of the Rhodian Epikrates (Livy 37.13.11–14.2). The Delians honored Epikrates for forbidding forces acting as pirates against the enemy (οἱ πει[ρατεύ]οντες τοὺς πολεμίους, *IG* XI 4.751.12–13 = *Choix,* 67) from using Delos as a base.[32] Another Rhodian commander, Anaxibios son of Pheidianax, was honored at Delos at about the same time, ἀποσταλεὶ[ς ὑπὸ] τοῦ δήμου τοῦ ʽΡοδίων ἄρχων ἐπί τε [τῶν νή]σων καὶ τῶν πλοίων τῶν νησιωτικ[ῶν] (*IG* XI 4.752.3–5, cf. 753 = *Choix,* 63).[33] Rhodian ships and troops operated out of Tenos throughout the first third of the second century (*IG* XII 5.830.11–13, 913–14).[34]

Finally, in 168 B.C., during the Third Makedonian War, Perseus sent his admiral Antenor to the Kyklades "ut inde [i.e., ab Tenedo] sparsas per Cycladas insulas naves Macedoniam cum frumento petentes tutarentur" (Livy 44.28.2; cf. also App. *Mak.* 18.4). After operations around Tenedos and Khios, Antenor sailed to Delos with forty *lembi.* Attalid and Roman ships also appeared at Delos, but respect for the sanctuary prevented vio-

30. *IG* XII 5.824, with Etienne, 120–23 (his remarks at 119 need reconsideration); Christian Habicht, *Chiron* 19 (1989): 273–77; see also G. Reger, *CQ* 42 (1992): 379–81.

31. Livy 36.42.8, 43.1, 11, *ID* 442B86; App. *Syr.* 22. Berthold, 151.

32. See M.-F. Baslez and Claude Vial, *BCH* 111 (1987): 311. It is possible that *IG* XI 4.713 should be referred to these events, but the date of the inscription is not certain (see Roussel's comm., *IG* XI 4, p. 39).

33. It is not absolutely certain whether Anaxibios's command fell during the war with Antiokhos; Livy does not mention him, and his "long stay" on Delos (ll. 5–6) may imply a permanent stationing rather than war duty. Cf. also Hiller von Gaertringen, *JÖAI* 4 (1901): 164–66, no. III. *IG* XI 4.754–55 are too vague about the activities of Anaxibios son of Dionysios of Rhodos, who is otherwise unknown (but cf. *LGPN* I, s.v. [4], for a coin magistrate of the same name and date), to determine his beneficia to Delos. The decrees date from about 190 B.C.

34. See Etienne, 115–16.

lence; the enemy sailors even mingled at the temple (Livy 44.29.1, 3–4). From Delos, Antenor carried out his assignment, attacking and plundering freighters bound for destinations other than Makedon. Antenor's confederates signaled by mirrors when ships were putting to sea, and Antenor, who had stationed his fleet around the islands, intercepted them, evidently releasing any bound for Makedon and holding the rest. The Roman *legatus* C. Popilius also set up shop at Delos; unlike Antenor, who had moved to the promontory of Phanai on Khios (Livy 45.10.1, cf. 44.28.16 for the location of Phanai), Popilius was still on Delos trying to prevent shipping to Makedon when news arrived of Perseus's defeat at Pydna. Delos and the islands therefore must have seen the influx of well over fifty ships and their crews during these operations, which also interfered with the normal flow of traffic among the islands (one suspects that many of the ships intercepted by Antenor were bound for local destinations).

It is striking and emblematic that the fighting attested again and again in the islands was never directed at capturing or controlling the Kyklades for their own sakes. From Antigonos Monopthalmos to Perseus, armies fought over the islands in hopes of controlling the routes to other places. With the important exception of the Rhodian station at Tenos in the second century and the Ptolemaic garrison at Thera, the forces that invaded the archipelago during war retreated as soon as the fighting was done. But outside rulers did not mean this policy as an abandonment of the Kyklades; on the contrary, they were eager to maintain their control over the routes the islands represented. Instead of keeping permanent forces in the archipelago, however, they generally devolved the responsibility for representing their authority onto local institutions, chiefly the various Nesiotic Leagues.

SUPPRESSION OF PIRACY

Maintaining the Kyklades as a stopover between Greece and Asia necessarily entailed suppressing piracy. Pirates threatened shipping, raided islands, and readily enlisted as freebooters in war. In this last guise they presented a genuine threat to the ruling power. Both Demetrios and Antigonos Gonatas used pirates in their operations against adversaries who controlled the sea. Pirates fought against the Romans and their allies in the war with Antiokhos.[35]

35. Demetrios: Diod. 20.82.5, 83.1, 3–4, 97 (at Rhodos), 20.110.4 (at Pherai). Gonatas: Polyain. 4.6.18 (at Kassandreia), Heinen, 152–54 (Khremonidean War), cf. Buraselis, 57 n. 72 (W. W. Tarn, *Antigonos Gonatas* [Oxford, 1913], 86–88, assumes all pirates operated under Antigonid instructions). War with Antiokhos:

Both claims and acts to suppress or end piracy recur again and again. The founding document of Monophthalmos's Hellenic League of 302 B.C. contains a clause that has been restored as a promise to keep the sea free of pirates.[36] Ptolemaic forces actually acted on a number of occasions to punish pirates, including a spectacular night action on Thera against pirates who had landed at Oia and kidnapped locals (*IG* XII 3 suppl. 1291; cf. also 3.328). Ptolemaic officialdom on Keos worked to recover property (perhaps slaves?) removed from a rural house in the territory of Karthaia by one Epiteles, who was perhaps a pirate (*IG* XII 5.1061). The Rhodians chased Demetrios of Pharos out of the Kyklades in 219 and fought a war against the Kretans a decade and a half later in part to end piracy. Philip V's propaganda in the Aegean just before the Second Makedonian War stressed his hostility to the Aitolians in particular and pirates in general (*IG* XII 5.125; *IG* XII 3.91 = *SIG*³ 572), despite his own support of the notorious Dikaiarkhos. In the official Roman and Akhaian propaganda reflected in Polybios (13.8.2), Nabis, king of Sparta, was a pirate who worked with Kretans, notorious for the practice; in the name of suppressing piracy, his seaports and possessions on Krete were taken away in 195 and he himself crushed two years later (see Livy 33.44.8, 34.32.18, 34.35.9, 36.3).[37]

This sword, however, cut two ways. While it was assuredly to the advantage of the hegemonic power to have safe seas, and no doubt residents of little villages on Keos, Ios, Naxos, Thera, Syros, Siphnos, Amorgos, Astypalaia, and Tenos were relieved to be free of sudden raids, the destruction of crops, kidnapping, and murder,[38] piracy had a positive aspect for the islanders as well. Not only did it provide a kind of alternative employment for poor farmers and fishermen, but pirates sold their wares on Delos, at Eretria on Euboia, and no doubt in other places too. The suppression of piracy worked in the interests of the *hegemon,* but not necessarily in those

---

Livy 37.13.11–14.2, 37.28.1–11 (cf. Polyb. 21.12.1), *IG* XI 4.751.12–13 = *Choix,* 67. The notion of policing states is common; for example, I cite Petropoulou, 41; Berthold, 98–99; H. A. Ormerod, *Piracy in the Ancient World* (Liverpool, 1924), 132–40, esp. 137. Cf. Petropoulou, 39–41, on booty.

36. *IG* IV² 1.68, II.38–39 (= Moretti, *ISE,* I.44). Cf. Will I², 78–79. Buraselis, 87–86.

37. *IG* XII 5.1066, Koresia (Arsinoë) on Keos, may report a Ptolemaic official repressing piracy, but the matter is hardly clear.

38. Syros: *IG* XII 5.653. Astypalaia: *IG* XII 3.171. Siphnos: Diodoros 31.45, τήν τε πόλιν ἐξηνδραποδίσαντο καὶ τοὺς τῶν θεῶν ναοὺς συλήσαντες, perhaps around 154 B.C.; cf. Hiller von Gaertringen *apud IG* XII 5, fasc. 2, p. xix, *testimonium* 1360. For the rest, see n. 79 below.

of at least some of the Kykladic locals. Asklepiades' remark about the names of two Samian prostitutes may imply the presence of pirates in the harbor of his hometown; the islands off Lade by Miletos provided anchorage for corsairs. And Alkiphron surely reflects reality when he depicts a poor fisherman debating with his wife whether to join a group of pirates who promise to make him rich. The suppression of piracy therefore also blocked a kind of economic activity, which may have had some importance. We shall return to this issue in chapter 7.[39]

METHODS OF CONTROL: THE NESIOTIC LEAGUE AND OTHER OFFICIALS

The evidence for the Nesiotic League is confined to inscriptions, except for a brief mention in Diodoros. He writes that the generals of Antigonos Monophthalmos who swept through the Aegean in 314 and again in 313 B.C. created a συμμαχία of the islands (19.62.9). This alliance, which incorporated most of the islands (whether Delos belonged remains controversial), most probably formed the basis of τὸ κοινὸν τῶν νησιωτῶν (*IG* XI 4.1036.2 = *Choix,* 13), dubbed by modern historians the Nesiotic or Island League.[40] The organization of this earliest incarnation of the league is obscure. The Antigoneia was founded on Delos as the common religious festival of the league and to celebrate the freeing of Delos and the other islands; perhaps Antigonos received the title Σωτήρ at the same time. In 312, following Dioskourides' expedition in the Aegean, Antigonos assigned control of the archipelago, along with other sites in Greece and Thrake under his authority, to his nephew Polemaios. Presumably the league and whatever functionaries it may have had reported directly to him.[41]

Polemaios's unreliability pointed up the unsatisfactory character of the arrangements Antigonos had promoted in the Aegean, and soon after Demetrios recovered the islands in 307, he (or his representatives) undertook

39. Asklepiades of Samos, *Anth. Pal.* 5.44; Strabo 14.1.7 (C635); Alkiphron 1.8. I owe these references to my former student M. Vandall. For the economic role of piracy, see chapter 7, pp. 261–63.

40. Buraselis, 41–44, 60–67, for details; cf. also Billows, *Antigonos,* 220–25. For the chronology of Dioskourides' activities at Diod. 19.62.9, see R. M. Errington, *Hermes* 105 (1977): 496–97.

41. Antigoneia: *IG* XI 4.1036.4–5 (= *Choix,* 13) with G. Reger, *ZPE* 89 (1991): 153 n. 12, contra Bruneau, 564–68. Soter: *IG* XII suppl. 168.7 of Ios, [τῶι βασιλ]εῖ Ἀντιγόνωι Σωτῆρι (who must be Monophthalmos despite Christian Habicht, *Gottmenschentum und griechische Städte*[2] [Munich, 1970], 65–73, 256–57, cf. Buraselis, 63–64 n. 105; cf. Moretti, *ISE,* I.7.16–17: [ὑπὲρ βασιλέως Δημητ]ρίου καὶ Δημητρίωι Σωτῆρι θύειν), and see now Billows, *Antigonos,* 224, with n. 98.

a reorganization of the league. It is probable that Apollodoros of Kyzikos was appointed that year as the first νησίαρχος of the league to serve as a civilian representative of the sovereigns; he may also have presided over the συνέδριον of the league, the deliberative body in which member states were represented. The league had a common fund, paid taxes, and had authority to punish members that did not make their payments (*IG* XI 4.1036.12, 14–17 = *Choix*, 13). In 307 B.C., the league instituted another federal festival, the Demetrieia, in honor of Demetrios. Perhaps that same year, but at any rate before the battle of Ipsos in 301 B.C., the Delians passed an expansive decree, unfortunately very badly perserved (*IG* XI 4.566), awarding Antigonos (l. 6) a bronze statue and gold crown (ll. 8–9), apparently thanking him for reestablishing democracy, freedom, and the ancestral constitution (ll. 12–13, 17), and declaring him ἀρχηγέτην τοῦ δήμου ("founder of the demos," l. 15).[42] After the death of Antigonos at Ipsos, Demetrios continued to depend on the islands to connect his regions of interest and to supply funds. K. Buraselis has characterized the league after 302 as undergoing a *Schattenleben*, but the importance the islands claimed during the years when Demetrios was a king without a kingdom make this unlikely.[43]

The Ptolemies took over the league ca. 288 B.C.; the most abundant testimony about it comes from this period. The Ptolemies retained the organization the Antigonids had created. Bakkhon and Hermias served as *nesiarkhoi*, the *synhedrion* continued to meet on Delos, the league passed honorary decrees and even awarded league citizenship (*IG* XI 4.1039b4, 1046.11). The duties of the *nesiarkhos* in this period are clearer. He acted to summon the *synhedrion* to its meetings (*IG* XII 7.506.2–4 = SIG³ 390), dispatched instructions and judges to settle disputes within member states (*IG* XII 5.1065, Holleaux III 32), and gave orders to military officials operating in the Kyklades (*IG* XII 5.1004.2). The Ptolemies instituted some modifications, however. Above the *nesiarkhos* they installed Philokles, king of the Sidonians. He participated with Bakkhon in calling the league meeting on Samos (*IG* XII 7.506.2–4) and confirmed Bakkhon's decisions about Karthaia on Keos (*IG* XII 5.1065.5). The Delians appealed to him to compel the islands to repay loans owed to Apollo (*IG* XI 4.559 = *Choix*, 18, Migeotte, 166–67, no. 47). His range of authority extended beyond the

42. G. Reger, *GRBS* 32 (1991): 229–37; Billows, *Antigonos*, 221–22. For the date of *IG* XI 4.1036 (= *Choix*, 13), see Buraselis, 67–75, with E. Will's restoration of ll. 45–46 as παρὰ τὸν βω[μὸν τῶν Σωτήρω]ν (Will, *Le Dodekatheon* [Paris, 1955], 170) instead of παρὰ τὸν βω[μὸν τῶν βασιλέω]ν, which would require the inscription to follow the battle of Salamis in 306 B.C.

43. Buraselis, 86.

Kyklades, as his activities on Samos and orders to Miletos, Myndos, and Halikarnassos show (*SEG* 1.363). The Ptolemies also apparently created the office of οἰκονόμος τῶν νήσων (*IG* XII suppl. 169.4), who is likely to have had financial functions.[44]

The arrangements the Antigonids and the Ptolemies instituted to govern the Kyklades clearly demonstrate the subordinate status of the islands in the hierarchy of authority. Antigonos entrusted their government in the first instance to local polis governments (if we could be certain that Delos was not a league member it would be the best illustration), then to the Nesiotic League, which was composed of locals, met locally on Delos, and took responsibility for collecting taxes and administering the league's common religious life. Over the league was appointed first Polemaios, a military official whose responsibilities reached well beyond the archipelago, and then from 307 B.C. on, a *nesiarkhos* who probably lived on Delos and served as liaison between the league and the sovereign. Antigonos never had his son run the islands directly, and even after his father's death, Demetrios preferred to reside in Athens or Asia Minor; the Kyklades continued to serve largely as stepping-stones, left in my view to the administration of the league and its *nesiarkhos,* Apollodoros. The Ptolemies were even more remote, for in Philokles they added another layer of bureaucracy separating the islands from the court. The island that provides the most evidence for Ptolemaic administrative activity, Keos, also had a Ptolemaic garrison during the Khremonidean War; this is not likely to have been a coincidence.[45] In other words, neither of these sets of outside *hegemones* did anything to integrate the Kyklades tightly into their kingdoms; if anything, their leagues reinforced the political isolation of the islands, forcing them to rely on each other and on local officials for the resolution of problems and reducing the frequency with which they could appeal directly to the sovereigns. Requests for settlement of disputes by individual islands and the contact the league had with the court illustrate this nicely. It was to Bakkhon and Philokles, local officials, that the islands appealed for help, not to the sovereign. The league most likely honored the court official Sostratos during a visit to Delos, perhaps in 287 B.C. in connection with his embassy to Athens to negotiate Demetrios's surrender and withdrawal.[46] At court the league sought the help of Theon son of Philiskos (*IG* XI 4.1042 =

44. Irwin L. Merker, *Historia* 19 (1970): 141–60; Hauben in *Studia Phoenicia V,* 413–28; Bagnall, 146–47 (*oikonomos*).

45. *IG* XII 5.1061, 1065, 1066, 541 + Ch. Dunant and J. Thomopoulos, *BCH* 78 (1954): 336–38, no. 13 (= *SEG* 14.543). Cf. Bagnall, 141–45.

46. *IG* XI 4.1038 (= *Choix,* 21); cf. 563 (= *Choix,* 22), a Delian decree for him, 1130, 1190 (= *Choix,* 23–24; dedications). Shear, ll. 32–43 for the embassy.

Choix, 26). Among honorands, Thrasykles was apparently a local official (*IG* XI 4.1043, cf. *I.G.* XII suppl. 169); others were citizens of foreign cities who had assisted the league in one way or another (*IG* XI 4.1040, 1044). The contrast with, say, the cities of Asia Minor or Syria, which had intimate and direct contact with their sovereigns, could not be stronger.[47]

The situation under the Rhodian incarnation of the league was somewhat different. In the first place, the headquarters were established on Tenos, not Delos. The military responsibilities of the league are much clearer, and the Rhodians sent out Rhodians as officials. The best example of the latter is the naval commander Anaxibios son of Pheidianax, who was "sent out by the demos of the Rhodians as commander [ἄρχων] over the islands and the ships of the islands" (*IG* XI 4.752.3–5, cf. 753 = *Choix*, 63). Several such officials are attested on Tenos (*IG* XII 5.830.11–13; cf. also 913–14). The league controlled a fund that was used at least once to buy grain (*IG* XI 4.759, *IG* XII 5.817 with *testimonium* 1349); the grain may have been wanted for military purposes. The Rhodians also interfered with the constitutions of Tenos and Syros.[48]

The Rhodians were far more directly involved in the administration of the league than were either the Ptolemies or the Antigonids. But this closer involvement does not imply a change in the regional status of the political situation of the islands. Contact with Rhodian officials generally occurred in the Kyklades; despite the relatively short distance to Rhodos and the wealth of Rhodian epigraphical evidence, only fifteen Kykladic islanders are attested on Rhodos, and several of them date to after the end of Rhodian control of the islands.[49] Moreover, Rhodos belonged to the Aegean world; it was, to borrow a term from urban geography, hardly a city of the first order, or perhaps even of the second. The Rhodians did not enjoy the range of wealth and power that allowed the great sovereigns to devolve the administration of the Kyklades onto lower-ranking bureaucrats, and their closer contact with the islanders did not pull the Kyklades out of their own Kykladic world.

GARRISONS

On the whole, sovereigns planted remarkably few garrisons on the islands, and in general this was a means of control far more attractive to rulers who

47. W. Orth, *Königlicher Machtanspruch und städtische Freiheit* (Munich, 1977), passim; John D. Grainger, *The Cities of Seleukid Syria* (Oxford, 1990), 137–69.

48. Garrison on Tenos suggested by P. M. Fraser and G. E. Bean, *The Rhodian Peraea and Islands* (Oxford, 1954), 168. *IG* XII 5.652 (Syros); Etienne, 117–18.

49. Donato Morelli, *Studi classici ed orientali* 5 (1956): 126–90, Guila Sacco, *Rendiconti Lincei* 35 (1980): 517–28.

did not control the entire archipelago, or who simply wanted to protect travel routes, than to those who had at their disposal a comprehensive league. Antigonos Monophthalmos planted a garrison on Andros before 308 B.C. (Diod. 20.37.1), but that was very early in his Aegean hegemony and was no doubt a step toward the capture of Athens. Andros was also the site of a Ptolemaic garrison in 287, and of Antigonid garrisons from before 250 to 199 as part of the Antigonids' desire to protect the entrance to the Saronic Gulf. Gonatas's garrisons on Kythnos and Kimolos, if genuine, had the same purpose.[50] Ptolemaios I probably stationed troops on Melos during his expedition against the Peloponnesos in 308 B.C.[51] Patroklos stationed troops at Arsinoë (= Koresia) on Keos during the Khremonidean War, surely as a base camp to support his more forward posts near Sounion and on the Attic mainland. The establishment of Ptolemaic forces at Koresia entailed the imposition of a governor (ἐπιστάτης), who had full authority even in local matters (*IG* XII 5.1061). Philip's garrisons on Andros, Kythnos, and Paros were, as we have seen, designed to guard his route to Asia.

Only two permanent garrisons were established in the Kyklades by hegemonic powers controlling a league. The first was the Ptolemaic garrison at Thera, which, as I have already argued, served to guard the routes south to Krete and beyond to Egypt. While it no doubt imposed a considerable burden on the local population,[52] it belongs not in the category of mechanisms of Kykladic control but rather in the same class as the Ptolemaic naval base at Samos, whose strategic importance is perfectly clear. The separation between Thera and the other mechanisms of Kykladic control is reflected in the fact that the Ptolemies retained the island even after they lost the Kyklades.

The other garrison was that established on Tenos by the Rhodians sometime after 199 B.C. It was associated with the headquarters of the new league and served as the base of the Nesiotic fleet. In this sense it was not analogous to the Ptolemaic garrison at Thera, which was manned by foreign mercenaries.[53]

The relative rarity of permanent garrisons on the islands suggests that rulers who governed through leagues could rely on them to keep the Kyklades in line. Once again, this implies relatively little contact between the

50. Shear, ll. 20–21; Plut. *Aratos* 12.2–3 (cf. G. Reger, *Historia* 43 [1994]: 48–50); Livy 31.15.

51. Holleaux, I.32, 34–35.

52. Cf. Bagnall, 123–34.

53. Louis Robert, *Noms indigènes dans l'Asie-Mineure gréco-romaine* (Paris, 1963), 388–89, 411–18.

sovereign and the islands and no impetus to draw the archipelago more tightly into the political orbit of the ruling center. This impression of relative isolation and laissez-faire finds confirmation in the strikingly light demands of outside *hegemones* in the way of military service.

MILITARY SERVICE

It is very difficult to find any clear evidence of regular military obligations imposed on the islanders. An inscription from Nemea that lists Keian, Kythnian, and Mykonian foot soldiers probably represents island contingents under Polemaios in 312 B.C. Melian contingents are attested under Ptolemaios I in 308. A Tenian probably employed as a mercenary died at Athens early in the third century, and Tenians may have participated in Demetrios's capture of Athens in 307 B.C. Early in the period of Ptolemaic control, an inscription speaks of Zenon "left in charge by the *nesiarkhos* Bakkhon" as commander of some undecked ships (*IG* XII 5.1004.2, 4–5), but it is hardly certain that these were "naval forces apparently supplied by the League." A festival at Koresia on Keos included military exercises and prizes for military skills. We find a Keian serving in the garrison at Eleusis probably after 240 B.C. and two Keians, one from Ioulis and one from Koresia, at Khios (?) in the third century. An Astypalaian served Olos on Krete as a mercenary.[54]

Kykladic soldiers were rare in Egypt. Marcel Launey counted one Naxian in 218/17 B.C., one Siphnian in 228/7, and a possible Astypalaian. A more recent count added none. Thera was the only island that produced even a handful of soldiers serving the Ptolemies: by Launey's count, six or seven in Egypt, one in Asia Minor, and perhaps one on Rhodos.[55] The Theran connection comes as no surprise, given Thera's Ptolemaic garrison; but equally interesting, studies of the names of the soldiers of that garrison, unfortunately preserved without ethnics in a list of 164/3–161/0 B.C., have yielded not one certain islander.[56]

54. Daniel J. Geagan, *Hesperia* 37 (1968): 381–84, no. 1, ll. 4–6, cf. Diod. 19.77.2. Holleaux, I.32, 34–35, with the inscription at p. 2, l. 24 (Melians). *IG* II^2 1957.9, see Reger, *CQ* 42 (1992): 366–68. Billows, *Antigonos*, 222 n. 93 (the "naval forces" quotation). *IG* XII 5.647.27–31. *IG* II^2 1958.15 (the ethnic Κεῖος suggests a date after the creation of the Keian federation; see G. Reger and M. Risser in *Landscape Archaeology*, 305–17); Georgios Zolotas, *Athena* 20 (1908): 214, no. 13, ll. 12–13, see also *LGPN* I, s.v. Ἀριστοφῶν 31. *IC* I Olos 4B40–42.

55. Launey, 235–36, cf. 81–83, and the remarks in the Addenda, p. 617, on pp. 89–90. Roger S. Bagnall, *BASP* 21 (1984): 7–20. Louis Robert, *Collection Froehner:* I. *Inscriptions grecques* (Paris, 1936), 94 l. 4; *Lindos* 121.4.

56. *IG* XII 3.325, with pp. 230, 283, and *IG* XII 3 suppl., p. 85. Robert, *Noms indigènes*, 388–89, 411–18. P. M. Meyer did identify Kallistagoras (l. 52) as a

Although it is hard to believe that the islanders had no military obligations as members of the Antigonid or Ptolemaic Nesiotic League, they have left virtually no trace in the sources. The simplest explanation would seem to be that when islanders served, they tended to soldier near home. Probably Nesiotic troops participated in the Khremonidean War, although the apparent absence of islanders among the Theran garrison warns against the easy assumption that Keian troops "must" have served under Patroklos on their home island. The Ptolemies seem to have preferred foreign troops for such duties. In any case, military service cannot have been frequent or onerous.

Once again the situation was different under the Rhodians. The islands were obligated to provide ships for a fleet under Rhodian command, stationed at Tenos. This obligation embroiled the Tenians and other islanders in fighting during Antiokhos III's retreat from Greece, and island ships may well have participated in the Rhodian war against Eumenes II to keep the straits open. The war most likely ended in 180 B.C.; island participation would explain the peace mentioned on Delos in 179.[57] As we have seen, the archipelago also saw a good deal of action in the war against Perseus; perhaps islanders fought then too.

In general, military obligations were light in the third century, and even when the Rhodians imposed stricter requirements in the second century, military service rarely took islanders outside the Kyklades. Military obligations did not break the insularity of the islands, whose inhabitants rarely served even as individuals. The contrast with Kretans could not be stronger; they appear all over the Greek world, in considerable numbers,[58] whereas their northern neighbors mostly stayed at home.

TRIBUTE AND TAXES

As a rule the payment of tribute was the most obvious consequence of domination by an outside power. The Kyklades had paid tribute to the Athenians in the fifth century; disgruntlement over these imposts led to the assurances in the foundation document of the Second Athenian Confederation that members would not pay tribute (φόρος, *IG* II² 43.23), al-

---

Tenian (*Das Heerwesen der Ptolemäer und Römer in Aegypten* [Leipzig, 1900], 21–22, *non vidi*), but there is no sure basis for this.

57. Polyb. 27.7.5, the date inferred from 25.2, which relates under 180 B.C. the treaty that ended the war. Cf. Strabo 12.3.11 (C545); Diod. 29.24; *IOSPE* I², 402; Will II², 288–90. Erich Ziebarth in *Mélanges Gustave Glotz* (Paris, 1932), II.914, dates the expedition to 181 precisely. *IG* XI 2.130.1 (179 B.C.): [ὑγίεια] καὶ εὐετηρία καὶ εἰρ[ήνη].

58. Launey, 248–86.

though soon enough members were paying a "contribution" (σύνταξις). Antigonos and Demetrios showed some sensitivity to this issue in 307 B.C., when Demetrios, crossing the Aegean to take Athens, brought with him a war chest of 5,000 talents and lavished gifts on the liberated Athenians (Plut. *Dem.* 8.4, 10.1 with *IG* II[2] 1492B120–22). But the Nesiotic League required contributions as early as 307 (*IG* XI 4.1036.12–16 = *Choix,* 13), even though the document attests explicitly only to funds used for religious purposes. These contributions were called εἰσφοραί (l. 44). Demetrios's imposts no doubt rose after Ipsos; his exactions were sufficiently resented for Ptolemaios I to brag that he had "abolished (or reduced) the contributions" (τῶν εἰσφορῶγ κουφίσας, *IG* XII 7.506.16 = *SIG*[3] 390) when he took control of the Kyklades. It has often been suggested that the loans the islanders sought from Apollo on Delos were borrowed to pay tribute to Demetrios. A recent attempt to estimate the amount of the tribute depends on many unsupported assumptions (not least that all loans taken out by some cities on Amorgos were used to pay it), but there can be no doubt that the Kyklades paid dearly under the Antigonids.[59]

The Ptolemies surely exacted monies too, although the mechanism may have been different and, at least at first, arrangements for collecting it seem to have been ad hoc. Karthaia on Keos honored one Philotheros "under orders of king Ptolemaios" ([τετ]αγμένος ὑπὸ τὸν βασιλέα Πτολεμαῖον) who had come to their city frequently about "the payment of the money" (ἐπὶ τὴν κομιδὴν τῶν [χρημά]των, *IG* XII 5.1066.2–3, 4). It seems most likely to me that tribute, whether regular or special, is meant.[60] The islanders were ordered in 279 B.C. to pay their contributions for a crown for Ptolemaios "to whomever Bakkhon may appoint" (*IG* XII 7.506.57–61 = *SIG*[3] 390). Voluntary payments in the form of crowns may have taken the place of, or supplemented, formal tribute; in the second century Delos deployed the awarding of crowns financed by loans from Apollo as part of a clever international diplomacy. Four loans known for 269 B.C.—just before the Khremonidean War—may have had an analogous purpose. Moreover, the league itself controlled a fund to pay for crowns for honorands and inscriptions. The military obligations imposed by the Rhodians surely entailed financial responsibilities as well. That there was a common island

59. *IG* XI 4.559 = *Choix,* 18, Migeotte, 162–66, no. 47, with further references. If *IG* XII 5.570 could be dated to Monophthalmos and Poliorketes, it would show taxes paid to the kings; but unfortunately the dating problem is intractable. See Buraselis, 87 n. 201, G. Reger, *Historia* 43 (1994): 51–52. Thomas W. Gallant, *Journal of Interdisciplinary History* 19 (1989): 393–413.

60. Cf. Migeotte, 220–21, with references for the restoration [χρημά]των in place of *IG* XII's [δανεισμά]των.

fund appears from the inscription honoring the banker Timon of Delos; the money in it at the time was Rhodian (*IG* XII 5.817). The Delians twice voted funds to pay for contributions to the Rhodians, once at least in the form of a crown; the Ietans had voted the Rhodians a crown during their brief Kykladic adventure in the 250s.[61]

There was a definite financial impact to control by outside *hegemones;* more important, a fair share of the money paid out by islanders left the archipelago, although obviously it is impossible to quantify. Tribute was probably the most obvious and onerous aspect of domination by an external power.

INTERFERENCE IN INTERNAL AFFAIRS

Intervention in the government of cities often accompanied changes of ruler during the Hellenistic period, and the Kyklades were no exception. The first appearance of Monophthalmos's forces in the Aegean in 314 B.C. entailed the expulsion of the Athenians from Delos, the establishment of an "independent" democracy on the island, and the creation of the Nesiotic League. Antigonos's interventions set the pattern. In the decree announcing the establishment at Alexandria of the Ptolemaieia for his father Ptolemaios Soter, Philadelphos remarked that he had "freed the cities [i.e., of the islands] and restored the laws and reestablished the ancestral constitution" (*IG* XII 7.506.13–15 = *SIG*[3] 390). This was no idle boast. A raft of inscriptions attest to interventions in the internal affairs of the islands not only by Soter but by his son as well. Through the *nesiarkhos* Bakkhon, who was acting "according to the instructions of King Ptolemaios" and of the Nesiotic League, the Naxians received "dikasts and reconcilers" (διαλ[λακτῆρας]) "to judge about disputed contracts" (Holleaux III.27, ll. 2–4 with p. 32). The Karthaians on Keos suffered from severe internal problems (ταραχή according to Hiller's restoration), requiring intervention, again mediated through Bakkhon, so that the Karthaians "could inhabit the city in harmony" (ὁμονοοῦν[τες]) and "do the things advantageous to the king Ptolemaios" (the last phrase is uncertain; *IG* XII 5.1065.2, 4, 5–12). Bakkhon's arrangements proved insufficient, however, and Philokles had to confirm his orders and send dikasts. Another decree from Karthaia honoring "Athenaios under orders of King Ptolemaios . . .

61. *IG* XI 2.203A74, A75–76, A76–77, A77–78; for the second-century crowns, see M.-F. Baslez and Claude Vial, *BCH* 111 (1987): 281–312, full list at 282, unfortunately without figures. League funds: *IG* XI 4.1039b14–16, 1040.24–28, 1041.17–21, 1048.13–16. Timon: *IG* XII 5.817, cf. Bogaert, 176–78. *ID* 406B64, 442A63–65 and A24–26. *IG* XII 5.1009.6, with *IG* XII suppl., p. 96; for the date, see n. 5 above.

as dikast" could be either part of the same business or of a separate board.[62] Ios had suffered a civic disturbance, [τῆς κατὰ τὴν] πόλιν γενομένης ταραχῆ[ς] (*IG* XII 5.7.2). The disturbances in these documents (except perhaps the decree honoring Athenaios) date to between 286 and 280 B.C. During the Khremonidean War, Thera received dikasts from Ioulis thanks to the intervention of the general Patroklos.[63] Antigonos Gonatas's intervention in the constitution of Syros likewise seems to go best in the immediate aftermath of his victory over the Ptolemies at Andros in 246 or 245 (*IG* XI 4.1052 = *Choix*, 45).

The Rhodians followed this long tradition of interference. During their intrusion into the Kyklades in the 250s, they exacted an alliance from the Ietans, who thanked them for securing Ietan freedom.[64] During the Second Makedonian War, the Karthaians on Keos responded to slanders against them suggesting disloyalty to the Rhodian cause and promised fidelity to their "good disposition and friendship and alliance" with the Rhodians.[65] The Rhodians intervened in the constitutions of both Syros and Tenos. To Tenos they seconded Philotimos, adoptive son of Teisikrates, to be "in charge of the soldiers and for the care of the city" (ἐπί τε τῶν στρατιω[τῶν καὶ ἐπὶ τὴν τῆς πόλ]εως ἐπιμέλειαν [*IG* XII 5.830.12–13]), clear evidence of the subordination of the Tenians to the Rhodian military commander on the island.

Some general observations are justified. As a rule, it was islands with garrisons—whether permanent, as on Thera, or temporary, as on Keos—that felt the hand of the *hegemon* most heavily; this was as true under the Rhodians as in the third century. Otherwise, the payment of tribute was undoubtedly the clearest regular evidence of the archipelago's subordination to outside authority. At the beginning of a new reign there was often a spate of interference by hegemonic officials in local governments. These interventions, however, were almost certainly not orchestrated by the *hegemon*, but rather responded to requests from within the cities themselves. Changes in authority permitted factions in the cities to try to gain an advantage over their local opponents; certainly groups within the cities also competed to show their loyalty to their new masters. However heavily the outside power weighed on the islands, it did not act to drag islanders out of

62. *IG* XII 5.541 + Ch. Dunant and J. Thomopoulos, *BCH* 78 (1954): 336–38, no. 13, ll. 1–2 (= *SEG* 14.543).

63. *IG* XII 3.320.7–8, 8–10.

64. On *IG* XII 5.1009, see n. 61 above.

65. Chr. Dunant and J. Thomopoulos, *BCH* 78 (1954): 338–44, no. 14, quotation from l. 13 (= *SEG* 14.544); BE (1955): 180. Cf. also Berthold, 128–29.

the archipelago. Control by outsiders did not entail deeper commitment on the political or military level outside of the central Aegean, and this was true even under the Rhodians, whose own relatively restricted sphere of action made their interests and activities in the Kyklades different from those of their greater predecessors.[66]

The Independent Kyklades: 245–200 B.C.

The contrast could not be greater between the political situation of the Kyklades under Antigonid, Ptolemaic, and Rhodian domination and that of the years 245 to 200 B.C. Scholars have offered ingenious arguments for a new hegemony by the Antigonids under Gonatas and/or his successors, by the Rhodians after ca. 230 B.C., or even by the Ptolemies,[67] but in fact the existence of any one *hegemon* is entirely excluded by the absence of any of the mechanisms of control that characterize all three other periods: a league, payment of tribute, the imposition of garrisons, the presence of officials representing the external power, the suppression of piracy, and interference in internal affairs. There is no need to argue the point here, which would in any case carry us far afield into very technical issues.[68] Instead, I would like to discuss briefly some of the political implications of this freedom from outside control. The economic repercussions will be dealt with later, especially in chapter 7.

For the Kyklades, the absence of an outside *hegemon* spelled genuine freedom for the first time in many years. In the political life of the islands, this freedom manifested itself in several ways; perhaps the most striking

66. Cf., e.g., the Ptolemaic treatment of the cities of Lesbos, recently elucidated by Patrice Brun, *ZPE* 85 (1991): 99–113.

67. Antigonid: Holleaux, III.55–73; J. Delamarre, *Rev. Phil.* 26 (1902): 301–325; Tarn, *Antigonos Gonatas*, 469–72; Huss, 213–37; Buraselis, 168 with n. 195; more cautiously F. W. Walbank in *Philip II, Alexander the Great, and the Macedonian Heritage* (Washington, D.C., 1982), 222. Rhodian: Fraser and Bean, *Rhodian Peraea*, 158–59; H. van Gelder, *Geschichte der alten Rhodier* (The Hague, 1900), 112; Delamarre, *Rev. Phil.* 26 (1902): 325, cf. Holleaux, III.68–73; Rostovtzeff, III.1485 n. 94; Roger B. McShane, *The Foreign Policy of the Attalids of Pergamum* (Urbana, 1964), 47–48; Berthold, 142. For Huss, 215–16 n. 288, 217–18, Rhodos seems to act as an agent of the greater powers, Makedon and the Ptolemies. Ptolemaic: Huss, 218, on the views of K. J. Beloch, *Griechische Geschichte* (Strassburg, 1904), III.2.281–83, cf. Holleaux, III.69–73; cf. Buraselis, 175 with n. 214.

68. I follow the penetrating remarks of Pierre Roussel, *Journal des Savants* (1924): 114–15. For a full treatment of the subject, see G. Reger, *Historia* 43 (1994): 32–69.

are the minting of silver coins, the creation of individualized or idiosyncratic political arrangements, the reemergence of piracy, and the striking by individual islands of their own arrangements with neighboring states.

COINAGE

During most of the third century, the Kykladic islands did not issue silver money. The bronzes they struck throughout the third century, which are generally hard to date (the Keian federal coins of the 240s–220s B.C. are an exception), were surely intended for local use; the immobilization in the storerooms of Apollo on Delos of such examples as happened to come into the god's possession show their uselessness outside their cities of origin.[69]

Probably around 230–220 B.C., however, several islands, including Paros, Tenos, Naxos, and Andros, minted silver coins. The coins are beautifully engraved and skillfully struck; some of the best examples come from hoards on Euboia, which proves their acceptability away from home. No specimens, however, have been found any farther away from the Kyklades; no Rhodian hoards, for example, have yielded Kykladic coins. The striking of silver coins in the Hellenistic period outside of Athens generally indicates either permission of a sovereign or a certain degree of independence. The latter is the case for the Kyklades. The source of the silver remains something of a mystery, although it need have originated no farther away than Athens, Thasos, or even residual mines on Siphnos or Keos.[70]

NEW POLITICAL ARRANGEMENTS

The independence of the Kyklades during the second half of the third century brought some new political arrangements. Sometime between 221 and 200 B.C., the Samians colonized the small city of Minoa on Amorgos and settled on the island of Ikaria. J. Delamarre has suggested that the Ptolemies may have sponsored this Samian expansion, but given Ptolemaic uninterest in the central Aegean after about 245 B.C., it is more likely that the Samians exploited the absence of greater powers to abuse their neighbors.[71]

69. Reger and Risser in *Landscape Archaeology*, 305–17. Robert, *Etudes de numismatique grecque*, 143–78; J. R. Jones, *ANS Museum Notes* 17 (1971): 127–36.

70. Robert Bauslaugh, *ANS Museum Notes* 24 (1979): 1–45. I am not convinced by the arguments of Etienne, 225–38, who wants to put some Tenian silver in ca. 315–250 B.C. My die study indicates that the coins all were issued over a very brief period. See, provisionally, *AJA* 91 (1987): 272. For the mines, see above, n. 11.

71. *IG* XII 7.237 + 245 + *IG* XII suppl., p. 144 (cf. BE [1970]: 147); 226 (cf. BE [1977]: 79), 231 (cf. *IG* XII suppl., p. 144), 240, 269, and 235, and *IG* XII 5.38 (with Robert, *Op. min. sel.*, I.541): on the Samians at Minoa, see generally Louis Robert, *REG* 42 (1929): 20–32 (= *Op. min. sel.*, I.530–42), BE (1979): 426, and Georges

In the 240s or a little later, three of the four poleis of Keos created a new federation, which seems to have been established in order to deal with the Aitolians, after whose own federal arrangements it was modeled and who were the only body with which the federation is known to have dealt.[72] The Keians were hardly the only Aegean state to deal with the Aitolians. The Delians received a guarantee of *asphalia* from them, probably in 250 (*IG* XI 4.1050 [= *Choix,* 41], 1051 with 2.287A80–81). Mytilene on Lesbos struck an *asylia* agreement (*IG* IX 1² 189–90). Magnesia on the Maiandros has left several documents (*IvMag,* 16, 18–64, 66, 68–73, 78–84). Athens dealt with them ca. 220 B.C.[73] Typical and telling is the agreement struck between Khios and the Aitolians, which guaranteed the security of the island from Aitolian piracy. Since Khios was probably independent at this time, the deal exemplifies the arrangements small insular Aegean states made to effect their safety.[74]

There is also abundant evidence to prove contact with Kretan cities. An inscription from Allaria on Krete dated either to ca. 200 B.C. or to the years after the war with Lyttos (ca. 220 B.C.) refers to renewal of an *asylia* decree with Allaria by Paros and the establishment of *isopoliteia.* In the early second century, the Parians borrowed money on Krete, probably from individuals.[75] The Tenians sought protection from Lebena, Gortyn, Lappa,

---

Rougement in *Les Cyclades,* 131–34, 236–39. On Ikaria, see Louis Robert, *REG* 46 (1933): 437–42 (= *Op. min. sel.,* I.563–568). *IG* XII 7, p. 50: "quo tempore Ptolemaeorum fuit Samos, dubitari vix potest, quin Ptolemaeo Philopatore favente Samiorum haec colonia deducta sit." Followed by W. Dittenberger, *SIG*³ 562 n. 16, Walter Ruppel, *Klio* 21 (1927): 315, Louis Robert, *REG* 46 (1933): 442 (= *Op. min. sel.,* I.568), applying the same "opinion raisonnable" to the Samians on Ikaria; see also Shipley, *Samos,* 205–7, and Anthony J. Papalas, *Ancient Icaria* (Wauconda, Ill., 1992) 119–20. The date is based on identifying the Antigonos of *IG* XII 7.221–23 as Doson; see Reger, *Historia* 43 (1994): 55–56. The Naxians came to Arkesine no earlier than the second century, the Milesians to Aigiale still later: W. Ruppel, *Klio* 21 (1927): 315–16.

72. *IG* XII 5.526–27 (= Schmitt, *Staatsverträge,* III.508), cf. 532–34; Reger and Risser, *Landscape Archaeology,* 305–17.

73. *IG* IX 1² 176 (= Schmitt, *Staatsverträge,* III.470), which R. Flacelière, *Les Aitoliens à Delphes* (Paris, 1937), 190–91, and in *Athenian Studies Presented to William Scott Ferguson* (Cambridge, Mass., 1940), 475, put in 274 B.C., but the letter forms point to ca. 220 B.C., as Klaffenbach in *IG* (cf. Gauthier, *Symbola,* 172). Generally, see Gauthier, *Symbola,* 245–66, 270–74.

74. Georges Daux, *BCH* 83 (1959): 475–77; cf. Bauslaugh, *ANS Museum Notes* 24 (1979): 20–21.

75. *IC* II Allaria 2B4–26; the later date is favored by Guarducci in *IC,* the earlier by Henri van Effenterre, *La Crète et le monde grec* (reprint, Paris, 1968), 255 n. 3; cf. Polyb. 5.63.12, 65.7, and *IG* II² 844 (229/8 B.C.), an agreement about returning Athenians taken in a raid. Loans: Migeotte, 215–18, no. 62; *SEG* 32.825.

and Tylisos (or perhaps Axos or Aptera) from the second quarter of the third century on. The numerous Kretan proxenies recorded in *IG* XII suppl. 304 probably reflect these relations.[76] An Andrian inscription of the second century attests contact with four Kretan cities, including Gortyn (*IG* XII 5.723). Melos had an *asylia* agreement with Polyrhenia, and Anaphe with Gortyn. Keian and Kimolian *proxenoi* are known from Gortyn. Other littoral states also courted the Kretans.[77]

This flowering of relations city by city with other states is new in the second half of the century. It reflects the absence both of a hegemonic power and of an organizing authority, such as the Nesiotic League, through which islands could deal collectively with outsiders. Further, these activities confirm the existence of a kind of political vacuum in the islands, and with the absence of any single state to police the seas, this vacuum drew in people like Demetrios of Pharos, who raided the Kyklades in 219 B.C.[78] It was to prevent such raids—and also to guarantee profit from them, as we shall see in chapter 7—that the Kykladic states made deals with the two most notorious pirate groups, the Aitolians and the Kretans.

THE RISE IN PIRACY

There is abundant evidence to demonstrate a rise in piracy in the central Aegean after ca. 250 B.C. Polybios and Diodoros describe the raids of Demetrios of Pharos and of Dikaiarkhos, although the latter was admittedly

76. *IC* I Lebena 1; IV 166 (= Schmitt, *Staatsverträge,* III.562); *IG* XII 5.868A1–12 = *IC* II Lappa 2 (Guarducci's date [comm., p. 196] seems much too early in view of van Effenterre, *La Crète et le monde grec,* 135–37; cf. Etienne, 93–97, 119, who at 93, with n. 36, stresses the possible role of the Ptolemies in promoting *asylia* for Tenos in the second quarter of the third century); *IG* XII 5.868B = *IC* I Tylisos 2, on which see van Effenterre, 136 n. 8, 138, 156 n. 6 (date). Cf. also *IC* I Phaistos 1, which Guarducci puts at 280–260 B.C. but Etienne, 95, thinks may belong after 250 B.C.; see pp. 184–85 on the Kretan proxenies.

77. Melos: *IC* II Polyrhenia 2 (= Schmitt, *Staatsverträge,* III.577); Anaphe: *IC* IV 197 (dated by reference to the κοινόν to 210–200 B.C., cf. R. F. Willetts, *Aristocratic Society in Ancient Crete* [London, 1955], 228 n. 3 [continued from p. 227]); *proxenoi* at *IC* IV 206H, 209B. Other states include Kos (unpublished inscription, cf. *IC* I, p. 100, III, p. 20; Sherwin-White, *Ancient Cos,* 113 n. 156; Petropoulou, 216 n. 89); Miletos (*IC* II Aptera 16); Magnesia on the Maiandros (*Iv Mag,* 20); Teos (long series of documents, cf. Petropoulou, 36, 216 n. 94); Athens with an unknown city (*IG* II^2 1130 = *IC* II xxx 3); Mylasa (*IK* 34 Mylasa 1.641–59, cf. *IC* IV, pp. 248–49).

78. Polyb. 4.16.6–8, 19.8. Political "vacuum" in the Aegean also in Berthold, 97–98, cf. Etienne, 124. On Parian-Pharian relations, see esp. Louis Robert, *Hellenica* 11–12 (1960): 504–41.

sponsored by Philip V for political purposes. The village of Aulon on Naxos was raided by Aitolians sometime after 240 B.C.; 280 persons were captured. At Aigiale on Amorgos over 30 women, single and married, free and slave, were kidnapped by pirates. The city of Arkesine on the same island honored a woman, who may have been Kretan, for her zeal "to recover all the citizens who had been kidnapped" (εἰς τ[ὸ ἀνασ]ωθῆναι τοὺς πολίτας πάντας [τοὺς ἀχθ]έντας), which sounds like a case of piracy. Allarians from Krete raided Thera; unidentified pirates who attacked Oia at the eastern end of the island were defeated by the Ptolemaic garrison in a daring night raid. Tenian citizens ransomed by a fellow citizen at Karystos on Euboia may have been victims of pirates. The capture at Koresia on Keos of persons both free and slave has reasonably been attributed to pirates. The Kretan pirate Boukris was welcome on Delos, and citizens of Theangela in Asia Minor captured by pirates were sold into slavery there. King Nabis of Sparta, who was accused of engaging in piracy with Kretans, also had good relations with Delos.[79]

The islanders could not depend on a policing state to help them out with these problems. The Rhodians intervened once, when Demetrios of Pharos appeared, but Demetrios, who enjoyed the confidence of Philip V, undertook his raid in the context of Philip's war against the Akhaians and Spartans. The Rhodians no doubt wanted to prevent mainland fighting from creeping eastward while they were engaged in their "trade war" with Byzantion.[80] The Rhodian προστασία of the sea, twice mentioned by Poly-

79. Naxos: *IG* XII 5.36 (= *SIG*³ 520), after 240 B.C. (alphas with bowed crossbars; autopsy, summer 1990). Aigiale on Amorgos: *IG* XII 7.386, esp. ll. 4–8 (= *SIG*³ 521), second half of the third century (bowed crossbars, cf. photo in *IG*). Arkesine on Amorgos: *IG* XII 7.36.13–15 and 32 with J. Delamarre, *Rev. Phil.* 27 (1903): 111–21, Brulé, 58–60, Migeotte, 197–98 (but see below). Thera: *IG* XII 3.328 and 3 suppl. 1291. Tenos: *IG* XII 9.6.11–14 with D. Knoepfler, *BCH* 96 (1972): 294 n. 32. Koresia: Robert, *Hellenica* 11–12 (1960): 134. Boukris: *IG* XI 4.692 = *Choix*, 42, *IG* II² 844 (= *SIG*³ 535) of 229/8 B.C. (B. D. Meritt, *Historia* 26 [1977]: 177). Theangelians: *IG* XI 4.1054 with *SEG* 3.666. Nabis: *IG* XI 4.716 = *Choix*, 58. Generally Polyb. 4.3.1–5.10, 16.2–4, 25.1–4. For important discussion of the relation between Aitolian piracy and the promulgation of *asylia* decrees, see Gauthier, *Symbola*, 245–66. For contacts between the Aitolians and Kretans, see Petropoulou, 40–41. While *IG* XII 7.386 clearly deals with piracy, I am less sure about the other documents Delamarre alleges in this context. *IG* XII 7.387 seems to me clearly to refer to war, not piracy: καὶ τοὺς μὲν ἐπιθεμένους [αὐτοῖς τῶν πολε]μίων ἐνίκησεν μαχόμενος, τοὺς δ[ὲ ἁλόντας ἔσ]ωσεν, τὴν δὲ πολιου[ρκί]αν [ἔλυ]σεν (ll. 4–6).

80. Polyb. 4.19.8; cf. Niese, *Geschichte der griechischen und makedonischen Staaten*, 2: 385–86 n. 6; Berthold, 95.

bios (4.47.1, 5.90.5), had nothing to do with controlling piracy. For the rest, with the exception of Thera, with its resident Ptolemaic garrison, the Kyklades were thrown back on their own resources to deal with this rising incidence of piracy. They responded by making treaties with the main perpetrators, the Aitolians and the various cities of Krete, and by opening their ports to them.

The last half or so of the third century B.C. thus saw the central Aegean relatively free of outside authority. The Nesiotic League had disintegrated; a few islands from time to time experienced the temporary presence of Antigonid or Rhodian authority, but nothing endured. This has important consequences for understanding the economic development of Delos and its neighbors in these years.

Politics and Economy

A regional approach to the political history of the Kyklades helps to clarify the relations among the islands and between the islands and their *hegemones.* The inward-looking character of the archipelago is perhaps most explicit during the second half of the third century, when it was free of outside domination. But even when important outside powers were in control, the very mechanisms the outsiders put into place to run the islands helped guarantee that they continued to focus on local issues. Tribute flowed out, of course, and officials and garrisons imposed from the outside strained the islands, but they nevertheless failed to create any important or lasting political connections with the outside world. As all too often in antiquity, the most frequent intersections of the Kyklades with the larger Greek world occurred when armies, mobilized for reasons unrelated to the islands, fought their way across the Aegean.

This isolation raises important questions about the economy. No casual reader of today's newspapers will doubt the intimate connections between contemporary political and economic activity. The Greek poleis acted vigorously to intervene in their own economic life; besides the obvious, continuous interest in the trade in grain exhibited by Athens, Samos, and hundreds of smaller cities, Greek states passed legislation regulating the prices and quality of goods, put up barriers to certain economic activities by certain persons, policed marketplaces through officials like *agoranomoi,* taxed, and coined. As we shall see, the Delians were no exception in the interest they took in these matters. But whereas today the links between political and economic actions are often patent—and especially so, in the United States, during a national election—the interconnections in antiquity are rarely so clear. Matters apparently as simple as the Athenian legislation regulating the retail trade in grain attested by Lysias have provoked continuing debate,[81] and every reader of the pseudo-Aristotelian tract *Oikonomikos* has been puzzled by the seemingly senseless measures sometimes recommended to states that wanted to increase their revenues.[82]

But if the Kykladic political world was restricted largely to the central Aegean, it is a short step to wondering whether the Kykladic economy was similarly restricted. Claims that political changes at great distances affected the economy of Delos become suspect. Fritz Heichelheim postulated the great growth of Greek populations in the Greek East as the engine driving up the prices of wheat, olive oil, wine, and other goods in heavy demand, which price rises he believed he could read in the Delian data. Others have supposed that Delian ties with the cities of the Black Sea meant that those cities supplied Apollo's folk with the grain they needed. In turn, any Delian regulation affecting grain—like the creation in the late third century of a permanent *sitonia* fund—would have had its impact on the shores of the Khersonesos.[83] But these presumptions now will require careful consideration before they can be accepted.

Claims about politico-economic influence flowing the other way require similar careful consideration. Gustave Glotz argued in an elegant article, still cited as standard, that Makedonian political interests dictated the price of pitch on Delos. During years when the island was under Egyptian control, the Makedonian kings refused to export pitch to the Delians, who used it as a sealant on altars and roofs, in order to deny this "strategic good"—it was also a crucial component of warships—to their inveterate Ptolemaic enemies. In contrast, when Delos was friendly to the Makedonians, or at least not under Ptolemaic control, the Makedonians gladly supplied it; indeed, Glotz suggested that a remarkably low pitch price in 179 B.C. reflected an attempt by Perseus, the new king of Makedon, to curry favor with the Delians.[84]

These claims depend on several presuppositions about the nature of commerce as well as the character of the interactions between political and economic interests. In the next chapter, I explore the evidence for the extent of Delian trade and commerce in an attempt to delineate the typical boundaries of its economic world. As we shall see, a regionalist model works very well in this context too.

81. T. Figueira, *Phoenix* 40 (1986): 149–71; Philippe Gauthier, *Revue historique de droit français et étranger* 59 (1981): 5–28; Robin Seager, *Historia* 15 (1966): 172–84.

82. For commentary, see B. A. van Groningen, *Aristotele: Le Second Livre de l'Economique* (Leiden, 1993).

83. Heichelheim, *Wirt. Schw.*, 48–56. Chapter 4, pp. 111–13, below. Reger, *Classical Antiquity* 12 (1993): 320–29.

84. Glotz, *REG* 29 (1916): 299–302.

Chapter 3
Delos and the Kyklades: A Regional Economy

The framework used here for analysis of the Delian economy during the years of the island's independence is regional. In contrast to more traditional approaches, which have regarded Hellenistic Delos as tied into a great trading network and price-setting market reaching from Greece, or even southern Italy, to the Black Sea, the Levant, and beyond, I focus on the connections and interrelations among the Kyklades themselves. Much of Delian economic history, especially prices and rents, can be explained perfectly adequately by appeal to entirely local phenomena.

For Delos, the key economic issues were its size, its natural facilities for trade, the presence of the sanctuary, and its location along a normal route of movement of people and goods. The economic situation of the Kyklades involved their ability to feed themselves, their relation to Delos, the presence (or absence) of trade goods, and the movement of people, whether visitors, traders, pirates, or soldiers.

Before proceeding further, however, we need to define "the economy" of the Kyklades. Too often the word is used as if what lay behind it were a unity. In fact, it would be better to speak of Kykladic "economies," some overlapping, some isolated, with constantly changing relations among them. In the ancient world, all economic activity was grounded ultimately in the household economy, the economy of the οἶκος. The goal of the peasant household was self-sufficiency: the ability to supply as many wants as possible from the activity of the members of the household itself. Landholdings suitable for grain and a garden plot, a few olive trees, and some goats could satisfy most food needs. For ceramics and the few metal tools a farmer needed, a handful of local village specialists sufficed. This microcosm, which numerically was undoubtedly the predominant unit of economic activity in the ancient world, had few points of contact with a larger trading economy. I do not mean to exaggerate: at civic festivals, peasants enjoyed publicly provided meat and other things they could rarely afford for themselves; they celebrated births, weddings, and funerals, requiring expenditures well beyond the normal daily round; they patronized local markets; they paid taxes; and they felt the costs of war, whether as raids by enemies—pirates in particular would have threatened the islanders—or as demands by the local authority on the household's manpower. Nonetheless, in order to understand ancient economic activity overall, an evaluation of the role of peasant self-sufficiency is crucial.[1]

For Delos, no such evaluation has ever been done. Scholars have been satisfied to point to the island's limited surface area of about 6 km^2 (about 600 ha) and to its supposed sterility. Waldemar Déonna, quoting Lucien Cayeux's description of *modern* Delos as a "hilly, rocky place, denuded and without water," was prompted to wonder whether Delos in antiquity was "less sterile" than today.[2] The answer is, of course: the island was thickly inhabited, and human habitation demanded efficient exploitation of an environment less than ideal. The Delians dealt with the problem of water by constructing capacious cisterns, both those that underlie the courtyard of every Delian house and the great public cistern near the theater dating from the third century B.C.[3] Scholars have tended to assume that the whole arable surface of Delos outside the city was owned by Apollo, divided up into the estates Apollo rented out.[4] In this view there would have been no room at all for cultivated private property on the island, and its economy then would have been radically different from that of any other known polis. In fact, however, the important recent work of Michèle Brunet has revealed private farmsteads; she estimates that Delos probably supported about fifty private farms.[5] Delos did indeed rest on a substratum of local farmers. Their numbers may have been small, and their produce a minor contribution, but they were there. Their presence helps, to some degree, to recover Delos from the abyss of "uniqueness" that precludes any real analysis or understanding of its situation.

The size of the local farming population leads directly to the next

1. See, most recently, Gallant, 1–10.

2. W. Déonna, *Vie privée des Déliens* (Paris, 1948), 89, quoting L. Cayeux, *Description physique de l'île de Délos* (Paris, 1911), 1.

3. J. Chamonard, *Le Quartier du Théâtre* (Paris, 1922–24), 323–56 (private); Vallois, I.265–68. Cf. *GD*[3], 178–79, 248.

4. Kent, 252–55, with fig. 5.

5. Brunet, 149. Cf. also Claude Vial in *L'Origine des richesses dépensées dans la ville antique* (Aix-en-Provence, 1985), 47–49 and G. Reger, *Phoenix* 46 (1992): 322–41.

"economy," that of local production and consumption mediated through a market. It goes without saying that Delos had its own agora, at which local producers and consumers exchanged goods. This exchange included locally produced foodstuffs; otherwise it would have been impossible for the *hieropoioi* to sell grain seized from delinquent renters of Apollo's estates, for the temple to buy feed for its holy geese, or for the city to require the sale generally of confiscated goods.[6] A good grasp of the operation of this local market economy is crucial, since it determined the degree to which Delos was self-sufficient. It is a mistake to suppose that the island was entirely dependent on imports.

Although obviously unable to compete in size or importance with Athens, Rhodos, or even Ephesos, Stratonikeia, or any of the other moderately large cities of Asia Minor, Delos grew as never before after 167, and particularly after the 140s B.C. The domestic ruins the visitor sees today date from these later years of the Athenian domination, when a local population of perhaps 20,000 rivaled that of Ephesos.[7] The third and early second centuries never saw that scale of habitation. While Delos's population surely exceeded those of many of its Kykladic neighbors either absolutely or at least in density, it fell into the range of small towns like Keramos in Asia Minor, with its 1,095 or so adult male citizens and a free population of about 6,500. The total local population of Delos in the years of its independence, counting citizens of both sexes and all ages, permanently resident metics, slaves, and the average number of transient visitors, cannot have exceeded about 9,100 persons, and may have been much smaller.[8] To estimate the importance of the local exchange network in the Delian economy, we need a sense of the needs of a population of this size. To give some perspective, two estimates of fourth-century Athenian grain demand amount to the cargoes of 96–192 and 600 ships per year, respectively.[9] By contrast, Delian demand could have been satisfied by the cargoes of one or two ships *per month.*

Delos sits in the middle of the Kyklades, surrounded by larger islands

6. *IG* XI 2.142.7, 11; 287A45, etc.; *ID* 503.34.

7. Chamonard, *Quartier;* Alexandre Papageorgiou-Venetas, *Délos: Recherches urbaines sur une ville antique* (Munich, 1981), 114–15; Pierre Roussel, *BCH* 55 (1931): 438–49.

8. Eberhard Ruschenbusch, *ZPE* 59 (1985): 253–63. *IK* 30 Keramos 9 with comm. there; cf. D. M. Lewis, *CR* 38 (1988): 124–25 and A. G. Woodhead, *JHS* 109 (1989): 244.

9. David W. J. Gill, *JHS* 111 (1991): 36; Signe Isager and Mogens Herman Hansen, *Aspects of Athenian Society in the Fourth Century* (Odense, 1975), 62.

(at least six of which can be seen from the top of Mt. Kynthos).[10] These islands are often dismissed as poor and unproductive, but in fact there is considerable variation among them. Andros, the northwesternmost, exposed to westerly winds, has enough moisture to yield running water part of the year. Naxos, the largest Kyklas, boasts high mountains, woods, and several substantial agricultural plains. Keos was rich enough to support four independent poleis for much of its history; Amorgos similarly had three. The central plain of Paros, although dusty, remains well-farmed today. Some islands produced specialty crops as well. Keos was famous for an expensive cheese and for its sheep, and we hear of wines from a number of islands. But such tales must not cloud our view: no matter what, the Kyklades, like the rest of the Greek world, depended first and foremost on grain. And although the islands were often too dry for wheat, they usually received enough rainfall for barley, which, as has now been universally recognized, was the staple cereal crop in the classical and Hellenistic Greek world.[11]

The larger local exchange network that included the Kyklades must therefore also be taken into account. Rough estimates of the population and productivity of the Kyklades as a unit support the proposition that Delian needs were generally supplied first by a minimum Delian production (which, however, never came even close to meeting demand) and second by local Kykladic output. Imports from farther away, like Egypt or the Black Sea, were needed not at all or only marginally in the regular cycle of production and consumption. Matters might of course look very different in a year of shortage, but this was true of any Greek city: there is no need to appeal to the "uniqueness" of the Delian situation.

In order for the Kykladic exchange network to have worked, Delos had to have a way to pay for the goods it got from its neighbors. The primary mechanism for generating local wealth was the sanctuary. Because Apollo and Artemis had been born on Delos,[12] its temple drew visitors and dedications from all over the Greek world, and the wealth so collected not only funded the purchase of goods like food but also flowed into the hands of contractors and workers from both Delos itself and its neighbors. The temple was thus an important element in the Kykladic economy, for it brought in wealth created elsewhere for local redistribution. Indeed, the relative prosperity of the Hellenistic Kyklades compared to, say, the islands

10. ἡ Δῆλος καὶ αἱ περὶ αὐτὴν Κυκλάδες (Strabo 10.5.3 [C 485]); "circa Delum in orbem sitae, unde et nomen traxere, Cyclades" (Plin. *Nat. hist.* 4.22). I count Rheneia, Mykonos, Tenos, Syros, Naxos, and Paros.

11. Chapter 4, p. 87, below.

12. *Homeric Hymn to Apollo* 14–18.

under the Turks, or even in the first four centuries A.D., must partly be attributed to the magnetism of the sanctuary. Along with Delos's central location in the islands and the ἀσυλία it enjoyed,[13] this wealth and the local demand for goods that could not be supplied by local production helped to make the island "a center of redistribution for the central region of the Archipelago."[14]

Typical claims for Delos's economic role, however, depict something far more spectacular than a local exchange center for the central Kyklades. The island "was a centre of commerce closely connected with Rhodes and Alexandria," a "thriving commercial city" that served as a center for the grain trade under the Ptolemies and again after 250 B.C. under Antigonid sponsorship, controlling as well the distribution of Black Sea grain in the Aegean.[15] In the third century, Delos "became one of the greatest markets for cereals in the Mediterranean," which "could not only supply its own needs but become one of the great entrepôts of cereals and sometimes underwrite the needs of others."[16] Or again:

> In the second half of the third century, at a time when the volume of goods which entered the port was increasing, the cereals arriving at Delos surpassed the needs of the inhabitants [of Delos] and of the neighboring islands. . . . From this date the *emporion* of Delos was—at least for grain—more than a center of redistribution for the central region of the Archipelago.

The emphasis, of course, remains on grain: "The *emporion* of Delos lived principally from commerce in cereals," although "we do not know . . . whether cereals were the *only* product of value to transit Delos in important quantities."[17] Delos then becomes an element in a great price-setting market: "The rise in prices, and thus the decrease in buying power of money, are attested at Delos and also in Egypt: there is, therefore, every reason to believe that the entire eastern Mediterranean basin (without going farther . . .) was affected" by the high prices read from Delian documents for the late fourth and early third centuries.[18]

These are bold claims. Speaking of the Delians' situation in the fifth and

13. Cf., e.g., Livy 44.29.3–4. I do not mean to confuse this with Delos's supposed neutrality, on which see most recently Philippe Bruneau, *BCH* 114 (1990): 583–91.

14. Vial, 341.

15. Rostovtzeff, 235, 221, cf. 231–32. Shear, 30–31.

16. *Choix*, pp. 57–58.

17. Vial, 339–43, quotations at 341, 342 (emphasis added). P. M. Nigdelis, Πολίτευμα και κοινωνία (Thessaloniki, 1990), 311–18. Cf. chapter 4, pp. 116–25, below.

18. Will I², 35 (his ellipsis).

fourth centuries B.C., Jacques Coupry notes wisely that "a great sanctuary tends only secondarily to become an economic force as such, whether national or international."[19] What kind of evidence is there for Delos's role in the long-range trade of the third and second centuries?

In the first place, a realistic assessment of Delos's natural advantages is called for. Lionel Casson offered an important judgment on the qualities and attractions of the Delian port some years ago:

> [The port] was no doubt perfectly adequate for the island trading vessels which probably were not very different from those that ply the Aegean today. Delos, then, was a natural choice as center for the trade of the nearby islands and, since they all were importers of grain, she very likely became the focus of a local traffic, servicing her neighbors' needs as well as her own. . . . So much can be said for the island's role. To consider it a major center, one that could compete with Rhodes in its own right, is to distort the facts. Where grain was concerned, Rhodes called the tune.[20]

Second, the fact that Delos and its neighbors are islands imposed a severe restriction on their trade. The Greeks were very reluctant to sail as merchants at any other time than the summer (although the exigencies of warfare might, of course, impose very different imperatives on navies). At other times, the Delians might well have taken advantage of a few days of suitable weather to make runs to nearby neighbors, but for all practical purposes, Aegean commercial traffic shut down between October and April. Even during the normal season, winds and weather could unpredictably stop sailing for days or even weeks at a time.[21] Everything needed over the winter and not available in sufficient abundance on the island thus had to be imported by October in amounts to last until the following spring. Any unexpected disaster—a winter slightly harsher than normal; the postponement of the opening of the sailing season because of spring storms; the loss of a shipload of goods to a shipwreck, pirates, or expropriation by an-

19. Jacques Coupry in *Atti del terzio congresso internazionale di epigrafia greca e latina* (Rome, 1959), 68.

20. Casson, "Grain Trade," 76. See, still, J. Paris, *BCH* 40 (1916): 5–73. Marasco, 129, with n. 14 for further references. Cf. also Berthold, 52–53.

21. Demos. 33.23; Casson, *Ships*, 270–72. While agreeing that Aegean shipping shut down during the winter—in part because cloudiness impeded navigation—M. Zimmermann makes an exception of the Egypt-Rhodos route (*ZPE* 92 [1992]: 205–6). On Hesiod *Op.* 663–65, see G. L. Snider, *AJAH* 3 (1978): 129–33. Henry Fanshawe Tozer, *The Islands of the Aegean* (Oxford, 1890), 1–3, 78, 94, 110–11, 117. E. Y. Kolodny, *La Population des îles de la Grèce* (Aix-en-Provence, 1974), 67–71. Note [Aiskhines]' experience trying to sail from Athens to Rhodos, *Ep.* 1.1. On conditions today, see Kolodny, *Population*, 68–71.

other state; the declaration of war and arrival of a military fleet—could wreak temporary but major havoc in the local price structure.

Third, as we have seen in chapter 2, Delos lay on an important route between Greece and Asia Minor, used by travelers, *theoroi*, ambassadors, and—most important—troops. The 1,500 cavalry, 8,000 Makedonian troops, 15,000 mercenaries, 25,000 allied troops from the Greek cities, 8,000 lightly armed troops, and unspecified number of "pirates" that Demetrios Poliorketes brought "through the islands to Ephesos" in 301 B.C. were exceptional, but there are plenty of instances of 1,000 or so troops visiting Delos or its neighbors. In some cases, the strain these influxes put on the local economy can be read in violent, but transient, price rises. In every case, the increase of 10 percent or more in the local population that these troop levels represented must have wreaked economic havoc, even if speculators may have profited.[22]

Delos therefore lacked many factors that drew merchants to other great centers of transit trade in the Greek world, such as high local demand (Athens) or highly desirable local products, good harbors, and connections with important producers (Rhodos).[23] The boom Delos enjoyed in through trade after 167 B.C. had other causes, among them the Roman decision to abolish Delian transit duties, the increasing establishment on Delos of Italian traders, who began to use the island as a marshaling point for trade coming out of Asia and the East and headed for Rome (including, but certainly not limited to, slaves), and, as Strabo emphasizes, the destruction of Korinthos by the Romans in 146 B.C.[24] In contrast, independent Delos made its contribution to the local Kykladic economy, which it both fed and depended upon.

The Scope of Delian Economic Connections

Early studies of the Delian economy were influenced by a "modernizing" model of the Hellenistic world that saw capitalism everywhere and emphasized long-distance trade and strong market interconnections. This model favored an internationalist view of Delos, especially as the great runs of prices I analyze further below provided the only semi-statistical economic

22. Diod. 20.110.4, 111.3. Ca. 1,000 troops on Andros in 287, Shear, ll. 20–21; 1,100 on Delos in 197, *ID* 425.11, 442B67–68 with Livy 33.18.5.

23. Similarly Marasco, 149–50.

24. Polyb. 30.31.12, with F. W. Walbank, *A Historical Commentary on Polybius* (Oxford, 1979), III.458–60; Strabo 10.5.4 (= C486), 14.5.2 (= C668); *ID* 2589 (= *SIG*[3] 657); Paus. 3.23.3; Roussel, *Délos colonie athénienne* (Paris 1916, rep. 1987), 7–18; rightly stressed by Déonna, *Vie privée*, 25–26. Cf. also A. N. Sherwin-White, *Roman Foreign Policy in the East, 168 B.C. to A.D. 1* (Norman, Okla., 1984), 31–32, Marasco, 150–53.

data for the Hellenistic world; they served as a solid substratum on which to build a history of economic change over time for the entire Greek East.

The evidence Delos has preserved is far from unambiguous. Delian inscriptions offer a very wide variety of testimonies about the economic connections of the island during the years of independence. Decrees honor benefactors who provided grain, ran banks, or offered other services to merchants; the temple accounts record the activities of bankers, the purchase of grain and other goods, and the employment of contractors and day laborers; decrees granted by foreign cities or kings recount the assistance their representatives received when buying grain or carrying out other activities on Delos. These documents have often been read to show the scale of Delos's economic net, which is supposed to have reached regularly to the Black Sea or the Levant.

This material is not always easy to interpret. Let me cite two examples. For religious purposes, the temple needed supplies of exotic goods, including frankincense and ivory, purchases of which recur frequently in the accounts.[25] These items came from very far away, but unfortunately we know virtually nothing about how the trade was organized. Did Herakleides of Tyre, who in 269 B.C. sold Apollo two elephant tusks weighing 1 talent, 32.5 *mnai,* and a fraction, for a grand total of 771 dr 5 ob, travel himself to Africa or the East for this ivory? Did he buy it on the Levantine coast, or was he a metic merchant established on Delos who found the tusks in a nearby market like Rhodos or Ephesos? There is no way to tell.[26] Wood provides another example. Wood bought for construction was chosen for its suitability for its purpose, whether beams or rafters or door frames, and the Delians sought it at the sources where it was available. As Russell Meiggs suggests, oak and fir were likely to have come from Makedon; the "Makedonian wood" of 274 B.C. probably conceals one or both of these varieties. Cedar, widely used on Delos, could only be obtained in Lebanon. But this alone does not prove that the Phoenicians who appear in the Delian accounts were engaged in this trade (*IG* XI 2.199A57, 78–79),[27] and neither can such high-weight, high-cost goods, demanded by the temple for quite specific purposes, for which no substitute would do, stand in for Delian trade in general, which in terms of volume must have concentrated far more on staples like grain, olive oil, firewood, and wine.

25. E.g., *IG* XI 2.287A43, 65, 73, *ID* 290.48, 372A74 (frankincense); *IG* XI 2.287A113–14, 203A71 (ivory).

26. *IG* XI 2.203A71; Jean-Paul Rey-Coquais, *Mélanges Beyrouth* 37 (1960–61): 250. Cf. also Rostovtzeff, *Klio* 30 (1937): 1–7.

27. Meiggs, 441–57, cf. Marasco, 144–45.

The second example centers on a family of Phoenicians from Arados. Iason son of Theogeiton was honored by the Delians for his services to the temple, the city, and individual Delians (*IG* XI 4.776). An exedra erected on Delos in the second half of the third century names eight members of the family, including a Sillis and Iason's son Straton (*IG* XI 4.1203). A Straton of Arados, probably this same man, donated a *phiale* to Apollo in 235 B.C.[28] M.-F. Baslez, arguing that Iason had lent money to the city of Delos and connecting a Straton involved in the transport of building stone for the temple with this family (*IG* XI 2.199A78–79), posited "a family enterprise whose members exercise complementary economic functions."[29] This family would thus attest both to the general role of Phoenicians as traders and bankers in the Hellenistic economy and to the ties of the Delian economy with the rest of the Greek world (for here we have trade, not in exotica like frankincense, but in something mundane and in great demand: building stone).

Unfortunately, Baslez's construction stands on foundations less secure than Straton's stone. In the first place, while she maintains that Iason was established on Delos, in fact the language of his decree makes it clear that he lived in Arados, not on Delos.[30] Second, she takes χρεία to mean "loan." But the decree is surely less explicit: συνεργε[ῖ μετὰ] πάσης προθυμίας ἐν οἷ[ς ἂν τυγχά]νωσι χρείαν ἔχον[τες], "he works with all enthusiasm among those who should happen to have need" (*IG* XI 4.776.15–17). This language could cover a multitude of needs, and cannot be invoked to prove that Iason lent Delos money. Third, while the attestations for Iason's family all date to after 250 B.C., and indeed in the case of his son Straton to 235 B.C., Straton the shipper was active in 274 B.C. Fourth, despite Baslez's assertion that the name Straton was not common on Delos, seven native Delians bore it in the third century alone.[31] This trading and banking family with roots both on Delos and in the Levant dissolves; it is much more likely that they were prominent Aradians whose dealings with Delos had political or religious significance. Clearly, Iason's family enjoyed high status on Delos and important relations with the city and its deity, but we cannot claim that these relations grew out of economic activity. Indeed, like almost all Delian proxeny decrees, Iason's emphasizes his devotion to the sanctuary and his great piety (cf. esp. ll. 5, 6–8). This statement should be

28. *ID* 313a9; for the date, see J. Tréheux, *EAC* 5 (1976): 89 n. 29.

29. M.-F. Baslez, *Studia Phoenicia* 5 (1987): 275–76, 281 n. 93.

30. *IG* XI 4.776, cf. ll. 9–15, esp. 14–15, τοῖς ἀφικνουμ[ένο]ις τῶν πολιτῶν of Delos.

31. *LGPN* I, s.v. Στράτων (26)–(28), (30), (31), (35), (36).

taken seriously. It was Delos's sanctity, not its economy, that generated the respect it received from all over the Greek world: Iason and his family fit this pattern.

In contrast, the people who can be identified positively as having benefited economically from their relations with Delos tend to come from a much more limited geographical setting. These people included not only traders, who have perhaps received more attention than they deserve, but also building contractors, renters of property, borrowers of money, bankers, and ordinary laborers.

ORIGINS OF PEOPLE ENGAGED IN ECONOMIC ACTIVITY ON DELOS

The sanctuary carried out an active building program, including not only the construction of new structures but also the repair and upkeep of existing buildings. As at most Greek temples, the Delians hired private contractors to carry out this work.[32] The accounts name almost a hundred contractors. Unfortunately, only in twenty-eight cases can we identify their origins. Of these, a total of twenty-one came from Kykladic islands or from Karystos on Euboia, which may be regarded as a Kykladic city for our purposes. Of the remaining seven, one came from Lemnos and one from Mytilene on Lesbos. One each are attested from Thebes, Korinthos, Knidos, Rhoiteion in Asia Minor (near Ilion), and Athens. Thus the vast majority of identifiable contractors came from the immediate Kykladic neighborhood.[33] Some of these men enjoyed long and profitable careers with the temple. For example, Nikon son of Nikokles of Syros signed contracts with Apollo by himself or in consortium with others, including other foreigners, from 304 to 269 B.C.; over these thirty-five years he collected at least 31,850 dr. It would not be surprising, given his income, if he were the metic Nikon who sponsored a comic chorus in 261 B.C.[34] Another

32. See, generally, Alison Burford, *The Greek Temple Builders at Epidauros* (Toronto, 1969).

33. Figures derived from a compilation of "entrepreneurs" from *ID Index*. Tréheux, 7, supposes that most contractors were foreigners, but this is far from assured when ethnics are absent.

34. *ID* 500; *IG* XI 2.145.10–11, 158A55–57, 161A55–56, A58–59, 165.6–7, 36–37 (the latter contract seems to have been embroiled in difficulties which may have led to a lawsuit, cf. 163Bg16–18), 199A24, 203B17–18, 219A57. Cf. Maurice Lacroix, *Rev. Phil.* 38 (1914): 329, with reservations. *IG* XI 2.114.16. The Nikon who appears doing labor personally for small payments is likely in my view to be a different person: *IG* XI 2.144A110, 111, B6; 148.69; 153.10–11; perhaps 157B4; 159A54, provision of a stele (but compare Kharisthenides in 147A19); 161A70–71, with his son; 163Aa13–14, perhaps also l. 59; 165.19 (?), 48; 161A49–50.

foreign contractor, Damasias son of Kypragoras of Paros, dedicated a *phiale* to Apollo, and Philandrides son of Ekhesthenes of Paros, who received 3,500 dr in 269 B.C. as a first payment on a contract to deliver marble for the theater, was declared *proxenos* and *euergetes* and awarded freedom from taxation (ἀτέλεια) and the right to own property. These honors may be connected with his gift of ἧρος (possibly a kind of earth) in the same year.[35]

Apollo owned agricultural estates and urban houses, which he rented out. Five foreigners are known to have rented estates. Four were from Rheneia (two may have been homonymous father and son); the other was a Kretan.[36] Some of the houses were rented to foreigners from the islands, including a Parian, a Theran, and perhaps a Tenian. A Phoenician appears as a guarantor in 192 B.C.; he must have enjoyed the right to own property. Another foreigner, Kleinodemos son of Lebotos of Siphnos, exercised his award of the right to buy property, perhaps after 167 B.C. under the new Athenian domination (although the grant of *enktesis* had been made under independence).[37]

The ability of these foreigners to serve as contractors and to rent property implies strong ties within the Delian community. The temple required as guarantors for all contractors and renters men who owned real property. Most Delians found their guarantors among their relatives; foreigners had

35. *ID* 502A24 with *IG* XI 2.150A6–8 (199B8 and other entries for the *phiale*, an ἀστερωτή, cf. *ID Index*, s.v.). *IG* XI 4.616; 2.203A95–96, A39–40. On the mysterious Parian ἧρος, cf. *IG* XI 2.144A72–73, with comm., p. 26; there it costs 37 dr. Marek, 274, suggests that Menestratos of Karystos, honored in *IG* XI 4.516 (with Lacroix, *BCH* 48 [1924]: 409), followed the same career as his father, the contractor Theophantos (*IG* XI 2.161A52).

36. *IG* XI 2.161A10–11, C120–25 (Kent, 331, no. 151); *ID* 353A7–8, 374Aa10–15 (Kent, 331, no. 152); *IG* XI 2.287A159–61 (Kent, 328, no. 111); *ID* 374A10–15, 399A81 (Kent, 337, no. 241); *IG* XI 2.161C111–15, 162A8, 199A4 (Kent, 335, no. 218). I reject Gnosidikos son of Herakleides as a foreigner (M. Lacroix in *Mélanges Gustave Glotz* [Paris, 1932], 2:519). Khion son of Lykophron falsely taken as a Khian by Th. Ch. Sarikakis in *Chios: A Conference at the Homereion in Chios* (Oxford, 1986), 128; he is gone from Th. X. Sarikakis, Χιακὴ Προσωπογραφία (Athens, 1989).

37. *IG* XI 2.161A24, 162A20 (Tolmides son of Leophon of Paros); 224A19–20 (Alexipolis [?] of Thera; not in Appendix IV below because his rent is missing); *ID* 459.35 (Pathon son of Euporion of Tenos) with 442B225 and Durrbach's note at p. 236; *ID* 400.11 with M.-F. Baslez, *Studia Phoenicia* 5 (1987): 280. *ID Index*, s.v. Ἀρκέων Σωτᾶ Κρῆς lists him as a Kretan (*IG* XI 2.199B94), but in fact he was the renter and former proprietor of a house (cf. Appendix IV, 2, "House that used to belong to Arkeon"), hence a Delian. Kleinodemos: *IG* XI 4.840 and *ID* 1408A, II.46 with M.-F. Baslez, *REG* 89 (1976): 351.

to have recourse to Delians.[38] The success of these foreigners in obtaining Delian guarantors bespeaks close ties of either wealth and friendship or—perhaps more likely—intermarriage and more distant kinship.[39]

Apollo served also as a bank, lending money to both private persons and to cities.[40] When the beneficiaries were not Delians, they were exclusively Kykladic. The best-preserved account of the fourth century, the so-called Sandwich Marble (*ID* 98 = *IG* II^2 1635 = Tod II.125), gives the interest paid on loans by thirteen neighboring states (including Karystos on Euboia) amounting to a borrowed capital of 260,600 dr, over 43 talents. Several other accounts over the period add to the picture. These loans should not be connected with "contributions" due under the Second Athenian Confederacy,[41] but with the chronic cash-flow problems of Kykladic states. Paros borrowed money in the fourth century; all three cities on Amorgos were forced to borrow in the fourth and third centuries; Ios likewise borrowed funds for various public purchases; and on Keos, Ioulis borrowed money in the third century, and another city, perhaps Karthaia, had to borrow pathetically small sums month to month.[42] Likewise individuals who borrowed from Delian Apollo during the Amphiktyonia came from Tenos, Karystos on Euboia, Andros, and Galessos on Syros.[43] During independence foreigners were essentially excluded from the bank: only two are known, one of whom, Apollodoros of Kyzikos, was *nesiarkhos* of the

38. All Delian guarantors at *ID* 500B14–16, 502A25. Vial, 292–301, esp. 293. Even the privileged Philandrides of Paros, who had been accorded ἔγκτησις (*IG* XI 4.616), must have used Delian guarantors, since the right to own property was restricted to himself.

39. For two families from Delos and Keos that use the name Pherekleides and may have been related, see Vial, 332–33, Stemma XXXIV. It was this problem of guarantors, and not lack of return (Lacroix in *Mélanges Glotz*, 519), that kept more foreigners from renting estates or houses.

40. Bogaert, 126–92.

41. Ibid., 126–30; Migeotte, 141–47, 151–56. Coupry in *Atti*, 64–66, has emphasized that the records do not correspond with the foundation and collapse of this organization—Mykonos, Paros, Syros, and some other unidentified states had borrowed by 393/2 B.C., and interest payments continued until at least 341/40 B.C.

42. Paros: *IG* XII 5.112 (= Migeotte, 213–15, no. 61), 113 (with Migeotte, p. 155); Amorgos: *IG* XII 7.5 (= Migeotte, 166–68, no. 48), 67B (= Migeotte, 168–77, no. 49), 69 (= Migeotte, 177–83, no. 50), 67A (= Migeotte, 183–87, no. 51), 66 (= Migeotte, 187–88, no. 52), 70 (= Migeotte, 188–89, no. 53), 68 (= Migeotte, 189–92, no. 54, with discussion at 192–94), 221 (= Migeotte 194–96, no. 55), 388 (= Migeotte, 196–98, no. 56); Ios: *IG* XII 5.1011 (= Migeotte, 210–12, no. 60); Keos, *IG* XII 5.1102 (= Migeotte, 218–21, no. 63), *IG* XI suppl. 236.

43. *ID* 98A20, 23, B15 (Tenos), B17 (Karystos), B18 (Andros), B19 and 104–9.11 (Syros).

Island League in the last decade of the fourth century and came about his debt by buying a garden already hypothecated to Apollo.[44] The other, Xenon of Hermione, who must have been granted *enktesis* like Apollodoros, had a native Delian guarantor, Teleson son of Autokles, a member of a rich and powerful family.[45]

Gifts to deities sometimes also reveal foreigners who made money off the temple; again, these people often came from neighboring islands. The Tenian Ktesias son of Apollodoros offered Osiris an ἀπαρχὴν ἀπὸ τῆς ἐργασίας δεκάτην and paid for construction for Sarapis, Isis, and Anoubis (*IG* XI 4.1248.3–4, cf. 1247); Roland Etienne regards him as settled on Delos engaged in commercial activity.[46] Citizens of Amorgos, Kerkyra, and Mylasa who likewise dedicated tithes were probably established in business on Delos (*IG* XI 4.1220, 1241, 1243). The Naxian Polymnestos son of Thibron honored at Delos may have donated a *phiale* to Apollo in the mid third century; whether his piety flowed from business interests, like the Khian Eutykhos's, cannot be determined.[47]

Identifying other foreigners who made money off the temple entails many difficulties. For modest laborers—masons, carpenters, smiths, haulers, and practitioners of countless other trades—the *hieropoioi* rarely give more than a simple name—Νικίαι ἐπισκευάσαντι θύραν ἐν τῶι Ἀφροδισίωι καὶ ὅσων προέδει ⊢⊢⊢ (*IG* XI 2.287A74)—and sometimes not even that: τὸγ κόπρον ἐξενέγκασιν ἐκ τοῦ ἱεροῦ μισθωτοῖς ΔΔ⊢⊢⊢ (*IG* XI 2.146A77). The same is true for the dozens of men who sold Apollo pigs or firewood or other goods. When their names appear, which is rarely enough, the *hieropoioi* almost never say whether they had imported the goods they sold, and even when we have a name, the rarity of patronymics and ethnics makes it almost impossible to sort out homonymous persons or to identify workers or traders with the same name in different years. For these reasons, many of the identifications offered by Maurice Lacroix rest on very fragile bases.[48]

44. G. Reger, *GRBS* 32 (1991): 229–37.

45. *IG* XI 2.161A35, D85–86. On the formula for payments by third parties with ὑπέρ as indicating payments by guarantors, see Bogaert, 148; on Teleson's family, Vial, 301–4.

46. Bogaert, 179; Etienne, 181 (cf. ibid., 180–81 for other Tenians at Delos, 182–83 for Delians at Tenos).

47. *IG* XI 4.701, cf. *ID* 298A12. On Eutykhos, see p. 71 below.

48. For example, his "family of dealers in wood" (*REG* 33 [1916]: 188–237) has been demolished by Jean-Paul Rey-Coquais, *Mélanges Beyrouth* 37 (1960–61): 249–54 (but still in Marasco, 138). I have not seen M.-F. Baslez, "Les Etrangers à Délos: Formes et évolution de la vie de relation dans un sanctuaire panhellénique" (diss., Université de Paris IV, 1982).

There is, however, some evidence. Two citizens of Thera worked for the temple on smallish projects; whether they were contractors in the sense discussed above is not clear. The first at any rate had a partner who was probably a Delian.[49] In 297 B.C., a Tenian mason was selected to engrave the contracts of contractors granted that year; *ID* 500 and 502 are his work (*IG* XI 2.150B8-10). In 250 B.C., a Khian—identified only thus, by a purchase παρὰ τοῦ Χίου—provided roof tiles (*IG* XI 2.287A113–14). An entry for 276 B.C. shows Astypalaians providing fine fabric (σινδόνες); their fellow citizens imported wood in 296 B.C.[50] One item of particular interest is pitch, which was used as a sealant on roofs, altars, and other structures exposed to moisture. We hear of importers from Khios, Klazomenai, Karystos, Naxos, and probably Byzantion.[51] The funeral monuments of Rheneia, which have yielded disappointingly few specimens from the years of independence, attest to two men from Paros and women from Thasos and Thera, the latter perhaps wives of Delians, as the family of Pherekleides on Delos seems to have had a Keian branch.[52] Finally, besides those already mentioned, there are another twenty-nine proxeny decrees for assorted islanders. Unfortunately, these decrees rarely give any indication of the benefits performed.[53]

The temple consumed Kykladic products. Besides the oil, wine, pigs, firewood, and grain that, I shall argue, came predominately from his neighbors, Apollo bought roof tiles from Syros and the mysterious ἦρος from

49. *IG* XI 2.161A66–68 (the partner Theodemos is not listed in *LGPN* I); 203A46.

50. *IG* XI 2.163A43, cf. also 156A41–42. We hear of Amorgian clothing under the Amphiktyonia, but the actual origin of the items is disputed, *ID* 104–26*bis*C7–11, with comm. p. 104. For a plant used to make red dye that may have been abundant on Amorgos, see G. M. A. Richter, *AJA* 33 (1929): 27, with 27–28 n. 4, on *Etymologicum magnum* 129.

51. *IG* XI 2.144A94 and 154A48, 203A47–48, 219A41, 144A112, 163A5.

52. Marie-Thérèse Couilloud, *Les Monuments funéraires de Rhénée* (Paris, 1974), no. 451, 88, 419. For the epitaphs of independence, see ibid., pp. 243–44, 307, with n. 3 there. The family of Pherekleides: Vial, 332–34. *BCH* 114 (1990) 812 reports the discovery of the funeral stele of one Kallistion of Paros at Rheneia; the name is not otherwise attested for the island (*LGPN* I, s.v.).

53. Andros, *IG* XI 4.833–34; Ikarios, 539, 811–12; Karystos on Euboia, 516, 673; Keos: Karthaia, 592 (cf. *IG* XII 5.544B2, 4, 1076.117, 135, and 610.22 perhaps for the family), 769, Keos only, 693 (doctor, cf. *IG* XII 5.820); Khalkis on Euboia, 706; Melos, 513, 749; Naxos, 552, 611, 656, 832; Paros, 841 (cf. *IG* XII 5.379); Pholeangros, 612; Seriphos, 639; Sikinos, 511, 688; Siphnos, 587, Syros, 591 (perhaps a relative at *IG* XII 5.652.1), 633 (doctor); Tenos, 655, 828; Thera, 709–10 (cf. *IG* XII 3.330.86).

Paros.[54] The cheese, wax, and *miltos* that appear in the accounts almost certainly came from close neighbors like Syros, Kythnos, Keos, and Rheneia.[55] Besides building stone quarried on Delos itself, the temple imported marble from Paros and Tenos.[56] Finally, it is worth noting that Karystos, Naxos, Keos, Mykonos, and Andros maintained treasuries (οἶκοι) on Delos.[57]

THE SCOPE OF DELIAN TRADE

Perhaps it is not surprising that the overwhelming majority of contractors and workers on Delos whose origin can be determined came from nearby islands, or that the beneficiaries of the Delian banks, whether sacred, public, or private, were neighbors. But (it will be objected) the preponderant role of locals in these sectors of the economy hardly eliminates from trade persons of more distant origin. And one category of Delian evidence speaks unequivocally of ties between Apollo's island and a widespread net of Greek cities: the proxeny decrees. Several hundred survive in better or worse states of preservation, passed in honor of citizens from all over the Greek world, from Lebanon and Palestine to Italy, from Kyrene to Olbia and Pantikapaion.[58]

These decrees are not easy to deal with. In the first place, unlike Athenian decrees of the same period, they have no dating formula; particularly frustrating is the absence in all but two cases of the name of an *arkhon*, which would have given a precise date. We are therefore reduced to guessing dates from the careers of the proposers and letter forms.[59] In

54. *IG* XI 2.161A73–75, cf. J. A. O. Larsen, *CP* 36 (1941): 156–66; for the ἦρος, *IG* XI 2.203A40, cf. 144A72–73, with comm. p. 26.

55. Cheese: *ID* 440A69, 445.14; wax: *IG* XI 2.154A36, 161A111, 287A54, 62, *ID* 316.84; *miltos: IG* XI 2.287A62; these lists are not complete. For honey from Syros and Kythnos, see Roufos in Oribasios, *Collectionum medicarum reliquae*, ed. Johannes Raeder, *Corpus medicarum graecarum*, vol. 6, pt. 1, fasc. 1 (Leipzig, 1928), ii.63; for bees as a type on Keian coins (both federal and city), see G. Reger and M. Risser in *Landscape Archaeology*, 305–17. For cheese from Keos, see Aiskhylides in Aelian 16.32; cheese from Rheneia and Kythnos, see chapter 7, n. 46.

56. *IG* XI 2.165.38, 47, 199A77 for stone quarried at Kestreion, evidently a site on Delos. Quarries are abundant on the island; see now Philippe Fraisse and Tony Koželj, *BCH* 115 (1991): 283–96. For Tenian and Parian marble, see *IG* XI 2.199A39, 203A70 and A95. Cf. Gustave Glotz, *REG* 32 (1919): 240–50.

57. Vallois, I.55–64, esp. 62–64.

58. *IG* XI 4.510–857. Marek, 71–73, 247–80. For a newly discovered part of *IG* XI 4.844, the proxeny decree for Apollonides of Khersonessos, see *BCH* 115 (1991): 722 and 723, fig. 4.

59. *IG* XI 4.576 (*arkhon*'s name lost), 769 of 180 or 176 B.C. For careers, see Vial, passim; on letter forms, G. Reger, *Historia* 43 (1994): 35–39.

the second place, individually they tend to be depressingly uninformative. Brief, formulaic, stripped of any detail, most simply give the Delian who moved the inscription, the honorand, his father's name, his ethnic, and a bald statement that the honorand "continues to be a good man concerning the temple and the city of the Delians and honors the temple on Delos and continues to do the Delians good" (ἀνὴρ ἀγαθὸς ὢν διατελεῖ περὶ τὸ ἱερὸν καὶ τὴν πόλιν τὴν Δηλίων καὶ τιμᾶι τὸ ἱερὸν τὸ ἐν Δήλωι καὶ ποιῶν εὖ διατελεῖ Δηλίους [*IG* XI 4.595.3–6]), or some equally colorless variant. Rarely are any specific benefactions named. For the majority of these decrees, we can say nothing about the honorand or his relations to Delos; in particular, as Christian Marek has observed, from proxenies alone we can neither affirm nor exclude economic relations. Of nearly 350 decrees known from Delos, only three were passed for persons certain or fairly certain to have been involved in commerce or trade, while I count 72 others passed for people involved in political, military, religious, civic, or artistic activities.[60] But usually we would have no idea why individuals were being honored without further evidence. The decree in favor of the famous Athenian Kallias of Sphettos says only that he was a "good man": not a word about his brilliant military exploits and court connections at the highest levels (*IG* XI 4.527; cf. Shear, passim). The same situation prevails for Dionysios son of Potamon of Naukratos, whose role in the Ptolemaic court is invisible in his Delian decree (*IG* XI 4.561; *OGIS* 724).[61]

Nevertheless, the uninformativeness of these documents has not stopped commentators from drawing economic inferences. Felix Durrbach went so far as to affirm that all proxeny decrees for citizens of Hellespontine states must have related to the trade in grain between Delos and the Black Sea; that Rhodian theoric visits had a commercial component; and that, even without explicit proof, the many decrees for Khians must have attested to an interest in Delian commerce.[62] It is therefore worthwhile to consider the implications of these documents. In general I want to explore two approaches. First, I want to consider what relations in fact lie behind

60. Marek, 71–73, for Delian decrees, with map facing p. 72, 332–81, esp. 359–64, on the economic function of *proxenoi,* with 359–60: "Handelsbeziehungen können zwar durch das Ethnikon des Honoranden allein ebensowenig ausgeschlossen wie unterstellt werden." Further, Christian Marek, *MBAH* 4.1 (1985): 67–78. *IG* XI 4.510–857 for the decrees; I exclude 858–1021 as too incomplete for analysis. Commerce or trade: *IG* XI 4.627 (= *Choix,* 46), 691 (= *Choix,* 43), 840 (cf. *ID* 1408A, II.46 and M.-F. Baslez, *REG* 89 [1976]: 351).

61. Cf. Bagnall, 153.

62. *Choix,* pp. 57–58 (followed by Vial, 341, Marasco, 131–32, with n. 30; criticized already by Casson, "Grain Trade," 174–76), 46, 36. Cf. also Nigdelis, Πολίτευμα και κοινωνία, 314.

the proxeny decrees. Many, we shall see, sprang from benefits in the political or religious spheres, not the economic. Second, specific regions that provide numerous decrees need to be considered for possible economic connections. There are some independent tests we can apply to these groups of documents to help ferret out such relations.

The Purposes of Individual Proxeny Decrees In some cases, it is possible to identify the honorand and guess the occasion for his award despite the silence of the decrees. Political activity often seems to lie behind the honors. Apollodoros of Kyzikos and Hermias, both *nesiarkhoi* of the Nesiotic League, resided on Delos and served as liaisons between the island and its outside *hegemones.*[63] Kallias son of Thymokhares of Athens commanded the Ptolemaic troops at Andros who participated in the liberation of Athens in 287 B.C. and oversaw the transfer on Delos of grain to representatives of the Athenian demos.[64] Demaratos son of Gorgion the Lakedaimonian, whose family had long-standing connections with Delos, represented Delian interests before Lysimakhos and his court (*IG* XI 4.542). The great Ptolemaic courtier Sostratos son of Dexiphanes received his honors in conjunction with a decree of the Nesiotic League, whose first few lines, although unfortunately mutilated and incomplete, nevertheless make it clear that he had taken some action beneficial to the league in conjunction with its then *nesiarkhos,* Bakkhon (*IG* XI 4.563 [= *Choix,* 22], 1038 [= *Choix,* 21]). Another Ptolemaic court official, Sosibios, may have been honored because he was on Delos in 246 B.C. to found a new Ptolemaic religious festival.[65] In other cases, such as that of Dikaios son of Diokles, the honorands may have facilitated access or a favorable hearing for Delian ambassadors at the hegemonic court (*IG* XI 4.631 [= *Choix,* 34], cf. esp. ll. 2–3). Representatives of many other monarchs appear, and with the turn of the century, Roman officials like Publius Cornelius Scipio take their place in the ranks of the honored.[66]

63. *IG* XI 4.562 (= *Choix,* 20), 565; cf. G. Reger, *GRBS* 32 (1991): 229–37. See Marek, 251–63, on political honorands; 263–69 on honorands connected with cult, etc.; and 269–75 on traders, bankers, and contractors.

64. *IG* XI 4.527; Shear; Christian Habicht, *Untersuchungen zur politischen Geschichte Athens* (Munich, 1979), 45–67; Michael J. Osborne, *ZPE* 35 (1979): 181–94.

65. *IG* X14.649 (*Choix,* 44), with Glotz, *REG* 29 (1916): 316 n. 7.

66. *IG* XI 4.649 = *Choix,* 44; 561 (with *OGIS* 724), 563 (= *Choix,* 22), 588 (cf. P. M. Fraser, *JRS* 39 [1949]: 56), 631 (= *Choix,* 34), 677 (Ptolemies); 585 (with W. Heckel, *ZPE* 70 [1987]: 161–62), 666 (= *Choix,* 48), 679–80 (= *Choix,* 47), and probably 681–82 (Antigonids); 765–66 (Attalids); 712 (Scipio).

In some cases, political connections may be suspected, not because of the names or origins of the honorands, but because of the name of the proposer of the honors. During the first third of the second century, one Telemnestos son of Aristeides dominated Delian politics; he was responsible for the passage of over seventy decrees, including one in honor of Herakleides son of Xeinias of Byzantion, who may have been the ambassador of Antiokhos III.[67] Telemnestos passed two decrees for Khians (*IG* XI 4.767 and 793) otherwise unknown. The decrees honoring Timon son of Nymphodoros, a banker on Delos who aided the Nesiotic League in the purchase of grain, and Tharsagoras son of Polykles of Siphnos, who had represented the league in the business, were also from his pen.[68] His many other decrees surely also flowed from political motivations.[69]

In every case about which we can say something, these "political" honorands obtained their honors either on account of local activities or because they had rendered assistance to Delian ambassadors at a foreign court. These honors imply no great, long-distance economic connections; rather, they reflect the quite parochial political worries of the Delians themselves. Furthermore, at least some of these men came to Delos primarily for religious reasons, perhaps including the dedication of monuments of thanksgiving, such as that of Attalos after his defeat of the Gauls in 241 B.C. or Antigonos Doson's dedication after his victory at Sellasia.[70] Or the honors may reflect simple acts of piety. Many of the decrees honoring citizens of individual cities must have been passed for *theoroi,* who visited Delos each year by the dozens, like Philodamos, a Rhodian *arkhitheoros* of around 280 B.C. (*IG* XI 4.614; cf. *IG* XI 2.161B17, 162B13). Asklepiodoros son of Kraton of Karystos is probably identical with the Asklepiodoros honored at Epidauros; perhaps he visited both sanctuaries as a *theoros?*[71] Kings, too, might send representatives for religious reasons, as in the case of Antigonos Gonatas honoring his sister Stratonike, who herself was ardently devoted to the Delian deities.[72] Some of the private persons who came for

67. Etienne, 107–10; M.-F. Baslez and C. Vial, *BCH* 111 (1987): 300–301; Vial, 279. *IG* XI 4.778, Polyb. 21.13.3, 14, 15.12, cf. *Choix,* p. 76.

68. *IG* XI 4.759 and 760, cf. *IG* XII 5.817.31 with *testimonium* 1349.

69. Cf. also Roland Etienne in *L'Etranger dans le monde grec* (Nancy, 1988), 164–66.

70. *IG* XI 4.1109 (= *Choix,* 53), 1110 with Holleaux, II.164 n. 1; *IG* XI 4.1097 = *Choix,* 51.

71. *IG* XI 4.605; W. Peek, *Inschriften aus dem Asklepieion von Epidauros* (Berlin, 1969), 67, no. 101.2.

72. Bruneau, 561–62; K. J. Beloch, *Griechische Geschichte* IV^2 (Berlin and Leipzig, 1927), 2.199–200. For her piety, see Bruneau, 546–50.

religious reasons include Ktesippos son of Ktesippos of Khios, who was *melanephoros*.[73] The Delians also honored tragedians, comic poets, artists, actors, musicians, philosophers, and athletes drawn to the island by its festivals.[74] Behind the hundreds of anonymous or unidentified honorands must lurk many others who came to the island for political or religious reasons. The cases in which it has been possible to suggest plausible noneconomic reasons for some individuals whose homes were far away to have been honored on Delos undermine any facile assumption even that a body of decrees honoring men who originated in one region, like the Black Sea, must reflect economic activity. Rather, these documents must be examined individually to see what, if any, reasons can be detected.

Decrees from Specific Geographic Regions and the Delian Economy

Two regions have often been pinpointed as having important commercial relations with Delos. Rhodos, which ruled the Kyklades in the first third of the second century (a fact that complicates the interpretation of the evidence), was both a great trading center and the source of the thousands of Rhodian amphorae found not only on Delos but elsewhere in the Greek world. Byzantion guarded the gateway to the Black Sea, whose resources included animals, slaves, honey, wax, and dried fish, and sometimes grain (Polyb. 4.38.4–5); the cities of the Hellespontos and of the Black Sea itself can be examined in the same context. In addition, it will prove enlightening to look at another site, much closer than either Rhodos or Byzantion, which sat at the end of the normal route of travel that ran from Athens through Delos to the East: Khios.

Rhodos. Seventeen proxeny decrees honoring Rhodians are known.[75] Four of them honor individuals involved in military activities.[76] Two more almost certainly have no economic aspect. Kleombrotos son of Leonides (*IG* XI 4.690) is listed in a catalogue of Delphic *proxenoi*, and another Rhodian who may be his son served in Delphi as a foreign judge (*SIG*^{3} 585.221;

73. *IG* XI 4.819–20, 1249–50, cf. M.-F. Baslez, *Chronique d'Egypte* 50 (1975): 297–303, with BE (1977): 316.

74. *IG* XI 4.544 (poet), 567, with 2.105.18 (actor, cf. Paulette Ghiron-Bistagne, *Recherches sur les acteurs dans la Grèce antique* [Paris, 1976], 360), 615 with 2.115.21 (actors), 572–73 (poets), 594 (artist), 646 (musicians), 613, 624 (philosophers), 744 (probably athlete). This list is far from exhaustive.

75. *IG* XI 4.580, 589, 596, 614, 648, 651, 683, 690, 711, 714, 751–55, 839, 842.

76. *IG* XI 4.596 (= *Choix*, 39), for a Rhodian *nauarkhos* and his *trierarkhoi;* 751 (= *Choix*, 67), for Epikrates, a fleet commander (cf. Livy 37.13.11, 14.1–2, 15.6); 752–53 (= *Choix*, 63), for Anaxibios, another military commander.

614). Kleombrotos's activities seem likely to have had a religious (or political) purpose. Even more intriguing is Praxon son of Aristonymos. Polybios (28.23.1) mentions a Rhodian embassy to Alexandria sent to reconcile Antiokhos IV and Ptolemaios Philometer, which, however, arrived too late to be of any use. It was headed by a Praxon. Unfortunately, Polybios does not give his patronymic. One other honorand, Philodamos, was *arkhitheoros*.[77] At least seven of the seventeen decrees honoring Rhodians have noneconomic explanations. This is particularly striking, since Rhodos's well-attested commercial interests ought to have made Rhodians prime candidates for business-related honors. But Rhodos also had noncommercial reasons for maintaining contact with other cities in the Greek world, and these reasons—piety and politics prominent among them—obtained for Delos as much as for any other city.[78]

The Hellespontos and the Black Sea. The one proxeny undoubtedly awarded for commercial reasons went to Dionysios of Byzantion, who was honored for supplying Delos with grain at a reasonable price (*IG* XI 4.627 = *Choix*, 46). As was also true of Rhodian merchants,[79] Dionysios's city of origin had nothing to do with the source of his goods. Athenian decrees provide abundant corroborating examples: the citizen of Kypros who imported grain from the Black Sea to Athens in the late fourth century; the Milesian who brought grain from Kypros; the Sicilian merchant who intended to sell olive oil (from Sicily?) in the Black Sea and buy grain to import to Athens. Dionysios's honors therefore do not have anything to say about commercial ties between Delos and Byzantion. Furthermore, many of the numerous decrees honoring citizens of Byzantion, Khalkedon, Lampsakos, Kyzikos, Abydos, Rhoiteion, Olbia, and Pantikaipon, like many of those honoring Rhodians, had noncommercial motivations.[80] The single decree for a Kyzikenos honored Apollodoros son of Apollonios, the *nesiarkhos* of the Island League. Kyzikos also had religious connections

77. *IG* XI 4.614, *IG* XI 2.161B17, 162B13.

78. Marek, 257–59 (with reservations); M.-F. Baslez and Claude Vial, *BCH* 111 (1987): 281–312. Other Rhodians whose honors may have had political or religious reasons: Praxidamos son of Arkhinomos, *Lindos*, I.87, ca. 267 B.C., *IG* XI 4.648; Anaxidikos son of Dionysios, coining official, 200–275 B.C., B. V. Head, *A Catalogue of Greek Coins in the British Museum*, vol. 18, *Caria and the Islands* (London, 1897), p. 253 no. 246; 754–55; Anaxibios son of Pheidianax, *JÖAI* 4 (1901): 164–66, no. III; 752–53 (= *Choix*, 63).

79. *IG* II^2 360.35–40, 407.6, 12, 903.6–9 with Philippe Gauthier, *REG* 95 (1982): 275–90, and *SEG* 32.132. Alain Bresson, *Index* 9 (1980): 144–49.

80. *IG* XI 4.510, 530, 570, 627 (= *Choix*, 46), 778, 779–80 (Byzantion); 618, 645 (Khalkedon); 518, 571, 708 (Lampsakos); 562 = *Choix*, 20 (Kyzikos); 517 (Abydos); 582 (Rhoiteion); 813–14 (Olbia); 609 (Pantikaipon).

with Delos, as two important decrees demonstrate.[81] Herakleides son of Xenias of Byzantion may be identical with the Herakleides of Byzantion sent by Antiokhos III to treat with Scipio in 190 B.C.[82] Th. Homolle conjectured that Metrodoros of Lampsakos (*IG* XI 4.708) was the man who captured Thasos for Philip V in 202 B.C., but as Pierre Roussel has pointed out, this must remain uncertain (*IG* XI 4, p. 37). Antiokhos son of Theodikos of Lampsakos, known from an unfortunately fragmentary Delian document (*IG* XI 4.518), was also honored at Eretria on Euboia (*IG* XII 9.216), although in language too vague to support any inferences about his benefactions. Finally, the decree for Herakleitos of Khalkedon (*IG* XI 4.618) honors him specifically for his accomplishments as a poet.

Potentially, then, five out of the sixteen documents honoring citizens of these Hellespontine or Black Sea cities reflect ties other than commercial ones. The results are not different from those obtained for Rhodos and do not support the contention that the interests of these cities in Delos were exclusively or primarily economic. It might be possible to argue that commerce lies veiled behind the bland language of the decrees were it not for the decree honoring Dionysios of Byzantion, which shows the Delians had no compunction about expressing economic benefactions quite bluntly. The rarity of business explanations in a very large corpus of decrees, however, cannot be attributed just to chance. Rather, we must assume that the Delians rarely had occasion to honor anyone with *proxenia* purely on the basis of his economic activities. This does not mean that merchants did not frequent Delos, or that the Delians did not benefit from their presence. But the Delians as a corporate body honored men for other benefactions, typically connected with either politico-military activities or generosity to the temple. Even for premier "trading states," this must have held true.

Khios. There are nearly as many decrees preserved for Khians as for Rhodians or for the Byzantines and their neighbors, and some positive evidence for trading by Khians on Delos exists. Khians supplied Apollo with pitch and roof tiles, and although it is hazardous to assume that Khians necessarily traded in Khian products, Khios did in fact produce pitch. Moreover, as we shall see in chapter 4, the islands off the coast of Asia Minor produced

81. *IG* XI 4.1027 and 1298, an oracle granted the Kyzikenoi by Apollo at Delphi; improved text at L. Robert, *BCH* 102 (1978): 466 (= *Documents d'Asie Mineure* [Paris, 1987], 162).

82. *IG* XI 4.778, Polyb. 21.13–15; cf. Eckart Olshausen, *Prosopographie der hellenistischen Königsgesandten. Teil I: von Triparadeisos bis Pydna* (Louvain, 1974), 193–94, no. 137, who does not, however, mention the possible identification (see Roussel, *IG* XI 4, p. 51); *Choix*, p. 76. Cf. Nymphaios of Byzantion, *IG* XII 5.802, with Etienne, 93, 187.

good grain crops. Delos may well have looked to them for supplies when the Kyklades suffered shortages, especially as the more easterly islands seem often to have escaped droughts that afflicted the central Aegean.[83]

When we look at the decrees, however, we find the same pattern as for Rhodos and Byzantion. One Khian was honored for religious reasons, another as a poet; a third, whose name appears on Khian coins, may perhaps have had political connections. A fourth, Kleandros son of Themistos, held a prominent position on Khios, where he served on a board to erect a statue honoring a Koan. (The Khians also honored Teleson son of Autokles, a member of one of Delos's richest families.)[84] The Khian Theon son of Straton, who dedicated two gold *phialai* in 195 B.C. or a little earlier, also set up a statue to his wife, Nikokleia daughter of Aristodemos.[85] A prominent family of Khians is also attested on Delos. The parents, Dexios son of Philon and Parmo daughter of Attinas, were honored by their sons Philon and Biottos with an exedra, and their daughter Parmo dedicated a frankincense burner to Apollo. Son Philon offered Apollo a chorus for the Deliades in 182 B.C. It is possible that the family had connections on Amorgos.[86] No evidence exists as to the nature of this family's involvement with Delos, but by analogy with Iason's family from Arados, whose dedications were very similar, we may suspect that Dexios and his relatives were wealthy Khians who expressed their piety on the sacred island.

Two Khians have very interesting proxeny decrees. Philistos son of Philistos received *ateleia, enktesis,* and *politeia* (with the right to choose his own phratry), *prodikia, asylia, ephodos,* and *proedria* (*IG* XI 4.547.10–17 = *Choix,* 28); the other, Polianthos son of Aristes, received *ateleia, proedria, politeia, enktesis,* and *prodikia* (*IG* XI 4.599.8–10, 13–14). The

83. *IG* XI 4.541, 547 (= *Choix,* 28), 572, 597–99, 628, 691 (= *Choix,* 43), 715 (?), 767, 793, 819–20. Polykrates of *IG* XI 4.604 is not a Khian; the X at l. 2 is the remnant of his patronymic (contra Sarikakis in *Chios,* 129), and in Sarikakis, Χιακὴ Προσωπογραφία, 383, no. 150. Traders: *IG* XI 2.144A94 (cf. Glotz, *REG* 26 [1913]: 27), 154A48 for pitch, 287A113–14 for roof tiles. On trade in "home products," see Meiggs, 424, 437, and 438, who assumes that traders from Krete, Knidos, and Samos were automatically bringing Kretan, Knidian, and Samian products (*IG* IV^2 1.102.26; *IG* II^2 1672.8, 14–16). For Khian pitch (called "mastic"), see Dioskourides 1.77.

84. *IG* XI 4.819–20, 572, 599 (with comm. p. 18), 597, with *SEG* 18.333.12, and G. Dunst, *Klio* 37 (1959): 66; 1022, with Vial, 302–3.

85. *ID* 442B74–75, cf. 1429A, II.10, 1432Aa, I.38; *IG* XI 4.1195.

86. *IG* XI 4.1197–98; the daughter at *ID* 1417A, II.128–29; Philon's chorus at 407.21 *IG* XII 7.84: Σιληνὸ[ς] Αὐτοκλ[έ]ος, Παρμὼ Δεξίου τὸν υἱὸν Αὐτοκλῆν Εἰλειθυίηι. But if this inscription really dates to the third century, this Parmo is too early to be the Khian Dexios's daughter.

award of *politeia* is rare on Delos, that of *prodikia* unexampled except in these two inscriptions, and that of *asylia* to an individual known only from Philistos's award. Christian Marek proposes that this mix of privileges, which cannot be coincidental, points to metics established on Delos, for whom *prodikia* and *asylia* would be particularly useful "if they were entangled in legal conflicts on Delos and their possessions were threatened with seizure."[87] But as we shall see below, the Delians did not grant *prodikia* or *politeia* to persons definitely settled on Delos as metics. The analysis must also take into account the award of citizenship, *politeia.* This rare privilege normally went to men who had high political connections with Delos's *hegemones:* the Antigonid *nesiarkhos* Apollodoros of Kyzikos; Sostratos of Knidos, the great Ptolemaic court official; and Dikaios of Kyrene, another Ptolemaic official.[88] This makes it very likely that despite our ignorance of the exact circumstances of these Khians' awards, they played some very important political role, probably in connection with one of the great hegemonic powers.

In fact, as for Byzantion, Khios can boast only one citizen whose commercial interests on Delos are unequivocally attested. Eutykhos son of Philotas was a banker resident on Delos who financed shipping: Εὔτυχος Φιλώτου Χῖος, οἰκῶν ἐν [Δή]λωι καὶ συνεργαζόμενος ἀπὸ τοῦ δικαίου [τοῖς τὴν θά]λατταν πλέουσιν (*IG* XI 4.691.4–6 = *Choix,* 43). In 230 B.C., or a little earlier, he established a festival, the Εὐτυχεία, with a capital of 3,500 dr, and in 196 B.C. he dedicated a silver *phiale* to Apollo.[89]

Once again, the ties between the citizens of Delos and Khios are religious and political obligations, not commercial ones. The "international" importance of Delos derived from its religious position, which in turn entailed certain political consequences; its location on routes between Greece and Asia also had consequences, but neither of these circumstances led to the development of a great trading center on the island. Comparison with neighboring Tenos, which like Delos had an important sanctuary, corroborates these results. A large number of Tenian proxenies were awarded for political or religious reasons. Those with religious implications—the award or renewal of *asylia* for the temple—had the greatest geographical reach, although they also included important neighbors like the Kretans, whose avidity for piracy made their acceptance especially important. The political

87. Marek, 249.

88. *IG* XI 4.562.14 = *Choix,* 20 with Reger, *GRBS* 32 (1991): 229–37; 563.11 = *Choix,* 22; 631.19–20 = *Choix,* 34. Cf. *Choix,* p. 37.

89. *ID* 320B58, 396A30, 442B71–72, 425.15. Cf. E. Schulhof, *BCH* 32 (1908): 107–8; E. Ziebarth, *Hermes* 32 (1917): 430; M.-F. Baslez, *REG* 89 (1976): 352; Marasco, 140–41.

proxenies show less geographical range; Athens, Rhodos, and Rome figure prominently. Very few can be identified as having certain commercial causes. Roland Etienne's concluding remark on Tenian economic activity applies equally to all the Kyklades: "The activities of the Tenians who lived on Delos show that economic motives are no less important for the movement of persons at a short distance in the Kykladic area than on a greater scale," with decided emphasis, however, on the "short distance."[90]

Grants of Privileges and the Role of Honorands Typically, the Delians granted their proxenies a mix of privileges that often included freedom from taxes (ἀτέλεια), access to the *boule* and demos first after religious matters (ἔφοδος, πρόσοδος), the right to own property (ἔγκτησις), and front-row seats at religious festivals (προεδρία). More rarely they awarded freedom from seizure (ἀσυλία), access to courts (προδικία), the right to be taxed like a Delian (ἰσοτέλεια), and citizenship (πολιτεία).[91] Although many decrees also included the formula that "there is to exist for them [sc. the honorands] also the other privileges that have been given to the other *proxenoi* and *euergetai* of the temple and the Delians" (ὑπάρχειν δὲ αὐτοῖς καὶ τὰ ἄλλα ὅσα δέδοται καὶ τοῖς ἄλλοις προξένοις καὶ εὐεργέταις τοῦ τε ἱεροῦ καὶ Δηλίων, or a variant [*IG* XI 4.745.23–27]), it is certain that this language did not automatically entail other privileges than those specifically stated; the language of *IG* XI 4.623 makes this clear: "they [i.e., the honorands] are to be given on Delos everything that has been given to other *proxenoi* and *euergetai* of the temple and the Delians and access to the *boule* and demos first after religious matters" (δεδόσθαι αὐτοῖς ἐν Δήλωι πάντα ὅσα καὶ τοῖς λοιποῖς προξένοις καὶ εὐεργέταις τοῦ ἱεροῦ καὶ Δηλίων δέδοται καὶ πρόσοδον πρὸς τὴν βουλὴν καὶ τὸν δῆμον πρώτοις μετὰ τὰ ἱερά, ll. 5–12). Since real differences subsisted among privileges given to different honorands (as in the case of the award of *politeia,* as discussed above), the possibility arises that we could identify persons engaged in trade or commerce from the privileges granted to them.

Unfortunately, this approach is fraught with difficulties. It might be thought, for example, that freedom from taxes (ἀτέλεια) would be particularly attractive to traders; on that assumption, the Sikinetan Kleagoras, awarded freedom from taxes and an invitation to a public dinner whenever

90. Etienne, 173–95, esp. 189–94, quotation 194–95.

91. *IG* XI 4.547 (= *Choix,* 28); 599; 627 (= *Choix,* 46); 547, 562 (= *Choix,* 20), 563 (= *Choix,* 22), 599, 631.

he was in town, makes a good candidate for a trader.[92] But in *IG* XI 4.573, which honors the comic poet Eukles of Tenos, the only named privilege is freedom from taxes. There is therefore no clear connection between this privilege and trade; indeed, the only unambiguous trader awarded a proxeny was granted not *ateleia* but ἰσοτέλεια, along with *enktesis* and *prosodos* (*IG* XI 4.627). We have three proxenies for bankers that include their privileges; Timon of Syracuse and Mantineus of Tenos received *enktesis* and *prosodos*, but Theon, whose benefactions to the Delians are obscure compared to his compatriots, was given *proedria* in addition.[93] The Parian contractor Philandrides was granted *ateleia* and *enktesis*, but Menestratos of Karystos, whose father was the contractor Theophantos, obtained *ateleia, proedria, enktesis,* and *prosodos.*[94] Not only is there no consistency in privileges within these groups, but each of these mixes of privileges can be paralleled for persons honored for political or religious reasons. Herakleides of Pergamon, an official of Eumenes II's, received *ateleia, proedria, enktesis,* and *prosodos,* just like Menestratos; Dionysios of Naukratos, likely a Ptolemaic official, received *ateleia* and *enktesis,* just like Philandrides; Nikomakhos the Athenian comic poet received *proedria, enktesis,* and *prosodos* like Theon; and Nabis, king of Sparta, had to be satisfied with only *enktesis* and *prosodos,* like Timon and Mantineus.[95]

M.-F. Baslez suggests that persons granted the right to own property on Delos, but no strictly honorary privileges, like *proedria,* or commercial ones, like *ateleia,* were foreigners coming to live on Delos; the increase in numbers of such awards in the second century would then attest to a growing metic population.[96] In fact, the disappearance of *ateleia* cannot be connected to any such phenomenon. As we have already seen, awards of particular privileges were not tied to the activities or status of the honorand. Rather, the kinds of honors typically awarded changed over time. In the decrees of the late fourth and third centuries, the Delians normally awarded explicitly *ateleia, proedria, prosodos* to the *boule* and demos, and *enktesis,* and they often also indicated that all other privileges granted to *proxenoi* and *euergetai* were granted to the individual in question as well (e.g., *IG* XI 4.513.16–19). Only rarely is one or another of these privileges

92. *IG* XI 4.511, restoring Σικ[ινήτης] at l. 7. Cf. also *IG* XI 4.534. On *ateleia* and trade, cf. Marasco, 163–64.

93. *IG* XI 4.759, 763–64, 779–80; cf. Marek, 272–73.

94. *IG* XI 4.616, 516 with Lacroix, *BCH* 48 (1924): 409; Marek, 274–75.

95. *IG* XI 4.583, cf. *IvPerg* 157A1; *IG* XI 4.561, cf. *OGIS* 724 and Bagnall, 153; *IG* XI 4.638 with Marek, 265 and 430 n. 329; *IG* XI 4.716 (= *Choix,* 58).

96. M.-F. Baslez, *Studia Phoenicia* 5 (1987): 276, *REG* 89 (1976): 351–52.

omitted, for reasons unrecoverable to us. But sometime between about 230 and 200 B.C., the Delians began to leave out certain privileges, sometimes *ateleia* (*IG* XI 4.667, 681, 693, 699, 701), sometimes *proedria* (*IG* XI 4.656, 699). By the early second century an entirely new formula developed, in which honorands were normally granted explicitly only *enktesis* and *prosodos.* Occasionally decrees from this period explicitly awarded *proedria* in addition to *prosodos.*[97] Baslez's view implies that the addition of *proedria* guarantees a truly "honorary" decree, as opposed to those intended to entice metics to settle on Delos by awarding *enktesis.* But in fact the presence or absence of an explicit grant of *proedria* looks arbitrary. Why would the Delians refuse *proedria* to Nabis, king of Sparta, and the banker Timon, who helped grain buyers for the Nesiotic League, while granting it to a Spartan official, a representative of Eumenes II, and a doctor from Halikarnassos?[98]

Moreover, it is very difficult to see how the award of *enktesis* is supposed to reflect the influx of persons wanting to live on Delos when every single decree passed after 200, and all but four passed before 200, contained this provision.[99] These include decrees honoring men who would never live on Delos, like Nabis of Sparta and the Pergamene court official Demetrios son of Apollonios. Indeed, there is positive evidence that the award of *enktesis* cannot really have helped metics to settle on Delos. Two of the honorands awarded *enktesis* are explicitly said to have been living on Delos for a long time.[100] The grant of *enktesis* was not their inducement to stay on the island, for they had clearly already committed themselves to that, but rather their reward for benefactions to the Delians and their god. The bankers provide a good example. Timon, Mantineus, and Theon all did business with the temple; Eutykhos may well have been honored for his establishment of a sacred fund.[101] Proxeny decrees expressed recognition by the Delians of people who had benefited the city and temple; those benefactions may sometimes have been financial or commercial, but the decrees themselves were not passed as inducements to economic activity, but for good works. Christian Marek has sensibly written: "Generally, foreigners became proxenoi who lived on Delos and were active in the branches of the

97. *IG* XI 4.717, 765, 769, 775, 777, 825, 826, 842.

98. *IG* XI 4.716 (= *Choix*, 58), 759, 717, 765, 775.

99. Absent from *IG* XI 4.511, 573, 623, 636; it should probably be restored in 534 and 842.

100. *IG* XI 4.759.6 (= *Choix*, 66), [δι' ἐ]τῶν ἐπι [δημῶν] ἐν Δήλωι; 789.6–7, παρεπιδημῶν ἐν τεῖ πόλει πλείω χρόνον.

101. Cf. Marek, 273–74, with further references.

economy typical for the island. They attained this honor in most cases because they had done a benefit to the polity of Delos and to the temple; their occupation gave them the opportunity, and they were able to afford it because of their wealth."[102]

The Ancient Economy and Regionalism

If Delos cannot be regarded as a center of a pan-Hellenic trade, where prices were regulated by a general Aegean market, the existence of a general Aegean market is itself called into question. This problem is inextricably connected with larger issues in the ancient economy, including the nature of trade, the character of polis demand, and the relation between partly or largely closed local economies and the pan-Mediterranean trade in staples and luxuries.

I cannot do more here than adumbrate some of the implications of my study for these problems and outline my sympathies in the larger issues, which have been and continue to be vigorously debated.[103] The idea that the Hellenistic Aegean saw an extensive price-setting market has appealed to many scholars. Fritz Heichelheim argued forcefully for it in his *Wirtschaftliche Schwankungen.* Johannes Hasebroek accepted it implicitly in *Trade and Politics* when he wrote that "the great cleavage in ancient economic development comes with the beginning of the Hellenistic age. The importance of this *caesura* is much greater than has been supposed; and the remarkable economic progress achieved by this age cannot be duly appreciated until it is recognised how many of its characteristics were still absent in the fourth century."[104] Michael Rostovtzeff, whose formulations

102. Marek, 274.

103. For some recent work with bibliography, see Elizabeth Lyding Will, *Rei cretorice romanae fautorum acta* 26 (1987): 71–77; Lutz Neesen, *MBAH* 4.1 (1985): 49–66; H. W. Pleket, *MBAH* 3.1 (1984): 3–36; C. R. Whittaker, *Opus* 4 (1985): 49–76; P. W. de Neeve, *Opus* 4 (1985): 77–110; M. M. Austin and P. Vidal-Naquet, *Economic and Social History of Ancient Greece: An Introduction* (Berkeley, 1977); Peter Garnsey and C. R. Whittaker, eds., *Trade and Famine in Classical Antiquity* (Cambridge, 1983); M. I. Finley, *The Ancient Economy*^{2} (Berkeley, 1985); Domenico Musti, *L'economia in Grecia* (Rome and Bari, 1981); Peter Garnsey, Keith Hopkins, and C. R. Whittaker, eds., *Trade in the Ancient Economy* (Berkeley, 1983); Marasco, 125–81; Dominic Rathbone, *Economic Rationalism and Rural Society in Third-Century A.D. Egypt* (Cambridge, 1991), passim; Edmund M. Burke, *TAPA* 122 (1992): 199–226. This list is by no means exhaustive.

104. Johannes Hasebroek, *Trade and Politics in Ancient Greece,* tr. L. M. Fraser and D. C. MacGregor (London, 1933), vi.

are generally qualified and nuanced, also presupposed a large-scale price-setting market in his claims that in the world of Alexander the "demand for Greek goods of special types was large, the buying capacity of the market was continually increasing" and that "the successful efforts of the Hellenistic kings to intensify production . . . [led to] a steady fall of prices in the Aegean Sea."[105] His far more cautious remarks specific to Delos are worth quoting at length:

> Since Delos was a centre of commerce closely connected with Rhodes and Alexandria, we may safely assume that the fluctuation of prices in Delos reflects the movement of prices in the rest of Greece. But I hesitate to draw far-reaching conclusions from curves of prices at Delos based on statistical data that are far from complete. We know too little of the general history of the Aegean world in the third century and more especially of the history of Delos to be able to determine the causes of the fluctuations. It seems, however, reasonable to ascribe the gradual stabilization and fall of prices between 270 and 250 B.C. to the Ptolemaic hegemony in the Aegean. With the downfall of this hegemony there was a recurrence of trouble and prices began to rise. It is likewise reasonable to assume during the period 270–250 B.C. a certain correspondence between prices in Egypt and in the Aegean, particularly as regards grain and papyrus. We may perhaps see a certain relation between the prices of pitch, tar, timber and the vicissitudes of the Macedonian kings. Farther than this I hesitate to go.[106]

Despite the qualification and hesitancy, Rostovtzeff continues to see a limited Aegean price-setting market, operating only for certain goods at certain times and in certain parts of that world.

In *The Livelihood of Man,* Karl Polanyi argued that this price-setting

105. M. Rostovtzeff, *AHR* 41 (1935–36): 235, 239–40; cf. Rostovtzeff, II.1026–1312.

106. Rostovtzeff, 235–36. Thirty-five years later, the views of Rostovtzeff, Heichelheim, and others continue to frame interpretation of the Delian prices. For Edouard Will's view, see below; in her recent study of the Delian community, Claude Vial cites several of the publications I have mentioned, and remarks, "Ces études [of the Delian economy] ont l'intérêt de comparer les faits déliens aux faits du reste du monde hellénique, ce qui améliore la compréhension des uns et des autres, et de replacer certains phénomènes économiques déliens dans leur contexte réel, le monde égéen et méditerranéen" (Vial, 283–84). Oddly, she neglects Heichelheim, who went the farthest in trying to set "[les] phénomènes économiques déliens dans leur contexte réel, le monde égéen et méditerranéen."

market was the invention of Kleomenes of Naukratis, the man Alexander had left behind to govern Egypt after his own departure for the East. Polanyi defended Kleomenes from what he regarded as slanderous later opinions and hailed him as "surely one of the greatest and most influential men of the Alexandrian period." His great accomplishment was to create a "'world' grain market" (Polanyi's quotation marks) in which "[f]or the first time, the prices in the various Greek cities were closely related to one another on a consistent basis; we can speak here of a true market price for the eastern Mediterranean, with supplies being moved according to price ratios."[107] Polanyi's main evidence for this view—aside from the anecdotes in the pseudo-Aristotelian *Oikonomikos*—is the famous description of Kleomenes' trade network in the speech *Against Dionysodoros* ([Demos.] 56). The speaker is prosecuting Dionysodoros and his business partner Parmeniskos for violating the terms of a bottomry loan of 3,000 drachmas, which the speaker and his partners had lent on the condition that the ship return to Athens. Instead, the ship discharged its cargo (of grain, as becomes apparent) at Rhodos, left for Egypt, picked up another cargo, and returned to Rhodos (56.3):

> Parmeniskos sailed on the ship, while this one [i.e., Dionysodoros] waited here. For, gentlemen of the jury, they were—so that you should not be unaware of this fact—all underlings and operatives of Kleomenes who was in charge of Egypt. Since the time he took over the office he has done no little harm to your city, and even more to the other Greeks, by reselling and manipulating the prices of grain, both himself and those with him. For some of them send money to Egypt, others sail to the ports, and others who stay in them distribute the dispatched goods. Moreover those who stay put send letters about the current prices [τὰς καθεστηκυίας τιμάς] to those who are away, so that, if grain is expensive among you, they convey it here, but if it becomes cheaper, they sail down to some other port. Hence not least, gentlemen of the jury, has the grain business been price-rigged by means of such letters and cooperation. Now when they sent the ship out from here, they left with grain relatively expensive. That's why they allowed it to be written in the contract that they were to sail to Athens and not into any other port. But afterwards, gentlemen of the jury, when Sicilian imports came and the price of grain dropped and these men's ship arrived in Egypt, this man [i.e., Dionysodoros] straightaway sent somebody to Rhodos to report to his associate Par-

107. Karl Polanyi, *The Livelihood of Man* (New York, 1977), 238–51, quotations at 240, 241, 249–50.

> meniskos the current conditions at home [τὰ ἐνθένδε καθεστηκότα], knowing that it would be necessary for the ship to put in at Rhodos.

Parmeniskos received the message and, in full contempt of the contract, unloaded his cargo at Rhodos and sold it (56.10). The result of this arrangement, for Polanyi, was to create at Rhodos a grain price that "would tend to reflect the average prices in the Greek cities, i.e., the Rhodian price would tend to be a 'world' market price, the various local prices tending to differ by the amount of transport charges."[108]

Several problems emerge. However much Dionysodoros's creditor abhorred the system in which his opponent participated—and we must always bear in mind that we are confronted here with a forensic speech—even he would have had to admit that there were many traditional elements in it. Nothing was more common in the fourth century, and indeed long before, than the dispatch of ships and money from a consuming center like Athens to a producing one like Egypt for the purpose of buying grain to bring home.[109] One of the speaker's main fears, in fact, is, not of "market manipulation," but of his exposure, as a resident of Athens who has lent money for the purchase of grain, to prosecution for failure to ship that grain to Athens.[110]

Furthermore, no indication emerges from the plaintiff's case that a general price-setting market developed. The plaintiff does not complain that an Aegean grain price had emerged, which differed from place to place by the cost of transport, but that Kleomenes "has done no little harm to your city, and even more to the other Greeks, by reselling and manipulating the prices of grain": that is to say, Kleomenes schemed to *raise* prices. The *Oikonomikos* reports explicitly the same objective in Kleomenes' plan to buy up all Egyptian grain direct from producers and to sell it to foreigners at the outrageous fixed price of 32 dr (*Oik.* 2.33e, 1352b14–20). The context of this activity, like Dionysodoros's, was the great famine of 330–326 B.C., which gave Kleomenes the opportunity—as the author of the *Oikonomikos* explicitly tells us—to intervene.[111] The "great harm" Kleomenes is alleged to have perpetrated should be sought in his price-fixing—as indeed the plaintiff plainly states. In this Kleomenes stands at the head

108. Ibid., 249.

109. For a recent discussion, see Paul Cartledge in *Trade in the Ancient Economy,* 1–15.

110. [Demos.] 34.37, 35.50. Briefly, Douglas M. MacDowell, *The Law in Classical Athens* (Ithaca, N.Y., 1978), 158.

111. [Arist.] *Oik.* 2.33a, 1352a16–23. Cf. André Wartelle's remarks in the Budé edition, p. 31 n. 1.

of a long line of Hellenistic "price-fixers" in times of famine, among whom large landowners figured prominently.[112]

Moreover, Kleomenes' "distribution scheme," if I may call it that, seems to have required not a general price-setting market but a large number of relatively independent local markets. The operation exploited the difference between prices at relatively close range. These price differences were not simply the result of differing transportation costs, since otherwise there would have been no higher profit in moving the grain. On the arrival of a grain shipment from Sicily, prices in Athens crashed—proof enough that prices in the Peiraieus were set in the Peiraieus, not at Rhodos. A general price-setting market would have defeated Kleomenes, whose only apparently new element, it would seem, was his communication network: "Those who stay put send letters about the current prices [τὰς καθεστηκυίας τιμάς] to those who are away, so that, if grain is expensive among you, they convey it here, but if it becomes cheaper, they sail down to some other port." These prices represented real differences between independent or semi-independent local markets, where prices were set locally and were relatively impervious to the impact of price changes elsewhere.

The small scale of the trade is also striking. Dionysodoros and Parmeniskos, like so many other traders, have but one ship. The plaintiff depicts them as Kleomenes' creatures, but they depended on Athenians for financing. Their ties to Kleomenes' system may have been no more than that they bought their grain in Egypt and used other merchants to move around information about price changes in Athens. And the decision to winter at Rhodos may have been determined in part by the fact that it was possible to sail between there and Alexandria even in winter; goods could be stockpiled on Rhodos to be ready for transshipment as soon as the weather cleared in the spring.[113]

Finally, the outcome of this sordid business is worth stressing. At news of low prices at Athens as a result of the unexpected arrival of grain ships from Sicily, the traders completely abandoned their plans, and Parmeniskos unloaded his goods at Rhodos. This illustrates for us, as for the ultimate purchasers and consumers of the grain, the unreliability of the supply network, and helps to explain the concern that so many states show in the Hellenistic period about assuring grain supplies. If a major consumer like Athens could be so victimized, it is easy to imagine how little pull a small city like Delos or its Kykladic neighbors would have. Chance variations in

112. Pleket, *MBAH* 3.1 (1984): 3–36.
113. M. Zimmermann, *ZPE* 92 (1992): 212–13.

price could drive suppliers quite suddenly away. The whole crucial matter of food supply must therefore have involved a great degree of uncertainty, which in turn would make the Delians and their neighbors strive for self-sufficiency, or at least the ability to supply oneself from sources known, local, and therefore easier to control.

Generally speaking, discussions of markets in the Hellenistic economy have not shown much sophistication. A large-scale, long-range, unified price-setting market for a good like grain requires the reliable exchange of local price information, available to all participants; reliable, reasonably quick transportation to respond to local changes caused by local conditions; redistribution and storage centers; and indifference on the part of consumers as to the origin of the goods they buy and on the part of producers as to the ultimate destination of their products. The Hellenistic Aegean met only some of these conditions, only in part, and only some of the time. The prosecution of Dionysodoros certainly shows that some merchants attempted to exchange price information. But that information was clearly only partial and tended to arrive only slowly; by the time it reached an interested trader, it might already be obsolete. Parmeniskos sold his cargo at Rhodos in response to news that prices had collapsed at Athens, *not* because prices were highest at Rhodos. The difference is important, for Parmeniskos's information was only partial. He knew prices were poor at Athens, but he evidently did not know where they were better, or else he surely would have sailed there to sell the grain. This circumstance gains interest for us when we recall that Dionysodoros and Parmeniskos were operating in the context of the very widespread grain shortage of 323/2 B.C.[114] The speech really only demonstrates the transmission of information about prices at Athens; the more general claim of the plaintiff that "those who stay put send letters about the current prices [τὰς καθεστηκυίας τιμάς] to those who are away, so that, if grain is expensive among you, they convey it here, but if it becomes cheaper, they sail down to some other port" is not only not substantiated, but apparently contradicted by the narrative the speaker himself provides.

The other conditions such a market requires are likewise only partially or conditionally met. Transportation clearly constituted a serious problem. The huge grain ships attested to by Moskhion and Lucian were rarities, and the bloated demand of an overpopulated Rome that made them necessary had no counterpart in the Hellenistic Aegean, not even in Athens.[115]

114. Garnsey, 154–62.
115. Casson, *Ships*, 184–89.

The constraints of the sailing season, which largely confined the movement of goods to the months between May and October, forced traders to do most of their buying and selling at a time of year when prices were often least favorable (the grain harvest fell in May–June). Although we know precious little about these aspects of the trade, there were certainly some redistribution and storage points in the Aegean—Rhodos being the most prominent—but for many poleis, including Athens and Delos, the point of attracting grain was not to export elsewhere but to supply local needs. Finally, there was a strong prejudice in the ancient world in favor of civic *autarkhy:* the notion that a polis ought to be self-sufficient to the extent possible, especially in foodstuffs. People preferred locally produced goods, and poleis worked to try to assure crops sufficient to feed their own populations.[116]

It turns out, then, that some evidence cited in favor of a general Aegean market in fact speaks against it. The interpretations of Delian economic history offered in the following chapters proceed in the same direction. This is not to deny the existence of long-distance trade in staples as well as luxuries, but rather to put that trade in perspective. The scale of pan-Mediterranean and pan-Aegean trade was small; and when Delos's role grew in the late third and second centuries, it was not to become "plus qu'un centre de redistribution pour la région centrale de l'Archipel,"[117] but rather to assume its full role as exactly that: a center of redistribution for the Kyklades.

Perhaps the best test of this view is the contention, first argued by Heichelheim, that high Delian prices around 314–270 B.C. reflect demand for Greek goods by new settlers in the Greek East. As we shall see in chapter 5, this claim rests in fact on only a handful of prices for olive oil (high estate rents in 314–290 B.C. must be attributed to completely different causes, as I show in chapter 6). Since no other goods show elevated prices, the notion of a general inflation because of high eastern demand—I leave aside the "flood of bullion" from Alexander's conquests, which also proves to have no connection with price changes (see chapter 7)—becomes untenable. There are better explanations for the high olive prices, which do not require a world market and have support both in the Delian documents themselves and in the political situation in the central Aegean in the late

116. As one example out of dozens, consider the lengthy struggle between Priene and Samos over the possession of agricultural territory on the mainland, Plut. *Mor.* 295f–296b, *IvPriene* 37 = *SIG*³ 599.

117. Vial, 341.

fourth and early third centuries.[118] The other economic phenomena on independent Delos will also be seen to be most easily explained by appeal to local conditions and a strictly limited local market.

118. Heichelheim, *Wirt. Sch.*, 55–56; Rostovtzeff, 158–59; see esp. Larsen, 380: "It is well known that the flood of currency let loose by Alexander the Great caused a general rise in prices." Rostovtzeff, 165–66, dissents somewhat from this view, attributing the main cause of the general rise in prices under Alexander and the Epigonoi to a "rapid increase in the demand for Greek commodities both for home consumption and export," with the infusion of Persian money as a subsidiary cause. On Alexander's foundations, see—magno cum grano salis!—Plut. *De fort. Alex.* 1 (*Mor.* 328E); App. *Syr.* 57.

Chapter 4

The Grain Supply of Delos and the Delian Grain Trade

As for every other Hellenistic polis that could not grow enough grain to satisfy local demand,[1] it was essential for Delos to supply its own requirements through a healthy and secure *import* trade. Interest in the import trade is well known for the cities of the Hellenistic period, and has recently received considerable attention.[2] For Delos, however, this aspect of Hellenistic statecraft has been almost entirely neglected.[3] An appreciation of the role of imports in the local economy presupposes estimates of local Delian demand, which is the subject of the following discussion.

The Population of Delos

An estimate of the aggregate annual demand for grain on Delos requires estimates of the total Delian population and of the average annual consumption of an individual (or family). The first question poses formidable difficulties. Robert Sallares has recently argued forcefully against the tendency of ancient historians to assume that ancient populations were stable. In his view, Greece as a whole saw important changes in population size between the tenth and third centuries, with a peak in the fourth century that may have extended into the late third but was definitely followed by a

1. "La production céréalière de Délos et Rhénée était insuffisante" (Vial, 341); "agricultural hinterland . . . was not very fertile" (Jan Pečírka, in *Problèmes de la terre en Grèce ancienne,* ed. M. I. Finley [Paris, 1973], 140); "almost devoid of fertile land" (Rostovtzeff, 230). See Casson, "Grain Trade," 75, on imports for local consumption; W. Déonna, *La Vie privée des Déliens* (Paris, 1948), 89, on the sterility of the island, and 37–38 on the grain trade.

2. See Garnsey, 3–86, generally, and, with reservations, Thomas W. Gallant, *Journal of Interdisciplinary History* 19 (1989): 393–413.

3. Casson, "Grain Trade," 74–75; brief treatment at Vial, 138–40, 237–39.

significant decline in the second and first centuries.[4] Such a profile, if applied everywhere, would suggest that Delos's population was either at its highest, or declining, during the years of independence. But such large-scale trends, even if accepted, cannot simply be applied in toto to individual places and over much shorter time periods. Certainly, for the second century, the trend on Delos was in the opposite direction, toward strong growth. This increase resulted, of course, from factors that operated only locally, and it was followed by a disastrous depopulation in the latter part of the first century.[5] For simplicity's sake, I shall assume that the Delian population was essentially stable in the years of independence—that is, that rates of growth, mortality, immigration, and emigration remained roughly the same. This is *not* to say there was no change at all in the size of the population—there may well have been—but I do suggest that such changes were not so great as to affect substantially the arguments presented below.[6]

Recent estimates have put the adult male population at 1,800–2,100 (Philippe Bruneau) and 1,200–1,500 (Claude Vial). If adult males were about 30 percent of the population, these figures imply total free populations of about 6,000–7,000 or 4,000–5,000. Even the lower figures may be too high; something like 2,000–3,000 may be more likely. Whichever figure is preferred, we must add in estimates for metics, slaves, and the average number of transient visitors (likely to have varied greatly with the rhythms of the seasons and of festivals on Delos: there would have been more visitors during the summer sailing season than in the winter; more during months with festivals, like Artemision and Posideon, than during those without, like Panemos, Bouphonion, and Apatourion; and more for the athletic games, which in 269 B.C. attracted competitors from Byblos, Sidon, Alexandria, and neighboring Tenos). Surely, even together these three groups would not have added more than 30 percent to the population, giving a total ranging from 2,600–3,900 (my figures), through 5,200–6,500 (Vial's), to 7,800–9,100 (Bruneau's).

These figures are not very exact, but our purposes call only for a general idea of the order of magnitude of the population. Even 2,600–3,900 people

4. Sallares, 1–107, esp. 62–73.

5. On the Athenian period (after 167 B.C.), see Pierre Roussel, *BCH* 55 (1931): 438–49, and Alexandre Papageorgiou-Venetas, *Délos: Recherches urbaines sur une ville antique* (Munich and Berlin, 1981), 114–15, with table 4 at 65.

6. See Bruneau, 262–63; Vial, 17–20. I hope to return to this issue and justify my lower figures elsewhere. Bruneau, 506–9, for the Delian liturgical calendar insofar as it has been reconstructed; athletes at *IG* XI 2.203A68–69; on the second century, cf. Strabo 10.5.4 (C486).

would be a sizeable population for Hellenistic Delos. The four cities of Keos probably supported no more than about 5,000 citizens, or say 7,500 persons in all.[7] Figures for guests at the festival Itonia at Arkesine on Amorgos imply no more than about 700 citizens of both sexes, or (say) 950 people in all; the entire island with its three poleis would thus probably have had no more than about 3,000 inhabitants.[8] Eberhard Ruschenbusch's recent comprehensive survey of the Greek world (the mainland, Aegean islands, the littoral of Asia Minor, and Krete) suggests that 85 percent of all known Greek poleis are unlikely to have had more than about 1,300 free inhabitants apiece.[9] Compared to its neighbors, Delos must have seemed overpopulated even in the early Hellenistic period. Even with only 2,600 inhabitants, its population density would have been roughly 720 persons/km^2, a figure almost five times the upper range of Ruschenbusch's estimates. Population density at that level, on an island poor in resources, would have posed serious problems of supply unknown to more traditional poleis with substantial agricultural territories and lower population densities.

Levels of Individual Grain Consumption

Broadly speaking, two kinds of data are required to estimate individual grain consumption in antiquity: figures for minimum daily caloric intake needs and a sense of the social factors that governed diet in the ancient world.[10] For the first category, recent studies have calculated basic needs from modern recommendations for caloric intake and from the behavior of modern peasant populations. The results of these studies, begun by Lin Foxhall and H. A. Forbes, have been remarkably consistent. Starting with figures for caloric need and the energy values of modern wheat and barley published by the United Nations Food and Agricultural Organization (FAO), and making adjustments to account for the slighter build of ancient Greeks, Foxhall and Forbes calculated that a Greek adult male probably required about 3,350 cal/day and an adult female about 2,450 cal/day. An

7. Eberhard Ruschenbusch, *ZPE* 48 (1982): 184; Robin Osborne in *Landscape Archaeology*, 319–25.

8. *IG* XII 7.22. Eberhard Ruschenbusch in *Aux origines de l'Hellénisme: La Crète et la Grèce* (Paris, 1984), 265–66, arrives at a total population for the island of about 3,200 persons by slightly different reasoning. See Philippe Gauthier, *BCH* 104 (1980): 197–220, and, in general on the Amorgan cities, M.-F. Boussac and G. Rougemont in *Les Cyclades*, 113–20. 235.

9. Eberhard Ruschenbusch, *ZPE* 59 (1985): 262, with reservations about the methodology in Philippe Gauthier, *BCH* 114 (1990): 438 n. 63.

10. Luigi Gallo, *Alimentazione e demografia della Grecia antica* (Salerno, 1984), 32.

analogous calculation for children (which Foxhall and Forbes did not make) yields about 2,560 cal/day.[11] Thomas Gallant recently went over the same ground and arrived at figures of 3,000 cal/day for an adult male, 2,200 cal/day for an adult female (2,500 if pregnant), 2,857 cal/day for an adolescent male, 2,383 cal/day for an adolescent female, and 2,010 cal/day (on average) for pre-adolescent children of either sex.[12] Studies of modern peasant populations give figures of the same general magnitude. Thus Leland Allbaugh's work on Krete just after World War II reckoned an average intake of about 2,550 cal/day, and a study of Near Eastern peasants yielded a figure of 876,000 cal/year, or 2,400 cal/day, for mature adults.[13] The differences among these figures are hardly worth arguing over, especially given the uncertainties that taint the rest of our data. For convenience, I shall accept Gallant's results, with the caveat that the calculations that follow have no pretense of precision, but are intended only as a guide to help us estimate total demand for Delos.

The remaining issues, related to the social factors governing consumption, are much more problematic. First is the structure of the Delian population. On this crucial question, which determines the distribution of demand over age and sex, we can only make some educated guesses. Gallant has recently exercised a great deal of ingenuity in trying to trace the life cycle of a typical ancient peasant family. His calculations imply that a population made up of such families would consist, on average, of 29.7 percent adult males, 29.8 percent adult females, 8.1 percent adolescent females, 8.1 percent adolescent males, and 24.3 percent pre-adolescent children, distributed equally between both sexes. Such a population distribution can be paralleled from calculations in model life tables.[14] I shall assume that urban and rural families had about the same structure, and that the population of Delos was stable over the period of independence—that is to say, that none of its important parameters, such as gross reproductive rate, was chang-

11. Foxhall-Forbes, 46–49; my figures vary slightly from those given in ibid., 46.

12. Gallant, 28, fig. 2.1, and 73, table 4.5. Gallo reckoned about 2,800 cal/day (*Alimentazione e demografia,* 41).

13. Leland G. Allbaugh, *Crete: A Case Study of an Underdeveloped Area* (Princeton, 1953), 97–134, esp. 97, 118–20; Royal Statistical Society, *Food Supplies and Population Growth* (London, 1963), 28 (*non vidi*); cf. Malcolm Wagstaff, Siv Augustson, and Clive Gamble in *Island Polity,* 174.

14. Gallant, 28, fig. 2.1, and 73, table 4.5. Cf. Ansley J. Coale, Paul Demeny, and Barbara Vaughan, *Regional Model Life Tables and Stable Populations*[2] (New York, 1983), and, in defense of the use of these tables, Tim G. Parkin, *Demography and Roman Society* (Baltimore, 1992), 67–90.

ing[15]—in order to use Gallant's implied typical population structure as a model for Delos. But about 30 percent of the Delian population consisted of slaves, metics, and transient visitors. On the assumption that they were virtually all adults, and that men predominated over women by 70 percent to 30 percent (at least among slaves and visitors), we can make an adjustment to the population structure. The final result, calculating need for calories according to Gallant's figures, suggests that the average per person caloric intake per day was about 2,460 calories. I shall use this figure in all the estimates that follow, but the reader should always bear in mind that it is only a gross estimate, probably on the high side. Given the uncertainties, however, it would seem to me to be false precision to try to refine it further.

The next question is what percentage of the total caloric intake is likely to have been satisfied by grain. Recent work seems to have settled virtually unanimously on 65–70 percent.[16] Because several new studies have cast doubt on the supposed monotony of the ancient diet, emphasizing the availability of other food sources than grain,[17] I have followed Gallant again and reckoned that 65 percent of caloric needs were satisfied by grain. That means that the average Delian would have consumed about 1,800 cal/day in wheat or barley.

At this point we can almost calculate very roughly the minimum annual grain demand on Delos; the only missing quantity is the relative weight to be given wheat and barley. There can be no doubt that barley remained the preponderant grain in the Hellenistic period, even though a growing taste for wheat seems detectable as the period wore on. Simple necessity must have encouraged the Kyklades, which as we shall see were far more suitable for barley culture than for wheat, to remain largely dependent on barley.[18] Nevertheless, for purposes of illustration, it is worthwhile to present calculations based on demand entirely for wheat, entirely for barley, and for a mixture of 30 percent wheat and 70 percent barley (table 4.1). The barley figures are for barley meal (ἄλφιτα).[19]

15. Sallares's criticism of this assumption (42–50) applies to the much longer term.

16. W. K. Akroyd and J. Doughty, *Wheat in Human Nutrition* (Rome, 1970), 31; Foxhall-Forbes, 56 and 65–68, analyzing data from Allbaugh, *Crete,* 95–134; Garnsey, 91 n. 6; Gallo, *Alimentazione e demografia,* 25; Gallant, 72.

17. J. K. Evans, *AJAH* 5 (1980): 19–47, 134–73; R. Etienne, *Index* 10 (1981): 66–77; G. D. R. Sanders, *BSA* 79 (1984): 259; Gallant, 62–68. On the "monotony" of the diet, see Gallo, *Alimentazione e demografia,* 35.

18. See A. Sarpaki in *Agriculture in Ancient Greece,* 69.

19. I use the following conversions, all from Foxhall-Forbes: 1 *med*/wheat = 52.176 l (Attic standard; see p. 84) = 40.280 kg (p. 44); 1 *med*/*alphita* = 52.176 l

Table 4.1. Annual Grain Consumption on Delos

	Per Person		*In* medimnoi *for a Population of:*		
	kg/yr	med*/yr*	*2,600*	*5,850*	*9,100*
Wheat	194	4.8	12,480	28,080	43,680
Alphita	195	5.8	15,080	33,930	52,780
Mixed	195	5.5	14,300	32,175	50,050

NOTE: Mixed consumption = .70 barley + .30 wheat.

These results are all internally consistent and agree as well as can be expected with the various recent studies devoted to the question of the ancient Greek diet. There is however one problem: they do not agree at all with such data on consumption as survive from antiquity. Although not perfectly consistent, many ancient sources from all periods point toward a "standard ration" of one χοῖνιξ of grain per day, or 7.6 *med*/yr (304 kg).[20] A *khoinix* of wheat provides 2,800 cal, far more than an adult male requires from grain (1,950 cal/day). Various explanations have been offered for this discrepancy. Foxhall and Forbes, for example, suggest that, as the Greeks tended to round figures up, the figure is prescriptive, not normative.[21] This solution explains neither why the figure is so consistent—shouldn't some authors have rounded up to another unit?—nor why no ancient authority remarks on the gross discrepancy between how much grain one actually needed to eat and how much the ration was. We are talking, after all, about almost half again as much grain as necessary. A better solution might take into account the context of these figures. Virtually all of them occur in military contexts: they are allotments to soldiers. Troops in antiquity

= 33.549 kg. For calories: 1 kg/wheat = 3,340 cal; 1 kg/"extracted barley" (*alphita*) = 3,320 cal (Foxhall-Forbes, 46). I reckon 3,330 cal/kg as an average for both grains. For the mixture in table 4.1, see H. J. van Wersch, in *MME* 185; see also Paul Halstead and Glynis Jones, *JHS* 109 (1989): 51, on the consumption of maslin (a mixed sowing of wheat and barley) on Amorgos.

20. Sources collected at Jardé, 129 nn. 6–13, with Pierre Ducrey, *BCH* 94 (1970): 638–42, no. 2, A23–25, cited by Foxhall-Forbes, 52. Accepted as reasonable by Jardé, 129; Carl Roebuck, *CP* 40 (1945): 159–61; Michael Jameson, *CJ* 74 (1977–78): 131 n. 51.

21. Foxhall-Forbes, 56–57, 73; Gallant, 67. Gallo has argued that the Greeks compensated for a monotonous diet dominated by cereals with generous rations (*Alimentazione e demografia*, 35; criticism by Sanders, *BSA* 79 [1984]: 259).

rarely traveled or fought alone. In the classical period, a hoplite usually had a batman or servant; in the Hellenistic period, mercenaries frequently had spouses, girlfriends, or other dependents. A standard ration of a *khoinix* per day may then have been intended partly to cover the needs of another unnamed party, whether free or slave, male or female, or might have been tradable for clothing, lodging, or other provisions.

The Delian documents themselves provide another instance of this problem. In 282 B.C., Apollo bought first wheat, then barley (as *alphita*), for three (later two) τεχνῖται (craftsmen) whom the god employed. They received in wheat 1.5 *khoinikes*/day (0.9375 *med*/month = 11.25 *med*/yr), and later in barley 3 *khoinikes*/day (1.875 *med*/month = 22.5 *med*/yr). These amounts represent daily rations of 4,175 and 6,950 calories, respectively 114 percent and 256 percent more than the 1,950 calories calculated as the typical daily requirement of an adult male.[22] In the case of these figures, there can be no doubt whatsoever that the rations go far beyond anything a person could consume in a day.[23] The solution, it seems to me, is to postulate an assistant for each worker, whether slave or apprentice, whose needs were also satisfied out of the allowances. Slave assistants are mentioned on Delos, including an instance in the very same year. The *hieropoioi* paid "Deinokrates and his slave [παῖς]" for work in the sanctuary (*IG* XI 2.158A71–72). Naturally, the full amount of the wage was paid to Deinokrates, who would have decided whether to turn any part over to the slave. Likewise the *tekhnitai* received the full grain allotment, which they divided as they saw fit.[24]

The contradiction between modern derived consumption figures and ancient data is therefore more apparent than real. It does, however, emphasize a very important point. The actual amount of grain demanded by a person was conditioned by factors beyond the simple biological need to stay alive. Soldiers and skilled workers evidently expected their employers to support

22. *IG* XI 2.158A48–50. These figures have been discussed many times: Gustave Glotz, *Journal des Savants* 11 (1913): 19–20; Jardé, 169–70; Larsen, 383–84; Heichelheim, *Wirt. Schw.*, 51, and "Sitos," cols. 857–58; Carl Roebuck, *CP* 40 (1945): 159–61; K. Clinton, *AE* (1971): 110–11; Foxhall-Forbes, 53–55.

23. Cf., however, Jardé, 135, who accepts the figures.

24. Partly already in Foxhall-Forbes, 57–58. For other slave workers, see *IG* XI 2.146A74–75, 154A26–27, *ID* 291b22, 446.9 + Γ 766β (unpublished; see *ID Index*, s.v. Παράμονος), 401*bis* A2, 13, 403.7, 443Bb148 (see *ID Index*, s.v. Παρμένων, pp. 69–70). The "woman," ἡ ἄνθρωπος, at *IG* XI 2.161A83, to whom 120 dr (10 dr/month) was provided εἰς τὰ ἐπιτήδεια, was almost surely the slave of the architect whose annual salary is given immediately preceding this entry. On the status of the *tekhnitai* (free not slave), see Appendix I.

their slaves or other hangers-on. For our purposes this is not important, since estimates for slaves, wives, other females, and children have already been reckoned into our figure for the population of Delos. But it should alert us to the possibility that undiscovered social factors may have affected the demand for grain. In fact, there is one such factor that deserves some attention: the need to store grain against bad years.

Bad years were inevitable in ancient as in modern Greece. Greece is a semi-arid country, although wetter in the west than in the east, and rainfall during the growing season frequently falls below the minimum of 300 mm necessary for wheat and even below the 240–200 mm minimum for barley. In Attike, for example, the wheat crop fails on average more than one year in four, the barley crop in one year in ten; and on Samos, wheat and barley crops fail almost every other year. Thessalia too shows a tendency toward failure every third or second year, and rainfall on Melos fell below the minimum needed for wheat in twenty-two out of forty years in this century, or oftener than every other year. During the years 1952 to 1980, rain at Herakleion on Krete during the growing season (roughly December–May) failed to meet wheat requirements in one year out of three. The failure rate at Limnos reached 51.7 percent. The climate does not appear to have been any different in antiquity, and indeed ancient evidence speaks eloquently about the frequency and impact of crop failures.[25]

In the second half of the second century B.C. in Boiotia, we hear of shortages "frequently" (πλεονάκις); during the reign of Augustus, an inscription from Lykosoura in the territory of Megalopolis speaks of times "whenever the city suffers a shortfall of harvests"; and the citizens of Kios

25. On the aridity of Greece, see H. Forbes in *Bad Year Economics*, 89; Oliver Rackham in *Greek City*, 88–91; I. Arnon, *Crop Production in Dry Regions* (London, 1972), II.4, 74 (rainfall requirements); Garnsey, 10–11 (Attike), 13 (Samos); Peter Garnsey, Tom Gallant, and Dominic Rathbone, *JRS* 74 (1984): 30–35, esp. table 11, and Paul Halstead, in *Bad Year Economics*, 73, both on Thessalia; Malcolm Wagstaff and Clive Gamble in *Island Polity*, 100–101, on Melos. For Herakleion and Limnos, see U.S. Dept. of Commerce, *World Weather Records, 1951–1960*, vol. 2, *Europe* (Washington, D.C., 1966), 143, 147; id., *World Weather Records, 1961–1970*, vol. 2, *Europe* (Washington, D.C., 1979), 133, 137; id., *World Weather Records, 1951–1960*, vol. 2, *Europe* (Washington, D.C., 1987), 131, 135. On the climate in antiquity, see Isager-Skydsgaard, 9–18; Eberhard Zangger in *Agriculture in Ancient Greece*, 15–16, 19; H. Lohmann in ibid., 31–33; Oliver Rackham in *Greek City*, 88 with n. 10; Anthony Snodgrass, *An Archaeology of Greece* (Berkeley, 1987), 67–72; Garnsey, 8–9, with the bibliography at his nn. 1–2; Claudio Vita-Finzi, *The Mediterranean Valleys: Geological Changes in Historical Times* (Cambridge, 1969), 113.

in Asia Minor, begging toward the end of the third century B.C. to be released from religious obligations toward their mother city, Miletos, write of a crisis resulting from "a shortage [ἀφορία] in the countryside that has persisted for many years."[26] Closer to home, literary sources speak of droughts and attendant crop failures at Naxos, Syme, Keos, and Khalkis on Euboia. Failure of fruit trees was said to be the cause of the Theran colonization of Kyrene. Epigraphical evidence from Nesos attests to a σιτοδεία soon after 320 B.C. (and therefore not part of the great shortage known from Tod II.196 and other sources). A shortage has been restored very plausibly in an Ietan inscription of the mid third century. A Greek city, almost certainly Kykladic, had occasion to thank its *proxenos* on Delos for releasing ships seized for debt; the cargo was grain, carried during a σπανισιτία. A Tenian inscription of the imperial period reports a shortage and gives reason to suspect hoarding. Under these conditions it is hardly surprising that even cities with productive agricultural hinterlands might show both a "superabundant harvest" and a failure of the grain crop *propter hiemis asperitatem* in different years.[27]

Warfare also took a heavy toll. Practically constant in the ancient world, fighting disrupted both local production and imports and devoured local resources even in years of good harvests. An honorary decree found at Brousse in Asia Minor and dated to 189–150 B.C. reports that "when the citizens were undergoing a famine because of the war, [the honorand] provided grain for seed and consumption" (ἐνδεῶς ἀπαλλασσόντων τῶν πολιτῶν διὰ τὸν πόλεμον [the honorand] ἐξεπορίσατο σῖτον εἰς σπέρμα καὶ διατροφήν). In Athens ca. 229/8 B.C., the countryside was left unseeded because of war. The war against Aristonikos in Asia (133–130 B.C.) brought disaster to Methymna on Lesbos and to Sestos, which had also suffered earlier under attacks by the Thrakians. Delos and its neighbors saw frequent military activity throughout the Hellenistic period, and it is a safe assumption that at least sometimes movements of troops

26. *IG* VII.4132.8–9; *IG* V 2.515.13–14; *Milet* III.147.7 (= H. W. Pleket, *Epigraphica*, vol. 1 [Leiden 1964], 35).

27. Diod. 5.51.3, 53.2; Schol. Apollon. Rh. II 498–527a; Herakleides Lembos frg. 55 (Dilts); Herod. 4.151; *IG* XII 2.645; *IG* XII 5.1011; *IG* XI 4.1049 (see further p. 118 below); *IG* XII 5.947. W. M. Ramsay, *JRS* 14 (1924): 178–79, no. 5 (early second century or ca. 50 A.D., 179 n. 4), ll. 4–5, [*ex superabundant*]*i messe;* 179–84, no. 6 (91/2 or 92/3 A.D.), ll. 6–7, for Antiochea Caesaria in Galatia. On shortages in the Greek world, see also Giangiacomo Panessa, *ASNP* 12 (1982): 905–15, an excellent, well-documented article, to which I owe a number of my examples.

and war interrupted supplies or disrupted the agricultural calendar. (In chapter 5 we shall see some direct evidence for economic disruption on Delos owing to military operations.)[28]

In some parts of Greece and until recently, storage continued to be a constant factor in the calculations of modern Greek peasants, for whom "arguably the most effective household-level mechanism for coping with crop failure was to store surplus from good harvests for use in bad years." This strategy called for consistent overproduction: households aimed to plant and harvest at levels that assured returns adequate for subsistence in poor years, beyond need in typical years, and abundant in good years. At Methana, for example, peasants typically produced surpluses of 63 percent over household needs. In general, modern Greek rural families aim to keep in storage at least two years' supply of grain, and four years' supply of olive oil in areas like Methana where olives, which produce only every other year, are also synchronized.[29]

These surpluses were "surplus" only in a relative sense, since they insured peasant farmers against frequent poor years and rarer, but inevitable, disasters. Overproduction was therefore really part of normal production. If the same considerations operated in antiquity, ancient consumers should also have sought to acquire grain in amounts that *included a buffer against bad years.* If this view is right, then modern estimates of caloric requirements, while valuable as theoretical models of minimal subsistence needs, must nevertheless be modified to take into account a social factor—the need to "overproduce"—that was built into the fabric of ancient attitudes toward grain consumption. Population estimates based on minimum need and the supportive capacity of polis territory, for example, will tend to be exaggerated because of underestimation of individual demand.[30]

28. Holleaux, II.74–75, ll. 13–14, 17–18, see for the translation pp. 95–100. *IG* II² 834.7–8. Cf. Chr. Habicht, *Studien zur Geschichte Athens in hellenistischer Zeit* (Göttingen, 1982), 79–93, on the historical circumstances. *IG* XII suppl. 116 (= *SEG* 3.710). *OGIS* 339.53–59.

29. Paul Halstead in *Bad Year Economics,* 73 (quotation); H. Forbes in ibid., 91, 93, and Lin Foxhall, *History Today* 36 (July 1986): 38, both on Methana; Paul Halstead and Glynis Jones, *JHS* 109 (1989): 52, for Amorgos in 1982; Christopher Connell, *In the Bee-Loud Glade* (Nafplion, 1980), 26, on wine storage on Amorgos. Gallant, 94–98.

30. Foxhall and Forbes come close to this position when they notice that the *khoinix*/day ration seems like "the sort of rule according to which a farmer might have calculated the amount of grain he needed for a year's food for his family" (Foxhall-Forbes, 56–57, with 57 nn. 51–52); but when they go on to stress that "Greek and Roman 'standard' rations were not minimum consumption allowances . . . [but,] in fact, distribution allowances," and that "rations cannot be considered

Investigation of modern Greek peasants' storage behavior reflects recent practice in the countryside. Since the ancient Greeks faced the same environmental constraints, it is reasonable to suppose they responded in the same way and there is indeed some evidence to suggest that they did.[31] Urban families may have responded somewhat differently. Delians without farms may generally have bought their bread already baked, like the Parians who honored an *agoranomos* for keeping the price down (*IG* XII 5.129). Alternately, they may have bought raw grain and entrusted it to local bakers to turn into bread; such was evidently Apollo's habit at his festivals. Failure of town-dwellers to store grain in quantities comparable to their rural cousins could account for the heightened vulnerability of the urban poor to shortages.[32]

How much was enough? Once again we are virtually without guides. An inscription of the late second century from Thessalia suggests that just before the new spring harvest, 30–50 percent of the previous year's crop was still in the hands of the original producers; this amount might have fed the local population for roughly a year.[33] A law at Selymbria permitted landowners to store no more than one year's supply ([Arist.] *Oik.* 2.2.15a–17 [1348b1–1349a3]). Presumably, they would have held on to more if they could have; part of the intention here must have been to prevent hoarding, a common practice, which accounts in part for the desire to store, since the opportunity to make money arises during shortages, at least for wealthier landowners. In addition, the city of Delos itself must have stored grain, at least in the later third and second centuries, when a *sitonia* fund was in operation.

Modern rainfall data help a bit. In general, the Kyklades receive too little rain to support a barley crop about every three years out of ten. Wheat is far more problematic, as we shall see. Roughly speaking, then, a society that aimed to overproduce by about 50 percent per year would be prepared for most shortages. That suggests in turn that we should raise our estimate

---

identical with consumption" (73), they obscure the very important result for historians of the ancient economy and demography that rations are better estimators of demand (and hence for use in calculation of the carrying capacity of a territory) than a putative, constructed "consumption."

31. Gallant, 95–96, 98, and esp. Garnsey, Gallant, and Rathbone, *JRS* 74 (1984): 30–35. Ausonius 3.1.27 and Sidonius *Carm.* 22.170 report storage of two years' supplies of grain on Gaulish estates of the fourth century A.D..

32. *ID* 442A223, 445.15, 440A70. On the Delian cooks at temple festivals, see Guy Berthiaume, *Les Rôles du mágeiros* (Leiden, 1982), 27–28, 39. On urban vulnerability, see Garnsey, 69–86; H. W. Pleket, *MBAH* 3.1 (1984): 3–36.

33. Garnsey, Gallant, and Rathbone, *JRS* 74 (1984): 30–35.

Table 4.2. Annual Grain Consumption on Delos Allowing for a Surplus of 50 Percent

	Per Person		*In* medimnoi *for a Population of:*		
	kg/yr	med*/yr*	*2,600*	*5,850*	*9,100*
Wheat	290	7.2	18,720	42,120	65,520
Alphita	290	8.7	22,620	50,895	79,170
Mixed	290	8.25	21,450	48,262	75,075

NOTE: Mixed consumption = .70 barley + .30 wheat.

for annual aggregate demand per person by roughly the same amount, or to about 290 kg/yr. The resulting demand for Delos appears in table 4.2. It is these figures we shall reckon on in trying to determine where Delos could have found the grain it needed.

On this basis the annual aggregate demand for grain on Delos would have approximated 19,000–66,000 *medimnoi* of wheat, 23,000–80,000 *medimnoi* of barley as *alphita,* or in combination 22,000–75,000 *medimnoi.* These very rough estimates are intended only as a guide to the scale of demand on Delos, and even if they are too low by half, they still evoke the small scale of grain demand on Delos compared to a really large market like fourth-century Athens, which probably had an aggregate annual demand on the order of 1,000,000 *medimnoi.*[34]

These figures must obviously be taken with a grain of salt. The assumptions on which the calculations rest are open to obvious objections: ancient grains were not genetically identical to modern grains and probably had a different caloric content; modern nutritional standards are normative, whereas much of the ancient population may have been chronically malnourished by modern standards; the exact weight of a given volume of ancient grain is unknown; a given *medimnos* might contain more or less than standard capacity; rations must have varied considerably with social class, level of activity, time of year, and cost of grains; dietary supplements

34. On Athenian demand, see Isager-Hansen, 19; Garnsey, 90, gives a population for fourth-century Athens of from 120,000–150,000 to 200,000 and an annual consumption of 600,000–1,000,000 *medimnoi* at ca. 200 kg/person = 5 *medimnoi* (cf. 104–5; reckoned at 40 kg/*med,* p. xiv). Cf. also Peter Garnsey in *Crux: Essays in Greek History Presented to G. E. M. de Ste. Croix* (London, 1985), 62–75.

that might have reduced demand for grain, including vegetables and locally available vetches and legumes, are largely ignored.[35]

The point, however, is not to establish some definite figure for Delian grain consumption, but to estimate the order of magnitude of the annual aggregate Delian demand for grain. On this matter, the figures are reasonable and invite some confidence. If we suppose that Delos needed something between 19,000 *medimnoi* of wheat and 88,000 *medimnoi* of *alphita* per year to feed its population, we shall probably not be far wrong; I am inclined to seek the true figure somewhere between those extremes, perhaps at about 30,000–50,000 *med*/yr inclusive of barley and wheat.

Now that we have some sense, however rough, of the aggregate annual Delian demand for grain, we can try to estimate the extent of its dependence on imported food and determine the sources from which that food might have come.

Production at Home

To begin, it is necessary to jettison the long-held assumption that Delos is "almost devoid of fertile land."[36] The appearance of Delos today is the result of recent neglect, partly owing to its use in the nineteenth century as communal pasture for Mykonite sheep and more to its current artificial status as an archaeological park. But even in the nineteenth century, Mykonites kept gardens on the island,[37] and there is no reason to suppose that Delos was not exploited to its fullest potential when it was heavily inhabited in the Hellenistic period. Apollo owned ten agricultural estates on Delos. In the third century B.C., there is documentary evidence for seven privately owned estates and three gardens; other gardens known only from later inscriptions certainly existed earlier. Of Delos's total area of about 360 ha, Michèle Brunet has recently reckoned that 250 ha were cultivated in antiquity, and that this Delian *khora* supported about fifty farms. Traces of terracing, which Brunet has dated tentatively to the fifth and fourth centuries, still lace the island, and her excavation of a putative farmhouse

35. On some of these points, see Evans, *AJAH* 5 (1980): 19–47, 134–73; L. A. Moritz, *Grain Mills and Flour in Classical Antiquity* (Oxford, 1958), 151–58, 184–94; N. Jasny, *AHR* 47 (1941–42): 747–64 (but cf. Gallo, *Opus* 2 [1983]: 452); Carolyn G. Koehler and Malcolm B. Wallace, *AJA* 91 (1987): 49–57; Gallant, passim; Sallares, passim. The preoccupation of the Athenians with guaranteeing standard weights and measures through the board of *metronomoi* may indicate frequent fraud; see Phillip V. Stanley, *Ancient World* 2 (1979): 18–19.

36. Rostovtzeff, 230.

37. Philippe Bruneau, *BCH* 103 (1979): 92, fig. 1.

has revealed evidence of ancient agricultural activity, including ancient threshing floors.[38]

There is some inscriptional evidence for Delian grain culture. To cover back rent for two estates whose renters were dispossessed in 307 B.C., the *hieropoioi* seized raw barley (κριθαί) from one estate valued at 140 drachmas and 300 drachmas' worth from the other, together with a pair of oxen worth 150 drachmas (*IG* XI 2.142.7, 11). There are no further records of seizures for back rent, but other evidence implies continued cultivation of cereal crops. Barley was bought regularly to feed holy geese or for animals reserved for sacrifice,[39] and it is a reasonable guess that the small amounts needed were found locally. The so-called *hiera syngraphe*, which regulated the rental of the estates after 300 B.C., stipulated the seizure and sale of "harvests" (καρποί) for failure to pay rent (*ID* 503.33–34). The word καρπός would have covered all crops, including not only grain but also grapes and olives, which were grown on some estates.[40]

As part of their duties, the *hieropoioi* inventoried the estates every ten years. The inventory for 250 B.C. survives essentially complete. Ten of the estates listed had an ἀχυρών, or storage facility for chaff. Four had a μύλων, or mill, and one a σιτοβόλων, or granary. All but two estates had a βούστασις, or stable for keeping a pair of plowing oxen.[41] These facilities quite clearly suggest grain cultivation probably on every estate. It is interesting that the two estates known to have produced barley at the end of the fourth century (Hippodromos and Soloe) lacked the capital equipment needed to process it by 250: this might mean that barley growing had ceased—we know that viticulture was drastically curtailed on some estates in the late third century—but more probably that milling and storage simply took place elsewhere. From the accounts and estate inventories, J. H. Kent has reckoned that at least eight of the estates produced some grain.[42]

38. See Kent, 252–58, on Apollo's estates; on private farms and gardens, see G. Reger, *Phoenix* 46 (1992): 322–41, and Bruneau, *BCH* 103 (1979): 89–99; on Cicero *Ad Attic.* 9.9.4, see Philippe Bruneau, *BCH* 112 (1988) 569–73, who argues that this passage refers to a private estate owned or leased by Atticus. On the size of Delos, Lucien Cayeux, *Description physique de l'île de Délos* (Paris, 1911), 188 with nn. 9–10 (generally *GD*[3] 15–16). Brunet, 149, 133–36 (terraces), 124, 126, 127–31, 140, 182 (threshing floors). For her excavations of a Delian farmstead, see ibid., 163–77, *BCH* 114 (1990): 906, *BCH* 113 (1989): 754–61, *BCH* 112 (1988): 787–91, and *BCH* 111 (1987): 644–46.

39. See Appendix III, p. 306.

40. For grapes, see Kent, 299–300; olives attested only for estates on Mykonos (*ID* 366B18–23 of 207 B.C.; Kent, 287–88).

41. *IG* XI 2.287A136–74; conveniently summarized by Kent, 299–300.

42. Kent, 309–12; 310, cf. 299–301.

Given the ancient preference for polyculture, the practice of sowing grain between rows of vines, and the facilities for plow teams, probably every estate grew grain.

We can try to estimate Delian yield. Barley prices ranged from 2 to 5 dr/*med* on Delos in the third century. At the higher end of the scale, prices of 4 and 5 drachmas are recorded for *alphita* in 282 B.C., which implies that unmilled barley (κριθαί) cost 2.6 or 3.75 drachmas.[43] At this rate, the barley confiscated in 307 B.C. amounted to 117–170 *medimnoi* of *krithai*. Processing into *alphita* would have yielded about 75–110 *medimnoi*. If the seven remaining sacred estates on Delos (excluding Kerameion) and the estimated fifty private farms all produced comparable crops, Delos might have grown 2,200–3,245 *med*/yr, enough grain to feed roughly 250–375 people per year (including amounts immobilized in storage).

Local production can also be estimated in a very theoretical fashion by applying estimates for typical yields to estimates of Delian arable. Naturally, there is virtually no ancient evidence to help with this problem, so we are forced to rely on recent data. The difficulties of this approach are numerous, including the usually unstated assumption that yields of the late nineteenth and early twentieth centuries must have been similar to those of antiquity because both were achieved with premodern technology. But it is not only technological changes, like the introduction of modern fertilizers, that affect yields, but also social and demographic factors. Declining population, greater integration of once isolated regions into a market economy, the creation of new employment opportunities, and changes in taste are only some of the nontechnological factors that can change cropping patterns, level of agricultural activity, and hence yields.[44] The great variability in rainfall both interannually and from region to region further makes it desirable to use only data covering a long span and only from the same region as is being investigated. Recently Eberhard Ruschenbusch compiled data on yields for the Kyklades for the years 1921–32, the only

43. No figures are preserved for the cost of turning κριθαί into ἄλφιτα. The barley was bought processed in 282. For wheat the temple bore a substantial milling cost of about 2 dr/*med* to 2 dr 2 ob/*med* (*IG* XI 2.158A37–47), paid to a σιτοποιός. In the second century, at the festival of the Posideia, Apollo paid an ἀρτοκόπος 1 dr, 2 dr, and 2 dr 3 ob to process a *medimnos* of wheat (*ID* 442A223, 445.15, 440A70). On the Delian cooks at temple festivals, see Berthiaume, *Rôles du mágeiros*, 27–28, 39.

44. Cf. Gallant, 76–78; E. Ruschenbusch, *ZPE* 72 (1988): 151–52 n. 19 (fertilizer); S. B. Sutton in *Landscape Archaeology*, 383–402; T. M. Whitelaw in ibid., 403–54. See Sallares, 372–89, 79–80, for an estimate of the productivity of Attike using slightly different yields (600, 500, and 400 kg/ha).

period for which reliable data exist for the archipelago.[45] They illustrate the extreme interannual variability of grain yields in Greece; between 1921 and 1932, for instance, the Kyklades yielded in wheat a maximum of 980 kg/ha and a minimum of 200 kg/ha, a variation of almost 400 percent. Barley ranged from 1,080 to 450 kg/ha, or 240 percent. As Ruschenbusch argues, such variability renders useless any figure for a single year, since the "normal" or "typical" yield can vary over such a wide range. Ruschenbusch's figures do provide some corrective to broad conclusions taken from too-limited data, and they at least offer average yields—450 kg/ha for wheat and 680 kg/ha for barley—that have the virtue of being based on a fairly long run of data. But they themselves are not without problems as models of ancient productivity. In particular, they come from a period (1921–32) of general population decline in the archipelago, although, as always, the details vary from island to island and even between different communities on the same island.[46] It is therefore possible that Ruschenbusch's figures, although accurate, reflect a lower rate of exploitation of the countryside than would have been achieved in antiquity. I have included in table 4.3 calculations based on data from Greece as a whole and from Krete for 1911 to 1950, with the caveat that these data clearly include yields improved by the application of artificial fertilizer. It should also be noted that these yields presume a two-field fallow system.

The production for Delos estimated from modern yield/ha figures corresponds extremely well with the figures worked up from estimates based on the putative production of two Delian estates in the late fourth century. The latter figures, roughly 2,200–3,245 *medimnoi* of *alphita*, lie comfortably within the range of 2,450–3,500 calculated from modern data. While this agreement cannot be claimed to prove or confirm either set of figures, the independence of the two calculations (they share no assumptions) cer-

45. Ruschenbusch, *ZPE* 72 (1988): 141–53. I reject his figures for yields from 1933 to 1938 since, as he himself clearly shows (151–52 n. 19), these improved figures were the result of increased application of artificial fertilizers. The Kykladic yields for 1916 of 460.8 kg/ha for wheat and barley yields of 716.8 kg/ha (= 465.9 kg/ha *alphita*) quoted by Wagstaff, Augustson, and Gamble, in *Island Polity,* 172–80, fall well within the normal range of Ruschenbusch's data; see also Peter Garnsey in *Agriculture in Ancient Greece,* 149, for average yields in Attike in 1911–51 of 629.1 kg/ha for wheat and 793.7 kg/ha for barley, and generally on the constraints on barley yields, see D. E. Briggs, *Barley* (London, 1978), 301, 314–15. I have not seen M. Saloni, Ἱστορία τῆς Τήνου (Athens, 1888; orig. Paris, 1809), said to have information on yields on Tenos in the nineteenth century. On a recent attempt to derive yields from some data for Melos in 1670, see Appendix I.

46. Gallant, 78, but cf. Sutton in *Landscape Archaeology,* 385, table 20.1; 391, table 20.3; 396, table 20.4; and 400–401.

Table 4.3. Delian Productivity Estimated from Modern Yield Data from the Kyklades (1), Krete (2), and All Greece (3)

	Cultivated surface (ha)	*Yield/ ha (kg)*	*Net yield*[a] *(kg)*	*Net yield* (*med*)	*% Population Fed*[b]		
					2,600	*5,850*	*9,100*
Wheat							
(1)	250	450	68,750	1,719	9.2	4.0	2.6
(2)	250	748	143,250	3,530	18.9	8.4	5.4
(3)	250	673	124,500	3,068	16.4	7.3	4.7
Barley[c]							
(1)	250	680	82,062	2,446	10.8	4.8	3.1
(2)	250	903	118,300	3,526	15.6	6.9	4.4
(3)	250	732	90,512	2,698	11.9	5.3	3.4

SOURCES: Kykladic yields, 1921–32: E. Ruschenbusch, *ZPE* 72 (1988): 141–53; Krete and Greece, 1911–50: Gallant, 77, table 4.7.

[a]In each case, net yield is gross yield (cultivated surface × yield/ha) minus 43,750 kg reserved for seed at a rate of 175 kg/ha.

[b]For wheat: 7.2 *med*/per/yr; barley: 8.7 *med*/per/yr.

[c]Yield/ha and seed figures are of course for raw barley, not *alphita*. To obtain the net yield (kg) I have reduced the result of 250 × yield/ha less seed by 35 percent to account for milling loss to produce *alphita;* thus net yield (kg) and (*med*) both reflect *alphita.*

tainly does lend confidence that the results are not likely to be radically wrong. I think it would be reasonable to postulate on the conservative side that ancient Delos probably produced in the long run something like 2,000–3,000 *medimnoi* of consumable grain each year. Depending on the exact mix of barley and wheat—although I do not doubt for a moment that barley predominated—the island could have fed 230–350 people per year. These figures might represent as few as 2.6 percent or as many as 13 percent of the population. On the whole, I think we shall not be far wrong to suppose that, on average, Delos could, very roughly, feed 10 percent of its total average population.

PRODUCTION ON RHENEIA AND MYKONOS

The Delians were clearly left with a sizable deficit of grain, and I think it is a fair assumption that like the population of any other ancient city, they preferred to seek the balance locally.[47] The nearest source was, of course, the sacred estates on Rheneia. To judge from the numbers of vines kept,

47. J. H. M. Strubbe, *EA* 13 (1989): 108; Pleket, *MBAH* 3.1 (1984): 21.

the Rheneian estates were considerably bigger than their Delian counterparts. If the estates really covered all of Rheneia south of the isthmus and the territory north up to the acropolis, as Kent believed, they would have accounted for perhaps three-fifths of the island, or about 840 hectares.[48] If virtually all of this land was sown in barley, then the ten Rheneian estates might have added 9,000 *medimnoi* of *alphita* to Delos's budget, enough to feed over 1,000 people. Of course, even with intensive intercropping of grain between vines, some of these 840 hectares would have been unavailable for cultivation; as a guess, we may reduce the figure by 30 percent to 6,300 *medimnoi*, or food enough for about 725 persons. Rheneia as a whole might have produced 8,430 to 9,030 *medimnoi*. Some of this food would clearly have gone to the local Rheneian population (whose size remains unknown; the island would repay careful exploration north of the isthmus), but Rheneia might nevertheless have had surplus enough to send (let us say) food for perhaps 500–700 persons to Delos. Combined with Delos's own budget, as reckoned above, these two islands alone could have fed 730–1,050 people, or 8 to 40 percent of the total average Delian population. It does not seem unlikely to me that in an average year the Delians could have counted on Delos and Rheneia for enough grain to accommodate about 25 percent of the inhabitants.

The other potential supplier nearby was Mykonos, where Apollo owned three estates probably located on the isthmus on the western side of the island, which included the only olive trees inventoried for any of the god's possessions. Mykonites were prominent on Delos, where they served as contractors and were honored with proxeny decrees. Their home island, which covers 87.3 km^2, is flat and easily cultivated.[49] Assuming that 20–40 percent of its surface was devoted to cereals, it could have produced a usable barley crop (measured as *alphita*) on the order of 573,124 to 826,207 kg (at 20 percent) or 1,146,249 to 1,652,414 kg (at 40 percent). These amounts could feed between 1,960 and 5,660 persons. Once again, we have virtually no idea of the population of Mykonos. A recent estimate has suggested 1,047 persons. Even if, on reasonable assumptions, we raise this figure by half again, to 1,625,[50] the island should have had a surplus the Delians could appropriate. As a very rough estimate, let us suppose Mykonos regu-

48. An average of 1,821 vines on Rheneian estates versus 451 on Delian; see Kent, 299–300, and chapter 6, p. 194. And see Kent, 248, fig. 3 for the location of the Rheneian estates; also Marie-Thérèse Le Dinahet-Couilloud in *Les Cyclades*, 135–40, rejected by J. Tréheux, *BCH* 110 (1986): 427–32. See now R. Charre et al., *Recherches dans les Cyclades* (Lyon, 1993), 126–32.

49. For estates, see chapter 5, pp. 169–70. For Mykonites on Delos, see *ID* Index, 105–6. For area, see ΣΕΕ 1937: 32.

50. See E. Ruschenbusch, *ZPE* 59 (1985): 259, with discussion below at pp. 108–9.

larly produced a surplus sufficient to feed 750–1,000 persons. Delos's two nearest large neighbors, separated by only a brief sail, might have fed 1,250–1,700 of Delos's population. Adding Delos's own production, the three islands could have fed from 16 percent (assuming 1,480 fed out of 9,100) to 79 percent (2,050 fed out of 2,600) of the Delian population. The conclusion seems inescapable that roughly half of the regular annual aggregate Delian demand for grain could have come out of the surpluses of Apollo's immediate neighborhood.

PRODUCTION IN THE REST OF THE KYKLADES

For the rest, Delos must have looked first to its other Kykladic neighbors. We know that these islands produced grain, sometimes in quantity. Modern data certainly suggest their potential productivity. For example, in three consecutive years, between 1936 and 1938, the Kyklades produced 9,608,800, 17,639,100, and 16,575,500 kg of grain, equivalent (assuming the crop was virtually all barley) to roughly 186,000, 341,750, and 321,100 *medimnoi.*[51] Early modern data collected by B. J. Slot point in the same direction. In 1670, Naxos produced the equivalent of about 8,200 *medimnoi* of grain, Paros about 19,000, Thera about 14,350, Melos about 10,680, Andros about 10,000, Syros about 4,900, or a total for just these islands of 67,130 *medimnoi.* From 1700 to 1718, an average of 42,813 pounds of wheat arrived from "the Archipelago" in Marseille; "the Archipelago" embraced more than just the Kyklades, but the figure gives a general sense of the availability of surpluses in the islands. This figure is the equivalent of about 480 *medimnoi.* Visiting the Kyklades at about the same time, J. Pitton de Tournefort reported exports in grain from Ios, Sikinos, and Naxos. Between the 1830s and 1911, Keos produced an average of 1,250,780 kg of barley, of which 110,000 kg were exported in 1906, equivalent to 24,230 *medimnoi* produced and 2,130 exported.[52] These figures have no statistical value, but they suggest a small, but genuine, exportable surplus. Recent travelers and researchers continue to report the production of barley and wheat on the islands.[53]

51. ΣΕΕ 1937: 112; 1938: 112; 1939: 112.

52. B. J. Slot, *Archipelagus turbatus* (Istanbul, 1982), I.302–6, 321–24. J. Pitton de Tournefort, *A Voyage into the Levant* (London, 1741), I.266, 270, 228. Sutton in *Landscape Archaeology,* 390. Cf. however Sallares, 316.

53. See Connell, *In the Bee-Loud Glade,* 18, 22–25; Wagstaff and Augustson in *Island Polity,* 110–12; Wagstaff, Augustson, and Gamble in ibid., 177–79; Wagstaff and Gamble in ibid., 98, 101; Halstead and Jones, *JHS* 109 (1989): 41–55; Sanders, *BSA* 79 (1984): 251–62; R. N. L. Barber, *The Cyclades in the Bronze Age* (Iowa City, 1987), 7. On soil types on Naxos and Paros, see J.-Y. Empereur and M. Picon, *BCH* 110 (1986): 496–98.

For an estimate of the potential productivity of the Kyklades, however, it is necessary to consider the factors that governed productivity over the long term. One of these, yield per hectare, has already been discussed, and I shall continue to use the figures in table 4.3. The other two are rainfall and area cropped. Although already discussed, the effect of insufficient rainfall on crops must be considered in more detail here because (1) rainfall is sufficient for barley production most of the time in the Kyklades, and (2) we can trace variability not only among years but also among islands, which implies that shortages on one island because of insufficient rain need not have meant shortages elsewhere. Area cropped is crucial, because the Kyklades today are apparently grossly underexploited compared to antiquity; the potential for grain production is certainly considerably greater than the rather neglected present appearance of many of the islands would suggest.

Rainfall. Rainfall is important not only because the amount of rainfall determines the success or failure of a crop, but also because it gauges the relation of social expectations of consumption (discussed above) to actual production. If a region produces more grain than social constraints demand, there will be a genuine surplus: that is to say, a surplus that can be regularly absorbed by a local nonfarming urban population or exported.

For 1951–70, Naxos received a mean rainfall during the growing season (December–May) of only 208.5 mm, enough rain to support a wheat crop only 44 percent of the time (seven years out of the sixteen for which data are available). Barley fared much better: in only two years of sixteen (12.5 percent) did rainfall fall outright below 200 mm, and in two (or possibly three) others (12.5 percent [18.75 percent]) was rainfall marginal for barley culture (200–240 mm). A culture dependent primarily on barley would therefore typically have experienced stress every third year (table 4.4).

Thera probably experiences similar conditions, although lack of data makes inference dangerous: for five years for which we have seasonal data (1933–37), there was always too little rain for wheat, and too little for barley in three years; but this could be the same kind of pattern that prevailed on Naxos in 1972–77.[54] Some data for eleven earlier years (1896–1907) illustrate extreme small-scale variability of precipitation. Rainfall at the town of Phira (= Thera) fell short of the minimum for wheat in eight years out of eleven, while it sufficed for barley in all but three years (27 percent). The pattern is thus virtually identical to that on Naxos. At Gonia on Thera, in contrast, rain was more than sufficient for both crops in all five years for which data were recorded (1901–5), while on the slopes of

54. ΣΕΕ 1937: 17–18; 1938: 17–18; 1939: 17–18.

Table 4.4. Rainfall on Naxos, December–May, 1967–1982

Year	*Rain (mm)*	*Wheat*	*Barley*	*Year*	*Rain (mm)*	*Wheat*	*Barley*
1982	540.0			1974	229.6	F	M
1981	460.4			1973	340.3		
1980	355.0			1972	251.8	F	
1979	181.8	F	F	1971	364.5		
1978	436.6			1970	356.6		
1977	105.8	F	F	1969	257.6	F	
1976	268.5	F		1968	214.5+	F?	M?
1975	231.0	F	M	1967	246.4	F	

SOURCE: ΣΕΕ, 1968–84.
KEY: F = failed crop, M = marginal crop (barley only, for rainfall = 200–240 mm).
NB: No rainfall recorded for December 1967.

Table 4.5. Rainfall on Thera, December–May, 1901–1905 (mm)

	1901	*1902*	*1903*	*1904*	*1905*
Gonia	301.1	399.0	302.0	503.0	461.5
Phira	179.9	273.3	203.9	313.3	382.3
Profitis Elias	189.0	278.0	247.2	427.2	385.1

Profitis Elias in the same period, the wheat crop would have failed three times (60 percent) and the barley crop once (20 percent).[55] Phira sits on the western ridge of the island, Gonia lies about 4.5 km inland to the east, and Profitis Elias rises to 564 m about 1.75 km SSE of Gonia. Within a range of barely six kilometers, therefore, rainfall varied enormously (table 4.5). Years that saw crop failures at Phira brought quite enough rain to support farmers near Gonia. This local variability is crucial for understanding the extremely localized stresses that ancient farmers underwent and the frequent reports in our sources of apparently quite localized shortages or failures. Disaster at Phira (as in 1901) did not necessarily spell disaster a few kilometers away.

55. P. Wilski, *Klimatologische Beobachtungen aus Thera* (Berlin, 1902), 89; partially reproduced in table 4.5.

These results are important. They suggest that the Kyklades could have supported a reliable barley culture, although wheat would typically have been more problematic. Considerable variability from island to island, and even from place to place on a single island, is also to be expected. This confirms the picture early travelers paint. Tournefort's detailed discussion of the condition of individual islands shows great variability among them in their productivity, but with a few exceptions—Ios and Sikinos—they had far more success with barley than wheat. Some, including Ios, Sikinos, and Naxos, are specifically said to have exported grain.[56] These results are also very much in harmony with the recent emphasis among scholars of ancient Greek agriculture on the importance for ancient farmers of exploiting micro variations in weather, soil conditions, and other variables by holding small plots in different locations. Theran farmers who held land only at Phira would certainly have had cause to rue it early in this century; there is no reason to suppose conditions were any different elsewhere in the islands, or indeed in antiquity.

Another important implication of the rainfall data relates to the extensiveness of crop failures because of lack of precipitation. Given not only the great interannual variability, but also the potential for extremely localized variability, great general failures are likely to have been rare. Each year some communities on some islands must have faced shortages, but typically they could expect to make them up from the surplus of luckier neighbors. Long experience would have built this factor into the calculus of production. Storage and the short-range movement of grain were the mechanisms that helped the islanders cope; no doubt, too, they provided a large part of the status and wealth that the island elite enjoyed.[57]

Area cultivated. In the 1930s, typically only about 6–8 percent of the total surface area of the Kyklades was under cultivation in cereals.[58] If comparable areas were cropped in antiquity, the islands' production could have satisfied only a very small population, approaching a high percentage of

56. Tournefort, *Voyage*, I.192, Seriphos produces only a small barley crop; I.228, Naxos exports barley; I.266, Ios exports wheat, likewise Sikinos (I.270); I.273, Pholegandros is self-sufficient in grain, with a population of 120 families (perhaps about 600–720 persons); I.284, Thera grows mostly barley (not surprising, given modern rainfall statistics); II.8, Kythnos grows lots of barley but little wheat; II.16, Keos "abound[s]" in barley; II.32, Andros has plenty of barley but imports wheat from Volos; II.41, Tenos again has plenty of barley but little wheat.

57. Cf. Gallant, 143–96.

58. ΣΕΕ 1937: 112; 1938: 112; 1939: 112: in 1936, 14,401 ha (6.4 percent); in 1937, 17,198 ha (7.6 percent); and in 1938, 18,581 ha (8.2 percent).

Delos's estimated population (see table 4.6). Three considerations, however, suggest that considerably more of the islands' land was under cultivation in antiquity.

Recent study of the Melian countryside has found at least 17 percent, and up to 58 percent, of land suitable for cultivation on the criterion of surface slope, although only 13.95 percent of the island was cropped in 1971.[59] Anything from 18 to 75 percent of potentially arable land was therefore idle. It is reasonable to suppose that much of this land would have been brought under cultivation in antiquity. Furthermore, this area was land arable as it was, without improvement. As any visitor to the Kyklades knows, even the steepest slopes have been rendered suitable for crops by terracing. Unfortunately, terrace walls are notoriously difficult to date, and study of the landscape archaeology of the islands remains in its infancy.[60] However, M. Brunet's careful examination of terracing on Delos suggests that the system there was in place by the fifth or fourth century B.C. The Delian system brings the arable surface of Delos up to about 250 ha, nearly 70 percent of the total area.[61] If the Delian system was created in response to the same needs as the terraces of its neighbors, then it would be safe to assume that the Kykladic system as a whole was in place by the early Hellenistic age at the latest. Many terraces are idle today, largely because of emigration in the face of declining opportunities for local employment and inability of local farmers to compete with imported foods, but if brought into use, they would considerably raise the total potential arable surface in the islands. The existence of the terraces thus provides a strong argument for much higher ancient rates of cropping than attested today.

In 329/8 B.C., Skyros, which covers 20,900 ha, produced 9,600 *medimnoi* of wheat and 28,800 of barley; Lemnos, with a total area of 47,600 ha, produced 56,750 *medimnoi* of wheat and 248,525 of barley. If only 8 percent of the surface of these islands were under cultivation, Skyros would have enjoyed yields of roughly 1,122 kg/ha and Lemnos of 3,960 kg/ha!

59. Wagstaff and Gamble in *Island Polity,* 101; Malcolm Wagstaff and Siv Augustson in ibid., 106–7.

60. See, e.g., Donald Davidson and Catriona Tasker in *Island Polity,* 82; Colin Renfrew in ibid., 274; T. M. Whitelaw in *Landscape Archaeology,* 407–8; J. Cherry, J. Davis, and E. Mantzourani in ibid., 59, 237; J. Bennet and S. Voutsaki in ibid., 377–78 (difficulty of dating); Oliver Rackham and Jennifer Moody in *Agriculture in Ancient Greece,* 123–30, with a typology of terraces (124–25) and brief discussion of the possibility (it seems very likely to me) that the τειχία of *IG* XII 7.62.17–19 were terraces, and of the discovery on Krete of an olive tree dating to the late fourth century B.C. rooted in a terrace wall (128); Lohmann in ibid., 51, on Attike.

61. Brunet, 149 with n. 27.

Table 4.6. Estimated Yields for the Kyklades, with 10–60 Percent of Surface Cropped
Kyklades (1), Krete (2), All Greece (3)

A. 10% cropped = 22,510 ha; seed = 3.94 mil kg (175 kg/ha)

	Yield/ha[a] *(kg)*	*Net Yield (mil kg)*	*Net Yield (mil* med*)*	*Population Fed*[b]
Wheat				
(1)	450	6.19	0.155	21,500
(2)	748	12.90	0.320	44,470
(3)	673	11.21	0.278	38,650
Barley				
(1)	680	7.39	0.220	25,310
(2)	903	10.65	0.317	36,490
(3)	732	8.15	0.243	27,920

B. 20% cropped = 45,020 ha; seed = 7.88 mil kg (175 kg/ha)

	Yield/ha[a] *(kg)*	*Net Yield (mil kg)*	*Net Yield (mil* med*)*	*Population Fed*[b]
Wheat				
(1)	450	12.38	0.309	42,915
(2)	748	25.79	0.640	88,940
(3)	673	22.42	0.556	77,300
Barley				
(1)	680	14.78	0.440	50,620
(2)	903	21.30	0.635	72,980
(3)	732	16.30	0.486	55,840

C. 40% cropped = 90,040 ha; seed = 15.76 mil kg

	Yield/ha[a] *(kg)*	*Net Yield (mil kg)*	*Net Yield (mil* med*)*	*Population Fed*[b]
Wheat				
(1)	450	24.76	0.619	85,970
(2)	748	51.59	1.281	177,880
(3)	673	44.84	1.113	154,600
Barley				
(1)	680	29.55	0.881	101,250
(2)	903	42.60	1.270	145,970
(3)	732	32.60	0.972	111,680

Table 4.6. *(Continued)*

D. 60% cropped = 135,060 ha; seed = 23.64 mil kg	*Yield/ha*[a] *(kg)*	*Net Yield (mil kg)*	*Net Yield (mil* med*)*	*Population Fed*[b]
Wheat				
(1)	450	37.14	0.928	128,890
(2)	748	77.38	1.921	266,830
(3)	673	67.25	1.670	231,900
Barley				
(1)	680	44.33	1.321	151,900
(2)	903	63.91	1.905	218,950
(3)	732	48.89	1.457	167,500

SOURCES: Kykladic yields, 1921–32: E. Ruschenbusch, *ZPE* 72 (1988): 141–53; Krete and Greece, 1911–50: Gallant, 77, table 4.7.

[a] (1) = Average yield/ha for the Kyklades; (2) = average yield/ha for Krete; (3) = average yield/ha for all Greece.

[b] For wheat: 7.2 *med*/per/yr; barley: 8.7 *med*/per/yr.

Clearly such figures are impossible. Yields per ha become reasonable only by assuming 20–50 percent of the total surface was cropped in grains. This result also strongly reinforces the view that considerably more of the islands' land was planted with grain in antiquity than modern figures suggest.[62]

Table 4.6 presents estimates for the productivity of the Kyklades, Krete, and Greece as a whole, based on these considerations. For total area of the islands, I use the figure for the modern *nomos* of about 2,251 km^2, or 225,100 ha.[63]

At a conservative cropping of 20–40 percent of total surface, Kykladic production could have supported very roughly 50,500 to 100,000 persons. It must be born in mind that these figures represent, not maxima, but a population that the mean production of the archipelago could support over the long haul. Consumption estimates have already taken into account social storage of surplus food, so that in good years there would be an excess

62. Contra, Eberhard Ruschenbusch, *ANSP* 13 (1983): 172, 174, who offers no argument for his pessimistic views. For an unpublished Athenian inscription extracting taxes in grain from (probably) Imbros, Skyros, and Lemnos in 374/3 B.C., see Isager-Skydsgaard, 140.

63. ΣΕΕ 1981: 2–3, table I.3. Exact figures differ in different sourcebooks; I have used the most recent official Greek figures readily available to me.

available for appropriation—whether by the elite, the government, the military, or outside powers—and in poor years imports would be necessary. Local shortages would be made up from local sources whenever possible, as at Phira and Gonia on Thera.

For a population of 2,600–9,100 persons, Delian demand represents 18.2 percent of the total typical supply on pessimistic assumptions, only 2.5 percent on optimistic, 7–8 percent on the mean. Could the Kyklades have provided this much grain?

The population of the Kyklades in the Hellenistic age can be estimated roughly. Ruschenbusch calculates a total population of 22,092 for fifteen Kykladic islands.[64] This figure may be low. It reckons the ratio of adult males to the full population at 1:4, which is probably too pessimistic; if we figure instead 1:5, we get 27,615 persons. Ruschenbusch regards slaves as an unimportant component of island populations, but even if only the upper 7 percent or so of the population could afford them,[65] that still implies 1,933 slaveholders in the islands; if each held on average just two slaves, they would have added almost 3,870 persons to the population. There must also have been some permanent metic population. During the great siege, the Rhodians counted 1,000 able-bodied adult male metics in contrast to a citizen population of 6,000 (Diod. 20.84.2). The Kyklades, less prosperous, must have attracted proportionally fewer resident foreigners: let us say no more than 10 percent of the citizen population, including wives and children; this would add another 2,750 persons. Finally, there would have been a steady population of transients: merchants, travelers, *theoroi*, ambassadors, soldiers, dramatic artists—perhaps another 10 percent. These adjustments yield a total population of about 37,000.

It should be emphasized that there are many uncertainties in these estimates. Beside the technical objections, corrections, and adjustments that may be applied to Ruschenbusch's figures and methodology, the larger structural issues Sallares has raised, to which I have already alluded, come into play. The two important Kykladic surveys that have been published (for Melos and part of Keos) agree that population reached its height in the fourth century and had suffered a retreat by the late second and first. On Keos this shrinkage can be traced also in the polis center of Koresia, which may have first begun to suffer during the Khremonidean War.[66] Unfortu-

64. E. Ruschenbusch, *ZPE* 59 (1985): 258–59.

65. Ruschenbusch in *Aux Origines de l'Hellénisme*, 265–69; *ANSP* 13 (1983): 176–79, reckoning slaves at 1.5–3 percent of the total population.

66. Sallares, 62–73. Malcolm Wagstaff and John F. Cherry in *Island Polity* 145–46, 252–53; T. M. Whitelaw and J. L. Davis in *Landscape Archaeology* 265–81.

nately, the third century remains generally obscure. In general, there are two possibilities: either population stayed high throughout the years of this study, so that whatever figures are accepted should be regarded as rough maxima; or population began to decline during our period, which would imply either a rising surplus[67] (and so relief for Delos, dependent as it was on appropriating such surpluses) or, assuming that production declined in tandem with the population, a roughly unchanging situation.

Given these caveats, two inferences are clear. First, the Kyklades must normally have been more or less self-sufficient in grain. This should come as no surprise. Most Greek poleis were self-sufficient; it is the rare cities chronically dependent on imports, like Athens, that are the exception. Even if we have underestimated the Kykladic population by half, a doubled total of 74,000 still falls within the high end of the range of estimated carrying capacity.[68] In general, ordinary Delian demand could be satisfied out of the marginal surpluses of its Kykladic neighbors. Second, even at the lowest levels estimated, Delos's population made it unique in the Kyklades. Its role in the islands as a religious center and an economic focus lent it special status, which in turn probably helped to attract the goods its inhabitants needed from its Kykladic neighbors. The most important implication of these calculations, however, is that Delos normally depended only on its nearest neighbors for its supplies of grain. The island had no need regularly to seek supplies from distant producers like the states of the Black Sea, or even Egypt; we shall see below that there is in fact virtually no evidence to suggest any dependence on the country of its Ptolemaic overlords for grain.

THE POTENTIAL OF FARTHER NEIGHBORS

Despite the general independence of the islands in grain, there were certainly occasional, if rare, general shortages that afflicted the archipelago as a whole, or even a larger geographical region, like the famous shortages of the 330s that required many Greek states to seek help from distant Kyrene (Tod II.196). When such problems arose, where were the Delians (and their neighbors) likely to have turned?

We need look no farther than the islands off the coast of Asia Minor. From Lemnos in the north through Lesbos, Samos, Khios, and Kos to Rhodos in the south, these islands, lying but a short sail east of Delos on the customary route, were remarkably productive. Modern rainfall statistics

67. Sallares, 316, explains the difference between ancient, grain-importing, and mediaeval, grain-exporting, Greece thus.

68. Tournefort, *Voyage*, I.159, 185, 216, 233, 273, 285, 296, II.1, 9, 13, 32, 40, 42, and 43, gives figures for the populations of most of the Kyklades that total 65,800, assuming his families or households consist of five persons.

for Samos show a mean accumulation during the growing season in 1952–80 of 646.5 mm, already double the amount necessary for wheat. Indeed, excessive rainfall brings problems of its own; too much rain can waterlog the soil, leaching out nutrients and retarding growth, and heavy rain just before harvest can promote rusts. Modern Samian wheat crop failure rates of nearly 50 percent may be attributable to these factors. Diodoros reports a period when too much rain "for many years" (ἐπὶ πολλοὺς χρόνους) ruined crops and brought about a plague (Diod. 5.82.1).[69] Nevertheless, in years when rainfall was generally low, these islands had enough to produce bumper crops. Only once in 1952–80 did a drought on Samos correlate with a shortage on an island to the north (Lemnos). A similar pattern emerges during the great shortages of 330–326 B.C. The great donation of grain to the Greek states by Kyrene included most of the Kyklades (Keos, Kythnos, Paros, Thera, and perhaps Tenos), but only Rhodos and Kos certainly appear of the islands off the coast of Asia. Samos and Khios are notably missing, and Lesbos is in my view very doubtful.[70] Indeed, the northerly islands seem not just to have been spared but to have enjoyed a normal or even good harvest. In 329/8 B.C., Imbros, Skyros, and two communities on Lemnos, all of them subject to Athens, produced at least 26,000, 28,800, and 248,525 *medimnoi* of barley, and 44,200, 9,600, and 56,750 *medimnoi* of wheat.[71] The combined wheat crop of these three islands could have fed roughly 15,350 persons, and the combined barley crop 22,650, or a total of 38,000 people. They clearly enjoyed a substantial surplus; no doubt all of it went to Athens. But these islands, not terribly far from the Kyklades, would have been a reasonable target for Kykladic islanders seeking crops when general shortages struck at home. Their large size, abundant rainfall, and convenient location made them perfect suppliers. We can estimate

69. U.S. Dept. of Commerce, *World Weather Records*, vol. 2, *Europe, 1951–1960*, 150, *1961–1970*, 140, *1971–1980*, 138. Arnon, *Crop Production in Dry Regions*, I.31 (excess rain), II.7 (rust). Garnsey, 13, on Samos. Cf. also Diod. 12.58.3–4 on a rainy Attike winter that led to crop failure and the purification of Delos in 450 B.C. Livy 37.27.1 on Khios; Theoph. *Hist. pl.* 8.2.9 on Khalke.

70. Tod II.196 (= *SEG* 9.2+), with Tod's comm., 274–76. The absence of other islands—for example, Kythnos and Keos appear but not Seriphos, Siphnos, Melos, or Andros—may reflect the regional variability in drought that we have seen so often; even a "general" drought may skip individual localities.

71. *IG* II^2 1672.297–98, 275, with Jardé, 41; cf. Garnsey, 99–101 and 98, table 5. Garnsey makes an airtight case for good harvests on the islands and bad harvests in Athens. If there was cheating (cf. Josiah Ober, *Fortress Attica* [Leiden, 1985], 23–24), these figures may underrepresent the real harvest; but see now Isager-Skydsgaard, 172, and Garnsey in *Agriculture in Ancient Greece*, 147–48. Cf. K. J. Beloch, *Opus* 4 (1985): 9–28, with Carmine Ampolo, *Opus* 4 (1985): 7–8.

their productivity using the same figures for yield and area cropped as for the Kyklades and a total surface area of 5,421 km^2 (= 542,100 ha).[72] At cropping levels of 40 percent, the islands would produce roughly 97,578,000 to 162,196,320 kilograms of wheat, or 2,422,492 to 4,026,720 *medimnoi,* enough to feed 336,450 to 559,260 people; in barley, production would be roughly 95,843,280 to 127,724,230 kilograms of *alphita,* or 2,856,814 to 3,793,681 *medimnoi,* enough to support 328,370 to 436,000 people. Cropped at a rate of 60 percent, the same islands could have fed half again as many people.

Perhaps Diodoros deserves the last word:

> The islands, exposed to breezes, supplying their inhabitants with wholesome air, and lucky in their crops, were filled with greater and greater abundance and quickly made the inhabitants happy. Therefore they have been named the islands of the blessed, the abundance they enjoy of good things being the reason for the name. . . . (3) In general, the islands just mentioned enjoyed a happiness far beyond their neighbors not only in antiquity but also in our age; for being the finest of all in richness of soil, excellence of location, and mildness of climate, they are reasonably called beautiful and truthfully happy.[73]

LONG-DISTANCE IMPORTS

The considerations advanced above show how limited Delian demand for grain originating outside the Kyklades really was. It should now come as no surprise that the entire body of documentation from Delos reveals only a single decree specifically honoring a dealer in grain, for Dionysios of Byzantion, who in the first half of the third century sold 500 *medimnoi* of wheat to the city at a price the city requested (*IG* XI 4.627 = *Choix,* 46). We have already seen that it is a mistake to construct on this single decree and on Dionysios's ethnic a superstructure of regular grain imports from the Black Sea.[74]

There are, however, two other pieces of evidence that deserve brief discussion. Throughout the years of Delian independence, the island bought grain from time to time to distribute to the local inhabitants. In the later third century, and certainly by 209 B.C., this practice had become institutionalized as a σιτωνία fund. The Delian government borrowed funds from a revolving account to pay for the grain, which was then resold at a

72. Figures for Karpathos, Khios, Kos, Lemnos, Lesbos, Rhodos, and Samos from Kolodny, *Population des îles,* 695–720.

73. Diod. 5.82.2–4, Loeb trans. by C. H. Oldfather, slightly modified.

74. As do Durrbach, *Choix,* p. 57; Shear, 30; Marasco, 130–35. Cf. chapter 3, pp. 53, 64, 68–69, above.

moderate price and the funds replenished. Several analogous funds are attested from other cities. The significance of this practice is not easy to gauge. The rising wealth of Delos in the later third century, combined with a modest growth in population, may have spurred the Delians to assure themselves of cheap grain out of public funds. The timing of the purchases and sales, however, adds another dimension: it seems evident that the Delians were working to guarantee the availability of affordable grain in the spring, just before the harvest and the opening of the sailing season. Rising wealth may have provided the opportunity to regularize a function that the city had undertaken occasionally in the decades before. The creation of the *sitonia* fund certainly attests to an interest in the grain supply—itself hardly unusual among the Greek cities. Unfortunately—with one exception, dealt with just below—we know absolutely nothing about the origin of this grain. Everything said so far leads me to suspect that the vast majority of it came from very nearby sources, not excluding Delian farmers themselves. The mere existence of the fund proves nothing about long-distance imports.[75]

In one case, however, we do happen to know the origin of grain sold cheaply to the Delians, and in this case the grain did come from a distant source. In 180 B.C., Massinissa of Numidia donated almost 2,900 *medimnoi* of grain (σῖτος, almost surely wheat),[76] which were sold in one lot for 3 drachmas and three other lots for 4 drachmas 1 obol per *medimnos*,[77] considerably below the market price for wheat. There is no indication whatsoever that Delos was in need of grain at the time, or that Delos had ever imported grain from Numidia before. The accounts mention the involvement of a Delian ambassador, ὁ πρεσβευτὴς Ῥόδων (*ID* 442A101).[78] The Delians had also voted Massinissa a crown; the accounts record the

75. G. Reger, *Classical Antiquity* 12 (1993): 320–29.

76. *ID* 442A100–106, cf. Larsen, 384, and Vial, 138–40, 238–39. Philippe Gauthier, in *CICG*, 61 n. 1, cautiously refuses to choose wheat or barley, but the price would have been no bargain for barley. Gauthier supposes that the original shipment consisted of 3,000 *medimnoi*, of which a little over 200 would have been lost in shipping, measuring, and so on. Loss of over 100 *medimnoi* seems high; perhaps some was diverted for temple or public use before the sale. See Appendix I for Massinissa's dedications on Delos.

77. Although the last entry cites a price of 4 dr/*med*, the actual price must have been 4 dr 1 ob, as Larsen, 384 n. 2, demonstrates.

78. As Philippe Gauthier has recently shown, Durrbach's restoration, Ῥοδ[ί]ων (*Choix*, p. 92), created a nonexistent Rhodian ambassador. I adopt Gauthier's emendation (*CICG*, 64–68), now confirmed by Tréheux (*ID Index*, s.v. Χαρμύλος Νικάρχου Ῥόδιος, p. 87).

repayment of the loan for this honor in Poseidon 179 B.C.[79] Philippe Gauthier thinks a Numidian ambassador may have passed through Delos early in 180 B.C. and assured the Delians of Massinissa's good will, and that the Delians might have dispatched Rhodon soon thereafter with the crown, who returned accompanied by the gift of grain.[80] It seems more likely to me, however, that Massinissa's gift was spontaneous. The proceeds of the sale of the grain were deposited in four lots, the first of which fell in Lenaion of 179 B.C. (*ID* 442A100). Given the exigencies of the sailing season, the grain must have arrived in 180 B.C., probably by October, as Gauthier suggests.[81] The first deposit is entered in the name of the three regular *sitonai* of 179 B.C. and the ambassador Rhodon. The remaining three deposits occurred in Artemision, perhaps under the aegis of a special committee appointed to dispose of the rest of the king's gift (see *ID* 442A102–6). What was Rhodon's role in the first deposit? Despite the absence of direct evidence, he had probably served on the board of *sitonai* of 180 B.C. who received the grain; if the first lot was sold in Poseidon, he may have handed over the proceeds to his successors for deposit early in 179 B.C. His role in dealing with the gift in 180 B.C. would then explain his designation, after his term of office as *sitones* had ended on the last day of Poseidon 180 B.C., as ambassador to Massinissa to convey the Delian demos's thanks and the crown to the king as soon as possible in 179 B.C. (*ID* 442A41–43, 65–67). Massinissa's gift thus probably belongs among the innumerable gifts of grain by potentates to Greek cities, reflections of political circumstances or simple piety whose details are lost to us.[82] It says nothing about local Delian demand or typical sources of supply. Indeed, the fact that the grain was a gift, not bought, forbids any inferences about the normal origin of grain on Delos.

The evidence from Delos's neighbors does not change the picture. Arkesine on Amorgos awarded citizenship to a Theran, Epianaktides, who

79. *ID* 442A41–43, 65–67. See also M.-F. Baslez and Claude Vial, *BCH* 111 (1987): 284–93.

80. Gauthier in *CICG*, 68–69, with 69 n. 30.

81. Ibid., 68.

82. "[Le] don de grain numide . . . vient seulement grossir la liste des libéralités que les rois firent aux cités ou aux sanctuaires panhelléniques" (Gauthier in *CICG*, 67). "L'episodo è stato giustamente interpretato come un'inziativa di Massinissa al fine di assicurarsi uno sbocco sui mercati ellenistici per il grano del su regno e la partecipanzione di un'ambasciatore rodio è prova del particolare interesse dei Rodi, i quali, data la carenza di novi da parte di Massinissa, avrebbero potuto trarre lauti guadagni dal commercio del grano numidico," thinks Marasco, *Prometheus* 11 (1985): 143–44, following Casson, 177–78. This seems very unlikely.

σεσιτήγηκεν εἰς τὴμ πόλιν τὴν ᾿Αρκεσινέων (*IG* XII 7.11.6). The same city also honored an Agathokles, who has been identified with a Rhodian honored at Ephesos for selling grain at a reduced price; his benefactions to Arkesine may have been along the same lines. Three Rhodians honored in *IG* XII 7.8 have also been regarded as traders in grain.[83] Money apparently left over from the purchase of public grain on Ios went to buy a crown for Antisthenes of Rhodos; it is a reasonable assumption that he had imported grain at a cut rate.[84] None of these inscriptions gives the slightest indication of the origin of the grain; just because Egyptian trade was largely in Rhodian hands does not mean that all Rhodians traded in Egyptian goods.[85] The Rhodians might just have been local traders, moving around the Kyklades and the coast of Asia Minor; perhaps the Theran honored by Arkesine was the same kind of small fry.

Nor do the islands' *sitonia* funds help. Their existence is hardly surprising, given the wide distribution of such institutions in the Hellenistic world—they certainly do not imply that the Kyklades were usually susceptible to shortages—and the documents that attest to them say nothing about the sources of the grain they bought.[86]

The evidence supports a picture of trade in grain around Delos not much different from that which Tournefort drew for the seventeenth century:

> There is however some difficulty to lade Corn in the Levant; being often forced to run from one Island to another, before you can get a full Cargo, and then it must sometimes be half Wheat, half Rye. In 1700, the Turks of Volo and Thessalonica being under apprehensions

83. *IG* XII 7.9, esp. ll. 3–6 = *SIG*³ 354. Cf. Alain Bresson, *Index* 9 (1980): 144, and Erich Ziebarth in *Mélanges Gustave Glotz* (Paris, 1932), 2: 916.

84. *IG* XII 5.1010.5–6. Ugo Fantasia, *Civilità classica e cristiana* 5 (1984): 298 n. 34 and 306 n. 61, suggests that the Areates who bought the grain and gave money for Antisthenes' crown was not a *sitones* but just a merchant.

85. See Will I², 181–91, and further discussion in chapter 5, pp. 159–65, below.

86. For Delos, see Reger, *Classical Antiquity* 12 (1993): 326–27. Paros, *IG* XII 5.135; Keos, *IG* XII suppl. 234, and Werner Peek, *Ath. Mitt.* 59 (1934): 63–64, no. 20 (the stone was found in the Epigraphical Museum in Athens with no indication of provenance; for doubts about its origin, see G. Reger and M. Risser in *Landscape Archaeology*, 315 n. 13). The decree *IG* XII 5.817 represents a purchase at Delos by representatives of the Island League; military needs may lurk behind it. Public purchase of grain occurred at least occasionally on Ios and at Arkesine on Amorgos (*IG* XII 5.1010; 7.11, 40). *Agoranomoi* on Astypalaia and Paros were responsible for regulating bread prices: *IG* XII 3.169 + 3 suppl. p. 278, 170 + XII suppl. p. 79; *IG* XII 5.129. A Syrian inscription from early in the third century A.D. (*IG* XII 5.658.30–31) mentions τὴν [κ]οιν[ὴν] ἀγορὰν τ[ῶν] σ[ιτ]ίων.

> of a famine, would not suffer the People of this place [i.e., Sikinos] to sell Corn to Strangers, any more than in Candia: but as the Mussulmans will do any thing for Money, they let the Provensals ship it off by night.[87]

Delos was no insatiable consumer of grain brought in from long distances, whether from the Black Sea or even Egypt. Delian production clearly played a role in feeding the local population, even if the figures reckoned above give only the roughest approximation of Delian production. When the surpluses of her Kykladic neighbors are figured in, Delos probably subsisted in normal years entirely or largely on grain shipped in from very nearby. As "the greater part of the grain that flowed into the *sitoboleia* [storage facilities of the Greek cities] must have been of local origin, produced by the farmers of the *khora*,"[88] it would be surprising if Delos were an exception. It is much more likely, as Garnsey, Gallant, and Rathbone have remarked in another context, that the attested "trade" in grain in the Hellenistic world reflects not ongoing operations of commercial exchange, but spontaneous, temporary responses to transient local shortages and surpluses.[89]

These results are also important for the view that Delos was a transit port for grain. Great local demand normally led to heightened local concern with the trade, which sometimes issued in regulations and improvements meant to attract the traders. The process is familiar from Athens, whose expanding demand—especially in the fourth century—promoted great growth in the city as a harbor and transit town.[90] No similar process can be assumed at Delos: sporadic and unpredictably varying annual demand for *long-distance* imports would not have encouraged the development of a transit trade business. That came later and was owing to other factors.

87. Tournefort, *Voyage*, I.270–71.

88. Luigi Moretti in *Storia e civilità dei Greci*, vol. 4, *La società ellenistica*, pt. 8, *Economia, diritto, religione* (Milan, 1977), 355. Cf. Pleket, *MBAH* 3.1 (1984): 21; Strubbe, *EA* 13 (1989): 108; Garnsey, 74–79 (on dealing with local speculators and hoarders).

89. Garnsey, Gallant, and Rathbone, *JRS* 74 (1984): 30–44, cf. 42. Cf. also Garnsey, 13; Robin Osborne, *Classical Landscape with Figures* (London, 1987), 97; Peter Garnsey and Ian Morris in *Bad Year Economics*, 104; Halstead and Jones, *JHS* 109 (1989): 54. In general, see M.-T. Le Dinahet in *L'Origine des richesses dépensées dans la ville antique* (Aix-en-Provence, 1985), 39–45.

90. See Garnsey, 107–64, and Robert Garland, *The Piraeus from the Fifth to the First Century* B.C. (Ithaca, N.Y., 1987), 58–100, esp. 72–83, on the administration, and 83–95 on the *emporion*.

Transit Trade in Grain

I have often noted the view that Delos was a great center of the grain trade. It is time now to consider some of the evidence on which this view is based.[91]

THE THIRD CENTURY TO ca. 240 B.C.

We must begin with an instance of "history from square brackets."[92] An inscription of 281 B.C. includes the entry Ἀρτίμαι καὶ Δεινί[αι (or -ωνι) οὗ ὁ πτολεμαϊ?]κὸς σῖτος ἔκειτο κλεῖδας ποιήσασι καὶ ἐπιθεῖσι, 4 dr ("to Artimas and Deinias [or Deinion], 4 dr, for making and installing the keys where the Ptolemaic grain used to lie").[93] In combination with the new Kallias decree, which mentions that "Kallias himself sailing at his own expense to Cyprus and there conversing earnestly with the king in behalf of the city brought back fifty talents of silver for the Demos [of Athens] and a gift of twenty thousand medimnoi of wheat, which were measured out from Delos to the agents sent by the Demos,"[94] this evidence appears to support the views that "the island became one of the great centers of the Aegean grain trade during the third century B.C." and that "the royal monopolies of Egypt had begun to develop Delos as a clearing-house for their grain trade from the earliest years of Ptolemaic control."[95]

Despite apparently universal acceptance,[96] the restoration [ὁ πτολεμαϊ?]κὸς σῖτος rests on no evidence whatsoever. It is the only attestation for Ptolemaic grain on Delos; the Kallias decree cannot be used to "confirm" it, since the decree itself says only that the grain was measured out on Delos, not that it was stored there. There are numerous other possible restorations for the passage. For example: [ὁ δημοτι]κὸς σῖτος, "the demos's grain," perhaps rather unlikely in view of τὸν σῖτον τὸν δημόσιον attested for Ios and Amorgos (*IG* XII 5.1010.6, *IG* XII 7.40.9); [ὁ πολιτι]κὸς σῖτος, "the city's grain," an adjective commonly used for polis

91. Larsen, 350–51; Rostovtzeff, 221, 231–32; Shear, 30–31; Vial, 341–42; Marasco, 142–47. Contra: Casson, "Grain Trade," 76. See too chapter 3, p. 53, above.

92. Ernst Badian, *ZPE* 79 (1989): 59.

93. *IG* XI 2.159A53–54. I confirmed the kappa on the stone and saw the possible trace of an iota before it in July 1990.

94. Shear, ll. 50–55; Shear's tr., p. 5. For the date I follow Christian Habicht, *Untersuchungen zur politischen Geschichte Athens* (Munich, 1979), 46–47, with n. 5 there. Cf. also Michael J. Osborne, *ZPE* 35 (1979): 181–94.

95. Shear, 30, echoing Rostovtzeff, 231. Cf. BE (1981): 230, at p. 396.

96. Shear writes simply that Durrbach's restoration is "only one of several possibilities, even if the most likely" (32–33 n. 76).

property, as with πρόσοδος, χώρα, or even σῶμα; or [ὁ ἐμπορι]κὸς σῖτος, "the imported grain."[97] Best however in my view are either [ὁ ξενι]κὸς σῖτος, which is attested in an Andrian inscription of the mid third century and probably refers to grain bought for a foreign garrison (*IG* XII 5.714.3, with *IG* XII suppl., p. 119), or, better still, [ὁ συναγοριστι]κὸς σῖτος or [ὁ ἀγοριστι]κὸς σῖτος, "grain for sale,"[98] which fits the space better than [ὁ ξενι]κός. Since Delos was buying grain at public expense as early as 301 B.C. (*IG* XI 2.146A20–21), the city must have needed storage space, which it could have rented from private owners or provided in one of its own buildings, including a building in the temple. The entry at *IG* XI 2.159A53–54 probably has nothing whatever to do with "Ptolemaic" grain.

Even without the traditional restoration, however, one might argue from the passage in the Kallias decree quoted above that the Ptolemies did indeed use Delos as a grain storage and transfer point. This evidence has in my view been grossly misinterpreted. In the first place, the passage does not say that the grain was stored on Delos, only that it was there transferred to the Athenians (l. 54). The grain may in fact have come from Kypros, where Kallias had spoken with the king. *OGIS* 56.17–18 attests to imports of grain (σῖτος) into Egypt from Syria, Phoinike, and Kypros (the demotic version of the text specifies Salamis, see Dittenberger's n. 34 there) by Ptolemaios III at a time of high prices (τιμῶν μειζόνων). There is abundant evidence as well for movement of grain in the other direction, from Egypt to Kypros and Asia Minor, both in Hellenistic and Roman imperial times.[99] We have already seen that the interest the Ptolemies had in the Kyklades was strategic, not economic. They lay on the route to mainland Greece. Projection of power onto the mainland required (among other things) reliable provisioning. The Ptolemaic intervention into Greece of 308 B.C. foundered for lack of supplies (Diod. 19.37.1). Troops in the Kyklades always stressed local supplies, as we shall see in chapter 5; any sensible government that had experienced the headaches of provisioning in the

97. For [ἐξ ἱερῶν κα]ὶ πολιτικῶν προσόδων, see *IvPerg* 246.41; πολε[ιτικὴγ] χώραν, Pergamon, *OGIS* 338.6; *IG* XII 5.1010.5–6, 7.40.8–9, and *IG* XII 7.386.25–26 (= *SIG*³ 521), σῶμα μηθὲν πολιτικόν; cf. the σιτικὸν ἐμπόριον at [Arist.] *Ath. pol.* 51.4 (I thank my colleague A. D. Macro for the suggestion [ὁ ἐμπορι]κὸς σῖτος).

98. On *IG* XII 5.714, see G. Reger, *Hesperia,* forthcoming. For συναγοριστικός and ἀγοριστικός, see H.-J. Drexhage, *Preise, Mieten/Pachten, Kosten und Löhne im römischen Ägypten* (St. Katharinen, 1991), 22.

99. Zimmermann, *ZPE* 92 (1992): 208 n. 35, 215–16; cf. M. Wörrle, *Chiron* 1 (1971): 325–40.

islands would surely have taken steps to assure supplies. Delos, centrally located and protected from raiding by its sacred status, offered a perfect location for a storage depot. Grain was probably stockpiled for use of the troops that liberated Athens in 287 B.C.

The second piece of evidence cited to show Delos's role in the transit trade is an inscription erected on Delos in the first quarter of the third century honoring the Delian Mnesalkos son of Telesarkhides: "during the dearth of grain [ἡ σπανισιτία] he got released grain that had been twice seized by Delians to whom the city owed money."[100] Unfortunately, the identity of the city honoring Mnesalkos is lost. Maurice Holleaux suggested perhaps a city on the Black Sea, which Jardé rejected because "these great cereal-producing countries" would not have needed to import grain.[101] If we assume that the debt was public—that is, that the "Delians" of the inscription were the corporate body of Delos, not private persons[102]—then it is impossible that the indebted city be located anywhere but in the Kyklades or close by. In the fourth and third centuries, Apollo lent money to Kykladic states, and in the third to Hermione in the Argolid and Peparethos. That was the geographical extent of his generosity; it is out of the question that the debtor here should have been farther away.[103] Most probably the grain seized was being moved from one Kykladic island to another and happened to pass through Delos; it is less likely, in my view, that the grain was bought on Delos. In either case, this was certainly a local operation, quite in line with the movement of grain at Delos depicted above.

In general, the very skimpy evidence for the first seventy-five years of Delian independence does not support the idea that the island served as a central transfer or transit point for the long-distance trade in grain. Delian

100. *IG* XI 4.1049.6–7: ἔν [τε] τῆι σπανισιτίαι σῖτογ καταχθέντα ὑπὸ Δηλίω[ν] δὶς οἷς ὤφειλεν ἡ πόλις. For the character and general procedures of such seizures, which fall under a type of σῦλον, see Philippe Gauthier, *Symbola* (Nancy, 1972), 220–21. Pierre Roussel dated the inscription to 300–275. It certainly belongs before 257 B.C., the last possible year of Mnesalkos's death. Cf. *IG* XI 2.161A29 and 162A23; Vial, 136. I agree with Bogaert, 171, that Mnesalkos was not a banker (cf. Bogaert's n. 205). Marasco, 141–42.

101. Holleaux, I.372; Jardé, 175 n. 3. On the false view that the Pontic countries were primarily grain exporters, see Will I², 187–91, esp. 190–91, discussing Polybios 4.38.4–5; Alexandra Stefan in *Hellenische Poleis: Krise, Wandlung, Wirkung* (Berlin, 1974), II.648–63.

102. Léopold Migeotte has recently argued that a similar locution in *IG* XI 4.559 (= *Choix*, 18, Migeotte, 161–66, no. 47) refers to the city as a corporate body (Migeotte, 163–64, contra Larsen, 337–40, 370).

103. For the Amphiktyonia, see chapter 6, pp. 215–17, below; *IG* XI 4.559 (= *Choix*, 18, Migeotte, 161–66, no. 47). Hermione: *IG* XI 2.144A18 and 162A27. Peparethos: *IG* XI 2.156A20 (shortly before 282 B.C.).

trade must have focused virtually exclusively on making up the deficit that Delian, Rheneian, and Mykonian production left; that deficit was sought in the regular, although small, surpluses of Delos's neighbors, and more rarely from farther away. Dionysios, honored for selling his grain at a discount—perhaps as part of a public purchase for resale—may stand in for the type of small-scale local merchant moving around the islands on whom Delos depended; his peers were men like the Theran Epianaktides and the Rhodian Agathokles honored on Amorgos.

AFTER ca. 240 B.C.

In contrast to the earlier period, there is more positive evidence for trade in grain on Delos after about 240 B.C. Sometime in the 230s or 220s, Histiaia on Euboia dispatched *sitonai* to Delos, where a Rhodian named Athenodoros son of Peisagoras lent them money at no interest (*IG* XI 4.1055 = *Choix*, 50). The Histiaians enjoyed a continuing relationship with Athenodoros, but we should not suppose that they sent buyers to Delos simply to deal with him.[104] They did not buy grain from Athenodoros, who is being honored for help with the financing. Rather, the Histiaian *sitonai* went to Delos because they expected to find grain there for sale. This does not take us out of the Kykladic orbit: the cities of Euboia had long-standing tight relations with Delos.[105]

Another important document dated 239–229 B.C. is often cited as proof of the role of Delos in the general transit trade in grain, where, it is claimed, grain from Egypt and Sicily would have been readily available.[106] An honorary decree was passed by the Delians in favor of Aristoboulos son of Athenaios of Thessalonike (*IG* XI 4.666 = *Choix*, 48). Aristoboulos, who spent a good deal of time on the island, "was sent by king Demetrios as grain buyer (σιτώνης)" (l. 6). Despite the closeness in date of this text to the Histiaian decree just discussed, it is important to avoid the temptation to treat them together as complementary or corroborating testimony on the importance (whether new or continuing) of Delos as an international market for grain in transit. Their contexts are in fact quite distinct, and they provide evidence for two very different functions that Delos played in this period.

Interpretations of Aristoboulos's activities on Delos have generally assumed that Demetrios II sent him there because grain was hard to find in Makedonia. Most recently, Gabriele Marasco has argued that the depreda-

104. As Vial, 341 n. 118, sees it. I do not see why Déonna, *Vie privée*, 38, writes, "La ville d'Histiée envoie *souvent* ses sitones à Délos" (emphasis added).

105. G. Reger in *Proceedings of the VIIth International Conference on Boiotion Studies* (Amsterdam, 1994), forthcoming.

106. Marasco, 146, for the claim; cf. Rostovtzeff, 232, Shear, 30, Vial, 341.

tions of the war of Demetrios II against the Aitolians and Akhaians occasioned severe shortages throughout central Greece; Demetrios therefore stationed his own *sitones* on Delos semi-permanently to divert to Makedon grain available on the market there from sources like Egypt and Sicily. Others have posited a cross-trade in grain from Delos and pitch and wood from Makedon that Demetrios was eager to foster so as to guarantee reliable grain supplies.[107] But this inscription needs to be placed in a wider context. Athenodoros was not Demetrios's only representative on Delos. The Delians honored Autokles son of Ainesidemos of Khalkis, φίλος ὢν τοῦ βασιλέως Δημητρίου, as *proxenos* and *euergetes* of the Delians and Apollo (*IG* XI 4.680.3–5, cf. 679 [= *Choix*, 47]); he was also awarded a proxeny by Oropos (V. I. Leonardos, *AE* [1892]: 49–50, no. 79). His son Autokles received similar honors from the Delians (*IG* XI 4.681–82). Admetos son of Bokros of Thessalonike, whose father may have been buried on Rheneia, is not explicitly associated in the texts with Demetrios, but the lavishness of his honors both on Delos and in his hometown make a connection with the royal house likely.[108] Demetrios II also advertised his victory over the Spartan king Kleomenes III on Delos (*IG* XI 4.1097 = *Choix*, 51). His interests in Delos clearly extended well beyond the purchase of grain or the promotion of trade between Makedon and Apollo's homeland.

The key to understanding these interests, I suspect, lies in the larger political context. At the start of his reign, Demetrios broke with his father's policy in northwestern Greece by contracting a marriage alliance with the ruling house of Epeiros. Hostilities—the so-called "War of Demetrios"—followed with the Aitolians and Akhaians, which led to troubles throughout central Greece. Because after 237/6 B.C. Demetrios held Boiotia and the Megarid, however, Athens was spared land raids by the Akhaians or Aitolians; the latter were able only to raid Attike by sea. As we have already seen in chapter 2, the Aitolians had taken advantage of the absence of a hegemonic power in the Aegean to establish relations with many island

107. Marasco, 144–46, and *Studi classici ed orientali* 36 (1986): 46–49. Cross-trade: Marek, 271–72; Casson, "Grain Trade," 75–76; Déonna, *Vie privée*, 37; Larsen, 395; *Choix*, p. 60; Glotz, *REG* 29 (1916) 289–94. Contra Marasco, 144–46; Meiggs, 454. F. W. Walbank in *Philip II, Alexander the Great and the Macedonian Heritage* (Washington, D.C., 1982), 216, thinks Aristoboulos was on Delos to sell grain: an unexampled interpretation of σιτώνης, which always designates a grain buyer.

108. *IG* XI 4.664, 665, 1053 (= *Choix*, 49); *IG* X 2.1028–29. See Marek, 256–57, against the view that this Admetos was identical with the Admetos executed by Philip V (Polyb. 23.10.9–11, Livy *Per.* 40.3.7; and see further Marek, 427 n. 285); as Marek notes, Rostovtzeff's notion (255) that Admetos was a businessman is entirely unfounded.

and littoral states in the 240s. Delos itself had enjoyed an *asylia* agreement with the Aitolians since 250 B.C. The benefits of these arrangements became apparent now. The Aitolian Boukris, who took captives in Attike, disposed of them at Kydonia on Krete and was honored by the Delians as *proxenos*.[109]

Demetrios clearly needed to counter the Aitolians at sea. He struck an agreement with Gortyn on Krete,[110] which provided him with a base of support on the island where Boukris sold his Athenian captives, and with a ready source of allied troops (some served at Sellesia a few years later; cf. Polyb. 2.66.6, 4.71.11, 5.23.2). Despite its "neutrality," Delos often played a crucial role in the naval struggles between opposing powers in the Aegean; the best example comes from the war with Perseus, when Delos saw Makedonian and Roman forces stationed on the island and even mingling in the sanctuary (Livy 44.29.3–4, cf. 45.10.1). I have already remarked on the importance of stockpiling supplies for military operations in the archipelago, which, although capable of supporting its own population, inevitably had difficulty feeding large influxes of troops.[111] Demetrios's grain purchases through his agent Aristoboulos do not, therefore, reflect the promotion of trade, or even attempts to recoup shortages created in Makedon by the war, but the military need to support the naval side of Demetrios's struggle against the Aitolians.

With Aristoboulos's activities set in their proper context, the mission of the Histiaian *sitonai* on Delos becomes easier to understand: they were undoubtedly sent by their home state to try to buy grain during a shortage. The little we know about the situation has all the earmarks of one of the transient, local shortages so common among the Hellenistic states. There is no evidence for grain shortages in neighboring states at this time,[112] and the fact that the Histiaians expected to find grain on Delos makes it very unlikely that the problem extended much beyond Histiaia itself; there is certainly no reason to suppose that Makedon was suffering a famine.[113] It

109. Will I², 343–47. Chapter 2, p. 43; *IG* XI 4.1050 = *Choix*, 41. *IG* II² 844 (= *SIG*³ 535), cf. also *IG* II² 746, 833, 858, with Adolf Wilhelm, *Attische Urkunden III* (Vienna and Leipzig, 1925), 55–59; *IG* XI 4.692 (= *Choix*, 42).

110. *IC* IV 167. Cf. Kostas Buraselis, *AE* (1981): 114–25; G. Reger, *Historia* 43 (1994): 58–59.

111. See chapter 2, pp. 26–29; chapter 3, pp. 116–18, above. Cf. also chapter 5, pp. 181–87; Gallant, 180, citing the texts in C. B. Welles, *AJA* 42 (1938): 245–60.

112. Cf. the wise remarks of Durrbach, *Choix*, 66–67.

113. Marasco, 143–44, responding to Casson's view ("Grain Trade," 75–76) that the interest-free loan offered by the Rhodian, and not the possibility of finding grain for sale, drew the *sitonai* of Histiaia to Delos, with id., *Studi classici ed orientali* 36 (1986): 48. The notion that the Histiaians should have gone to Athens either

seems to have remained unremarked that the Histiaians came to Delos without any money to buy grain, for they praised their Rhodian benefactor because he "conducted everything with the *sitonai* sent to Delos by the city [of Histiaia] enthusiastically and advanced money without interest and became the reason the *sitonai* completed their business expeditiously, putting the gratitude of the city [τὸ πρὸς τὴμ πόλιν εὐχάριστον] ahead of his own profit" (*IG* XI 4.1055.9–14 [= *Choix,* 50]). This is absolutely typical of the public impoverishment of the Greek cities of the Hellenistic period, when they were frequently incapable of financing their needs.[114] This document, then, simply attests to the attempt by a state on the Kykladic margin to find grain on Delos during a local shortage. It does not demonstrate the existence of an international market, but rather reinforces the picture of Delos as a developing transshipment point for grain being moved around the Kyklades.

In the 190s B.C., probably before 192, the reconstituted Island League sent grain purchasers to Delos. They arrived with Tenian money unacceptable to the sellers, and Timon of Syracuse, a banker, came to their rescue by exchanging their funds without charging a markup. The two Siphnian representatives of the league were also honored on Delos.[115] The involvement of the Island League suggests a military purpose behind this transaction. As part of its responsibilities, the league provided ships to a fleet under Rhodian command headquartered on Tenos, where the Rhodians also maintained a garrison. Treaties governing the requisitioning of soldiers from one city by another often required the home city to provide maintenance for the first part of the campaign (e.g., for the first thirty days). The league may therefore have been buying grain for its sailors or for the garrison.[116]

These documents build a coherent picture of the grain business on Delos. Delos's strategic situation in the Kyklades, and the Kyklades' role as

---

to procure grain (Casson, "Grain Trade," 75) or for financing to buy grain (Marasco, 143) founders on the fact that Athens imported grain. There is no reason to suppose that the late fourth-century laws had been rescinded that forbade the reexport of grain brought into Athens ([Arist.] *Ath. pol.* 51.4), cf. Philippe Gauthier, *REG* 95 (1982): 275–90, and *Revue historique de droit français et étranger* 59 (1981): 5–28; Heichelheim, "Sitos," 849–51.

114. See the documents collected by Migeotte and the analysis of Philippe Gauthier, *Les Cités grecques et leur bienfacteurs* (Paris, 1985), 7–75.

115. *IG* XII 5.817; cf. Bogaert, 176–78. *IG* XI 4.760.

116. For Rhodian presence on Tenos, see chapter 2, pp. 19–20, 34–35, 40, above; also Donald V. Sippel, *Ancient World* 13 (1986): 35–40, 41–46. For a typical Rhodian treaty governing provisioning of soldiers, see IC III Hierapytna 3A22–35 (= *SIG*[3] 581; Schmitt, *Staatsverträge,* III.551).

stepping-stones between mainland Greece on the one side and western Asia Minor and Egypt on the other, drew the interests of powers that had more than regional ambitions. The actions of the Ptolemies illustrate this admirably; Demetrios II's grain purchases—if indeed military in inspiration—seem to belong to the same category.

The character of the island played its role in determining the nature of its economy, which in turn had an impact on the trade in grain. Delos imported grain from its Kykladic neighbors, and sometimes from farther away. It also drew in merchants and contractors who did business with its temple, which was an important local economic engine. Grain importers could never have known precisely how much grain Delos needed, and since its demand for imported grain must proportionally have been the highest among the group—every other Kykladic island had a much larger χώρα in relation to its population—Delos must have become a natural place for regional exchange: for unloading surpluses and making up shortfalls. Public and private banking supplied the crucial loans for the risky enterprises of "those who sail the sea" (*IG* XI 4.691.5–6 = *Choix,* 43). This role may help to explain why Dionysios of Byzantion was the only grain importer honored by the Delians: Delos's role as a local distribution center radically reduced the locals' need to encourage or compel imports, at least until the changes of the late third century.

Although we can trace this kind of activity from the first quarter of the third century, when Mnesalkos helped a neighboring city during a shortage of grain (*IG* XI 4.1049), the amount of evidence rises considerably after ca. 230 B.C. It is in the last quarter of the third and first quarter of the second centuries that the activities of the Histiaians, Demetrios II, Eutykhos, and the Island League belong. The range of Delos's economic reach had not extended—it was still confined to the Kyklades, including Euboia—but its intensity had grown.

THE PRICE OF GRAIN AND LONG-DISTANCE TRADE

To the positive evidence limiting to the Kyklades Delos's role in the movement of grain can be added some negative considerations. If Delos had played an important part in the trade in grain outside the islands, then prices on Delos for grain should have been affected by conditions that set prices in supplying or purchasing regions.[117] But evidence for such impacts is very hard to find.

Egyptian traders are largely absent from Delos, which should be no surprise if, as Edouard Will and others have argued, the Ptolemies depended

117. Just as Kleomenes' manipulations of Egyptian prices affected both Rhodos and Athens: cf. [Demosth.] 56.7–8, [Arist.] *Oik.* II.2.33e (1352b14–20).

on the Rhodians to move their goods around.[118] The abundance and price of Egyptian grain was determined almost entirely by the character of the flood of the Nile. When the flood was poor, prices should have been high; when the flood was normal, prices should have been normal; and when the flood was good, they should have been normal or low. We happen to know the character of the flood for many years, and in the few cases in which we can match a flood with grain prices on Delos, the prices show no relation either for wheat or for barley.[119]

Even more revealing is the shortage of ca. 174–173 B.C. along the Euripos. Four or five inscriptions from a number of cities on both Euboia and the mainland attest to troubles with the grain supply in these years just before the Third Makedonian War. (Another inscription is generally

118. Will I² 181–91, esp. 191; Rathbone, 50–52. The rest of Rathbone's arguments unfortunately often rest on inadequate or misinterpreted evidence. Contra: Marasco, 127–28.

119. Drexhage, *Preise*, 21–22; Danielle Bonneau, *Le Fisc et le Nil* (Paris, 1971), 217–58. For wheat purchases for the Posideia in the second century: flood of 170, abundant, price of wheat 10 dr/*med* (Bonneau, *Fisc*, 226; *ID* 461Bb53 [169 B.C.]); flood of 175 ? ("perhaps good?": land along the desert was seeded, cf. *P. Teb.* III 826.47), price of wheat 11 dr/*med* (Bonneau, *Fisc*, 225; *ID* 440A69 [174 B.C.]). Unfortunately no data on the flood are available for the years before the Posideia of 190 and 178 B.C. (*ID* 401.22, 445.13). Barley: flood of 259, abundant, barley on Delos, ca. 5.1 dr/*med* (Bonneau, *Fisc*, 221; *IG* XI 2.224A29 [258 B.C.]); flood of 252, normal or good, barley on Delos declining from ca. 5.1 in Lenaion and 5.0 in Thargelion (April–May) to ca. 4.6, 4.1, 3.6, and 3.1 in Panemos–Bouphonion (May–September) (Bonneau, *Fisc*, 222; *IG* XI 2.287A45, 59–60, 64, 66, 67–68, 71 [250 B.C.]).

Fritz Heichelheim has suggested that the Athenian Kephisodoros's service in 203/2 B.C. as secretary of the *sitonia* was related to a devaluation of Egyptian currency in 204 B.C. that disrupted the grain market (*Aegyptus* 17 [1937]: 61–64; the Kephisodoros decree, B. D. Meritt, *Hesperia* 5 [1936]: 419–28, no. 15, at ll. 13–15 = *ISE* 33; a grain shortage accepted by Will II², 123, "à expliquer aussi bien par la situation en Egypte que les opérations de Philippe dans le Nord"). A. H. McDonald and F. W. Walbank, *JRS* 27 (1937): 184, relate Kephisodoros's service to Philip V's attack on the Hellespontos in 202 B.C. (Walbank repeats this view in *Philip II, Alexander the Great, and the Macedonian Heritage*, 230), an argument that is unconvincing on chronological grounds. More important, Tony Reekmans, *Studia Hellenistica* 7 (1951): 67–69, 83–85, 94–95, 104, detects devaluations in 221–216, 183–182, 173, and 130–128 B.C., and a reorganization in 211–210 (75–80), but not in 204 B.C. Moreover, he dates a crucial piece of evidence for Heichelheim's argument, *P. Mich.*, III 173, to 170 B.C., much later than Heichelheim, and argues that Heichelheim misconstrued the number of copper drachmas to the stater (92 n. 2, 93); cf. now also W. Clarysse and E. Lanciers, *Ancient Society* 20 (1989): 117–32. The connection Heichelheim drew between Kephisodoros's activities and changes in the price of Egyptian grain evaporates.

Table 4.7. Wheat and Barley Prices on Delos, Second Century B.C. (dr)

Source	*Year*	*Month*	*Barley*	*Wheat*
401.18, 22	190	12	4 (5.333)[a]	10
442A220	179	12	4 (3)[a]	
445.4–5, 13	178	12	3.75 (5)[a]	10
440A62–63, 69	174	12	4	11
461Bb51, 53	169	12	3.875 (5.167)[a]	10

[a] Price reconstructed by Larsen, 347–48. Prices in parentheses are alternative prices, offered by Larsen based on a different set of assumptions about the relation between wheat and barley prices.

thought to belong to the period of the Third Makedonian War itself.[120]) Wheat and/or barley prices are preserved from Delos for the Posideia in 179, 178, 174, and 169 B.C., right during the period of this shortage (table 4.7).

These prices can hardly be said to reflect the storage on the Euripos. The minor variation in prices for barley in 178 and 169 B.C. (both, be it noted, lower than typical) and for wheat in 174 B.C. are perfectly in line with typical year-to-year fluctuations. The serious shortage, which led cities near Thisbe to embargo exports of grain, makes no mark here (*ISE*, 1.66 = Migeotte, 41–44). If Delos had really become an important center for the grain trade by the 220s B.C., we would expect its prices to rise during nearby shortages as supplies were diverted to areas in need and *sitonai* of the cities spread out looking for grain. The absence of any impact at Delos of the shortage along the Euripos reinforces the view that limits Delos's role as a distribution center for grain to the Kyklades even as late as the 170s B.C.[121]

Delos relied virtually entirely on production in the Kyklades for its grain supplies. No doubt the frequent, although irregular, movement of grain

120. Most recent discussion with the date in Denis Knoepfler, *BCH* 114 (1990): 490–91; generally, Will II², 262–64. For the evidence, see Appendix I.

121. It makes no difference that the shortage may not date precisely to 175–174 B.C. The 170s are certain enough, and we have prices for three years in that decade. The market disruption of a serious shortage should ripple across several years, as farmers, dealers, and townsfolk competed to replenish stocks. There ought to have been some effect on Delos. Moreover, the prices of 190 B.C., clearly long before the shortage, are identical to those of the 170s, again suggesting no important impact.

from the other islands to the port of Delos for sale and consumption there promoted a localized trade in grain and the creation of a transit trade among the islands. Delos certainly became a convenient center for neighboring islands to sell surpluses and to make up shortfalls, and such trade must have resulted in a varying but continuous exchange on Delos among merchants who did not plan on leaving their grain on the island. This exchange in turn encouraged outsiders, like the Histiaians and the representatives of Demetrios II, to seek grain on Delos on occasion, although their activities cannot have been constant or large in scale. By the last third of the third century, however, evidence accumulates that local transit trade in grain had increased along with a rising public interest in grain provisioning for the Delian population that resulted in the creation of a permanent local *sitonia* fund. I attribute these changes to the generally rising prosperity of the islands during this period of independence from any outside *hegemon;* we shall explore this in more detail in chapter 7.

Chapter 5

The Prices of Olive Oil, Pigs, and Firewood

Short-term fluctuations and long-term trends in the prices of commodities, especially of basic consumer goods, offer indications of the level of economic activity, economic health, and change in the economy over time. For much of the ancient world, lack of data prevents discussion of these matters from proceeding beyond the grossest generalities, but Delos is an exception. For 145 years the accounts kept on stone by the ἱεροποιοί who administered the temple of Apollo on behalf of the citizens of Delos provide scrupulous records of the income and outgo of the temple. This information was not compiled as economic data, as (for instance) the U.S. Bureau of Labor Statistics tracks the prices of goods and services to produce its Consumer Price Index; like most ancient accounting, the records were meant to assure, and their publication to advertise, the responsibility with which the administrators had discharged their office.[1]

As a consequence, the majority of the thousands of prices recorded in the inscriptions are useless for economic analysis. Every month, year in, year out, the *hieropoioi* bought charcoal (ἄνθρακες) for the cult. Prices sometimes vary, sometimes remain rock steady. It would be fascinating to be able to compare these prices with those for firewood, also bought every month, since charcoal was made out of wood and both were treated together by a famous Delian law regulating prices (*ID* 509 [*SIG*[3] 975]); but because the amount of charcoal bought is practically never recorded, there is no way to know whether the quantity or the price was changing.[2]

For dozens of other goods, the accounts provide too little information to permit comparison over time. A spade bought in 303 B.C. cost 21 dr, while

1. On the goals of ancient accounting, see the works cited in chapter 1, n. 17.

2. The exception that proves the rule: *IG* XI 2.203A59 of 269 B.C., 9.5 dr per κάλαθος.

another cost 7 dr 2 ob in 269. Perhaps this drastic decline represents far-reaching structural changes in the price of metals or the cost of labor, but since we know absolutely nothing about these two spades, it is just as likely that they were so different that comparison of their costs is unwarranted. These examples could be multiplied by the dozen.[3]

There are three goods for which the *hieropoioi* regularly provide all the information necessary for comparison of cost over time: olive oil (ἔλαιον), firewood (ξύλα), and pigs (χοῖροι). Monthly purchases for ritual and personal use, always giving the quantity and the total or unit price, and sometimes all three, permit us to track the movement of prices across the seasons and across the years. Price changes within a year reflect the seasonal cycles of the olive and the pig and the exigencies of the sailing season; changes over the short term also sometimes illustrate strikingly the impact of political or military events. Over the long term, permanent movement in average price levels reveals profound changes in the economic history of Delos; these changes do not always find their echo in the rent histories for Apollo's agricultural estates and houses, as we shall see in chapter 6.

Character and Limitations of the Data

Olive oil, firewood, and pigs were bought every month to satisfy cult requirements. Typically, the full monthly allotment of oil was entered under a single rubric, "ἐλαίου χόεις [number], [price]." There are, however, other entries as well. Sometimes oil was bought specifically for use in the Hieropoion, the office of the *hieropoioi.* Another entry records oil εἰς χέρνιβον, and still another the mysterious ἔλαιον ταῖς ε.εσιν. Very large quantities were bought for the athletic games held on Delos each year.[4]

Sometimes the *hieropoioi* did not indicate quantity. There are dozens of entries for wood like that of 304 B.C., ξύλα ⊢⊢III (IG XI 2.144A83). In 269 B.C. the *hieropoioi* recorded an oil purchase as εἰς ἔλαιον III (*IG* XI 2.203A49); more frequently they wrote simply "oil" (ἔλαιον), followed by a price.[5] It is impossible to do anything with the laconic wood

3. *IG* XI 2.144A85, 203A42. See, e.g., on labor costs, Heichelheim, *Wirtschaftsgeschichte,* 451 (contra, J. A. O. Larsen, *CP* 36 [1941]: 162–63). The impossibility of comparison of so many objects mentioned in the accounts renders useless Gustave Glotz's suggestions, *REG* 45 (1932): 241–49.

4. *IG* XI 2.154A14–15, 161A108 (280 B.C.), εἰς ἱεροποιόν; 144A32; 147A3; athletics: 161A108 (prob. 279 B.C.), 203A64–65 (269 B.C.), 287A131–32, 133 (250 B.C.), cf. M.–C. Amouretti, *Le Pain et l'huile dans la Grèce antique* (Paris, 1986), 184–85. For religious use on Kos, see Paton-Hicks, 38.24–25; generally, Amouretti, *Pain,* 194–95.

5. E.g., *IG* XI 2.142.60 (307–305 B.C.), *ID* 440A63–64 (174 B.C.). Full details in Appendix III.

entries, but for oil it is usually obvious from the price that a χοῦς was meant, and I have treated these entries as if the amount were specified. In some instances, however, the figures are suspicious. In 174 B.C., oil sold in the months from Lenaion to Aresion for prices ranging between 1 dr 1.5 ob and 5.5 ob/*kh*. Suddenly, in Posideon, oil was bought for 2 and then 3 dr. It is possible that some disaster—harvest failure or shipwreck, war or piracy—suddenly and dramatically forced up prices. This oil, however, was not acquired for the usual reasons; it was destined for the Posideia, a festival celebrated each year at this time, which revolved around a major public feast paid for out of Apollo's pocket. Since the entire Delian population was invited, it is very possible that this account records the purchase of several *khoes*.[6] It is also possible that, in keeping with the sumptuousness of the celebrations, which provided ordinary folk with the kind of food that rarely graced their tables (beef, mutton, goat, pork, and Koan and Knidian wines),[7] a better quality of oil was bought, too: we do not know, since of the many kinds of olive oil available in the Greek world, the *hieropoioi* identify only one variety, "white oil" (ἔλαιον λευκόν), which was apparently put to the same uses as ordinary oil and cost only marginally more.[8]

These matters of variation in quality or variety plague the other two products as well. Firewood probably came from one of two main sources. Coppicing—the harvesting of scrub, underbrush, and branches, especially for fuel—which was practiced in antiquity in Greece and continues today on Naxos, Amorgos, Ios, Samos, and other Aegean islands, provided a steady supply of wood throughout the year.[9] The other source was more

6. On the Posideia, see Bruneau, 260–64; Vial, 18–20.

7. For example, *ID* 445.1–3, 9–10; full list at Bruneau, 260–61.

8. *IG* XI 2.203A39 (269 B.C.), regular 1 dr 2–3 ob, white 1 dr 3.5 ob; *ID* 372A79, 81 (200 B.C.), regular 1 dr 2 ob, white 1 dr 3 ob; all per *khous*. Cf. the document quoted at Louis and Jean Robert, *Claros I: Décrets hellénistiques* (Paris, 1989), 58 n. 308. On varieties of oil available in Egypt, see Andreas Wittenburg, *ZPE 38* (1980): 185–89, and id. in *Produccion y comercio del aceite en la antigüedad* (Madrid, 1983), 501–14; generally, D. Brent Sandy, *The Production and Use of Vegetable Oils in Ptolemaic Egypt* (Atlanta, 1989), 72–82; Amouretti, *Pain*, 179–81.

9. [Demos.] 42.7, 9 for Attike, with stress on the *daily* production of firewood; Theophr. *Hist. plant.* 2.2.2 on Krete. Discussion in Meiggs, 352–53, 441–57; Larsen, 395; Gustave Glotz, *Journal des Savants* 11 (1913): 23–24. Meiggs, 353, regards Naxos, Khios, Lesbos, and perhaps Euboia as the most likely sources for Delian firewood, but even little islands like Peparethos may have made a contribution: "This island is good for wine and wood, and bears grain" (Αὕτη ἡ νῆσος εὔοινός ἐστι καὶ εὔδενδρος, καὶ σῖτον φέρει [Herak. Lembos, ed. Dilts, frg. 41]. In 250 B.C. Aratos and his companion escaped Makedonian soldiers on Andros by fleeing "into a place full of woods" (εἴς τινα τόπον ὕλης γέμοντα [Plut. *Aratos* 12.3]). Contra A. J. Papalas, *Platon* 35–36 (1982–83): 53 n. 3, Arrian 7.20.5 does not refer to a "thick forest" on Ikaria in the Aegean but (at 7.20.3) to Failaka at the mouth

seasonal. Olive prunings might be burned for fuel or baked into charcoal, but would only have been available from the time of harvest in September–December.[10] This extra infusion of firewood at the beginning of winter may have helped to moderate prices, but the *hieropoioi* never identify the variety of ξύλα they buy.

For pigs the problems are different. Because of their important role in the cult, the *hieropoioi* distinguished carefully among pigs by age and condition. The Thesmophoria, which was celebrated on Delos in Metageitnion, required pigs of three different conditions: a pregnant sow (ὗς ἐγκύμων), sacrificed to Demeter herself; two castrated pigs (δελφάκια), offered to Kore and Zeus Euboulos; and a simple piglet to purify the sanctuary (χοῖρος, τὸ ἱερὸν τῆς Δήμητρος/τὸ Θεσμοφορίον καθάρασθαι).[11] The *hieropoioi* occasionally called the δελφάκιον simply ἱερεῖον, "victim" (*IG* XI 2.287A69), but *ID* 290.88–89 makes it clear that the terms were synonymous. The prices paid for these different types of pig also clearly separate the varieties. Pregnant sows sold typically for 20–40 dr, δελφάκια for 14–33. Χοῖροι, by contrast, regularly fetched 2–6 dr, prices perfectly in line with those paid for χοῖροι bought for the monthly purification of the temple of Apollo. The evidence of the Thesmophoria makes it certain that all χοῖροι in the accounts were animals of approximately equivalent age, size, and condition, including both those acquired τὸ ἱερὸν καθάρασθαι at the beginning of each month and those sacrificed irregularly κατὰ νόμους καὶ ψηφίσματα to carry out purifications: commonly, when someone died within the sacred precinct; once after a strange portent.[12]

---

of the Euphrates, known as Ikaros. On use of different varieties of wood for fuel, see Theophr. *Hist. plant.* 5.3.4, 9.6 and *De caus. plant.* 1.21.7. Oliver Rackham in *Archaeological Aspects of Woodland Ecology* (London, 1982), 177–97; Malcolm Wagstaff and Clive Gamble in *Island Polity,* 104. See *IG* XII 5.606 for an interest-free loan to a *thiasos* of Sarapis worshippers on Keos for ξυλωνία (l. 6).

10. On pruning in conjunction with the harvest in modern Messenia, see Aschenbrenner in *MME,* 54.

11. *IG* XI 2.287A68–69; full citations at Bruneau, 287; see 285–90 on the Delian Thesmophoria. See also Varro *Res. rust.* 2.4.6 on *porci sacres,* pigs just weaned and regarded as ideal for sacrifice. On the meaning of δελφάκιον, see David Schaps, *JHS* 111 (1991): 208–9.

12. See Walter Burkert, *Greek Religion* (Cambridge, Mass., 1985), 242–46, on the Thesmophoria generally. For the monthly sacrifice, see Bruneau, 93; cf. also Robert Parker, *Miasma: Pollution and Purification in Early Greek Religion* (Oxford, 1983), 30 n. 66; death, *IG* XI 2.199A50: ὅτε ἐτελεύτησε Στέφανος, χοῖρος⊢⊢⊢, with Bruneau, 49–51; portent, *IG* XI 2.153.8–12, with pig sacrificed at l. 11. The restoration at *IG* XI 2.148.62, [τῆι Κόρ?]ηι ὑὸς, is unlikely on grounds of terminology: in this matter, the *hieropoioi* are admirably consistent.

This is not to say, however, that pigs were interchangeable. Even generally similar animals are likely to have fetched different prices depending on the tastes, needs, and perceptions of buyer and seller. Temples typically imposed more stringent requirements than common buyers, since animals obtained as offerings to the gods had to be "perfect." Despite the absence of explicit testimony, there can be no doubt that Delian Apollo enforced a similar requirement.[13]

In other circumstances, consistency of terminology was not one of the virtues of the *hieropoioi,* who, for example, also called the Neokoros of the Arkhegeton the Neokoros εἰς θεόν (cf. *IG* XI 2.144A28, 142.52–53). The ἰνωποφύλαξ and the κρηνοφύλαξ were the same official, although not so recognized until quite recently.[14] Sometimes δᾶιδες are called φάνοι (*IG* XI 2.144A31–32; *ID* 316.76–80, 87, 101). The *hieropoioi* of 247 B.C. consistently lumped together the costs of the pig bought for the monthly purification and the wood (ξύλα) and pine bough (πεύκη) or torch (δᾶις) also needed for the ceremony: χοῖρος τὸ ἱερὸν καθάρασθαι καὶ εἰς τὰ λοιπά· price (*ID* 291b9–10, 20–21, d5). In this case, it is possible to estimate the cost of the accessories, which are listed separately in *ID* 290 of the preceding year, and recover a pig price. The wholly unique entries ἔλαιον καὶ ἐλλύχνια τοῖς φανοῖς in 231 B.C. cannot be disarticulated, for we have no independently attested prices for wicks.[15]

Such are the limitations of the evidence.[16]

One final matter. Prices from Delos are recorded in drachmas, obols (= one-sixth of a drachma), and fractions of obols as small as one-twelfth. These figures are cumbersome to manipulate. To ease the task, I shall quote all prices below in an *indexed form.* The index is constructed very simply by dividing all prices by a *base-year* price, which for our purposes will be the price of an item in the month of Metageitnion (= July–August) 250 B.C., and multiplying by 100. The base-year price for all goods is 100 (since the price in that year divided by itself is 1, which, multiplied by 100, equals 100). The price for oil (for instance) in 281 B.C. is 219, or (2 dr 5.5 ob/1 dr 2 ob) × 100. This procedure has the added advantage of ex-

13. "Perfect": Burkert, *Greek Religion,* 51. For some regulations, see *SIG*³ 1024.6, 9–10, 13 (Mykonos); *IG* XII 5.647.7–9 (Koresia on Keos); Paton-Hicks, 37 (= *SIG*³ 1025), pigs in 40B2–3 (both Kos). For further references to prices and regulations, see Herbert Graßl, *MBAH* 4.2 (1985): 85–86.

14. Philippe Bruneau in *Etudes déliennes* (Paris, 1973), 121–23, refuting Vallois, I.202–203 n. 10.

15. *ID* 316.76–80, 87, 101.

16. For full details of the evidence, with citations and commentary, see Appendix III.

pressing all prices in relation to the cost of the same goods in currency of a single moment, namely, July–August 250 B.C.[17]

Analysis of the Price Data

The three sections that follow try to answer different sets of questions about the price history of the three commodities. The first section explores the fluctuations of price within a year. Several interesting patterns emerge, which can be accounted for by appeal to the structure of the seasonal market for each good; as we shall see, harvest dates and the sailing season prove crucial for the seasonal price curve for some commodities.

In the second section I study the long-run trend of prices over the whole period of independence. For these purposes I use mean annual prices to dampen the impact of large but transient fluctuations in monthly prices, and to permit the inclusion of years preserving only a few (or even only one or two) individual prices. The results, which depend in part on the application of techniques of linear regression, partly support and partly refute traditional interpretations of price histories.

The discoveries of the second section lead directly to a brief examination of the interrelations among the price histories of all three goods. On the basis of the available data, I propose a set of hypotheses that may account for price movements and relations among the prices of the three commodities. In particular, there seems good reason to postulate a break in earlier interconnections around 220–200 B.C. The transformation fits well with certain other indications of a changed economic scene on Delos by ca. 220 B.C., a matter that will come in for further treatment in chapter 7.

MONTH-TO-MONTH FLUCTUATIONS AND SEASONAL CYCLES

Olive Oil The accounts give eleven years with at least three monthly prices (table 5.1). The first series comes from 304 B.C., for which the accounts preserve three prices for the first three months, and then, after a gap of five months, two consecutive prices in Metageitnion and Bouphonion. The early prices are the highest known from Delos, but after the gap the price has plummeted 41 percent, and it suffers a further staggering fall in the next month of 44 percent. The total decline for 304 B.C. amounts to

17. I ignore many intricacies here. For an introduction to the construction of economic indices, see S. N. Afriat, *The Price Index* (Cambridge, 1977); Jacqueline Fourastié, *Essai sur la mesure des quantités économiques* (Paris, 1972); and U.S. Department of Labor, Bureau of Labor Statistics, *BLS Handbook of Methods*, vol. 2, *The Consumer Price Index* (Washington, D.C., 1984). See also Kent, 309 with n. 209; Roger Bagnall, *Currency and Inflation in Fourth-Century Egypt* (Atlanta, 1985), 1–8.

Table 5.1. Indexed Olive Oil Prices on Delos, 304–174 B.C.

Year	*Month*	*Price*	*Change (%)*	*Year*	*Month*	*Price*	*Change (%)*
304	1	337.6	—		3	87.6	0.0
	2	337.6	0.0		5	112.5	+28.4
	3	337.6	0.0		6	112.5	0.0
	8	200.1	−40.76		8	112.5	0.0
	9	112.5	−43.80	200	1	100.0	—
250	1	100.0	—		2	100.0	0.0
	2	100.0	0.0		3	100.0	0.0
	3	100.0	0.0		3	112.5	+12.5
	4	100.0	0.0		4	100.0	−11.1
	5	150.0	+50.0		5	100.0	0.0
	6	100.0	−33.3		6	100.0	0.0
	7	100.0	0.0		7	100.0	0.0
	8	100.0	0.0		8	100.0	0.0
	9	100.0	0.0		9	100.0	0.0
	10	112.5	+12.5		10	100.0	0.0
	11	112.5	0.0		11	100.0	0.0
	12	100.0	−11.1		12	100.0	0.0
246	1	87.6	—	194	1	112.5	—
	3	87.6	0.0		2	112.5	0.0
	4	87.6	0.0		4	112.5	0.0
	6	87.6	0.0	179	1	106.2	—
	6 (2)[a]	87.6	0.0		2	100.0	−5.8
	7	87.6	0.0		3	106.2	+6.2
	8	93.8	+7.1		6	100.0	−5.8
	10	100.0	+ 6.6		7	100.0	0.0
	11	100.0	0.0		8	100.0	0.0
	12	100.0	0.0		9	100.0	0.0
231	2	112.5	—		10	112.5	+12.5
	4	106.2	−5.6		12	106.2	−5.6
	7	106.2	0.0	174	1	93.8	—
224	2	100.0	—		5	93.8	0.0
	3	100.0	0.0		6	81.2	−13.4
	4	100.0	0.0		6 (2)[a]	81.2	0.0
	7	100.0	0.0		8	81.2	0.0
	9	75.0	−25.		9	75.1	−7.5
218	1	87.6	—		11	68.7	−8.5
	2	87.6	0.0				

[a] Intercalary Panemos.

about 67 percent. Of the remaining ten years, six offer a series of prices well distributed across the year. Five show a distinctive pattern in which prices undergo an adjustment in the late summer or early fall (250, 246, 224, 179, and 174 B.C.). In 250 and 246 B.C., prices rise; in 224 and 174 B.C., they fall; 179 B.C. shows a mixture of the two patterns. Six years show another adjustment in the late winter or spring. In 250, 218, 200, and 179 B.C., prices rise once in Galaxion or Thargelion and then return to former levels. In Artemision 231 and Panemos 174 (already early summer), prices fall for a month and then resume previous levels. Exceptionally, the prices of 218 B.C. remain elevated after a rise in Thargelion. Finally, three years have a slight but interesting drop in price toward the end of the year (250, 179, and probably 174). I shall postpone discussion for the present (see pp. 136–38 below). The year 200 B.C. is unexampled in its stability.[18]

The spring and fall price adjustments are probably best seen as reflections of the exigencies of ancient transportation and of the seasonal cycles of the olive. As we saw in chapter 3, the sailing season "par excellence is from 27 May to 14 September . . . and . . . the outside limits are 10 March to 10 November."[19] Except for occasional forays to and from nearby neighbors, enabled by a spell of good weather, the Delians could not count on imports outside the sailing season. Supplies sufficient to tide them over the winter must have been on the island by the end of the autumn at the latest.

The annual cycle of the olive, which has not changed since antiquity, is well known.[20] Collection of fruit fell into three periods: fallen olives were picked up in August, green fruit was taken in September, and the real har-

18. I can offer no good account of this year. It stands out among all the series by its absolute stability of price. Perhaps a benefactor provided oil for the year at a fixed rate (although there is no mention of such benefactions anywhere in the documents); perhaps the *hieropoioi* experimented with contracting a year's supply from a single supplier at a fixed price, as they did for the sharpening of tools in 279 B.C. (*IG* XI 2.161A107–8); or perhaps prices were simply extraordinarily steady. The remark that under the *arkhon* of 200 B.C. "there was health and prosperity" (*IG* XI 2.128.2) means nothing, since the sentiment is commonplace (cf. e.g., *IG* XI 2.105.2, 108.2, 109.1, etc.).

19. Casson, *Ships*, 270–72, quotations from 270–71. See chapter 3, pp. 54–55, above. This chapter is in part a modest response to Casson's remark that an "important subject that has never been treated is the extent of the economic dislocation that all port towns had to suffer because of the limited sailing season" (271 n. 4).

20. See A. S. Pease, *RE* 17 (1937), s.v. Oleum, 2454–74, and s.v. Ölbaum, 1998–2022. Amouretti, *Pain*, 177–95, catalogues the many uses of olives and their oil in great detail. The bibliography on ancient olioculture is large and growing; for

vest of ripe olives ran from October through December. In the modern Kyklades, the harvest typically lasts from late September through November.[21] The "market year" for olive oil thus lasted from autumn to autumn. Two additional factors affected the pricing of olives. Trees produce good yields only every other year; during off years, the crops tend to be only half of the previous year's yield. Moreover, orchards over vast regions tend to synchronize: biennial fluctuation in yield can be seen in harvest figures for the Peloponnesos, and even for the whole of Greece. Finally, although mature olives are generally reliable producers, regional shortages were not unknown, and once trees reach the age of about 200 years, as Theophrastos remarked (*Hist. plant.* 4.13.5), production tends to fall off markedly.[22]

Delos must have expected its first cargoes of the new sailing season each year in the period between March and May, which so frequently shows an adjustment in price level. Price rises may, therefore, reflect the final sales of depleted local stocks just before the arrival of fresh shipments; consumers would be willing to pay higher prices in the face of immediate local but temporary "shortages" and of uncertainty about prices of oil to come (250,

---

recent contributions, see Amouretti, *Pain,* passim; Sandy, *Production and Use of Vegetable Oils in Ptolemaic Egypt,* 72–82, with 82 n. 18; M. Helzer and D. Eitan, eds., *Olive Oil in Antiquity* (Haifa, 1987); H. Camps Fabrer, ed., *L'Huile d'olive en Méditerranée* (Aix-en-Provence, 1985); brief overview, Isager-Skydsgaard, 33–40. On the life cycle of the olive, see Raymond Lousset and Gérard Brousse, *L'Olivier* (Paris, 1978), 47–77.

21. *Geoponika,* ed. Beckh, 9.17.1; Pliny *Nat. hist.* 15.4; Theophr. *Hist. pl.* 1.11.4 and *De caus. pl.* 1.20.4. Amouretti, *Pain,* 73. For Greece, Theophrastos (*De caus. pl.* 6.19.3, 8.1, 8.5) indicates that olives ripen after the rising of Arcturus, which falls in September; cf. also Pliny *Nat. hist.* 15.3: "Augetur oleum ad Arcturi exortum a. d. XVI Kalendas Octobris: postea nuclei increscunt et caro." For the modern agricultural calendar in Messenia, see Aschenbrenner in *MME,* 51 (olive harvest November–January); for Melos, Malcolm Wagstaff and Siv Augustson in *Island Polity,* 121, fig. 10.7 (olives in November–January); for Amorgos, Christopher Connell, *In the Bee-Loud Glade* (Nafplion, 1980), 47.

22. Aristotle knew the pattern (*De plant.* 1.7 [821b15–17]); his student and successor Theophrastos observed a three-year cycle at Olynthos (*De caus. pl.* 1.20.4). For modern data, see Aschenbrenner in *MME,* 53. On the shortage at *IG* II^2 903, see Philippe Gauthier, *REG* 95 (1982): 275–90. "The notorious uncertainty of the olive crop might account for fluctuations in price in antiquity as in modern times, when a good harvest may be followed by a complete and utter failure,—a few days of rainy weather at the critical time of blossom may bring disaster," says W. K. Pritchett (*Hesperia* 25 [1956]: 184 n. 34). On senescence, see Marie-Claire Amouretti in *Agriculture in Ancient Greece,* 80; Lousset and Brousse, *L'Olivier,* 63.

218 [but see further below], 200, and 179). If the previous year had been good, expectation of reduced yields might also contribute to upward pressure. Since olives were harvested and processed in the late fall and early winter, after the sailing season had closed, Delians probably lacked complete information about the size and quality of the harvest. Arrival of the first shipments calmed the market in those years when harvests were typical; in years with good harvests, or simply of higher preseason anxiety, the appearance of fresh oil may even have depressed the price temporarily (231, 174).

Of the two patterns, price declines are clearly more important. Except for 250 B.C., the rises are of little importance (about 12 percent) and of brief duration; in 200 B.C., the change affected only a single spot purchase in the month of Galaxion: another purchase the same month cost the same as in the preceding and following months. The declines of 231, 179, and 174 B.C. persisted through the summer. This difference suggests that years in which the price fell and stayed down were benefiting from a good harvest the previous autumn, which had only come onto the market and affected prices with the opening of the spring sailing season. We can guess that harvests in 232, 180, and 175 B.C. had been abundant. Conversely, poorer harvests preceded those springs in which the opening of the sailing season led to no permanent downward readjustment of prices (251, 219, and 201 B.C.). This further implies that Kykladic olives followed a cycle of good-poor harvests in even-odd years (by the Julian calendar), with the occasional exception like 175 B.C.

In 218 B.C., prices did not readjust after the rise in Thargelion. The persisting price of 112.5 is the highest summer price for any year except 304 B.C. (whose prices are exceptional: see below); it is matched only by prices from the late autumn or winter of 250, 179, and 169 B.C. This unique pattern probably represents a poor harvest year. The cycle derived above would make 219 B.C. a year of low yields anyway, but these high prices imply that it was poorer than usual.[23]

The adjustments of the late summer or early fall correspond to the olive harvest and the closing of the sailing season. Merchants typically returned to winter ports in September, although again some might continue to sail as late as November. The olive harvest was at its height from late September till December, with oil produced continuously. If harvesting began long enough before the sailing season ended, increasing supply might have

23. The shortage of 218 B.C. was trivial, however, compared to the prices of 304 B.C. These prices, which form a crucial piece of evidence in the inflation-demand theory espoused by Fritz Heichelheim and others, receive detailed discussion below.

brought prices down. Conversely, if the harvest of the olives or the processing of the oil was delayed until after the merchants had put their ships up for the winter, tight supplies and the anticipation of no new imports till spring might have fueled a price rise. The data seem to reflect these patterns perfectly. For all years, the price adjustments are permanent, unlike those of the spring; this reflects the combined impact of the harvest and the end of sailing (and incidentally makes it very unlikely that these adjustments should be attributed to the adventitious arrival of a winter shipment made possible by temporarily favorable weather). Three years show rises in the fall (250, 246, and 179), which probably mean either that the sailing season was effectively over by the time the harvest was well under way, or that the harvest was poor (247 B.C., for which we have only two prices, also follows this pattern; see table 5.2). In the two years showing declines (224 and 174), a good and early harvest probably overlapped with the sailing season enough to permit distribution of some new oil before winter set it.

There is one additional factor that must be taken into account, and that is local production. The conventional view is that Delos lacked olive trees. The inventories taken every ten years by the *hieropoioi* of the capital equipment of the estates owned by Apollo show no olives until after 237 B.C., when new estates on Mykonos came into the god's possession. The early traveler J. Pitton de Tournefort, who visited Delos in the middle of the eighteenth century, remarks on its grain crop but says nothing about olives; they were, he observes, "peu" on Mykonos. No olives grow on Delos today.[24]

But these arguments are hardly conclusive. No inventories have been preserved for three estates, so that we do not know what was cultivated on them, and the Delian χώρα certainly hosted perhaps as many as forty or fifty private farms, about whose products we know nothing.[25] Nor is it true

24. Philippe Bruneau and Philippe Fraisse, *BCH* 108 (1984): 721; Brunet, 147; Isager-Skydsgaard, 197; Alison Burford, *Land and Labor in the Greek World* (Baltimore, 1993), 110, following Kent, 288. For Kykladic oil production, see *ID* 366B18–23 (Mykonos); Galen *De simp. med. temp.* 11.872K; Herak. Lembos, ed. Dilts, frg. 41 (Peparethos); Athen. 67a (Samos). For some modern accounts, see Wagstaff and Augustson in *Island Polity* 111–13 (Melos); Paul Halstead and Glynis Jones, *JHS* 109 (1989): 51, and Connell, *In the Bee-Loud Glade,* 43–47 (both Amorgos). The rarity of olives on early modern Keos, often noted by travelers, may have been because of concentration on commercial production of acorns (*velanidia*); see J. Bennet and S. Voutsaki in *Landscape Archaeology,* 377, S. B. Sutton in ibid., 387, and T. M. Whitelaw in ibid., 447–49.

25. There are no inventories for Akra Delou, Lykoneion, and Sosimakheia. On Phytalia, see chapter 6, pp. 207–8. For private farms, see P. Bruneau, *BCH* 112 (1988): 569–73; Michèle Brunet, *BCH* 114 (1990): 706, 113 (1989) 754–61,

that the accounts preserve *no* mention of olives before 237 B.C., for Apollo himself owned at least one olive tree. Under Apatourion 250 B.C., the *hieropoioi* report an income of 3 dr 2 ob from two sales "of wood from the wild olive" (τῶν ξύλων ἀπὸ τοῦ κοτίνου [*IG* XI 2.287A22]; the absence of this tree from Delos today shows that olives, however long-lived, can disappear). The time of year makes it tempting to suppose that Apollo was selling off prunings from his tree after the harvest (see below).

Price drops in 224, 179, and 174 B.C. may thus reflect a good local harvest; the same decline in Poseidon 250 B.C. may also belong to this pattern, and olive yields in the Kyklades may have been synchronized to give good harvests in even-numbered years and poor in odd. Furthermore, the occasional association of declining winter wood prices with low early winter olive prices—250 and 174 B.C.; in 179, wood prices remained stable (see table 5.3)—lends credence to the view that Delos did have some olives. Another argument, explored below, also implies that Delos ought to have had some olives.

The data speak quite eloquently and in considerable detail about the character of the annual market for oil. Prices correspond well with the behavior of olives (and their producers) in conjunction with the exigencies of supplying a small island far from self-sufficient in oil and subject to closure to merchants for a good part of the year. The patterns we have seen also justify some guesses about seasonal price changes for years with only limited data (table 5.2). In both 272 (or 271) and 247, prices reflect typical end-of-year changes. For 279, 269, and 265–255, prices look instead like those before and after a spring adjustment (assuming they are reported in chronological order). In this context, it might be interesting to estimate the total annual demand for oil on Delos. Much of this demand must have been met by imports, and an estimate will help to delineate the scale of trade in oil.

In a number of cases in the accounts, the *hieropoioi* record oil bought for the Hieropoion (εἰς ἱεροποιόιον), which was surely destined in the first instance for religious celebrations to which the *hieropoioi* were bound, although some probably went for their personal consumption as well, even if the accounts do not show this explicitly.[26] If this oil covered all the personal needs of the *hieropoioi*—cult, lighting, consumption—they consumed about 1.3 *kh*/mo. Reckoned at the same ratio of adult male grain

112 (1988): 787–91, and 111 (1987): 644–47; Brunet, passim; G. Reger, *Phoenix* 46 (1992): 322–41.

26. E.g., *IG* XI 2.154A14–15, 161A108; *ID* 316.79, 354.59. On the religious duties of the *hieropoioi* (quite limited), see Vial, 216–32. On the Hieropoion, see now Jacques Tréheux in *Stemmata*, 377–86, esp. 383–86.

Table 5.2. Olive Oil Price Changes in Years with Fewer than Three Prices or Lacking Months of Purchase (dr)

	With Months		*Without Months*	
Year	*Month*	*Price*	*1st*	*2d*
279			175	150
272 or 271	1	125.1		
	9?	137.5		
269			112.5	100
265 or 255			125.1	106.2
247	8	100.0		
	11	150.0		

consumption to the average per person for the population as a whole established in chapter 4, this comes to 1. 08 *kh*/mo/person, or 13 *kh*/yr.[27] This figure corresponds well with an independent estimate offered by Marie-Claire Amouretti, who, beginning from rather different suppositions, puts the annual consumption of a "free man, citizen, who frequents the gymnasion" at 55.5 liters, or 17.8 *khoes* (= 1.5 *kh*/mo). Adjusted to account for less consumption by women and children, Amouretti's figures yield an annual demand per person of about 15.6 *khoes*, or about 1.3 *kh*/mo. This figure is only 18 percent higher than my estimate, and, as Amouretti herself admits, her figure "must be taken as an unusual consumption."[28] At my lower estimate of 13 *kh*/person/yr, the estimated Delian population of 2,700–9,100 would have had a total annual demand of 2,925–9,860 *metretai*.

But this estimate is probably too high. Because the *hieropoioi* came from the highest social levels of Delos, their standard of living must have surpassed that of most of their fellow citizens.[29] Oil was expensive in antiquity, so the level of consumption was no doubt linked to social standing. Poorer citizens, without the resources, leisure, or responsibilities of their wealthier fellows, must have consumed appreciably less oil. We can figure consumption minima by reckoning from caloric intake. We saw in chapter 4 that

27. See purchases for 279, 250, 231, and 218 B.C., all years when only two *hieropoioi* served (Vial, 163–64, with discussion at 172–83). For the ratios, see chapter 4, pp. 85–86, above.

28. Amouretti, *Pain*, 195, approved by D. J. Mattingly, *J. of Roman Arch.* 1 (1988): 159.

29. On the social level of the *hieropoioi*, see Vial, 187–91, 253–61, 262–69.

a reasonable guess for the average daily caloric intake of the Delians is 2,460 cal/day/person. Thomas Gallant has estimated that roughly 5 percent of a person's needs were satisfied with oil, which implies a monthly per capita consumption of about 0.15 *khous* and a total Delian demand of 405–1,365 *met*/yr.[30] These results are not even one-sixth of those calculated on the basis of the purchases of the *hieropoioi*. As in the case of grain, for which ancient rations consistently outstrip modern estimates of caloric need, other factors are likely to intervene. Oil served other purposes than food; it was used for lighting, washing, perfumes, medicines, ritual, and in other contexts.[31] Demand estimates based purely on consumption as food will ignore these important uses. Moreover, Gallant's caloric estimate of roughly 5 percent seems low. Diets in which about 28 percent of daily caloric needs were satisfied with oil are attested for modern Greece; consumption at such levels in fact comes very close to 13 *kh*/person/yr. Other surveys yield, rather consistently, a consumption of about 12.6–12.9 percent of calories in oil.[32] Granted that the *hieropoioi* who bought oil for themselves—and Amouretti's "free man, citizen, who frequents the gymnasion"—consumed considerably more oil than the typical Delian, let us strike a compromise and reckon that, very roughly, minimum consumption was about 4.5 *kh*/yr (corresponding to 12.6 percent of calories in grain) plus half again as much for other needs, for a total of 6.75 *kh*/yr/person. Taking the consumption at the level of the *hieropoioi* (13 *kh*/yr/person) as a maximum, and assuming that only 10 percent of the population consumed at this level, gives a typical annual consumption of 7.4 *kh*/person, or, for Delos as a whole, roughly 1,665–5,611 *met*/yr.

Figures compiled by Lionel Casson for the carrying capacity of ancient merchant ships suggest typical cargoes of about 1,500 *metretrai*. A wreck of about 275 B.C. recently recovered off the southwestern coast of Turkey carried at least six hundred amphorae in two sizes, with mean capacities of 38.0 and 10.87 liters, for a total minimum cargo of about 580 *metretrai*. (These amphorae may not have been typical; a recent study of capacities found standard Rhodian containers to hold 24–26 liters.) By Casson's reckoning, this was a small ship; but annual Delian demand would have filled

30. See chapter 4, pp. 85–86, above; Gallant, 72–73. On the caloric value of olive oil (8,073 cal/l, or about 25,188 cal/*khous* for a *khous* of 3.12 l), see Catherine F. Adams, *Nutritive Value of American Foods in Common Units* (Washington, D.C., 1975), 102; Foxhall-Forbes, 85, table 1.

31. Amouretti, *Pain*, 181–95.

32. Reckoned from Gallant, 65, table 4.1. For the 28 percent figure, see Leland G. Allbaugh, *Crete: A Case Study of an Underdeveloped Area* (Princeton, 1953), 100–111, 131; criticized at Gallant, 64, but see Lousset and Brousse, *L'Olivier*, 22, giving an annual per capita consumption in Greece of 18.9 kg, the highest they cite.

only 3–13 such vessels, and at Casson's typical cargo capacity, as few as 2–4 shiploads could have satisfied the annual Delian demand.[33]

It is also possible roughly to calculate the number of trees that would have been required to meet Delian demand. At a biennial average of 4 kilograms of oil per tree, 16,848 to 56,777 trees would have sufficed. Planted at 40 trees per hectare, they would have covered only 421–1420 ha, a maximum of about 0.6 percent of the total area of the Kyklades; even at a much less dense planting of 6 trees/ha, which would have left almost all that land free for cereals, they would have occupied no more than 9,463 ha, or 4 percent of the islands' surface. No doubt Kykladic olives were clustered in orchards much more rarely than their cousins in North Africa (source of the planting densities) and were far more integrated into a small-scale, diversified economy.[34]

As we have already seen of cereals in chapter 4, total Delian demand for oil was a trivial portion of the local Kykladic demand, to say nothing of that of the Aegean as a whole. A handful of shipments sufficed to cover Delos's total annual need. This situation helps to explain the general stability of price across any one year. Once local oil retailers had sufficient stock to cover a year's demand, wholesale prices on Delos would drop. Merchants with oil for sale would divert elsewhere, perhaps until close to the end of the sailing season, when local dealers would want to replenish stocks before winter set in (and take advantage of the harvest if possible). Any fluctuations in the wider market for oil would bypass Delos, where prices would tend to be set across the whole year by the prices that had obtained when the original shipments arrived.

Firewood Month-to-month price changes for firewood appear in table 5.3. Two patterns are detectable. Many years show a shift, usually a decline, within the first few months of the year. Prices in 250, 231, 224, and 174 B.C. fell in Hieron, Galaxion, Artemision, or, in 174, after Thargelion. Two years (200, 179) have rises early in the year. Another adjustment occurred in the late summer or fall. In 250, 246, 231, 224, 200, and

33. Çemal Pulak and Rhys F. Townsend, *AJA* 91 (1987): 31–49; Carolyn G. Koehler and Malcolm B. Wallace, *AJA* 91 (1987): 49–54; recent study: M. B. Wallace in *Recherches sur les amphores grecques* (Paris, 1986), 87–94, at 93; Foxhall-Forbes, 84; Casson, *Ships*, 184.

34. Amouretti, *Pain*, 204; D. J. Mattingly, *J. of Roman Arch.* 1 (1988): 160. Ibid., 45. Amouretti in *Agriculture in Ancient Greece*, 79–80; Forbes in ibid., 93–98. Chapter 4, p. 107, above. At the planting ratios cited at Sallares, 475 n. 41 (present-day planting at 190 trees/ha and a figure of 100–130/ha for dry farming area with minimum annual rainfall of 500–650 mm, after Loussert and Brousse, *L'Olivier*, 10, 178), the surface covered would have been even smaller.

Table 5.3. Indexed Firewood Prices on Delos, 272 or 271–170 B.C.

Year	Month	Price	Change (%)	Year	Month	Price	Change (%)
272 or	6	199.8	—	218	1	224.9	—
271	11?	162.4	−18.7		2	224.9	0.0
	12?	149.9	−7.7		3	199.8	−12.6
268	7	153.1	—		5	199.8	0.0
	8	149.9	−2.1	200	1	224.9	—
	9	149.9	0.0		2	224.9	0.0
250	1	175.0	—		3	249.9	+11.1
	2	162.4	−7.2		4	224.9	−10.0
	3	100.0	−38.4		5	249.9	+11.1
	4	124.9	+24.9		6	249.9	0.0
	5	100.0	−19.9		7	249.9	0.0
	6	100.0	0.0		8	249.9	0.0
	6	124.9	+24.9		9	249.9	0.0
	8	100.0	−19.9		10	224.9	−10.0
	8	112.4	+12.4		11	249.9	+11.1
	9	112.4	0.0		12	249.9	0.0
	11	100.0	−11.0	179	1	187.4	—
	11	100.0	0.0		2	224.9	+20.0
	12	112.4	+12.4		3	224.9	0.0
246	5	199.8	—		4	224.9	0.0
	6 (2)[a]	193.7	−3.0		5	224.9	0.0
	9	193.7	0.0		7	224.9	0.0
	11	208.2	+7.5		8	224.9	0.0
	12	210.3	+1.0		9	224.9	0.0
231	2	224.9	—		10	224.9	0.0
	3	175.0	−22.2		11	224.9	0.0
	7	149.9	−14.3		12	224.9	0.0
	8	175.0	+16.7	174	3	224.9	—
	11	175.0	0.0		5	224.9	0.0
224	2	187.4	—		7	199.8	−11.2
	4	149.9	−20.0		8	199.8	0.0
	5	149.9	0.0		9	188.6	−5.6
	6	149.9	0.0		10	224.9	+19.2
	7	149.9	0.0		11	233.9	+4.0
	8	149.9	0.0		12	191.9	−18.0
	10	157.4	+5.0		12	196.8	+2.5
				170	2	224.9	—
					3	224.9	0.0
					6	224.9	0.0

[a] Intercalary Panemos.

174, prices rose between Metageitnion and Posideon, with rises most common in Bouphonion–Aresion. In only one case, 272 or 271 B.C., did prices fall, by 7.7 percent from Aresion to Posideon. But 250 and 174 B.C. also showed declines in Aresion or Posideon after the more typical rise in the fall. Prices tended to stabilize in the late spring and summer, although subject to occasional monthly fluctuations (268, 250, 246, 231, 224, 218, 200, 179, and 174).

These patterns are amenable to explanations based on the seasonal demand for firewood, the exigencies of the sailing season, and the "harvesting" patterns for scrub. The demand for wood was certainly higher in the winter than in the summer; the nodes of change fell in the spring and the fall. Spring declines, which appear in four out of six cases, clearly fit the supposition of a reduced demand with the onset of warmer weather. The opening of the sailing season would have added to the downward pressure on prices, since now supplies from elsewhere could be brought in to replenish stocks depleted over the winter. The pattern appears nicely in 250, 231, 224, and 174 B.C.[35]

The summer pattern of lower prices subject to fluctuations responds to a reduced demand met by occasional imports; the transient price changes that occur across months, as in Panemos of 250 or Hekatombaion of 231 B.C., probably reflect temporary changes in supply. The fact that these fluctuations are transient and do not follow a clear pattern lends further support to this view. In the fall, demand changed again. The approach of winter and the impending closure of the sailing season would have led to increased stockpiling, hence increased demand; six years reflect this change with increased prices at exactly this time.

How can the declines at the end or very beginning of some years (272 or 271, 250, 179 [Lenaion], and 174) be accounted for? I see three possibilities, which should be supposed to have acted in conjunction and in different combinations in different years. Some years must have had milder winters than others, just as the winter of 169–168 B.C. was exceptionally severe (Livy 44.20). In such years, Delians may have overstockpiled firewood and then sought to unload the excess in midwinter: hence occasional price declines in Aresion or Posideon. In other years, transient declines may have resulted from unexpected shipments from neighboring islands during a

35. This view is not affected by the disagreement about the use for which wood was bought for the Hieropoion between Philippe Bruneau, *BCH* 105 (1981): 94 (wood for heating and cooking), and Jacques Tréheux in *Stemmata,* 385 (ritual only). The accounts cannot settle the matter, but the *hieropoioi* did not *always* buy wood for themselves each month, which may mean that their needs varied; some personal use may therefore be supposed.

spell of good weather. Perhaps 250 B.C. offers the best candidate in the strikingly anomalous price of 100 in Galaxion.

The third possibility has a structural aspect. As noted above, coppices could be harvested at any time of year. Olive prunings, which were also an important source of fuel, became available only during and immediately after the harvest. Olive presscake—the residue left after the fruit has been pressed for oil—was another important energy source also available in quantity only immediately after the harvest.[36] In years of heavy pruning and/or good harvest, these materials would begin to reach the market at the end of the Delian year, in Apatourion, Aresion, or Posideon. In sufficient quantity, they may have acted to counter the normal winter pressure keeping prices high. In conjunction with a mild winter, the sudden availability of olive by-products might account for the 12–25 percent price decline seen in these three years. Moreover, our investigation of oil prices suggested that the olive cycle in the Kyklades brought good harvests in even years, poor harvests in odd. In modern practice, pruning is heavier in years with good harvests. All four years showing wood price declines at the end of the year should also have produced good harvests (counting the low price of Lenaion 179 as evidence for 180 B.C.).[37]

The level of olive production on Delos must have been low, at least compared to the total demand for oil. It is possible that the reduction in price of firewood at the end of many years reflected the availability to the temple of prunings from its own trees; this would account for the absence of other instances of sale of cuttings.[38] In any case, year-end declines in both oil and firewood prices are rare enough that local production can have covered only a fraction of the demand, and it is probably appropriate to imagine that, in the years where we see such reductions, harvests were especially good and other factors—like a mild winter—also helped.

36. Aschenbrenner in *MME*, 54, on pruning in a contemporary Messenian community: "Some of the prunings are burned green soon after pruning, but most remain to dry and are used through spring, summer, and the next fall." For advice on presscake I am indebted to Lin Foxhall (per. comm.); cf. also Frederick R. Matson, *Advancement of Science* 23 (1966): 152.

37. Aschenbrenner in *MME*, 54: "If the [olive] tree is loaded [with fruit], the pruning is very severe and several large limbs . . . are cut off, as well as many smaller ones." Pruning is necessary because olives bear fruit only on branches two years old; see also Sandy, *Production and Use of Vegetable Oils in Ptolemaic Egypt*, 73. Although *IG* XI 2.219 + 220 might belong to either 272 or 271 B.C., J. Tréheux considers the early date more likely: *REG* 99 (1986): 301.

38. At the prevailing prices for Bouphonion and Aresion 250 B.C., Apollo had sold off between 4.3 and 5 talents of wood (*IG* XI 2.287A73, 80). No purchase of firewood for the temple is recorded in Apatourion itself. Could this mean that Apollo was able to supply all his own needs that month from prunings?

The great exceptions to this model for the annual price history of firewood are 200 and 179 B.C. Both years showed prices *rises* at the beginning of the year, high but stable prices across the spring and summer, and no further rise in the fall. Below I explore the possibility that, for 200 B.C., prices may have been affected by the constant military activity in the central Aegean. For 179 B.C., however, military operations cannot be invoked, since the Delians celebrated the year as one of peace (*IG* XI 2.130.1). Another possibility, also treated below, relates to the structural change in mean annual firewood prices that occurred around 218 B.C.; it is possible that these structural changes in long-term price trends overwhelmed the annual pattern typical for the first eight decades of the third century.

In general, however, annual firewood prices conform with very satisfying consistency to a price model based on a typical annual demand fluctuation, the exigencies of the sailing season and of summer trade, and the occasional infusion of additional supplies at the end of the year after the olive harvest.

Pigs Monthly pig prices (table 5.4) show less patterned behavior than either of our other two goods. Fluctuations are sometimes extreme, sometimes mild; prices may rise or fall in two or three consecutive months, or they may zigzag; occasional stability across two or three months may give way to wild fluctuations.

As with our other two goods, at least some pigs are likely to have been imported to Delos,[39] but evidence for any impact of the opening and closing of the sailing season is elusive. Some years in which prices fall begin with low prices, others with high. Three years show high end-of-year prices compared with prices earlier in the same year (250, 174, and 171), which might be attributed to the closure of the sailing season, except that eight years show high prices in the summer (269, 246, 224, 218, 200, 179, 174, and 169), and in four of those years, prices declined in the fall (246, 224, 200, and 174). There is therefore no persuasive evidence for price changes in response to the close of the sailing season.

The opening of the season may have left rather more, although still tenuous, traces. Six years registered a price decline across either Galaxion–Artemision or Artemision–Thargelion, and no year recorded a price rise

39. On the trade by sea in pigs and other animals, see Graßl, *MBAH* 4.2 (1985): 77–88, esp. 80–83. Some examples of such shipments: Demos. 22.167, Diod. 8.7.2, Paus. 4.4.6; *ISE* I.55.18 (237/6 B.C.?). During the period of the Athenian Amphiktyonia on Delos in the fourth century, payment of the πεντηκοστή proves that sacrificial oxen were imported (*ID* 98A38).

across both pairs of months (250, 231, 224, 200, 179, and 174). This pattern looks promising as evidence for a price decline at the opening of the season except for one major problem: in only two (218 and 179), or possibly three (including 174), years did prices stay down. In the others they rose in the very next month, usually to levels at least as high as if not higher than they had occupied before. While the opening of the sailing season may have had some effect every year—and certainly seems visible in 218 and 179, when prices fell and stayed down—other effects that kept prices up seem generally to have swamped it.

The impression of atypical price behavior at the usual nodes for change is reinforced by the level of prices at other times of the year. High summer and low winter prices are particularly unamenable to explanation by the ebb and flow of the sailing season. Of the several factors that may have intervened to overwhelm the pattern seen with our other commodities, two are difficult to evaluate, although they are bound to have had their impact. Swine are especially prone to disease, a fact of which Aristotle was fully aware. Swine diseases spread rapidly and may wipe out most of the animals in an infected herd. On small islands like Delos and Rheneia, however, the population may not always have been large enough to sustain a disease, whether epidemic or endemic. Thus while there may have been occasional

Table 5.4. Indexed Pig Prices on Delos, 269–169 B.C.

Year	*Month*	*Price*	*Change (%)*	*Year*	*Month*	*Price*	*Change (%)*
269	1	100.0	—	250	4	112.5	+22.8
	2	137.5	+37.5	(*cont.*)	5	100.0	−11.1
	3	150.0	+ 9.1		6	91.7	−8.4
	4	175.0	+16.7		7	91.7	0.0
	5	175.0	0.0		8	100.0	+ 9.1
	6	175.0	0.0		8	116.7	+16.6
	7	150.0	−14.3		9	83.3	−28.6
	8	225.0	+50.0		10	91.7	+10.0
	8	200.0	−11.1		11	125.0	+36.4
	9	158.3	−20.8		12	100.0	−20.0
	10	200.0	+26.3	247	7	125.0	—
	11	200.0	0.0		8	125.0	0.0
	12	225.0	+12.5		12	116.7	−6.6
250	1	91.7	—				
	2	75.0	−18.2				
	3	100.0	+33.3				
	4	91.7	−8.4				

(*continued*)

Table 5.4. Continued

Year	Month	Price	Change (%)	Year	Month	Price	Change (%)
246	1	70.8	—	200	7	200.0	0.0
	6	75.0	—	*(cont.)*	8	200.0	0.0
	6(2)[a]	125.0	+33.3		9	216.7	+8.3
	7	79.2	−36.7		10	175.0	−19.2
	8	125.0	+57.9		11	175.0	0.0
	9	83.3	−33.4		12	175.0	0.0
	10	100.0	+20.0	194	1	225.0	—
	11	150.0	+50.0		2	133.3	−40.7
	12	116.7	−22.2		4	200.0	+50.0
	12	100.0	−14.3	179	2	241.7	—
231	2	150.0	—		4	225.0	−6.9
	3	158.0	+ 5.6		5	200.0	−12.3
	4	125.0	−21.1		6	200.0	0.0
	5	125.0	0.0		8	225.0	+12.5
	7	191.7	+53.3		1	225.0	—
224	1	175.0	—		3	150.0	−33.3
	2	150.0	−14.3		4	175.0	+16.7
	3	166.7	+11.1		5	150.0	−14.3
	4	195.8	+19.2		6	150.0	0.0
	5	150.0	−23.4		7	150.0	0.0
	7	233.3	+55.5		8	200.0	+33.3
	9	200.0	−14.3		8	225.0	+12.5
218	1	166.7	—		10	150.0	−33.3
	2	166.7	0.0		11	150.0	0.0
	3	166.7	0.0		11	250.0	+66.7
	4	175.0	+5.0	171	12	200.0	+20.0
	5	166.7	−4.8		8	150.0	—
	6	175.0	+5.0		8	300.0[b]	
	8	179.1	+2.4		11	150.0	0.0
200	1	208.3	—		12	250.0	+66.7
	2	183.3	−12.0	169	6	225.0	—
	2	300.0[b]			8	233.3	+3.7
	3	191.7	+4.6		8	250.0	+7.2
	4	183.3	−4.4		12	250.0	0.0
	6	200.0	+9.1				

[a] Intercalary Panemos.

[b] These prices are so high compared to their neighbors that they have not been included in the treatment of price history. I suspect either some inconsistency in terminology or that the *hieropoioi* imposed unusually stringent requirements of "perfection" (see chapter 5, n. 13).

epizootics that wiped out swine on Delos or its neighbors and so raised prices, in general the fluctuations we see are probably not to be attributed to this cause.[40]

The second matter has to do with requirements for sacrifice. Sacrificial animals had to be "perfect."[41] If different administrators at different times and under different circumstances imposed different standards, widely varying numbers of animals might qualify; very picky *hieropoioi* might feel justified in paying substantially higher prices for animals they judged to be better suited to Apollo. Particular circumstances might also have an effect. Early in the third century, a strange portent occurred "when grape cuttings appeared in the spring" (κλήμ̣α̣τ̣α σ̣ταφύλης ξ . . . . ὅτ' ἐ[ν τ]ῆι κρηνῖδι ἐφάνη [*IG* XI 2.153.8–9]). The χοῖρος bought for expiatory sacrifice cost eight drachmas, making it the most expensive such animal attested on Delos. Under the circumstances, it would not be surprising if the *hieropoioi* had sought out the most perfect animal they could find: there had been another portent that same year, although a lacuna in the text prevents us knowing how it was dealt with.[42] Such variations in quality surely affected price, but the impact is impossible to quantify.[43]

Two other possible factors seem more important to me, because they would have been structural and cyclical: the impact of the life cycle of the pig, and the unusual demand structure for pigs as opposed to oil or firewood.

Pigs were reckoned in antiquity to be able to produce two litters a year, with a gestation period of about four months and two months for weaning.[44] A χοῖρος was a "piglet," an animal already weaned but not yet adult

40. *Hist. anim.* 8.21. Sallares, 221–93.

41. See n. 13 above. On the Delian *boonai,* appointed to buy oxen for sacrifice, see *ID* 399A7, 14, 17, 18, and Vial, 243–44. Although explicitly attested only in this one year, these boards are likely to have functioned throughout independence, since the sale of hides and payments to priests—two of the duties of the *boonai*—are attested frequently: see *IG* XI 2.274.24, 287A24, A113–14.

42. *IG* XI 2.153.6–7: "When the signs occurred around the eyes," ὅτε τὰ περὶ τοὺς ὀφθαλμοὺς [of the statue of Leto?] ἐγένετο σημε[ῖ]α. There is another portent a few years later at *IG* XI 2.159A41.

43. Prices for older pigs also show violent month-to-month fluctuations. Two animals both bought in the same month in 246 B.C. cost 14 and 8 dr; in 247 B.C., 18 and 16.5 dr; and 20 dr in 224 B.C. (*ID* 290.88, 291b23–24, 338Aa59).

44. Arist., *Hist. anim.* 8.6; cf. Orth, *RE,* n.s., II.2 (1923), s.v. "Schwein," 801–15. This corresponds very well with modern experience: see W. J. Carmichael and John B. Rice, "Variations in Farrow, with Special Reference to the Birth Weight of Pigs," University of Illinois Agricultural Experiment Station Bulletin no. 226 (Urbana, 1920), 68–71; Dennis L. Meadows, *Dynamics of Commodity Production*

and younger than the δέλφαξ or δελφάκιον.[45] This life cycle means that over the course of a year, there would be two times directly after weaning when χοῖροι were especially abundant, and so cheap, and two other periods between birth and weaning when χοῖροι were relatively scarce, and so more expensive. These periods of highest and lowest price should be separated by only a month or two, while in between prices should gradually rise. The result is a sawtoothed price curve of sharp drops and gradual rises with a periodicity of about six months. Price patterns in 224, with rising prices from Lenaion to Artemision and a sharp drop in Thargelion, and in 200, where prices rose from Lenaion through Bouphonion and then fell precipitously in Apatourion, seem to follow this cycle; prices in 269 and 231 may repeat the pattern, although less consistently. If, however, this pattern connected with the life cycle of the pig really did affect prices on Delos, its impact must have been modulated, dampened, and sometimes swamped by other factors. Demand fluctuations are likely to have played a more important role.

Fish aside, pork was probably the commonest meat consumed in the ancient diet,[46] and young pigs were the least expensive pork. They were also a favored offering, especially for poorer people.[47] Demand for pigs,

---

Cycles (Cambridge, Mass., 1970), 54; J. L. Krider, J. H. Conrad, and W. E. Carroll, *Swine Production*[5] (New York, 1982), 172 (111–17 days, with average of 114).

45. Athen. 375a, quoting Aristophanes of Byzantion: τῶν δὲ συῶν τὰ μὲν ἤδη συμπεπηγότα δέλφακες, τὰ δ᾽ ἁπαλὰ καὶ ἔνικμα χοῖροι. Cf. David Schaps, *JHS* 111 (1991): 208–9.

46. Plut. *Quaest. con.* 4.5.1 (*Mor.* 669F) calls pork τὸ δικαιότατον κρέας; Athen. 375a–e; Polyb. 2.15.2–3 on consumption in the Roman army; Theophr. *Hist. pl.* 9.20.5; Pliny *Nat. hist.* 27.120.145; Hippokrates, ed. Littré, vol. 2, pp. 492–95; Galen *Peri trophon dynamenon* 3.2, ed. Kühn, vol. 6, p. 661; cf. Sallares, 458 n. 313. Plato *Rep.* 373c includes "swineherds" among the occupations needed in his more luxurious city, which Michael H. Jameson in *Pastoral Economies in Classical Antiquity* (Cambridge, 1988), 99, cites among the evidence that pigs played a limited role in sacrifice in the classical city. On the consumption of pork in late antique Rome and the *Testamentum porcelli,* see Edward Champlin, *Phoenix* 41 (1987): 174–83. Nor can I resist a reference to the now famous epitaph for a pig dated to the second or third century A.D.; see Nicos Nikolaou, *REG* 98 (1985): 147–52, with text and further references.

47. Plato *Rep.* 378a; cf. also Herod. 2.48, Xenoph. *Anab.* 7.85; [Demos.] 54.39, Hippon. fr. 40 (Bergk), Heniokh. fr. 2 (Kostel-Austin) = Athen. 9.396D. For scenes of household sacrifice on Delos, see W. Déonna, *La Vie privée des Déliens* (Paris, 1948), 103, citing M. Bulard, *La Religion domestique dans la colonie italienne de Délos d'après les peintures murales et les autels historiés* (Paris, 1926), 18, 57–58, 86 (which was unavailable to me). See also A. Plassart, *BCH* 40 (1916): 176, fig. 10;

however, may have been very sensitive to small price changes; that is to say, the demand for pigs may have been relatively price-elastic. If so, demand would have responded quickly to small price variations, leading to a quick price rise. High prices will naturally attract sellers, and may force the price back down if the supply exceeds the demand. The year 250 B.C. offers an excellent example of such a pattern.

The year begins in Lenaion with a price of 91.7. Suppose poorer buyers abstain, and by Hieron the price has fallen by 18.2 percent to 75. The low price attracts buyers, and demand pushes the price up again to 100. A high price encourages producers—this early in the year we should think of Delians, not importers—to bring more pigs to market, so that by Artemision the price has fallen to 91.7, but rises again within a week to 112.5 (for a pig bought for the Artemisia). Demand slackens again in the face of a high price, and by Thargelion pigs fetch only 100. This would be a perfect example of a price curve for a commodity whose demand curve is highly price-elastic.

Five other years show extended periods of similar response (224 for nine months; 200 for seven; 246, 231, and 174 for five); other years might also display the pattern if the data were complete (218, 179, and possibly 247). It seems evident that pig demand was extremely sensitive to price, and that this sensitivity overwhelmed the impact of both the natural cycle of the animals—hardly a serious problem, since producers could easily afford to withhold animals for a month or two if prices were low—and of the opening and closing of the sailing season, which seems to have exhibited no more than a modest and occasional effect in the spring and hardly any at all in the fall.

The failure of pig prices to show much response to the sailing season has important implications. It seems very likely that much of the local demand was satisfied, not from imports, but out of local production. Some pigs were clearly raised on Delos. Although the inventories of temple-owned estates, which are rich in words for agricultural buildings, never mention pigsties, a chance reference in another context proves Apollo's responsibility for at least one. This building may have belonged to one of the estates for which we lack inventories. Livestock, including pigs, were surely raised on private estates on Delos; Michèle Brunet has recently suggested that the peninsula of Patinioti at the northeastern tip of the island was

177, fig. 11; and esp. 213, fig. 29; and, most recently, *BCH* 112 (1988): 765–66, with fig. 36, a private votive plaque dating to before 69 B.C.

entirely devoted to ranching.[48] We also happen to know the names of a number of persons who sold pigs to the temple. Two, Timesidemos and Aristodikos, who sold a pig each in Bouphonion and Apatourion 269 B.C., may well be identical with the brothers who shared the lease of Khareteia in 269–260 B.C.[49] It is tempting to suppose that they raised the pigs there. In any case, the ἱερὰ συγγραφή that regulated the lease of Apollo's estates envisioned raising livestock (*ID* 503.19–30). There is no reason to suppose this did not include pigs.[50]

At the same time, total demand on Delos may well have been relatively low. The temple is a poor guide here. Its demand was largely inelastic, for the *hieropoioi* had to buy and sacrifice a pig on the first of every month. It is exactly where some slight "elasticity" in temple demand emerges, however, that some very striking corroborating evidence arises for the sensitivity of price to demand. The Delian Thesmophoria was held every Metageitnion, and this ceremony required the *hieropoioi* to buy four pigs of different condition, one of which was a χοῖρος.[51] Preserved are five years with prices for both the χοῖρος bought on the first of the month to purify the temple and the χοῖρος bought later in the month for the Thesmophoria. In all cases but one (269), the second pig was more expensive, sometimes substantially so (250, by 17 percent; 174, by 25 percent; 171, by 100 percent;[52] 169, by 4 percent). Marginal increase in total demand thanks

48. E.g., "ox shed" (βούστασις) and "sheepfold" (προβατών); see *IG* XI 2.287A143–174. Χοιροτροφεῖον is attested in Eupolis (*CAF*, vol. 1, fr. 453) and in Phrynichos (ibid., fr. 43). For the Delian "pigsty"—really more a place to keep adult swine—see *IG* XI 2.154A41: τὸγ καπρῶνα ἐπισκευάσαντι · ⊢. For the three estates for which we lack inventories, see n. 25 above. On the terminology, see briefly Robin Osborne, *BSA* 80 (1985): 119–28. Brunet, 141–42, and id., Τόποι 2 (1992): 40–42.

49. *IG* XI 2.203A52, 53–54; 203A20. Cf. Kent, 335, no. 223, 323, no. 44; Vial, 218–19. As Khareteia had vines (see chapter 6, p. 194, below), I am reminded of Varro's advice (*Rust.* 2.4.6) on raising *porci sacres* for sacrifice: "Si fundus ministrat, dari solent vinacea ac scopi ex uvis."

50. See the discussion of these clauses at Kent, 277–78. The term for livestock, πρόβατα, often refers particularly to sheep and goats (see Herod. 1.133.1, 8.137.2; *IG* V 3.14; *IG* II^2 1672.289), but it can include animals generally, especially those destined for sacrifice (Herod. 6.56). In my view the authors of the contract are more likely to have understood the term as comprehensively as possible, to avoid evasion by renters; this interpretation is supported by the inclusion of oxen, βοές, under the general word (see ll. 20–21, 25–27).

51. *IG* XI 2.287A68–69. Full citations at Bruneau, 287; see 285–90 on the Delian Thesmophoria.

52. This rise is so great that I suspect some other factor, such as especially picky *hieropoioi*, must also have been at work.

to an increase in temple demand from one to five pigs apparently delivered a substantial boost to the price.

This price behavior also reinforces the notion that the total monthly demand for pigs on Delos could not have been very large. Except for the rarified stratum who could afford meat on a regular basis, individual Delians probably bought pigs only very rarely: for household sacrifice, for public ceremonies in which they participated,[53] and for feasts. Total demand cannot have approached that for firewood or olive oil, both staples in every Delian household.

In many respects the behavior of pig prices, tied partly of course to the natural history of the animals, has changed remarkably little in the past 2,300 years. This constancy suggests a possible explanation for high summer pig prices. Modern pig farmers, who also get two litters a year from their animals, prefer to avoid farrowing in cold weather. They therefore arrange for sows to farrow in May and September. Piglets born in May will not be weaned until July or August. If ancient farmers also favored late spring farrowings, χοῖροι would have been relatively rarer in the summer. Such a pattern might account for high summer prices on Delos.[54]

LONG-TERM PRICE HISTORIES

By "price history," I mean the history of fluctuations in price levels over the 147 years of Delian independence. Since transient monthly variations are not at issue here, I use for each available year a mean price constructed from all available monthly prices. The base data for these mean prices are very uneven. Some years have twelve or more monthly prices, while for others we depend on three, two, or even a single price. Despite the possibility of distortion, I have preferred to keep these data as at least partly representative of the price level for their years. I have, however, rejected data from inscriptions so poorly dated that they might fall on either side of a securely dated inscription (for instance, *IG* XI 2.275 of 259 B.C. or 256–251 B.C.) and from inscriptions whose dates might vary by more than two or three years (for instance, *IG* XI 2.147, dated only 296–290 B.C.). To inscriptions imperfectly dated but ranging over only two or three consecutive

53. In the Athenian Thesmophoria, in which participation was mandatory for Athenian women, their husbands or other κύριοι were obligated to cover the costs: Isaios 3.80; Men. *Epitr.* 749–51 (Sandbach). Pork distributed at a public feast in Syros in the third century A.D., *IG* XII 5.667.14, 20.

54. Meadows, *Dynamics of Commodity Production Cycles,* 39. Modern management techniques allow for wide variation in age at weaning; see Krider, Conrad, and Carroll, *Swine Production*[5], 248–49.

years, I have arbitrarily assigned the earliest possible date; e.g., *ID* 314 is treated as 233 B.C., not 232. Since the range in no case exceeds three years (e.g., *ID* 459), the convenience in handling and analyzing the data more than compensates for any slight error that may creep into the time series.

The purpose here is to identify long-term price trends for our three Delian commodities and to try to account for these trends. One method used both here and in chapter 6 to analyze the data is regression analysis. Regressions give information about the degree of correlation between two or more variables and a sense of how likely or unlikely it is that such correlations are due to chance. The reality of apparent trends can be tested quite readily by regression analysis; for instance, the supposed long-term decline in olive oil prices after ca. 270 B.C. proves chimerical. Such analyses may also be designed to test a hypothesis about the relationship between changes in prices and outside factors; regression strikingly confirms the reality of a deep fall in rents for Apollo's estates in 290 B.C. (chapter 6). Regressions may also suggest relationships or trends not previously suspected, such as the link between firewood and pig prices after ca. 220 B.C. However, regression analysis alone cannot either guarantee or explain a *causal* connection between purely statistical correlations. For that, we must depend on our understanding of the natural history of the products studied, the operation of the economy, the impact of social practices, and the role of historical circumstances and developments, such as the effect of military activity on the local economy. For example, whereas the link between firewood and pig prices can be explained by the ways in which pigs were raised and fed, the strikingly low prices for several goods in 250 B.C., while statistically valid, have no readily apparent explanation. Throughout I have tried to bear in mind the limitations of both the data and the method. It should also be clear that the obscurities of the history of independent Delos and of its Kykladic neighbors set limits of their own; I have tried to respect them.[55]

In searching for hypotheses, I have also tried to stand by the principle enunciated and justified in chapter 3 of looking first and foremost for local causes. The hierarchy of preference for purchase of goods runs always from indigenous suppliers (Delians or resident metics) through neighbors, first close (Rheneia, Mykonos) then farther away (Tenos, Paros, Andros,

55. Readers unfamiliar with regression analysis, or to whom tables 5.6 through 5.9 say nothing, may wish to consult the brief explanation in Appendix II. For a good, cautionary introduction to the pitfalls and value of correlation analysis, see Stephen Jay Gould, *The Mismeasure of Man* (New York, 1981), 239–55.

Table 5.5. Mean Annual Indexed Prices on Delos for Olive Oil, Firewood, and Pigs, 307–169 B.C.

		Prices		
Year	*Adj. Year*	*Oil*	*Firewood*	*Pigs*
307	8	262.6		
304	11	277.2	187.4	
302	13			250.0
301	14			350.0
300	15		188.3	
281	34	219.5		158.3
279	36	162.5	199.8	
277	38			137.5
276	39			200.0
274	41		212.3	150.0
272 or 271	43	131.3	171.8	
269	46	110.4	175.0	174.7
268	47	123.5	151.0	162.5
260–259	55	100.0		
258	57		140.6	
250	65	105.8	117.3	97.9
247	68	125.0	175.0	122.2
246	69	91.5	201.1	102.5
233 or 232	82			150.0
231	84	108.3	180.0	150.0
224	90	95.0	156.3	181.5
218	97	100.0	212.3	170.9
200	115	101.0	241.6	200.7
194	121	112.5	224.9	186.1
179	136	103.5	221.5	218.3
178	137	103.2	224.9	
177	138			245.8
174	141	82.1	209.5	188.5
173	142	70.8	224.9	191.7
171	144			212.5
170	145	93.8	224.9	216.7
169	146	137.5	199.8	239.6

Naxos), to distant sources. Since, as I have argued, local sources generally satisfied most of Delos's needs, local causes for unusual events should first be investigated and eliminated before appeal to distant happenings like the closure of the straits.[56]

56. For instance, it is appealing to attribute the high prices of firewood in 173 B.C. to the impact of Perseus's expedition to Byzantion, usually dated to about

One final preliminary matter. As I have repeatedly emphasized, the price series are frustratingly lacunose. Were they treated, for purposes of analysis, as regular time series, most years would show missing data (see table 5.5). To avoid this problem, I have treated the data as if contiguous, and compensated by creating data sets for time in which the time value of each datum point represents the actual time elapsed since the next earlier datum. Thus for olive oil the first price value, 278.2, of the year 304 B.C., corresponds to the time value "11" (from 315 to 304); the next price value, of 281 B.C., corresponds to the time value "34" (these time values are given in the column headed "Adj[usted] Year" in table 5.5). In this way the actual chronology of the data is preserved. The main consequence is to moderate the degree of change over time; it does not affect the character or significance of the relations. The mean prices used in the following sections are given in table 5.5.

The Price History of Olive Oil A glance at a graph of mean annual olive oil prices over time (fig. 5.1) immediately suggests that oil prices declined steadily and significantly over the years from 304 to 279 B.C. and thereafter fluctuated within bounds provided by the prices of 279 and 173 B.C. A second decline from 194 to 173 and the rise thereafter to 169 are exceptional and require comment, but pale compared to the much higher price levels before 279, and nothing indicates that the high value for 169 B.C. marks the beginning of an extraordinary new upward trend.[57] A dummy variable constructed to distinguish the data before and after 279 B.C. confirms this hypothesis (table 5.6), which accounts for fully 80 percent of the variation in oil prices. No other hypothesis or combination of hypotheses comes near this success.

The results of the analysis suggest that the history of oil prices on Delos falls into two broad periods: (1) high but declining prices from the begin-

---

that year (Livy 42.13.7, 40.6, 42.4; App. *Mak.* 11.1; cf. Will II[2] 267). With Delos under Rhodian tutelage, and Rhodos allied with Rome and Pergamon, politics may have favored cancellation of deliveries from Makedon even if Perseus's activities did not close the straits. But in fact (1) nothing proves that Delos depended on Makedon for firewood; (2) nothing shows any Delian dependence on suppliers north of the straits; (3) Perseus would have found it very difficult indeed to stop shipments to specific buyers; and (4) our knowledge of the king's activity derives entirely from one reference (going back ultimately to Polybios) in the litany of complaints Attalos delivered before the Roman Senate in 173 B.C., the repetition of the charge by a Roman envoy, and Perseus's *apologia.* See further discussion below.

57. Contra Heichelheim, *Wirt. Sch.*, 48–56; Larsen, 388–90. Local military events and an exceptionally harsh winter suffice to explain it; see p. 169 below.

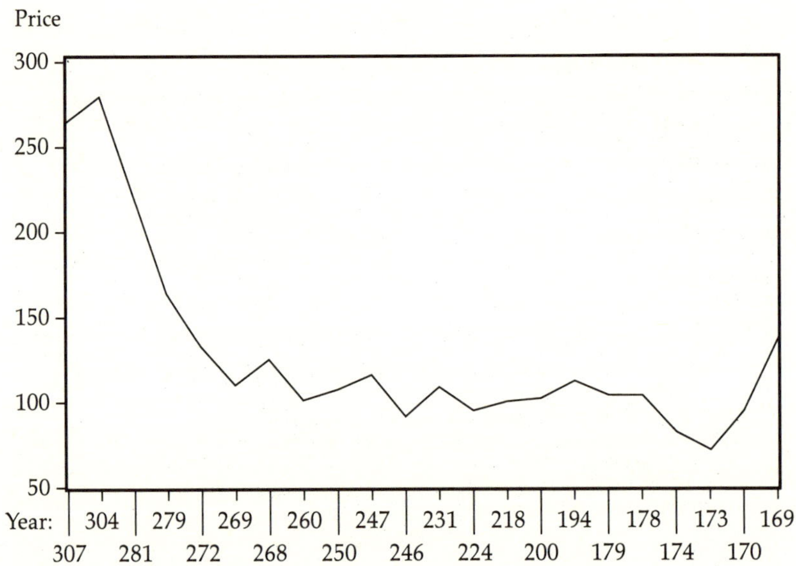

Figure 5.1. Indexed Olive Oil Prices, Delos, 304–169 B.C.

ning of the evidence in 307 B.C. to 279 B.C., and (2) a long period of fluctuating, but steady, prices thereafter. Within the second period, three possible subperiods may be distinguished: (a) 279–224 B.C., marked by sharp rises and declines covering up to about a decade; (b) a slow but steady rise from 224 to 194 B.C.; and (c) a rapid decline from 178 to 173 B.C. The price of 170 B.C. looks like a return to rising prices, while the high price of 169 B.C.—higher than any price in 110 years—is an anomaly owing to transient local conditions.

Table 5.6. Olive Oil Prices, Sorted before and after 279 B.C.

Dependent Variable is OIL
Number of observations: 22

Variable	*Coefficient*	*Std. Error*	*T-Stat.*	*2-Tail Sig.*
C	*105.28889*	*5.9430513*	*17.716302*	*0.000*
279 B.C.	*125.16112*	*13.937691*	*8.9800467*	*0.000*

R-squared	0.801274	Mean of dependent var	128.0455
Adjusted R-squared	0.791338	S.D. of dependent var	55.19809
S.E. of regression	25.21423	Sum of squared resid	12715.15
Durbin-Watson stat	1.731431	F-statistic	80.64124
Log likelihood	−101.1712		

Period 1. The declining prices of 307–279 B.C. have not escaped attention.[58] An interpretation first offered by Fritz Heichelheim attributes these high prices to Alexander's conquest of the East. One facet of this view—that a general inflation swamped the old Greek world as gold and silver captured from the Persians made its way west[59]—cannot be sustained from the Delian evidence, which flatly contradicts it.[60] The other facet is more plausible. It argues that as the Greeks established themselves in the East, demand grew for traditional Greek products not available locally. Chief among these were olive oil and wine, whose prices rose in the entire Greek world, Delos included. In time, the new settlers planted olive orchards and vineyards and the pressure on Greek products relented. The response was a general decline in prices, to which the Delian data attest.

This view depends on a number of assumptions about the economy of the early Hellenistic world. It requires a unified world market in staple goods, which could draw on the production of all important agricultural centers. It assumes prices set universally by a universal market, so that olive oil prices on Delos would represent the cost of oil—without additional transportation expenses, of course—anywhere in the Hellenistic world. Even quite local transactions—the sale, for instance, of wine produced on the Delian estate of Epistheneia on the market in Delos—would be modulated through this universal market. It presupposes a very sophisticated transport system, capable of moving enormous quantities of goods over long distances (including a good deal of land transport for the Greek settlements in the old Persian Empire).

This model of the Hellenistic economy has come in for a great deal of criticism in the past fifty years; it is now generally discredited, although some scholars have recently begun a retreat from the more radical version of the "primitivist" economy erected in its place.[61] Yet the specifics of Heichelheim's argument about oil and wine prices still command adherents, who have evidently not considered that the presupposition that there

58. Gustave Glotz, *Journal des Savants* 11 (1913): 20–21, 29; Heichelheim, *Wirt. Sch.*, 53 (cf. 55); Larsen, 389 (cf. 388–90, 380–83); Rostovtzeff, 158–59, although his remark (at 235) that "The general tendency of prices in the first period [ca. 310–270 B.C.] is upwards" is generally wrong. He discusses Delos at 190–91, 230–36, with notes.

59. Heichelheim, *Wirt. Sch.*, 55–56; Larsen, 380; H. Michell, *Canadian Journal of Economics and Political Science* 12 (1946): 1–17; Bruno Cavagnola, *Istituto lombardo (rend. lett.)* 107 (1973): 538–40. Cf. Will I², 35.

60. See chapter 7, pp. 250–52 below.

61. For discussion and some basic bibliography, see chapter 3, pp. 75–82, above, with nn. 103–4, 106, 107, 109.

was a unified world economy, at least in staples, undergirds his interpretation of the data.[62]

Not all the Delian data can be accounted for easily by this model, however. The oil price of 112.5 for Bouphonion 304 B.C., coming just before the harvest, when oil should have been particularly scarce, fits comfortably with oil prices common after the 270s. A single low price in a time of high price levels might merely be an anomaly, but the Heichelheim model (for want of a better expression) cannot easily account for such anomalies; and the appearance of this low price in the very year that provides the highest attested oil prices is especially troubling. The oil price of 307–305 B.C. also presents a problem. On Heichelheim's model, prices should decline over time, yet this price is almost 30 percent lower than the prices of 304 (discounting the price of Bouphonion).

Finally, Heichelheim's model offers no account of the timing of oil price stabilization in the 270s. The date seems arbitrary. Alexander's settlements had been established by 323 B.C. At his death, twenty thousand of the settlers who had hoped to return to Greece were massacred at Babylon, and thereafter the settlements were permanent. Presumably, the survivors would have begun to plant olives and vines then, assuming they had not done so before; Alexander had seen to it that his colonies had both sufficient agricultural territory and the labor to till it. New vineyards require about seven years to become productive, olive orchards ten to twenty. Even on the most pessimistic assumptions, plantings put in in ca. 320 B.C. would have begun to produce by the end of the fourth century, or by the 290s at the very latest.[63] On the other hand, the creation of new cities (or settlements) in the East did not stop with Alexander; his Seleukid successors pursued the policy vigorously, and well beyond 270 B.C. If Alexander's settlers had needed Greek goods, the same should have held for their Seleukid counterparts, yet oil prices fell by 272 to levels that persisted through the rest of the century.[64]

62. See Will I², 34–35; Vial, 283–84, 330; Cavagnola, *Istituto lombardo (rend. lett.)* 107 (1973): 538–40; Robin Osborne, *Chiron* 18 (1988): 301; perhaps also Meiggs, 455. D. W. Rathbone, in *Eighth International Economic History Congress, Budapest 1982, ser. B12* (Budapest, 1982), 44–51, at 48, suggests that price changes were linked to the price of wheat, which was declining owing to the introduction of cheap Ptolemaic wheat into the Aegean market.

63. Diod. 18.7.1 (massacre); Arr. 4.22.5; Q. Curt. 7.6.25–27, Arr. 4.4.1; Q. Curt. 7.10.15, 11.29, Arr. 4.16.3. See the convenient recent summary in A. B. Bosworth, *Conquest and Empire: The Reign of Alexander the Great* (Cambridge, 1988), 245–50; and on the revolt, see now Paul Bernard, *BCH* 114 (1990): 529–31 (preliminary version in *CRAI* 1989: 301–2), with further references.

64. Evidence for Seleukid colonies includes Diod. 18.25.5; Jos. *AJ* 12.147–53;

It is possible, in my view, to account for the prices of 304 B.C. and the trend of 307–279 B.C. without appeal to eastern demand and the theoretical substructure it supposes. The responsiveness of olive oil prices to the sailing season has shown that Delos imported much of its oil. On the assumption that before 314 B.C., Athens was the main source, the price history of olive oil can be interpreted as the replacement of Athens by Rhodos until Delos could develop local sources in the neighboring islands that guaranteed a stable price and replaced Rhodian imports.

In the sixth and fifth centuries, Athens exported olive oil and wine. Solon's legislation had encouraged the expansion of olive culture, and a rental contract for a parcel of land dated to 418/7 B.C. confirms the owner's interest in expanding production of olives.[65] The importance of oil exports for the Athenian economy persisted throughout the fourth century. Even if the Peloponnesian War had interrupted production—and Victor Hanson has shown the difficulties attendant on "economic warfare," particularly against olives—any damage caused by the war was repaired within a decade or two, and no one doubts that, down to the end of the century, oil remained an important Athenian export.[66] Especially after the Social War,

---

App. *Syr.* 1; Welles, *RC,* 51. For his refoundation of Lysimakheia, Antiokhos III provided settlers with βοῦς καὶ πρόβατα καὶ σίδηρον ἐς γεωργίαν (App. *Syr.* 1.1); see also *IvMag.* 61.18–19 (= *OGIS* 233), describing colonists dispatched from Magnesia to Antiokheia in Persis at royal request as ἄνδρας πλήθει ἱκανοὺς καὶ ἀρετῆι διαφέροντας, which refers to their farming skills, not their moral characteristics (P. Bernard, *BCH* 114 [1990]: 539). Cf. Getzel M. Cohen, *The Seleucid Colonies* (Wiesbaden, 1978), 47–50; Heinz Kreissig, *Wirtschaft und Gesellschaft im Seleukidenreich* (Berlin, 1978); John D. Grainger, *The Cities of Seleukid Syria* (Oxford, 1990). Susan Sherwin-White and Amélie Kuhrt, *From Samarkhand to Sardis* (Berkeley, 1993), 141–87.

65. A. French, *The Growth of the Athenian Economy* (New York, 1964), 123–24, 131; Plut. *Solon* 24.1. Peter Garnsey and Ian Morris argue in *Bad Year Economics,* 103, that if the Solonian law is genuine, "it is best interpreted in the same way as the Teian regulation" (Meiggs-Lewis 30, ca. 470 B.C.), "as an attempt by the state to limit the power of the large landowners to dispose of their food surplus overseas in circumstances in which the inevitable harvest fluctuations periodically exposed many domestic consumers to hunger"; this view considers only the ban on other agricultural exports, however, not the positive support for olive oil export; *IG* I^3 84.33–34 (= *IG* I^2 94). Isager-Skydsgaard, 201, with references to studies of the SOS amphoras.

66. Victor Davis Hanson, *Warfare and Agriculture in Classical Greece* (Pisa, 1983), 47–56, 113–43; Paul Harvey, *Athenaeum* 64 (1986): 205–18. Barry S. Strauss, *Athens after the Peloponnesian War* (Ithaca, N.Y., 1986), 44–45, exhibits some skepticism: "There was, however, a serious depression, if not a universal one, in the post-war / Corinthian War period. . . . A small number of olive trees would

Athens became even more dependent on income from trade; Euboulos and other Athenian officials strove to increase the attractiveness of the city to merchants by expanding the docks and instituting the ἐμπορικαὶ δικαί. Encouragement of export of local products such as olive oil must have continued.[67] One neglected aspect of this trade, which has recently received attention, involves the "export" of Athenian oil in Panathenaic victors' amphorae. Amphorae of 316/5 B.C., for example, have been found at Eretria, Melos, and Rhodos. The amount of oil could be considerable; winners received from 50 to 140 amphorae, containing 1,300–5,000 liters: enough to satisfy the annual needs of 30–120 persons.[68] I should perhaps stress that I do not envision an organized "export industry" in olive oil, but rather a regular surplus from the whole territory of Attike, which individual landowners sought to dispose of. They no doubt sold to middlemen in the Peiraieus, or even to local rural jobbers, who then arranged export themselves.

As we have seen, Delos needed imported oil, since local production was never sufficient to cover demand. From 394 to 386 and 377 to 314 B.C., the Athenians controlled the temple of Apollo on Delos, which they ran through an *amphiktyonia* that sometimes included Andrians, but from which Delians were excluded (*ID* 97.5; 97bis1, 2; 98A63, 64, 75, 96; 100.7, 8, 10). They integrated themselves deeply into Delos's economy. There is good evidence that they either dominated or controlled a good share of the estate and house rentals on the island, and in the 370s B.C., they freely lent temple funds to many Kykladic states. Delians enjoyed borrowing privileges from the temple, but so did private persons from Andros, Tenos, Karystos on Euboia, Syros, and perhaps Seriphos.[69] Given stable De-

---

have sustained partial damage, in some cases enough to interrupt production for seven or more years." On the importance of oil to the Athenian economy, see, e.g., Hans Lohmann in *Agriculture in Ancient Greece*, 42, 51–56; Sallares, 304–9; Josiah Ober, *Fortress Attica* (Leiden, 1985), 27–28; Claude Mossé, *La Fin de la démocratie athénienne* (Paris, 1962), 63–65. V. F. Gajdukevič, *Das bosporanische Reich* (Berlin, 1971), 57, 103, documents Athenian olive oil exports to the Black Sea in the fourth century. The tendency for oil from Sinope to predominate after ca. 350 B.C. (ibid., 104, 182 n. 37) should perhaps be attributed to Athens's declining position after the Social War (cf. ibid., 89).

67. Edmund M. Burke, *Classical Antiquity* 9 (1990): 1–13, and *TAPA* 114 (1984): 111–20; Claude Mossé in *Trade in the Ancient Economy* (Berkeley, 1983), 53–63. The driving force behind all of this was of course the growing Athenian dependence on imported grain, on which now see Garnsey, 134–64.

68. Panos Valavanis, *Recherches sur les amphores grecques* (Paris, 1986), 453–60; G. R. Edwards, *Hesperia* 26 (1957): 320–21.

69. *ID* 98A11–15, B1–10 (= *IG* II^2 1635); *ID* 100.15–17; *ID* 104–9.7–10

lian demand, continuing Athenian export of oil, and Athenian control of Apollo's temple, Athenian citizens and metics must have been perfectly aware of local sacred and profane requirements for oil. Delos would have offered an ideal nearby market for the disposal of exported Athenian oil.

The Delians chafed at foreign control of Apollo's patrimony. The city had remained Delian, and Delian officials participated to some extent in the administration of the temple, but without representation on the Amphiktyonia. For a few years early in the fourth century (386–378 B.C.), they regained authority over the temple, only to lose it again. In 377/6 B.C., a group of wealthy, prominent Delians struck the Athenian amphiktyonic officials and chased them from the temple. The offenders were punished with fines of 10,000 drachmas each, permanent exile, and (probably) the confiscation of their property. After 367 the Athenians became more imperious in administration of the temple, although the details remain obscure. In 345/4 B.C., the Athenians won a case put before the Delphic Amphiktyone, which confirmed their rights over the temple; the next year, the Delian Peisitheides, forced to flee Delos under a death threat, was awarded Athenian citizenship for his support of Athens and granted a pension of a drachma a day "so that he would not lack food" until he could return to Delos. No doubt he had lost his property on Delos.[70] When Antigonos granted Delos its freedom and returned control of their temple to the Delians in September of 314 B.C., they immediately cancelled leases in force on the estates and the τέλη and offered new contracts exclusively to Delians. They reorganized the administration of the temple, putting temple business in the hands of the *hieropoioi,* who seem to have played only a passive role under the Amphiktyonia. A new ἱερὰ συγγραφή governing the rental of temple estates was issued. Jacques Tréheux has recently sug-

(= *IG* II^2 1637); loans to individuals, *ID* 98A15–24, 50–56, 78–94, B10–23. Tréheux, "Dernières années," 1020–22; Jack Cargill, *The Second Athenian League* (Berkeley, 1981), 37–38; J. Coupry in *Atti del terzio congresso* (Rome, 1959), 65–66.

70. Delian officials under the Amphiktyonia, *ID* 98A97, 104–26*bis*B8 (*hieropoioi*), 104.1–7 ("the *boule* of the Delians and *hieropoioi*" witnessing transfer of temple treasures from one board of Amphiktyones to its successor); 98B24–30: attack, fine, exile, B31–52 for confiscations. For increasing imperiousness after 367 B.C., see Coupry, *Atti*, 61; for difficulties, *ID* 104–22, with comm., pp. 89–90, 104–26C, perhaps 104–19A1–6; case before Delphic Amphiktyonia, Demos. 22.134, Hypereides fr. 13, cf. Th. Homolle, *BCH* 15 (1891): 153, W. A. Laidlaw, *A History of Delos* (Oxford, 1933), 84–85, Athens had retained Delos "by force": William Scott Ferguson, *Hellenistic Athens* (London, 1911), 50; Peisitheides, *IG* II^2 222. Cf. also *Choix*, 12, for some "national" feeling.

gested that they also confiscated the *oikos* of the Andrians as punishment for Andrian cooperation in the Athenian administration.[71]

It would not be surprising if the reaction against the Athenians included the search for non-Athenian sources for necessary imports, including olive oil, after 314 B.C.[72] The Rhodians, whose increasing penetration of Aegean trade in the late fourth and early third centuries has been well documented,[73] would no doubt have been only too happy to step in. Rhodos produced and exported olive oil from its own territory and from the Peraia. Rhodos also had a hand in the transshipment of goods from other parts of the Greek world; we know of shipments of Samian oil through its port.[74]

Dependence on Rhodos in the early period could also explain the shortage of 304 B.C., for that was the second and final year of the famous siege that earned Demetrios his epithet "Poliorketes."[75] Economic disruption played a large part in the war, in part because of Rhodos's close economic ties to Egypt (Diod. 20.81.4), and in part because of the requirements of

71. Tréheux, "Dernières années," 1008–32; id., *BCH* 68–69 (1944–45): 293 ("il serait difficile de concevoir qu'une administration purement délienne, fière de son indépendance recouvrée, eût continué longtemps à se fonder, pour la gestion des biens du dieu, sur une ordonnance athènienne"); id. in *Stemmata,* 386, and cf. the confiscation by the Athenians of the *oikos* of the Karystians after 167 B.C., which Tréheux attributes to the good relations of the Karystians with the Delians (ibid., 389–90 n. 78, 387 n. 53).

72. If this suggestion is right, it might help to account for the apparent collapse of the rural economy of the Attic deme Atene at the end of the fourth century: cf. Lohmann in *Agriculture in Ancient Greece,* 56.

73. Lyk. *Leok.* 14–15, 18; [Demos.] 56.3–13, esp. 10; Diod. 20.81.4. Cf. Berthold, 44–45, 47–50 (at 59–60 he suggests that Rhodos avoided the Lamian War partly in hopes that a defeat might cripple an economic rival); Erich Ziebarth in *Mélanges Gustave Glotz* (Paris, 1932), 2: 912–13; Michael Rostovtzeff in *CAH,* VIII (Cambridge, 1930), 622–23; Rostovtzeff, 169–73; H. van Gelder, *Geschichte der alten Rhodier* (The Hague, 1900), 101–3; on the Rhodians' commercial relations with Egypt, Will I², 180–200 (passim).

74. Local production: [Aiskhines], *Ep.* 5.2, who found Rhodian oil slightly less desirable than Athenian; Athen. 67a on Karian oil (fourth century B.C.); *Milet* I.3, 149.18–20 (182 B.C.?), oil at Pidassa; cf. David Magie, *Roman Rule in Asia Minor* (Princeton, 1950), I.50; F. Hiller von Gaertringen, *RE* suppl. 5 (1931), s.v. "Rhodos," 736–37; van Gelder, *Geschichte,* 427 (whose reference to Pollux 1.105 has, however, nothing to do with Rhodian oil). For Rhodos as a transshipment point for Samian oil (praised at Athen. 67a), cf. *P. Cair. Zen.* 59012–015, with Rostovtzeff, 229, and Michael Rostovtzeff, *Klio* 30 (1937): 1–7; Claire Préaux, *Le Monde hellénistique* (Paris, 1978), 495; Rostovtzeff, 1268. For *ateliers* of amphora manufacturers, see J.-Y. Empereur and N. Tuna, *BCH* 113 (1989): 277–99.

75. Diod. 20.81–88, 91–100.4; Will I², 70, 73–74. For the date of *IG* XI 2.144, see Jacques Tréheux in *CICG,* 30.

besieging an island state. Antigonos had provoked the war in part by seizure of merchant ships (Diod. 20.81.2), and according to Polyainos (4.16.6) made every effort to prevent Rhodian traders in the East from returning home. As soon as Demetrios put in on Rhodos, he dispatched pirates to raid by land and sea (Diod. 20.83.3). During the siege the Rhodians sent out men and ships to raid and harass local merchant shipping (Diod. 20.93.5, ἐπὶ νήσων, 20.84.5, 93.2–3, 97.5–6), while Demetrios's men cut trees and cannibalized farmsteads for his encampment (Diod. 20.83.4). Rhodos received grain from Egypt, Kassandros, and Lysimakhos (Diod. 20.96.1, 96.3, 98.1, 99.2). The economic disruption the war entailed may have prompted the embassies sent on various occasions by Knidos, by Athens and at least fifty other Greek cities, and finally by the Aitolians, to try to settle the dispute.[76] Oil would surely have been largely unavailable and its export stymied. By Metageitnion and Bouphonion, the siege had ended and goods should have begun to flow again. The very low price of Bouphonion may show Rhodian merchants eager to recapture markets lost or endangered during the siege and to unload stored supplies before the end of the sailing season.

From a Delian point of view, dependence on Rhodos would have been as undesirable as dependence on Athens, if freighted with fewer political overtones. Still better would have been sufficient and reliable local supplies. High local prices should have encouraged local Kykladic plantings (and indeed the gradual price decline can be interpreted as evidence that they did). Because olives take many years to produce their first crop, planting a new orchard one year could not affect prices the following year. High prices would continue to encourage plantings year after year until the first new orchards began to contribute to the supply and to drive prices down. Prices should have fallen gradually as orchards planted in previous years began to bear. Eventually an equilibrium would be achieved, prices would stabilize, and the need for long-distance imports would dry up.

Data for Rhodian stamped amphorae from Delos support this interpretation. J.-Y. Empereur has recently warned of the dangers of marshaling amphora data as evidence for economic developments without due consideration of the chronology of the amphorae and of the excavations that produced them, the relation between numbers of stamped and unstamped handles, and the relation between number of handles and number of complete

76. Diod. 20.95.4–5, 98.2, 99.3; on the Knidian embassy, see Berthold, 74 n. 32: "with its territory adjoining the Rhodian Peraea and its economy employing the Rhodian standard since 400 . . . , Cnidus was completely in the Rhodian economic sphere and must have suffered considerable economic difficulties during the siege."

jars;[77] but cautious use of only data available for Rhodian handles on Delos as compiled by Empereur may suggest some trends. Of the stamped and dated Rhodian handles so far published, 53 belong to about 331–275 B.C. (0.95 handles/yr) and 32 to about 275(?)–220 B.C., or a little later (0.58 handles/yr).[78] If these figures represent the real relative abundance of Rhodian handles on Delos for these two time periods—not an unreasonable assumption, given that continuing excavation on Delos has not modified the relative proportions of handles very much,[79] and that one would expect to migrate into later contexts more handles from more recent third-century levels than from late-fourth- / early-third-century levels—then we may posit a drop of about 40 percent in stamped Rhodian handles on Delos over this period. This may mean that Rhodian imports were relatively more important before about 275 B.C. than after. The change suggests a decline in demand for Rhodian products after the first quarter of the third century. In the absence of full publication—which can only follow much further excavation—these results can only be regarded as preliminary but suggestive.

The insufficiency of Delian production of olive oil to meet local demand is clear from the relative absence of olive trees on the island (discounting of course the single tree owned by Apollo and any trees that may have graced private farms) and the large size of the population compared to the island's limited arable surface. But the same cannot be said for its Kykladic neighbors (excluding, of course, Rheneia), which certainly must have produced at least some oil; indeed, the model I propose to account for the price history of olive oil after the 270s demands increased Kykladic production. This raises several important questions: why did Delos not import olive oil from its immediate neighbors, rather than from Athens, in the fourth cen-

77. J.-Y. Empereur, *BCH* 106 (1982): 222–33, 225; cf. Etienne, 213–15.

78. Virginia R. Grace and Maria Savvatianou-Pétropoulako in *L'Ilot de la Maison des comédiens* (Paris, 1970), ch. 14, with corrections at Virginia Grace, *Ath. Mitt.* 89 (1974): 200; cf. also Virginia Grace, *BCH* 76 (1952): 514–40; John H. Kent in *Studies Presented to David Moore Robinson* (St. Louis, 1953), 2: 127–34; Empereur, *BCH* 106 (1982): 219–33; *GD*[3] 97–98.

79. Empereur, *BCH* 106 (1982): 223 n. 19. Cf. Y. Garlan in *Trade in the Ancient Economy* (Berkeley, 1983), 185 n. 19: "Brashinsky [cf. Y. Garlan, *DHA* 8 (1982): 145–52] has shown convincingly that conclusions derived from a sample are generally not seriously undermined by further work. From my own experience, even simple surface finds are often representative enough of buried material." See further Susan Alcock, *Graecia Capta* (Cambridge, 1993), 52 with 238 n. 30. Etienne, 216, fig. 4, does not seem to correspond with Empereur's figures; I have preferred Empereur. Etienne promises (217 n. 46) a treatment of Rhodian amphorae in a forthcoming *MBAH*.

tury? What local changes could have driven an increase in Kykladic production sufficient to meet local Delian demand and drive Rhodian imports out of the market? Why did the *hieropoioi* not plant olives on the estates to take advantage of the high prices and heavy unsatisfied demand for oil in the late fourth and early third centuries? It is not possible to give definitive responses to any of these questions, but we must consider some hypotheses, if only to test the plausibility of the larger model.

For the Kyklades, it will not suffice to cite the oft-repeated observation that the islands were too windy for olives. Variation in topography provides niches today for olive culture on most islands, even the smallest, and olives and oil certainly were produced in antiquity as well.[80] There are really two separate questions here. The Kyklades may simply not have produced enough local surplus to satisfy Delian demand; in this case, new plantings would have been necessary if the islanders did indeed take over from the Rhodians in the 270s and 260s. For Paros and Naxos, some evidence points toward increased production of amphorae in the third and second centuries.[81] On the other hand, the problem may have been one of organization rather than production. If the Athenians controlled Delos in the fourth century as tightly as I have argued they did, then there may have been little room for islanders to operate. Despite the Andrians' occasional benefits from their association with the Athenians and Apollo's loans to the rest of the Kyklades, there is very little evidence to suggest any economic activity by the islanders on Delos. When the expulsion of the Athenian masters in 314 B.C. afforded the Delians the opportunity to look elsewhere for their supplies, the islanders may have lacked both the tradition and the organization for harvesting, collecting, and exporting surpluses to their nearby neighbor. It would have required time for the necessary economic and social structures to evolve; the Rhodians, better organized, stepped into the breech.

Two further factors may have been at work. Before 314 B.C., the Kyklades do not seem to have functioned as a single economic unit. Especially the western islands, including Keos, Andros, and Melos, enjoyed strong ties with Athens and the cities of Euboia. These ties dropped off markedly after the end of the fourth century, only to resume from about the middle of the second century. The same years saw growing contact between the islands and Delos. It is no coincidence that this period corresponds roughly

80. Amouretti in *Agriculture in Ancient Greece,* 78. For modern olive production, see E. Y. Kolodny, *La Population des îles de la Grèce* (Aix-en-Provence, 1974), 71–72, 77, 85–92; ΣΕΕ 1937: 112, 1938: 113, 1939: 113.

81. J.-Y. Empereur and M. Picon, *BCH* 110 (1986): 495–510, 647–53.

to the years of Delian independence, for it was (in my view) the concomitant formation of the Nesiotic League that first tied the Kyklades together into a region focused on Delos.[82] The emergence of a regional outlook in political and military life should have fostered new economic ties, which helped promote Delos as the local exchange center for Kykladic products, and, not incidentally, permitted the Delians to reap the benefits of the local surpluses of their neighbors.

Second, it *may* be that the Kyklades themselves depended to some degree on imported oil in the fourth century. Recent archaeological survey work in both the southern Argolid and the Athenian deme of Atene has revealed a period of prosperity in the fourth century. In both cases, this prosperity has been attributed to the production of olive oil for an export market.[83] This notion has come in for some severe criticism, focused especially on its failure to consider other factors that might account for population change in the rural landscape and for its reliance on too simplistic a "modernizing" model of economic activity based on the exploitation of export markets.[84] The latter criticism, at least, is justified, especially as against an inclusive and sufficient explanation for economic growth in the southern Argolid from the Neolithic to modern times. Yet the presence, both there and in Atene, of olive processing equipment in fourth-century contexts lends some credibility to the suggestion that, for that period alone, rising oil production *may* have contributed to local prosperity. Ties especially of the western Kyklades to Athens and Euboia suggest a western orientation for these islands in the fourth century; this in turn might reflect the existence of an economic region incorporating the Attic peninsula, the southern Argolid, and the western islands, and thus of a natural (and nearby) market for locally produced surpluses. Such a model does not require a massive, centralized economic organization; individual merchants operating independently and on a small scale would suffice, especially given the relatively small amounts involved (annual Delian olive oil demand, for example, would fill only 2–4 ships, as we have seen). These reflections must remain speculative, but they do suggest avenues for further explora-

82. G. Reger in *Proceedings of the VIIth International Conference on Boiotian Studies* (Amsterdam, 1994), forthcoming.

83. For the southern Argolid, the view is expressed most clearly in Tjeerd H. van Andel and Curtis Runnels, *Beyond the Acropolis* (Stanford, 1987), 105–9, but see also Curtis N. Runnels and Tjeerd H. van Andel, *Hesperia* 56 (1987): 326–27, and Tjeerd H. van Andel, Curtis N. Runnels, and Kevin O. Pope, *Hesperia* 55 (1986): 117–18. On Atene, see Hans Lohmann in *Agriculture in Ancient Greece,* 56, with further references.

84. Sallares, 103–5, but cf. the comments of Alcock, *Graecia Capta,* 243 n. 84. Thomas W. Gallant, *CJ* 86 (1990–91): 184–86.

tion; if they turn out to be right, they would shed welcome light on the transformation of the economic scene in Greece during the early Hellenistic period.

It may also seem somewhat surprising that the Delians did not do more to increase supplies of oil on Delos itself. The island has spots sheltered from the winds, and as I have argued above, there can be no doubt that there was some local production in antiquity, although it has left frustratingly little trace. In the case of the sacred estates, a reason lies to hand for the failure to plant olives: the short lease period. Renters restricted to ten-year leases (and even shorter terms before 300 B.C.) had no motivation whatsoever to plant trees that would not yield at all for seven to ten years, and required much longer still to return the initial investment. If Apollo decided to plant olives himself, he would have had to make the investment out of his own funds without hope of recouping them in rent, since the renters, who bid for the estates in a closed auction and had no hope of benefiting from the plantings, would not bid enough to compensate his outlays.[85] Since the *hieropoioi* were in office only one year, during which their main aim was to show at the end of their term of office that they had been faithful stewards of Apollo's patrimony, they had no incentive to tie up the god's money in a long-term, expensive investment either. It is certainly telling that, with the single exception of the extirpation of some vines on Nikou Khoros between 180 and 178 B.C. (*ID* 445.16–24), the *hieropoioi* made no improvements of any kind to the estates over the century and a half of independence.

These considerations did not apply private landowners, and I remain convinced that some of them anyway must have planted olives. There may, however, have been factors working to discourage them, even in the face of high prices. The long lead time for the first crop meant that only those wealthy enough to tolerate a very postponed return could afford to plant olives. Demand may well also have encouraged landowners to plant other crops whose return could be realized in a season. Grain stands naturally at the head of the list; far less expensive to produce, grains were ready in a few months and in very high demand. Indeed, since olive oil may have been something of a luxury, making up far less of the diet than grain, it would always have been more reliably profitable to have produced barley or wheat. Livestock are another commodity that may have squeezed out olives. While the extent of herding on sacred estates has been exaggerated (see chapter 6), virtually every one of Apollo's estates had facilities for sheep or goats; stock raising must have had an important role on the island

85. Details in chapter 6.

and certainly occurred on private farms.[86] Like grains, pigs and sheep are ready for market within a year or less, and so repay the initial investment far faster than olives. In the eighteenth and nineteenth centuries, the island of Keos was remarkably devoid of olives, producing generally only enough to satisfy local peasant household demand. The reason was perhaps that concentration on *velanidia* (acorns), which were used for curing and dyeing leather, squeezed olives off the landscape.[87] Something analogous may have helped prevent Delos from planting the olives she needed to supply her own demand. Local production from other islands ultimately made it up.

This model has some more general implications as well. The Athenians clearly understood and exploited the economic possibilities their control of Delos offered. The men who served there as administrators in the fourth century all came from the upper reaches of Athenian society; it would be naive to suppose that these opportunities would have escaped men who derived income from mining in Attike or shipping, not to mention ordinary landowning.[88] This is not to say that there was a simple and direct connection between politics and trade; rather, the Athenians simply acted to gain what they could. The same pattern recurs in the rental of sacred estates, as we shall see in chapter 6.

The model I have advanced is plausible but hardly sure. In the current state of the evidence, it cannot be tested. Some research that might help to support or disprove it:

1. Careful study of the countryside of Delos. Preliminary reports from a survey on Delos reveal the existence of widespread terracing, which the investigator dates from the late fourth century on. This might be consistent with the planting of new orchards.[89]

2. Full publication of Delian amphorae. Such a study would help us decide whether the very preliminary results adduced here reflect the reality of imports.

3. Surveys of the countryside of other Kykladic islands. A recent survey of Keos has revealed extremely interesting changes in the patterns of rural settlement that could correspond to changes in land-use practices;

86. See Brunet, 141–42, on Patinioti.

87. See n. 24 above.

88. Epikrates son of Menestratos of Pallene (*ID* 98A10–11, 62–63; J. F. Davies, *Athenian Propertied Families* [Oxford, 1971], 4909A + B), mining interests, *Hesperia* 10 (1941): 14, no. 1, ll. 70–71. Demades (I) son of Demeas (I) of Paiane may have been a *naukleros* or *emporos: ID* 104–33B9, Davies, 3263.

89. See now O. Rackham and J. Moody in *Agriculture in Ancient Greece,* 124–25.

greater olive culture could have had a profound impact on the character of the countryside, since olive planting is capital-intensive and requires owners able to absorb many years without return before the first crop.

Period 2. The second period encompasses the years 279–169 B.C. On the model for Delian oil trade elaborated above, it is fairly easy to account for the post-272 prices. Their history suggests a nicely balanced market, with supply and demand in equilibrium, and shortages or surpluses, although perhaps common, never extreme. The rise and fall of average prices over time around a stable center may reflect olives' natural tendency to produce bigger crops every other year. Given a relatively stable body of trees, and a relatively stable (and confined) geographic area for the sources, the average of the whole would eventually have found its own rhythm of yield.

Such a local rhythm perhaps accounts for the prices of the two subperiods of 224–194 and 178–173 B.C. The apparently climbing prices of the first of these periods are an illusion. Chance has preserved data only from those years regulated by a poor harvest: it is not surprising that they show generally higher prices, and it is more important that the average prices are perfectly typical for the whole period after 272 B.C. The second subperiod is more interesting, for it does show a genuine price drop. This decline, which seems to span about five years (178–173 B.C.), ends abruptly by 170 B.C. with a return of price to an entirely typical level. In my view, these low prices probably represent a happy coincidence of several good harvests. The good harvest inferred above for 175 may be an element: perhaps the regional rhythm in oil yields (even years = good; odd years = poor) was changing, and a series of abundant harvests were a side effect?

Following Larsen, I would attribute the clearly anomalous price of 169 B.C. (which depends particularly on high prices at the end of the year) to a poor harvest that fall. Inspectors from Rome who visited the Roman fleet at its winter quarters at Khalkis and Oleos on Euboia reported that the winter had been so harsh that part of the crews had succumbed to disease and others had gone home.[90]

The temple may have enjoyed the additional benefit of "captive" producers. In 237 B.C., the god acquired two estates on Mykonos: Thaleon, which supported 147 olive trees (ἐλαίαι), 87 "bud-grafted olives" (ἔλαιοι ἐνωφθαλμισμένοι), and at least 200 wild olives (ἔλαιοι), for a minimum total of 434 plants; and Dorion-Khersonesos, which had at least 25 wild olives.[91] The acquisition of these estates cannot have caused the price sta-

90. Livy 44.20; Larsen, 390, who, however, doubts the high end-of-year prices.

91. *IG* XI 2.287A142–74 (inventory of 250 B.C.); *ID* 366B18–23. On the acquisitions, see Kent, 286–88; inventories at *ID* 346A13, 353A33–34, 366A99–

bility of the later period, which had been achieved much earlier; rather the acquisition may have been a consequence of that stability. If the grafts and the wild olives on Thaleon indicate a new planting, the owner may have decided that the estate would not produce enough income in the current market, and so have deeded it (perhaps by testament) to Apollo. An alternative explanation, that it was put up as guarantee for a loan and reverted to Apollo after a default, is not very likely.[92]

It is possible to estimate, very roughly, the productivity of Thaleon.[93] The Melian harvest of 1973 is estimated to have produced about 17.5 kg/tree; in the 1960s in Messenia, yields/tree ranged from 50 kg for a "large mature tree" to 15–20 kg for a tree 30–40 years old and 7–15 kg for a young tree. Fifteen to 20 kg of fruit yield conservatively 4 kg of oil, roughly 1.4 *khoes.*[94] Given a young orchard in Thaleon, yields might have fallen in the range of 600 *khoes:* not even 2 percent of Delian demand. This is apparently a trivial figure. However, Melos in 1971 supported 19,910 olives,[95] which would yield roughly 79,640 kg of oil/yr, which falls within the estimated range of total Delian demand (ca. 57,000–192,000 kg/yr). It is therefore not unlikely that Delian needs beyond local production could have been supplied from the marginal exportable surplus of many nearby neighbors.

It is also important to consider how, in this model, olive oil from outside Delos might have arrived there. In general, I see two broad possibilities. Merchants from outside Delos may have brought oil in either because prices were grossly high compared to nearby markets, virtually guaranteeing easy sale and high profit; or they may have shipped the oil on speculation, hoping to find a good price on Delos, and willing to try elsewhere if

---

102, B8–23, 440B22–27, 452.26–29, 461Bb55–57. Kent's translation of ἔλαιοι ἐνωφθαλμισμένοι as "grafted" olives (p. 288) is incomplete. The procedure involves implanting budded sprouts in a host trunk; see *Geoponika* (Beckh) 10.77. The host need not be of the same species (Theoph. *De caus. pl.* 5.5.4). See generally Amouretti, *Pain,* 59–62. I am indebted to John Scarborough for advice on this matter.

92. Kent, 286–88, does not speculate on how these estates came into Apollo's hands; on defaults see Kent, 256–58, but if by default the acquisition of Thaleon would be unique after ca. 290–280 B.C.; cf. Brunet, 50–54 and chapter 6, pp. 220–30. I thank Lin Foxhall for discussion on the character of the plantings.

93. The production of Dorion-Khersonesos must have been low; moreover, we do not know how many trees it supported. See Kent, 288.

94. Wagstaff and Augustson in *Island Polity,* 132; Aschenbrenner in *MME,* 54, table 4-2; Amouretti, *Pain,* 204; D. J. Mattingly, *J. of Roman Arch.* 1 (1988): 160. Modern extra-virgin Greek olive oil from Kalamata runs about 1.08 l/kg.

95. Wagstaff and Augustson in *Island Polity,* 111, table 10.8.

not. The first case would have occurred most commonly during severe local shortages. If the high price of 169 B.C. was indeed the result of a bad winter, then presumably it would have attracted sellers from around the Aegean. To this extent, there was something like an "international" market for staples like oil, but only, as I have stressed (see chapter 3), under transient conditions of localized shortage. Substantial price differentials between regions can persist over long periods only if markets are local and relatively decoupled. In the case of Delos, the smallness of its demand also acted against it. Since the arrival of even two shiploads of oil simultaneously, or roughly simultaneously, would have swamped the market, it was a very bold merchant who would sail into the harbor of the island with oil for sale. Centers of greater demand, where prices were likely to have been more stable (although even Athens could have problems in this regard, as we saw in chapter 3), drew merchants away from more hazardous markets like Delos. This helps to explain why higher prices persisted on Delos for several decades instead of being equalized by the movement of goods.

Oil might also be supplied by merchants living on Delos or in the Kyklades who purposefully went out seeking it elsewhere to sell at home, whether on their own volition or with public support (as in the case of grain, which could be sold to the public *sitonia* fund after 209 B.C.). These merchants were in a rather different position to the outsiders. Experienced in the local market, they must have had some sense of the typical fluctuations in price, the arrival times of shipments, and other factors that affected profit. They also knew local tastes. Since Delians resented the Athenians—as they clearly did, at least in the early years of independence[96]—these men would have known to seek goods needed on Delos elsewhere than in Athens. It was they, presumably, who headed to Rhodos, and, later, moved oil and other goods around the Kyklades, through the local exchange center for the archipelago that Delos became.

The Price History of Firewood Mean annual prices for firewood appear in figure 5.2. It is obvious that mean prices fluctuated considerably. Two aspects of figure 5.2, however, stand out. Prices seem to fluctuate around a mean lower before than after 218 B.C., and the prices of the 250s, especially of 250 itself, are strikingly low. A model constructed on these observations accounts fairly well for the data (table 5.7).

This model picks out nicely the highly anomalous prices of 250 B.C., which average 61 units (about 2.4 obols) lower than all other prices. Prices after 218 B.C. average 42 units (about 1.7 obols) higher than those before

96. See further chapter 6, p. 217.

Figure 5.2. Indexed Firewood Prices, Delos, 304–169 B.C.

the break. These results give a general picture of the price history of firewood. Price behavior displayed the same general volatile behavior throughout Delian history, but prices fluctuated around a lower average level before 218 than after. The year 250 B.C. showed unusually low prices. Nothing in the model lends support to the view that prices were higher in

Table 5.7. Firewood Prices, Sorted for 250 B.C. and before and after 218 B.C.

Dependent Variable is FIREWOOD
Number of observations: 22

Variable	*Coefficient*	*Std. Error*	*T-Stat.*	*2-Tail Sig.*
C	*178.21667*	*5.2057205*	*34.234774*	*0.000*
250 B.C.	*−60.916665*	*18.769492*	*−3.2455148*	*0.004*
218 B.C.	*42.261108*	*7.9518695*	*5.3146129*	*0.000*

R-squared	0.710267	Mean of dependent var	192.7364
Adjusted R-squared	0.679769	S.D. of dependent var	31.86689
S.E. of regression	18.03314	Sum of squared resid	6178.692
Durbin-Watson stat	1.325688	F-statistic	23.28881
Log likelihood	−93.23266		

the late fourth and early third centuries. It remains to account for these results.

Assuming for the moment that the wood supply is likely to have been relatively stable from year to year, variation ought to have come from demand, which would depend especially on the severity of winters. Because of the restrictions of the sailing season, demand ought to affect prices with a lag: after a mild winter, supplies would be larger and demand lower; after a bad winter, supplies would be depleted and demand high. (It would be very interesting to have a wood price for the severe winter of 168 B.C. [Livy 44.20].) If this hypothesis is correct, it could account for the behavior of prices apparent in figure 5.2.

The change in price structure ca. 218 B.C. requires more consideration. Even discounting the low price of 250 B.C. and the high one of 173 B.C., the average of all prices before 218 is 40 price units lower than for prices after 218, representing a 22 percent rise. I would like to consider three possible explanations.

Sometime between 250 and 200 B.C., but most likely between 235 and 220 or a little later, the Delians passed an important law regulating the import and pricing of wood and wood products, including charcoal.[97] Among other things, the law forbids importers to sell wood products—ʼἌνθρακας μηδὲ ῥυμοὺς μη[δὲ ξύλα] (l. 1)—at prices above or below those declared to the πεντηκοστολόγοι and interdicts resale of imported wood.[98] Most commentators have regarded the law as a kind of "consumer protection act,"[99] but it is hard to see how consumers would be served by a law that forbade them to negotiate a *lower* price from importers.[100]

97. *ID* 509 = *SIG*³ 975. On the date, see H. W. Pleket, *Epigraphica* (Leiden, 1964), 18; *ID* comm., p. 325.

98. Lines 8–11, 2–4. On the duties of the *pentekostologoi* and *agoranomoi*, see Vial 232–35 (at 233 she seems to infer that the registers [σανίδες] mentioned at l. 30 recorded declared prices; in fact, they record the names of malefactors from whom the *agoranomoi* charged with enforcing the law were not able to exact the penalty). Generally on the transportation of wood in antiquity, see Dominique Mulliez, *BCH* 106 (1982): 107–18.

99. Larsen, 353–54; Philippe Gauthier, *BCH* 101 (1977): 207: "Le législateur veut protéger les consommateurs" and "Le but est d'assurer aux consommateurs les prix moins élevés possible (les législateurs sont les consommateurs)"; and Meiggs, 453 (evidently without benefit of Gauthier's article): "This [regulation] is a gallant attempt to protect the consumer"; Déonna, *Vie privée*, 39, says the law "assure la stabilité du prix . . . [et] cherche à empêcher l'accaparement par l'achat en gros"; John Perlin, *A Forest Journey* (New York, 1989), 96–97. Generally, Isager-Skydsgaard, 146.

100. Cf., e.g., Larsen, 354. The passage from the comic poet Alexis quoted by Athenaios (6.226a–b), which appears comparable at first glance, arises out of differ-

In my view, the law was intended to guarantee the full collection of the *pentekoste* (5 percent tax) on imported wood. The regulations require importers to use public wood scales, which prevented under- or overweighing (ll. 1–2). A dealer who bought wood was not allowed to resell it (ll. 2–3), which would have resulted in a transaction on which no tax was paid. Sale directly from the ship, which would have made use of the public scales impossible, was prohibited (ll. 3–4). Possibilities of fraud were reduced by requiring sellers to register on their own behalf (ll. 4–5). Philippe Gauthier has shown that the next clause forbade persons who had bought wood sold by the state to resell it (ll. 5–8).[101] The clause preventing sale at prices higher or lower than declared, which follows, must be understood in this context: such sales might allow merchants to circumvent the prohibition of resale by claiming that the different price proved that the lot of wood was different from that declared, even if its variety and weight were identical. (It is easy to imagine two merchants colluding to declare a purposefully high price on a lot that was then resold for less, with the second merchant reimbursing his coconspirator for the excess tax. If suspected, they could always argue that no one would *intentionally* overpay a tax!)[102]

Such a regulation might well have had an adverse impact on the price of wood on Delos. Since importers were required to make a declaration of value before they could offer their goods for sale (ll. 11–14), they must often have done so without a clear notion of the current market. (We have seen both from monthly and from annual prices how widely prices could fluctuate.) Sellers would therefore prefer to set prices high. And since sale at lower than declared prices was not allowed, buyers would have little recourse but to pay the higher prices. Delian officials in charge of enforcing the regulations would be little concerned, since high prices meant greater tax income.

It might be objected that since the Delian government was in the hands of its citizens, they would surely not have tolerated a regulation that damaged their interests as consumers. Aside from the anachronism built into

---

ent circumstances: fish go bad, so sellers may be inclined to reduce prices as the day goes on.

101. Philippe Gauthier, *BCH* 101 (1977): 206–7, translating as "Il est interdit (à l'importeur) de vendre, après en avoir été déclaré acquéreur, des marchandises (bois et charbons) vendue aux enchères publiques."

102. This law would probably have had a dampening effect on any transit trade, since it essentially forbade the development of middlemen to buy imported wood and store it for later resale to exporters. This casts a rather different light on some claims about the Delian desire to encourage trade and the development of an entrepôt, which is explored further in chapter 7.

this notion of "consumers," several points deserve to be made. First, the causal connection between law and price was probably not obvious; it would not have been apparent without careful study of a long set of price data, since transient annual or monthly fluctuations would often have swamped long-term trends. Second, Delians engaged in trade (although they may have been few)[103] would have benefited and seen no need to oppose the law. Third, the Delian magistracies were in the hands of the wealthier strata of Delian society, who were less likely to be troubled by moderate price rises. Fourth, the period of time over which the rise occurred was long. Fifth, other factors (as I shall argue) were also working to push up wood prices.

It would be nice to be able to test this view against the prices of wood for construction, but unfortunately the accounts rarely provide enough information. A few prices for oak (see Meiggs, 455–56) may show price increases for ten-foot pieces from 9 dr in 246 B.C. to 10 dr 2 ob in 189 B.C. (*ID* 290.211, 403.23), and for eight-foot pieces from 7 dr 1 ob in 246 to 7 dr 3 ob in 207 and 9 dr 4.5 ob in 189 (*ID* 290.221, 336A38, 403.24), if some assumptions are made. The trend is right but the data are very slim indeed.

The reason for the passage of the law is not known directly, but one possibility connects with the second possible explanation for the rise in firewood prices. The wood-product import regulation imposes heavy penalties on violators, including a 50 dr fine (ll. 14–16), equivalent to 37.5 talents of firewood at the prevailing price in 218 B.C. of 1 dr 2 ob. The state clearly believed it was losing money on wood undervalued at declaration, which suggests that upward pressure on wood prices had already begun.

This pressure could be associated with some other evidence from Delos and its neighbors for a period of economic expansion in the 230s, 220s, and 210s. We have already seen that a local transit business in grains is first attested in these years. Other indicators include a rise in the number of Rhodian amphorae; expansion of the docks; new construction north of the *temenos* of Apollo; and issuance of new coinage by Paros, Naxos, Tenos, and Andros. If this activity, which on Delos is largely confined to the port, led to increased building (of warehouses, for instance), the rising demand for wood for construction could have pulled up the prices of all wood products. This "new prosperity" is not universally attested in the evidence—oil prices do not rise, and neither, as we shall see, do rents for most of Apollo's estates—and therefore demands further discussion, which it will receive in chapter 7.[104]

103. See Claude Vial in *L'Origine des richesses dépensées dans la ville antique* (Aix-en-Provence, 1985), 47–53; Vial, 317–56.

104. Chapter 7, pp. 257–64.

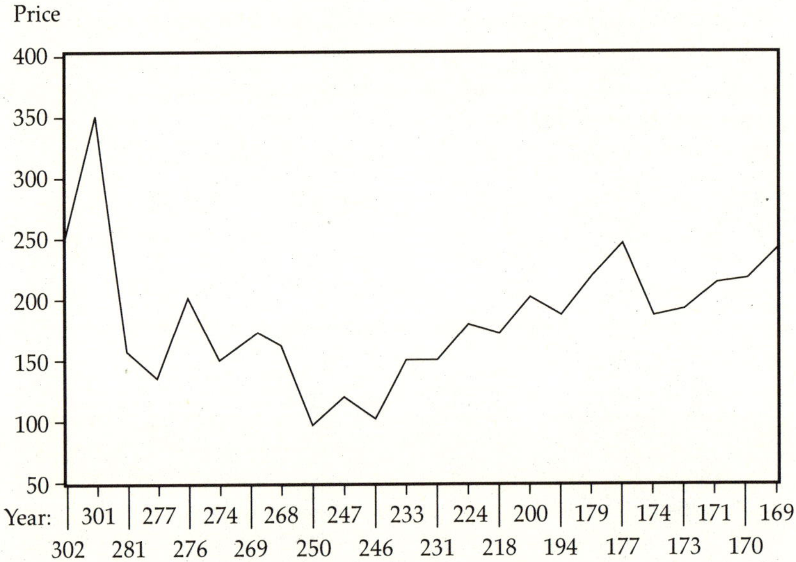

Figure 5.3. Indexed Pig Prices, Delos, 302–169 B.C.

Finally, it is possible that firewood prices were responding to deforestation on the immediately neighboring islands. This is a difficult topic, where research is in its infancy; but it is already clear that different islands may have had very different histories, depending on microclimate, geology, soil type, land use, settlement patterns, and numerous other factors. The modern visitor soon notices the contrast between largely denuded Tenos and Keos and the relatively abundant scrub of Andros and especially Naxos.[105] Some threshold may have been reached toward the end of the third century that required wider search for or greater import of firewood; but much basic research needs doing before such a hypothesis can be adequately evaluated.

The Price History of Pigs Mean annual prices for pigs appear in figure 5.3. The curve resembles that for wood prices: fluctuation from year to year around a low mean before 200 B.C. and a higher mean thereafter. Two anomalies come in 302 and 301 B.C., when prices were extraordinarily high.

105. On deforestation in general, see Meiggs, 371–403, and John L. Bintliff, *Natural Environment and Human Settlement in Prehistoric Greece* (Oxford, 1977), I.59–86. Malcolm Wagstaff and Clive Gamble in *Island Polity,* 97, reckon that Melos was basically treeless by the fifth century B.C., whereas Naxos still had woods into the nineteenth century. Rhodos still had wood to cut in 305 B.C. (Diod. 20.83.4). Rackham gives much useful information about the Kyklades in *Archaeological Aspects of Woodland Economy,* 177–97, and *Greek City,* 85–111.

Table 5.8. Pig Prices, Sorted for 302–301 B.C. and before and after 200 B.C.

Dependent Variable is PIG
Number of observations: 24

Variable	*Coefficient*	*Std. Error*	*T-Stat.*	*2-Tail Sig.*
C	*150.61538*	*8.4256927*	*17.875727*	*0.000*
302–301 B.C.	*149.38462*	*23.074710*	*6.4739543*	*0.000*
200 B.C.	*60.484617*	*13.173334*	*4.5914434*	*0.000*

R-squared	0.712101	Mean of dependent var	185.7458
Adjusted R-squared	0.684682	S.D. of dependent var	54.10070
S.E. of regression	30.37927	Sum of squared resid	19380.90
Durbin-Watson stat	1.811940	F-statistic	25.97111
Log likelihood	−114.3824		

A model based on two dummy variables set to capture (1) the years 302 and 301 B.C. and (2) the years from 200 offers an excellent account of these prices (table 5.8). The prices of 302/1 B.C. are almost 150 units (about 3 dr) above typical levels for the rest of the era of Delian independence. The change at 200 B.C. of 60 units (about 1.2 dr) is strong and clear, parallel to that for firewood of some years earlier.[106]

The history of pig prices must therefore address three questions: (1) why should prices for 302 and 301 B.C. be so much higher than those for any other year; (2) what accounts for the change in average price level around 200 B.C.; and (3) is there a causal connection between higher firewood prices after 218 and higher pig prices after 200 B.C.?

The high pig prices of 302 and 301 B.C. appear at first glance to support the view advanced by Heichelheim and others of inflated prices in the Aegean after Alexander's conquest of the East. In fact, however, there is a clear, transient local phenomenon that can account easily for prices in both years: the presence of troops.

In 302 Demetrios Poliorketes, who had been in Athens since 304, was recalled to Asia Minor by his father, Antigonos, in preparation for the conflict that would culminate in the battle of Ipsos. Demetrios passed with full army and fleet directly through the Kyklades. The following year, 301 B.C., after the defeat at Ipsos, as he fled back to Athens through the islands, he

106. While prices respond to a model postulating a change in 218 B.C., the results are far better for 200 B.C.

stopped at Delos with an army of 9,000 men; he stayed long enough, probably residing in the temple of Apollo itself, to receive ambassadors from Athens. Additional evidence for economic strain in 301 comes in the form of a loan of 1,000 dr the Delians took out to buy grain (*IG* XI 2.146A20–21); if loans for grain purchase early in the third century imply periods of stressed price, then this loan adds to the evidence that 301 was a bad year for Delos.[107]

Although there is no direct statement in any of our sources that Demetrios's presence entailed economic problems, the conclusion is nevertheless inescapable. The passage of armies always brought local economic strain, and in this case the presence of perhaps 10,000 troops, a body of persons at least as large again as the entire population of Delos, must have devoured local food supplies and sent prices skyrocketing. The two extraordinary pig prices of 302 and 301 B.C. attest eloquently to the impact of armies on the market balance of local economies.[108]

Since firewood prices (but not oil prices) show a clear jump around 218 B.C., there is reason to suspect other goods might show the same behavior; this suspicion is now confirmed. Moreover, like firewood, pig prices on either side of the threshold are fairly stable; there is no indication of a trend up or down with respect to time. The mean annual price for pigs in 302–218 B.C. is 141.6, or 120.5 excluding 302–301 B.C.; the same mean price from after 200 B.C. is 211.1, an increase of 50 or 75 percent.

Furthermore, pig and firewood prices generally behave in a similar fashion: both fluctuate around mean levels but show no particular tendency to rise or fall except for the striking and rapid adjustment at about 218 and 200 B.C. A graph of prices only from those years that have both pigs and wood reinforces this impression (fig. 5.4). Figure 5.4 also suggests a lag between the prices—that is to say, pig prices moved in the same direction as wood prices from year to year, but only after a delay. A regression to test this impression gives good results (table 5.9). This lag indicates that it was not pig but firewood prices that drove the system; the rise in mean pig prices after 200 seems to be only a response to high wood prices.

What could account for the conjunction of pig and firewood prices?

107. See Plut. *Dem.* 30.2 for the troop figures; 30.4: γενομένῳ περὶ τὰς Κυκλάδας αὐτῷ πρέσβεις Ἀθηναίων ἀπήντησαν; residence in the temple itself may be inferred from *IG* XI 2.146A76–77, and Demetrios had also lived in the Parthenon three years before (Plut. *Dem.* 23.5). Jacques Tréheux, *CRAI* 1987: 384, suggests that Demetrios may have dedicated the Neorion during this stay on Delos. On patterns in public grain-buying on Delos, see G. Reger, *Classical Antiquity* 12 (1993): 300–34.

108. See further pp. 181–87 on the impact of military presence.

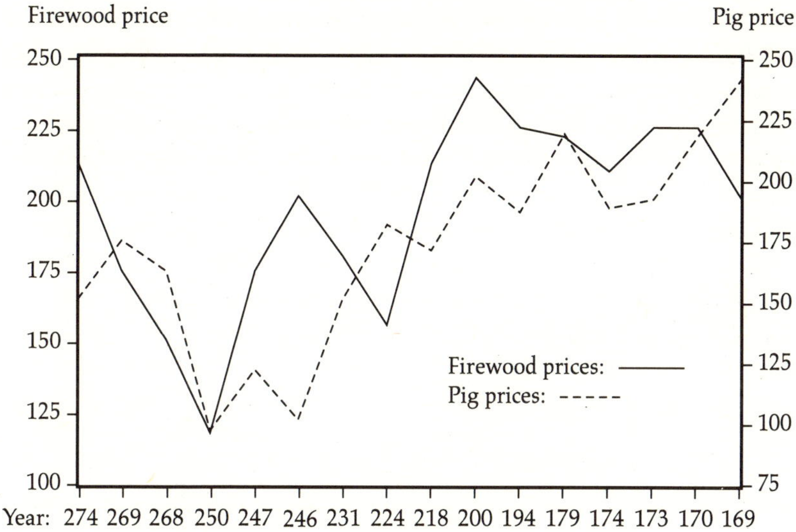

Figure 5.4. Indexed Firewood and Pig Prices, Delos, 274–169 B.C.

Table 5.9. Pig and Firewood Prices, Lagged One Period

Dependent Variable is PIG
Number of observations: 15

Variable	*Coefficient*	*Std. Error*	*T-Stat.*	*2-Tail Sig.*
C	*−1.2522150*	*42.822360*	*−0.0292421*	*0.977*
LAGGED FIREWOOD PRICE	*0.8958134*	*0.2162328*	*4.1428183*	*0.001*

R-squared	0.569008	Mean of dependent var	173.5867
Adjusted R-squared	0.535854	S.D. of dependent var	41.25766
S.E. of regression	28.10811	Sum of squared resid	10270.86
Durbin-Watson stat	1.896217	F-statistic	17.16294
Log likelihood	−70.25170		

Pigs "take care of themselves, day and night," writes a modern observer; they are "self-feeders."[109] Aristotle and other ancient commentators were no less aware of their virtues, which included heartiness, adaptability, and

109. Verlyn Klinkenborg, *Making Hay* (New York, 1986), 48. Cf. Burford, *Land and Labor*, 146–47.

fecundity.[110] In the matter of feeding, ancient agricultural writers recognize pigs' appetite for almost anything, but Columella recommends they be driven into "groves" (*nemora*) that provide a wide variety of trees and bushes or, less desirably, ground cover (*terrenum pabulum*, 7.9.7). He recommends storage of mast (*glans*) against periods when there is little forage outside, presumably winter. Varro too favors summer pasturing.[111]

This method of feeding pigs, to which Homer and other ancient sources attest,[112] is called "pannage" and has been practiced since the Neolithic. In a highly developed form, it created the tight bond between pig raising and forest management that has been a predominant aspect of the rural economy in southwestern Spain and Portugal.[113] On the assumption that pannage figured among the approaches to raising pigs in the Kyklades, it is possible to offer a tentative account of the connection between pig and firewood prices. As the mechanisms already discussed exerted pressure on wood prices, coppices and other woodlots in the Kyklades would have been more intensively worked. But this would have reduced the acreage available for pannage, making raising pigs more expensive and forcing prices up. Since pigs can eat a wide variety of foods, not just the acorns from Kykladic oaks and other woodlot forage, the impact would be delayed and moderated.[114] The result would be rising or falling average pig prices that trailed

110. Arist. *Hist. anim.* 8.6.2; see esp. Columella 7.9, passim.

111. According to Aristotle (*Hist. anim.* 8.6.2, 21.4) they prefer a varied diet and fatten best on chick-peas and figs (ἐρέβινθοι, σῦκα). Acorns (βάλανοι), which they especially enjoy, make the meat "wet" and can cause miscarriages in pregnant sows who eat too many. For fattening Aristotle also recommends raw barley, millet, figs, acorns (ἄκυλοι), the wild pear, and cucumbers. (On the difference between βάλανοι, which are acorns of the true oak [δρῦς] and ἄκυλοι, which according to some are the acorns of two varieties of holm oak, πρῖνος and φελλόδρυς, see Theophr. *Hist. pl.* 3.16.3.) Columella *Rust.* 7.9.6: "nemora sunt convientissima, quae vestiuntur quercu, subere, fago, cerris, ilicibus, oleastris, termitibus, corulis, pomiferisque silvestribus, ut sunt albae spinae, Graecae siliquae, iuniperus, lotus, pampinus, cornus, arbutus, prunus et paliurus atque achrades pini." Varro *Rust.* 2.4.6.

112. Hom. *Od.* 14.5–22, 24–26, 409–12, 524–33. Cf. Phereklides fr. 186, Amphis fr. 38 (*CAF*, vol. 1, 145; vol. 2, 236); Polyb. 2.15.2–3 on Italy; Longus *Daphnis and Khloe* 3.3.

113. James J. Parsons, *Geographical Review* 52 (1962): 211–35; Caroline Grigson in *Archaeological Aspects of Woodland Ecology*, 279–315; J. G. Lewthwaite in ibid., 217–30 (I am indebted to Oliver Rackham for directing my attention to this article). For a slightly different view, see Michael H. Jameson in *Pastoral Economies in Classical Antiquity* (Cambridge, 1988), 98–99.

114. Oaks are among the commonest trees in the Kyklades today and in the few pollen analyses conducted for the past. See Rackham in *Archaeological Aspects of Woodland Ecology*, 182–83, 189, 192, 193–94. Rackham cautions, however,

the changes in wood price levels. I should emphasize that this mechanism accounts for the long-term connection between wood and pig prices, not for short-term fluctuations, which as we have seen and shall see further below, are better accounted for by other means.

There is no significant relationship between pig and oil prices or between oil and firewood prices.

The Impact of Military Operations

The Greeks were quite aware that military operations in the vicinity of a city could raise prices.[115] The most obvious circumstance was, of course, the direct siege of a city by an enemy; as an example it will suffice to cite Plutarch's report of prices of 40 dr/*med* for salt and 300 dr/*med* for wheat during Demetrios's siege of Athens in 295/4 (*Dem.* 33.6). Less direct mechanisms were also familiar. In the fourth century, Lampsakos in Asia Minor raised prices for *alphita* and oil from 4 to 6 dr/*med* and from 3 to 4.5 dr/*kh* in anticipation of the arrival of a fleet of enemy triremes; the city pocketed the difference between the market and the inflated price. When the city of Herakleia Pontika commenced naval operations against the Bosporus, it effectively commandeered "all the grain and the oil and the wine and other goods" in the hands of merchants. In 366–365 B.C., Timotheos of Athens, besieging the Samians, sold them the crops in the fields to raise money to pay his soldiers; he also found large numbers of soldiers gathered in a camp so difficult to provision that shortages arose and the sale of foodstuffs had to be regulated. Feeding soldiers off the crops of the enemy was, of course, standard practice, which could not help but raise prices for the victims. Military commanders might also impose new or higher taxes on the local population to cover war costs, like Khabrias in Egypt in the 360s B.C.[116]

The presence of foreign troops, whether in the form of a garrison, as on Andros in the third century, or simply awaiting operations elsewhere, as in Epidauros before the Kretan War (*IG* XII 5.714; *IG* IV^2 1 66), could also

---

against assuming too great a connection between woodlots and pigs (per. comm., 31 December 1989).

115. See general remarks by Luigi Moretti in *Storia e civilità dei Greci,* vol. 4, *La società ellenistica,* pt. 8, *Economia, diritto, religione* (Milan, 1977), 358–59. Launey, II.724–812, has scattered information but no analysis from this point of view. On the occasional advantages of having troops quartered nearby, see Burford, *Land and Labor,* 191–92.

116. [Arist.] *Oik.* 2.7, 1347a32–b2; 2.8, 1347b3–16; 2.25a, 1350b33–1351a12; 2.23c, 1350b4–7; 2.23d, 1350b7–15; 2.24a, 1350b15–16. Cf. B. A. van Groningen, *Aristote: Le Second Livre de l'Economique* (Leiden, 1933), passim.

drive up prices. *SIG*[3] 495.176–79 directly links wars and shortage: "all those in the city were doing badly on account of the wars and the shortages" (τῶν δ' ἐν τῆι πόλει κακῶς διακειμένων πάντων διά τε τοὺς πολέ[μ]ους καὶ τὰς ἀφορίας). Khios provides some striking testimony; its citizens honored one of their own, a man of exceptional wealth, whose name has not been preserved, for taking on himself the cost of supporting Roman soldiers on the island during the war with Antiokhos III. This included giving each soldier an amphora of wine, which may have come from his own stores. His generosity must have insulated the market against what would have otherwise been a devastating rise in demand. Methymna on Lesbos suffered severe and continuing shortages of grain as a direct result of the Romans' war against Aristonikos in the late 130s B.C. Repeated testimony of grain shortages in Boiotia in the 170s has been linked to the Third Makedonian War.[117]

Raiders often targeted crops in the fields or rural habitations, as in Mylasa during the war with Labienus in 40 B.C.: "both concerning the land, which had been plundered, and the farmsteads, which had been burned, so that in all matters you had been unlucky" (καὶ περὶ τῆς χώρας τῆς λελεηλατημένης καὶ τῶν ἐπαύλεων τῶν ἐμπεπρησμένων ὥστε ἐμ πᾶσιν ὑμᾶς ἠτυχηκέναι).[118] "Economic warfare" against shipping was also frequent. Antigonos Monophthalmos and his son attacked shipping during the siege of Rhodos; ten years later, Demetrios interdicted a grain ship bound for Athens in 295/4 B.C. and hanged some of the crew; Delos itself experienced disruption of the sea lanes during the Second Syrian War. No wonder hundreds of proxeny decrees guarantee freedom to sail in and sail out "during peace and war."[119]

A number of difficulties plague the investigation of possible relations between military activity and price trends on Delos. The testimony for military and political activity in the islands is exceptionally poor, especially for the third century. The other problems stem from the exiguousness of the prices themselves. It is not always easy to say that a price is "unusual." The variations of season, sailing schedules, harvests, shipwrecks, piracy, and natural disasters may have forced prices up without any military

117. Luigi Moretti, *Rivista di filologia e di istruzione classica* 108 (1980): 36–47, ll. 3–4, 12–14, and on the source of the wine, 40–41; *IG* XII suppl. 116; Denis Knoepfler, *BCH* 114 (1990): 491; cf. also L. Moretti, *ISE,* I.64, p. 162, who prefers the war against Antiokhos.

118. *IK* 34 Mylasa I.602.17–20 (= *SIG*[3] 768), cf. Strabo 14.2.24 (C660), Dio Cassius 48.26.3–4. Another example: Polyb. 4.3.10.

119. Diod. 20.81.2, 82.5, 83.3, 84.5, 93.2–3; Plut. *Dem.* 33.5; *IG* XI 4.751 (= *Choix,* 67).

Table 5.10. Mean, Mode, and Range of Indexed Prices for Olive Oil, Firewood, and Pigs on Delos, 307–169 B.C.

	Period	*N*	*Mean*	*Mode*	*High*	*Low*
Oil	307–297		—	—		
	272–224	9	110.1	100–109	131.3	91.5
	218–194	3	104.3	100–109	112.5	100.0
	179–170	5	90.7	100–109	103.5	70.8
	272–170	17	101.8	100–109	131.3	70.8
Firewood	304–224[a]	17	173.5	170–179	212.3	117.3
	218–169	9	220.5	220–229	241.6	199.8
Pigs	281–218[b]	13	150.6	150–159	200.0	97.9
	200–169	9	211.1	180–189, 210–219	245.8	186.1

[a] Includes the prices for 250 B.C.
[b] Includes the prices for 276 and 250 B.C.

presence at all, or may have conspired with a military presence to raise prices. Disentangling the responsibility of the various causes is virtually impossible.

In general, I have identified prices as unusual if they meet two criteria: (1) they must be substantially above both the mean and mode prices for that commodity during the period in question, and (2) other explanations—closure of the sailing season, poor harvest, and so forth—must be excluded. For example, the olive oil prices of 272 or 271 B.C. are about 25 percent above the mean and mode for the period (110.1, 100–109), but they fall at the end of the long decline to ca. 270 B.C., which may mean they were simply the end of that trend; furthermore, the two prices occur in Lenaion after a presumed poor harvest (for 273 B.C.) and in Bouphonion (?), when supplies in any case should be shortest and pressure of the approaching end of the sailing season greatest. Even though the First Syrian War, which has left some evidence on Krete and may have involved operations in the Bosporus,[120] was raging in these years, the presence of other potential explanations precludes invoking a military one for these prices.

The mean, mode, and range of prices are set out in table 5.10.

OLIVE OIL

The candidates for unusually high prices are 307–306, 281, 279, and 259 or 256–251 B.C.

120. Will I², 146–47, 149. Krete: *IC*, II, Lisos 1, I, Lyttos 8. Pontic expedition: Steph. Byz., s.v. "Ankyra"; cf. also *FGrHist*, 434, Memnon F 10–11.

The first three years belong to the period of decline from generally high prices; this, with the rarity of prices from the whole period from 307 to 273 B.C., makes it very difficult to decide whether a price is in fact high. There was military activity in the Kyklades in 307 and 306. Demetrios Poliorketes, who besieged Athens during the winter of 307/6, passed through the islands traveling between Athens and Asia Minor; although the inscription giving the prices does not assign them to a particular month, they may nevertheless well be associated with Demetrios's activities. The prices of 304, I have argued above, can be explained by the impact of Demetrios's siege on Rhodos, and thus are related to military activity. The price of 281 does seem quite elevated in comparison to prices just two years later, but in view of the scarcity of figures it is impossible to know for sure. Finally, the price of 279 B.C. might also be related to military activities. That year saw a war between Ptolemaios II and Antiokhos that resulted in the acquisition of Samos and parts of Ionia by the Egyptians. Since the Ptolemies had controlled the Kyklades for eight years or so, operations may have been staged from the islands.

That leaves only a single unusually high oil price of 125.1, 13.6 percent above mean, from an inscription that can only be dated to 259 or 256–251 B.C.[121] The period is that of the Second Syrian War, which Rhodos exploited to seek connections in the Kyklades, including on Delos, against her long-time Egyptian allies. The price *might* be attributable to the presence of the Rhodian fleet, but without a more precise date for the inscription it is impossible to be sure.

With but one exception, all the many other years that show a military presence in the Kyklades—260–258, 246, 200, and 170 B.C.—yield oil prices that are either perfectly normal or low. The exception is 169 B.C., with a price 51.6 percent above the mean for 179–170 B.C. (or 35.1 percent above the 272–170 B.C. mean). I have already argued that this price from Posideon represents a poor harvest owing to the bad winter of 169–168 B.C., but if troops were stationed on Delos itself, as in the following year, they may have contributed additional stress.

These results can be explained by the model for Delian oil supplies worked out above. Before 272 B.C., Delos was dependent on supplies brought in from relatively great distances, but by the 260s the temple could satisfy its needs from sources on Delos itself and on very close neighbors. Only disruption of trade in the neighborhood—say between Delos and Rheneia, Mykonos, and perhaps Tenos—would affect its supplies. Hence the complete absence of any impact by fleets or troops even as close as

121. See discussion in Appendix III, p. 299.

Andros, and even when—as we shall see presently—those troops did cause the prices of other commodities to rise.

FIREWOOD

Six groups of wood prices meet both criteria (279, 274, 272 or 271, 246, and 200). All fall in years for which military activity in the Kyklades is attested or very likely. In 279 B.C., when wood sold for 15.1 percent above the mean, Ptolemaios II and Antiokhos were fighting a war that, as we have just seen, may have involved the Kyklades. Two wood prices for 274 B.C. of 15.1 and 29.6 percent above the mean may be associated with the First Syrian War, which affected Krete and may have involved an expedition by Egyptian forces to the Pontos; the Kyklades may have served as a staging ground for this expedition. Unfortunately, we do not know to what months the prices for these years applied. It therefore remains possible that they might be explained by seasonal factors. For the rest of the prices, months are attested, and we are on commensurately more solid ground.

In 272 (or 271) B.C., another wood price of 15.1 percent above mean appears in Panemos. This price cannot be attributed to seasonal variation, since it falls in the summer in the middle of the sailing season, when demand for wood was low and availability high. The First Syrian War continued until 271 B.C. It seems at least plausible to blame this rather high wood price on the presence of troops in or around the Kyklades. It would be nice to know whether this price corresponds with the Pontic expedition of Ptolemaios II, but its exact date, like other details, remains an enigma.

For 246 B.C., we have a series of high summer prices for firewood, spanning Thargelion, Second Panemos, and probably Metageitnion. Because the year was intercalary, Thargelion and Panemos must have fallen about a month earlier than usual, that is, in March–April and April–May. The prices, about 11.6–15.1 percent above mean, thus spanned spring and early summer. The Third Syrian, or Laodikean, War began this year, and there is now convincing evidence to put a Ptolemaic fleet in the Kyklades in the spring and early summer; it fought a battle at Andros and then liberated Ephesos from Seleukid control.[122] It is very tempting to suggest that the naval operations conducted as part of the war both raised local demand for basic goods like firewood and grain and disrupted the local trade network. With its small demand, Delos was especially susceptible to the distrainment or diversion of cargo ships.

Finally, 200 B.C. recorded two wood prices 13.3 percent above mean in

122. On the details, see G. Reger, *Historia* 43 (1994): 43–46. For a possible parallel, see Appendix I.

Thargelion and Panemos. Prices on either side of these months were perfectly in line with average prices. The spring of 200 B.C. saw widespread activity in the islands. Philip V returned to Greece from Karia, where he had wintered, early in the spring, and following an award by Athens, also in the spring, of *isopoliteia,* the Rhodians put a fleet to sea, visited Keos, and obtained alliances with all of the islands except Andros, Paros, and Kythnos, which had Makedonian garrisons. The high spring wood prices could well be a consequence of this activity.[123]

Unfortunately, the years of the war against Perseus, which saw an almost continuous Roman and allied naval presence not only in the islands but also on Delos itself, and in 168 B.C. included attacks on shipping by both sides, report either normal (171) or low (169) wood prices.[124]

Despite the troubling exception of the war against Perseus, the evidence seems to support the view that wood prices were affected by military activity. This activity did not need to be centered directly on Delos, as with the pig prices of 302 and 301 B.C., to exercise its influence; it seems to have sufficed that fleets or troops moved through the islands or operated in the vicinity.

As we have seen, armies were most likely to raise prices either directly through blockades and sieges or indirectly by competing with local consumers or disrupting supplies. Since direct measures can be ruled out for Delos—as a sacred precinct it was exempt from direct military intervention, and fighting was banned there[125]—troops could have raised prices there only by their demand or by interrupting supplies. In none of the cases we have examined is a military presence on Delos itself explicitly attested (although presumably any military commander who passed through the islands would have stopped to pay his respects to the god and make a dedication),[126] but twice, in 246 and 200 B.C., military actions are reported for the vicinity of Delos (Andros; the Kyklades generally). This situation can be accounted for by assuming that firewood reached the island from sources that, while not distant, did embrace most of the Kyklades. The picture of the trade in firewood that emerges from an examination of seasonal price variations finds confirmation in the reaction of prices to military activity.

123. Meiggs, 456, objects on the basis of stable charcoal prices, but as we have seen (and as Meiggs admits) no quantities for charcoal purchase are recorded.

124. See chapter 2, pp. 28–29.

125. Paus. 3.23.3–5 (locus classicus); for a recent statement (with parti pris) on this controversial topic, see Philippe Bruneau, *BCH* 114 (1990): 583–91.

126. See, e.g., the list of Roman magistrates who visited Delos or the Kyklades in Etienne, 253–64.

PIGS

Three years give candidate pig prices: 281, 171, and 169 B.C.

The pig price of 281 B.C. is 21.7 percent above the mean, but unfortunately I have not been able to identify any military activity in the Kyklades in that year, except for the flight of Arsinoë II from Samothrake to Egypt after the murder of her husband, Ptolemaios Keraunos. If her hasty escape brought her through Delos—likely by reason of geography—it left her no time to make an offering to Apollo to mark her passage.[127] Nor does any evidence assign her a substantial escort of troops, or even of courtiers.

The other two sets of prices fall during the war with Perseus. For Posideon 171 B.C. is recorded a single pig price of 18.4 percent above mean. Perhaps military activity could account for it, but since the month before saw a remarkably low price of 150—28.95 percent below mean—the typical monthly cycle in pig prices we have seen year after year seems sufficient.

The case for 169 B.C. is rather better. Prices of 10.5 and 18.4 percent above mean occur in Metageitnion and Posideon, which at least suggests a trend (the price for Panemos is 6.6 percent higher than mean). Since there was a military presence on Delos itself and a bad winter affected oil prices, this year seems likely to have experienced high pig prices owing to military activity.

It is interesting to compare these results with prices for two years during which we can be certain, or virtually so, that Delos was at peace: 218 and 179 B.C. For both years, wood prices are either perfectly normal (Lenaion–Hieron, 218; Hieron–Posideon, 179) or actually low (Galaxion and Thargelion, 218; Lenaion, 179, although there is a good explanation for this price). On the contrary, oil and pig prices behave as in any other year, showing seasonal fluctuations and, in the case of pigs, some unusually high prices (Artemision, Panemos, and Metageitnion, 218; Hieron [14.5 percent] and Metageitnion [16.1 percent], 179). This is very satisfying confirmation that high wood prices really are attributable to the military operations that coincided with them, and that oil and pig prices were generally unaffected by war, unless troops were actually on Delos. Moreover, pig prices may show quite extraordinary but very transient elevations that are best attributed to the preferences of farmers and the natural history of the pig, as we have seen.

The results of this study nicely confirm the inferences drawn from the examination of seasonal price fluctuations and long-term price trends. Of

127. Bruneau, 518.

the three goods, only firewood was drawn from a relatively broad trade network, and that was limited to the Kyklades and, perhaps, Samos and a few other northerly islands. Olive oil (after 272 B.C.) and pigs came from sources so nearby that only troops on Delos itself could affect their prices. Independent Delos was no great entrepôt, transshipping goods from and to all over the Aegean; it was a Kykladic backwater, very unlike its subsequent incarnation under the Athenians in the late second and early first centuries B.C.

Chapter 6

The Rent Histories of Estates and Houses

Delian Apollo owned about twenty properties, called τεμένη in the accounts and conventionally referred to in scholarship as "estates," which were located on Delos itself, on Rheneia, and, after 237 B.C., on Mykonos. Most of them were farms, producing grain, livestock, figs, and wine, but unfortunately (except for the Mykonian holdings) no olive oil. For most of the years of independence, the estates were leased after secret bidding for ten-year periods. Except for a few gaps, the most serious of which covers 240–220 B.C., records of the rents of the estates are fully preserved. Every tenth year, before the next rental period, the *hieropoioi* recorded detailed inventories of the estates' capital equipment, including plantings of vines and fruit trees, which permit some inferences about the strategies of exploitation followed on each estate.

This unusually rich material offers a counterpoint to the price data studied in the previous chapter. Land rents can be compared to the movement of prices for agricultural goods, an enterprise impossible virtually everywhere else in the Hellenistic world except Egypt. While Delos was not part of a large-scale, pan-Aegean price-setting market, there was clearly a local market for agricultural products, and the impact of that market can be read in changes in the rents for the estates; we can sometimes even make inferences, tentative though they may be, about conditions in the neighboring Kyklades. We can explore the differing impact of specialization in viticulture, stock raising, and cereal culture in rents over time, as local economic conditions changed. Even some of the noneconomic factors that entered into decisions by the Delian elite to rent Apollo's estates can be elucidated.

The accounts also preserve records of a series of "sacred houses" (ἱεροὶ οἶκοι) owned by Apollo and rented on five-year leases by private persons. Unfortunately, the rents of these buildings, although fairly well-preserved across the years of Delian independence, cannot be subjected as easily and directly as the estate rents to economic analysis. Nevertheless, they provide important evidence about the economic situation in the city of Delos itself as opposed to the countryside, and open a window on changes in the urban economic situation, which did not always move in conjunction with the rural one.

The Origin and Character of the Estates

We can only surmise how the first estates came into Apollo's possession. In 523 B.C., Polykrates of Samos captured Rheneia and gave it to Apollo, and John Kent has reasonably conjectured that this gift was the origin of some or all of the god's Rheneian estates. Those on Delos may likewise have been gifts or dedications; Kent's suggestion that Hippodromos was a gift from the Athenian general Nikias in the fifth century seems to have won general acceptance.[1] Several more estates seem to have come into Apollo's possession as a result of seizure of property of Delians convicted of sacrilege in 375 B.C.; the origin of yet other estates, which first appear in the accounts between 297 and 282 B.C., is treated below.[2] However Apollo came to own them, the estates constituted an important part of his wealth, as shown by the scrupulous regulations that govern their rental (*ID* 503, the ἱερὰ συγγραφή, on which further below).

For the amounts of the rents I generally follow the figures given by Kent,[3] except that for several estates in the early period I have omitted rents reconstructed on the assumption that some missing rentals were renewed without competitive bidding by the application of a 10 percent increase, the ἐπιδέκατον. Kent is usually probably right in his reconstructions, but since they do not affect the rent history I have preferred to set them aside. I have also used the original of two rents when a renter defaulted in the middle of a lease and the estate was rerented. Sometimes these estates fetched considerably less in rerental, but not, I think, for economic reasons: the new renters were no doubt taking advantage of an unexpectedly vacant estate to pick it up at a bargain rate.

Beginning with the year 299 B.C., table 6.1 shows rents for each ten-

1. Thuc. 1.13.6, 3.104.2 for Polykrates, with Kent, 245; Plut. *Nik.* 3.7, Thuc. 3.104.6, Kent, 255–56, Brunet, 31–32, Isager-Skydsgaard, 183, for Hippodromos.

2. See *ID* 98B24–52 for the confiscations; Kent, 256–58, 286–89; Tréheux, "Dernières Années," 1016 n. 2; Brunet, 31–35, 49–64.

3. Kent, 303–4, still the standard treatment. There is, however, much to correct; see Jacques Tréheux, *Rev. Arch.* 31/32 (1948): 1008–32, esp. 1011–22; Brunet, passim; Heichelheim, *Wirt. Sch.*, 82–83; Larsen, 402–7, esp. 403, 406. And see Appendix IV, pp. 309–38, below.

Table 6.1. Indexed Estate Rents by Rental Period, 314–179 B.C.

	Rental Periods								
Estate	*314*	*307*	*304*	*301*	*299*	*289*	*279*	*269*	*259*
Hippodromos	109	139	153	—	151	83	92	111	77
Leimon	353	271	271	294	299	136	149	158	137
Soloe/Korakia	57	79	—	—	76	71	98	89	95
Pyrgoi	89	—	130	165	165	111	122	134	102
Kharoneia	95	—	95	—	132	73	73	100	80
Rhamnoi	145	—	—	—	131	68	78	85	105
Porthmos	117	—	161	—	158	117	129	142	91
Limnai	224	172	192	—	181	105	116	167	140
Panormos	124	—	153	—	170	109	116	137	121
Dionysios	93	—	164	124	171	75	82	87	70
Kharetia	157	202	222	—	280	162	162	162	126
Nikou Khoros	169	162	212	163	231	134	104	135	123
Epistheneia	—	—	—	—	—	69	81	84	91
Phoinikes	124	—	169	169	169	111	109	111	92
Skitoneia	107	—	164	—	190	118	112	118	102
Akra Delos	—	—	—	—	—	68	114	116	91
Lykoneion	98	—	171	164	180	66	123	125	90
Phytalia	—	—	—	—	—	124	124	149	91
Sosimakhia	—	—	—	—	—	73	124	55	91
Kerameion	—	—	—	—	—	48	56	66	68

	249	*239*	*229*	*219*	*209*	*199*	*189*	*179*
Hippodromos	100	—	—	88	94	87	95	99
Leimon	100	—	—	92	95	105	—	129
Soloe/Korakia	100	—	—	48	84	68	—	59
Pyrgoi	100	—	—	60	49(?)	52	—	47
Kharoneia	100	—	—	38	—	36	27	41
Rhamnoi	100	—	—	54	52	58	—	63
Porthmos	100	—	—	54	79	66	53	58
Limnai	100	—	—	102	62	61	—	82
Panormos	100	—	—	63	64	47	—	55
Dionysios	100	—	—	50	49	49	—	42
Kharetia	100	—	—	75	82	59	65	72
Nikou Khoros	100	—	—	74	66	31	—	37
Epistheneia	100	—	—	58	59	48	—	57
Phoinikes	100	—	—	73	—	90	—	75
Skitoneia	100	—	—	42	66	48	—	70
Akra Delos	100	—	—	77	—	—	—	34
Lykoneion	100	—	—	125	—	106	—	141
Phytalia	100	—	—	103	103	107	—	62
Sosimakhia	100	—	—	73	55	76	—	65
Kerameion	100	—	—	105	—	—	114	121

year rental period.[4] The figure given under 299 B.C. was that submitted by the winning bidder (estates were leased by sealed bid; see further below) in 300 B.C. for a lease beginning in Lenaion 299 B.C. and running through Posideon 290 B.C. This term was the result of the implementation of a new rental contract, the ἱερὰ συγγραφή, which called for ten-year rental periods.[5]

Before 300 B.C., rental periods were very irregular. In the fall of 314 B.C., when Antigonos Monophthalmos and his son Demetrios freed the island from Athens, the Delians cancelled leases then in force and replaced them with new four-year leases that ran until 310 B.C. Four Delians were apparently allowed to renew their leases by paying 10 percent more rent (the ἐπιδέκατον); the other estates, which had probably been in Athenian hands, now fell to Delians.[6] Over the next few years, leases were renewed several times. In 310, the estates were put up for five years (*IG* XI 2.143B1–2), but the lease period that began in 305 B.C. cannot have lasted longer than three years, for the payments in *IG* XI 2.144A9–17 (304 B.C.) are different from those of *IG* XI 2.146A9–12 of 301 B.C. There were therefore four separate leasing periods between 315 and 300 B.C. Table 6.1 dates the earlier ones by the dates of the inscriptions to which we owe our knowledge of the rents, and not by the dates of the leases:

1. Four-year lease, 314–310 B.C.
2. Five-year lease, 310–305 B.C.
3. One-, two-, or three-year lease, 305–304/3/2 B.C.
4. Two- to four-year lease, 304/3/2–300 B.C.

For purposes of analysis, it is useful to try to sort the estates into groups that share important characteristics. Groupings based on the primary products of each estate would clearly be interesting for economic analysis. In the years when the estates were put up for lease, the *hieropoioi* made a

4. For discussion of individual figures, see Appendix IV, pp. 309–38, below. Unfortunately, in some respects the data collected there are provisional. Several important new discoveries await publication: the join of *ID* 456 + 440 (photograph at J. Tréheux, *BCH* 109 [1985]: 486, fig. 1); a new reading of 356*bis;* and the join of 374B with a new frag. Γ761, for all of which see J. Tréheux, *BCH* 110 (1986): 430–31 (Brunet, 45). For *ID* 452 + 467, see M. Brunet, *BCH* 114 (1990): 678–79, and for the date G. Reger, *Hesperia* 63 (1994): 105–10.

5. On the date, see Appendix I.

6. Tréheux, "Dernières Années," 1028–31, 1011–12, with n. 4, for the ἐπιδέκατον; four-year leases at *IG* XI 2.135.1–2.

thorough inventory of the capital goods of each estate. The results were incorporated into the accounts as part of the contract between Apollo and the renters. Using these inventories (especially the very well preserved one for 250 B.C. in *IG* XI 2.287A134–74), Kent posits four estate groups based on product. His first group consists of eight estates that produced grapes, grain, and livestock. The second group comprises three estates primarily devoted to livestock, with some vines. The four estates of his third group lacked vines altogether, and the products of the five estates of the fourth group could not be identified. Kent's groupings were especially interesting in view of his hypothesis that declining wine prices in the second half of the third century depressed the rents for estates that were dependent on wine.[7]

Unfortunately, close inspection of the evidence for estate products fails to support Kent's groupings. His third group indeed includes only estates that clearly lacked vines—Hippodromos, Kerameion, Leimon, and Soloe-Korakia—but one of them, Kerameion, is by Kent's own description "a potter's establishment."[8] It clearly should be eliminated from the group, whose other members are agricultural enterprises. Two of the three estates in Kent's second group, devoted mainly to livestock but with some vines, each have a βούστασις and one, Phoinikes, has an ἀχυρών, both of which suggest grain production—said by Kent to be characteristic of his first group.[9] Moreover, Rhamnoi, although placed in this group, supported 1,978 vines, almost three times as many as the 700 that qualify Nikou Khoros for placement in Kent's first group. One of the estates Kent puts in his fourth group, whose products are said to be unidentified, is Skitoneia, which in fact had 629 vines but no προβατών or ἀχυρών, which would seem to make it preeminently dependent on wine production.

In fact, capital equipment in the form of buildings may in general offer a poor guide to the products of the estates. Every estate but Dionysios had a βούστασις, implying that they all produced at least some grain; and Dionysios in fact had an ἀχυρών, which means that it produced "chaff" in some manner. Two estates known to have produced barley in the late fourth century—Hippodromos and Soloe-Korakia—both lacked ἀχυ-

7. Kent, 310, 299–301; 309–13.

8. Kent, 254, with n. 25.

9. The products of the third estate in the group, Episthenelia, known to Kent only from the very fragmentary *ID* 373A8–13 (cf. Kent, *BCH* 68 [1939]: 242) and 467.1–4 (cf. Kent, *BCH* 68 [1939]: 245), have now become clear thanks to Tréheux's join of *ID* 452 and 467 (*BCH* 110 [1986]: 430–31), published by M. Brunet, *BCH* 114 (1990): 678–79.

ρῶνες. The absence of προβατῶνες on Limnai and Skitoneia, then, cannot prove that neither estate supported herding.[10]

There is, however, one factor that can be used unambiguously to sort the estates, and that is the presence or absence of vines. *IG* XI 2.287 proves conclusively that—at least in 250 B.C.—Hippodromos, Leimon, and Soloe-Korakia had no vines at all. The three estates therefore make a clear group, which I shall call Group I. Of the remaining sixteen estates, twelve are known to have had vines, but in considerably different numbers. Three estates supported more than 1,900 vines: Pyrgoi with 2,250, Kharoneia with 2,187, and Rhamnoi with 1,978. These I call Group IIA. Four estates, Group IIB, had between 1,550 and 1,000 vines: Porthmos with 1,535, Limnai with 1,514, Panormos with 1,298, and Dionysios with 1,056. A final set, Group IIC, consists of estates with 700 or fewer vines: Nikou Khoros with 700, Skitoneia with 629, Phoinikes with 596, Khareteia with 560, and Epistheneia with 487.[11] This sorting will allow a close test of Kent's hypothesis that declining wine prices depressed estate rents after the mid third century. (The estates are arranged by group in table 6.1.) For our purposes I have calculated indexed values for each estate's rents and then derived an aggregated average rent for each group in each rental period. The aggregated data appear in table 6.2.[12] It is these aggregated data that we shall use in our analysis. The same data are displayed graphically in figure 6.1.

Figure 6.1 offers graphic illustration of the decline rents underwent in 290 B.C.; as we shall see, analysis confirms the reality of this change. Another, more modest adjustment can be detected around 220 B.C. Various hypotheses have been suggested to explain these changes, including Kent's view, already mentioned, that declining wine prices after 250 B.C. were to blame for the loss in value of the estates after 220 B.C. These earlier views are tested below. First, however, I would like to explore another approach, which, strangely enough, has not been tried. As we saw in chapters 4 and 5, we have series of prices for several important agricultural commodities,

10. On the terms, see Brunet, 180–81, 187–98; Robin Osborne, *BSA* 80 (1985): 121; Vallois, I.213; Kent, 292–301; and see generally, Jan Pečírka in *Problèmes de la terre en Grèce ancienne* (Paris, 1973), 137–40.

11. For three remaining estates—Akra Delos, Lykoneion, and Sosimakheia—no inventories survive. On Phytalia, see below. The evidence is conveniently set out at Philippe Bruneau and Philippe Fraisse, *BCH* 105 (1981): 141–44, with a table at 143 (missing however Epistheneia).

12. For full data, see Appendix IV.

Table 6.2. Aggregated Average Indexed Estate Rents, by Group and Rental Period, 314–170 B.C.

Rental Period	*Groups*			
	I	*IIA*	*IIB*	*IIC*
314–311	173	109.7	139.5	139
310–305	163	—	—	182
304	212	112.5	167.5	192
301	294	—	—	166
299–290	175	142.7	209.5	218
289–280	97	84	101.5	119
279–270	113	91	110.75	114
269–260	119	106.3	133.25	122
259–250	103	91.3	105.5	107
249–240	100	100	100	100
239–230	—	—	—	—
229–220	—	—	—	—
219–210	76	50.7	67.25	64
209–200	91	50.5	63.5	68
199–190	87	48.7	55.75	55
189–180	95	—	—	—
179–170	96	50.3	59.25	62

KEY: Group I = Estates without vines
Group IIA = Estates with more than 1,900 vines
Group IIB = Estates with 1,550–1,000 vines
Group IIC = Estates with 700 or fewer vines

including barley, olive oil, firewood, and pigs. Since some of these goods (especially barley) were produced on many, if not most, of the estates, nothing is more natural than to see whether the rents renters paid were determined by the prices of agricultural commodities.

Commodity Prices and Estate Rents, ca. 280–169 B.C.

The estates produced a variety of agricultural commodities—grain, wine, livestock, figs—of whose local prices the renters must have been perfectly aware. Since much of the Delian demand for these goods was satisfied by local Delian or neighboring Kykladic production, renters who wanted to dispose of products on the local market would have had to take these prices

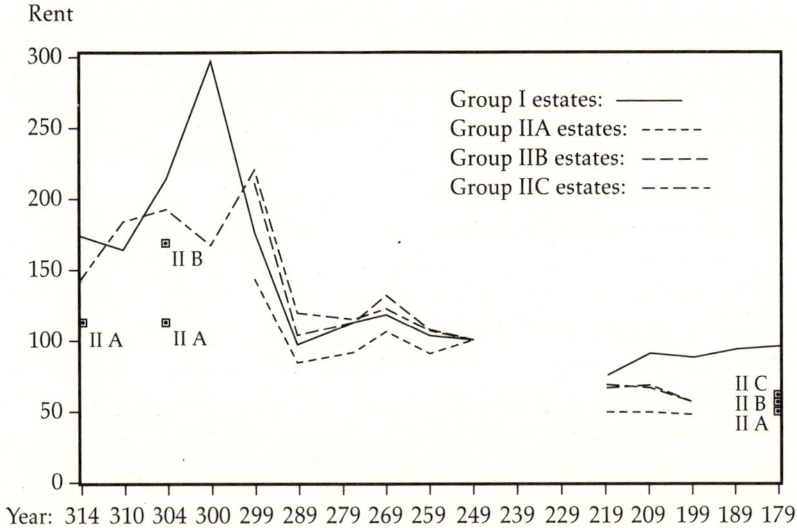

Figure 6.1. Average Aggregated Indexed Rents of Apollo's Estates, by Group, 314–179 B.C.
Note: No data available for years 248–220, or for Group II for 198–180.

into account when reckoning the level at which they were willing to bid for an estate. Once the *hiera syngraphe* had eliminated the less wealthy and more speculative bidders, whose interest in the estates may have had a considerable social component (as we shall see below), rents ought to have centered increasingly on economic considerations.[13]

Unfortunately, several difficulties stand in the way of testing this hypothesis. For the most important agricultural commodity, grain, we possess only a handful of prices (see table 6.3), and only a few of these date to years when the estates were up for rental. The situation with olive oil prices is considerably better, since we have a very long series of prices for that commodity, and many that date to years when estates were bid out; but unfortunately not a single estate except on Mykonos had any olives. Firewood

13. On the "commercial" character of these enterprises, see Claude Vial in *L'Origine des richesses dépensées dans la ville antique* (Aix-en-Provence, 1985), 47–53; Vial, 317–38; and Robin Osborne, *Chiron* 18 (1988): 302–304, who writes that "the pattern of agriculture on the temple estates made an openended commercial attitude to farming possible: the turn-over of estate leases makes it look as if some, at least, [of the renters] took advantage of that possibility" (302) and observes that on Delos "agricultural activity seems to have become devoid of social value" (304). For another approach to the relation between grain prices and rents, see Robin Osborne, *Classical Landscape with Figures* (London, 1987), 46–47.

prices are likewise abundant, but it may fairly be doubted whether the collection and sale of firewood was of any real economic importance to estates without copses. Sheep prices are far too rare to be of any help, whereas the long series of pig prices presents its own problems, as we shall see.

The earliest years of Delian independence present even worse problems. While we can document a relation between commodity prices and rents for each rental period from 280 to 250 and again from 220 to 180 B.C., there are only one usable oil price and one usable pig price for the period of high rents (314–291 B.C.). Scholars have long argued for a connection between these rents and prices, but this view cannot be tested for want of data. I shall therefore postpone treatment of this period and concentrate here on the years after 280 B.C.

For this analysis, I have compared rents with prices for goods from the year in which new bids were submitted, from the closest year immediately preceding, or, in a few cases, when no other data were available and prices were relatively steady over time, from the immediately following year. This procedure assumes that bidders were most likely to be affected by prices current when they offered bids. There may, of course, have been fluctuations unknown to us that affected rents, but we have no way to control for these. In any case, there are some interesting relationships between rents and prices that help to alleviate worries about the potential inadequacy of the data.

GRAIN PRICES AND RENTS

As grain, and especially barley, was the staple food in the Kyklades, it is reasonable to begin with a comparison of grain prices with estate rents. Unfortunately, grain prices are scarce for Delos, and those for wheat are too rare to use here; the few barley prices are given in table 6.3 in the form of cost of processed *alphita.* Any comparison between *alphita* prices and rents must be treated with extreme caution, because so few comparable data points are available (only six for Group I and five for Group II estates), but the results are extremely interesting. For Group I estates, the correlation is almost perfect. To the extent it is possible to test, estate rents move in exact conjunction with *alphita* prices (fig. 6.2; table 6.4).

For Group II estates, the connection is considerably less definitive (fig. 6.3, table 6.5). Although Groups IIA and IIB show a correlation—47 and 49 percent respectively of the variation in rents can be explained by changes in barley prices—the relation is not very significant (in both cases

Table 6.3. Mean *alphita* Prices on Delos, 282–169 B.C. (dr/*med*)

Date	*Price*/med	*Alternative Price*	*Use*
282	4.67	—	H
258	4.62	—	G
250	4.25	—	G
224	3.08	—	G
190	4	5.333	P
179	4	3	P
178	3.75	5	P
177	4	3	P
174	4	—	P
169	3.875	5.167	P

KEY: Alternative Price = from Larsen, 386.
H = human consumption.
G = feed for geese.
P = for the Posideia.

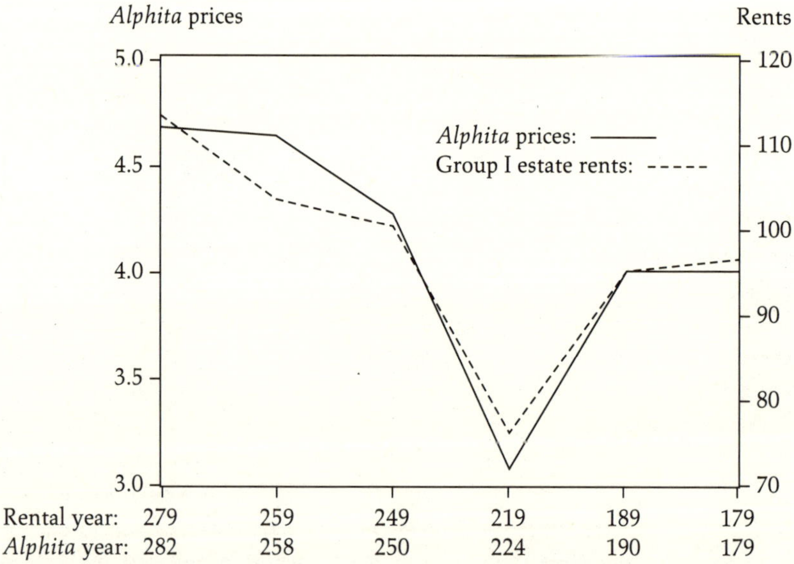

Figure 6.2. Movement of Group I Estate Rents in Relation to *alphita* Prices, 279–179 B.C.

Table 6.4. Group I Estate Rents and *alphita* Prices

Dependent Variable is GROUP I ESTATES
Number of observations: 6

Variable	*Coefficient*	*Std. Error*	*T-Stat.*	*2-Tail Sig.*
C	12.992485	10.347748	1.2555858	0.278
ALPHITA *PRICES*	20.516111	2.5014444	8.2017057	0.001

R-squared	0.943874	Mean of dependent var	97.16667
Adjusted R-squared	0.929842	S.D. of dependent var	12.22157
S.E. of regression	3.237163	Sum of squared resid	41.91691
Durbin-Watson stat	2.474831	F-statistic	67.26798
Log likelihood	−14.34542		

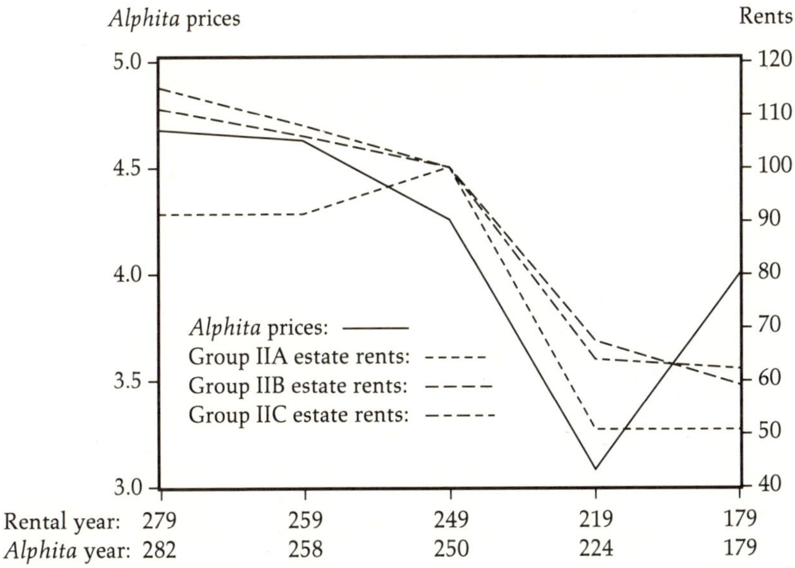

Figure 6.3. Movement of Group II Estate Rents in Relation to *alphita* Prices, 279–179 B.C.

Table 6.5. Group II Estate Rents and *alphita* Prices

A. Dependent Variable is GROUP IIA ESTATES
Number of observations: 5

Variable	*Coefficient*	*Std. Error*	*T-Stat.*	*2-Tail Sig.*
C	*−43.204734*	*56.712658*	*−0.7618182*	*0.502*
ALPHITA *PRICES*	*29.065164*	*13.619148*	*2.1341396*	*0.123*

R-squared	0.602888	Mean of dependent var	76.66000
Adjusted R-squared	0.470518	S.D. of dependent var	24.15312
S.E. of regression	17.57514	Sum of squared resid	926.6567
Durbin-Watson stat	1.459022	F-statistic	4.554552
Log likelihood	−20.15006		

B. Dependent Variable is GROUP IIB ESTATES
Number of observations: 5

Variable	*Coefficient*	*Std. Error*	*T-Stat.*	*2-Tail Sig.*
C	*−29.924729*	*54.285249*	*−0.5512497*	*0.620*
ALPHITA *PRICES*	*28.728111*	*13.036223*	*2.2037143*	*0.115*

R-squared	0.618144	Mean of dependent var	88.55000
Adjusted R-squared	0.490858	S.D. of dependent var	23.57660
S.E. of regression	16.82289	Sum of squared resid	849.0290
Durbin-Watson stat	1.445195	F-statistic	4.856357
Log likelihood	−19.93133		

C. Dependent Variable is GROUP IIC ESTATES
Number of observations: 5

Variable	*Coefficient*	*Std. Error*	*T-Stat.*	*2-Tail Sig.*
C	*−42.869520*	*49.645926*	*−0.8635053*	*0.451*
ALPHITA *PRICES*	*32.073114*	*11.922122*	*2.6902185*	*0.074*

R-squared	0.706953	Mean of dependent var	89.40000
Adjusted R-squared	0.609271	S.D. of dependent var	24.61300
S.E. of regression	15.38517	Sum of squared resid	710.1108
Durbin-Watson stat	1.475606	F-statistic	7.237276
Log likelihood	−19.48465		

the two-tailed significance is greater than 0.1). Group IIC is another matter: 61 percent of its rent variation can be explained by variation in barley prices, and the correlation is significant.

Based though they are only a handful of data, these results are striking and important. There is a clear relationship between the absence of vines and the degree to which estate rents are linked to *alphita* prices; this link becomes almost absolute for Group I estates, which lacked vines entirely. No one can doubt that the renters of these estates had a clear idea of the local market value of the goods the estates produced, and that they calculated their bids accordingly. Furthermore, the increasingly strong correlation between rent and barley prices as one moves from Group IIA estates through Groups IIB and IIC to Group I casts doubt on the supposition, offered by Kent, Brunet, and others,[14] that herding was the main income-producing activity of estates without vines. In fact, it would seem that barley culture, not herding, was their chief business (although there was doubtless some herding on all of them, as they all had sheep shelters).[15] As I show below, there is no correlation of rents with pig prices except perhaps for Group I estates after ca. 220 B.C., which may represent a change in patterns of exploitation. But until then, and certainly always for Group IIC estates, barley was likely to have been their most important agricultural product.

OLIVE OIL PRICES AND RENTS

Even though none of the estates had any olives, some of their rents do show striking correlations with oil prices. The results for Group I estates are set out in figure 6.4 and table 6.6. Figure 6.4 makes it quite clear that, with the exception of the decade between 280 and 270 B.C., oil prices and rents for Group I estates were tightly linked. Indeed, 74 percent of the variation in rents can be explained simply by variation in oil prices (table 6.6). While we must be cautious about the implications of the single datum point available for before 290, there can be no doubt that from about 270 B.C. on, changes in the price of oil predict the changes in rent levels for these estates very well.

The story becomes more complicated in Group II estates. Figure 6.5 appears to reflect relations between oil prices and rents very like those iden-

14. Kent, 301 (no. XI, Hippodromos; XII, Leimon; XIV, Soloe-Korakia), 309–10; Brunet, 140–42; Bruno Cavagnola, *Istituto lombardo, rendiconti, Class. di lett. e sc. mor. e. stor.* 107 (1973): 513; Isager-Skydsgaard, 196–98 (less precise about which estates).

15. Kent, 300.

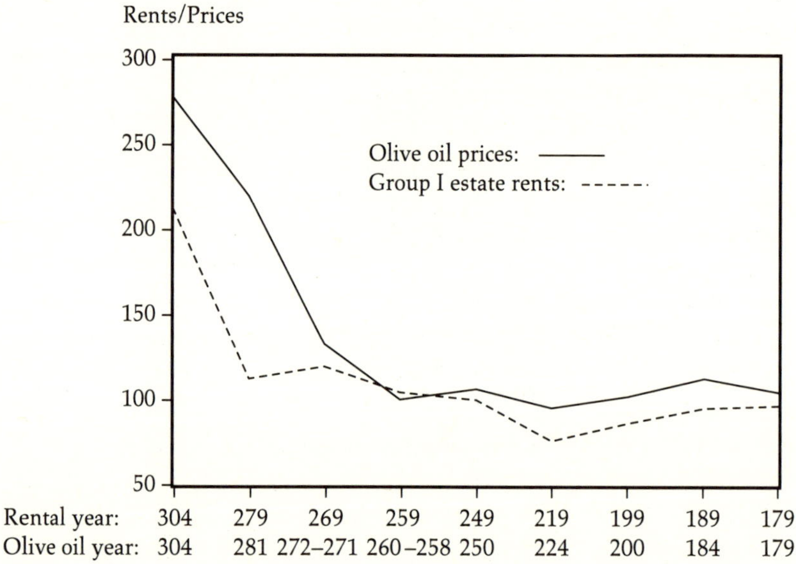

Figure 6.4. Correlation of Olive Oil Prices with Group I Estate Rents, 304–179 B.C.

Table 6.6. Group I Estate Rents and Olive Oil Prices

Dependent Variable is GROUP I ESTATES
Number of observations: 9

Variable	*Coefficient*	*Std. Error*	*T-Stat.*	*2-Tail Sig.*
C	*36.475718*	*16.909916*	*2.1570608*	*0.068*
OIL PRICES	*0.5399892*	*0.1117580*	*4.8317726*	*0.002*

R-squared	0.769327	Mean of dependent var	111.2222
Adjusted R-squared	0.736374	S.D. of dependent var	39.89918
S.E. of regression	20.48604	Sum of squared resid	2937.745
Durbin-Watson stat	2.704366	F-statistic	23.34603
Log likelihood	−38.81723		

tified for Group I estates; very interesting again, but difficult to interpret because of the extreme paucity of data points, are the apparent correlations between high prices and high rents (304–303 B.C.) and the rise in rents in the decade 280–270 while oil prices fell. For the decades after 270 B.C.,

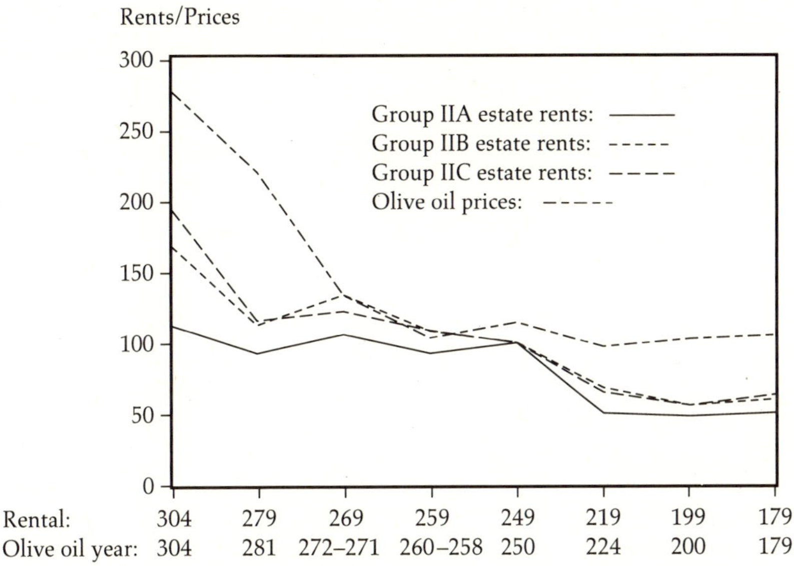

Figure 6.5. Correlation of Olive Oil Prices with Group II Estate Rents, 304–179 B.C.

however, the subgroups of Group II, although showing at least some correlation with oil prices, diverge from one another and from Group I in a very interesting way: the degree of correlation between oil prices and rents varies inversely according to the number of vines (table 6.7). Group IIA estates, which depended heavily on wine production, show poor correlation with oil prices. Only 23 percent of rent variation can be accounted for by changes in oil prices, the significance of the correlation is poor, and the amount of auto-correlation as measured by the Durbin-Watson is unacceptable. An attempt to correct for the latter eliminates all significance from the relationship.[16] In other words, decisions about the level of rents renters were willing to pay for Group IIA estates were essentially independent of oil-price levels. Rents for Group IIB and IIC estates, on the other hand (table 6.7 B, C), moved in conjunction with oil prices. Half of the variation in Group IIB estates, with a moderate number of vines, is linked to oil-price change; and fully 66 percent of the variation in Group IIC can be attributed to oil-price changes. This last figure approaches the result for Group I estates.

The first two patterns apparent for Group I estates seem reasonable.

16. As seen when the Cochrane-Orcutt procedure is applied, giving a two-tailed significance of 0.501 (!) and an adjusted R-squared of only 0.23.

Table 6.7. Group II Estate Rents and Olive Oil Prices

A. Dependent Variable is GROUP IIA ESTATES
Number of observations: 8

Variable	*Coefficient*	*Std. Error*	*T-Stat.*	*2-Tail Sig.*
C	*48.683496*	*20.288891*	*2.3995148*	*0.053*
OIL PRICES	*0.2305939*	*0.1304922*	*1.7671090*	*0.128*

R-squared	0.342298	Mean of dependent var	81.35000
Adjusted R-squared	0.232681	S.D. of dependent var	26.99820
S.E. of regression	23.64954	Sum of squared resid	3355.806
Durbin-Watson stat	1.089352	F-statistic	3.122674
Log likelihood	−35.50753		

B. Dependent Variable is GROUP IIB ESTATES
Number of observations: 8

Variable	*Coefficient*	*Std. Error*	*T-Stat.*	*2-Tail Sig.*
C	*38.254365*	*22.906971*	*1.6699879*	*0.146*
OIL PRICES	*0.4352026*	*0.1473309*	*2.9539128*	*0.025*

R-squared	0.592546	Mean of dependent var	99.90625
Adjusted R-squared	0.524637	S.D. of dependent var	38.72751
S.E. of regression	26.70128	Sum of squared resid	4277.751
Durbin-Watson stat	1.394123	F-statistic	8.725601
Log likelihood	−36.47847		

C. Dependent Variable is GROUP IIC ESTATES
Number of observations: 8

Variable	*Coefficient*	*Std. Error*	*T-Stat.*	*2-Tail Sig.*
C	*24.368805*	*22.322686*	*1.0916610*	*0.317*
OIL PRICES	*0.5480010*	*0.1435729*	*3.8168826*	*0.009*

R-squared	0.708293	Mean of dependent var	102.0000
Adjusted R-squared	0.659675	S.D. of dependent var	44.60301
S.E. of regression	26.02022	Sum of squared resid	4062.310
Durbin-Watson stat	1.605108	F-statistic	14.56859
Log likelihood	−36.27177		

High oil and high estate prices might be linked before 290 B.C., as many scholars have thought (but see below), but the data points are so few that it is very difficult to say. That rents and oil prices should move in different directions in the 270s occasions no surprise, since the estates had no olives and therefore their rents should not have been affected by oil prices.

But the results for the years after roughly 270 B.C. are striking. The pattern virtually reproduces the results for barley: the fewer the vines, the greater the link between oil prices and rents. These results seem strikingly to confirm D. Rathbone's view that "agricultural prices in general, including that of olive oil, are likely to have followed similar price trends in the long term."[17] But the linkage between oil and grain prices implied by the correlation of both with rents is itself puzzling. No clear mechanism accounts for it. The natural history of the two crops is very different (grain was planted in the fall/winter and harvested in the spring/summer; olives were harvested in the fall); their demands on labor fall at different times of year and at different levels; their rainfall requirements are strikingly different as regards both amount and timing. Most important, they cannot have been substitute goods, like wheat and barley. When wheat was scarce, consumers turned to barley, and the rising demand drove the price up. But it is hard to see why consumers unable to get barley would turn to oil, especially as oil was a relatively expensive product in antiquity anyway.

This correlation presents many questions, and it is impossible to offer a definitive solution. Reflection on the local situation on Delos and the neighboring Kyklades, however, may suggest a tentative hypothesis. In chapter 5, I argued that, after a period of dependence on extra-local sources for olive oil in the late fourth and early third centuries, Delians and their immediate neighbors planted olives and began to supply local needs from local sources. (The failure of the *hieropoioi* to plant olives on Apollo's estates must be attributed to reluctance to make the long-term investment on rented property.) This development reduced and stabilized oil prices. It would also have had an effect on the local price of land, for once the olives began to produce, their yields would have become part of the income-producing capital of the property they grew on. Oil prices would then generally have become a factor in the equation by which land values, and so rents, were set. This linkage would be still stronger if it was customary in the Kyklades—as would seem very likely—not to plant olives in dense orchards but to scatter them about the landscape with enough space in between to grow grains. Such a mechanism could explain why even rents for

17. D. Rathbone in *Eighth International Economic History Congress, Budapest 1982, ser. B12* (Budapest, 1982), 48.

Apollo's estates, which had no olives, followed oil prices. The power of this explanation must not be exaggerated. Unlike the correlation between rents and barley prices, that between rents and olive oil prices breaks down on occasion. This indicates that the tie is not direct, as I have argued for barley, but indirect, perhaps through the mechanism suggested here. Indeed, it seems likely that, rather than trying to explain rents as a dependent function of oil prices, we should seek a larger explanation to encompass both. My suggestion that planting olives helped to stabilize land prices is such a larger explanation, but, as we shall see in chapter 7, there are still other, more general, factors that need to be considered.

FIREWOOD PRICES AND RENTS

Not surprisingly, goods that moved in a different economic sector, with different constraints on production, show no price correlation with the estates: firewood prices fail entirely as predictors of rents. Firewood, of course, was produced in a very different way from grain or oil; and the estates entirely lacked copses where wood would have been gathered. It is therefore no surprise that firewood prices do not correlate with rents in any significant way.

LIVESTOCK PRICES AND RENTS

Livestock would seem to have been a different matter. The estate inventories assure us that many estates were equipped to run livestock, and Kent and others have supposed that herding was an important generator of income for many estates, including especially those of Group I. It is, however, difficult to test for a connection between livestock prices and rents. There can be no doubt that the majority of the estates' πρόβατα were sheep and goats, but prices for these animals are too few to try testing for a connection. Pig prices, of course, are abundant, but I hesitate to use them as a substitute. As I argued in chapter 5, pig prices were tied to firewood prices for reasons that seem to stem from the methods of raising hogs. This means that pig prices were set, at least in part, by mechanisms that had little or no impact on rents. Moreover, pigs and sheep or goats cannot be regarded as substitute goods. Whereas hogs provided only meat (and, of course, sacrificial victims), sheep and goats were raised primarily for milk and (in the case of sheep) wool; only secondarily did they themselves serve as food. Finally, pig prices were extremely volatile; they might fluctuate by 40 percent, 50 percent, or more from month to month. Such frequent and extreme changes may have made their prices useless for gauging the profitability of an estate.

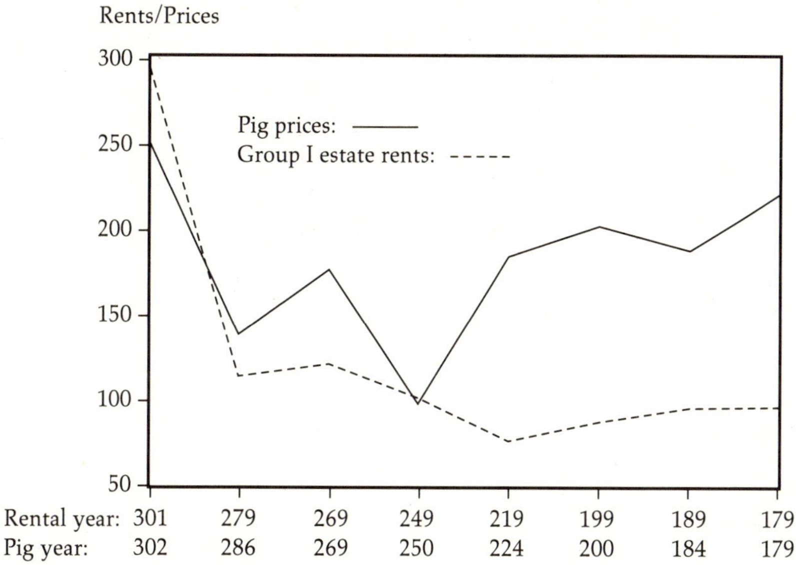

Figure 6.6. Correlation of Pig Prices with Group I Estate Rents, 301–179 B.C.

Yet pigs were surely raised on at least some estates (see chapter 5), and although over the whole period of independence, pig prices do no better than firewood as predictors of rents, they may have left a trace in the rents of Group I estates. Unlike the estates of Group II, these show a slight but definite rise in rent in the later third and second centuries. This period after ca. 220 B.C. is exactly the time when mean annual pig prices (following firewood) climbed to a new and permanently higher level (fig. 6.6). Although it is impossible to be sure, it may be that the renters of these estates, which were devoid of vines and had previously been devoted largely to cereal culture, began, in response to the rising price of pigs, to run more hogs, and thus to reckon the value of these enterprises in part in terms of pig prices. If this is right, it points to yet another shift in the economy of Delos in the late third century, to which I shall return in chapter 7.[18]

I cannot leave this topic without discussing one other issue, and that is the character of Phytalia, an estate that was regarded as an orchard until the recent join of *ID* 452 and 467 provided the first inventory for it, showing that it was devoid of any capital equipment at all.[19] Its rents show no

18. See the somewhat similar view expressed at Isager-Skydsgaard, 196–98.

19. W. Déonna, *La Vie privée des Déliens* (Paris, 1948), 96, and *BCH* 70 (1946): 160; Kent, 254 n. 25; Vial, 323 (a *jardin*). For the join, see n. 9; for the inventory, see ll. 24–25.

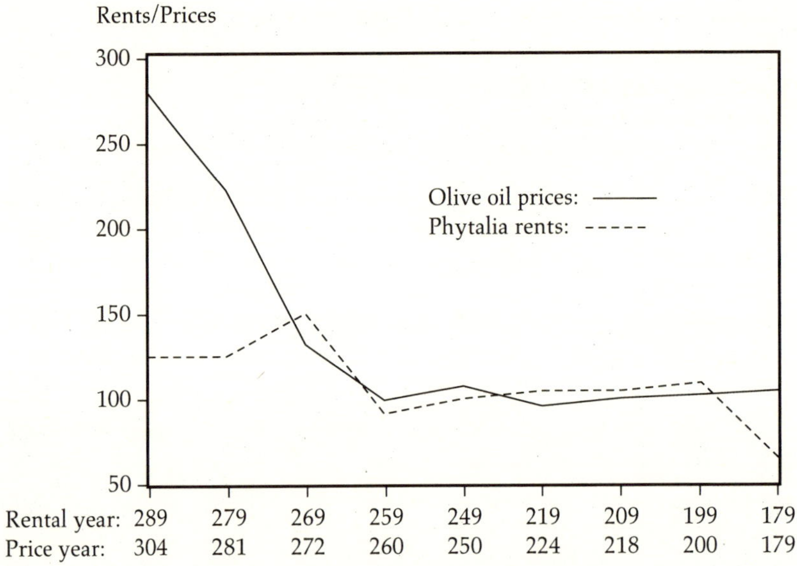

Figure 6.7. Olive Oil Prices and Rents for Phytalia, 290–179 B.C.

important correlation with barley prices and a correlation of about 40 percent with oil prices (fig. 6.7, table 6.8). The absence of any correlation with barley prices makes it very unlikely that Phytalia was, as Brunet suggests, γῆ ψιλή devoted to barley culture,[20] and the moderate correlation with oil (roughly between the responses of Group IIB and IIC) reflects only the general impact of oil prices on the rent of land on Delos. What was Phytalia then? It may be that here, and here only, we have a true ranch: a tract of land without capital equipment, used by renters to run sheep, goats, or other livestock, which were housed elsewhere.

The results of this section are very important, for despite the few data points on which they rest, they are remarkably consistent: the rents fetched by agricultural land on Delos were linked to and in part determined by the price levels of important agricultural commodities. This linkage expressed itself most strongly in the estates of Groups I and IIC, and to a lesser extent Group IIB, which had no, or relatively few, vines. Barley culture provided the direct connection, since these estates in fact produced barley. The tie with olive oil, at first sight surprising, can probably be explained by the

20. Brunet, 146; cf. *BCH* 114 (1990): 679.

Table 6.8. Rents for Phytalia and Olive Oil Prices, 272–169 B.C.

Dependent Variable is RENTS FOR PHYTALIA
Number of observations: 7

Variable	*Coefficient*	*Std. Error*	*T-Stat.*	*2-Tail Sig.*
C	*−56.948398*	*71.652776*	*−0.7947829*	*0.463*
OIL PRICES	*1.5120537*	*0.6771778*	*2.2328754*	*0.076*

R-squared	0.499286	Mean of dependent var	102.1629
Adjusted R-squared	0.399143	S.D. of dependent var	25.62244
S.E. of regression	19.86123	Sum of squared resid	1972.342
Durbin-Watson stat	1.508424	F-statistic	4.985732
Log likelihood	−29.67630		

role oil played on land in private possession on Delos and its nearest neighbors.

These two basic staples, barley and olive oil, which were locally produced and locally consumed, were thus closely linked in the local economy, and rents were tied to them. This sheds welcome light on a very important aspect of the local economy. In contrast, growing grapes and running livestock seem to have taken place in a different sphere. Livestock have left surprisingly little impact in our data, although the picture might be quite different if we had a set of prices for sheep or goats comparable to those for pigs. Viticulture, of course, was aimed mostly at wine production, and we shall have to test Kent's idea that declining wine prices after 250 B.C. depressed the values of Group II estates. Whether we can say a "universal price-setting market" for wine existed will depend in part on the results of that investigation.

Rent History until 290 B.C. and Kent's Wine Hypothesis

Two important phenomena in the rent histories of the estates have long been noticed: the drastic collapse of rents in 290 B.C., and a slower decline after 220 B.C., which Kent attributes to depressed wine prices.[21] Both of these phenomena can be confirmed by statistical analysis, which

21. Kent, 302, Larsen, 401–7, Heichelheim, *Wirt. Schw.*, 82–83, Gustave Glotz, *Journal des Savants* 11 (1913): 19–20. Kent, 310, 299–301; 309–13.

however also reveals new and important differences among the groups of estates.

The rent history of Group I estates responds very nicely to a model that attributes almost all of the change in their rents to a turnaround in 290 B.C. This model explains fully 72 percent of the variation in rents and indicates an extremely strong response to the watershed; rents decline by almost 106 units (table 6.9). There is, however, no improvement in explanation if the model is modified by adding a dummy variable for the period after 220 B.C. This is an important result, since it seems to confirm Kent's view: these estates without any vines at all are not affected by his proposed decline in wine prices over the second half of the third century.

For Group IIA estates the best model incorporates dummy variables for both 290 B.C. and for Kent's wine factor, taken as a watershed at 220 B.C. This model accounts for fully 88 percent of the variation in rents with good statistics (the Durbin-Watson is marginal but acceptable). It is interesting that the coefficient for 290 B.C. represents a much more modest response than that for Group I estates (table 6.10).

Group IIB estates, which had 1,550–1,000 vines, follow a pattern similar to that of Group IIA estates (table 6.11). Eighty-three percent of their rent variation can be attributed to the two factors, 290 B.C. and Kent's wine hypothesis. The response of rents to the watershed years, however, is rather different from those for the IIA estates. The decline in 290 B.C. amounts to 61 units, or 2.25 times greater than for IIA estates, while the decline in 220 B.C. of 48 units is essentially the same as that for IIA estates.

The same pattern obtains for Group IIC estates (table 6.12). Again, the

Table 6.9. Group I Estate Rents, Sorted before and after 290 B.C.

Dependent Variable is GROUP I ESTATES
Number of observations: 15

Variable	*Coefficient*	*Std. Error*	*T-Stat.*	*2-Tail Sig.*
C	*203.40000*	*14.146106*	*14.378515*	*0.000*
290 B.C.	*−105.70000*	*17.325370*	*−6.1008796*	*0.000*

R-squared	0.741143	Mean of dependent var	132.9333
Adjusted R-squared	0.721231	S.D. of dependent var	59.91001
S.E. of regression	31.63165	Sum of squared resid	13007.30
Durbin-Watson stat	1.967533	F-statistic	37.22073
Log likelihood	−72.02320		

Table 6.10. Group IIA Estate Rents, Sorted before and after 290 B.C., and by Kent's Wine Price Factor

Dependent Variable is GROUP IIA ESTATES
Number of observations: 12

Variable	*Coefficient*	*Std. Error*	*T-Stat.*	*2-Tail Sig.*
C	*121.63333*	*6.0072939*	*20.247608*	*0.000*
290 B.C.	*−27.113330*	*7.5986925*	*−3.5681573*	*0.006*
WINE	*−44.470001*	*6.9798448*	*−6.3712020*	*0.000*

R-squared	0.905525	Mean of dependent var	86.47500
Adjusted R-squared	0.884530	S.D. of dependent var	30.61999
S.E. of regression	10.40494	Sum of squared resid	974.3647
Durbin-Watson stat	2.597124	F-statistic	43.13145
Log likelihood	−43.40854		

Table 6.11. Group IIB Estate Rents, Sorted before and after 290 B.C., and by Kent's Wine Price Factor

Dependent Variable is GROUP IIB ESTATES
Number of observations: 12

Variable	*Coefficient*	*Std. Error*	*T-Stat.*	*2-Tail Sig.*
C	*172.16667*	*11.040772*	*15.593716*	*0.000*
290 B.C.	*−61.966667*	*13.965595*	*−4.4370947*	*0.002*
WINE	*−48.762500*	*12.828218*	*−3.8011905*	*0.004*

R-squared	0.864641	Mean of dependent var	109.4375
Adjusted R-squared	0.834561	S.D. of dependent var	47.01549
S.E. of regression	19.12318	Sum of squared resid	3291.264
Durbin-Watson stat	1.945140	F-statistic	28.74485
Log likelihood	−50.71198		

model accounts for 87 percent of the rent variation, and the coefficients that represent the response to each factor are close to those of the Group IIB estates. On the evidence of these results, Groups IIB and IIC clearly belong together. Group IIA estates stand apart in their more moderate response to the change in 290 B.C.

Table 6.12. Group IIC Estate Rents, Sorted before and after 290 B.C., and by Kent's Wine Price Factor

Dependent Variable is GROUP IIC ESTATES
Number of observations: 14

Variable	*Coefficient*	*Std. Error*	*T-Stat.*	*2-Tail Sig.*
C	*179.40000*	*8.3960489*	*21.367193*	*0.000*
290 B.C.	*−67.000000*	*11.873806*	*−5.6426725*	*0.000*
WINE	*−50.150000*	*12.594073*	*−3.9820318*	*0.002*

R-squared	0.889515	Mean of dependent var	122.0000
Adjusted R-squared	0.869426	S.D. of dependent var	51.95560
S.E. of regression	18.77414	Sum of squared resid	3877.150
Durbin-Watson stat	1.844195	F-statistic	44.28038
Log likelihood	−59.23173		

RENT LEVELS, 314–290 B.C.

The results show unequivocally that important adjustments in estate rent levels occurred on Delos for all estates around 290 B.C. Before 290, rents were extraordinarily high, and they collapsed in that year; they never again reached levels even approaching the dizzying heights of the late fourth century. Several hypotheses have been offered to account for these extraordinarily high rents. Fritz Heichelheim and others have pointed to the high prices for agricultural commodities for the same period and suggested that these prices, attributed to the great demand for "Greek goods" by the new settlers in the East, drove up rents.[22] The close tie found above between agricultural prices and estate rents would seem to support this view, and indeed it must be admitted that oil prices at least were very high in this period.

There are, however, some problems with this view. Consider first the link between prices and rents. Group I estates show the tightest correlation with *alphita* prices (fig. 6.2). This correlation can be used to work out a very rough formula for calculating putative barley prices from rents (multiplying the rent by about 0.0422 gives an *alphita* price in dr). By this formula, barley prices in 314–290 B.C. ought to have ranged from a low of 6.9 dr/*med* in 310 to a high of 12.4 dr/*med* in 301 B.C.; the average price would have been 8.6 and the median 7.3 dr/*med* (cf. table 6.3). These prices

22. Heichelheim, *Wirt. Sch.*, 55–56; Larsen, 380; Rostovtzeff, 165–66; cf. also H. Michell, *Canadian Journal of Economics and Political Science* 12 (1946): 3–7.

are extraordinarily high; indeed, the highest *alphita* price actually attested on Delos is only 5 dr/*med*, in a year generally considered to have seen a severe shortage.[23] Such prices, persisting over twenty-five years, would have represented a disaster of enormous proportions, far more serious than the shortages that beset Athens in the 330s and 320s.[24] It is hard to believe that such a situation would have left no traces in the sources at all.

Furthermore, it is difficult to understand how exactly the high commodity prices are supposed to have raised land rents. Barley was produced in abundance in the Greek East, sown certainly from the first day the colonists arrived (see App. *Syr.* 1.1). It is hard to imagine an eastern demand for barley lasting twenty-five years that could drive up prices at Delos to as high as three or four times the typical price level in the mid third century. Oil is another matter, since trees require many years to produce new crops; but here is a puzzle too. The Delian estates produced no oil. The tie elucidated above between oil prices and rents works well in a market of relatively stable oil prices, in which olive-bearing land is priced in the same local market as land without olives, but these relations would be broken in a market in which oil prices were high and rising, especially if grain prices were relatively unaffected. Under those conditions, it would be much more profitable to rent property with olives, and Apollo's estates would *lose* value. Appeal cannot be made to vines as the decisive crop (like olives, vines need some time to begin producing once planted) because Group I estates, which entirely lacked vines, show the highest rents before 290, and Group IIA estates, which had the most vines, show the least decline in 290 B.C. Moreover, the telltale data of 280–270 B.C. deserve close attention. In that decade, rents rose while oil prices declined. This strongly suggests that the link between oil prices and rents that obtained after 270 may not have prevailed before; that is to say, the high oil prices and high rents may not be causally linked. Finally, our study of oil prices in chapter 5 has found an alternative explanation for the high and declining oil prices of 314–270 B.C.

Jacques Tréheux has offered a quite different explanation for the rent collapse of 290 B.C.[25] Renewal of four estates in Bouphonion 314 B.C. by Delians, evidently for a 10 percent increase in rent, suggests that ἐπιδέκατον renewals practiced during independence were also permitted un-

23. See Appendix IV, p. 306, below. Glotz, *Journal des Savants* 11 (1913): 19–20, with *REG* 31 (1918): 214; Jardé, 169–70, 170 (cf. Shear, 31); Larsen, 383–84; Heichelheim, *Wirt. Schw.*, 51, and "Sitos," cols. 857–58; Roebuck, *CP* 40 (1945): 159–61; Kevin Clinton, *Arch. Eph.* (1971): 110–11; Foxhall-Forbes, 53–55; Garnsey, 25. But see G. Reger, *Classical Antiquity* 12 (1993): 304–14.

24. Garnsey, 154–62.

25. Tréheux, "Dernières Années," 1011–22.

der the Amphiktyonia. Applying successive 10 percent increases to rents known for some estates in 350 B.C. (*ID* 104–11A8–21 [= *IG* II^2 1638]) yields rents close to those attested for the same estates in 315 B.C., the last year of the Amphiktyonia (*IG* XI 2.135). From this, Tréheux argues that renters accepted 10 percent increases at renewal because the real rental value of the properties had risen by more than 10 percent. Thus, prices must have been rising too since at least the late 340s, well before the Greek expansion to the East. The Delian rises of early independence would just continue this phenomenon.

But this view is not wholly satisfactory either. First, for most of the estates, the really impressive rises occurred, not on the cusp of independence, but between 310 and 300 B.C., when rises of 20–40 percent were typical and 75 percent not unknown (see table 6.1). Thus it seems evident that the truly dramatic rise in estate rents was not connected with the late Amphiktyonia, but with the early years of independence. Second, if a substantial number of renters were Athenians, rents may have been set in part by comparison with costs in Athens. Third, factors other than purely economic ones may have predisposed renters to retain their estates; there may have been some prestige associated with renting land on sacred Delos. In the absence of detailed knowledge of the rent histories of 340–320 B.C., it is impossible to sort out such considerations. Fourth, this explanation begs the question to some extent, for it still fails to present the reasons why rents should have been rising.

J. H. Kent and Michèle Brunet have taken related approaches to the problem. Kent argued that defaults by renters before 290 led the *hieropoioi* to try to protect Apollo's interests by proceeding against other persons who had borrowed money from the temple and failed to repay it. They seized their property, hypothecated as security, and these processes discouraged other renters. He explains the high rents themselves by suggesting that the Delians were "possibly moved as well by a false optimism engendered by their newly acquired independence."[26] Brunet, who saw how unsatisfactory this account was, postulated instead that a rising demand for estates after 314 (more on this later), which fueled the rise in rents, drove the *hieropoioi* to seize insolvent debtors' property as a mechanism to satisfy demand for more estates to rent.[27] But her view, no more than Kent's, fails to explain the connection between high rents and the failure of debtors. In an "inflationary" economy (Brunet's term), debts should

26. Kent, 284–85; 308 (quotation), followed by Cavagnola, *Istituto lombardo, rendiconti* 107 (1973): 539–40.

27. Brunet, 62–64; cf. esp. 63.

be easier, not harder, to pay, especially for estate owners presumably benefiting from high agricultural prices.[28] Moreover, she offers no explanation for this expanded demand for the estates, although she does properly insist on looking for it in local circumstances, and not, like Heichelheim and his followers, in some general universal price rise.

Most important, none of these views really comes to grips with the two most puzzling aspects of the problem: why should the collapse have occurred exactly in 290, and why did different groups of estates behave differently? I would like to explore a very different kind of explanation. I argue that the Delians, "locked out" of investment in sacred properties during the Amphiktyonia, rushed to seize the opportunity once the Athenians departed. (The fact that the greatest rent rises occurred between 310 and 300 B.C. supports this view.) Rapid turnover of renters coupled with the desire to have property pushed estate values up precipitously until some defaults occurred. The Delians, realizing that the estates were overvalued, promulgated new regulations for estate rental, the *hiera syngraphe* (*ID* 503), to protect Apollo's interests. These regulations greatly decreased the desirability of the estates, and hence lowered the rents; in exchange, Apollo's interests were strongly protected, and only the wealthiest and best-connected families would be able to compete for the estates.

RENTAL PRACTICE IN THE LATER AMPHIKTYONIC PERIOD (350–315 B.C.) AND DURING EARLY INDEPENDENCE (314–290 B.C.)

Estate rents had very probably been rising on Delos since about 350 B.C. Jacques Tréheux has offered a persuasive, although not conclusive, argument that most estates were renewed for an ἐπιδέκατον (a 10 percent rise in rent) in 340, 330, and 320 B.C. Even though it does not follow that the "real value" of the estates must have been substantially higher, such renewals would have established a pattern of increases at renewal that might have persuaded Delian bidders after 314 B.C. that even higher rents were reasonable, laying the groundwork for the really spectacular rises of 310–300 B.C.

Since the Athenians (with, from time to time, the help of Andrians) controlled the sanctuary in this period, it seems reasonable to ask whether the Athenian administrators favored their countrymen in renting the estates. At first sight, the evidence for the origins of renters (whether of estates or houses) does not seem to support the view that Delians had trouble renting Apollo's property. The evidence is unfortunately exigu-

28. Kent, 302 n. 199; Brunet, 62.

ous;[29] only a handful of inscriptions give ethnics for renters. In the case of the sacred houses, one document (*ID* 104–8B1–51) shows probably a total of seventeen Athenian renters (including one Athenian metic) against nine Delians.[30] The six inscriptions that offer some evidence about the estates yield only four Athenian renters as opposed to nine or ten Delians and one Tenian.[31] Delians seem to have done well against their Athenian competition.

But it would be a mistake to conclude from this evidence that there was no pent-up demand on Delos for Apollo's property. The ratio of Delian to Athenian renters seems to have changed from rental period to rental period. *ID* 104–21, which dates to about 346 B.C.,[32] reports only one Athenian renter against five Delians. But *ID* 104–26, which may date to 350 B.C.,[33] has three Athenians and two or three Delians. Tréheux has pointed out that four estates seem to have been in the hands of Delians in 314 B.C., for they were allowed to accept a rent rise of 10 percent in return for not having to bid competitively for the estates.[34] The rest of the estates passed into new hands. It may be that some of the other estates were in the hands of Delians who preferred to take their chances in the bidding and lost out, but it seems more reasonable to me to suppose that the renters had been Athenians, now dispossessed. The pattern of renewals by ἐπιδέκατον that Tréheux reconstructs would have made the procedure seem normal to those in a position to take advantage of it, like the four Delians.[35] There is evidence of tightening Athenian control after midcentury, and particularly

29. The discussion of the evidence by Tréheux, "Dernières Années," 1021–22, has been superseded now that the texts of *ID* are available; cf. also J. Coupry in *Atti del terzio congresso* (Rome, 1959), 63–64. Unfortunately, the detailed treatment promised by Coupry in his *Athènes et Apollon Délien: Recherches sur l'histoire de Délos, de l'époque de Pisistrate à l'époque d'Alexandre le Grand* has not yet appeared.

30. Cf. Coupry's comm. at *ID*, p. 64. Tréheux's conclusions ("Dernières Années," 1021) depend on the less reliable text at *BCH* 29 (1905): 423–24, no. 140. On the date, see J. Tréheux, *EAC* 5 (1976): 92 n. 56.

31. *ID* 98Ab105, 104-19A7–14, 104–20 (rerental after a default, cf. Coupry, *ID*, p. 83, and Brunet, 26–27), 104–21bA10, 12 and bB5–21, 104-26A9–24, 104-26*bis*A'. Cf. Coupry, *ID*, pp. 87, 104.

32. See J. Coupry, *Atti*, 64.

33. Brunet, 36.

34. Tréheux, "Dernières Années," 1011, 1022. The practice is permitted by the *hiera syngraphe* (*IG* XI 2.287A174; the apposite clauses of *ID* 503 have been lost, but see Kent, 270), and was evidently already allowed under the Amphiktyonia if Tréheux is correct; cf. also Kent, 260 n. 49, who suggests that the rent figures of *ID* 102.8–9 (ref. to *BCH* 8 [1884]: 313, no. 15) may reflect 10 percent renewals.

35. The study of names in individual documents yields meager results; see Tréheux, "Dernières Années," 1021–22. For example, *ID* 104-11A8–21 (= *IG* II²

after the decision of the Delphic Amphiktyonia in 344 B.C. confirming the Athenians' right to control the temple.[36] It is therefore quite possible that only four estates were in Delian hands in 314 B.C. The impact of even a few Athenian renters should not be underestimated. Apollo's patrimony included only eight or ten estates under the Amphiktyonia, and the right of Athenians to rent them reduced the number available to locals. The fierce competition among Delians after 314 B.C. strongly suggests that even a modest Athenian contingent would have restricted the locals.

There is another, even more important factor. As Jacques Coupry has emphasized, all guarantors certainly identified, whether acting for renters of estates or renters of houses, were Athenians.[37] Since no one could rent sacred property without guarantors, all Delians without strong ties in the Athenian community were effectively debarred from Apollo's property. Only Delian "collaborators" could exercise the theoretical right of Delians to rent from the god. We know from documents like *IG* II^2 222 the hostility that a Delian's friendliness to the Athenians could provoke among his fellow citizens. It would not be surprising if only a small minority of those Delians wealthy enough to rent property had the taste for collaboration—and the connections in Athens—necessary to indulge themselves.

In any case, there can be no doubt that the Delians moved aggressively in the fall of 314 B.C. to extirpate every remnant of Athenian control from their newly liberated island. As Tréheux has shown, they cancelled leases in force in late 314 for the τέλη that had been let out under the Athenians in 315 B.C. and replaced them with temporary leases good only until the beginning of the next Delian year in Lenaion. Estate leases were cancelled as well and replaced with new four-year leases that ran until 310 B.C.[38] Tréheux has even suggested that the Delians may have confiscated the Andrian οἶκος as punishment for Andrian cooperation with the Athenian masters.[39]

1638) lists individual estates and renters, but the names are given without patronymics or ethnics, except for an entry reading "Renter, Phoinix the Tenian" ([μισθωτ]ὴς Φοῖνιξ Τήνιος, A20). The other documents give only sum total rents. In one case, however—*ID* 98Ab101–111 (= *IG* II^2 1635Ab) of 376/5–375/4 B.C.—a few fragments of rental agreements are preserved. These show the rental of an estate by someone, son of Stesimbrotos, Delian, with perhaps at least one Delian guarantor (*ID* 98Ab104, 105 = *IG* II^2 1635). These examples suggest—but do not prove—that the names recorded without patronymic or ethnic elsewhere in this inscription may have belonged to Athenians.

36. Cf. *ID* 104–22, with Coupry's comments, pp. 89–90.

37. Coupry in *Atti*, 64. One possible exception at *ID* 98 Ab105.

38. Tréheux, "Dernières Années," 1011–12, 1028–31.

39. Jacques Tréheux in *Stemmata*, 386.

Over the next few years, leases were renewed on a quite irregular basis, as we have seen, with four different leasing periods between 315 and 300 B.C. The irregularity of rental strongly mitigates, in my view, against the presumption that the regulations that had covered estate rentals during the Amphiktyonia continued in force after 314 with little break.[40] Although the *hieropoioi* accepted renewal with an ἐπιδέκατον certainly once, and possibly twice more,[41] the abandonment of the ten-year leases of the amphiktyonic period, the relative rarity of 10 percent renewal, and the apparently ad hoc procedures followed during foreclosures for failure to pay the rent (see below) strongly suggest that the *hieropoioi* had abandoned Athenian administrative practice. Their willingness to do so may be related to the dramatic rises in rents after 314 and especially 310 B.C.

Competition among renters for the estates was fierce during these two decades. It is unusual for the same man to rent an estate for two consecutive lease cycles (only three or four instances out of seventy-five rental periods [fifteen estates × five rental periods each]). Table 6.1 shows how often and by how much competing renters were willing to bid each other up for control of the estates on very short-term leases.

The lessees belonged to the highest circles of Delian society. Twenty-eight out of fifty-nine different renters for the estates between 314 and 282 B.C. can be assigned with certainty or high probability to wealthy, highly placed Delian families. Among them are Lysixenos son of Aristoboulos, *arkhon* of 301 B.C. and renter of Lykoneion; Skymnos, another

40. Tréheux, "Dernières Années," 1012: "les hiéropes de l'Indépendance n'ont fait, le plus souvent, en matière juridique, que reprendre à leur compte les méthodes des administrateurs athéniens et les différences qu'on observe entre les deux gestions sont moins de principe que d'application." Cf. also Tréheux, *BCH* 68–69 (1944–45): 294–95. I do not see how Tréheux can claim that "the *hieropoioi* must have followed [the amphiktyonic *hiera syngraphe*] up to the publication of the new text" (i.e., the *hiera syngraphe* in *ID* 503) when, as he himself admits, they violated the ten-year lease provisions of that regulation again and again after 314 B.C. (ibid., 293). On the amphiktyonic ten-year lease, see also Kent, 259–260 (probable but not certain); Tréheux, "Dernières Années," 1012 (implicitly accepted); Durrbach, *BCH* 29 (1905): 443, and 35 (1911): 19.

41. See table 6.1. In two cases, however, the "renewer" is in fact a different person; in two more (*IG* XI 2.142.1–4) the names of the renters are not preserved (although the rents increase by 10 percent between this lease and the one represented in *IG* XI 2.144), and given the first two cases, there is no warrant to assume that the same persons were renters. The only solid case is that of Panormos, rented by Maisiades in 304 B.C. for 925 dr and again in 300 and later for 1,030 (*IG* XI 2.144A12, 149.5–6, 147A15–17). On the practice, see Maurice Lacroix, *BCH* 56 (1932): 373; J. H. Kent, *BCH* 63 (1939): 233; and Tréheux, *BCH* 68–69 (1944–45): 285.

renter of Lykoneion, who is probably the homonymous *hieropoios* of 298 B.C.; Empedokles, renter of Nikou Khoros, who guaranteed a state loan; and Amnos son of Dexikrates, who moved two decrees in the assembly and rented Skitoneia. These were the people who controlled Delian political life; for them, as a traditional Greek aristocracy, investment in land was an important social desideratum. As soon as the opportunity arose, they rushed to capture sacred leases, and the competition was apparently fierce.[42]

This competition must at first have appealed to the *hieropoioi* charged with the administration of the sacred estates. They could offer quite short leases—perhaps as little as two years—permitting rapid turnover in renters, and usually guaranteeing increasing revenues for Apollo. Already by the second lease period, however, some potential difficulties had begun to emerge. Sometime during that lease period, two renters failed to fulfill their obligations and were dispossessed (*IG* XI 2.142.5–12). In neither case were the *hieropoioi* able to exact the full rent due by sale of crops and farm animals, or by exaction from guarantors; Apollo took a loss of at least 645 dr. Additional payments, called ἐπαναβληθέν in *IG* XI 2.142.2–4, may indicate difficulties with other estates; the year was unusual enough to be remembered almost twenty years later as τὸν ἐνιαυτὸν τοῦ ἐπαναβληθέντος.[43] In 304 B.C., there was another default, but because the crucial figures are missing, it is not possible to know whether the *hieropoioi* succeeded in exacting the full amount from the renter's guarantors.[44] Four years later, yet another renter defaulted; the *hieropoioi* record his guarantor's partial payment of the back rent (*IG* XI 2.147A15–17). The record shows four defaults in ten years.

It is not difficult to imagine the problems these losses posed for the Delian community. On the one hand, Apollo's interests wanted protection. The god looked for steady, reliable income from his estates, and that meant above all renters and guarantors wealthy enough to cover any potential losses. On the other hand, the Delian aristocrats who rented the estates, and especially any belonging to levels of Delian society under the very top, had social and economic interests in the prevailing system, which permit-

42. Kent, 330, no. 145 (*IG* XI 2.145.46); Kent, 334, no. 211, Vial, 263, Stemma XXI; Kent, 326, no. 83, Vial, 334; Vial, 133, with n. 31. For full details of the renters, see Kent, 320–38; Vial, passim; and Bruno Cavagnola, *Istituto lombardo, rendiconti, Class. di lett. e sc. mor. e stor.* 106 (1972): 51–115, esp. 90–110. Cf. also Robin Osborne, *Chiron* 18 (1988): 299–300. On the social position and attitudes of upper-class Delians, see the detailed and definitive study by Vial, 253–74, 283–306, 317–56.

43. *IG* XI 2.156A14; Tréheux, *BCH* 68–69 (1944–45): 284–85.

44. *IG* XI 2.144B13, 78–81. The estate has evidently been rerented at ll. A13 and B78–81; cf. J. H. Kent, *BCH* 38 (1939): 235.

ted many different people to profit from Apollo's holdings, albeit at rather high risk.

THE IMPACT OF THE *HIERA SYNGRAPHE* (*ID* 503)

The *hiera syngraphe,* first put into effect with the leasing period of 299–290 B.C.,[45] seems to have been designed to solve these problems. The text preserved sets out in great detail regulations to govern the rental of Delian estates. Among the provisions are stricter requirements for guarantors (who now must be renewed annually) and detailed regulations covering payment of rent and default. As Kent suggested many years ago, these regulations seem clearly intended to prevent further serious defaults.[46] In particular, two strong, broad clauses subjected all the belongings of the renters and their guarantors to seizure: εἰὰν ⟨ειαν⟩ δέ, κ[αὶ] τούτων (crops, plow oxen, livestock, and slaves) πραθέντων, ἔτι ἐλλείπει τι τοῦ μισθώματος, εἰσπρασσόντων [the *hieropoioi*] τὸ ἐλλεῖπον ἐκ τῶν ὑπαρχόντων τοῖς μεμισθωμένοις καὶ ἐγγυηταῖς and ὑποκεῖσθαι δὲ τῶι θεῶι τὰ βοσκήματα καὶ τὰ ἀνδράποδα καὶ τὰ ἐνοικεῖα [καὶ] τὰ [ὑπάρχοντα] πάντα, ὅσα ὑπάρχει τοῖς μεμισθωμένοις, and ὑποκεῖσθαι δὲ καὶ τὰ τοῖς ἐγγυηταῖς ὑπάρχοντα πάντα τῶι θεῶι καθάπερ τὰ τοῦ μεμισθω⟨σα⟩μένου.[47] Had the *hiera syngraphe* been in effect in the 300s, this clause would have permitted much more comprehensive action against the defaulters of *IG* XI 2.142.5–12, whose personal goods were not expropriated, even though Apollo failed to get full restitution after the seizure of Hermadas's barley crop and Arkhandros's barley crop and plow team. Under the *hiera syngraphe,* a renter and his guarantors who failed to pay the full rent, or violated certain other regulations, might theoretically find not just the investment in the estate—crops, oxen, livestock, and slaves—but their entire personal fortunes in jeopardy. The threat alone might have made rental of estates seem riskier after 300 B.C. But did the *hieropoioi* ever in fact proceed with such vigor against defaulters?

45. On the date, see Appendix I.

46. Pierre Roussel, *Délos colonie athénienne* (Paris, 1916), 73 (on the attitude of the Athenian administrators); Kent, 279–80, 285; Tréheux, *BCH* 68–69 (1944–45): 290–92, 295 (pointing out however that not all provisions were strengthened, only those covering default); Kent, 267–89; Marie-Françoise Baslez, *REG* 89 (1976): 347–48; Dieter Hennig, *Chiron* 13 (1983): 442–43 n. 71. Brunet, 62; contra, Erich Ziebarth, *Hermes* 61 (1926): 96–97, whose views Tréheux answers, however. Cf. also Felix Durrbach, *BCH* 35 (1911): 25–29, and René Vallois, *BCH* 55 (1931): 290–91.

47. *ID* 503.34–36, 46–48; cf. Kent, 282.

A good deal of circumstantial evidence strongly hints that they did.[48] I argue that the efforts of the *hieropoioi* to prosecute defaulters under these new and stronger regulations had two important consequences: (a) the possessions of Apollo were increased by seizure of land and houses from defaulting renters, which (b) helped considerably to reduce the appeal of the estates, and hence the rents to which renters were willing to commit.

Let us consider three cases.

(1) In 297 B.C., one Autosthenes was renting Dionysios for 1,372 dr. His guarantor was Kleokritos son of Hermon (*IG* XI 2.149.6–7, 11–12), whose prominent and wealthy family counted among its members a *hieropoios* of 297 and a *khoregos* in 255 B.C. The family had extensive interests in the sacred estates, three members having rented four different estates at different times.[49]

In 314 B.C., Kleokritos's father, Hermon son of Kleokritos, paid interest of 150 dr on behalf of one Sosimakhos (*IG* XI 2.135.26–27). Hypothecated land or a house or both must lie behind this payment. Payments "on behalf of someone" were usually made either by guarantors or heirs (the guarantors themselves often being relatives with an interest in the hypothecated property) or by outsiders who bought the hypothecated property and assumed the debt that accompanied it.[50] Thus it is fairly certain that Sosimakhos's property had come into the hands of Hermon's family by 314 B.C.

If Autosthenes had defaulted at a time during his rental of Dionysios when Kleokritos was his guarantor, Kleokritos's property would have been "subject to the god" under the rules of the *hiera syngraphe*. If Autosthenes' debt could not be collected from his livestock and slaves, the *hieropoioi* would have proceeded against his real goods and those of his guarantors.

48. Vial, 224, rejects the possibility: "il est peu vraisemblable que les hiéropes aient jamais saisi les biens personnels du fermier et de ses garants" and at n. 137 cites the *hieropoioi*'s failure to seize the personal property of Hermadas and Arkhandros in 305 B.C. or slightly earlier. But the *hiera syngraphe* was not in force before 300 B.C., and Vial's parallels—failure to act against defaulting house renters, tax-farmers, or borrowers—founder on our ignorance of the conditions that governed these transactions. (If *ID* 499 is a regulation governing loans, it remains unfortunately too fragmentary to be very informative.) The evidence outlined below, if correctly interpreted, outweighs these theoretical considerations.

49. See Vial, 322, Stemma XXXI, for full details and references.

50. For inheritance, see, e.g., *IG* XI 2.135.19–20 and 142.14; 199A11 and many other entries, with Vial, 82–83, Stemma XII, 372, no. 124; for the case of Apollodoros of Kyzikos, who bought a hypothecated garden (*IG* XI 2.142.14–15), see G. Reger, *GRBS* 32 (1991): 229–37; another example at *IG* XI 2.287A15 with Vial, 295, Stemma XXV.

In this way, Sosimakhos's land, now in Kleokritos's family's possession, might have fallen into the hands of Apollo, becoming the sacred estate Sosimakheia, known first from the rental period of 289–280 B.C.[51]

There is more. It would be strange if the *hieropoioi* had foreclosed on Kleokritos without also acting against the renter himself. Among the renters of the sacred houses appears the name of Autosthenes, who rented "the house that belonged to the children of Aristoboulos" (τῆς οἰκίας ἣ ἦν τῶν παίδων τῶν Ἀριστοβούλου) in 279 and 278 (*IG* XI 2.161A18–19, 162A18). Like many other houses, this one is not attested during the Amphiktyonia, appearing first only in the 280s (*IG* XI 2.156A1, 158A23). It was not unknown for former owners whose houses had, for whatever reason, gone over to Apollo, to continue to occupy and rent them.[52] If Autosthenes had done the same, then this house could have been his contribution to his debt to Apollo.

This reasoning makes of Autosthenes a son of Aristoboulos. In fact, an Aristoboulos, who is twice specified as Aristoboulos son of Lysixenos,[53] rented the same house—undoubtedly originally his own—from 269 to 246 B.C. This man, who probably also leased one of the τέλη in 262 B.C. and failed to pay his rent,[54] was a prominent personage with important temple connections: he was priest of Asklepios in 279 and may well have

51. First attested in *IG* XI 2.156B16–20 (not 157, as in Brunet, 54) as τὰ Σωσιμαχεία. Kent, 286, with n. 149, argued that this estate was confiscated for debt, relying on *IG* XI 2.135.27; concurring, Bogaert, 152 n. 112, Vial, 224 n. 139. It is possible that the estate was not rented until the year to which 156 dates. The entry reads simply, Τὰ Σωσιμαχεία ἀνεμισθώσαμε[ν] Ἀμφιστράτωι HH[⊢]. The verb is that typical for all new or rerentals. But for rerentals the *hieropoioi* typically indicate the reason: failure to renew guarantors, failure to pay rent, or, as in 157B7–9, the death of the previous renter. This argument suggests placing 156 as early as possible, although clearly even if the estate had come into Apollo's possession many years earlier, there may have been reasons to delay rental; cf. the case of the Sosileia house discussed below.

52. The house of Antigonos, *IG* XI 2.158A20; the house of Arkeon, 158A16–17, 161A23, 162A17, 199B94; perhaps the house where Ephesos had his shop, 161A13–14, although it was rented by Aristolokhos in the 280s (157A14, 158A21): perhaps Aristolokhos was Ephesos's owner and manumitted him sometime between 282 and 279 B.C.?

53. *IG* XI 2.226A19, 287A36; further 203A27, 204.34, 224A20–21, *ID* 290.23.

54. *IG* XI 2.223A53. Vial, 349, notes that in 192 B.C. the "house of Aristoboulos" (as it was later designated) contained facilities for producing purple dye from the shellfish murex (*ID* 400.7), and cautiously raised the possibility that Aristoboulos might also have run such a business. Could then his τέλος in 262 have been the murex beds, which were later consistently rented by Exekestos? For the documents, see the list at Philippe Bruneau, *BCH* 93 (1969): 760–63; further at *BCH* 102 (1978): 110–14, and *BCH* 103 (1979): 83–88.

been the Aristoboulos who served as an *epimeletes* in 274 B.C. He rented Soloe in 289–280 B.C.[55]

Finally, it was typical for guarantors to have some connection with renters. The very first attested renter of the house of Aristoboulos was one Diakritos (*IG* XI 2.156A1, 158A23). The name recurs, and prominently: it belongs to Kleokritos's brother, who was *hieropoios* in 297 B.C., the very year Kleokritos was named by Autosthenes as his guarantor (*IG* XI 2.148.77, perhaps for the first time).

None of this is proof, of course; what we most sorely lack is direct evidence of a default by Autosthenes. The circumstantial evidence, however, is strong, and a default and procedure by the *hieropoioi* (obviously not the board with Diakritos on it!) against Autosthenes and Kleokritos would explain neatly the appearance of two new properties among the possessions of Apollo.

(2) The renter of Nikou Khoros in 297 B.C. was a man named Sosilos (*IG* XI 2.149.5). Like Kleokritos and Autosthenes, he belonged to an important family.[56] Through a close relative (perhaps his cousin?) and his son Gorgias, the family bought up, between about 282–279 and 274–250 B.C., a piece of property at Passiros (or Passiron) that had belonged to the family of Eurymanthes.[57] It is tempting to connect this family, and Sosilos in particular, with a series of houses owned by Apollo and called collectively ἡ οἰκία ἡ Σωσιλεία. They first appear in the 280s, although one had collapsed and was not rented until 252.[58] If Sosilos suffered a default in the 290s on Nikou Khoros, his family may have lost their house(s), and the purchase of Eurymanthes' family's land at Passiros may have been designed, in part, to make up for the loss.

(3) Phytalia is another estate that first appears in the accounts during the rental period of 289–280 B.C.[59] On the basis of a restoration in an account of the Amphiktyonia, some have thought that Phytalia was one of the estates confiscated in 375 B.C. and returned to its owner's family in

55. *IG* XI 2.161D3–12; 199A82–83 with Vial, 165 n. 9; 157A3, 158A12–13.

56. Vial, 136–37, Stemma XVI, cf. also 326–28.

57. Vial, 326–28, with Stemma XXXII, p. 327. Sosilos was the son of Mnesalkos, a name that recurs in the family of Stemma XVI. If this Mnesalkos was Telesarkhides' brother, then Sosilos and Mnesalkos I would be cousins (cf. Vial, 136, Stemma XVI).

58. *IG* XI 2.156 + 170 + 173A29, A33, A55–56 (join announced by Philip A. Davis, *BCH* 59 [1935]: 78–79, text at Vallois, I.218 n. 3), 199A68–69, *ID* 296A30 for repairs, first rental at 287A35–36; two other parts of the house first rented at 158A20–21, 226A15. Cf. Hennig, *Chiron* 13 (1983): 436–38; on the κρηπίς, Vallois, ibid., with n. 1.

59. *IG* XI 2.158A14, rented by Philtes.

314 B.C. Tréheux and Brunet have expressed doubt.[60] Kent thought that, like Sosimakheia, it had come into Apollo's hands as a result of unpaid debt. As we shall see, this view cannot be supported, but the evidence Kent adduced does point to the solution. In 250 B.C., Diaktorides son of Theorylos borrowed 400 dr from Apollo ἐπὶ ὑποθήκει τῶι χωρίωι ὧι γειτονεύει τὸ χωρίον ὃ ἦν Φερεκλείδου καὶ ὃ καλεῖται Φυταλιὰ καὶ τοῖς ἄλλοις τοῖς ὑπάρχουσιν Διακτορίδει πᾶσιν καὶ ἀναδόχοις Καλλισθένει Θεωρύλου, Ἀντιγόνωι Διδύμου (*IG* XI 2.287A129–31).[61] Kent's view, that this entry shows that Phytalia was seized for debt, is insupportable: the property called Phytalia used to belong to Pherekleides, but nothing is said about how he lost it. Indeed, Claude Vial thinks "Phytalia" has nothing to do with Pherekleides at all. She understands the relative clause ὃ καλεῖται Φυταλιά to refer not to the same χωρίον as ὃ ἦν Φερεκλείδου but to the τῶι χωρίωι: "on the hypothecation of land [τῶι χωρίωι] that borders land [τὸ χωρίον] that used to belong to Pherekleides, and that is called Phytalia."[62] This understanding is forced against what seems to me the plain meaning of the whole sentence: Diaktorides borrows 400 dr "on the hypothecation of [a] the land on which borders the land that used to belong to Pherekleides and that is called Phytalia, and on [b] all other things that exist for Diaktorides, and [c] on his guarantors Kallisthenes son of Theorylos, Antigonos son of Didymos."[63] Phytalia, which once belonged to Pherekleides, has been used to delimit a neighboring property in private hands that has been hypothecated for a loan.

If this is right, it is easy to find circumstances under which Pherekleides

60. *ID* 104–11A18–19, Ἡ Φ[υταλία], cf. already *IG* II² 1638; Coupry, comm. p. 70, is cautious but accepts the restoration. Tréheux, "Dernières Années," 1016 n. 11; Brunet, 50, 52–53, rejects the restoration and supposes rather that Ἡ Φ[- - -] represents an otherwise unattested estate confiscated in 375 and returned in 314, whose name we do not know because it remained private thereafter.

61. Kent, 286, with n. 149, where he restores the same expression at *ID* 287*bis*20. Vial, 326 n. 56, mentions this entry without Kent's restoration.

62. Vial, 326, followed by Brunet, 58–59. Bogaert, 152 n. 112, cited by Vial and Brunet, writes only, "Phytalia a en effet appartenu à un certain Phérécleidès . . . que M. Kent identifie avec le débiteur dont nous avons parlé *supra* p. 150. Mais il faut remarquer que ce domaine était devenu propriété du dieu avant 290 et que la dette de Phérécleidès existait encore en 250. Il ne peut donc s'agir de la même créance." His refutation of Kent proves only that Pherekleides' own personal debt cannot have been the cause of the loss of Phytalia, not that the estate cannot have come into Apollo's hands by the route I lay out below.

63. For a parallel repetition of the relative pronoun, see Xenoph. *Anab.* 1.7.3; Gustave Simonson, *A Greek Grammar: Syntax* (London, 1911), 84, par. 1541. Compare also the use of the expression τὸ χωρίον ὃ καλεῖται for the estates Rhamnoi and Skitoneia at *IG* XI 2.287A136, 137.

could have lost his property. In 297 B.C., his two brothers Proxenos and Khares independently rented Leimon and Phoinikes. The default of either one could have led to the seizure of Pherekleides' land.[64]

Two other estates, Korakia and Akra Delos, also appear for the first time, and Epistheneia reappears,[65] in this decade. It may fairly be suspected that Apollo obtained them by the same route.

If these seizures are real, they would certainly have made a severe impression on potential renters. The threatened—and sometimes all too real—loss of personal property must have frightened both renters and their guarantors. The greatly lengthened leases of ten years, at least double the terms that had prevailed in 314–300 B.C., added more uncertainty: who could be confident that a decade would not see at least one year when unexpected losses would make meeting payments difficult, if not impossible? After 290 B.C., most of the defaults we hear of resulted from the failure of renters to renew guarantors; given the potential losses for guarantors in a bad year and the absence of any benefits during good ones, the problem is not surprising.

Unfortunately, the seizures I have postulated to explain Apollo's acquisition of new estates in the 290s are only hypothetical. Is there any positive evidence for such procedures during 299–290 B.C.? The very poor state of the inscriptions for that decade renders definite conclusions difficult, but luckily a few indications do survive.

The most important is *IG* XI 2.152. In the absence of an *arkhon*'s name or other definite indicators, it must be dated on style of writing, internal grounds, and other criteria. In style it fits well with other documents of the 290s; the few names point to the 290s or the 280s.[66] Of these, Diaitos may be identical with Diaitos son of Apollodoros, known from *ID* 502A29 of 297 B.C. and other documents of the next twenty years.[67] Diaitos is recorded here as a renter of an estate. Since no such renter is known from any period, he must have rented an estate for only part of a decennium: either he took over from a defaulter after 297 or he rented an estate in 290 and defaulted before 282 B.C. (I leave aside other imaginable, but more complicated, scenarios.) Of the two possibilities, I prefer the first. The few

64. *IG* XI 2.149.3–4; Vial, 295, Stemma XXV. Starting in 289, Pherekleides himself rented Leimon, which Proxenos had held in 299–290.

65. Korakia, first attested in *IG* XI 2.157A4–5 as τῶν ἐγ Κο[ρακίαις] (see also, e.g., 161A12), but cf. 158A12–13, τῶν ἐγ Κορακίαι. Kent, 286, suggests that it was confiscated for debt. On Epistheneia, see Appendix I.

66. Theophile Homolle, *Les Archives de l'intendance sacrée à Délos* (Paris, 1887), 119, no. XI.

67. *IG* XI 2.161A41, D82, 83; 203D77, 78; perhaps 199C85.

words of 152A7, [γ]ῆν ἣν Δίαιτος ἐμισθώ[σατο], more closely resemble the language the *hieropoioi* use of rerenters than that for defaulters.[68] This would put 152 in the 290s, but this argument is very tenuous.

The content of the document is arresting. Despite the very fragmentary state of the text, it clearly records judicial proceedings against renters: it mentions the *boule* (μετὰ βουλῆ[ς], A3); a debt and a law court ([ὀφεί]λειν αὐτοὺς ἐν τῶι δικα[στηρίωι], A5–6); perhaps interest of 10 percent, but perhaps better a reference to 10 percent renewals ([τόκ]οις ἐπιδεκάτοις in *IG*, which may be better restored as [τ]οῖς ἐπιδεκάτοις, A8); at least three estates, including Kharoneia ([κ]αὶ τὸ ἐγ Χαρωνείαι, A9); the renters (τοὺς γεωργοῦντας, A10; cf. *IG* XI 2.147A18); the deprivation of something (ἀποστερήσει τῆς, A12); rental (πρὸς τὴν μίσθ[ωσιν], A13–14); at least 1,400 dr ([δραχμ]αῖς χιλίαις τετρα[κοσίαις], A14–15); a total figure (κεφάλαιον, A15); and a payment by a someone in the first person singular to the *hieropoioi* ([παρέδ]ωκα ἱεροποιοῖς, A16).

In my view, this text records the trial and conviction of renters who violated the rental contract, payment of fines and/or back rent, and the seizure of property from those who could not or would not pay. Restoration at A12 as ἀποστερήσει τῆς [γῆς], someone "will deprive [the renter?] of his [land]," is almost unavoidable. The last phrase may belong to an oath the condemned were forced to swear about payments.

Unfortunately, the absence of the names of all but one of the estates involved in *IG* XI 2.152 stymies further inquiry. For Kharoneia we have only hints. The figure at A14–15, 1,400 dr, might refer to the rent: one Xenomedes was paying 1,450 dr/yr for it in 297 B.C. (*IG* XI 2.149.7–8). His name recurs twice in contemporaneous documents. A Xenomedes son of Apatourios served on the commission of Eleven in 297 B.C. overseeing certain contract work done for the temple. The name also occurs as a purchaser, with two guarantors, in *IG* XI 2.153.[69]

IG XI 2.152 does not stand alone. Another account, probably of almost the same date, attests to a similar disaster, in which at least three renters defaulted (*IG* XI 2.153.21–27). The guarantors are explicitly included in the proceedings; we have the names of two, Aristodikos and Hypselos (ll. 22, 23), unfortunately not otherwise attested in connection with the

68. See *IG* XI 2.142.5–6, Τὴν γῆν τὴν ἐν Σολόει ἀνεμισθώσαμεν οὐ καθιστάντος τὸν ἐγγυητὴν Ἑρμάδ[ου] (. . .)· ἐμισθώσατο Ἀριστόδικος Ἀρ[ι]στοκράτους; also 9–10.

69. *ID* 502A27; see Vial, 116–19, on the board; *IG* XI 2.153.17. It is not possible to trace the guarantors, Kallimos son of Patrokles and Dionysodoros son of Lysileos, farther, although Kallimos was perhaps the synonymous *arkhon* of 268 B.C. (*IG* XI 2.110.17–18). Neither Vial nor Brunet discusses *IG* XI 2.152.

estates.[70] The miserable fragment *IG* XI 2.151 may preserve a third reference to this business at l. 6 in the word [ε]ἰσπρᾶξαι.[71]

These cases are not unique.[72] In 247 B.C., two renters were tried and convicted, one by unanimous vote of the jury. The one defendant had failed to pay rent, [ὦ]φλεν ἔρημον, and the other had destroyed something, κατέσπασ[ε]; Vial thinks of either buildings or trees.[73] Unfortunately, it is not possible to recover the name of either defendant; one is lost completely, and the other, [——]ράτωι Ἰκαρίου, is not among the renters for the decennial 249–240 B.C., fully preserved at *IG* XI 2.287A142–180; he probably took over from another defaulter in 249 or 248.[74] In another similar case in 206 B.C., probably three renters were fined one and a half times the rent owed (τὸ ἡμιόλιον). Here again, it seems likely to me that these men did not have sufficient property to cover the full rent owed.[75] These examples show indisputably that the *hieropoioi* had both the authority and the will to proceed by law against renters who had violated the terms of the *hiera syngraphe*.[76]

In the most generally accepted view, however, the new estates of the early third century came into Apollo's hands through a very different process: they were seized from borrowers who had hypothecated them to Apollo for loans they failed to repay. The evidence to support this view comes from *IG* XI 2.135, where one Tharsynon son of Hierognotos paid 200 dr interest ὑπὲρ τῆς γῆς τῆς Ἐπισθενείας (ll. 22–23), clearly private property. The inference that this land became the estate Epistheneia after

70. A Hypselos appears as a contractor in *IG* XI 2.145.18.

71. Erich Ziebarth, *Hermes* 61 (1926): 97, proposed for l. 4 [καρπῶ]ν πρα[θέντων?], which if accepted would reinforce the impression of confiscations.

72. I do not accept Ziebarth's very speculative restorations for *IG* XI 2.225b7 and 199D32–35 (ibid.).

73. *ID* 291d35, 33, with Vial, 156, 230; cf. Brunet, 71.

74. Γοργίας Ἰκαρίου may indeed be his brother (*LGPN* I, s.v. Ἰκάριος [2]), but Gorgias's debt (*IG* XI 2.287A195, *ID* 291d32) has nothing to do with ——ratos's default.

75. *ID* 369A40–41, cf. Brunet, 71. For what may be a similar case under the Amphiktyonia, see *ID* 104–19A.

76. Although the surviving clauses of the *hiera syngraphe* contain no provisions about the maintenance of capital goods on the estates, numerous parallels make it virtually certain that there was such a stipulation: *IG* II^2 1241.30–33, 2492.14–17, 2494.11–16, 2496.15–17 (renter to repair structures as necessary), 2499.14–18 (Athens), *IG* XII 5.568.11–14 (Poiessa on Keos), *IG* XII 7.62.8–13 (Arkesine on Amorgos; care enjoined rather than cutting prohibited); cf. Kent, 272; Robin Osborne, *Classical Landscape with Figures* (London, 1987), 42–43. Vial, 230, claims that the *hieropoioi* carried out repairs on the estates, but can cite no evidence (cf. ibid., 144).

default on the loan is not hard to draw. The interest paid ὑπὲρ Σωσιμάχου (ll. 26–27), which I have already discussed, is supposed to provide another example.[77]

There is one insurmountable objection to this view: never in the entire history of the island did the *hieropoioi* proceed against private debtors who had defaulted on their payments. The leniency with which Apollo treated slackers extended even to conferring new loans on defaulters; no one who failed to pay his annual interest payments was ever, to our knowledge, debarred from further traffic with the temple, whether as contractor or renter or official; and certainly, no property can be shown ever to have come into Apollo's possession because of action against a defaulting borrower.[78] Indeed, the owner of the property Sosimakhos had hypothecated may have himself benefited from this leniency. *ID* 104-8A15, which can be dated only to 360–330 B.C., carries a payment ὑπ[ὲ]ρ Σωσιμάχο : ΔΠ. If this refers to the same loan recorded in 313 B.C., Tharsynon paid off ten years' back debt (or 150 dr), covering presumably 322–313 B.C. Yet during those ten years, while unpaid interest mounted up, neither the Athenian administrators nor their successors acted to seize the security.

To see the seizures of Akra Delos, Epistheneia, Korakia, Phytalia, and Sosimakheia[79] as a consequence of the *hiera syngraphe,* high rents for the estates, and subsequent defaults permits a very satisfying reconstruction of the events of the decade from 300 to 290 B.C. The defaults of the 300s must have frustrated the *hieropoioi.* Their inability to seize property prevented recovery of unpaid rent, and the relatively low risks to renters, who gambled only the investment made directly in the estates, did nothing to discourage the ever-increasing competition for the estates. By 301 or 300, the Delians at last extended the power of the *hieropoioi* to move against defaulters by the publication of the stricter regulations of the *hiera syngra-*

77. Jardé, 147 n. 1 (with his minority view that the Epistheneia of independence had no relation to the Epistheneia confiscated in 375 B.C.), cf. Heichelheim, *Wirt. Sch.,* 134–35 n. 1, G. Glotz, *REG* 45 (1932): 243, Larsen, 405; J. Tréheux, "Dernières Années," 1016 n. 2; Kent, 256–57, 286 n. 149, with however the notion that Epistheneia and Kerameion were confiscated in 375 B.C. and never returned but registered among the houses (impossible for Epistheneia: see Appendix I; Kent explains *IG* XI 2.135.22–23, unconvincingly, as perhaps "interest on a loan that was raised on other security in order to avoid forfeiture of the lease of Epistheneia" as a house [Kent, 257 n. 38]); Bogaert, 152 n. 112; Vial, 224 n. 139; Brunet, 61–63.

78. Bogaert, 138–65, esp. 151–52: "Pour aucun immeuble acquis depuis l'indépendance, nous ne possédons un document qui permette d'affirmer qu'il aurait été confisqué pour dettes"; Vial, 374; Brunet, 60–61.

79. Always excepting Kerameion, which had evidently remained in Apollo's possession ever since 375 B.C.

phe. At first, having no experience with the new rules, renters proceeded as before: they bid high for estates in 300 B.C., driven, as I have argued, as much by social as economic motives. But now the situation had changed. When the first inevitable defaults ensued, the *hieropoioi* took the renters to court, secured their condemnation, and seized real estate belonging to them and to their guarantors. A few such cases—recorded in the laconic but allusive inscriptions *IG* XI 2.151–53—chilled demand: fear of loss of property in the case of default dampened prices, since default would be less likely if rent was lower, and scared off potential guarantors, whose interests in the whole business were marginal anyway. The paradoxical result was to make the estates appealing only to the richest members of Delian society: men whose personal wealth reduced the likelihood of default, and whose connections with other wealthy men (especially their immediate relatives) eased the problem of finding guarantors.[80]

We can read the impact of these events in the rents of the estates. As figure 6.1 and table 6.1 show, between 297 and 290 B.C. rents plummeted by an average of more than 43 percent. For the rest of the third century, rents tended to be stable; moreover, the same renters often rented the same estates for more than one rental period or passed estates on to relatives. Over the following 110 years (to 180 B.C.), there were eleven renewals by families and twenty-six by individuals out of two hundred rental cycles (twenty estates and ten rental periods each), a rerental rate of 18.5 percent, as opposed to 5.3–4.0 percent before 290 B.C.[81]

Defaults do not seem to have become any rarer, as the record shows thirty-one certain or probable instances from 290 to 175 B.C., but their character changes: in the vast majority of cases where details are preserved—and that accounts for most of the defaults—the renter defaulted because of failure to renew his guarantors. In every case the *hieropoioi* found some-

80. I think this account of the decline in rents far more plausible than Brunet's notion (61–64) that the new estates just exactly matched unsatisfied demand, and so depressed rents. The coincidence that six new estates exactly balanced demand seems incredible (there were then only six or seven unsatisfied bidders in 300?). Moreover, if this were so, one would expect the renters of 300 B.C. to continue renting in 290 (since there were now plenty of estates to go around), but in fact only one renter of the 299–290 period, Aristeides who held Hippodromos, continued in 289–280 B.C. Moreover, would not the expelled owners of confiscated estates, now deprived of their property, enter the bidding for estates (like ex-proprietors of the sacred houses) and thus increase demand, counteracting the expanded supply?

81. See Appendix IV, pp. 309–38, below. I do not see how Robin Osborne, *Chiron* 18 (1988): 300, arrives at only eight cases of renewal by individuals and three by families.

one else to assume the lease, although sometimes for a reduced rent. In these cases the former renters (or their guarantors) were held responsible for the difference. The regulations seem to have protected Apollo's financial interests well.[82]

This stability had advantages for both Apollo and the Delian aristocracy. By eliminating the fierce and expensive competition that had prevailed in the two decades after independence, it minimized the impact of defaults and losses for Apollo. Renters were now able to hold estates over longer periods, and the ten-year lease, which virtually guaranteed that renters would face bad years during its term, would doubtless have discouraged speculators from bidding too high. The losers in the game were probably the less wealthy members of the Delian upper class who had neither wealthy relatives to stand surety nor the resources to cover rents in years when crops failed.[83]

Aside from its inherent probability, this reconstruction of events has the advantage of looking to local circumstances for an explanation of the boom and fall in prices of land, and is independent of any (possibly specious) account of prices for agricultural commodities on Delos or elsewhere in the Aegean. Local prices for agricultural commodities were, however, another issue: they mattered crucially to renters, as we saw above.[84]

82. Defaults are recorded or inferred for Epistheneia in 288–283, 206?, 178–175 B.C. (*IG* XI 2.156B7–15, *ID* 369A41, 467.1–3); Hippodromos in 262, 189 (204.8 [cf. 290.9–11], 403.51–53); Kerameion in 257 (226A36); Leimon in 257, ca. 190 (226A34–35, 406B80–83); Lykoneion in 218, 209–200 (354.35, 356*bis*B22); Phytalia in 207, 177 (368.26–27 [cf. 371A26, 372A18], 452.24–25); Soloe-Korakia in 177 (452.31–32, but there are problems: see Appendix IV, p. 321 below); Sosimakheia in 288–283 (156B16–20); Khareteia in 257, 250 (224A14 [cf. 226A30, 225a8–9], 287A30, 139–142); Kharoneia in 250, 189 (287A29–30, 138–39, 403.48–51); Dionysios in 207, 206, 192 (366A104–5, 369A40); Nikou Khoros in 279, 210, 178 (161A9, C116–20, 356*bis*A12, 445.16–24); Panormos in 279, 207, 192, 177 (161A9, C111–15, 366A105–6, 399A79–80, 452.20–21 [cf. 456A18, 440B17–20]); Porthmos in 274, 207 (199A3–4, 14, 366A102–3); Rhamnoi in 250 (287A25, 136–37); Skitoneia in 250 (287A26, 137–38, D27–28). I have not distinguished certain defaults from probable ones or counted defaults on estates whose rents are not known.

83. Cf. Vial, 331, for a partial account of the control of the estates by individual families over more than one rental period after 290 B.C.

84. This view does not really conflict with that of Robin Osborne, *Chiron* 18 (1988): 302–4. Osborne is analyzing data from the later third and second centuries, not from 314–290 B.C. Moreover, *commercial* attitudes toward farming need not preclude a *social* value to estate rental. I find Osborne's conclusion rather too categorical. That, however, there may have been substantial changes in attitudes in the later third century seems very likely to me.

THE DIFFERING RESPONSES OF GROUP I AND II ESTATES

The threat that the *hiera syngraphe* delivered to renters and their guarantors was the confiscation of personal property. I have concentrated on real property, houses and land, because it was the seizure of such property on a grand scale in the 290s that had such a devastating effect on the interest of potential renters. But the *syngraphe* envisions the confiscation of other kinds of property as well: εἰὰν δέ τι ἐλλείπει τοῦ μισθώματος, πραθέ(ν)των τῶγ καρπῶν, [ἀπ]οδόσθων πρὸς τὸ ἐλλεῖπον τοὺς βοῦς [κα]ὶ πρόβατα καὶ τὰ ἀνδράπ[οδα] (*ID* 503.33–34).[85] Crops, plow oxen, livestock, and slaves: these "movables" represented a renter's personal investment in his estate.

Now, although the rents all four groups of estates (I, IIA–C) fell drastically in 290 B.C., the degree of change varied considerably from group to group. Group I estates responded most strongly, with a change of about 105 units. The three subgroups of Group II range from a mere 27 for IIA to 62 for IIB and 67 for IIC (tables 6.3, 6.5, 6.6, 6.7, "coefficient"). These results reconfirm the contention that Group I belongs apart from the others, Group IIA weathered the change with only minimal loss of appeal, and Groups IIB and IIC responded very similarly: much more strongly than Group IIA, but much less vigorously than Group I.

Not only did Group II estates respond less vigorously to the *hiera syngraphe,* but their rents had also risen much less before 290 B.C. than the rents for Group I estates. Indeed, the more vines an estate had, the less its rent rose during 314–300 B.C. The effect is most apparent for Group IIA estates, whose high average rent in the period is only 143. Groups IIB and IIC lie close together, as we might expect, but even here there is a noticeable difference; Group IIC average rents are invariably higher than Group IIB rents (cf. fig. 6.1, table 6.2). The sum effect of vines, then, was to dampen the swings in estate rents. In my view, two factors may be at work: the stability of the crop, and hence the income, that the vines offered; and the relatively low capital investment required of renters of estates with large vineyards.

Like olives, established vineyards can be expected to yield an approximately consistent harvest—given, of course, interannual variation owing to changes in rainfall, incidence of disease, and other factors—over the long run. As a result, renters could easily estimate the approximate income from these estates, assuming that wine prices were relatively stable. Expec-

85. Cf. Kent, 279–80, 282. Robin Osborne, *Chiron* 18 (1988): 301–2, misses the significance of this clause in his discussion of the "pastoral bias" among renters.

tations of profit would not have varied much before or after 290 B.C., and so the estates with vines would have been much less sensitive to the impact of the new rental regulations.

Capital investment in the production of wine would likewise have been relatively small. The vines were already there; they needed only tending, including occasional replacement of senescent stock. Cato the Elder's agricultural manual, which was written around 160 B.C. and reflected current Hellenistic thinking about farming techniques, recommends sixteen slaves for a vineyard of 100 *iugera*.[86] This figure may be a bit high in comparison to later writers, who reckon one slave per 7–10 *iugera*, but for our purposes it can stand, implying one slave per 6.25 *iugera* of vineyard.[87] Columella, who admittedly wrote at a period much later than ours, and for a specifically Italian audience,[88] gives simple formulae for calculating plantings. He recommends placing vines at the intersections of lines laid out in the fields from 3 × 5 to 10 × 10 Roman feet. His closest planting (3 × 5) allows 2,025 vines per *iugerum*, his most generous (10 × 10) only 325 vines per *iugerum* (*Rust.* 5.3.1–8). If we assume that the Delian estates' vines were laid out with plenty of space to allow for the care required by the dry climate and for the cultivation of grain between rows,[89] then for purposes of illustration, and without any claim to precision, we can estimate the manning requirements at Columella's moderate (5 × 5) and most generous (10 × 10) planting ratios (table 6.13). The latter figure corresponds roughly with Kent's own estimate of 10 m^2 per vine derived from observation of modern vineyards on Mykonos and Syros.[90] Even if these estimates are low by a factor of two (which I do not regard as likely), the

86. Cato *De agri cult.* 11.1. On Cato *De agri cultura,* see Alan E. Astin, *Cato the Censor* (Oxford, 1978), 189–203 (ignoring, however, the technical issues); and Silvano Boscherini, *Lingua e scienza greca nel "De agri cultura" di Catone* (Rome, 1970), esp. 23–91. See also Hanson in *Agriculture in Ancient Greece,* 161–66, on the use of slaves in viticulture.

87. Richard Duncan-Jones, *The Economy of the Roman Empire: Quantitative Studies*[2] (Cambridge, 1982), 39, 327–33; Andrea Carandini, *Opus* 2 (1983) 177–204. The criticism of Carandini in M. I. Finley, *The Ancient Economy*[2] (Berkeley, 1985), 180–81, is not relevant here.

88. See Carandini, *Opus* 2 (1983): 186–87.

89. See Theophr. *De caus. pl.* 3.11–12, 10.3 (Theophrastos recommends barley). Ox sheds and other equipment related to grain production are attested for almost every estate with vines; see Kent, 299–301. Marie-Claire Amouretti in *Agriculture in Ancient Greece,* 83 n. 17 (planting ratios).

90. Kent, 291–92, n. 173. For vineyards at Kydonia on Krete, cf. *IC,* II, Kydonia 1: 2 plots of 2 *plethra,* 6 of 4 *plethra,* 1 of 10 *plethra,* 1 of 20 *plethra,* and 1 of 22 *plethra.* I have not seen A. Chaniotis, "*Vinum creticum excellens:* Zum Weinhandel Kretas," *MBAH* 7.1 (1988): 62–89.

Table 6.13. Planting Ratios and Personnel for Delian Vineyards

Group	*5 × 5*	*Slaves*	*10 × 10*	*Slaves*
IIA	1.5–1.8	0.2–0.3	5.8–7.0	0.9–1.1
IIB	0.8–1.3	0.1–0.2	3.1–4.8	0.5–0.8
IIC	0.4–0.6	0.1	1.4–2.1	0.2–0.3

labor requirements for the vineyards are strikingly modest. Only if vines in Group IIA estates were planted at Columella's greatest ratio would vine tending absorb the full-time labor of even one slave. Since the vines themselves and the capital equipment necessary to care for them were already present on the estates, a renter's initial investment would be confined to the cost of a single slave, whose labor might well be available much of the time for other tasks, and to a handful of other equipment, like stakes.

Group I estates present the extreme case. Entirely without vines, they offered none of the security to the renter of even Group IIC estates. Virtually all the income a renter could expect from them came from money he invested, whether as barley seed, plow oxen, and labor, or as sheep, goats, or pigs.[91] Under the terms of the *hiera syngraphe*, all of this investment, along with the renter and his guarantors' personal property, was subject to seizure and loss in the event of default. Stripped of the protection afforded by the heady years of early independence, renters fled from these estates, which, it must be admitted, had a history of defaults.

The high rents and collapse of early independence can thus be explained by appeal entirely to local conditions. Social factors, always important in antiquity, take a place beside economic ones in elucidating these events. Moreover, we can now offer a very satisfactory account of why the high prices and collapse occurred when they did.

WINE PRICES AND RENTS FOR GROUP II ESTATES

As we have seen above, estates of Group II all show a drop in rents after about 220 B.C. that was directly proportional to the number of vines on

91. Although he might also be responsible for looking after animals belonging to the temple: *ID* 503.21–27, cf. Kent, 277–78. For branding of sheep owned by Apollo, see *IG* XI 2.287A58. Individual animals were expensive. Pigs, as we have seen, might run 2–4 dr each; a προβάτιον sacrificed in the 280s B.C. cost 15 dr (*IG* XI 2.156A16); an ἀρήν might fetch 3.5 to 7.5 dr (142.59, 154A11), a κάπρος or κριόν, 16 dr (199A71). Cf. Cavagnola, *Istituto lombardo, rendiconti* 107 (1973): 511–45.

them. As I have noted on a number of occasions, Kent attempts to explain this decline by linking it to a drop in the price of wine:

> The pronounced and prolonged drop in the rentals of the vineyard estates shows that after 220 B.C. the vines yielded little or no profit, but were able to bring in merely enough revenue to pay for the expenses of maintaining them . . . yet there is evidence to show that there was no deliberate destruction of vines. . . . Since the loss of revenue by the vineyard estates was not due to loss of vines, we are obliged to conclude that the decrease was caused by a sharp drop in the value of wine.[92]

There is certainly a great deal of truth in this view. Our results have confirmed the declining rents for "vineyard estates" after 220 B.C. and clarified the differences in rent histories arising from differing numbers of vines, a very important result. There can be no doubt that, generally speaking, estates with vines became less desirable by the last quarter of the third century, and indeed less desirable in proportion to the number of vines each had. It is far from clear, however, that this situation was a consequence of "a sharp drop in the value of wine." In fact, the evidence available for wine prices on Delos cannot be said to show any such drop at all.

For the second century, two sources offer wine prices: the accounts of the festivals of Posideia and Eileithyaia. Posideian accounts preserve three prices for Knidian wine, two for Koan, and one unidentified variety. The wines were purchased by the κεραμίον, which J. A. O. Larsen identifies with the Egyptian measure of the same name of eight *khoes* capacity.[93] Prices must therefore be multiplied by 1.5 to obtain the equivalent of the standard Delian *metretes* of 12 *khoes*. The results, set out in table 6.14, prove clearly that Knidian wine was more expensive than Koan by one and a half to two times. To sustain Kent's view, however, it is necessary to show, not a differential between varieties of wine (as perfectly familiar in antiquity as today),[94] but that there was an absolute drop in price over time that depressed the price of wine produced locally on Delos and its neighbors.

For this we need a series of wine prices over time, and it does not exist. The only earlier wine price preserved from Delos—a healthy 11 dr/*met*—dates to 296 B.C. No variety is indicated. Gustave Glotz restored two more prices at about the same level (11 dr 4.5 ob, 10 dr 3 ob) for 304 and 279 B.C.,

92. Kent, 311.

93. Larsen, 392, 394.

94. For example, Athen. 25f–34e, esp. 28d–f on Khian, Thasian, and Lesbian, 30b–e on Ikarian, 30f on Naxian and Skiathian.

Table 6.14. Delian Wine Prices, Early Second Century B.C. (cf. Larsen, 393)

		Posideia		*Eileithyaia*	
Year	*Source (ID)*	*Knidian*	*Koan*	*Unknown*	Οἶνος
190	401.18	7.5			
179	442A223				8.5
178	445.4, 445.9–10, 445.16	8.25	4.285		8.0
177	452.12			3.66–4.185	
174	440A62, A66–67, A71	6.5	4.965		5.5
169	461Bb54				11.0

but as Larsen remarks they are nothing better than "plausible guesses."[95] Even if a decline is assumed, these three prices are separated by over a century from those for the Posideia. It is impossible to know when the decline occurred. The example of oil might suggest putting it earlier rather than later: say by 270 at the latest; but this is exactly the period when Group II estates show a recovery in rents (see fig. 6.1 and table 6.2). In fact, nothing assures Glotz's two prices, and nothing justifies even the assumption that the wine bought in 296 B.C. was at all comparable to the Knidian and Koan vintages favored 100 years later at the Posideia.

Wine was also bought for the Eileithyaia.[96] As Larsen observes, no measure is recorded,[97] but the designation οἶνος may mean that a *metretes* was bought. Table 6.14 is constructed on this assumption. Philippe Bruneau and Philippe Fraisse have suggested that the wine bought for the Eileithyaia may have been local. They may well be right: it is identified only as οἶνος in two inscriptions (*ID* 440A71, 62, 66; 445.16, 4, 9–10) that specify Knidian and Koan wines (as οἴνου Κνιδίων or Κνίδια and οἴνου Κῴου or

95. *IG* XI 2.154A15; Glotz, *Journal des Savants* 11 (1913): 20, for restorations in *IG* XI 2.144A30, 199A22; Larsen, 392. On Delian viticulture in general, see Bruneau and Fraisse, *BCH* 105 (1981): 127–53, 108 (1984): 713–30, Philippe Bruneau, *BCH* 111 (1987): 339–41. See also the brief treatment of prices for Khian, Delian, Kyprian, and some other wines in Luigi Moretti, *Rivista di filologia e di istruzione classica* 108 (1980): 41.

96. Cf. Bruneau, 217–18.

97. Larsen, 393.

Κῷια) in the same year in the immediately preceding accounts for the Posideia. If Bruneau and Fraisse are right, local wine was obviously no cheaper than Knidian or Koan, and it is hard to believe that producers at Kos and Knidos could survive making wine that sold at 4–5 or 6–8 dr/*met* but Delians could not.[98]

More to the point, in my opinion, is the price differential between Knidian and Koan wines. If the οἶνος of the Eileithyaia was local, then imported Koan wine was cheaper than either Delian or Knidian even in Posideon, three months after the close both of the sailing season and of the vintage. In the incomplete state of evidence for amphorae on Delos,[99] only provisional inferences are possible, but Jean-Yves Empereur has recently shown that stamped Knidian amphora handles do not begin to appear on Delos in appreciable quantity until the 140s B.C.[100] Rarity could then account for the prices of the Knidian purchases. But Delian wine cannot have been "rare," or at least was no "rarer" in the 170s B.C. than it had ever been.[101] It seems more likely to me that the prices for οἶνος reflect on the one hand the restricted availability of local Delian vintage and on the other the greater productivity of islands like Kos and Khios. Modern travelers in the Kyklades know how difficult it is to get local vintages, although this is owing in part to loss of vineyards to phylloxera in the 1960s and the abandonment of productive orchards as inhabitants emigrated; in antiquity production must have been much higher. Yet Delos, for all that, was small, and the local product cannot have come near to satisfying demand. Under such conditions, the appeal of a far cheaper, quality wine like the Koan would be self-evident; furthermore, the increase in numbers of stamped Rhodian amphora handles on Delos from 220 B.C. on strongly suggests the increased availability of yet another desirable but cheaper foreign vintage. The difficulty for renters of the vineyard estates, I submit, was not a "price decline" but "cheap foreign competition."[102]

98. Bruneau and Fraisse, *BCH* 105 (1981): 141. The Eileithyaia took place in Posideon (*IG* XI 2.287A84, cf. Bruneau, 217); wine bought for it and the Posideia must therefore have been subject to similar, if not identical, market conditions.

99. See chapter 5, pp. 163–64, above, and chapter 7, pp. 263–64, 266, below.

100. J.-Y. Empereur, *BCH* 106 (1982): 224–25. For Tenos, see Etienne, 217–18.

101. Vines on the estate of Nikou Khoros were extirpated between 180 and 178 B.C., but this was a unique case: the destruction occurred after the renter Akhaios son of Zelomenes defaulted by failing to post new guarantors. There was no change at all in the rent it fetched, but since rerentals after such defaults often fetched the same rent, it is far from certain that the presence or absence of the vines had any impact (*ID* 445.16–24).

102. For Rhodian handles, see again Empereur, *BCH* 106 (1982): 224–25.

This competition could also have been quite local. As with other foodstuffs, Delian production certainly failed to cover local demand. Given an annual consumption of about 150 liters per adult, the Delians would have needed very roughly 262,500 to 787,500 l/yr. If 10 percent of Delian land were under vines, the annual yield would have amounted to about 84,000 l, or 11–32 percent of demand. Sacred estates on Rheneia might have added another 34,000 l, for a total of 15–45 percent. Kykladic neighbors probably made up the bulk of the shortfall: a recent calculation suggests that a single Tenian vineyard in 1950 produced 460,000 l, which could have covered much or all of ancient Delian demand. Ateliers that manufactured amphorae have been identified on Paros, Naxos, and Antiparos, and Columella knew Kykladic vintages.[103]

There is further evidence to corroborate this view. From 290 to 250 B.C. (see fig. 6.1), Delos was relatively isolated: a small market, dependent mostly on its close Kykladic neighbors and its own production. The wine-growing Group II estates enjoyed local demand for their product, which probably made them popular with renters; some competition among renters would then account for the gradual, steady rise in rents. Trouble arose, as in so many other areas, around 220 B.C. Mean annual firewood and pig prices rose about 40 percent over former levels, a permanent *sitonia* fund was established, and many other indicators of a changing economic scene are evident.[104] Probably in these years—although we have no evidence until the 170s—foreign wine began to make inroads on Delos. It may be that religious conservatism is to blame for our lack of evidence: tastes for and availability of Koan and other wines may have developed from the 220s on, but the *hieropoioi* may have resisted the new vintages for the Posideia until the 190s or so. It is perhaps not just coincidence that the first attestation of Koan wine for the Posideia comes soon after the Rhodians established their new Island League, through which they dominated the Kyklades. Unlike the earlier league, this one counted Delos as a member.[105]

There is one more consideration. Group I estate rents enjoyed a recovery after 220 B.C.; I have suggested, on the basis of rising pig prices, that

103. Etienne, 219 n. 56; A. Tchernia, *Le Vin d'Italie* (Paris, 1986), 26, 200, 360, for consumption and production estimates, cf. also Amouretti in *Agriculture in Ancient Greece*, 83 n. 17; Jean-Yves Empereur and Maurice Picon, *BCH* 110 (1986): 495–511, 647–53; Columella, *Rust.* 1 *praef.* 20; Plin., *Nat. hist.* 14.6.54.

104. See chapter 4, pp. 111–14, and chapter 5, pp. 171–81, above.

105. Etienne, 101–24; see further chapter 7, pp. 264–67, below. On inferring local taste from amphora remains, see Yvon Garlan in *Trade in the Ancient Economy* (Berkeley, 1983), 30–32, and *DHA* 8 (1982): 145–52.

renters may have begun to turn to herding to take advantage of these price rises. That in turn would have rendered Group I estates more desirable. It would have been far easier to expand herding on these estates than on any Group II estate, since Group I estates were essentially vacant land, γῆ ψιλή, suitable either for barley culture or for stock. Despite the presence on most Group II estates of sheep shelters,[106] which indicates some herding, renters could not run stock through vineyards, which they were obligated to maintain. If the late third and early second centuries were a period of higher stock prices, renters of Group I estates would have enjoyed an advantage. This may also have contributed to the decline in rents for Group II estates.

The rent histories of the estates of Delian Apollo have proven a rich vein of economic information. Rents of estates were tied to the movement of prices of barley and olive oil, a very satisfying result. Since these prices were set in a local market, rents too must have been determined in light of local conditions. This result makes good sense, given the restricted range of trade for the goods in question in all but the most exceptional circumstances. We have also seen that the varying character of the estates and products they yielded helped to determine the way they responded to changes in the economic scene. Sometimes, however, changes resulted not from economic considerations, but from local social and political preferences. The expulsion of the Athenians in 314 released an enormous pent-up demand for estates, which propelled rents far beyond anything justified by economic conditions; to correct the situation, the Delians passed the *hiera syngraphe,* with its stringent procedures against defaulters. Finally, we have yet another piece of evidence for important economic restructuring on Delos in the last third of the third century. We shall return to these matters in chapter 7.

The Rents of Sacred Houses

Along with the estates, Apollo also rented out a number of houses. They included buildings used as a smithy, by a porphyry processor, and for other productive purposes; a shop; *andrones;* and probably at least a few residences. Some, like the houses that used to belong to Episthenes, came into Apollo's hands as a result of the confiscations of 375 B.C.; others were dedicated to the god by private persons, like the house of Stesileus, which was apparently beyond repair and sold. Others may have passed to Apollo by

106. Kent, 299–301.

testament, and some were probably confiscated from defaulting renters of estates in the 280s.[107]

By 207 B.C., the houses were rented on five-year contracts. For the earlier parts of the century, the evidence is less secure. *IG* XI 2.226, which has new leases (see A11), probably dates to 257 B.C. That date would correspond to the five-year cycle attested later. The date of *IG* XI 2.268, which also has new leases, has been disputed; Molinier thought he could set it in 267 B.C. exactly, but because of doubts about the five-year cycle during this period, Dieter Hennig argues only that it fell sometime in the 260s—in 268 at the earliest.[108] One objection to holding that the five-year cycle was in force earlier than 257 is the absence of new leases in *IG* XI 2.158, which dates to 282 B.C. and so should have fallen in a new lease year. But this is not decisive. The inscription is not complete, and there is no reason why new leases could not have been recorded on the lost portion of the stone (cf. *ID* 366A94–99) or, as sometimes happened, on a separate stele (see *ID* 399 and 400, both of 197 B.C.).[109]

The real problem with postulating a five-year lease on the same pattern before 257 B.C. comes with a new lease period that must have fallen between the rents paid in *IG* XI 2.158A15–23 (282 B.C.) and 161A16–24 (279 B.C.). The house formerly of Antigonos, rented by Antigonos himself in 282 B.C. for 30 dr but by Arkhepolis in 279 for 60 dr, is still in Antigonos's hands in 281 B.C. For Hennig this is the decisive evidence that a five-year lease cycle based on years ending in 7 and 2 is impossible for the early third century.[110]

The form of the entry at *IG* XI 2.162A39–40, however, suggests a par-

107. *ID* 400.7–8 for the manufacturer of porphyry, cf. also Sylvain Molinier, *Les 'Maisons sacrées' de Délos* (Paris, 1914), 21–22, and Vial, 341 (who is cautious); *IG* XI 2.158A21 for a shop; one certain residence, "the house πρὸς τῆι Βρέμπι," *ID* 356*bis*A18, 355A98, 369B1–3, etc. (cf. Molinier, *Maisons*, 34; Hennig, *Chiron* 13 [1983]: 424), and probably "the house where Antigonos lives" (*IG* XI 2.158A20, despite the silence of Hennig, 420–21); on Arkeon's house, see Appendix I. Cf. the brief, dense treatment of Vallois, I.216–20. Stesileus's house at *IG* XI 2.162A42–43. For a general introduction to the Delian houses (to be used with care), see Wolfram Hoefner et al., *Haus und Stadt im klassischen Griechenland* (Munich, 1986), I.241–46. For the important join, *IG* XI 2.156A33–41 + 170.5–12 + 173, see n. 58, above.

108. *ID* 366A94–99, 400.1–31, esp. 1. 2: εἰ[ς] τὴν πενταετί̣α̣ν. Cf. Hennig, *Chiron* 13 (1983): 444–46; Molinier, *Maisons*, 45–47.

109. Molinier, *Maisons*, 48. Hennig, *Chiron* 13 (1983): 447 n. 77, 444 n. 72.

110. *IG* XI 2.158A20, 161A20–21, 162A39–40, cf. Hennig, *Chiron* 13 (1983): 446–47. Molinier, *Maisons*, 48–50, postulates a four-year cycle based on 285–281 and 281–277; objections at Hennig, 447 n. 78.

tial default: [ἐπ' ἄρχοντος] Χάρμου · ΔΔΔ · ἃς κατέβαλεν Ἀντίγονος ὁ Τιμοκράτους τὸ προσώφειλεν τοῦ ἐνοικίου ἐπ' ἄρχοντος Γλ[αυκιάδου] ("under the *arkhon* Kharmos [280 B.C.], 30 dr, which Antigonos son of Timokrates paid, he owed in addition as part of the rent under the *arkhon* Glaukiades [281 B.C.]").[111] Apparently Antigonos had owed an *additional* 30 dr (προσώφειλεν) of the rent (τὸ . . . τοῦ ἐνοικίου) for 281 B.C., which he paid in 280 B.C. But this would mean that the rent in 281 B.C. was more than 30 dr, therefore proving a new rental in 282 B.C.[112] His rent in 281 may well have been the 60 dr attested for 279 B.C. The presence of a new renter by 279 B.C. would indicate that Antigonos had failed to renew his guarantors or perhaps had died and his heirs had either failed to provide guarantors or decided not to take up the lease.[113] Thus there is no reason to doubt a five-year rent cycle in the early third century.

There is no direct evidence attesting to the manner in which the houses were leased. The automatic renewal with a 10 percent increase (the ἐπιδέκατον) available to renters of estates did not apply to houses.[114] Sylvain Molinier presumed that sealed bids were accepted on the model of the estates. Hennig suggests that the rents could also have been preset by the *hieropoioi*, but his argument, based on occasionally drastic rises in rents, has no force, since the same phenomenon appears among the estates.[115] No *hiera syngraphe* for the houses survives; whether one existed is debatable, although *IG* XI 2.226A11 certainly proves the use of some kind of contract. The only question is whether there were also general regulations, as for the estates.[116]

Although the accounts preserve records of literally dozens of houses, the information is much harder to use than that for the estates. The *hie-*

111. Compare, for example, *ID* 442D2–11: Ἐγγράφομεν δὲ καὶ Εὐφράνορα καὶ τὸν ἔγγυον αὐτοῦ Ἀριστείδην Ἀπιστείδου ὃ οὐκ ἀπέδωκεν τοῦ ἐνοικίου τῆς ἱερᾶς οἰκίας τῆς Ἐπισθενείου 24 dr $\frac{2}{3}$ ob.

112. Compare the case of Apemantos son of Leophon, who rented the first house of Episthenes for 51 dr, of which he apparently paid only half in 279 B.C. (*IG* XI 2.161A22, D69–72), but retained possession (162A17–18, 278 B.C.).

113. Both common problems; examples at Hennig, *Chiron* 13 (1983): 447–51; on the responsibilities of heirs, see Hennig, 449, esp. n. 84; Molinier, *Maisons*, 52–54, argues that heirs had to take up the lease. Hennig, 451, doubts the annual renewal of guarantors, in my view on insufficient grounds. I thank my colleague A. D. Macro for discussion on these matters.

114. Hennig, *Chiron* 13 (1983): 443, 442–43 n. 71; Molinier, *Maisons*, 50–51.

115. Molinier, *Maisons*, 42; Hennig, *Chiron* 13 (1983): 443–44.

116. Hennig, *Chiron* 13 (1983): 441–43, dubious; Molinier, *Maisons*, 41–42, assumes general regulations.

ropoioi were not always scrupulous about distinguishing buildings; sometimes they recorded rents one year for several *andrones* that were obviously different buildings, but without indications that could help us identify them with the same buildings in other years. Houses also sometimes disappear from the record, only to recur years later. The "houses where Ephesos has his shop," for instance (*IG* XI 2.158A21: τῶν οἰκημάτων ἐν οἷς Ἔφεσος καπηλεύει), occurs regularly in accounts from the 280s to 268 but is mysteriously absent from the fully preserved account of 250 B.C., only to crop up again in 219 and continue down to the end of our records. It is possible that such gaps represent periods when a house was not rented out because it was undergoing repair, or for some other reason; but these lacunae do not help establish a consistent set of data.[117]

It is possible to estimate, in a general way, what proportion of the rental property on Delos was in Apollo's hands. In 250 B.C., the *hieropoioi* recorded income from the city of 1,690 dr, attributed to a 10 percent tax on rents, the ἐνοικίων δεκάτη. Since a 5 percent surcharge was added to the tax (the ἐπώνια), the actual total tax collected was 1,605 dr 3 ob, representing a total rent paid of just over 16,000 dr. Assuming that the monies turned over to the *hieropoioi* represent the total tax, and that the tax was levied on all rents, the rents Apollo collected that year for his houses—934 dr—account for just under 6 percent of all rents.[118] Since not all buildings belonging to Apollo appear in this account, the actual total percentage must have been higher, but probably no more than about 10 percent of the whole rental stock (as represented by money rents). Apollo may have been the chief landlord on Delos.

From all the houses recorded from time to time in the inscriptions, I have selected eleven to analyze. Rents for these buildings occur from the 280s to 179 or later, giving a full range of data, with the inevitable gaps. Full details appear in Appendix IV. As in other cases, I have constructed an indexed rent for each house on a base year, but unlike the commodities or the estates, the houses did not provide enough data points in 250 B.C. for a base year. Instead, I selected rents recorded in 269 or 268 B.C.—both from the same rental period, 271–267 B.C.—as the best available compromise. Since it was not possible to distinguish among uses of the houses as neatly

117. E.g., Ephesos's house, Orthokles' house, and Pythas's, all absent from *IG* XI 2.287A34–39 but attested in years prior and subsequent to 250 B.C. (see Appendix IV).

118. *IG* XI 2.287A9–10, 34–39.

Table 6.15. Aggregated Indexed Rents for Apollo's Houses, 287–182 B.C.
(numbers correspond to house numbers in Appendix IV)

	Rental Periods						
House	*287*	*282*	*277*	*272*	*262*	*252*	*247*
1	28.9	51.1	51.1	100.0	84.9	157.1	169.8
2	75.8	75.8	90.9	100.0	136.4	127.3	175.8
3	78.6	72.9	—	100.0	—	—	—
4.1	61.1	56.7	—	100.0	55.5	66.7	—
4.2	50.0	100.0	100.0	100.0	140.0	134.0	—
5	—	82.0	90.8	100.0	—	—	160.0
6	—	—	200.0	100.0	190.0	—	305.0
7	—	105.0	[100.0?]	100.0	100.0	135.0	—
8	—	—	95.4	100.0	—	35.4	—
9.1	—	—	—	100.0	—	60.0	194.0
9.2	—	—	—	100.0	—	80.0	—
N	*5*	*7*	*7*	*11*	*6*	*8*	*5*
Aggregate	58.88	77.64	104.02	100.0	117.8	99.44	200.92

House	*222*	*212*	*207*	*197*	*192*	*182*
1	169.4	—	136.3	67.5	154.3	109.8
2	—	—	106.1	—	151.5	151.5
3	171.4	85.7	100.0	—	165.7	157.1
4.1	56.7	77.9	76.7	51.5	116.7	74.6
4.2	100.0	130.0	210.0	90.0	120.0	160.0
5	80.0	101.3	190.0	74.0	—	218.0
6	150.0	—	255.0	—	350.0	340.0
7	105.0	—	110.0	—	125.0	148.0
8	41.7	—	86.2	63.2	92.4	113.2
9.1	108.0	—	158.4	—	—	—
9.2	104.0	—	60.0	—	—	—
N	*10*	*4*	*11*	*5*	*8*	*9*
Aggregate	108.62	98.73	135.34	69.16	159.45	163.58

as among the estates—those in the sample appear mostly to have been used as commercial enterprises—I have aggregated the data to produce a single average indexed rent for each possible rental year (table 6.15).

Inspection of figure 6.8 suggests that rents in general climbed over time. The figures for 247 B.C. and 197 B.C., however, look clearly out of line with the rest of the data. A model that makes house rents dependent on time, with dummy variables to pick out 247 and 197 B.C. and a correction for auto-correlation that appears in the initial regression (a poor Durbin-Watson of 1.15), yields very good results (table 6.16), accounting for fully 80 percent of the variation in rents.

Several questions arise. First, it is not immediately obvious why 247 and 197 B.C. should be so out of line with the other years. Second, the trend line of figure 6.8 suggests a closer periodization of the data. From 287 to 277, rents clearly rose; the same is true from 212 to 192, with the gross exception of 197 B.C. Between 277 and 212, however, except in 247, rents remained remarkably steady. They varied by no more than 12 percent from the average (104.76) in 262 B.C., and in every other year by less than 6 percent. What could account for these phenomena?

Let us consider first the exceptions, for which several explanations are conceivable. For both exceptional years we are dependent on only five rents for the aggregate. Perhaps the houses whose rents survived were somehow unusual? This however does not seem likely. Three other aggregates (287,

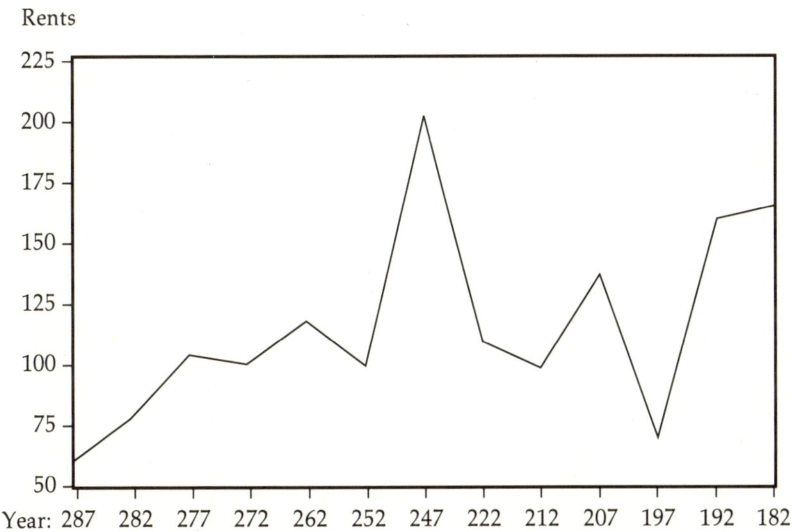

Figure 6.8. Aggregated Indexed Rents of Apollo's Houses, 287–182 B.C.

Table 6.16. House Rents, Sorted by Change over Time and for 247 and 197 B.C.

Dependent Variable is HOUSE
Number of observations: 12
Convergence achieved after 5 iterations

Variable	*Coefficient*	*Std. Error*	*T-Stat.*	*2-Tail Sig.*
C	*73.838575*	*24.887923*	*2.9668436*	*0.021*
TIME	*0.5745594*	*0.2539957*	*2.2620827*	*0.058*
247 B.C.	*98.552637*	*16.176367*	*6.0923838*	*0.000*
197 B.C.	*−77.655574*	*16.061950*	*−4.8347539*	*0.002*
AR(1)	*0.4267435*	*0.3201279*	*1.3330405*	*0.224*

R-squared	0.875363	Mean of dependent var	119.5583
Adjusted R-squared	0.804142	S.D. of dependent var	38.47129
S.E. of regression	17.02582	Sum of squared resid	2029.149
Durbin-Watson stat	1.854471	F-statistic	12.29075
Log likelihood	−47.81005		

262, 212) depend on only four to six rents, yet show nothing unusual. For three houses (1, 2, 9.1), 247 gives the highest rents ever recorded; for the others (5, 6) the only higher rents occurred 40–55 years later. In 197 B.C., two houses fetched their lowest rent ever (4.1, 5), and two others their lowest rents in 80 and 90 years (1, 4.2). Further, rents for most individual houses in 247 and 197 run against the trend for the years before and after. The exceptions are not the artifacts of scarce data.

Commodity prices showed some upward pressure in 247 B.C. Firewood prices were extraordinarily high, pig prices elevated compared to 250 B.C. (but that was an exceptional year), and oil prices too rose. For at least the latter two goods, these adjustments were returns to more typical price levels after the cheap year of 250. But perhaps additionally something was happening on Delos to raise firewood prices radically and to affect rents too. What it was, however, I am at a loss to say.

For 197 B.C. there may be an explanation. That year the Greek world, including the Aegean, was embroiled in the Second Makedonian War. Philip had taken the Kyklades in 201–200 B.C., but lost them in the summer of 200 to the Rhodians. Naval operations in the Aegean included an attack on Andros, held by a Makedonian garrison, which resulted in the temporary expulsion of the population and the delivery of the island into Pergamene hands.[119] More immediately important, exactly in 197 B.C., the Akhaian general Theoxenos, commanding 1,000 infantry and 100 cavalry, passed through Delos on his way to or from assisting the Rhodians in Asia Minor; he stayed long enough to dedicate a silver *phiale* (*ID* 425.11, 442B67–68; Livy 33.18.5). If Theoxenos had commandeered housing for his troops, as often happened in the Hellenistic world,[120] this might well have discouraged potential renters. At the end of the war, Rhodian interests in the Kyklades led to the reestablishment of the Nesiotic League, whose headquarters were set up on Tenos (not on Delos, as formerly), and to the imposition of military responsibilities on the Kyklades. In the aftermath of war and the creation of a new Kykladic *hegemon*, renters may have hesitated to commit themselves to rents at levels previously accepted. But five years of experience with the new situation convinced renters that economic circumstances had not changed, and rents resumed their climb.

What can we say about the long-term trend of rents? First, house rents have provided yet another indicator of an improved situation after ca. 220 B.C. Like firewood and pig prices and the rents for Group I estates, house rents rose—and strikingly—in the last quarter of the century (more specifically between 212 and 207 B.C.). The rise in rent occurred rather later than that for prices and land rents for Group I estates, which indicates that whatever was fueling the expansion worked first in those areas rather than on house rents. The inference is important, for it speaks against seeing international trade as the engine of the expanding economy. If prices for pigs and firewood were rising because of expanded trade, the impact ought to have appeared early in house rents, since merchants would have needed buildings on Delos both as warehouses and as residences. Inasmuch as the merchants would generally have been metics, they would have been compelled to rent, and the rising demand they created would have appeared early, not late, in house rents.

The rise in rents may be connected to the rise in firewood prices. I argued in chapter 5 that the wood price regulation the Delians passed prob-

119. See, generally, Will II², 149–60, with references. On Andros, see Livy 31.45.2–13, with John Briscoe, *A Commentary on Livy Books XXXI–XXXIII* (Oxford, 1973), 153–54; Theophil Sauciuc, *Andros* (Vienna, 1914), 83–87. The notice in one manuscript of Livy 33.30.11, taken from Valerius Antias, that Paros was given to the Athenians in 197 B.C. has been universally rejected: see *IG* XII 5.2, *testimonium* 1348, Otto Rubensohn, *RE,* 18.2 (1949), s.v. "Paros" 1824. Briscoe, *Commentary,* 307–08, does not mention the variant. Etienne, 114 n. 48.

120. See Launey, 695–713. Cf. also *IG* XI 4.1030.2–4, *Labraunda* III 2.46.7–9.

ably in the 230s or 220s may have provoked the rise in firewood prices seen from the last third of the century. We do not know for a fact whether the costs of wood for construction rose too, but it seems likely. Higher prices for building timber, which was used for roof beams in Delian houses, would certainly have led to higher buildings costs; that in turn would have put upward pressure on rents.

A different explanation may be offered for the rise in rents from 287 to 277. I argued above that the imposition of the *hiera syngraphe* for the estates in 300 B.C. led to a series of defaults and confiscations of property of renters; Delians who could not find guarantors under these circumstances were locked out of estate rentals. The exploitation of estates was an economic activity intended to turn a profit. Delians who could not rent them were likely to have looked elsewhere for economic opportunities; they may have found them in the sacred houses, which provided space to carry out all sorts of activities, as we have seen. And indeed, five men who rented one or more sacred estates in the years 314–290 also rented houses in the years 290–240 B.C.[121] The houses were substantially cheaper than the estates, ranging in the 280s and 270s from 25–55 dr (except house 8, 60–76 dr), and most were under 45 dr. The leases ran only five years, exposing renters to only half as many opportunities to default. The commercial businesses the houses housed were certainly less liable to uncontrollable fluctuations (like the weather) than agricultural enterprises. Best of all, the *hieropoioi* never seem to have proceeded against defaulters or cancelled their leases, but rather merely to have written them up with the rest of the debtors who defaulted on loans.[122] Houses provided an altogether safer investment. The flight of some former estate renters to them in the 280s could then account for that decade's rather substantial rise in house rents until an equilibrium was achieved.

With one known exception, that equilibrium lasted until the second-to-last decade of the century. Nothing serves better to indicate Delos's eco-

121. Ampheas son of Aristeas, Soloe-Korakia in 314, *IG* XI 2.287A36; Aristeas son of Aristeas, Hippodromos in 303, 199A8 (cf. Hennig, *Chiron* 13 [1983]: 475, no. 1); Aristeides, Rhamnoi in 297, 158A17 (Kent, 323, no. 40; Molinier, *Maisons,* 94, no. 24); Autosthenes, Dionysios in 301, Nikou Khoros in 303, 297, 161A19, 162A18 (his son Alexibios also rented a house, cf. Hennig, 479, no. 15); Makhon son of Praximenes, Kharoneia in 314, 203A25, 204.29. See Appendix IV. Other possible candidates include Aristodikos son of Aristokrates, Soloe-Korakia in 307–306, 290.26; Demeas, Pyrgoi in 301, if he is the Demeas son of Eumedes at 203A26, 224A21, 226A20, 287A37; Nikandros son of Xenomedes, Kharetia in 307–303, 287A35.

122. Molinier, *Maisons,* 66–68; Hennig, *Chiron* 13 (1983): 452.

nomic stability throughout the period. The arrival and departure of several *hegemones,* troop movements, and wars, while skewing or distorting prices in the short term, as we have seen in chapters 4–6, failed in the long run to disturb the character of the economy. Especially interesting is the absence of any impact of the end of Ptolemaic hegemony. House rents continued at the same levels as before—as did other indicators. Changes beyond the immediate sphere of the Kyklades had virtually no permanent impact on prices and rents on Apollo's birthplace.

Chapter 7

Toward a Delian Economic History

Summarizing the economic relations between the temple of Apollo and the city of the Delians in the fifth and fourth centuries B.C., Jacques Coupry wrote: "A great sanctuary tends only secondarily to be an economic power as such, whether nationally or internationally."[1] This judgment applies with equal force to independent Delos. The Delian economy, as we have seen, depended largely on local suppliers to satisfy its demands, and Delos could best be characterized as a center of the local Kykladic economy, extending to Karystos on Euboia, and sometimes fed by Rhodos or its allies.

The distinction between temple and island is not always easy to draw, however. The temple, which provides the economic data I have used to illuminate an economy confined largely to Delos's immediate Kykladic neighborhood, had international connections too. It dealt with other religious centers elsewhere in the Greek world; received embassies from kings and cities; enjoyed the patronage of wealthy public and private donors, who adorned its treasuries with gifts and its *temenos* with buildings; displayed treaties and decrees from many cities; hosted meetings of the Island League and the bivouacs of armies. The international scope of Delian Apollo's religious and political reach may obscure the very limited range of his economic authority, but it is crucial to distinguish between the two to assess the character of the Delian economy and to trace its development across the years of independence.

The History of Delian Economy

Despite many gaps and uncertainties, three separate periods of Delian economic history can be identified. Different kinds of economic activity, levels

1. Jacques Coupry in *Atti del terzio congresso internazionale di epigrafia greca e latina* (Rome, 1959), 68.

of price, and apparent strategies of investment characterize each. To some degree they correspond with the periods distinguished by Fritz Heichelheim, J. A. O. Larsen, and Michael Rostovtzeff,[2] but their characters and the explanations for them are quite different; and, of course, I make no claim for the validity of this "economic history" for any of the Greek world outside of Delos and its immediate neighbors.

The three periods are (1) the early years of independence (314–290 B.C.), characterized by high estate rents and declining oil prices; (2) a period of stability down to the late third century, when commodity prices were generally level, estate prices gradually declining, and house prices roughly steady (272–212 B.C.); and (3) a period from the late third century to 167 B.C., when firewood and pig prices rose to a new plateau, oil remained steady, estates except for Group I continued to fall, and house rents rose appreciably (207–167 B.C.). This last period seems to have been one of readjustment in the economy during a time of growth and change; perhaps misleadingly, I call it the "new prosperity."

PERIOD I (314–290 B.C.): UNCERTAINTY AND ADJUSTMENT

The removal of Delos from the Athenian orbit and the creation of the Island League seem to have spelled disruption for certain segments of the local economy, which needed years to recover and adjust. Athenian citizens had played an important role in the economy of the temple as renters of the sacred estates and houses, and perhaps (as I have suggested) as suppliers of the island's demand for olive oil. Once the Athenians were gone, locals competed vigorously for the estates. The competition to invest in landed property brought Apollo unexpected gains, but also unwelcome risks. Defaults climbed; renters' property did not always suffice to cover the losses. The situation must have provoked considerable debate among the Delian elites, who both profited from the business and, as temple administrators, felt responsible for protecting the god's patrimony. By 301 or 300 B.C., a compromise had been worked out and embodied in the *hiera syngraphe*. Henceforth estate rentals would be tightly controlled, and defaulters treated severely; a series of defaults and confiscations of property showed how serious these regulations were. Because the new regulations effectively debarred potential renters who could not find guarantors or whose personal wealth could not weather a default or a few bad crops, only the highest levels of Delian society—and a handful of Kykladic islanders who had connections among the Delian landholding elites—had any hope of renting the estates. The immediate results were a drastic decline in rents in

2. Heichelheim, *Wirt. Sch.*, 55–56; Larsen, 379–83, 402–7; Rostovtzeff, 235.

290 B.C. and a tendency for estates to remain in the same hands or the same families for years afterward.

The response of estate rents to this change depended radically on the products the estates produced. Group I estates, which required the heaviest investment from the renter because of their lack of vines, suffered the severest reduction in rents. Those estates that had vines, and therefore demanded a more modest commitment of funds up front from renters, weathered the transition better; the estates of Group IIA, which may predominantly have been vineyards, underwent only a very moderate decline. Presumably the predictable demand for wine coupled with low initial investment continued to make these properties an attractive investment.

Olive oil also showed a continuous, steady decline in prices from the late fourth century down to ca. 270 B.C. I have suggested that a dependence in the fourth-century amphiktyonic period on Athens for oil may have given way after 314 to imports from Rhodos, and that the desire to have local sources encouraged plantings on Delos and neighboring islands, which resulted finally in substantial, reliable local supplies and a steady, low price. The facts fit this view well, especially in view of the correlation between the great siege of Rhodos (305–304 B.C.) and extraordinarily high oil prices in 304 B.C. This interpretation also accounts in a satisfying way for the change in numbers of Rhodian amphorae recovered on Delos (always assuming that some of those amphorae contained oil). In contrast, the traditional view, which attributes high prices to the new demand of the Greek East for home products, looks much less appealing, especially because of its difficulty in explaining the low oil prices of the last months of 304 B.C.

Other sectors of the economy displayed little change. To the extent that pig and firewood prices can be traced, they do not seem to show levels much different from those common twenty or thirty years later. The exceptions, like the high pig prices of 302 B.C., were linked to military operations in the islands. Citizens of Kykladic islands worked on Delos as contractors and laborers, imported goods, rented property, and borrowed money. Apollo lent funds (and rued it) to members of the Island League and to some few small neighbors just outside the Kykladic orbit,[3] but Delian economic influence faded away at the boundaries of the Kyklades.

This reconstruction implies some interesting things about the Delian economy in these years. For one, rents for the agricultural estates display an ambiguous tie with local agricultural prices. We have seen that rents for Group I estates, and to a lesser extent Groups IIB and IIC, correlated well

3. *IG* XI 4.559 (= *Choix*, 18, Migeotte, 161–66, no. 47). Hermione, *IG* XI 2.144A18, 162A27; Peparethos, *IG* XI 2.156A20.

in later periods with barley and olive oil prices. Although the data are too exiguous to permit analysis for this period, it is an apparently reasonable supposition that the high oil prices of this first period encouraged renters to offer the high rent bids to which (I have argued) social considerations impelled them too. Yet none of the estates had olives, and neither did renters plant them. The failure of renters to do so is unsurprising: olives need seven to twenty years to produce their first crop, whereas rental periods in 314–300 B.C. were never longer than five years. Moreover, the great collapse in estate rents in 290 B.C. had no connection with oil prices, which underwent no comparable radical, discontinuous change. This shows quite clearly the operation of extra-economic forces, or at least forces that did not affect oil prices. It can be argued that the instability of this sector of the economy resulted from a partial decoupling of estate rent levels from their normal indicators among agricultural commodities.

The Delian evidence also casts new doubt on long-standing claims about generally high prices in the Greek world in the late fourth century. The facts that prices of individual goods did not move together and that rents for estates rose at least partly independently of prices and of each other undermine any attempt to attribute these "high prices" uniformly to inflation brought on by the influx of eastern wealth or other such causes. Moreover, many of the "data" from other parts of the Greek world are equally suspect. The evidence from Athens, collected long ago by William Ferguson and Rostovtzeff, does not hold up under close examination. "Prices" quoted by Theophrastos (*Char.* 3.3, 23.5, 8) have no claim to represent market prices, and the enormous dowries attested by New Comedy have been deflated by M. I. Finley's careful study of the Athenian *horoi*.[4] This whole subject requires reexamination.

These first few decades of Delian independence also saw the evolution of the Kyklades into an economic unit focused on Delos. While the archipelago certainly always formed something of a region, during the fourth century many of the islands enjoyed important relations with the outside world independent of their links to Delos. The western islands in particular cultivated relations with western neighbors, including the cities of Euboia and Athens. Especially before 350 B.C., Athens played an important role, running the second Athenian sea league, to which most Kykladic states belonged, and controlling the temple of Delian Apollo. Sometimes allies

4. See chapter 3, n. 118 and chapter 6, n. 22, above; cf., too, Brunet, 62. William Scott Ferguson, *Hellenistic Athens* (London, 1911), 65–69; Rostovtzeff, 161–65, 1353 n. 39. M. I. Finley, *Studies in Land and Credit in Ancient Athens, 500–200 B.C.* (New Brunswick, N.J., 1951).

like the Andrians participated in this Athenian control, and individual citizens of other Kykladic states also sometimes benefited from it. The establishment of the Nesiotic League in 314 B.C., however, entailed a marked reorientation of the Kyklades toward their center at Delos and away from the outside world. The political and military relations of the islands with their *hegemones*—first Antigonos Monophthalmos and Demetrios, then the Ptolemies—were mediated through the structures of the league and through the royal officials, such as the *nesiarkhoi*, the *oikonomoi*, and Philokles, king of the Sidonians, put in charge of it. The league knit the islands into a unit in a way that had not been seen before. Furthermore, the removal of Athens from the central Aegean seems to have opened economic opportunities for the islanders on Delos. The result was the creation of an economic region for which Delos became the natural exchange center through a combination of geographic centrality, religious magnetism, and housing the apparatus of the Nesiotic League.[5]

PERIOD II (CA. 290–230 B.C.): THE STEADY ECONOMY

By the beginning of this period—poorly defined as it is—the Delian economy began to achieve a balance that would persist for about half a century. Commodity prices were quite stable over the long run. Estate rents fluctuated, but in fact all four groups recovered after the debacle of 290 B.C., with rents in 269 B.C. higher than, and in 249 B.C. about the same as, those of 290 B.C. Group II estates, distinguished by their vineyards, benefited particularly from this recovery, a phenomenon I have attributed to the insularity of the Delian economy, which created a good market for local vintages. Except for the very unusual rental period of 247 B.C., house rents remained roughly steady.

The economy continued to be largely a local matter. Renters were Delians or their Kykladic neighbors; imports (where attested) came from nearby sources. Some years the Delian government intervened in the purchase of grain during the winter, but nothing indicates that this was anything but an irregular practice. Visitors and passing merchants were mainly from nearby islands. The economy felt the impact of military operations in the neighborhood—for instance, the naval battle near Andros in 246 B.C.—but was insulated from more distant disruptions. There was some transit trade in grain (*IG* XI 4.1049), but the amount does not seem likely to have been great, given the evidence we have for the level of port activity in the second quarter of the third century (see below), and the

5. Gary Reger in *Proceedings of the VIIth International Conference on Boiotian Studies* (Amsterdam, 1994), forthcoming.

unidentified city importing grain, as I have argued in chapter 4, was almost certainly a close Kykladic neighbor.

The accounts for 279, 278, and 250 B.C. give a measure of the port activity on Delos during this period. In 279 a portion of the 2 percent harbor tax, which was regularly farmed out, was paid to Apollo to cover debts the city owed. The amount was 14,910 dr, of which 5 percent was the ἐπώνια or "sales tax" charged on the 2 percent tax; the net 2 percent tax collected therefore came to 14,164 dr 3 ob. The payments for the next year totaled 18,800 dr, or 17,860 net. In 250 B.C. a tax called the πεντηκοστὴ ἡ ἀστία, which Vial interprets as the portion of the 2 percent tax on goods coming into or going out of the city, brought in 5,250 dr, or 4,987 dr 3 ob net. Vial concludes from these figures that two-thirds of the tax was collected on goods in transit and that the whole value of the farmed-out tax is represented.[6]

These inferences are far from certain. The payments of 279 and 278 were made to cover debts—probably loans—the city owed Apollo. Public loans were frequently secured on public income,[7] but nothing assures that the total amount collected went toward the debt. The actual income might have been higher. Nor is the identity of the πεντηκοστὴ ἡ ἀστία secure. It may, as Vial thinks, represent the 2 percent tax on the portion of the goods that came into or out of Delos itself, as opposed to purely transit goods, but it might also be an alternative name for the general 2 percent tax. The accounts are not consistent in reporting taxes and their names. While a grain tax (ἡ δεκάτη τοῦ σίτου) and a tax on rents (ἐνοικίων δεκάτη) are reported in both 279 and 250, the χορηγικόν appears only in 279. A tax called the ὑποτρόπιον, which was perhaps a "fishing rights tax," was recorded in 279 and 278, but a 10 percent tax on fish (ἰχθύων δεκάτη) in 250 (*IG* XI 2.161A26–27, 287A9–10). These two might be the same taxes under different names or different taxes imposed at different times. The law regulating the sale of wood products (*ID* 509 = *SIG*³ 975), which was passed probably in the 230s, makes no provision for separate recording of the *pentekoste* on wood sold in the city (ll. 13–14: πρὸ τοῦ πωλεῖν ὅσου ἂν ἀπογράψωνται [i.e., οἱ εἰσαγαγόντες] πρὸς τοὺς

6. *IG* XI 2.161A25–26 (279). Cf. Larsen, 354–55, and Vial, 339–40 (who rounds the figure up to 14,200 dr), accepted by Marasco, 156. *IG* XI 2.162A29–30 (278); 2.287A9, Vial, 235 n. 231. On the various taxes, see Théophile Homolle, *BCH* 14 (1890): 440–44. On *pentekostai* generally, see Siegfried J. de Laet, *Portorium: Etude sur l'organisation douanière chez les Romains* (Bruges, 1949), 47–48, n. 1; Christian Habicht, *Hermes* 85 (1957): 106, with n. 1.

7. E.g., *IG* XI 2.148.75–76: ὃ ἐδανείσατο ἡ πόλις κατὰ ψήφισμα τοῦ δήμου δραχμὰς ΜΧΧ ἐπὶ ταῖς προσόδοις ταῖς τῆς πόλεως.

πεντηκοστ[ο]λόγους). (Of course, the *pentekostologoi* may have known to register imports and transit goods separately.) The Delians reformed the administration of temple business several times during independence, and they may have done the same for city finances.[8] Even if Vial is right, the transit : import ratio must have varied considerably from year to year (figures for 279 and 278 B.C. prove that), and although it would in the long run have fluctuated around some typical value (assuming no sustained growth or decline), there is no warrant that the ratio of two to one for goods in transit to imports that Vial derives was typical.[9]

Moreover, if the figures for the πεντηκοστή do represent payments on goods *in transit,* then each unit of goods would have paid the tax twice, and the actual value of goods in transit would have been twenty-five, not fifty, times the amount of tax collected on transit goods. If Vial has inferred correctly that the tax value of goods imported into the city—thus paying the πεντηκοστή only once—amounted to one-third of the tax value of transit goods (paying the tax twice), then the total value of goods in transit would equal the tax paid divided by 0.06.[10] On this calculation, Delos saw 236,075 dr (= 39 talents) of transit goods in 279 B.C. and 297,667 dr (= 50 talents) in 278 B.C. If Vial's results are rejected, and the full value of the tax is treated as deriving from transit trade, the figures are 354,112 dr (= 59 talents) and 446,500 dr (= 74 talents). Finally, if the full value of the tax is treated as deriving from imports, the results are 708,225 dr (= 118 talents) and 893,000 dr (= 149 talents). The same considerations for 250 B.C. yield figures (for the transit trade) of 247,875 dr (= 41 talents) or 123,937 dr (= 21 talents), or, taking the full figure as imported goods, 232,875 dr (= 39 talents). Since however some of the goods coming to Delos must have been consumed there, some portion of the total tax collected must have been on those imported goods. If we accept Vial's distinction between the simple πεντηκοστή and the πεντηκοστὴ ἡ ἀστία as the best explanation of these terms, the total annual value of goods in transit on Delos would have remained fairly stable across the first half of the third century—roughly 39 talents in 279, 50 talents in 278, and 41 talents in

8. On *hypotropion, IG* XI 2.161A26–27, with comm., p. 53; Homolle, *BCH* 14 (1890): 442–43. Roland Etienne in *L'Origine des richesses dépensées dans la ville antique* (Aix-en-Provence 1985), 61–62.

9. Cf. Marasco, 156–57, 161.

10. Let T = the total tax paid, $.04t$ = the tax paid on goods in transit, and $0.2c$ = the tax paid on imported goods. Then, $T = .04t + .02c$. If one-third of the total tax should be attributed to imported goods, then $T/3 = .02c$, or $T = .06c$. Substituting for T, we get $.06c = .04t + .02c$, or $.06c - .02c = .04t$, which equation yields $T = .04t + .02t$, or $T = .06t$. For the observation, see already Marasco, 156.

250 B.C. Like all of our calculations, these must be taken with a grain of salt.

We must appreciate what a piddling trade these figures represent. Kaunos and Stratonikeia brought Rhodos 120 talents each in tribute in the second century. We do not know how these payments were calculated, but on the reasonable assumption that they cannot have been more than about 10 percent of total economic activity, these two cities each enjoyed a "gross city product" 24–40 times greater than that of Delos. Delos practically vanishes compared to truly great economic centers. For Athens, Andokides reports an Athenian *pentekoste* of 33 talents in 402/1 B.C. and just over 36 talents the next year, representing a transit trade worth perhaps 550 and 600 talents.[11] In 165/4 the famous embassy the Rhodians sent to complain about the creation of a free port at Delos claimed that before 167 B.C. their harbor dues used to fetch a million drachmas, representing 25 million dr worth of goods in transit alone (= 4,167 talents), or 83–106 times the Delian income.[12]

The other taxes recorded for these years are low. The ὑποτρόπιον brought in 530 dr 279, 543 dr in 278; the ἰχθύων δεκάτη, 1,850 dr in 250; the 10 percent tax on grain, 120 dr in 279, 410 dr 3 ob in 278, 120 in 250; the χορηγικόν, 2,056 dr 4 ob in 279; the ἐνοικίων δεκάτη, 600 dr in 279, 1,690 dr in 250. Each tax includes a surtax of 5 percent (the ἐπώνια) totaling 62 dr 3 ob in 279, 47 dr 4.5 ob in 278, and 445 dr in 250.[13]

These taxes give a sense of the level of economic activity on Delos in the second quarter of the third century. If the *hypotropion* really was a fishing rights tax, analogous to the funds collected from leasing porphyry fields, the full value of fish caught must have exceeded 600 dr in 279–278 B.C.; by how much it is impossible to know. The 10 percent tax on fish from 250 B.C. represents the sale of fish worth 17,575 dr. At the mean rent for Apollo's houses in 250 B.C. of 55 dr per annum, the tax on rents that year of 16,055 dr represents about 290 properties, which may have housed 20–80 percent of the population.[14]

11. Andok. 1.133–34. On the date, see Andokides, *On the Mysteries*, ed. Douglas MacDowell (Oxford, 1962), 158, 205. Imprecisely, Robert Garland, *The Piraeus from the Fifth to the First Century B.C.* (Ithaca, N.Y., 1987), 88, where 18,000 talents is a misprint for 1,800.

12. Polyb. 30.31.12. On the textual problems with this passage, see F. W. Walbank, *A Historical Commentary on Polybius* (Oxford, 1979), 3: 459–60; Vial, 342, accepts a dubious restoration.

13. *IG* XI 2.161A26–27 (with Lacroix, *BCH* 48 [1924]: 404, on the reading of the *eponia*), 162A30, 287A9–10.

14. On the fish tax, see Homolle, *BCH* 14 (1890): 442–443, with *SIG*^{3} 1024.9–11 (Mykonos); [Arist.] *Oik.* 2.3a (1346b20) (Byzantion); cf. Vial, 338. Homolle,

The first two periods of the Hellenistic Delian economy were characterized by three features: the adjustments consequent on the liberation of the island from the Athenians, the stability of prices for goods (like wood and pigs locally available) that had not been in Athenian hands, and a generally low level of economic activity. The population, although large by Kykladic standards, was nevertheless relatively small in the scale of Greek cities. Local needs could be satisfied largely from local sources. Aside from the situation with olive oil in the two decades after 314 B.C., there was certainly very little regular importing from farther away then nearby neighbors. Occasional dearths may have forced the Delians to rely on long-distance imports, although it must be admitted that there is virtually no evidence for such activity, in striking contrast to Athens, Samos, and many other similarly well-documented cities. Transit trade remained at a very low level even in comparison to inland cities like Stratonikeia, and such transit trade as there was certainly was moving through Delos from one Kykladic island to another. Delos's role as a pan-Hellenic sanctuary, visited and patronized by kings and wealthy citizens from all over the greater Greek world, had no noticeable impact on its economic life.

PERIOD III (CA. 230–167 B.C.): THE "NEW PROSPERITY"

From the 240s and especially the 230s, the economic scene on Delos began to show signs of change. On Delos itself, new residential building started after midcentury and seems really to have blossomed in the last third of the century in new construction north of the temple. Excavations there are not complete, and the material far from fully published, but the results that have appeared so far point consistently toward new growth. The sanctuary also shows new building, especially after 200 B.C.[15]

The crucial period for this change was the last third of the third century B.C. A frustrating gap in the data, a result of the loss of all but a few

441, uses the tax on rent to estimate a metic population of about 600 persons in 279 and 1,680 in 250 B.C., but his approach is methodologically flawed.

15. See provisionally, Philippe Bruneau, *BCH* 92 (1968): 633–709. For further excavations, see *BCH* 89 (1965): 981–91, 90 (1966): 988–97, 91 (1967): 870–82, 92 (1968): 1101–23, 93 (1969): 1031–44, 99 (1975): 716–23, 100 (1976): 799–821, 111 (1987): 629–44, 112 (1988): 755–78. On building in the sanctuary—the portico of Philip V, the stoa of the square agora, and the temple of Artemis—see René Vallois, *Le Portique de Philippe, EAD* 7 (Paris, 1923), and Vallois, I. 49, 65, 67–68, with n. 1. The decline in building on Tenos at the sanctuary of Poseidon and Amphytrite in 260–220 B.C. (Etienne, 97) reflects the absence of outside patronage, on which the sanctuary was very dependent; see Etienne and Braun, *Ténos I* (Paris, 1986), 309–11, on Rhodian patronage.

fragments of the accounts between *ID* 290 of 246 B.C. and *ID* 351 of 220 B.C., obscures the character of the changes evident from a comparison of the evidence from either side, but it is nevertheless apparent that the Delian economy underwent important adjustments in those years. Around 220 B.C., mean firewood and pig prices rose by about 20 percent. The rises in firewood and pig prices may be connected, and the rises in firewood prices are surely related to important new regulations governing the sale of wood and wood products on Delos. Both phenomena suggest a rising demand for wood, which would tie in nicely with new building. The import regulations suggest that the Delian government was eager to guarantee itself a full share of the higher profits.

Another set of evidence points to increased local transit trade. I have already reviewed the evidence for the grain trade, which increased in the last quarter of the third century. The permanent *sitonia* fund created by 209 B.C. may have reflected increased pressure on local supplies. The Delians also established a new commission to oversee renovation of the docks, spending almost 10,000 dr on the project between 217 and 171 B.C. Rents rose for sacred houses, most of which were probably devoted to commercial ends, and many of which were located in the harbor district. The first evidence for foreign financiers like Eutykhos of Khios and Athenodoros of Rhodos appears in this period. After 200 B.C., foreign bankers become more prominent.[16] The second century also saw an influx of new metics. Prominent among these were Phoenicians. In 187–175 B.C., "the warehousers and shippers in Laodikeia in Phoenicia" (οἱ ἐν Λα[οδικείαι] τῆι ἐν Φοινίκηι ἐγδοχεῖς καὶ να[ύκληροι]) erected on Delos a statue of Heliodoros, σύντροφος and minister of Seleukos IV (*IG* XI 4.1114.4–5 = *Choix*, 72; cf. 1112–13 = *Choix*, 71). This inscription offers evidence, far more dependable than the proxeny decrees, of real activity on Delos by merchants going back and forth between Delos and the Levant. Nevertheless, we must be cautious. The numbers involved are impossible to calculate; even if M.-F. Baslez were right that proxeny decrees awarding only *enktesis* represent metics who had come to live on Delos, the number preserved would reflect only a very modest growth. Yet this growth, a result of the new attractiveness of Delos as a local distribution center for the Kyklades, might account in part for some of the changes seen after 220 B.C., like the rise in rents for the sacred houses.[17]

Apollo's estates also show important adjustments at this time. The rents

16. *Sitonia:* G. Reger, *Classical Antiquity* 12 (1993): 320–29. Docks: *Choix*, p. 89; G. Reger, *ZPE* 74 (1988): 29–30; cf. also Vial, 340–41. Bankers: Bogaert, 171–82, with Etienne, 112, on Timon of Syracuse.

17. On metics and proxenies, see chapter 3, pp. 63–75, above.

for Group I estates, producers of grain and livestock, rise from 220 B.C. on. This corresponds so nicely with the simultaneous rise in pig prices that it is tempting to postulate an increased local demand for animal products. The vine-growing estates of Group II suffer a real decline in the same period, which has been attributed to changes in the demand for and availability of various vintages. The introduction of cheaper and more desirable Koan wines diminished the demand for local Delian products, which were not only less popular but rarer and therefore more expensive. Rhodian wines may have figured also in the equation, given the rise in numbers of amphorae after ca. 220 B.C. Local Kykladic vintages may also have benefited, if the evidence for some increased production of amphorae on Paros and some other islands has been interpreted correctly.

The economic changes Delos underwent in the last third of the third century transformed it from a consumer dependent on its neighbors to something of a local transshipment point, through which much of the local Kykladic traffic passed. This new role would have increased the availability of these other vintages, and probably also, although at first marginally, of Rhodian and other wines as well. If these imported wines were preferred to local vintages, then the rents for estates dependent on wine may have declined without any general fall in wine prices. Indeed, the great volatility of agricultural prices from year to year—well attested, too, for Koan and Knidian wines bought for the Posideia, whose prices could fluctuate by 100 percent—should have masked any gradual decline; only the availability of either cheaper or preferable wines on Delos can account for the fading appeal of Apollo's estates.

To what should the new prosperity be attributed? It seems clear to me that the economic changes I have catalogued are not consistent with a simple rise in local population, whether owing to natural local increase—unlikely on other grounds[18]—or to an influx of metics,[19] because population growth ought to prevent any agricultural decline. Higher population should fuel the demand for olive oil, wine, and grain, guaranteeing at least stability in prices, if not a rise. Yet oil prices remained low and fairly stable, and the demand for local wine evidently fell off. On the other hand, live-

18. See Vial's discussion (179; cf. 183) of the difficulties of filling local offices and the implications of this for the populousness of the island (Vial, 183, judges that, unfortunately, we cannot be sure whether the problem was because of "la faiblesse de la démographie locale").

19. M.-F. Baslez, *Studia Phoenicia* 5 (1987): 275–76, argues for growing numbers of Phoenicians on Delos in the second century (but cf. chapter 3, pp. 57–58, above). See also M.-F. Baslez, *REG* 89 (1976): 351–52, and *L'Etranger dans la Grèce antique* (Paris, 1984), 284–87, 327–28.

stock prices clearly rose, as attested directly by pig prices and indirectly by the rent histories of Group I estates. Unlike wine, sheep, goats, and pigs vary little in desirability according to their origin, and although they were often shipped by sea in antiquity, transportation of livestock was certainly more cumbersome and more expensive than that of wine.[20] This fact may explain the continuing appeal of Group I estates. But why should prices for livestock have risen when those of other agricultural products did not?

The answer may lie simply in increased local prosperity. The consumption in antiquity of domestic livestock, whether as food or for sacrifice, depended very much on social standing and wealth. If there was a real increase in local wealth on Delos after ca. 240–220 B.C., the demand for pigs and other livestock may have grown without a concomitant growth in the demand for oil and local wine, of which the Delians already consumed enough. A growth in the local transit trade could also account for the rising rents of warehouses Apollo owned, and increased local wealth could have prompted new construction—even of residences, as families that used to live in the harbor district moved away,[21] or as the increasingly wealthy demanded bigger, finer homes.[22] Both Claude Vial and Robin Osborne have argued that the Delian elite became more accepting of wealth generated through trade and business as opposed to agriculture. I would place the most important changes in their attitudes exactly in the period of the "new prosperity."[23]

Local political changes seem to have accompanied this economic transformation. Vial has carefully examined the political careers of Delians. Be-

20. On shipment of livestock by sea, see Herbert Graßl, *MBAH* 4.2 (1985): 80–83.

21. See, e.g., the house of Arkeon, which was situated by the harbor and may have been converted from a residence to a warehouse (*IG* XI 2.158A16–17 for its location: τῆς οἰκίας τῆς ἐν λιμένι ἣ ἦν Ἀρκέοντος παρὰ Ἀρκέοντος; Sylvain Molinier, *Les 'Maisons sacrées' de Délos* (Paris, 1914), 34, Hennig, *Chiron* 13 [1983]: 424).

22. Compare the transformation in the theater quarter in the late second and early first centuries B.C. I hope to address this phenomenon at another time.

23. Claude Vial in *L'Origine des richesses dépensées dans la ville antique* (Aix-en-Provence, 1985), 47–53, and Vial, 317–56, who, however, insists (356)—no doubt strictly correctly, although with too little consideration of the opportunities for landholding—that "Délos comme toutes les autres cités grecques accordait la primauté aux détenteurs de terres"; Robin Osborne, *Chiron* 18 (1988): 300–303. It seems very likely to me that the "freezing out" of many Delians from any hope of renting the estates after 290 B.C., and the unlikelihood that any Delian who owned private property on the island would sell it, predisposed the Delians to regard non-agricultural wealth as socially acceptable. When the opportunities came along in the last third of the century, they were prepared to seize them.

fore 240 B.C., the authors of public decrees—the men cited in the εἶπεν clause—came from many different groups: they were renters of estates, holders of office, *hieropoioi*. The number of different men attested as authors was high. After 230 B.C., the pattern was completely different. Very few individuals moved most of the decrees, and no renters or *hieropoioi* appear among them. The phenomenon culminates with the remarkable Telemnestos son of Aristeides, who completely dominated Delian politics after 200 B.C., no doubt thanks in part to his ties with Rhodos (see below).[24] The economic changes of the second half of the third century thus entailed political changes as well. The rising wealth the economic evidence implies seems to have concentrated political power too. Decline in the value of most estates (those of Group II) perhaps contributed to a loss of influence for the people who rented them, a group that—as we saw in chapter 6—tended to be rather closed after 290 B.C. The stronger local transit economy, moving goods in and around the Kyklades, bringing in traders from neighboring islands to buy or sell grain or slaves or wood, put money into the accounts of Delians who participated in the business. It may well have been these people who in turn began to flex their political muscle, replacing the more traditional landed, or agriculturally based, aristocracy in the halls of the *boule* or at the *bema* of the *ekklesia*. With wealth outstripping their rivals, they tended to monopolize policy decisions.

This analysis in turn suggests, as I have already argued, that the change in the Delian economy was owing to the growth of the Delian port into a local transshipment center for the Kyklades. The first decades of this growth, which did not alter the embeddedness of the Delian economy in the local Kykladic economy, fell during a period when the Kyklades were largely free of outside domination. The Ptolemies were gone, the Antigonids were preoccupied in Greece and in the islands ringing the Saronic Gulf, and the Rhodians were kept busy, first, dealing with the impact of the great earthquake, then with fighting Byzantion and the Kretans. Emblematic of both the absence of the Rhodians (whose active presence was always signaled by a campaign against pirates) and the prosperity of the islands is the rise in piracy, which I have already discussed in chapter 2.

There is, however, another element to the role of piracy in the Kyklades: piracy contributed to the economy. Pirates did not simply raid, kidnap, and flee; Demetrios of Pharos, whose purpose was indeed to withdraw wealth from the archipelago, provides a poor model for the full local impact of piracy. In the first place, pirates undoubtedly recruited heavily from the

24. Vial, 260–61, 333; Etienne, 108–9; M.-F. Baslez and C. Vial, *BCH* 111 (1987): 300–301; Roland Etienne in *L'Etranger dans le monde grec* (Nancy, 1988), 164–66; Vial, 279.

inhabitants of the islands. In early modern times, under the Tourkokratia, the Kyklades were notorious as nests of pirates. While we are virtually devoid of evidence for the origins of pirates, a handful of literary sources provide some hints. Alkiphron's letter of Eukolymbos to his wife Glauke, although obviously a literary production, nevertheless suggests the appeal of piracy to a poor fisherman who could hope to get gold and nice clothes without having to murder or stain his hands with bloodshed (1.8). Asklepiades' Samian prostitutes took names from types of boats often used by pirates.[25] The pirates who raided Syros and Siphnos in the early first century were probably based on the little island off Siphnos where they took refuge with their captives (*IG* XII 5.653.28–29). Probably around 154 B.C., Kretan pirates attacked Siphnos: they kidnapped people in the polis center and raided the temples (Diodoros 31.45).[26]

When these pirates wanted to dispose of their booty or ransom captives, they turned to local economic centers. In the 230s B.C., pirates who had captured citizens of Theangela in Asia Minor had recourse to Delos as a slave market, as we know from a fragmentary inscription in honor of the Delian Semos who ransomed the Theangelian captives from the block (*IG* XI 4.1054; cf. *SEG* 3.666). This sale need not, of course, imply a great "slave market" on Delos in the late third century comparable to the business Strabo describes in the wake of late-second-century Kilikian piracy (14.5.2, C668–669); there was plenty of local demand for slaves.[27] The Delians went so far as to honor Boukris son of Daitas of Naupaktos as a *proxenos* of the temple and the Delians for long-lasting good will toward them; he was the notorious pirate who raided Attike, captured "many citizens and others from the city," and disposed of them in Krete.[28] The king of

25. *Anth. Pal.* 5.44. On the κέρκουρος, see Casson, *Ships,* 163–66.

26. Cf. Hiller von Gaertringen *apud IG* XII 5, fasc. 2, p. xix, *testimonium* 1360 for the date.

27. *ID* 503.33–34; *IG* XI 4.1296A2–8, B2–7, 1054; *IG* XI 2.154A26–27, 156A71 (with Philip A. Davis, *BCH* 59 [1935]: 91), *ID* 291b22; *ID* 290.108–9, 113–15.

28. *IG* XI 4.692 = *Choix,* 42; *IG* II^2 844 = SIG^3 535. Durrbach, *Choix,* p. 50, dates the proxeny decree to 250–240 on the basis of the writing, but despite his confidence in the precision of such dating, we now know that conclusions drawn thus can be off by twenty years (cf. *ID* 440, dated to 190–180 B.C. on the basis of the writing by Durrbach [J. H. Kent, *BCH* 38 (1939): 244], but in fact of 174 B.C., cf. J. Tréheux, *BCH* 109 [1985]: 493 n. 29). I prefer to follow Roussel, who puts it ca. 230 B.C., which conforms better with the date for the Athenian decree (*arkhon* Heliodoros, 229/8 B.C., W. Kendrick Pritchett and B. D. Meritt, *The Chronology of Hellenistic Athens* [Cambridge, Mass., 1940], 44, 106; B. D. Merrit, *Historia* 26 [1977]: 177).

Sparta, Nabis, who figures in official Roman and Akhaian propaganda as a pirate who worked with Kretans (cf. Polyb. 13.8.2; Livy 33.44.8; 34.32.18, 35.9, 36.3), was a Delian *proxenos* (*IG* XI 4.716 = *Choix,* 58). Pierre Brulé has suggested that he and his Kretan friends sold booty on Delos; this is nothing but a guess, but on the face of it not an unreasonable one.[29] Piracy was part of the economic revival of the last third of the third century; emblematic of this upswing are the raids of the outsider pirates Demetrios in 219 and Dikaiarkhos in 205 or 204 B.C., both of whom found the archipelago satisfying hunting grounds.

This period of prosperity, which based on price rises must have begun between 250 and 230 B.C., corresponds perfectly with the years of Kykladic independence. As we have seen, the great powers retreated from Delos after 245 B.C., not to return until the Second Makedonian War. Of the many consequences the absence of overlords had, probably the most important was that wealth generated in the islands no longer migrated to royal coffers. Payment of tribute ended, or at least diminished (the Delians surely continued to award crowns from time to time to kings). Garrisons were withdrawn from some islands, although others still supported them. The wars of the second half of the century imposed far less frequently on the Kyklades, which probably contributed fewer soldiers, paid less money, and witnessed less fighting than they had under their former sovereigns.[30] The result was a period of prosperity unparalleled earlier in the Hellenistic period.

The role of the Rhodians in this remains difficult to assess. Rhodian traders certainly plied the Kyklades in these years, although they remain frustratingly hard to identify.[31] The striking rise in numbers of Rhodian amphorae on Delos after 220 B.C. or so attests explicitly to the import of

29. Brulé, 49, citing *IG* XI 4.716 (= *Choix,* 58), for Nabis and 719, proxeny for a Knossian. See, generally, on Nabis (with strong denial of the charge of piracy), Benjamin Shimron, *Late Sparta: The Spartan Revolution, 243–146 B.C.* (Buffalo, N.Y., 1972), 79–100; also Paul Cartledge and Antony Spawforth, *Hellenistic and Roman Sparta* (London, 1989), 71, 246 n. 19.

30. Only a handful of military incidents are attested. Doson's Karian expedition certainly passed through the Kyklades but has left no trace (Trog. *Prol.* 28; see discussion at Will I^2, 366–71). Attalos I stopped on Delos in 209 and dedicated a *phiale* on his way to claim his purchase of Aigina (Polyb. 22.8.10, *ID* 396B67–68, with 443Bb108 and Durrbach's comm., p. 42, following a suggestion of Holleaux; R. E. Allen, *BSA* 66 [1971]: 1–12). Bruneau, 573, thinks that this *phiale* may be part of the series for the Attaleia, founded by 216 B.C., but this is unlikely: Attalos's special *phiale* was stored in the Artemision (*ID* 396B58), while the *phialai* for the festival were kept in the temple of Apollo (*ID* 366A55–56).

31. Alain Bresson, *Index* 9 (1980): 144–49.

Rhodian products, whether or not they all were transported on Rhodian bottoms. Politically and militarily, however, the Rhodians maintained no permanent presence in the Kyklades until after 200 B.C. Their sweep against Demetrios of Pharos was just that, a sweep, mediated by larger political considerations. The First Kretan War, fought because of Kretan pirate raids against Rhodos and its immediate neighbors,[32] probably played a more important role in turning Rhodian attention toward the central Aegean. Philip's aggression against Asia Minor, which threatened Rhodian possessions there, made them only too happy to join Attalos and the Romans against him. The Kyklades were their prize.

The Rhodians

In his discussion of the preliminaries of the great siege of Rhodos that earned Demetrios Poliorketes his ironic nickname, Diodoros of Sicily treats the close economic connection between the Rhodians and Ptolemaic Egypt; the Rhodians, Diodoros claims, provided the bottoms to export Egyptian grain and import other goods. The speaker of the Demosthenic speech *Against Dionysiodoros* imputes similar ties in the late fourth century when Kleomenes was in charge of Egypt.[33] This tie with Egypt served as the foundation of the role Rhodos played in the economic life of the Hellenistic world.

But economic power (without being more specific about what that was) did not necessarily spell political influence, and neither can it be assumed that Rhodian political decisions were inevitably based on economic considerations. This point should be obvious, but modern commentators are fond of statements such as "It perhaps goes without saying that one mechanism of Rhodes' control [of the Kyklades in the second century] was its tremendous economic influence among the islands,"[34] which in fact are very hard to justify. The role of the Rhodians in the Second Syrian War offers a very good example of the embarrassments that arise from equating political and economic interests. The Rhodians chose to fight against their longstanding Ptolemaic allies, whom they defeated ca. 258 in the battle of Ephesos. This defection from "their most important trading partner" has issued in theories of a Rhodian policy to avoid a "world-monarchy": Rhodian "policy makers were farsighted enough to realize that the predominance of

32. Brulé, 35–61, Petropoulou, 35–45, Berthold, 98–99; Patrick Baker, *Cos et Calymna* (Québec, 1991), passim.

33. Diod. 20.81.4, cf. also 46.6; [Demos.] 56.3. See also chapter 3, pp. 76–80, above.

34. Berthold, 143 n. 45.

any one power, even Egypt, would almost certainly mean the end of the republic's autonomy and influence."[35]

This sounds as if the Rhodians had anticipated the outcome of the war against Perseus by almost one hundred years. Moreover, the Rhodians had no trouble supporting the Ptolemies during their remarkably successful years from 287 to 267, when they liberated Athens, controlled the Kyklades, seized Samos and bases in Asia Minor, held Koile Syria, and fought the Seleukids in the First Syrian War. Surely, if the Ptolemies looked about to recreate a world empire in 260 B.C., they had already started on that road by 279. Why did the Rhodians not act to stop them earlier? Or again, in the Third Syrian War, which started out looking like a sure defeat for the Seleukids, which would have delivered a huge land empire into Ptolemaic hands, the Rhodians stayed loyal. Given the assumption that economic considerations loomed large in Rhodian policy-making, choosing to oppose their premier trading partner would at any time have been exceedingly risky.

Once again, local political concerns are the better place to look for an explanation. Since 279, the Ptolemies had controlled numerous cities in Karia, Pamphylia, and elsewhere in littoral Asia Minor. The causes of the Second Syrian War remain very obscure, but it is clear at least that the revolt of Ptolemaios the Son resulted in the loss to the Ptolemies of many possessions in Asia Minor. When the war began, then, it looked, not as if the Ptolemies were about to recover Alexander's empire, but rather as if instability and unwelcome tyranny were spreading right in Rhodos's back yard, making the region ripe for exploitation. Antiokhos II had, of course, the same idea; by working together, he and the Rhodians could carve up former Ptolemaic possessions. This, it seems to me, provides a much better explanation of Rhodian opposition to the Ptolemies. It also, at least partly, decouples political and economic policy.[36]

Our examination of Rhodian activities in the Kyklades reinforces this position. In the late fourth and early third centuries, the Rhodians stepped in to replace Athenian suppliers of olive oil to the Kyklades. Yet throughout the years of these activities, there is not the slightest indication of Rhodian attempts to obtain political jurisdiction over the archipelago. There is no sign of Rhodian political or military activity either in 311, when Polemaios revolted from Antigonos Monophthalmos, or in 308, when Ptole-

35. Berthold, 92, 91. For "world-monarchy," see H. van Gelder, *Geschichte der alten Rhodier* (The Hague, 1900), 110.

36. Will I², 168–200, on Ptolemaic foreign policy.

maios I took advantage of the confused situation, or in 307, when Demetrios came back through the islands, or in 288, when control of the archipelago was up in the air.

The same is true for the last two decades of the third century. Amphora finds on Delos, although not yet fully published, demonstrate a striking interest in Delos beginning after 220 B.C. From ca. 275 to 220 B.C., an average of only 0.6 handles/yr has been found on Delos; for the years from ca. 220 to 175, the figure leaps to 9.9 handles/yr.[37] Yet again, this economic interest, which may have been fueled largely by a demand for better-quality wine (see above), led to virtually no political involvement. Rhodian interventions against Demetrios and Dikaiarkhos (in the context of their First Kretan War) are their only attested activities in the Kyklades before the decisive events of the Second Makedonian War. In the one case, they were acting to expel an outsider whose presence had larger political and military implications; in the other, they were expanding military activity that had begun as a result of Kretan raids in the immediate territory of Rhodos, not in the Kyklades.[38] These events may well have alerted the Rhodians that the central Aegean, a region close to their own shores, was essentially a political vacuum, absent any outside *hegemon*,[39] and that the islands had become fairly prosperous since the last Rhodian incursion. But such a realization, if indeed it occurred, did not eventuate in action until the support of the Attalids and the Romans facilitated intervention in the archipelago after 200 B.C.

The Rhodian domination of 199–167 B.C. had real political consequences. The Rhodians exacted alliances, reactivated the Island League, compelled the islanders to serve in a Nesiotic fleet, stationed troops on Tenos, encouraged or pressured islanders to adopt Rhodian-style constitutions, entangled the islanders in the wars they fought, and probably supported local figures like Telemnestos son of Aristeides on Delos, who has been implicated in a pro-Rhodian policy during the 190s and 180s.[40] But it would be a mistake to impute a clear *economic* aspect to this policy. Am-

37. Computed with adjustments from data published by Virginia R. Grace and Maria Savvatianou-Pétropoulako in *L'Ilot de la Maison des comédiens* (Paris, 1970), ch. 14; cf. Virginia Grace, *BCH* 76 (1952): 522–33; John H. Kent in *Studies Presented to David Moore Robinson* (St. Louis, 1953), II.127–34; and J.-Y. Empereur, *BCH* 106 (1982): 224. The numbers may well include an error of a few percent. One must be very cautious in interpreting this material; cf. the remarks of Empereur, 219–25, and chapter 5, pp. 163–64, above.

38. See n. 32, above.

39. "Political vacuum" in the Aegean: Berthold, 97–98, cf. Etienne, 124.

40. See chapter 2, pp. 19–20, 27–30, 34, 37, 40–41, above.

phora handles tell part of the tale: 92 handles dated ca. 220–210 have been found, or an average deposition rate of 9.2/yr; for ca. 210–175 the figure is 10.0/yr, a change of no significance.[41] Despite the wealth of epigraphical evidence from Rhodos, only fifteen Kykladic islanders are attested there, and several of them date to after the end of Rhodian control of the islands.[42] There was neither a "federal" coinage nor any attempt to impose Rhodian money on the islands. Unlike in the Peraia or at Kaunos and Stratonikeia, the Rhodians did not demand tribute or other payments. The development of the Delian and Kykladic economies antedated the Rhodian presence, and the forces that drove them continued to operate into the second century. The real break in Delian development fell not under the Rhodians—although there can be no doubt that the numbers of outsiders grew in the second century—but after 167 B.C., when Delos was made a free port to punish Rhodos, and especially after 146 B.C., when the destruction of Korinthos brought Delos's trade to levels it had not before experienced.[43]

Politics and the Economy

This review of the interests of the Rhodians in the Kyklades leads directly to consideration of the larger connections between politics and economics on Delos, in the Hellenistic Kyklades, and in the ancient Greek world generally. Certainly no single picture characterizes the relation. Consider the Ptolemies. On the one hand, some of their activities must have had an economic impact. The kings and their families and officials dedicated *phialai*, crowns, and other precious objects to the god; the offerings of the Ptolemies and their wives and relatives amounted to perhaps 1,000 dr in gold, or about two talents of silver.[44] Festivals they founded (several Ptolemaieia and a Theuergesia) used dedicated capital to make loans whose interest covered the cost of annual dedication of *phialai* or other gifts. The Ptolemaic official Philokles and the *nesiarkhos* Hermias created foundations with capital of 6,000 and 3,300 dr. Bakkhon the *nesiarkhos* and Patroklos the admiral of the Khremonidean War donated precious objects. In

41. Cf. n. 37 above.

42. See chapter 2, p. 34 n. 49.

43. Polyb. 30.31.10 on the troops; Pierre Roussel, *Délos colonie athénienne* (Paris, 1916), 1–3, 7–18; W. Déonna, *La Vie privée des Déliens* (Paris, 1948), 25–26; Erich S. Gruen, *The Hellenistic World and the Coming of Rome* (Berkeley, 1984), I.299, 311–12, and id. in *The Imperialism of Mid-Republican Rome* (Rome, 1984), 70–71; Rostovtzeff, 777–78; Will II^2, 298, 300–301. Cf. pp. 270–71 below.

44. Bruneau, 516–18, giving an actual total of 780.5 or 791.5 dr, but the weight is not recorded for some objects.

this they stood in a long tradition that included the Antigonid admiral Polykleitos, Androkles the Amathousian king, and the Spartan Lysandros.[45]

On the other hand, there is virtually no evidence that the Ptolemies attempted to integrate the archipelago into their economic circuit. Trade between the islands and Egypt seems to have been limited to small shipments of high-value goods, like Rheneian and Kythnian cheeses, Kimolian fuller's earth, or a few amphorae of Parian wine. The Ptolemies did not try to bring the islands into their monetary orbit, as they did with Thrake and Koile Syria, and neither did they build any important structures on Delos.[46]

Indeed, the strongest indicators of some kind of economic impact by the Ptolemies are negative. The passage of armies frequently stressed local systems of supply and disrupted prices and rents, although this was always transitory. More important were demands for tribute (however paid), which probably absorbed an appreciable, although unquantifiable, proportion of local wealth. Recent study of the territory of the Keian city of Koresia, renamed Arsinoë during the Khremonidean War, which was port to a Ptolemaic fleet, has documented the start of the polis's decline in exactly this period; in contrast to Thera, where the imposition of a garrison had positive effects, Koresia apparently suffered. We must be careful in our analysis. The evidence uncovered by work in Koresia is not well enough dated to prove that the beginning of Koresia's decline did not correspond with the withdrawal of the garrison rather than its introduction; but it is nevertheless certainly true that the *akropoleis* of the city show no new building in the third century, in strong contrast to Thera, with its extensive remains of the Ptolemaic fortress.[47]

These effects, or rather their absence, can be attributed to the nature of Ptolemaic interest in the Kyklades. As I have repeatedly argued, the Kyklades provided the Ptolemies with the necessary stepping-stones for project-

45. Ibid., 518–45; Ziebarth, *Hermes* 32 (1917): 429; Bogaert, 153–61. K. J. Rigsby, *AJP* 101 (1980): 194–96. *IG* XI 2.226B4, etc. *IG* XI 2.161B27, etc., 137.39, etc., 161B59, etc.

46. *P. Cair. Zen.* I.59110, r. 25–26 (cf. v. 35–36), about 26 Nov. 257 B.C. (cf. 59548, 59547, both of about the same date), IV.59704.18, not dated, I.59012, col. II.45, about May–June 259 B.C.; IV.59741.24, undated, and *PSI* 859 for the Parian amphora. For expensive Keian specialty cheese (which may serve as a model for Rheneian and Kythnian cheeses), see Aiskhylides in Aelian 16.32. J. R. Jones, *ANS Museum Notes* 17 (1971): 133–35; J. N. Svoronos, Τὰ νομίσματα τοῦ κρατοῦς τῶν Πτολεμαίκων II (Athens, 1904), pl. xxvii 11–14 = nos. 930–33; J. M. F. May, *Ainos: Its History and Coinage* (London, 1950). On building, Bruneau, 516.

47. T. M. Whitelaw and J. L. Davis in *Landscape Archaeology*, 265–81; J. F. Cherry, J. L. Davis, and E. Mantzourani in ibid., 327–47.

ing their power into Greece. Their intrinsic appeal was low. "Investment," in the sense of reconstructing the local economy or putting lots of money into building projects, made little sense. The Nesiotic League and Philokles bore the administrative responsibilities, freeing the court in Alexandria to devote its attention to its genuinely important possessions.

These two examples, the Ptolemies and the Rhodians, nicely illustrate the complexities that arise in the study of the interconnections between political activity and economic effects. Strict political hegemony involving taxation, garrisoning, recruitment of soldiers, and military operations can subsist perfectly comfortably with a commodious disinterest in economic matters. That the Ptolemies, who, despite some recent revisionism on the issue, did care deeply about the economic operation of their own country, evinced no concern whatsoever about the same issues in the Kyklades, shows perfectly the disjunctions between politics and economy with which Hellenistic rulers could happily live. The Rhodians illustrate the same disjunctions. They cared profoundly about the condition of their possessions on the mainland of Asia Minor, but despite being involved far more intimately and immediately in the Kyklades than the Ptolemies ever were, they too did virtually nothing to affect the Kykladic economy: they simply exploited the system already in place.

I have stressed the principle of discontinuity between politics and economics, but in the case of the Kyklades it must be admitted that strictly local considerations surely went a long way to encourage the disjunction. The islands formed an economic unit, largely self-sufficient in foodstuffs (especially after ca. 270, when local olive oil production seems to have risen enough to satisfy local demand), building materials (except for wood for construction), and other basic needs. The system yielded a surplus sufficient to support a large "parasitic" population on Delos, which paid for its needs by providing religious services (which in turn brought in external wealth in the form of dedications) and by acting as a convenient central point of exchange, a role that expanded once the islands were permitted after 245 to retain the wealth outside *hegemones* had formerly appropriated. But the islands must have been operating near the bounds of their carrying capacity. They supported large populations themselves, on land already thoroughly exploited, as recent surveys have made more and more apparent. Squeezing more wealth out of them would have been a taxing undertaking, hardly worth the effort. The impetus for greater exploitation simply was not there. This situation conspired with the interests of the outsiders—and here I am thinking especially of the Ptolemies—to mitigate against any intimate involvement with the local economic system.

I do not mean to say, however, that political actions did not frequently have unintended economic effects. The creation in the late fourth century of the Nesiotic League by Antigonos Monophthalmos, its central role among his son Demetrios's possessions after the battle of Ipsos, and the decision of the Ptolemies, once they had seized control of the archipelago, to retain it as their instrument of administration of the islands, played a determining role in defining the character of the regional Kykladic economy in the first half of the Hellenistic period. I do not however believe that either the Antigonids or the Ptolemies intended this result. For the *hegemones* of the Kyklades, the league simply provided a convenient mechanism for administering many small poleis and for disseminating the rulers' propaganda. Likewise, the powerful impact of military activity in the islands, whether through transient troop movements and fighting or through the establishment of permanent or semi-permanent garrisons, was a direct result of political decisions taken by the *hegemones* or their allies or enemies. But again, the economic effects of this activity on the Kyklades played no role in the decisions of whether to fight a war, or, on a smaller scale, whether to send troops through Delos or Tenos.

As a coda, it should be said that after 167 B.C. the rules of the game changed dramatically. When the Romans declared Delos a free port, they set in motion a process that ultimately decoupled Delos from the rest of the Kyklades.[48] The destruction in 146 B.C. of Korinthos, which had been an important mustering point for traders moving east or west, accelerated the process. Foreign traders had begun to appear on Delos in the first third of the second century, attracted by the new local prosperity, but their numbers swelled in the last fifty years of the century. The great expansion of city and port belong to this period—and well into the first century, until Mithridates' invasion and the pirate attacks of the midcentury drove away almost everybody. The wealth of this period came from well outside of the Kyklades, which themselves seem to have suffered a serious decline.[49] The flood of Italians, Phoenicians, and other traders devoted to moving goods west to Italy and uninterested in the local economic scene undoubtedly swamped the local traders who had traditionally moved goods around the archipelago. The loss of their central local entrepôt cannot explain the de-

48. This decision was certainly political, not economic: Delos sat at the center of the Nesiotic League, one of two important Rhodian possessions outside of the island (the other being the Peraia). Contra, H. Hill, *The Roman Middle Class in the Republic Period* (Oxford, 1952), 97–98: "The treatment of Rhodes in 167–166 B.C. . . . [was] the first clear example of a policy influenced by commercial considerations." See also Donald V. Sippel, *Ancient World* 12 (1985): 97–104. Will II^2, 300–301.

49. Cherry, Davis, and Mantzourani in *Landscape Archaeology,* esp. 341–44; Malcolm Wagstaff and John F. Cherry in *Island Polity,* 145–46, 252–53.

cline of the islands attested from ca. 200 B.C., since the abandonment of rural settlement and the shrinkage of population centers seems to have been widespread in Greece in the last two centuries B.C. But the decoupling of Delos from its traditional Kykladic base may help to explain the failure of the sacred island to recover from the depredations of Mithridates and the pirates of the mid first century. If the neighboring islands had undergone an economic decline in the intervening century, they might no longer have been able to support a local trade at Delos; when the long-distance merchants fled, there was no one in the archipelago to take their place.

Further Directions

Where do we go from here? In many ways, this study is only the first step on a long road to a more nuanced understanding of the character of the Hellenistic economy. I would like to end with a few of the lessons it has offered and some suggestions for future investigation.

One serious problem has remained largely unaddressed in the preceding chapters, although I have often alluded to it. The economic data we have for Delos come almost exclusively from the records of its great pan-Hellenic sanctuary. I have generally assumed that these data may be extrapolated to the city as a whole; in the case of commodity prices, I have tried to show that such prices must have been fair market prices (chapter 1). But we have also seen that the temple was constrained by some considerations that might not have affected secular consumers. It had to buy sacrificial animals, no matter what the price; if some scholars' suggestion is right, it may have sometimes refused to rent sacred houses that failed to fetch satisfactory rents (chapters 5 and 6). Beyond this, however, we know virtually nothing specific about either the economic relations between the sanctuary and the city or the impact of the sanctuary on the local economic scene.[50] There can be no doubt that the dedications of kings and their ministers and the stopovers of visitors great and humble brought in wealth (chapter 3); but how and to what degree did that wealth impinge on the local economy? Did any real local benefit flow from the *phialai* and crowns and thousands of other objects stored in the buildings of the sanctuary? Our understanding of these issues would be greatly helped by comparative study of other sanctuary sites. Delos was not the only small town in the Hellenistic world that had a great sanctuary nearby; besides the obvious case of Delphi, we may think of Samothrake, Tenos, and Labraunda near Mylasa. Elucidation of the economic impact of these sanctuaries on their cities would help us evaluate the situation on Delos.

50. Cf. Rostovzteff, 190.

Similar institutions at different places do not always produce the same results. The economic impact of garrisons illustrates this. On Thera the Ptolemaic garrison fostered prosperity, despite occasional conflict between the community and the soldiers; at Keos the imposition of a garrison either had no visible effect or may have correlated with the beginning of a period of decline. The difference may be explicable as the consequence of the permanence of the garrison at Thera compared to the transitoriness of the Keian one; the situation at Samos may have been comparable to that on Thera. But the point remains that it is dangerous to assume that every city reacted similarly to similar institutions.

It is a serious mistake to underestimate the carrying capacity of the land in antiquity. Typically, especially in the minor poleis that formed the vast majority of Greek states, the *khora* certainly did satisfy most local needs, even in apparently unproductive environments like the Kyklades. Regular consumption of barley, which requires much less rainfall than wheat, made an important contribution to the ability of the Kyklades to feed themselves. Intensive exploitation of the land by terracing, rotating crops, manuring fields, and constructing waterworks raised productivity enough to permit limited exports, which went to support the nonagricultural population of Delos. Regular long-distance importation of foodstuffs was not an important part of the economic scene, except during occasional periods of famine. Recent attempts to argue that trade in fact played a large role in creating income for many cities seem to me mistaken, although it may well be that the Kyklades were more prosperous in the fifth century than at any other time.[51] Self-sufficiency was not merely a slogan but a reality for many Greek cities, notwithstanding a certain level of necessary imports.

The links between politics and economics remain very obscure. Despite sources like Pseudo-Aristotle's *Oikonomikos,* we know very little about the economic policies of most Greek cities, especially as they relate to purely internal matters. The economic imposts of outside powers present similar obscurities. It is clear, however, that the connections that the modern world sees as a matter of course between the two may not have been so palpable in the Hellenistic world. *Hegemones* seem to have had a very limited sense of what they wanted to extract out of the Kyklades: taxes first and foremost; perhaps troops when necessary or possible. They appointed officials to oversee the collection of these monies and settled disputes within cities that might impede the flow of tribute, but that was about it. The gifts of precious *phialai* or other dedications to the sanctuary of Apollo on Delos enriched the temple and the city of the Delians, but this effect

51. Lucia Nixon and Simon Price in *Greek City,* 137–70.

was purely coincidental. The motive behind the dedications was religious, not economic.

The time has certainly come to stop seeing the "Hellenistic economy" as unitary. Differences were great from region to region, even from polis to polis. Within the Kyklades, variation in climate, resources, topography, and geography combined with differing social and political traditions to create substantial differences within a restricted and superficially uniform region. The divergent trajectories of the four poleis of Keos, an island covering only 103 km^2, elucidate the point nicely. But the examples can easily be multiplied: Andros, with its relatively abundant water and strategic location; Tenos, with its remarkably flat (hence easily cultivated) landscape and its sanctuary, second in importance only to Delian Apollo's in the islands; Naxos, with its high mountains, extensive woods, and tradition of local political dominance since the Archaic period; Thera, with its commodious harbor; Amorgos, split virtually into separate islands by its tortuous landscape, straddling the sea routes to Krete—in each case, we are presented with a unique combination of circumstances that helped determine separate economic fates for each island, however much the archipelago as a whole may look like a unit. In the same sense, individual poleis were not unitary. Delos certainly offers the best example, tied as it was to the entire Greek world through its sanctuary, while its economy was virtually entirely parochial. But the other islands present their own contradictions. Through its garrison, Thera maintained connections with distant parts of the Greek world; it might even serve as a retirement home for a citizen of distant Perge. Parian marble had an assured market outside the Kyklades, although in other ways the island retained its local ties (including selling stone to nearby Delian Apollo). The strategic situation of Andros assured constant attentions from foreign powers wanting to secure the entrance to the Saronic Gulf. Full elucidation of these differences is crucial for a nuanced understanding of the economic life of the Hellenistic period.

The research and writing of this book brought home to me with some force a list of desiderata for future study of the ancient economy. Difficult as they may be, there is a great need for more quantification studies. Many places offer no data, of course, and the desire to squeeze as much information as possible out of the sources that do exist certainly can lead to overinterpretation, distortion, and generalizations based on inadequate evidence. The envy historians of ancient Greek economies feel for historians both of ancient Mesopotamia and of early modern Europe will never go away. But there are some bodies of evidence. The most abundant, and still very inadequately studied, comes from Ptolemaic Egypt. A recent collection of data for the Roman period has been treated virtually without statistical analysis, despite tables of data that run in some cases literally for dozens of pages. I do not mean to trivialize the formidable difficulties the Egyptian material presents; I was lucky on Delos to have had data from a very limited time frame and all from one place, so that issues of comparability of prices did not arise. Nevertheless, the Egyptian data would reward close work.[52] Likewise, the Greek world presents some of the kinds of data that Richard Duncan-Jones exploited for his quantitative studies of the Roman imperial economy. Despite the limitations of his approach and the justifiable reservations one may have about it, similar work would be worth doing for the Hellenistic period.

Amphora data need to be published thoroughly and consistently. It is especially regrettable that we still lack complete data for great sites like Delos. The French amphora project, which aims to computerize all amphorae known from all sites, will be a great help when it finally becomes available. In the meantime, traditional publication of all finds must go on.[53]

The archaeological surveys of Melos and Keos cited so frequently in this book have been an invaluable aid to my understanding of the economic history of the Kyklades. There can no longer be any doubt that surveys have proven their value.[54] The Kyklades offer an especially attractive arena for further survey work. The islands are small enough to be covered in a relatively brief time, with relatively small teams, at relatively low cost. The publication of two previous surveys offers plenty of comparative evidence, and the results of these surveys suggest that the history of the islands was unexpectedly rich, varied, and interesting. I would hope, however, that future survey teams will be characterized by greater cooperation from the beginning between archaeologists and historians. For obvious reasons, the designers and directors of surveys tend to be archaeologists (and increasingly anthropologists and ethnoarchaeologists). Historians could learn a great deal by participating in surveys from the initial stages; in turn, their participation could help ensure that surveys are designed in part to explore specific historical questions, especially questions that might seem at first glance to be unamenable to archaeological investigation.[55]

One question that more surveys might help to answer comes immedi-

52. For a recent example of statistical work with Egyptian material—in this case toll documents—cf. Wolfgang Habermann, *MBAH* 9.1 (1990): 50–94.

53. Cf. recently Yvon Garlan, *CRAI* 1990: 490–507; Francine Blondé, Arthur Muller, and Dominique Mulliez, *BCH* 115 (1991): 213–42.

54. Anthony Snodgrass in *Greek City*, 113–36, esp. 118–19.

55. Ongoing work on several islands may help to clarify the picture. Besides the German research on Paros and Naxos, see, for Karthaia on Keos, Lina G. Mendoni, *Arkhaiognosia* 4 (1985–86): 149–84; for Amorgos, Lila Marangou in *Les Cyclades*, 121–29, 236.

ately to mind. The results of surveys conducted not only in the Kyklades but in many other parts of Greece point to a decline in the rural population in the later Hellenistic period.[56] There are two related problems here. One is the interpretation of the phenomenon. A decrease in rural habitation sites—which is really the evidence on which the proposition rests—is amenable to a number of explanations. Perhaps the rural population simply retreated to local polis centers, giving a nucleated settlement pattern. There need then be no actual decrease in the numbers of people. Recent work at Koresia on Keos, however, suggests a decline in this urban center at about the same time as the rural decline started.[57] This would appear to mean that the rural population did not retreat to urban centers; but in the absence of studies of the other poleis of Keos—especially Ioulis and Karthaia, which absorbed Koresia and Poiessa sometime in the Hellenistic period (cf. Strabo 10.5.6 [C486])—it is impossible to be sure whether Koresia's contraction was localized or a local example of a general phenomenon. Further survey work, especially surveys that cover the whole of an island, would help to settle this matter.

The other problem is the exact date of the population decline, which currently cannot be dated more closely than to the third to first centuries B.C. Now the late third century, as we have seen, is exactly the period when Delos and its Kykladic neighbors show a rising local prosperity. I have attributed this prosperity to the absence of outside control, and as far as it goes, the explanation is reasonable. If, however, it could be shown that a real fall in Kykladic population had begun in the third century, it might be possible to attribute Kykladic prosperity in part also to expanding carrying capacity of the land as the absolute numbers of mouths to be fed declined. As the process continued, however, loss of labor would have reduced production even as economic activity was expanding. This might help account for the appeal of Delos to the Rhodians and even to the decoupling of Delos from the local Kykladic economy after the mid second century: a depopulated Kyklades no longer offered the opportunities for enough local activity to support the Delian population; the solution was sought in long-distance trade. This in turn would account for the failure of Delos to recover as a local entrepôt after 69 B.C. The low population and low productivity of the islands could no longer support even the functions Delos had carried out in the third and early second centuries. But all this will remain speculation unless survey work can provide evidence to support or refute it.

56. For recent overviews, see Sallares, 62–64, with references, and Susan Alcock, *Graecia Capta* (Cambridge, 1993), 37–49.

57. Whitelaw and Davis in *Landscape Archaeology*, 265–81; John F. Cherry and Jack L. Davis, *BSA* 86 (1991): 9–28.

Finally, we need more regional studies. Only by piling up specific detail about limited regions can we hope to create a fully articulated, fully nuanced picture of the history of economic life and economic change in the Hellenistic world. The surveys of Keos and Melos, Roland Etienne's study of Tenos, Michèle Brunet's work on rural farmsteads on Delos and Thasos, Lila Marangou's excavations at Minoa on Amorgos, to mention only a few: these quite specific regional or polis studies are vital. In this regard, I think M. I. Finley was mistaken to condemn regional studies as uninteresting or largely antiquarian: they are, rather, the lifeblood of the study of the ancient economy.[58]

58. M. I. Finley, *Ancient History: Evidence and Models* (New York, 1985), 61.

Appendix I
Additional Notes

STATUS OF THE τεχνῖται OF 282 B.C.

These workers were surely free, not temple slaves, despite payment in kind of food and clothing, taken as a sure emblem of slave status by J. A. O. Larsen (399). The gap in payment of two months in early summer (*IG* XI 2.158A45–46) must represent a period when the *tekhnitai* were not employed, since there is no lacuna in the text. If the temple had owned them, the expense of upkeep would have continued (unless of course they were lent to the city or to some other entity for two months; Vial, 261–62, has suggested that the temple and the city shared a herald). Moreover the disappearance of the third *tekhnites* after two months makes better sense as the dismissal of an employee than the death or sale of a slave, since these events tend to show up in the accounts (burial expenses for a dead slave, *ID* 372A97–98, 113; sale of an unsatisfactory slave, *ID* 290.114). Finally, the word τεχνῖται is used in the accounts to describe two smiths working for the temple at a piece rate of one obol to sharpen tools in 281 B.C.: τοῖς τεχνίταις εἰς τὸν ἐνιαυτὸν τὰ σιδήρια ὀξύνασιν Ἡρακλείδηι καὶ Δεξίωι (*IG* XI 2.159A58). Dexios's subsequent negotiations with the temple over this business—he accepted a flat 40 dr/yr for all sharpening in 279 but in 274 returned to a piece rate of only half an obol (*IG* XI 2.161A107–8, 199A87; cf. Gustave Glotz, *Journal des Savants* 11 [1913]: 255–56)—suggest a free person, not a slave.

MELIAN YIELDS IN 1670

Guy D. R. Sanders, *BSA* 79 (1984):251–62, attempts to recover yields from a tax assessment made on the Kyklades in 1670 and summarized in B. J. Slot, *Archipelagus turbatus* (Istanbul, 1982), 1:294–309. Sanders's approach, however, founders on a confusion: he assumes that the Turkish assessor assessed crops by area (the *binek*, probably about 1,000 m^2 [cf. Slot, 296]) and adjusted the rate of assessment to match local conditions. In fact, crops were assessed at standard rates (listed in Slot, 299) per *binek* of volume (probably about 38 liters [Slot, 295–96]); it was the assessment rates for land that varied (Slot, 294–95). Figures for Naxos, the only island for which Slot gives fairly complete data, illustrate this. Slot details the assessments for the village of Khalki, with 853.5 *binek* (area) of cultivated land, which produced just over 570 *binek* (volume) of grains and vegetables (296–97). The gross yield for this village was therefore about 0.67 *binek* (volume) / *binek* (area), approximately 2.5 l/ha: not impressive. The whole island did little better, producing 0.88 *binek* / *binek*. It is, however, impossible to obtain yields for individual products, because the data cannot be made to yield an area cultivated for each product. For Melos, Slot notes that the land paid an average rate of 20 *akçe / binek* (296), from which Sanders correctly calculates that the Melians must have cultivated about 5,022 *binek.* (The *akçe* was a small silver coin.) This gives a gross yield for Melos of about 2.25 *binek / binek,* much better than Naxos's certainly, and in conformity with claims about the productivity of Melian soils, which "have long been regarded as exceptionally fertile, at least on the scale of the Kyklades" (Malcolm Wagstaff and Clive Gamble in *Island Polity,* 101); but nothing justifies Sanders's yield figures of 1,928.6 kg/ha for wheat and 3,000 kg/ha for barley.

DEDICATIONS TO MASSINISSA ON DELOS

There are several dedications to Massinissa known from Delos, including separate statues erected to him and his wife by Hermon the Delian and Kharmylos of Rhodos.[1] Felix Durrbach associates these dedications with Massinissa's gift of grain. Now that Philippe Gauthier has severed the "Rhodian connection," the connection of these statues with the gifts has become more nebulous.[2] There is perhaps no need to invoke special circumstances to explain them. As a supplier of grain to the Roman armies, Numidia had close relations with Rome, whose policy Rhodos supported in the Aegean in the 180s.[3] It is therefore reasonable that the statues of Massinissa, who remained Rome's friend his whole life, should be dated to the early 170s. Rhodos controlled the refounded Nesiotic League in the first quarter of the second century. The dedications may therefore simply reflect wider Rhodian political interests unrelated to Delos specifically.

DOCUMENTS RELATING TO GRAIN SHORTAGES IN BOIOTIA AND EUBOIA

The evidence includes:

(1) *IG* XII 9.900Aa, dated by Denis Knoepfler, *BCH* 114 (1990):491, to ca. 175, with Olivier Picard, *Chalcis et la confédération eubéenne* (Paris, 1979), 298–99.

(2) A decree of Oropos of the same date, *IG* VII 4262 (= *SIG*³ 547, *ISE,* I.64), with L. Robert, *Opera minora selecta* (Amsterdam, 1990), 7.746, with n. 2, and 751 with n. 6, and *REG* 94 (1981):342 (= *Opera minora selecta* (Amsterdam, 1989), 6.436), with the date at Roland Etienne and Denis Knoepfler, *Hyettos de Béotie et la chronologie des archontes fédé-*

1. *IG* XI 4 1115–16 = *Choix,* 68–69; cf. also *Choix,* 93, another statue, dated to 149/8 B.C., and *ID* 1578, mentioning his sons and dated to the 170s by M.-F. Baslez, *REG* 94 (1981): 160–65 (*SEG* 31.730). *ID* 442A104 for Hermon, cf. *Choix,* p. 92.

2. See chapter 4, pp. 112–13, above, and esp. Gauthier's remarks at *CICG,* 69.

3. On the deterioration of Roman-Rhodian relations in the following decade, see Gabriele Marasco, *Prometheus* 11 (1985): 137–50.

raux entre 250 et 171 avant J.-C. (Paris, 1976), 318, 350; it honors two Phoenicians who imported grain to Oropos and at the request of the *polemarkhoi* sold it at a reduced price (ll. 3–4). There is no explicit mention of a shortage.

(3) A decree of Khorsiai for Kapon of Thisbe, *ISE,* I.66 (= Migeotte, 41–44, no. 10), with, for the date, Etienne and Knoepfler, *Hyettos,* 243–44, with n. 908; cf. also Paul Roesch, *Rev. Phil.* 39 (1965):256–61, no. II. The decree refers to a σπανοσιτία (l. 4) in the *khora* that caused the cities (pl.) to embargo grain; Kapon responded with 200 *kophinoi,* equal to 37.5 *medimnoi* (l. 7; on the size of the *kophinos,* cf. Pollux 4.169; Moretti, *ISE,* I, p. 170 n. 3). If the 500 dr he released the city from paying (ll. 14–15) was the price of the grain (wheat, cf. l. 7), then the price/*med* was 13 dr 2 ob Aiginetan (cf. Moretti, *ISE,* p. 170 n. 7; for this interpretation, see ibid., 169, Philippe Gauthier, *Symbola* (Nancy, 1976), 382–83; Migeotte, 44, is not convincing).

(4) A decree of Thisbe on *sitonia, IG* VII 1719, with Michel Feyel, *Contribution à l'épigraphie béotienne* (Le Puy, 1942), 45–46; Paul Roesch, *Thespies et la confédération béotienne* (Paris, 1965), 223.

A decree of Athens is sometimes cited in this context (*IG* II^2 903, with Gauthier, *REG* 95 [1982]:278–90 and *SEG* 32.132), but it in fact records not a grain but an oil shortage. Oil and grain shortages had very different causes and fell at different times of year.

The fifth document has been assigned definitely to the Third Makedonian War:

(5) *Gonnoi II,* no. 41, dated 180–160, and related by B. Helly, *Gonnoi II* (p. 47) to the war with Perseus. This decree refers specifically to a shortage—σπανοσιτία—of one season, relieved by the sale of grain on credit to Gonnoi by the Thessalian Nikias.

THE DECREE FOR BOULAGORAS OF SAMOS AND THE THIRD SYRIAN WAR

The Samians passed a well-known decree in favor of Boulagoras (most readily available as *SEG* 1.366) in either 247/6 (which I favor) or 243/2 B.C.[4] Among Boulagoras's many beneficences was the provision of money to buy grain during a famine that was so bad that three citizens,

4. Brief treatment with reference to earlier literature in Werner Transier, *Samiaka: Epigraphische Studien zur Geschichte von Samos in hellenistischer und römischer Zeit* (Mannheim, 1985), 79–80. Graham Shipley, *A History of Samos, 800–188 B.C.* (Oxford, 1987), 189 n. 23, rejects a specific date in the 240s because it "rests on the assumption that [Antiokhos II] Theos had Samos continuously till c. 246, but since this is no longer certain we can only put the decree somewhere in the 250s or 240s." Yet Shipley himself in his text uses the decree as evidence that Samos "was once more Ptolemaic by the late 240s," implicitly rejecting a date before 246. In fact, however, *SEG* 1.366 cannot go before 247 B.C., for Boulagoras's

Boulagoras among them, were elected as grain buyers (ll. 36–49). These activities are related directly after praise for Boulagoras's performance at the Ptolemeiaia in Alexandria, which occurred in 246/5 or 243/2 and dates the inscription. Thus the famine that plagued the Samians fell during the Third Syrian War. Samos, which had been a Ptolemaic possession after 280 B.C. (*IG* XII 7.506.4 = *SIG*^{3} 390), was lost around 260 B.C. as a result of the revolt of Timarkhos in Miletos and Ptolemaios "the son"; their deaths may have led to Seleukid control after about 258 B.C., although a resumption of Ptolemaic influence or even Antigonid involvement may have intervened. By 253 B.C. or so, however, the Seleukids seem to have been installed.[5] Control must have passed back into Ptolemaic hands thanks to Ptolemaios III's great Aegean sweep in 246 B.C.; probably the "Ionia" of *OGIS* 54.14 includes Samos, which should also no doubt be counted among the "islands" inherited by Ptolemaios IV from Euergetes in 221 B.C.[6]

THE ESTATE EPISTHENEIA

Episthenia presents difficult problems. That the estate—as opposed to the houses—was confiscated, tardily, as part of the crackdown in 375 B.C., has been inferred from an entry in *ID* 98A24–25: Εἰσπράχθη μηνυθὲν ἐκ τῶν ᾿Επισθένος Δηλίο HH [H] 𐅄 ΔΔΔ. This statement is not unequivocal: it could refer to seizure and sale of property, including personal property like slaves or furniture; cf. the disposal of the goods of the Hermokopai in Athens (W. Kendrick Pritchett, *Hesperia* 22 [1953]:225–99, and 25 [1956]:178–328). However, the recurrence of an Episthenia among the rented estates during the Amphiktyonia assures that property was in fact confiscated (*ID* 98Ab108, 102.9, 104–3A2–3, 104–11A19, 104–19A12).

Yet in 313 B.C. Episthenia appears as hypothecation for a loan (*IG* XI 2.135.22–23). Jacques Tréheux and others (*BCH* 68–69 [1944–45]:1016 n. 2) have taken this to mean that it was returned in 314 B.C. as part of a reaction against the acts of the Athenian-led Amphiktyonia. Others have rejected this view (notably Jardé, 147 n. 1; in a modified form, Kent, 256–58). I see two problems. First, Tharsynon paid 200 dr on Episthenia in 313 B.C. We have seen that Hermon's payment on Sosimakheia may represent ten years' back interest. If the same is true for Tharsynon's payment,

generosities include money to cover the costs of Samian representation in Alexandria at the Ptolemaieia honoring "king Ptolemaios and his sister queen Berenike" (ll. 27–28). They were only married in 247 B.C. (cf. *OCD*^{2} [Oxford, 1970], s.v. Berenice (3)).

5. Frontinus *Strat.* 3.2.11; cf. Bagnall, 80–81, and, for full details with references, Shipley, *History of Samos,* 187–89.

6. Polyb. 5.34.7. Bagnall, 80–88, 170–75, gives a good account of Ptolemaic-Samian relations. Shipley, *History of Samos,* 189, confines Euergetes' gains in the Third Syrian War to southwestern Asia Minor.

then the loan on Epistheneia must have fallen under the Amphiktyonia. There is another reason for suspecting this. Every borrower in the rubric in which Tharsynon is recorded seems to be paying a preexisting debt; this is certain for Theophrastos son of Theophrastos (ll. 16–17, cf. Vial, 323–25). Nothing indicates the granting of a loan in 314 or 313 B.C. That strongly suggests that the loan on Epistheneia goes back also into the Amphiktyonia.

Second, it is generally agreed that Kerameion was not returned in 314 (Kent, 256–58; Brunet, 33–35). Why, however, would the Delians have seen fit to make right the confiscation of Epistheneia but not of Kerameion? Moreover, the failure of the Delians to restore the confiscated houses seems to add another problem: why would they return (some) property but not these? I raise these questions without having satisfactory answers for any of them.

ID 503: THE DATE OF THE *HIERA SYNGRAPHE*

Since the estates were offered for rental in years that ended, in the Julian calendar, with 0, the *hiera syngraphe,* which imposed this regulation, must have gone into force in a year ending in zero or soon before. Only two possibilities have been seriously defended: 300 by Jacques Tréheux and others[7] and 290 B.C. by J. H. Kent (Kent, 282–85). Kent's case rests on one important observation and several arguments from probability.

IG XI 2.147A18–19 includes the entry: [Εἰ]ς τὴν ἀ(να)γραφὴν τῶγ γεωργῶν στὴλη παρ' Ἑρμοδίκου καὶ βατὴρ Δ· γράψαντι Ἑρμοδίκωι ΔΔΠ. This "stele of the farmers," as Kent calls it, had seemed to Gustave Glotz to be best taken as a record of renters, guarantors, and inventories of estates made at the beginning of a new rental period. Since 147 was dated to 300 B.C., this put a new rental period in that year, and strongly suggested that the *hiera syngraphe* had been promulgated then (Gustave Glotz, *BCH* 44 [1920]:365–66 n. 1; *IG* XI 2.147 comm., p. 31). Kent however observed that 147A15–17 noted the failure of the renter Maisiades to pay his full rent on Panormos. Since Maisiades still occupied the estate in 297 B.C. (*IG* XI 2.149.5–6), Kent dated 147 to 296 B.C. or later. This date made a difficulty either for the view that the "stele of the farmers" represented a new rental period or for the view that the *hiera syngraphe* was issued in

7. Felix Durrbach, *REG* 32 (1919): 177–78; the uncertainties introduced by the views of Erich Ziebarth, *Hermes* 61 (1926): 96 and reflected at *ID* 503, comm., p. 316, answered by Tréheux, *BCH* 68–69 (1944–45): 289–95; followed by Brunet, 47. I have not been able to consult Jacques Tréheux, "Etudes critiques sur les inventaires de l'indépendance délienne" (diss., Paris, 1959), 229–37, which Brunet (47 n. 6) says answers Kent's view; see also briefly J. Tréheux, *Mus. Hel.* 48 (1991): 248. Signe Isager and J. E. Skydsgaard give "about the year 300" but note Kent's alternative (Isager-Skydsgaard, 194 and n. 324).

300 B.C. For if the "stele of the farmers" showed a new rental in the year of 147, then the ten-year rental period had still not been established in the 290s. If the *hiera syngraphe* was still put in 300 B.C., then the "stele of the farmers" could not be a record of a new rental period.

Part of the problem lay in the 25 dr paid to Hermodikos to make the stele. In 302 B.C., he was paid 1 dr per 100 or 130 letters to inscribe another inscription: γράψαντι Ἑρμοδίκωι τῆς δραχμῆς· Η· μισθὸς· ΠΔΔΠ (*IG* XI 2.145.27); γράψαντι Ἑρμοδίκωι τῆς δραχμῆς ἑκατὸν τριάκοντα· Η· μισθὸς· ΗΔΔ (l. 43). Twenty years later, other masons were paid at 300 letters per dr (*IG* XI 2.159A66–67, 161A118–19). Even at the lowest rate, the "stele of the farmers" must have had about 2,500 letters; if, as Glotz and Kent thought, pay rates for masons were declining, then the text of the stele might have been considerably longer. This made it impossible to see in the stele a simple annual record of rents like *IG* XI 2.149, for that required only about 500 letters.

Kent proposed to solve this problem by identifying the "stele of the farmers" with the text of the *hiera syngraphe* itself. Thus the *syngraphe* was issued in the 290s, probably close to 290 itself (Kent's view implies a date for 147 of as close to 290 B.C. as possible, probably 291).

But this is unlikely. First, the designation "stele of the farmers," which Kent uses repeatedly (Kent 283–84), is misleading. The inscription actually says, "For the registration of the farmers, stele from Hermodikos and base." This phrase cannot designate the *hiera syngraphe,* which was not a register but a general contract covering the rental of the estates. (This is supported by the payment to Hermodikos. Rates for inscription for 302, not for 281 or 279 B.C., are relevant for comparison. Thus Hermodikos carved about 2,500–3,250 letters. But the preserved text of the *hiera syngraphe* has about 4,335 letters, and much of the text is missing; the full original may well have had 7,000 letters.) I do not see how it could be anything but what Glotz thought: the register of farmers, guarantors, and rents, with full inventories, of each estate at the start of a new rental period.

Moreover, Kent's argument for the date of *IG* XI 2.147 is not decisive. Renters were not expelled from estates as long as the full rent was paid, whether by themselves or by their guarantors. The right parallel for Maisiades' situation is not that of Hermades or Arkhandros in 307, who were removed from their estates because of failure to renew guarantors or to pay the full rent (*IG* XI 2.142.5–12), but that in *IG* XI 2.135.23–26, where Lysixenos son of Aristoboulos paid 500 dr as his part of the rent owed on Porthmos by his father. Nothing indicates that Aristoboulos was expelled from his estate because of this. Maisiades should likewise have continued in possession, and if so, *IG* XI 2.147 can go in 300 B.C., not after 297 B.C.

Kent's other arguments are only from probability, and have much less force. He asks why the Delians would impose a new rental contract in 300, when rents were still high; better, he thought, was 290, when rents had fallen. This argument falls before two objections. First, nothing in the *hiera syngraphe* or elsewhere suggests that it owed its imposition to the decline in rents; it is as easy to suppose, for example, that the defaults of the 300s provoked it, or a desire on the part of the Delians to regularize the administration of the estates. Indeed, *ID* 499, which is probably a general regulation covering loans, was issued at about the same time; it looks as if the Delians were acting at the end of the fourth and beginning of the third centuries to establish ground rules for the administration of Apollo's goods (cf. Vial, 277–78). Second, the decline in rents occurred in 290 B.C.: even by Kent's account, after the *syngraphe* came into effect.

Kent points to the four new properties (by his count) of Akra Delos, Korakia, Phytalia, and Sosimakheia which, he believes, were confiscated for failure to pay interest on loans. He connects these confiscations, rather vaguely, with the *syngraphe*. But the *syngraphe* has nothing whatsoever to do with the terms of loans and hypothecations; this is a red herring.

Finally, he evokes some indications of a reorganization of the administration of the estates between 297 and 290, including the transfer of Epistheneia and Kerameion from the houses to the estates[8] and the increase in the number of *epitimetai* for the estates from two to three (Kent, 274 n. 95, citing *IG* XI 2.148.67 (298 B.C.) and 159A55, 203A62–63). But these changes could as easily be a response to new conditions brought about by the *syngraphe*, as accompaniments to the *syngraphe*. I am inclined to imagine that some years of experience with enforcing the *hiera syngraphe* convinced the *hieropoioi* that oversight was inadequate, and so they requested an expansion of the board of *epitimetai*.

WERE HOUSES 1 AND 2 RESIDENCES?

House 1, the house that "used to belong to the children of Aristoboulos" (see *IG* XI 2.158A23 and many other entries), seemed to Sylvain Molinier to have been an industrial concern, because it was leased in 192 B.C. by one Pyrros, described as a πορφυροβάφος (*ID* 400.7–8; Sylvain Molinier, *Les 'Maisons sacrées' de Délos* [Paris, 1914], 21–22). The inference is unimpeachable for the second century—Vial, 341 is overcautious—but it does not assure commercial use in the third as well. Two arguments can be offered. The rents for this house varied considerably over time. They remained less than 40 dr until 272 B.C., then rose substantially when Aristoboulos son of Lysixenos assumed the lease that year. He held on to the house for at least thirty years, paying generally rising rents. The rent de-

8. Kent, 257–58, thought Epistheneia, taken over in 375, was registered like Kerameion with the houses and remained permanently in the temple's possession. This position is no longer tenable.

clined again in the last third of the third century, then rose dramatically by 222 and stayed mostly high until the records run out. It is possible, then, that the house changed use from a residence early on (perhaps the first renters, Diakritos, Autosthenes, and Kharmos, were relatives of Aristoboulos?) to an industrial concern later. If so, the rising rents of midcentury may reflect this change, although it is, of course, impossible to know which occupation (if any) Aristoboulos son of Lysixenos pursued, or even whether Pyrros worked in the house he rented (see Vial, 341).

House 2, which used to belong to one Arkeon, was rented in 247 by one Ktesias; Molinier thought it was a residence, but Dieter Hennig has preferred to see it as a warehouse (*Lagerhaus*).[9] In this case, Hennig's view seems to me the less acceptable one. He argues for a warehouse on three grounds. The rent, he observes, is generally below the mean rate for the houses; from this fact he infers that the house of Arkeon is a *bescheidenes Gebäude*. Moreover, some rather expensive repairs were effected in 179 B.C.; too expensive, Hennig thinks, for a residence. Finally, its situation by the harbor seems inappropriate for a home (*ID* 442B251–53 for the repairs; *IG* XI 2.158A16–17 for its location: τῆς οἰκίας τῆς ἐν λιμένι ἥ ἦν Ἀρκέοντος παρὰ Ἀρκέοντος).

The relation of the level of its rents to those of other houses means little; indeed, low rent may imply a residence rather than a commercial property. The house by the *bremes* fetched 70 dr. Of the eight houses rented for less than 70 dr in 207 B.C., when the mean rent for sixteen buildings was 72.8 dr, at least six served commercial ends: *andron e* of the Khareteia complex; the house by the *sidereion;* the building called ἡ ἑτέρα Σωσιλεία; the two *xylones;* and a "stray *andron*" (for details and citation, see Appendix IV). The expensive repairs of 179 B.C. are the only work known to have been done on the building, and the document recording them is so badly mutilated that we know only that house 2 (the house of Arkeon) had some work done and that the second payment to the contractor amounted to 25 dr. Since the contractor, whose name is lost, probably received three equal payments, about 75 dr is involved (not certain, but cf. *ID* 442B226–27, where a contractor gets a second payment of 340 dr 4 ob and a third and final payment of 340 dr). This was not a great deal of money by temple standards; in 280 B.C., the *hieropoioi* paid out 40 dr to install a wall with a door in the house of Antigonos, which was probably a residence until at least 282 B.C. (*IG* XI 2.165.6–7; for Antigonos as renter, see 158A20). *IG* XI 2.161A23–24 of 279 B.C. reports Arkhepolis as renter. Perhaps when Antigonos died or vacated, the *hieropoioi* decided to improve the property, which fetched from Arkhepolis exactly double the rent Antigonos had paid (60 vs. 30 dr). Perhaps this reflects a change of purpose?

The location, too, would seem to have little significance. In the third

9. Molinier, *Maisons*, 34; Dieter Hennig, *Chiron* 13 (1983): 424.

century, Delos was not the trading emporium it later became, and residence in the harbor district might well have had attractions, especially for tenants who depended on the transit trade for business or had small shops at home. (Marco Bettalli, *Opus* 4 [1985]:32, 37–38, discusses shops on Delos and suggests that the κλείσιον attested frequently on Delos referred in country houses to slave quarters but in urban houses to an attached shop; cf. Robin Osborne, *BSA* 80 [1985]:122, and Brunet, 180–81, 187–89.) The "business boom" on Delos, such as it was, began in the late third century and really picked up with the Athenian reoccupation after 167 B.C. We should be willing to consider the possibility that buildings changed use under the pressure of expansion. The phenomenon is familiar today; I see no reason why it should not have occurred in antiquity too that a district that used to include residences should succumb under the pressure of rising population and real estate values to a redefinition of its use. It might be that Arkeon's house, once a desirable residence, fell before the need to serve the commercial demands of an expanded harbor district.

This view depends on rents; and for Arkeon's house these do not support it. The house earned a high rent of 58 dr in 246 B.C. and shortly before or after, when Ktesias was renting (*ID* 290.27 and perhaps *IG* XI 2.289.2). Thereafter the rent fell strikingly to 35 dr in 207 and 206 B.C. (*ID* 366A97 and 368.34). If commercial pressure on real estate driven by a boom were inflating the values of waterfront property, we would not expect so sharp a decline. The fall leads me to suppose rather that the house held little attraction for commercial renters and so continued to be occupied by residents. If Hennig's view that the house had been subdivided could be substantiated, my case would be refuted, for the building as a whole would be bringing in at least 70 dr. But the utter absence of any entries in the accounts like ἡ οἰκία Ἀρκέοντος, ἡ ἑτέρα, speaks strongly against subdivision. Such entries are very common for other subdivided properties (for example, the two *xylones* and the Epistheneia houses, both detailed in Appendix IV). I am therefore inclined to regard the house of Arkeon as a residence, at least in the third century.

Appendix II

Some Remarks on Statistical Analysis

The main statistical techniques employed to analyze the data may call for some comment. In most cases I have tried to subject the data to a *linear regression*.[1] A linear regression is a mathematical technique that finds the "best" straight-line fit to the sample data. It is "best" in the sense that it minimizes the sum of squared deviations (i.e., between observed and predicted values). The *dependent variable* in regression analysis is usually expressed, as a function of one or more quantitative *independent variables* (i.e., variables that can be measured or counted, like time). The procedure also allows the introduction of qualitative or *dummy variables* that indicate whether a dependent variable belongs to a particular category or possesses a particular quality.

Regressions are intended to test hypotheses about data. For instance, I might hypothesize about Delos that the price of olive oil changes as a function of time. A regression using oil as the dependent and time as the independent variable tests this hypothesis (table II.1). *C* is a constant required for the mathematics to work; it can be ignored as a rule.

In the example in table II.1, the COEFFICIENT shows that oil prices decline slightly on an average with each unit of time. (Time is treated in this model in such a way that the distance between the first and second data points for time equals the actual number of years between the first and second data points for oil; see table 5.6.) The T-STAT(istic) gives the likelihood that the coefficient is actually zero (that is, without significance); any t-statistic over 2.0 gives very good confidence that the value of the coefficient has not been generated by chance. The 2-TAIL SIG(nificance) tests the significance of the relation between the variables: anything less than 0.10 (= 10 percent likelihood that the relation is owing purely to chance) is acceptable. The R-SQUARED and ADJUSTED R-SQUARED measure the percentage of variation that the model explains. The adjusted measure is better since it takes into account the degrees of freedom lost when introducing independent variables; a perfect result is 1.0. The DURBIN-WATSON STAT(istic) measures the amount of auto-correlation in the data. (Auto-correlation occurs when the value of a datum at one point depends on the value of the datum at the previous point.) A perfect Durbin-Watson is 2.0; for our purposes the acceptable range will run generally from 1.4 to 2.4, 1.5 to 2.5, and 1.75 to 2.75, depending on how many independent variables we have. The SE OF

1. For discussion and explanation, see any basic statistics handbook; I have consulted Heinz Kohler, *Statistics for Business and Economics* (Glenview, Ill., 1985), 531–60, 583–97.

Table II.1 Olive Oil Prices and Change over Time

Dependent Variable is OIL
Number of observations: 22

Variable	*Coefficient*	*Std. Error*	*T-Stat.*	*2-Tail Sig.*
C	*115.64243*	*11.267425*	*10.263430*	*0.000*
Time	*−0.1185571*	*0.1057361*	*−1.1212549*	*0.280*

R-squared	0.077333	Mean of dependent var	103.7588
Adjusted R-squared	0.015821	S.D. of dependent var	15.89513
S.E. of regression	15.76888	Sum of squared resid	3729.865
Durbin-Watson stat	1.606918	F-statistic	1.257212
Log likelihood	−69.94472		

REGRESSION measures the magnitude of the residuals, that is, the differences between the actual and fitted values of the dependent variable. A lower SE of regression is better. The MEAN OF DEPENDENT VARIABLE simply gives the mean (average) of all values of the dependent variable. The S(tandard) D(eviation) OF DEPENDENT VARIABLE gives the standard deviation of the values of the dependent variable. The SUM OF SQUARED RESID(uals) is simply the sum total of the squares of all residuals. The F-STATISTIC is, like the t-statistic, another test of the hypothesis that all coefficients are actually zero. The higher the f-statistic, the better. The LOG LIKELIHOOD, which is used in forecasting, is not necessary for our purposes and has been included only for the sake of completeness. The results presented in table II.1 effectively demolish our hypothesis: the relation is without significance and explains barely 1 percent of the variation.

Appendix III

Prices of Firewood, Olive Oil, Pigs, and Grains (Barley and Wheat) on Delos, 314–169 B.C.

The tables below and in Appendix IV give the data on which the foregoing studies of the Delian economy are based. For each good, I cite the source (*IG* XI 2 or *ID*), the date (giving the range when no precise date is known), the month (where recorded and preserved or restored with certainty), the unit price, the quantity bought, the indexed price (based always on a price from Metageitnion 250 B.C., set below in italic type), and the mean annual indexed price used for price series calculations (cf. chapter 5, pp. 131–32, above). Prices marked with a raised "a" are not used in any calculations; for explanation, see the commentary following each table. Quantities enclosed in square brackets ([ ]) are fully or partly restored; I have made no attempt to indicate which portion of the figure is restored (thus [ΔΔΔ]Π or ΔΔ[ΔΠ] would be represented indifferently as [35]). The point at which restoration calls for comment is necessarily somewhat arbitrary, and I have made no effort to indicate minor restorations that are certain (for example, Π[⊢]⊢ becomes "7" without comment), or essentially so (but see commentary on specific cases). Nor have I indicated cases where the item purchased has been restored with certainty (e.g., firewood at *IG* XI 2.224A30).

For ease of calculation, I have converted fractions of a drakhma given in the inscriptions into decimals on the following system: 1 ob = .167; 1½ ob = .250; 2 ob = .333; 2½ ob = .416; 3 ob = .500; 3½ ob = .583; 4 ob = .667; 4½ ob = .750; 5 ob = .833; 5½ ob = .916; ½ ob = .083; ¼ ob = .042; $\frac{1}{12}$ ob = .014. The slight loss of precision is more than compensated by the greatly increased ease of manipulation of the figures. The original amounts in fractions can be recovered by breaking down the decimals below in accord with the equations just given. I have indicated the months simply by their number in order (1 = Lenaion, etc.; see table 1.3 above). Intercalary Panemos is designated as 6 (2).

There are still some unpublished accounts. In *BCH* 109 (1985): 483 and 488 n. 12, Jacques Tréheux reported the discovery of two new fragments, inv. no. Γ766 α and β, which join *ID* 446 + 463. Since 463A contains monthly accounts, full publication will probably add prices. I do not expect that they will modify the conclusions that I have come to. A third new fragment, Γ761, joins *ID* 374B (see p. 192 n. 4, above). Another unpublished fragment, which has been known for almost forty years (cf. Vial in *CICG*, 59 n. 37) and dates to 297 B.C. (reference at l. 2 to Pyrrides, *arkhon* of that year) is almost surely the account complementing *IG* XI 2.149 listing estate rent payments. The account will be published by Panayotes Chatzidakes, director of the museum on Delos. I am grateful to him and to Fotini Zafiropoulou, ephor of the Kyklades, for permission to examine this stone.

In addition, several joins of previously published fragments have unfortunately not yet been published. The joins of *ID* 291b + 292 + 306 + 291c + 291e + 294 were discovered by Philip H. Davis (*AJA* 41 [1939]: 109; cf. Vallois, I.37–38 n. 2, 233 n. 5), who however died before he was able to publish them. (*ID* 291d and 293 also join and are perhaps part of the same complex.) Tréheux discovered the join of *ID* 440 and 456 (*BCH* 109 [1985]: 485–86). In both cases I have reconstructed texts from which I derive my data. M.-F. Baslez and Claude Vial (*BCH* 111 [1987]: 290 n. 42) have shown that *ID* 460v and 465c date to the same year; I believe they along with 460t are in fact (nonjoining?) fragments of the same stele and have been able to derive some prices from a reconstructed text. Published joins are noted in the commentary below.

Table III.1. FIREWOOD (ξύλον)

Usually bought for the Hieropoion as firewood and/or for use on the altars. Under "Quantity," I have not distinguished between cases where a quantity was named but has been lost (e.g., 219A15) and cases where no quantity was recorded (e.g., 205bd14).

Source	*Date*	*Month*	*Price/ talent (dr)*	*Quantity (talents)*	*Indexed Price*	*Annual Mean*
144A29	304		1.250	120	187.4	187.4
147A12	300		1.256	90	188.3	188.3
161A108–9	279		1.333	85	199.8	199.8
199A49	274		1.333	1	199.8	212.35
199A71	274		1.500	7	224.9	
219A15	272 or 271	2	1.167		175.0	171.8
REG 99 (1986): 296, A30	272 or 271	6	[1.333]		199.8	
219Ab49	272 or 271	11?	1.083		162.4	
219Ab54	272 or 271	12?	1.000		149.9	
203A58–59	269		1.167	52	175.0	175.0
204.46	268	7	1.021	4	153.1	151.0
204.49	268	8	1.000	3	149.9	
204.63	268	9	1.000	7	149.9	
205Bd14	267		1.333		199.8	
224A30	258	2	1.042	8	156.2	140.6
224A31	258	3?	0.833	9	124.9	

Source	Date	Month	Price/ talent (dr)	Quantity (talents)	Indexed Price	Annual Mean
287A45	250	1	1.167	20	175.0	117.3
287A50	250	2	1.083	10	162.4	
287A52	250	3	0.667	5	100.0	
287A55	250	4	0.833	7	124.9	
287A61	250	5	0.667	6	100.0	
287A63	250	6	0.667	2	100.0	
287A65	250	6	0.833	22	124.9	
287A67	*250*	*8*	*0.667*	*6*	*100.0*	
287A70	250	8	0.750	5	112.4	
287A73	250	9	0.750	20	112.4	
287A80	250	11	0.667	1	100.0	
287A81	250	11	0.667	5	100.0	
287A82	250	12	0.750	5	112.4	
291b + 59	247	8	1.167	3	175.0	175.0
290.48	246	1	[1.333][a]	[40]		
290.73	246	5	1.333	13	199.8	201.1
290.81	246	6(2)	1.292	2	193.7	
290.85–86	246	8	[1.333][a]	[13]		
290.94	246	9	1.292	13	193.7	
290.99	246	11	1.389	21.5	208.2	
290.102	246	12	1.403	21	210.3	
316.80–81	231	2	1.500	30	224.9	180.0
316.85	231	3	1.167	22	175.0	
316.100	231	7	1.000	20	149.9	
316.104	231	8	1.167	10	175.0	
316.110	231	11	1.167	10	175.0	
338Aa22	224	2	1.250	20	187.4	156.3
338Aa26	224	3	[1.000][a]	18		
338Aa30	224	4	1.000	18	149.9	
338Aa34	224	5	1.000	18	149.9	
338Aa36	224	6	1.000	16	149.9	
338Aa39	224	7	1.000	[18]	149.9	
338Aa43	224	8	1.000	20	149.9	
338Aa48–49	224	10	1.050	20	157.4	
338Aa50	224	11	[1.000][a]	15		
354.58	218	1	1.500	15	224.9	212.3
354.61–62	218	2	1.500	[18]	224.9	

(*continued*)

Table III.1. (CONTINUED)

Source	Date	Month	Price/ talent (dr)	Quantity (talents)	Indexed Price	Annual Mean
354.65	218	3	1.333	18	199.8	
354.72	218	5	1.333	15	199.8	
372A74	200	1	1.500	20	224.9	241.6
372A76	200	2	1.500	21	224.9	
372A78	200	3	1.667	20	249.9	
372A80–81	200	4	1.500	18	224.9	
372A82	200	5	1.667	17	249.9	
372A83–84	200	6	1.667	17	249.9	
372A86	200	7	1.667	16	249.9	
372A87–88	200	8	1.667	17	249.9	
372A89–90	200	9	1.667	18	249.9	
372A91	200	10	1.500	20	224.9	
372A92–93	200	11	1.667	20	249.9	
372A95	200	12	1.667	18	249.9	
396A69	194	2	1.500[a]	[10?]		
396A71	194	3	1.500	10	224.9	224.9
396A76	194	5	1.500	16	224.9	
396A78	194	6	[1.5?]	13		
442A182	179	1	1.250	22	187.4	221.8
442A183	179	2	1.500	27	224.9	
442A184	179	3	1.500	20	224.9	
442A185	179	4	1.500	15	224.9	
442A186–87	179	5	1.500	[10]	224.9	
442A189	179	7	1.500	15	224.9	
442A190	179	8	1.500	10	224.9	
442A191	179	9	1.500	20	224.9	
442A192	179	10	1.500	15	224.9	
442A193	179	11	1.500	20	224.9	
442A194	179	12	1.500	20	224.9	
442A221	179	12	1.500	15	224.9	
445.5	178	12	1.500	10	224.9	224.9
456B11–12	174	3	1.500	15	224.9	209.5
456B18 + 440A4	174	5	1.500	12	224.9	
456B25–26 + 440A11–12	174	7	[1.333]	30	199.8	
456B28–29 + 440A14–15	174	8	1.333	21	199.8	

Source	*Date*	*Month*	*Price/ talent (dr)*	*Quantity (talents)*	*Indexed Price*	*Annual Mean*
440A17–18	174	9	1.258	20	188.6	
440A19–20	174	10	1.500	16	224.9	
440A21–22	174	11	1.560	18	233.9	
440A23–24	174	12	1.280	25	191.9	
440A63	174	12	1.3125	8	196.8	
BCH 109 (1985): 497, A9	173	6	1.500	10	224.9	224.9
459.45–46	170	2	1.500	22	224.9	224.9
459.46–47	170	3	1.500	19	224.9	
459.49–50	170	6	1.500	16	224.9	
461Ab13	169	9	1.333	15	199.8	199.8

[a] *I have regarded this price as too problematic to use in my analysis; see further in the lemma, below.*

IG XI 2.142.60: the entry ξύλα ἐπὶ βωμοὺς ⊢|| is likely to represent one talent, given the price; but to avoid circularity I have not included it. On the date of this document, see "Olive Oil" below, comm. on *IG* XI 2.142.

IG XI 2.144A29: for a date of 304 B.C., not 303 (Kent, 266), see *CICG*, 30.

IG XI 2.147: for the date, see pp. 281–82 above.

IG XI 2.199A71: read Δ[|]||; Glotz's suggestion (*REG* 26 [1913]: 37) of 5 dr 5 ob is wrong.

IG XI 2.219: this inscription joins 220, 221, and 229 and is dated to 272 or 271 B.C.; see Jacques Tréheux, *REG* 99 (1986): 293–301 (date already in Bruneau, 10). Tréheux's text (p. 296) must now be consulted for A18-37; at A30, however, restore χο[ῦς], not χο[εῖς], after A8 and A40.

The months are reckoned from the placement of the entry and the following month assignments: Lenaion, A7–14 (on the sacrifice to Apollo and Artemis that took place on the first day of Lenaion, which appears here at A7 and sets the beginning of the monthly expenses, see Bruneau, 91–93); Hieros, A15–18; Galaxion, A19–21; Artemision, A22–25; Thargelion, A26–29; Panemos, A30–33; Hekatombaion or second Panemos, A34ff. Cf. Tréheux, *REG* 99 (1986): 297–99.

REG 99 (1986): 296, l. 30 (= 219A30 + 229.13): Tréheux prints τιμὴ τοῦ ταλά[ντου · .]||, but ⊢ must clearly be restored.

IG XI 2.219Ab49: restore ξύλων τάλαν[τα ἕξ? εἰς Πύθιον, τὸ] τάλαντον. There is space in the lacuna for no more than about fifteen letters.

IG XI 2.219Ab54: restore [ξύλων τάλαντα fig. εἰς Πύθιον,] τὸ τάλαντον.

IG XI 2.205Bd14: Durrbach prints [τὸ τάλα]ṿτον ⊢||· ξ[ύλα?]. There is no other product bought by the talent at prices close to this, but the ξ[ύλα?] at the end seems suspicious.

IG XI 2.224A31: restore as [ξύλων τάλαντ]α ἐννέα, ἀνὰ·||[|]||· ἡ πᾶσ[α, 𐅃⊢⊢|||].

ID 291b+ (291b + 292 + 306 + 291c + 291e + 294), 59 = 291b29.

ID 290.48: τιμὴ 𐅄̣⊢̣⊢̣⊢̣[|||], with the obols added to yield a price/talent of 1 dr 2 ob (cf. l. 73) at [ΔΔΔΔ] talents, also restored; cf. comm. p. 12 (G. Glotz). A reasonable but completely arbitrary result, since many different prices are attested for this year.

ID 290.85–86: a likely but not certain restoration.

ID 338Aa26: price restored; there is no reason to prefer 1 dr/talent (cf. Aa30) to 1.25 dr/talent (cf. Aa22, comm. p. 108).

(*continued*)

ID 338Aa39: amount restored but certain, given steady price/talent across surrounding months.

ID 338Aa50: price restored; in view of the rise in the previous month, the restoration is uncertain.

ID 354.58: read, with some hesitation, Πύθιο[ν·] ΔΠ̣· τιμὴ ΔΔΔ.

ID 354.62: restore, with some hesitation, [ΔΠ]Ị Ị Ị · τιμὴ· ΔΔΠ⊢⊢.

ID 354.72: I read something that looks like Π̣Ị before τιμή; therefore restore [καὶ ἱεροποιοῦ·] Δ̣Π̣· τιμὴ ΔΔ.

ID 372A80–81: the figure for total cost corrected by Durrbach from 28 to 27 dr.

ID 372A84: I read an amount of ΔΔΠΙΙ, which must be an inscriber's error; interpret as Δ⟨Δ⟩ΠΙΙ.

ID 396A69: I read [τι]μὴ Δ̣Δ̣, which if correct would make a price of 1.5 dr/talent impossible.

ID 396A71: do not dot pi of price.

ID 442A189: do not dot second obol mark.

ID 442A221: purchase for the Posideia, which took place in Posideon (see Bruneau, 261).

ID 445.5: purchase for the Posideia.

ID 456B11–12: read Δ̣̄ΔΠ.

ID 456B25–26 + 440A11–12: for reasons of space a price of ΔΔΔΔ (= 1 dr 2 ob/talent) seems more likely than the alternative (ΔΔΔΔΠ = 1 dr 3 ob/talent).

ID 440A17–18: the price is difficult. Durrbach prints ΔΔΠ⟨X?⟩. I read either ΔΔΠ⊢̣ or ΔΔΠΙ. I have preferred the last price because ΔΔΠΙ seems best to account for the traces on the stone.

ID 440A19–20: Durrbach printed ΛΔΠ(ΙΙΙ), τιμὴ ΔΔ⊢⊢⊢⊢ on the assumption that 1 dr 2 ob/talent was the typical price. In fact, variation in this inscription is so marked, and uneven prices common enough, that this correction should be rejected. Far more likely is the omission of a single stroke, giving 16 talents purchased at 1 dr 3 ob each. This is the emendation I have accepted.

ID 440A23–24: read τιμὴ Δ[Δ]Δ⊢⊢.

ID 440A63: purchase for the Posideia.

ID 459: for the date of this inscription as 170 instead of 172 B.C., see M.–F. Baslez and C. Vial, *BCH* 111 (1987): 290 n. 42 (170 already preferred by R. Vallois, *BCH* 55 [1931]: 293–94).

ID 459.45–46: this entry is very difficult to read; I have seen ΔΔΔΠ, ΔΔΔΠ⊢, and ΔΔΔ⊢⊢. There is a mark at the end of the entry which Durrbach interprets as a half-obol (C) which in fact solves the problem. The correct reading must be ΔΔΔ⊢⊢⊢̣, yielding the perfectly reasonable price of 1.5 dr/talent.

ID 459.46–47: a difficult entry. Durrbach reads τιμὴ ΔΔΠ⊢⊢⊢ΙỊ[Ι or ΙΙC/], which would produce prices of 1.5 or 1.515; the former is obviously to be preferred. I read ΔΔΠ⊢⊢⊢· ἄ[νθρακες], which yields a price of 1.474 dr/talent, also very strange. I have preferred the simplest result, without however certainty that it corresponds to what was inscribed on the stone.

ID 459.50: restore ΔΔ⊢̣⊢̣[⊢⊢].

ID 459.51–52: of the price only Δ̣[is preserved, which cannot be the full price given the other prices/talent for this year; the price is not included in the table.

Table III.2. OLIVE OIL (ἔλαιον)

The quantity is always one *khous* unless specified otherwise. Bought for use of *hieropoioi* or for ritual, or for athletic events. At *ID* 354.67 the account specifies [ἐλαίου] λευκοῦ εἰς Ἀρτεμίσιον καὶ εἰς τὸν ναὸν τ[οῦ] Ἀπόλλωνος.

Source	*Date*	*Month*	*Price/* khous *(dr)*	*Quantity (in* khoes*)*	*Indexed Price*	*Annual Mean*
142.60	307		3.500		262.6	262.6
142.67	307		3.500[a]			
144A30	304	1	4.500		337.6	277.2
144A30–31	304	2	4.500		337.6	
144A32	304	2	2.251[a]			
144A33	304	3	4.500		337.6	
144A37	304	3	4.500	0.5	337.6	
144B21	304	8	2.667		200.1	
144B24	304	9	1.500		112.5	
147A3	300		4.667		350.1	350.1
159A14	281		2.926	9	219.5	219.5
161A92	279		2.333	1.5	175.0	162.5
161A108	279		2.000	12	150.0	
219Aa8	272 or 271	1	1.667		125.1	131.3
219Ab40	272 or 271	9?	1.833		137.5	
203A39	269	3	1.583	2	118.8[a]	110.4
203A49	269	8	0.500[a]			
203A59	269		1.500	12	112.5	
203A64–65	269		1.333	36	100.0	
204.45–46	268	7	1.251		93.8	123.5
204.74–75	268	11	2.042	2	153.2	
235b9–10	265–255		1.667		125.1	125.1
240.2	265–255		1.416		106.2	106.2
274.25	260 or 259		1.333		100.0	100.0
275A6	259, 256–51	12?	1.667	2	125.1	125.1
287A131–32	250		1.500	54	112.5	105.8
287A133	250		1.333		100.0	
287A43	250	1	1.333	2	100.0	
287A47	250	2	1.333	2	100.0	
287A53–54	250	3	1.333	2	100.0	
287A54	250	3	1.333	3	100.0	
287A58	250	4	1.333	1.5	100.0	

(*continued*)

Table III.2. (CONTINUED)

Source	Date	Month	Price/ khous (dr)	Quantity (in khoes)	Indexed Price	Annual Mean
287A58	250	5	2.000	1.5	150.0	
287A63	250	6	1.333	1.5	100.0	
287A65	250	7	1.333	2	100.0	
287A68	*250*	*8*	*1.333*	*1.5*	*100.0*	
287A74	250	9	1.333		100.0	
287A76	250	10	1.500	2	112.5	
287A79	250	11	1.500		112.5	
287A82	250	12	1.333	2	100.0	
291b + 53	247	8	1.333		100.0	125.0
291b + 83	247	11	2.000		150.0	
290.49	246	1	1.167	3	87.6	91.5
290.62	246	3	[1.167]	3	87.6	
290.65	246	3	1.167	3	87.6	
290.72	246	4	1.167	2	87.6	
290.78	246	6	1.167	2	87.6	
290.80	246	6(2)	1.167	2	87.6	
290.83	246	7	1.167	2	87.6	
290.93	246	8	1.250	2	93.8	
290.95–96	246	9	[1.250][a]	[2]		
290.97	246	10	1.333	3	100.0	
290.101	246	11	1.333	3	100.0	
290.104	246	12	1.333	3	100.0	
316.79	231	2	1.500	4	112.5	108.3
316.91	231	4	1.416	3	106.2	
316.99	231	7	1.416	2	106.2	
338Aa19	224	1	[1.375][a]	8	103.1	95.0
338Aa22	224	2	1.333	8	100.0	
338Aa26	224	3	1.333	6	100.0	
338Aa30	224	4	[1.333]	6	100.0	
338Aa39	224	7	1.333	4.5	100.0	
338Aa47	224	9	1.000	8	75.0	
354.59	218	1	1.167	[5]	87.6	100.0
354.62–63	218	2	1.167	5	87.6	
354.66	218	3	1.167	5	87.6	
354.67	218	3	[1.167][a]	3		
354.69	218	4	[1.167][a]	5		
354.72	218	5	1.500	4	112.5	

Source	Date	Month	Price/ khous (dr)	Quantity (in khoes)	Indexed Price	Annual Mean
354.75	218	6	1.500	4	112.5	
354.80–81	218	8	1.500	4	112.5	
372A74–75	200	1	1.333	9	100.0	101.0
372A76	200	2	[1.333]	[9]	100.0	
372A78–79	200	3	1.333	9	100.0	
372A79	200	3	1.500		112.5	
372A81	200	4	1.333	9	100.0	
372A82	200	5	1.333	8	100.0	
372A84	200	6	1.333	8	100.0	
372A86	200	7	1.333	8	100.0	
372A88	200	8	1.333	8	100.0	
372A90	200	9	1.333	9	100.0	
372A92	200	10	1.333	9	100.0	
372A93	200	11	1.333	9	100.0	
372A95	200	12	1.333	9	100.0	
396A67	194	1	1.500	10	112.5	112.5
396A69	194	2	1.500	[10]	112.5	
396A72	194	3	1.500[a]			
396A74	194	4	[1.500]	9	112.5	
442A182	179	1	1.416	12	106.2	103.5
442A183	179	2	1.333	12	100.0	
442A184	179	3	1.416	6	106.2	
442A188	179	6	1.333	[10]	100.0	
442A189	179	7	1.333	6	100.0	
442A190	179	8	1.333	6	100.0	
442A191	179	9	1.333	9	100.0	
442A192	179	10	1.500	12	112.5	
442A194	179	12	1.416	12	106.2	
443Ab104	178	7	1.375	[8]	103.2	103.2
445.6	178	12	8[a]			
456B8	174	1	1.250	12	93.8	82.1
456B10	174	2	1.333[a]	[3]		
456B16 + 440A2	174	4	[1.083?][a]	12		
456B18 + 440A4	174	5	1.250	4	93.8	
456B21 + 440A7	174	6	1.083	12	81.2	

(*continued*)

Table III.2. (CONTINUED)

Source	*Date*	*Month*	*Price/* khous *(dr)*	*Quantity (in* khoes*)*	*Indexed Price*	*Annual Mean*
456B23 + 440A9	174	6(2)	1.083	[12]	81.2	
456B26 + 440A12	174	7	[1.083][a]	[12]		
456B29–30 + 440A15–16	174	8	1.083	[6]	81.2	
440A18	174	9	1.0	12	75.1	
440A22	174	11	0.916	12	68.7	
440A63–64	174	12	2.000[a]			
440A40	174		3.000[a]			
BCH 109 (1985): 497, A7	173	4	0.944	6	70.8	70.8
459.56	170	11	1.250	12	93.8	93.8
461Ab6	169	4	[1.833]	8	137.5	137.5
461Ab12	169	8	1.833	[6]	137.5	
461Ab17	169	12	1.833	6	137.5	

[a] *I have regarded this price as too problematic to use in analysis; see further in the lemma, below.*

IG XI 2.142.67: Gustave Glotz, *REG* 26 (1913): 27, restored [ἔλαιον] on the basis of the price. For a probable date of 307 B.C., see G. Reger, *GRBS* 32 (1991): 234.

IG XI 2.144A30: read ⊢⊢⊢⊢ I I I · οἶνος.

IG XI 2.144A30–31: oil restored, [ἐλα]ίο(υ), but practically certain.

IG XI 2.144A32: this oil was bought εἰς χέρνιβον. The price very strongly suggests that only half a *khous* was bought, despite the simple ἔλαιον.

IG XI 2.147A3: read ⊢⊢⊢⊢ I I I I. For the date, see pp. 281–82, above.

IG XI 2.159A14: Glotz, *REG* 26 (1913): 33, argues for an engraver's error in the price and would read 27 dr to give an even price/*khous*, but Maurice Lacroix, *BCH* 48 (1924): 403, reads the two obol signs as certain.

IG XI 2.219: see note for 219 under "Firewood," above.

IG XI 2.203A39: price is for "white oil" (ἐλαίου λευκοῦ).

IG XI 2.203A49: the price is impossibly low for a *khous;* the entry reads εἰς ἔλαιον.

IG XI 2.203A59: Glotz, *REG* 26 (1913): 37, suggested the correction of the price from *IG*'s 17 dr 1 ob; confirmed on stone by Lacroix, *BCH* 48 (1924): 407.

IG XI 2.204.45–46: restore [ἐλαίου] χοῦς ⊢ I C.

IG XI 2.204.74–75: restore [ἐλαίου] χοεῖς δύο ⊢⊢⊢⊢ C.

IG XI 2.235b9–10 oil restored but certain.

IG XI 2.240.2: the figure was originally suggested as a correction from *IG*'s reading by Glotz, *REG* 26 (1913): 38, and confirmed by revision by Lacroix, *BCH* 48 (1924): 408.

IG XI 2.274.25. The correct date for this inscription has aroused some dispute. Vial, 42 n. 102, puts it between 267 and 258 without supporting argument. Bruneau, 67 n. 3, restores in l. 25 from Durrbach's ΑΥΓΝΕΙ the name Αὐτοκλεῖ. Since the same person won in the games of *IG* XI 2.203, dated to 269 B.C., Bruneau thought 274 likely to date close to 269 B.C. More precision is possible. In *ID* 290.11–12, one Amphias son of Demolytos pays 280 dr he was cited as owing in 261 B.C. as a guarantor for Radis son of Didymos: [παρ'] Ἀμφίου τοῦ Δημολύτου ΗΗΠΔΔΔ τὴν ἐγγύαν ὑπὲρ Ῥάδιος τοῦ Διδύμου ἥν ἐνεγέγραπτο ἠγγυημένο[ς Ῥάδιν ἐπὶ Θαρσύνοντος ἐν τ]ῆι στήλῃι ἥν ἔστησαν οἱ ἱεροποιοὶ Ξενοκλείδης καὶ Τιμοκλῆς. Since Radis owed 35 dr interest per year (cf. *IG* XI 2.226A25, 287A190, *ID* 291f11), Amphias's payment represents eight years' interest. Radis has therefore paid no interest between 268 and 261. As the payment of *IG* XI 2.274 is not in arrears, that inscription must date to after 261: to either 260 or 259 B.C.

Further confirmation for this date comes from *IG* XI 2.223Aa63. There Kraton son of Mnesiades pays 10 dr interest on a debt of 100 dr. He pays again at 274.22 (10 dr ½ ob). Since 223 dates to 262 B.C., 274 cannot date to that year; it belongs either to 267–263 B.C. or 261–258 B.C.

Bruneau's argument from the athlete's name is not decisive because athletes do sometimes enjoy long successful careers—and even so, the gap between Autokles' victories will not be greater than eleven years—and because we cannot be sure that Autokles refers in each case to the same person, or even that Bruneau's suggested reading is correct.

IG XI 2.275A6: the inscription must belong to 259 or 256–251 B.C., for it carries renters whose leases began in 260 (e.g., Pythokles renting Porthmos at A12, Kerkion renting Dionysios at A13); it cannot date to 260, because the account lacks inventories for the estates; and 258 and 257 are occupied (*IG* XI 2.224 and 226). The restoration [Νεοκροντίδη?]ς τοῦ Κε[ραμείου] at A16 is arbitrary: the original renter Ergoteles defaulted in 257 B.C. (226A36) and Neokrontides, who is attested paying the rent in 250 B.C. (287A33), probably took over, but it is impossible to know which person to restore here.

The oil entry probably fell in the month of Posideon.

IG XI 2.287A133: I have assumed the rate/unit to be the same as the total amount.

IG XI 2.287A58: read, at the end of the line, ⊢⊢⊢.

IG XI 2.287A82: read ⊢⊢IIII.

ID 291b+ (291b + 292 + 306 + 291c + 291e + 294) 53 = 291b23.

ID 291b+ (291b + 292 + 306 + 291c + 291e + 294) 83 = 291c11 + 291e10. The price is probably ⊢⊢.

ID 290.95–96: figures restored, but arbitrary.

ID 338Aa19: for the price, I read a small cross-stroke (–) after the delta, giving provisionally Δ⊢, but this is very uncertain. Perhaps the restoration in *ID* should be preferred (Δ[IIII]).

ID 354.67: price restored, but not certain; the purchase is of ἔλαιον λευκόν, which is sometimes slightly more expensive than ordinary oil: cf. *IG* XI 2.203A39 ("white oil") and 203A59 (ordinary oil), 269 B.C.

ID 354.69: price restored, not certain because price in the following month is higher than in the preceding (cf. ll. 66, 72).

ID 354.72: I read a price of ΔI, not Δ⊢, but this yields a very strange price/*khous*. I have preferred Durrbach's reading.

ID 354.80–81: read [χό]ες · III · τιμή· Π⊢.

ID 372A76: for the amount, read ΔIIỊ[I]. The restored price is certainly correct.

ID 372A78–79: *lapis*, eight *khoes* bought, corrected by Durrbach.

ID 372A79: purchase of ἔλαιον λευκόν.

ID 372A95: I thought I could read a trace of a letter, either ⊢ or I, at the end of the price, but this must be a mistake.

ID 396A67: the price looks like Δ⊢⊢ on the stone, but ΔΠ̣ must be right.

ID 396A69: read χόες Δ, [τι]μὴ Δ̣Π.

ID 396A72: the purchase is of ἐλαίου λευκοῦ, presumably one *khous;* but the price could be either ⊢̣ỊII or ⊢̣⊢̣II.

ID 396A74: the total price is fully restored; I could not read the pi of the amount.

ID 442A188: the amount is fully restored.

ID 442A191: *lapis,* four *khoes,* corrected to nine by Durrbach.

ID 445.6: purchase for the Posideia.

ID 440A2: the price is fully restored.

ID 456B10: restoration uncertain.

ID 456B16 + 440A2: of the two prices attested for a *medimnos,* 13 dr would seem more likely here.

ID 456B18 + 440A4: read ἐλαίου χό. | | ị |, ⊢Π.

ID 456B23 + 440A9: the entry reads ἐλαίου [μϵ. . . .]⊢⊢. In the lacuna we could restore either [⊢Δ] or [⊢Δ⊢], both of which are attested as prices for a *medimnos* of oil. I have preferred the latter because it seems to fit the available space better.

ID 456B26 + 440A12: [ἐλαίου μϵ. ⊢Δ̣⊢⊢⊢·]. There is not enough space (7–9 letters) for the alternative ἐλαίου χο. fig., τιμὴ fig. The price could be either 12 or 13 dr, but 13 fits the pattern better.

ID 456B29–30 + 440A15–16: although the amount is fully restored, it must be right because of the attested prices only 1 dr ½ ob divides 6 dr 3 ob evenly.

ID 440A63–64: purchase for the Posideia. In both this and the following entry, the prices are far out of line with those for the rest of the year. Probably either two and three *khoes* or a much higher than usual quality of oil were bought.

ID 440A40: ἔλαιον ἐπὶ ἀκ[ά]ν[θους]?

BCH 109 (1985): 497, A7: the reading can be confirmed easily on Tréheux's photograph, fig. 2, p. 487.

ID 461Ab6: the cost, fully restored, is likely but not certain.

ID 461Ab12: the amount, fully restored, is likely but not certain.

Table III.3. PIGS (χοῖρος)

Sacrificed at the beginning of every month at the temple of Apollo, more rarely at Demeter's or Artemis's temple, on the island (Νῆσος, *IG* XI 2.203A42), or at the Thesmophorion (*IG* XI 2.287A68–69).

Source	*Date*	*Month*	*Price (dr)*	*Indexed Price*	*Annual Mean*
145.5	302	8	5.000	250.0	250.0
145.9	302		5.000	250.0	
146A79	301		7.000	350.0	350.0
146A77–78	301		7.000	350.0	
146A80	301		7.000	350.0	
153.11	297–290		8.000	400.0	400.0
159A9	281		3.667	183.3	158.3
159A10	281		2.667	133.3	
165.16	ca. 277		2.500	125.0	137.5
165.46–47	ca. 277		3.000	150.0	

Source	Date	Month	Price (dr)	Indexed Price	Annual Mean
163Aa61	276		4.000	200.0	200.0
199A50	274		3.000	150.0	150.0
203A33	269	1	2.000	100.0	174.7
203A34	269	2	2.750	137.5	
203A36	269	3	3.000	150.0	
203A41	269	4	3.500	175.0	
203A42	269	4	3.500	175.0	
203A44	269	5	3.500	175.0	
203A45	269	6	3.500	175.0	
203A46–47	269	7	3.000	150.0	
203A48	269	8	4.500	225.0	
203A50	269	8	4.000	200.0	
203A52	269	9	3.167	158.3	
203A53–54	269	10	4.000	200.0	
203A55	269	11	4.000	200.0	
203A57	269	12	4.500	225.0	
204.56–57	268	9	3.500	175.0	162.5
204.76–77	268	12	3.000	150.0	
228.4–5	265–255		2.000[a]		
287A41–42	250	1	1.833	91.7	97.9
287A47	250	2	1.500	75.0	
287A50–51	250	3	2.000	100.0	
287A55	250	4	1.833	91.7	
287A55–56	250	4	2.250	112.5	
287A58	250	5	2.000	100.0	
287A61–62	250	6	1.833	91.7	
287A65	250	7	1.833	91.7	
287A67	*250*	*8*	*2.000*	*100.0*	
287A68–69	250	8	2.333	116.7	
287A70	250	9	1.667	83.3	
287A74	250	10	1.833	91.7	
287A76	250	11	2.500	125.0	
287A82	250	12	2.000	100.0	
291b + 39–40	247	7	2.500	125.0	122.2
291b + 50–51	247	8	2.500	125.0	
291d5	247	12	2.333	116.7	
290.47	246	1	1.416	70.8	102.5
290.71	246	4	0.333[a]		
290.76	246	6	1.500	75.0	

(continued)

Table III.3. (CONTINUED)

Source	*Date*	*Month*	*Price (dr)*	*Indexed Price*	*Annual Mean*
290.79	246	6(2)	2.500	125.0	
290.82	246	7	1.583	79.2	
290.85	246	8	2.500	125.0	
290.90–91	246	8	4.250[a]		
290.93	246	9	1.667	83.3	
290.96	246	10	2.000	100.0	
290.98	246	11	3.000	150.0	
290.101–2	246	12	2.333	116.7	
290.104	246	12	2.000	100.0	
314A81	233 or 232	4	3.000	150.0	150.0
316.73	231	2	3.000	150.0	150.0
316.82	231	3	3.167	158.3	
316.86	231	4	2.500	125.0	
316.92	231	5	2.500	125.0	
316.98	231	7	3.833	191.7	
338Aa17	224	1	3.500	175.0	181.5
338Aa21	224	2	3.000	150.0	
338Aa25	224	3	3.333	166.7	
338Aa29	224	4	3.916	195.8	
338Aa33	224	5	3.000	150.0	
338Aa38	224	7	4.667	233.3	
338Aa46	224	9	4.000	200.0	
354.57	218	1	3.333	166.7	170.9
354.61	218	2	3.333	166.7	
354.64–65	218	3	3.333	166.7	
354.67–68	218	4	3.500	175.0	
354.70–71	218	4	3.500	175.0	
354.71	218	5	3.333	166.7	
354.74	218	6	3.500	175.0	
354.80	218	8	3.500	175.0	
372A72	200	1	4.167	208.3	200.7
372A75–76	200	2	3.667	183.3	
372A77	200	2	6.000	300.0	
372A78	200	3	3.833	191.7	
372A80	200	4	3.667	183.3	
372A81	200	5	[3][a]		
372A83	200	6	4.000	200.0	
372A85	200	7	4.000	200.0	

Source	Date	Month	Price (dr)	Indexed Price	Annual Mean
372A87	200	8	4.000	200.0	
372A89	200	9	4.333	216.7	
372A91	200	10	3.500	175.0	
372A92	200	11	3.500	175.0	
372A94	200	12	3.500	175.0	
396A64	194	1	4.500	225.0	186.1
396A68	194	2	2.667	133.3	
396A70	194	3	4.[5?]		
396A73	194	4	4.000	200.0	
442A182	179	2	4.833	241.7	218.3
442A185	179	4	4.500	225.0	
442A186	179	5	4.000	200.0	
442A187	179	6	4.000	200.0	
442A198	179	8	4.500	225.0	
444A32	177	8	4.916	245.8	245.8
456B4–5	174	1	4.500	225.0	188.5
456B11	174	3	3.000	150.0	
456B14	174	4	3.500	175.0	
456B16–17 + 440A2–3	174	5	3.000	150.0	
456B19 + 440A5	174	6	3.000	150.0	
456B24–25 + 440A10–11	174	7	3.000	150.0	
456B27–28 + 440A13–14	174	8	4.000	200.0	
440A38–39	174	8	5.000	250.0	
440A48	174	8	5.000	250.0	
440A18–19	174	10	3.000	150.0	
440A21	174	11	3.000	150.0	
440A40	174	11	5.000	250.0	
440A23	174	12	4.000	200.0	
BCH 109 (1985): 497, A13	173	10	3.833	191.7	191.7
BCH 109 (1985): 497, A14	173	11	[3.833]	191.7	
460t53	171	8	3.000	150.0	212.5
460t67	171	8	6.000	300.0	
460v12	171	11	3.000	150.0	
460t62	171	12	5.000	250.0	
459.44	170	1	4.667	233.3	216.7

(continued)

Table III.3. (CONTINUED)

Source	*Date*	*Month*	*Price (dr)*	*Indexed Price*	*Annual Mean*
459.62	170	8	4.000	200.0	
461Ab8	169	6	4.500	225.0	239.6
461Ab11	169	8	4.667	233.3	
461Ab12	169	8	5.000	250.0	
461Ab16	169	12	5.000	250.0	
461*bis*13	ca. 170		10.333[a]		

[a]*I have regarded this price as too problematic to use in analysis; see in the lemma, below.*

IG XI 2.145.5: price, Π. The sacrifice (εἰς ἐχθυσίαν), associated with the Thesmophoria, took place in Metageitnion (see Bruneau, 285–87).

IG XI 2.153.11: pig sacrificed to Artemis, ἐνεθύσαμεν τῆι Ἀρτέμιδι χοῖρον.

IG XI 2.159A9: three pigs bought for 11 dr; this price casts some doubt on the reading of A10, which Durrbach read as ⊢⊢!̣III; perhaps ⊢⊢⊢̣III is correct?

IG XI 2.159A10: cf. comm., l. A9.

IG XI 2.165.46–47: "pig" almost surely a correct restoration; see my comments on *IG* XI 2.204.56–57, below. The date of this inscription is a problem. It probably belongs ca. 277 B.C. and not in 280 as in *IG;* see J. Tréheux in *CICG,* 30–31, who excludes 282 and 280. I likewise exclude 279 and 278 because we have inscriptions for those years, but it is not impossible that it belongs in 275. I have treated it as ca. 277 in my analysis.

IG XI 2.163Aa61: the price is complete; there is a trace of punctuation at the edge of the stone.

IG XI 2.199A50: the price is complete; there are traces of letters after it, perhaps ΑΔ.

IG XI 2.203A50: χοῖρος καθάρασθαι τὸ ἱερὸν τῆς Δήμητρος; the Thesmophoria with which this is associated took place in Metageitnion.

IG XI 2.204.56–57: restore [Βουφονιῶνος· χοῖρος παρὰ τοῦ δεῖνος τὸ ἱερὸν/γ καθάρασ]θαι.

IG XI 2.228.4–5: probably restore [χοῖρος κα]θάρασθαι δ̣ραχμῶν δ̣ύ̣ο.

IG XI 2.287A68–69: purchase of χοῖρος τὸ Θεσμοφόριον καθάρασθαι; see Bruneau, 285–87.

ID 291b+ (291b + 292 + 306 + 291c + 291e + 294) 39–40 = 291b9–10; 50–51 = 291b20–21; 291d5: entries reading (in various states of preservation and restoration) χοῖρος τὸ ἱερὸν καθάρασθαι καὶ εἰς τὰ λοιπά. "The rest" is certainly firewood (ξύλα) and a pine bough (πεύκη) or a torch (or lamp, δᾶις); cf., e.g., *ID* 290.79, 93. These items cost 2 ob in 246 B.C. I have therefore subtracted 2 ob from the prices given in the texts to arrive at the figures in the table.

ID 291d5: this stone joins 293, but the join does not affect the text at this point. On the character of the entry, see the preceding note. I strongly suspect that 291d is part of the complex 291b + 292 + 306 + 291c + 291e + 294; if so, this price must be from Posideon.

ID 290.71: the figure may well be wrong; there seems to be space available before the II, and I would not be surprised if the lines should be read as drachma marks.

ID 290.90–91: two pigs bought for sacrifice to Demeter and Zeus Euboles, as part of the Thesmophoria; see Bruneau, 285–87.

ID 316.92: for the price read ⊢⊢III, without brackets.

ID 316.98: Durrbach hesitates over the price because two figures are missing between the two drachma marks and the three obols, printing ⊢⊢⊢. . III; I assume two missing obols, yielding a price more in line with those of the inscription than 4 dr 4 ob, the other choice.

ID 354.80: read only ⊢⊢⊢III.

ID 372A77: χοῖρος τὴν Νῆσον καθάρασθαι.

ID 372A81: price fully restored, but not with certainty.

ID 372A92: read ⊢⊢⊢III.

ID 396A70: read ⊢⊢⊢⊢ị ị [I] or ⊢⊢⊢⊢ị ị ị.

ID 442A198: purchase τὸ Θ̣εσμοφόριον καθᾶραι, as part of the Thesmophoria, which took place in Metageitnion; see Bruneau, *CDH*, 285–87.

ID 444A32: purchase for Thesmophoria.

ID 456B11: price difficult to read. I was able to confirm only ⊢⊢, but there is probably another drachma.

ID 456B16–17+ 440A2–3: price fully restored.

ID 440A38–39: purchase καθά̣[ρασ]θαι τὸ ἱερόν as part of the Thesmophoria.

ID 440A48: purchase to purify the temple of Demeter as part of the Thesmophoria.

ID 440A18–19: for the price, read ⊢⊢⊢.

ID 440A40: purchase as part of the Nyktophylaxia, which was celebrated in Aresion; see Bruneau, 290–93.

BCH 109 (1985): 497, A14: price partly restored, but virtually certain.

ID 460t: M.-F. Baslez and C. Vial, *BCH* 111 (1987): 290 n. 42, have shown that 465c belongs in 171 B.C. On that basis, I have been able to reconstruct a text consisting of *ID* 465c, 460t, and 460v.

ID 460t53–63: these entries represent monthly expenses. Lines 66–67 give expenses for the Thesmophoria, which here are included in the monthly outlays; this means that the pig purchase for monthly purification at l. 63 belongs to Metageitnion. From that it follows that Hekatombaion begins at l. 60, Panemos at l. 59, Thargelion at l. 57, and Artemision at l. 53. Expenses for the Artemisia appear in l. 56, which may be restored to read: Π· λαμπάδες [καὶ ῥυμοὺς? το]ῖς χορο[ῖ]ς [Ἀρτεμισίοις, etc.], confirming the dating. This also corroborates the identification of 171 as a normal (nonintercalary) year; see R. Vallois, *BCH* 55 (1931): 294.

ID 460t53: the price may not be complete.

ID 460t67: purchase to purify the temple of Demeter as part of the Thesmophoria.

ID 460v12: Durrbach prints Δ⊢⊢⊢⊢· πε[ύ]κη, κληματὶ(ς) IIII. This should almost certainly be emended and restored as [ΑΡΗΣΙΩΝΟΣ· χοῖρος τὸ ἱερὸν καθᾶρ]α̣ι̣ ⊢⊢⊢ (or possibly Π̣⊢) · [πεύ]κη, etc.

ID 459.44: read ⊢⊢⊢⊢̣IIII.

ID 459.62: purchase to purify the temple of Demeter as part of the Thesmophoria.

ID 461Ab12: purchase to purify the Thesmophorion as part of the Thesmophoria.

ID 461*bis*13: purchase [χοῖρος καθᾶ]ραι τὴν Νῆσον.

Table III.4. BARLEY (ἄλφιτα [MARKED *] OR κριθαί)

The most interesting entries, *IG* XI 2.142.11 and 142.7 (307 B.C.), cannot be included because no quantity is indicated. The accounts note 300 and 140 dr obtained from the sale of barley (κριθαί, presumably standing) seized for unpaid rent on estates. T = food for *tekhnitai;* G = feed for geese; P = purchase for the Posideia.

Source	*Date*	*Month*	*Price/* medimnos (dr)	*Quantity* (med)	*Use*
158A48	282	10	4.000*	3.75	T
158A48–49	282	11	5.000*	3.75	T
158A49–50	282	12	5.000*	3.75	T
224A29	258	2	3.000	1	G?
287A45	250	1	3.333	3	G
287A59–60	250	5	3.223	3	G
287A64	250	6	3.000	3	G
287A66	250	7	2.667	3	G
287A67–68	250	8	2.333	3	G
287A71	250	9	2.000	3	G
291b + 55	247	8	2.500	3	G?
291b + 82	247	11	2.250	4	G
290.82	246	7	4.000	3	G
290.97–98	246	10	4.000	3	G
338Aa35	224	5	2.000	1	G
442A220	179	12	4.000[a]	3	P
445.4–5	178	12	3.750[a]	4	P
452.9	177	12	4.000[a]	3	P
440A62–63	174	12	4.000	1	P

[a] *Price reconstructed based on Larsen, 347–48 (who also offers alternative prices that are less likely in my view).*

IG XI 2.224A29: read κριθῶν μέδιμνος· ⊢⊢⊢.

ID 291b + (291b + 292 + 306 + 291c + 291e + 294) 55 = 291b25; 82 = 291c10 + 291e10.

ID 290.97–98: the figures are all restored.

ID 338Aa35: read [μέδιμν]ον χη[σ]ὶν κριθῶν · vac ⊢⊢.

ID 452.9: Durrbach restores Δ[Π], but this is unexampled. I prefer Δ[⊢⊢].

ID 464.4–5 (ca. 170 B.C.): entry reading ἀλφίτων μεδι. τέσσα[ρες]; not included in table.

Table III.5. WHEAT (πῦρος)

Provided for first three, then two τεχνῖται for seven months in 282 B.C., perhaps partly in lieu of wages, or bought for the Posideia.

Source	*Date*	*Month*	*Price/* medimnos (dr)	*Quantity*
158A37–38	282	1	7.000	2.8125
158A39–40	282	2	6.500	2.8125
158A41–42	282	3	6.000	1.8750
158A42–43	282	4	4.500	1.8750
158A43–44	282	5	6.833	1.8750
158A45–46	282	8	7.000	1.8750
158A46–47	282	9	10.000	1.8750
401.22	190	12	10.000	
445.13	178	12	10.000	
440A69	174	12	11.000	
461Bb53	169	12	10.000	

Appendix IV
Rents of Estates and Houses on Delos, 314–169 B.C.

TEMPLE ESTATES

The estates are thoroughly discussed in John Harvey Kent, "The Temple Estates of Delos, Rheneia, and Mykonos," *Hesperia* 17 (1948): 243–338, with the many new readings and restorations in id., "Notes on the Delian Farm Accounts," *BCH* 63 (1939): 232–45, and Brunet, passim.

The estates are ordered below alphabetically, sorted by the island on which they were located: Delos, Rheneia, and Mykonos. The ordering implies no acceptance of any theories about the location of the estates on each island; see the response of Jacques Tréheux, *BCH* 110 (1986): 427–32, to the views of M.-Th. Couilloud–Le Dinahet in *Les Cyclades,* 135–41.

As with goods, I have established the index for the calculation of indexed rents with the year 250 B.C. as the base. The figure I use as a base figure, however, is not the rent *paid* in 250 B.C. but the rent *bid* in 250 B.C. for the next rental period (the rent dated below as "249pro"). I use this because the rent actually paid in 250 B.C. represents the amount bid for the estates ten years earlier, in 260 B.C. All citations are from *IG* XI 2 or *ID.* The abbreviation "s." in the tables stands for "son of." In some cases in the commentaries I have discussed inscriptions not included in the tables for the sake of completeness.

ESTATES ON DELOS

1. AKRA DELOS

Source	*Date*	*Rent*		*Renter*
		Raw	*Indexed*	
158A12	282	300.000	68.18	Anapsyktides
161A13	279	501.000	113.86	Zopyros s. Automedon
162A11	278	501.000	113.86	Zopyros
199A6	274	501.000	113.86	Zopyros
200.5	ca. 274	501.000	113.86	Zopyros
203A21	269	512.000	116.36	Kharilas
204.16–17	268	512.000	116.36	Kharilas
224A14	258	400.000	90.91	Empedos s. Xenon
287A31	250	400.000	90.91	Empedos
287A175–76	249pro	440.000	100.00	Empedos

(*continued*)

1. AKRA DELOS (*continued*)

Source	Date	Rent		Renter
		Raw	*Indexed*	
290.14	246	440.000	100.00	Empedos
353A13	219	340.250	77.33	Empedes
354.37–38	218	340.250	77.33	Empedes
356bisA10–11	210	340.250	77.33	Empedos
399A74–75	192			Polyxenos
442A146	179	150.000	34.09	Pistos s. Pherekleides
456A9	174	150.000	34.09	Pistos s. Pherekleides

IG XI 2.203A21: rent correctly read by J. H. Kent, *BCH* 63 (1939):237.

ID 372A11–12, 374B19: Kent, 306–7, has suggested restoring Akra Delos in both places, yielding rents of 431 for 209–200 B.C. and 430 for 199–190 B.C. As Kent himself points out, these rents would be very much out of line with those for the preceding and subsequent rental periods (see above). Further doubts at Brunet, 45.

ID 399A74–75: rent given as [H..]⊢⊢.

ID 456A9: for the date, Jacques Tréheux, *BCH* 109 (1985):493 n. 29.

2. EPISTHENEIA

Source	Date	Rent		Renter
		Raw	*Indexed*	
156B7–15	288–283	500.000	68.87	Polykritos
158A12	282	500.000	68.87	Polykritos
161A14	279	590.000	81.27	Khoirylos s. Teleson
162A12	278	590.000	81.27	Khoirylos
199A6	274	590.000	81.27	Khoirylos
203A21	269	612.000	84.30	Xenon s. Teleson
204.16	268	612.000	84.30	Xenon
223A36–37	262	612.000	84.30	Xenon
224A15	258	660.000	90.91	Periandros s. Hegesagoras
287A31–32	250	660.000	90.91	Periandros
287A178–79	249 pro	726.000	100.00	Periandros
290.15–16	246	726.000	100.00	Periandros
351.13–14	220 pro	422.000	58.13	Diaktorides s. Tl——?
353A8–9	219	422.000	58.13	Diaktorides

Source	Date	Rent: Raw	Rent: Indexed	Renter
354.37	218	422.000	58.13	Diaktorides
356*bis*A12–13	210	[422.000]	58.13	Diaktorides?
372A11–12	200	431.000	59.37	Polyxenos?
374B15–16	200	345.000pro	47.52	Polyxenos s. Phokeus
399A75	192	345.000	47.52	Polyxenos s. Phokeus
373A9	180 pro	[411.000]	56.61	Menestratos s. Timostratos
442A146	179	411.000	56.61	Menestratos s. Timostratos
452.16–32 + 467.1–5	177	411.000	56.61	Meilikhides
456A9–10	174	[411.000]	56.61	Meilikhides s. Silenos

IG XI 2.156B7–15: the former renter, Teleutesas son of Kallisthenes, defaulted.

IG XI 2.199A6: rent read correctly by Kent, *BCH* 63 (1939):237.

IG XI 2.223A36–37: this entry is based on restorations, from a revision of the stone, in Maurice Lacroix, *BCH* 48 (1924):407–8, confirmed with new readings by Kent, *BCH* 63 (1939):238.

ID 369A41: the *hieropoioi* have imposed an *epiballon* of 1.5 ×. There is some question as to the identity of the estate.

ID 372A11–12: Epistheneia is fully restored by Durrbach; Kent, 304, gives no rent figure for this period because (306–7) he thinks Epistheneia falsely restored (Akra Delos is his alternative); but his argument that the rent here "does not tally well with the rental of Epistheneia in 199 B.C." (306) ignores the fact that it is the rent of that period, and not of 219–210 B.C. nor 209–200 B.C. nor indeed 179–170 B.C., that is odd.

ID 373A9: See Kent, *BCH* 63 (1939):242.

ID 452.16–32 + 467.1–5: this is a rerental after failure to provide guarantors, and not a regular new rental in 180 or 170, as Kent, *BCH* 63 (1939):245, thought. For the join, see Tréheux, *BCH* 100 (1986):431; text in Michèle Brunet, *BCH* 114 (1990):678–79; for the date, see G. Reger, *Hesperia* 63 (1994): 105–10.

ID 456A9–10: for the date, Tréheux, *BCH* 109 (1985):493 n. 29.

3. HIPPODROMOS (SOMETIMES WITH APHESIS; MARKED WITH *)

Source	Date	Rent: Raw	Rent: Indexed	Renter
135.6–7	314	720.000*	108.93	Sarpedon s. Karneios
142.9–12	307	920.000	139.18	Arkhandros
142.9–10	307	920.000	139.18	Nikomakhos s. Arkhandros
144A10–11	304	1,012.000	153.10	Ari[steas] s. Aristeas
149.2	297	1,001.000	151.44	Aristeides
158A11	282	550.000*	83.21	Aristeides
161A11	279	605.000*	91.53	Aristeides s. Aristeas
162A9–10	278	605.000*	91.53	Aristeides
199A5–6	274	605.000*	91.53	——— s. Aristeides
201A6	277–270	605.000*	91.53	Aristeides?
203A24–25	269	732.056*	110.75	Antikrates s. Timesidemos
204.8	268	732.056	110.75	Antikrates
224A17	258	510.000	77.16	———
287A32–33	250	510.000	77.16	Hierombrotos
287A143–44	249pro	661.000	100.00	Antigonos s. Telemnestos
290.16–17	246	661.000	100.00	Antigonos?
353A12	219	579.000	87.59	Xenomedes
354.38	218	579.000	87.59	Xenomedes
356*bis*A11	210	579.000	87.59	Xenomedes
362A15	209	622.000	94.10	Xenomedes
368.25–26	207	622.000	94.10	Alkimakhos
372A16	200	622.000	94.10	Alkimakhos
399A75–76	192	572.000	86.53	Amnos s. Hierombrotos
403.51–53	189	629.250	95.20	Menethales
442A146–47	179	655.500	99.17	Diaitos s. Diaitos
456A10	174	655.500	99.17	Diaitos s. Diaitos

IG XI 2.142.9–12: the renter defaulted. The rent was extracted as follows:

Seized barley:	300 dr
Two oxen, sold:	150 dr
Payment by Protoleos, $\frac{1}{2}$ of the balance:	235 dr
Owed by renter and Amphias:	235 dr
TOTAL:	920 dr

For the date, see "Olive Oil" above, comm. on *IG* XI 2.142.

IG XI 2.142.9–10: a rerental to the son of the defaulter.

IG XI 2.144A10–11: rent corrected from *IG*'s 1,200 by Lacroix, *BCH* 48 (1924): 401, followed by Kent, *BCH* 63 (1939):234. Renter's name should be restored as Ἀ[ρ]ι[στέας Ἀρ]ιστέου according to E. Schulhof, *BCH* 32 (1908):13, no. 3, and to Kent, *BCH* 63 (1939):234.

IG XI 2.146: Kent, 303, shows Hippodromos (as his estate XI) with a (supposed) rent of 910 dr for 301 B.C. This results from the assumption that the next rental period figure of 1,001 dr was obtained by exercise of the 10 percent increase option.

IG XI 2.183.15: Kent, *BCH* 63 (1939):236, is tempted to see in the figure HHΔΔΔ that he reads here part of the rent of Hippodromos because (see his n. 2) the rent for the next rental period, 269–260 B.C., is 732 dr $\frac{1}{3}$ ob, suggesting an extension by adding 10 percent. But this is impossible: a 10 percent increase would have called for a rent in 279–270 B.C. of 665 dr 3 ob, or 𐅅H𐅄Δ𐅃III. Kent's reading clearly cannot concur with that. It is much more likely, as Kent himself admits, that the stone has nothing to do with rentals at all (see the dative, already noticed by Kent, at l. 4).

IG XI 2.199A5–6: Lacroix, *BCH* 48 (1924):405 restores [ὁ δεῖνα] Ἀριστείδου, i.e., implying that Aristeides has died since 278 B.C. Lacroix's doubts about the rent are groundless.

IG XI 2.201A6: both the rent and the renter (restored by Durrbach) are very doubtful: Lacroix, *REG* 35 (1922):419.

IG XI 2.203A24–25: Kent, 304, gives 732.1 dr rent for this period; his $\frac{1}{10}$ dr presumably represents $\frac{1}{3}$ ob. (cf. Kent *BCH* 63 [1939]:236 n. 2).

IG XI 2.204.8: the name of the guarantor is from *ID* 290.9–11 of 246 B.C., where he pays 366.347 dr as his pledge on Hippodromos, under a contract struck in 262 B.C., under the *arkhon* Elpinos. Perhaps Aristothales was Antikrates' guarantor only in that year, and Antikrates only defaulted that year?

IG XI 2.224A17: Kent, *BCH* 63 (1939):238 (cf. Kent, 304) reads 510 dr.

IG XI 2.287A32–33: two guarantors are recorded as paying the *epiballon:* Kallagoras for 55 dr 5 ob, Philon son of Demoson for 86 dr 2$\frac{1}{6}$ ob, giving a total of 142 dr 1$\frac{1}{6}$ ob. Hiembrotos the renter has come up with only 367 dr 4$\frac{5}{6}$ ob.

ID 290.9–11: Aristothales is recorded in this inscription as paying up 366 dr 2$\frac{1}{12}$ ob that he owes as guarantor for Antikrates for 262 B.C., under the *arkhon* Elpinos. This implies a default in 262 B.C. and, presumably, a rerental that year. Aristothales' payment represents one-half of the rent.

ID 353A11: rent corrected to 289 dr 3 ob by Kent, 306.

ID 356*bis*A11: rent read more completely by Lacroix, *BCH* 56 (1932):379.

ID 403.51–53: this is a rerental after Amnos failed to renew his guarantors; the expression [τοῦ ἴ]σου (l. 52) is odd, since the *hieropoioi* patently obtained a higher rent.

ID 456A10: for date, Tréheux, *BCH* 109 (1985):493 n. 29.

4. KERAMEION

Source	Date	Rent: *Raw*	Rent: *Indexed*	Renter
158A13	282	120.000	48.00	Eteokleides
161A12	279	140.000	56.00	Hierombrotos s. Eteokleides
162A10	278	140.000	56.00	Hierombrotos
199A7	274	140.000	56.00	Hierombrotos
200.3–4	ca. 274	140.000	56.00	Hierombrotos
201A8	277–270	140.000	56.00	Hierombrotos
203A18–19	269	166.000	66.40	Hierombrotos
204.13	268	166.000	66.40	Hierombrotos
224A15	258	171.000	68.40	Ergoteles
226A36	257	171.000	68.40	Ergoteles
275A16	259 or 256–251	171.000	68.40	Neokrontides?
287A33	250	171.000	68.40	Neokrontides
287A145–46	249pro	250.000	100.00	Eudikos
290.17	246	250.000	100.00	Kosmiades
353A14–15	219	262.000	104.80	Lysixenos
354.36	218	262.000	104.80	Lysixenos
356*bis*A9	210	262.000	104.80	Lysixenos
399A76–77	192	200+		Boethos s. Orthokles
404.16	188	285.000	114.00	Anaxandros
442A150	179	302.500	121.00	Anaxandros s. Neokrontides
456A21	174	[302.500]	121.00	Neokrontides s. Neokrontides

IG XI 2.226A36: the renter is in default: he has paid 70 dr but owes the rest, presumably 101 dr; I take my information from *IG* XI2.224A15 of 258 B.C. There is some question as to the identity of the estate.

IG XI 2.275A16: on the date, see lemma under "Olive Oil" in Appendix III.

IG XI 2.287A145–46: failure on the part of Lyses son of Simis to put up guarantors led to rerental. This seems to have happened during the period of bidding; for Neokrontides was the renter in 250 B.C. The rent offered by these two was the same. Were both original bidders? Or did Eudikos take advantage of Lyses' misfortune to bid the same rent on the reoffer, and thus capture the estate?

ID 373B1, 374Ab1: Kent, *BCH* 63 (1939):243, suggested restoring Kerameion at both places; doubts, Brunet, 45–46.

ID 399A76–77: rent read as "HH . . .".

ID 404.16: Kent, *BCH* 63 (1939):244.

ID 456A21: for the date, Tréheux, *BCH* 109 (1985):493 n. 29.

5. LEIMON

Source	Date	Rent: Raw	Rent: Indexed	Renter
135.3	314	781.000	353.39	Hermon s. Kleokritos
143B1–4	310	600.000	271.49	Theodorides s. Epikrates
144A10	304	600.000	271.49	Theodorides
146A10	301	650.000	294.12	Pelops
149.4	297	661.000	299.10	Proxenos s. Eukleides
157A2–3	287–283	300.000	135.75	Pherekleides
158A11	282	300.000	135.75	Pherekleides
161A11–12	279	330.000	149.32	Pherekleides s. Eukleides
162A10	278	330.000	149.32	Pherekleides
199A6	274	330.000	149.32	children of Pherekleides
200.4	ca. 274	330.000	149.32	——doros
203A20–21	269	350.000	158.37	Hodoiteles
204.15	268	350.000	158.37	Hodoiteles
226A34–35	257	302.000	136.65	
287A32	250	300.000	135.75	Dionysodoros
287A148	249pro	221.000	100.00	Dionysodoros
290.14–15	246	221.000	100.00	Dionysodoros?
353A11	219	204.000	92.31	Eudemos
354.37	218	204.000	92.31	Eudemos
362A21	209	210.000	95.02	Demonous
368.28–29	206	210.000	95.02	
399A74	192	231.000	104.52	Demonous s. Sosidemos
406B80–83	ca. 190	See note		
442A147	179	284.000	128.51	Aresimbrotos s. Nikandros
456A11	174	284.000	128.51	Aresimbrotos s. Nikandros
459.40	172 or 170	[284.000]	128.51	Aresimbrotos s. Nikandros

IG XI 2.143B1–4: in *IG* XI 2.144A10 (of 304 B.C.) this same property is rented to the same person for 600 dr (the source of the restoration here). But this cannot be a 10 percent increase because the nearest amount, 545 dr, does not fit (not to mention that the *hiera syngraphe* is not yet in force). Yet there are definitely two different rental periods since Theodorides' lease here is set at five years. Either this is a case of renewal without an increase, or Theodorides took a chance by bidding for the same estate at the old price, and won out. For the date, see Vial, 205.

IG XI 2.203A20–21: Kent, *BCH* 63 (1939):237, reads the rent as 350 dr.

(*continued*)

IG XI 2.204.15: restored after Kent, *BCH* 63 (1939):237 (correction for rent in *IG* XI 2.203A21).

IG XI 2.226A34–35: the difference of 2 dr in rents between this entry and that at *IG* XI 2.287A32 is difficult to explain unless the original renter defaulted in 257 and Dionysodoros took over that year for a rent of 300 dr. Cf. the reading at this passage: [τῆς] γῆς τῆς ἐλ Λειμῶνι ἣν ἐ[μεμίσθωτο - - - - - - - -] ἀπέδωκε Πισ[τ]ῆς ὁ ἔγγυος [τ]ὸ ἥμυσυ τοῦ ἐνηροσίου Η𐅄⊢· τὸ δὲ λοιπὸν ὀφείλεται.

ID 362A21: cf. *ID* comm., p. 341, and Lacroix, *REG* 39 (1926):445, with Kent, 306.

ID 368.28–29: the rent is Kent's suggestion (Kent, 306) in place of the 250 dr 2 ob in *ID* read by Selden (cf. lemma at *ID* 368). The stone has disappeared, making confirmation impossible.

ID 406B80–83: very possibly a default, cf. l. 80, [οὐ καθιστά]ντος τοὺς ἐγγύους Δημ[- - -], restore Δημ[όνους?], after *ID* 399A74.

ID 456A11: for the date, Tréheux, *BCH* 109 (1985):493 n. 29.

6. LYKONEION

Source	Date	Rent: Raw	Rent: Indexed	Renter
135.3–4	314	120.000	98.28	Sarpedon s. Karneios
144A16	304	209.000	171.18	Lysixenos (?) s. Aristoboulos
146A11	301	200.000	163.80	Leonymos
149.3	297	220.000	180.18	Skymnos
157A3–4	287–283	80.000	65.52	Eumedes
158A13	282	80.000	65.52	Eumedes
161A14–15	279	150.000	122.85	Aristeides s. Aristeas
162A12–13	278	150.000	122.85	Aristeides
199A6–7	274	150.000	122.85	Aristeides
201A8	277–270	150.000	122.85	Aristeides
203A23	269	153.000	125.31	Hippakos s. Delikos
204.19	268	153.000	125.31	Hippakos
224A16	258	111.000	90.91	Akridion s. Dionysodoros
287A33	250	111.000	90.91	Akridion
287A179–80	249pro	122.097	100.00	Arkidion
290.17	246	122.097	100.00	Eukleides
351.18–19	220	153.000	125.31	Naxiades
353A14	219	153.000	125.31	Naxiades
356.13	217–211	153.000	125.31	Apollodoros
356*bis*B22	210pro	250.000	204.76	Apollodoros s. Ekhenikos

Source	Date	Rent		Renter
		Raw	*Indexed*	
372A15–16	200	231.000	189.19	
399A76	192	130.000	106.47	Nesiotes s. Dorieus
442A150	179	171.611	140.55	Neon s. Demetrios
456A19	174	171.611	140.55	Neon

IG XI 2.144A16: rent read correctly by Kent, *BCH* 63 (1939):234.

IG XI 2.146A11: rent read correctly ibid., 235.

IG XI 2.199A6–7: rent and renter restored ibid., 237, from new readings and comparison with *IG* XI 2.161A15 and 162A13.

IG XI 2.201A8: Gustave Glotz, *REG* 26 (1913):37, suggests at l. 2 the reading [Λυκων]είο[υ]. *Apud* Lacroix, *BCH* 48 (1924):406, Glotz offers, for l. 8, [τοῦ Λυκωνείου Ἀριστ]ẹίδης [Η∏]. Lacroix himself reads the epsilon and the figure 105, observing, however, that Glotz's earlier restoration at l. 2 could not be right if this was. After Kent, *BCH* 63 (1939):237, and *IG* XI 2.161A15 and 162A13, it seems sure to me that Glotz's second suggestion was correct and that Lacroix misread a pi for 50 (𐅄) as a simple 5. I restore the rent as 150 dr.

IG XI 2.203A23: rent correctly read by Kent, *BCH* 63 (1939):237.

IG XI 2.204.19: rent corrected after ibid., 237 for *IG* XI 2.203A23.

ID 354.38: in 218 B.C. Euthypolis paid 76 dr 3 ob on behalf of Naxiades. This may imply a default.

ID 356.13; for Apollodoros instead of Naxiades, cf. comm. on 356*bis* A9.

ID 356*bis*B22 and 372A15–16: the first figure is the winning bid for the 209–200 rental period, 250 dr. If the figure of 231 for 200 B.C. is correct, there must have been a default. But both figures are dubious; for 356*bis*B22, see Pierre Roussel *apud* Lacroix, *BCH* 56 (1932):381–82, who restores Lykoneion as the estate.

ID 456A19: for the date, see Tréheux, *BCH* 109 (1985):493 n. 29.

7. PHOINIKES

Source	Date	Rent: Raw	Rent: Indexed	Renter
135.5–6	314	810.00	124.42	Pasitimos s. Xenomedes
144A10	304	1,100.000	168.97	Hermon
146A9–10	301	1,101.000	169.12	Pistoxenos?
149.3–4	297	1,101.000	169.12	Khares s. Eukleides
158A11–12	282	720.000	110.60	Aristodikos
161A13	279	710.000	109.06	Theorylos
162A11–12	278	710.000	109.06	Theorylos s. Diaktorides
199A6	274	710.000	109.06	Theorylos
201A7	277–270	710.000	109.06	Theorylos
203A23	269	723.000	111.06	Kallisthenes s. Diakritos
204.18–19	268	723.000	111.06	Kallisthenes
224A15	258	600.000	92.17	
225a15	259–250	600.000	92.17	
287A31	250	600.000	92.17	Diaktorides
287A151	249pro	651.000	100.00	Antigonos s. Didymos
290.16	246	651.000	100.00	Antigonos
351.14–16	220	474.111	72.83	Xenokrates
353A4–5	219	934.111	143.49	Xenokrates
354.35–36	218	474.111	72.83	Xenokrates
356*bis*A7	210	474.097	72.83	Philon
374Aa15–16	200pro	[585.000?]	89.86	
399A77	192	585.000	89.86	S——kon? s. Philokrates
373A41	180pro	491.000	75.42	Parmikos s. Epikydos
442A145	179	491.000	75.42	Parmikos s. Epikydos
456A8–9	174	[491.000]	75.42	Parmikos s. Epikydos
459.39	172 or 170	[491.000]	75.42	Parmikos s. Epikydos

IG XI 2.146A9–10: rent and renter read and corrected by Kent, *BCH* 63 (1939): 235; cf. also *SEG* 1.340.

IG XI 2.153.9–10, 154A41: the *hieropoioi* pay workers to clean a sheep pen and to repair a pigsty (προβατών and καπρών). These structures no doubt belonged to sacred estates; otherwise, why would Apollo have been concerned about their condition? The sheep pen is said to belong to Diaktorides. A Theoryles son of Diaktorides rented Phoinikes in 280 B.C. (*IG* XI 2.162A11–12), and in ca. 277 B.C. a Diaktorides sold a pig to Apollo (*IG* XI 2.165.46–47).

ID 356*bis*A7: the two $\frac{1}{12}$ marks bracketed in *ID* are readable according to Lacroix, *BCH* 56 (1932): 379, but Kent, *BCH* 63 (1939): 241, could read only one. The difference is trivial.

ID 373A41: cf. Kent, *BCH* 63 (1939): 242.

ID 456A8–9: for the date, see Tréheux, *BCH* 109 (1985): 493 n. 29.

8. PHYTALIA

Source	Date	Rent: Raw	Rent: Indexed	Renter
158A14	282	60.000	123.85	Philtos
161A14	279	60.000	123.85	Kallisthenes s. Diakritos
162A12	278	60.000	123.85	Kallisthenes
199A7	274	60.000	123.85	Kallisthenes
203A22–23	269	72.000	148.62	Diakritos s. Kallisthenes
204.18	268	72.000	148.62	Diakritos
287A34	250	44.000	90.83	Eubios
287A177–78	249pro	48.444	100.00	Eubios s. Theodotos
290.15	246	48.444	100.00	Eubios
351.8	220pro	50.000	103.21	Kineas s. Dionysodoros
353A13	219	50.000	103.21	Kineas
354.38	218	50.000	103.21	Kritoboulos
362A18, 21	209	50.000	103.21	
399A77	192	52.000	107.34	Hegeas s. Mennis
373A31–32	180pro	[30.000]	61.93	Silenos s. Silenos
442A147	179	30.000	61.93	Silenos s. Silenos
452.24–25 + 467.9–10	177	30.000	61.93	Alkimakhos s. Antikrates
456A11–12	174	[30.000?]	61.93	Alkimakhos s. Antikrates
460u24	171	[30.000]	61.93	Alkimakhos s. Antikrates

ID 362A18, 21: Metonymos pays his share of an *epiballon* of 25.5? dr; another of the same amount (name lost) at l. 21. See also the following lemma.

ID 368.26–27 (207), 371A26 (202 or 201), 372A18 (200): these three entries represent payments of 25.5, 25.5, and 12 dr made by Metonymos as an *epiballon* on the estate for the difference between the old rent and the new after the former renter, who is probably Kritoboulos, defaulted.

ID 373A31–32: cf. Kent, *BCH* 63 (1939): 242.

ID 452.24–25 + 467.9–10: rerental after failure to renew guarantors, not a new rental period, as Kent, *BCH* 63 (1939): 245, thought. For the join, see Tréheux, *BCH* 10 (1986): 431; text in Brunet, *BCH* 114 (1990): 678–79; for the date, see G. Reger, *Hesperia* 63 (1994): 105–10.

ID 456A11–12: for the date, see Tréheux, *BCH* 109 (1985): 493 n. 29.

9. SOLOE AND KORAKIA

When the estates are rented as a unit, I have marked the rent with an asterisk (*). When rented separately by different people, the name of each renter is followed by "[S]" for "Soloe" or "[K]" for "Korakia."

Source	*Date*	*Rent* *Raw*	*Rent* *Indexed*	*Renter*
135.4–5	314	240.000	57.14	Ampheas s. Aristeas
142.5–9	307	330.000	78.57	Hermadas
142.6–7	307	120.000	28.57	Aristodikos s. Aristokrates
149.2–3	297	321.000	76.43	Agasikles
157A3, A4–5	287–283	300.000	71.43	Aristoboulos (S) Anapsyktides (K)
158A12–13	282	300.000	71.43	Aristoboulos (S) Anapsyktides (K)
161A12–13	279	410.000*	97.62	Teleson s. Autokles
162A10–11	278	410.000*	97.62	Teleson
199A6	274	410.000*	97.62	Teleson
203A20	269	372.000*	88.57	Teleson
204.14–15	268	372.000*	88.57	Teleson
225a13	259–250	400.000	95.24	
275A15	259 or 256–251	400.000*	95.24	Timoxenos?
287A31	250	400.000*	95.24	Timoxenos
287A149–50	249pro	420.000*	100.00	Philarkhos s. Theorylos
290.16	246	421.000*	100.24	Kallisthenes
351.11–12	220	201.000*	47.86	Konon
353A6	219	201.000*	47.86	Konon's heirs
354.36	218	201.000*	47.86	Konon's heirs
356*bis*A8	210	201.000	47.86	Demarkhos
368.31–32	206	354.000*	84.29	Empedos
372A17	200	354.000*	84.29	Empedos
374B11–12	200pro	286.000	68.10	
442A146	179	248.000	59.05	Aristion s. Phelys
452.31–32	177	See note		
456A20–21	174	[248.000?]	59.05	Apatourion s. Phelys

IG XI 2.142.5–9: Hermadas defaulted by failing to renew one of his guarantors. The *hieropoioi* exacted the rent as follows:

Seized barley:	140 dr
Owed by Hermadas:	190 dr
TOTAL:	330 dr

Hermadas and his guarantors also owed a fine of 1.5 × the rent. Because the land was then re-rented for only 110 dr, Santos son of Timon, a guarantor, owed 220 dr, the difference between the two amounts (cf. *ID* 503.18–19, which, however, was not yet in force).

IG XI 2.157A4–5 (287–283) and 158A12–13 (282): in this rental period Korakia was rented separately for 100 dr to Anapsyktides. I have added the rent in to the figures given for Soloe alone to get the composite rent reported above.

IG XI 2.224A14: the restoration in *IG* of Soloe and Korakia here is shown wrong in Kent, *BCH* 63 (1939): 238.

IG XI 2.275A15: for the date, see the lemma under "Olive Oil" in Appendix III.

ID 290.16: the extra ⊢ is sure.

ID 353A6 and *ID* 354.36: Konon died between the auction for leases which he won in 220 B.C. and the first payment of rents in 219.

ID 356 *bis* A8: rent is actually slightly more than 201, but no more than 202 (there is space for one more figure). Rent and renter read by Kent, *BCH* 63 (1939): 241.

ID 374B11–12: Kent, *BCH* 63 (1939): 243.

ID 399A75: the payment reported, 300 dr from the heirs of Polykrates, must include a partial payment or fine.

ID 452.31–32: possible rerental owing to failure to renew guarantors, cf. G. Glotz *apud ID* 452 comm., p. 211; see also G. Reger, *Hesperia* 63 (1994): 105–10.

ID 456A20–21: for the date, see Tréheux, *BCH* 109 (1985): 493 n. 29.

10. SOSIMAKHEIA

Source	*Date*	*Rent* *Raw*	*Rent* *Indexed*	*Renter*
156B16–20	288–283	201.000	73.09	Amphistratos
157A5	287–283	201.000	73.09	Amphistratos?
158A14	282	201.000	73.09	Amphistratos
161A15	279	340.000	123.64	Geryllos s. Pistoxenos
162A13	278	340.000	123.64	Geryllos
203A24	269	150.000	54.54	Polybos s. Diodotos
204.20	268	150.000	54.54	Polybos
223A35	262	150.000	54.54	Polybos
224A17	258	250.000	90.91	Apollonios
287A31	250	250.000	90.91	Apollonios
287A176–77	249pro	275.000	100.00	Apollonios
290.15	246	275.000	100.00	Apollonios
353A10	219	200.250	72.82	Kallisthenes
354.37	218	200.250	72.82	Kallisthenes
356*bis*A11	210	200.250	72.82	Kallisthenes
362A16	209	150.000	54.54	Kallisthenes
368.32–33	206	75.000	54.54	Kallisthenes
369A41	206	112.500	40.80	Kallisthenes
442A147–48	179	178.000	64.73	Geryllos s. Karystios
456A12	174	178.000	64.73	Geryllos

IG XI 2.156B16–20: the former renter must have defaulted, since the estate is being rented within the ten-year rental period.

IG XI 2.223A35: restored by Kent, *BCH* 63 (1939): 237.

ID 368.32–33: the guarantor has paid on behalf of the renter.

ID 369A41: the stone reads Ἐπισθενείας, but Durrbach, following Glotz, has made a good case for regarding this as an error for Σωσιμαχείων; cf. *ID* comm. at p. 181.

ID 399A77: the 210 dr paid by Antigonos son of Kharistios includes a penalty.

ID 456A12: for the date, see Tréheux, *BCH* 109 (1985): 493 n. 29.

ESTATES ON RHENEIA.

11. DIONYSIOS

Source	Date	Rent: Raw	Rent: Indexed	Renter
135.12–13	314	750.000	93.28	Onomakleides s. Mnesilas
144A13	304	1,321.653	164.38	Pasitimos
146A11	301	1,000.000	124.38	Autosthenes
149.6–7	297	1,372.000	170.65	Autosthenes
158A9–10	282	602.000	74.87	Parmenion
161A8	279	662.195	82.36	Parmenion s. Khoirylos
162A7	278	662.195	82.36	Parmenion
199A4	274	662.195	82.36	Telesandros
200.2–3	ca. 274	662.195	82.36	Telesandros
203A23–24	269	700.000	87.06	Telesandros s. Parmenion
204.7	268	700.000	87.06	Telesandros
224A13	258	560.000	69.65	Kerkion
275A13	259 or 256–251	560.000	69.65	Kerkion
287A26	250	560.000	69.65	Kerkion
287A159–60	249pro	804.000	100.00	Herakleides of Rheneia
290.18–19	246	804.000	100.00	Herakleides
353A9	219	402.000	50.00	Anektos
354.39	218	402.000	50.00	Anektos
356*bis*A10	210	400.333	49.79	Anektos
362A20	209		—	
366A104–5	207	390.000	48.51	Aristodikos s. Lykades
399A80–81	192	390.000	48.51	Althaimenes s. Althaimenes
442A148	179	341.000	42.41	Apollonios s. Kteson
456A14	174	341.000	42.41	Apollonios

IG XI 2.144A13: rent read and corrected by Kent, *BCH* 63 (1939): 234.

IG XI 2.161A8: rent read and corrected by ibid., 236.

IG XI 2.162A7: corrected after ibid., 236, on *IG* XI 2.161A8.

IG XI 2.199A4: corrected by ibid., 236–37, who, however, evidently misprints 661 dr $1\frac{1}{6}$ ob for 662 dr $1\frac{1}{6}$ ob.

IG XI 2.200.2–3: corrected after ibid., 236, on *IG* XI 2.161A8.

IG XI 2.203A23–24: ibid., 237, reading 700 dr plus space for one additional figure.

IG XI 2.204.7: corrected after ibid., 237, on 203A23.

IG XI 2.275A13: on the date, see the lemma under "Olive Oil" in Appendix III.

ID 362A20: a guarantor paid 84 dr.

ID 366A104–5: the former renter Pottos failed to renew his guarantors, and after the default the estate was evidently rerented for the same (τοῦ ἴσου).

ID 369A40: the *hieropoioi* imposed an *epiballon* of 1.5 × the rent; the stone records the amount owed, 102 dr. Evidently there had been a default.

ID 456A14: Kent, *BCH* 63 (1939): 244–45; for the date, Tréheux, *BCH* 109 (1985): 493 n. 29.

12. KHARETEIA

Source	Date	Rent: Raw	Rent: Indexed	Renter
135.7	314	1,750.000	157.23	Hegemon
142.2–3	307	2,250.000	202.16	Nikandros?
144A11–12	304	2,475.000	222.37	Nikandros s. Xenomedes?
149.9	297	3,111.000	279.51	Amphoteros
158A8	282	1,800.000	161.72	Straton
161A10	279	1,800.000	161.72	Empedokles s. Kharileon
162A8–9	278	1,800.000	161.72	Empedokles
200.1–2	ca. 274	1,800.000	161.72	Empedokles
201A5	277/270	1,800.000	161.72	Empedokles
203A19	269	1,800.000	161.72	Empedokles
204.13–14	268	1,800.000	161.72	Empedokles
224A14	258	1,400.500	125.83	Teleson s. Xenon; Ekephylos?
226A30	257	1,400.500	125.83	Teleson s. Xenon; Ekephylos?
225a8–9	259–250	[1,400.500]	125.83	See note
287A30	250	700.000	125.83	Diogenes
287A30	250	281.000		Xenokrates s. Hierombrotos
287A139–42	250	419.500		Mnesimakhos
287A169	249pro	1,113.000	100.00	Philonikos s. Pherekleides
290.20	246	1,113.000	100.00	Philonikos
351.6–8	220pro	832.000	74.75	Phanodikos
353A3–4	219	832.000	74.75	Phanodikos
354.35	218	832.000	74.75	Phanodikos
356*bis*A6–7	210	832.000	74.75	Phanodikos
356*bis*B40–41	210pro	915.195	82.23	——os s. Kharilas
362A17	209	915.195	82.23	Phanodikos s. Phanodikos
368.29–30	206	900.000	80.86	Phanodikos
372A11	200	915.195	82.23	Phanodikos
399A79	192	661.000	59.39	Phanodikos
373B8–10	180pro	799.806	71.86	Phanodikos
442A151	179	799.806	71.86	Phanodikos
456A16–17	174	799.292	71.81	Phanodikos
459.42–43	172 or 170	799.292	71.81	Phanodikos

IG XI 2.142.2–3: an additional payment was made (ἐπα[ναβληθέν]). The restoration of the renter comes from Lacroix, *BCH* 56 (1932): 374. For the date, see "Olive Oil" above, comm. on *IG* XI 2.142.

IG XI 2.144A11–12: patronymic suggested by Kent, *BCH* 63 (1939): 234.

IG XI 2.224A14: restoration corrected by Kent, *BCH* 63 (1939): 238.

IG XI 2.224A14, 226A30, 225a8–9, 287A30, 139–42: The history of this estate in the 250s is very complicated (cf. Kent, 250 n. 13). I reconstruct events as follows:

(1) In 260 B.C. Teleson and Ekephylos rented the estate together (not each a separate part, as Kent writes; see *IG* XI 2.226A30, [τῆς γῆς τῆς ἐν] Χαρητείαι ἣν ἐμεμίσθωτο Τελέσων Ξένων[ο]ς καὶ Ἐκέ[φυλος?]).

(2) In 257 B.C. the partners defaulted for reasons lost in lacunae, and their guarantors, among them Teleson's son Autokles and one Mnesimakhos, were required to pay up (*IG* XI 2.226A29–34).

(3) At this point the *hieropoioi* decided to rent the estate as two *separate* halves. One new renter was Mnesimakhos, almost surely identical with the guarantor. He agreed to pay 700 dr 3 ob for his half (*IG* XI 2.287A139–41). The other half was assumed by one Diogenes, who paid 700 dr (287A30); he may also have been a guarantor of the original renters. (Perhaps it was the guarantors who suggested the arrangement of splitting the estate?) That the two halves were treated quite separately is evident from 287A30.

(4) In the very last year of the contract (250 B.C., not 251 per Kent) Mnesimakhos defaulted by failing to renew his guarantors. Following the stipulations of the *hiera syngraphe*, the *hieropoioi* offered Mnesimakhos's half for rerental, and it was taken for only 281 dr by one Xenokrates son of Hierombrotos (287A140; his regular payment is recorded at 287A30). Along with his guarantors (from 251 B.C.) Mnesimakhos, whose business sense seems less than shrewd, was once again recorded as a debtor to Apollo (287A140–41).

(5) For the new lease period to begin in 249 B.C. the *hieropoioi* returned to their former practice of treating the estate as a unit, and the reunited Khareteia passed into the hands of Philonikos son of Pherekleides (287A169).

As Kent points out (250 n. 13), the only sure rents for Khareteia in the 250s are the figures from 287A30 and 139–41 of 700 and 700.5 dr for the two halves of the estate. *IG* XI 2.226A30 shows 1,200 dr (presumably the rent for Khareteia), but because the figure comes at the end of the line (already noted at Kent 250 n. 13), it need not be complete. Since rerental of estates generally fetched either the same rent or less (see, e.g., *ID* 403.48–49, 52; for an exception, cf. rents for Lykoneion in *IG* XI 2.287A1 and *ID* 290.17), it seems very unlikely that in this case the *hieropoioi* were able to find rerenters willing to pay almost 17 percent more, especially inasmuch as at least one of the two was himself a guarantor of the former renters. I therefore restore XHH[HHIII] at *IG* XI 2.226A30 and [XHHHHIII] at 224A14 (with Kent, *BCH* 63 [1939]: 238).

IG XI 2.225a9 remains a problem. Clearly Durrbach's restoration of 981 dr is wrong, but what is missing? Everything depends on the date of the inscription. If it belongs before 257 B.C. (i.e., 259), then it will simply record the full rent of 1,400 dr 3 ob of Teleson and Ekephylos. If after 257, then it must show the separate rents of the two halves. There is one piece of evidence suggesting it belongs after the breakup. In *IG* XI 2.226A30, referring to the full estate rented jointly by Teleson and Ekephylos, the *hieropoioi* write [τῆς γῆς τῆς ἐν] Χαρητείαι. They use the same locution in 225a10 to refer to Skitoneia. At 287A139, however, they write τῆς Χαρητείας τὸ μέρος ὃ ἐμεμίσθωτο Μνησίμαχος. (Unfortunately, at 287A25–34 they simply use the genitive for all estates.) It is therefore possible that the genitive in 225a9 was used because the *hieropoioi* were recording parts of the estate separately.

(*continued*)

ID 356*bis*B40–41: text by Roussel *apud* Lacroix, *BCH* 56 (1932): 381–82.

ID 362A17: there is some doubt about the restored rent.

ID 372A11: Durrbach puts "?" after the restoration of the rent.

ID 399A79: I follow Kent, *BCH* 63 (1939): 244, for the rent instead of Lacroix, *REG* 43 (1930): 377, or *BCH* 56 (1932): 386.

ID 373B8–10: this is a renewal by ἐπιδέκατον. I cite the rent given by Kent, *BCH* 63 (1939): 242 instead of 809.639 given by Lacroix, *BCH* 56 (1932): 386.

ID 456A16–17: for the date, see Tréheux, *BCH* 109 (1985): 493n.29.

13. KHARONEIA

		Rent		
Source	*Date*	*Raw*	*Indexed*	*Renter*
135.9–10	314	1,050.000	95.45	Makhon s. Praximenes
144A14–15	304	1,050.000	95.45	Hermodotos s. Aristeas
149.7–8	297	1,450.000	131.82	Xenomedes
158A9	282	800.000	72.73	Thesteas
161A10–11	279	800.000	72.73	Melesippos of Rheneia
162A9	278	800.000	72.73	Melesippos
199A5	274	800.000	72.73	Timesidemos and Aristodikos
203A20	269	1,100.000	100.00	Timesidemos and Aristodikos
204.9–10	268	1,100.000	100.00	Timesidemos and Aristodikos
224A13–14	258	872.000	79.72	Timesidemos
225a15–16	259–250	872.000	79.72	Timesidemos
287A27–9, 138–39	250	435.000	79.72	Timesidemos and guarantors
287A29–30, 138–9	250	437.000		Boulon s. Tynnon
287A164	249pro	1,100.000	100.00	Euktemon and Dexikrates s. Akhaios
290.20	246	1,100.000	100.00	Euktemon and Dexikrates
353A5	219	[421.028]	38.27	Pherekleides
354.35	218	421.028	38.27	Pherekleides
356*bis*A10	210	420.195	38.20	Pherekleides
374Aa1	200pro	400.000	36.36	Aresimbrotos s. Nikandros
399A80	192	400.000	36.36	Aresimbrotos
403.48–51	189	300.000	27.27	See note
442A149	179	451.000	41.00	Kassandros s. Katonandros
456A19–20	174	451.347	41.03	Kassandros
459.42	172 or 170	440.000	40.00	
460u25	171	440.000	40.00	

IG XI 2.135.9–10: estate name spelled Χαιρώνεια.

IG XI 2.144A14–15: rent read correctly by Kent, *BCH* 63 (1939): 234.

IG XI 2.161A10–11: Melesippos has assumed the rental of this property. The text of ll. 125–31 reads: "These [i.e., the renters listed above] have taken over the plants and the other things recorded on the stele that Hegias and Anaskhetos [the *hieropoioi* for 280 B.C.] erected." Unfortunately, the month in which Melesippos took over is not recorded.

IG XI 2.199A5: Lacroix, *BCH* 48 (1924): 405, reads all but the first two letters of the name Timesidemos on the stone.

IG XI 2.287A27–29, 138–39: eight guarantors were called upon to pay their portions of the balance owed (for Eukleides' figure, see Kent, *BCH* 63 (1939): 239 n. 1; for Mne(simakhos?), ibid., 240) on Timesidemos's portion of the rent, he having paid only 370.167 dr.

Polyxenos s. Alkimakhos	24 dr $2\frac{5}{6}$ ob
Dionysodoros s. Theotimos	16 dr $4\frac{1}{6}$ ob
Kleomakhos s. Pelagon	7 dr $3\frac{11}{12}$ ob
Eukleides s. ?Pyrrides	7 dr $5\frac{1}{4}$ ob
Polystratos s. ?Timothemis	2 dr $4\frac{1}{2}$ ob
Theokydes s. [patronymic never recorded]	1 dr $3\frac{1}{6}$ ob
Aristophilos s. Mne(simakhos?)	3 dr $\frac{1}{3}$ ob
Timokrates s. ?Lysanios	0 dr $4\frac{3}{4}$ ob
TOTAL	64 dr $4\frac{11}{12}$ ob

See the comments of Kent, *BCH* 63 (1939): 239–40.

IG XI 2.287A29–30, 138–39: like Khareteia, Kharoneia was divided during the 259–250 rental period, but the division persisted, for Boulon assumed only the half of the estate that Aristodikos, Timesidemos's brother, was farming. The rent recorded at l. 139 is 437 dr. The default was, however, the result of Timesidemos's failure to give guarantors. It looks almost as if Timesidemos was subletting half of the estate to his brother.

ID 353A5: the rent is restored differently from in *ID*, and correctly, by Lacroix, *BCH* 56 (1932): 378; cf. *ID* 354.35 and 356*bis*A10.

ID 354.35: amount of rent corrected from *ID* by Lacroix, *BCH* 56 (1932): 378.

ID 356*bis*A10: I record the rent Lacroix, *BCH* 56 (1932): 379, reads, with the correction of a misprint in Lacroix's text pointed out by Kent, *BCH* 63 (1939): 241, but Lacroix reports that Roussel continues to read 421.167. Kent does not comment on the discrepancy.

ID 368.27–28, 372A13–14: restorations of a rent of 150 at these lines arise from Durrbach's theory (see *ID* 368.28, comm., p. 177) that Pherekleides had taken his chances by bidding low for the estate he had rented in the previous period for over 420 dr. But Durrbach's reading of the stone at 368.28, το[ῦ] ἐμ Πανόρμου?, is manifestly wrong (cf. Glotz *apud* comm. p. 177), and we cannot rely on the accuracy of anything in this line. Just above, however, is the partial payment of rent for Nikou Khoros by the renter Kalliphantes' heirs. Since the payment here is by Pherekleides' heirs, we may suspect a partial payment.

ID 372A13–14: Lacroix, *REG* 43 (1930): 373 restores [Η𐅄. .] for the rent, allowing the possibility of up to 20 dr more.

ID 403.48–51: estate rerented after default because of failure to renew guarantors for [τοῦ ἴ]σου?, from which the rent.

ID 456A19–20: for the date, see Tréheux, *BCH* 109 (1985): 493 n. 29. The additional fractional payment is not explained.

14. LIMNAI

Source	Date	Rent		Renter
		Raw	*Indexed*	
135.13	314	770.000	224.49	Kleokritos s. Iphianax
142.3–4	307	600.000	171.93	Gnosidikos?
144A12–13	304	660.000	192.42	Gnosidikos s. Herakleides (?)
149.10	297	622.000	181.34	Epikydes
158A10	282	361.000	105.25	Aristeas
161A7–8	279	397.083	115.77	Aristeas s. Amphoteros
162A6	278	397.083	115.77	Aristeas
199A5	274	397.083	115.77	Aristeas
203A22	269	573.000	167.06	Khoirylos s. Teleson
204.10	268	573.000	167.06	Khoirylos
287A26	250	480.000	139.94	Kynthiados
287A157–58	249pro	343.000	100.00	Autokles s. Teleson
290.18	246	343.000	100.00	Children of Autokles
351.10	220pro	350.000	102.04	Hegias
353A6	219	175.000	51.02	Hegias
354.36	218	175.000	51.02	Hegias
362A18	209	212.000	61.81	Timosthenes
368.30–31	206	212.000	61.81	——nos
374Aa10–11	200pro	[208.000]	60.64	Melesippos and Philonikos of Rheneia
399A81	192	208.000	60.64	Melesippos and Philonikos
442A148	179	280.000	81.63	Antigonos s. Antigonos s. Telemnestos
456A13	174	280.000	81.63	Antigonos
459.41	172 or 170	[280.000]	81.63	Antigonos
460u23	171	280.000	81.63	Antigonos

IG XI 2.142.3–4: the rent range is 601–700 dr, but 600 is probably correct. For the renter, see Lacroix, *BCH* 56 (1932): 374. The ἐπαναβληθέν is 30 dr (after Kent, *BCH* 63 (1939): 232).

IG XI 2.144A12–13: rent corrected by Lacroix, *BCH* 56 (1932): 374.

IG XI 2.162A6: the rent comes from a new reading by Lacroix, *REG* 35 (1922): 417; there may be a / at the end, which would add .0139 to the rent.

ID 290.18: Autokles must have died between 250 and 246, after the estate rentals for the next ten-year rental period were recorded in 250 (*IG* XI 2.287A157–58) but before the rent was paid in 246.

ID 354.36: evidently Hegias paid only half of his rent.

ID 456A13: Kent, *BCH* 63 (1939) 244; for the date, see Tréheux, *BCH* 109 (1985): 493 n. 29.

ID 460u23: Kent, *BCH* 63 (1939): 245.

15. NIKOU KHOROS

Source	Date	Rent: Raw	Rent: Indexed	Renter
135.14	314	440.000	169.23	Gnosidikos s. Herakleides
142.4	307	420.000	161.54	Asteas
144A15	304	551.500	212.11	Autosthenes
146A13	301	425.000	163.46	
149.5	297	600.000	230.77	Sosilos
158A10–11	282	348.000	133.85	Empedokles
161A9	279	271.000	104.23	Dionysios s. Autokles
161C116–20	279	271.000	104.23	Hegesagoras
162A7–8	278	271.000	104.23	Hegesagoras s. Anaximenos
199A5	274	271.000	104.23	Hegesagoras
203A23	269	351.000	135.00	——os? s. Tharsydikos
204.8–9	268	351.000	135.00	Tharsydikos
287A26	250	321.000	123.46	Pythokles
287A155–56	249pro	260.000	100.00	Pythokles s. Pherekleides
290.18	246	260.000	100.00	Antirretos
353A7	219	191.250	73.56	Ekhekratides
354.35	218	191.250	73.56	Ekhekratides
362A16–17	209	171.000	65.77	Xenokrates
368.24–25	206	171.000	65.77	Nikomakhos
372A12–13	200	171.000	65.77	Xenokrates
399A79	192	80.000	30.77	Akhaios s. Zelomenes
373B2–4	180pro	96.806	37.23	Akhaios s. Zelomenes
442A150–51	179	96.806	37.23	Akhaios
445.16–24	178	96.806	37.23	Lykomedes s. Kritias and Kharistios s. Antigonos
456A17–18	174	96.806	37.23	

IG XI 2.142.4: the rent is 420 dr despite the text of *IG;* where the latter shows two missing letters we should restore *kai:* cf. Lacroix, *BCH* 56 (1932): 374. An additional payment of 56 dr is recorded (*epanablethen*). Renter's name read as Ἀστέας by Kent, *BCH* 63 (1939): 232.

IG XI 2.146A13: rent read correctly by ibid., 236. The name of the renter is not lost but omitted.

IG XI 2.161A9: Dionysios evidently reneged or defaulted this year, for a new renter is recorded at the same amount at C116–20.

(*continued*)

IG XI 2.203A23: rent correctly read by Kent, *BCH* 63 (1939): 237.

IG XI 2.204.8–9: rent corrected read by ibid.

ID 356*bis*A12: the figure of 40.667 dr paid by Sosidemos was probably a partial payment, perhaps by a guarantor; there may have been a default.

ID 368.24–25: the figure in the text is a combined total for this estate and Rhamnoi, which were now being exploited conjointly.

ID 373B2–4: Kent, *BCH* 63 (1939): 242.

ID 445.16–24: rerental after failure by Akhaios to renew guarantors.

ID 456A17–18: Kent, *BCH* 63 (1939): 245 erroneously restored 46, rather than 96, dr. For the date, see Tréheux, *BCH* 109 (1985): 493 n. 29.

16. PANORMOS

Source	*Date*	*Rent*		*Renter*
		Raw	*Indexed*	
135.8	314	750.000	123.76	Hieros s. Phanodikos
144A12	304	925.000	152.64	Maisiades s. Herakleides
147A15–17	300	1,030.000	169.97	Maisiades
149.5–6	297	1,030.000	169.97	Maisiades
158A8–9	282	660.000	108.91	Telesandros
161A9	279	704.000	116.17	Iekles
161C111–15	279	0.000	—	Sotadas of Krete
162A8	278	704.000	116.17	Sotadas
199A4	274	704.000	116.17	Sotadas
203A22	269	830.000	136.96	Aresimbrotos s. Polyxenos
204.17	268	830.000	136.96	Aresimbrotos
224A16	258	731.000	120.62	Polyxenos s. Aresimbrotos
275A14	259 or 256–251	731.000	120.62	Polyxenos
287A30	250	731.000	120.62	Polyxenos
287A167	249pro	606.000	100.00	Stesarkhos
290.20	246	611.000	100.82	Stesarkhos
353A8	219	384.000	63.37	Alkimos
354.36–37	218	384.000	63.37	Alkimos
366A105–6	207	390.000	64.36	Antigonos s. Anektos
368.29	206	390.000	64.36	Antigonos
374Ab1–2	200pro	285.000	47.03	——des s. Pol——

Source	Date	Rent: Raw	Rent: Indexed	Renter
399A79–80	192	285.000	47.03	Empedos s. Asbelos
442A149–50	179	332.000	54.78	Phelys s. Phelys
452.20–24 + 467.5–9	177	332.000	54.78	Kallias s. Kallias
456A18	174	332.000	54.78	Kharilas? s. Phanodikos
440B17–21	174	See note		

IG XI 2.147A15–17: Maisiades seems to have failed to pay all of his rent, and one Gnosidikos, presumably a guarantor, paid his share of 340 dr, or about 33 percent. Did Maisiades have three guarantors? For the date, see pp. 281–82, above.

IG XI 2.161A9, C111–15: Iekles defaulted in some way, because this estate is listed with Sotades as renter at C111–15.

IG XI 2.275A14: for the date, see the lemma under "Olive Oil" in Appendix III.

ID 290.20: the figure is sure, but is probably a stonecutter's error of Δ for Γ.

ID 366A105–6: the former renter Mikon failed to renew his guarantors.

ID 368.29: rent restored by Lacroix, *REG* 39 (1926): 460. The payment at ll. 27–28 has nothing to do with Panormos.

ID 399A79–80: there has probably been a default, for Empedos son of Asbelos was guarantor for the renter (cf. 374Ab1–2).

ID 452.20–24 + 467.5–6: this is a rental after failure to renew guarantors, not a new rental period, as Kent, *BCH* 63 (1939): 245 thought. For the join, see Tréheux, *BCH* 110 (1986): 431; text in Brunet, *BCH* 114 (1990): 678–79; for the date, see G. Reger, *Hesperia* 63 (1994): 105–10.

ID 456A18, 440B17–21: this must be a rerental after a default, and Kent's restoration for 440B17 must be mistaken (*BCH* 63 [1939]: 244); for the date, see Tréheux *BCH* 109 (1985): 493 n. 29.

17. PORTHMOS

Source	Date	Rent: Raw	Rent: Indexed	Renter
135.10	314	1,200.000	117.18	Theodoros s. Aristarkhos
144A11	304	1,653.000	161.41	Antikrates s. Xenomedes
149.8–9	297	1,622.000	158.38	Antikrates
158A7	282	1,200.000	117.18	Apollodoros
161A6–7	279	1,320.000	128.89	Apollodoros s. Xenomedes
162A5	278	1,320.000	128.89	Apollodoros
199A3–4	274	1,320.000	128.89	Apollodoros
203A19	269	1,452.000	141.78	Apollodoros
204.6–7	268	1,452.000	141.78	Apollodoros
224A12–13	258	931.000	90.91	Pytheas s. Pherekleides
225a11–12	259–250	931.000	90.91	
275A12	259 or 256–251	931.000	90.91	Pythokles
287A25	250	931.000	90.91	Pythokles
287A174–75	249pro	1,024.097	100.00	Pythokles s. Pherekleides
290.17	246	1,024.097	100.00	Pythokles
353A10–11	219	550.000	53.71	Nikandros
354.35	218	550.000	53.71	Nikandros
—	209 or 208	812.000	79.29	Aiskhron
366A102–103	207	691.000	67.47	Lampron s. Nikandros
368.29	206	641.000	62.59	Lampron s. Krittis
399A78	192	680.000	66.40	Tlepolemos s. Amnos and Tlepolemos s. Krittis
404.17	188	[539.000]	52.63	Tlepolemos
373B15–16	180pro	[592.944]	57.90	Tlepolemos
442A151	179	592.944	57.90	Tlepolemos s. Krittis
456A16	174	592.944	57.90	Tlepolemos s. K.

*IG*XI 2.144A11: rent corrected by Kent, *BCH* 63 (1939): 234.

IG XI 2.149.8–9: rent corrected by ibid., 236.

IG XI 2.199A3–4: there may be a default here. At l. 14 Eparkhides paid, on behalf of the guarantor Polyzelos, what appears to be one-half of the rent due on Porthmos.

IG XI 2.287A174–75: rent read more completely by Kent, *BCH* 63 (1939): 240, but there is no difference from amount in *IG.*

ID 366A102–3: the previous renter, Aiskhron, had failed to renew guarantors and defaulted. In the rerental recorded here, the estate fetched only 691 dr (the "500" restored by Durrbach with a "?" is read in part by Kent, *BCH* 63 (1939): 241, who prints the figure dotted and in brackets; I was able to read the left vertical stroke of the pi and both vertical strokes of the eta), which must have been 121 dr less than the original rent because of the penalty recorded. The original rent bid in 210 B.C. must have been 821 dr, which is entered in the table preceding this entry.

ID 368.29: the rent is fifty dr lower than 366A103; cf. Lacroix, *REG* 39 (1926): 459. The figure in the text could be a misreading; probably we should restore [𐅅H]𐅄̣ΔΔΔΔ⊢.

ID 373B15–16: Kent, *BCH* 63 (1939): 243 restores [Πορθμὸν· Τληπόλεμος Κρίττιος] 𐅄ΔΔΔΠ⊢[⊢⊢⊢T· καὶ σὺν τῶι ἐπιδ]εκάτωι̣ [Π⊢⊢⊢TIIII] /̣/̣. This is wrong. The rent in 442A151 is 592 dr 5 8/12 ob. As Durrbach comments (comm. at 404.17, p. 79), this looks like a renewal with a 10 percent increase, as indeed the preserved εκατωι̣ assures. Restore instead [Πορθμὸν· Τληπόλεμος Κρίττιος] 𐅅̣ΔΔΔΠ⊢[⊢⊢⊢⊢· καὶ σὺν τῶι ἐπι δ]εκάτωι̣ [𐅄⊢⊢⊢ΠC//].

ID 456A16: for the date, see Tréheux, *BCH* 109 (1985): 493 n. 29.

18. PYRGOI

Source	Date	Rent		Renter
		Raw	*Indexed*	
135.11–12	314	890.000	89.00	Menandros s. Praximenes
144A15	304	1,298.000	129.80	Herodes s. Theodoros
146A10–11	301	1,650.000	165.00	Demeas
149.5	297	1,650.000	165.00	Epikydes
158A7–8	282	1,110.000	111.00	Dorkon
161A7	279	1,222.097	122.21	Dorkon
162A5–6	278	1,222.097	122.21	Kleinias s. Dorkon
199A4	274	1,221.000	122.10	Kleinias
203A18	269	1,343.097	134.31	Kleinias s. Orthios
204.12	268	1,343.097	134.31	Kleinias
224A14	258	1,022.000	102.20	Kleinias
287A30	250	1,012.097	101.21	Kleinias
287A172	249pro	1,000.000	100.00	Eutheas s. Geryllos
290.20–21	246	1,000.000	100.00	Menyllos
353A4	219	602.500	60.25	Antigonos
354.39	218	602.500	60.25	Antigonos
356*bis*A7	210	602.500	60.25	Xenokrates
368.23–24	206	245.500	24.55	Kalliphantos's heirs
399A78	192	521.000	52.10	Xenokrates' heirs
442A179	179	472.000	47.20	Aphrodisias s. Sopatros
456A15	174	472.000	47.20	Aphrodisias

IG XI 2.144A15: renter's name read by Kent, *BCH* 63 (1939): 234.

IG XI 2.162A5–6: the renter is also identified as the *kleronomos*. For the rent, see Lacroix, *REG* 35 (1922): 417.

IG XI 2.224A14: rent correctly read by Kent, *BCH* 63 (1939): 238.

IG XI 2.287A30: the reading comes from a part of the stone that was no longer legible in 1909; I suspect an error for XΔ[Δ⊢⊢].

IG XI 2.287A172: renter read by Kent, *BCH* 63 (1939): 240.

ID 356*bis*A7: rent restored in *ID*; Lacroix *BCH* 56 (1932): 379 reads the first two figures.

ID 456A15: for the date, see Tréheux, *BCH* 109 (1985): 493 n. 329.

19. RHAMNOI

Source	*Date*	*Rent*		*Renter*
		Raw	*Indexed*	
135.15	314	800.000	144.66	Gnosidikos s. Herakleides
144B78–79	304			Khion s. Lykophron
149.8	297	725.000	131.10	Aristeides
158A10	282	375.000	67.81	Antigonos
161A8	279	429.000	77.58	Antigonos s. Anektos
162A6–7	278	429.000	77.58	Antigonos s. Anektos
199A4	274	429.000	77.58	Antigonos
203A21–22	269	471.389	85.24	Antigonos' heir Anektos
204.10–11	268	472.728	85.48	Anektos s. Antigonos
225a11	259–250	580.000	104.88	
226A28	257	580.000	104.88	
287A25, 136–37	250	580.000	104.88	Autokles s. Teleson
287A153	249 pro	553.000	100.00	Parmiskos s. Diodotos
290.18	246	553.000	100.00	Phanos
351.17–18	220 pro	301.000	54.43	Phanos
353A11–12	219	301.000	54.43	Phanos
354.37	218	301.000	54.43	Phanos
356.15	217–211	301.000	54.43	Phanos
356*bis*A6	210	301.000	54.43	Phanos's heirs
362A15	209	290.000	52.44	Nikomakhos
368.24–25	206	290.000	52.44	Nikomakhos and Xenokrates
372A10–11	200	290.000	52.44	Nikomakhos and Xenokrates
374Aa20–23	200 pro	319.000	57.68	Nikomakhos s. Nikomakhos and Xenokrates s. Antigonos

(*continued*)

19. RHAMNOI (*continued*)

Source	Date	Rent		Renter
		Raw	*Indexed*	
399A81–82	192	319.000	57.68	Nikomakhos and Xenokrates
442A148	179	351.000	63.47	Euelthon s. Nikias
456A12–13	174	351.000	63.47	Euelthon

IG XI 2.144B78–79: Khion has defaulted. The land was rerented to a renter whose name is missing. On the default, cf. ll. A13 (Ῥάμνους ἐγλιπόντος Χίονος ἀνεμισθώσαμεν) and B78–81, where the rent owed appears to have been extracted from Khion's guarantors. The amount owed by Khion has been lost. Kent, *BCH* 63 (1939): 235 n. 2, guesses 409 dr.

Something further has occurred with estates this year whose character eludes us. I give 144B78–81 in Durrbach's text:

- [τὴν γῆν] τὴν ἐν] (*sic*)
[Ῥάμν]οις ἐμισθώσα[το - - - - - - - - - -] - | N..
(I omit some text here) Ἐπ̣ικ̣ύ[δης? Λ]υκόφρ[ο-]
νος, Ἐπικύδης Ἀριστέου δραχμῶν 𐅅̣ Ḥ ⊢̣ - vac.

(Lacroix, *BCH* 48 [1924]: 401 has suggested 516 dr.) Perhaps this has something to do with the missing rents for Soloe and Rhamnoi? Cf. Kent, *BCH* 63 (1939): 235.

IG XI 4.203A21–22: Durrbach has dotted the two obols; there is probably some small error here.

IG XI 4.204.10–11: the *hieropoioi* have not bothered to note that the heirs were paying.

IG XI 2.226A28: read and restored by Kent, *BCH* 63 (1939): 238.

IG XI 2.287A25, 136–37: the rent is at least 580 dr; there are three unreadable figures at l. 25, so that the rent could be as high as 592. But at l. 137 the exact figure of 580 is preserved, so I believe that the following space was vacant. This is also the view of Kent, *BCH* 63 (1939): 239. Autokles rented the estate after the previous tenant, Xenomedes, failed to renew his guarantors.

IG XI 2.287A153: the original successful bidder was Kynthiades, who bid the same rent but could not secure guarantors.

ID 362A15: the figure in *ID* is mistakenly restored; it should read ΗΗ𐅄ΔΔΔ.

ID 368.24–25: this rental does not correspond to the figure restored in 362A16, supposedly on the basis of this passage. Note that our two renters are now associated; in the text, the full figure is a combined figure for this estate and Nikou Khoros.

ID 456A12–13: for the date, see Tréheux, *BCH* 109 (1985): 493 n. 29.

20. SKITONEIA

Source	Date	Rent: *Raw*	Rent: *Indexed*	Renter
135.8–9	314	506.000	106.98	Euelthon s. Lysagoras
144A14	304	774.416	163.72	Amnos? s. Dexikrates
149.6	297	900.000	190.27	Erotion
158A9	282	560.000	118.39	Khoirylos
161A9–10	279	530.000	112.05	Didymos s. Kallidikos
162A8	278	530.000	112.05	Didymos
203A19–20	269	560.000	118.39	Didymos
204.11–12	268	560.000	118.39	Didymos
223A34	262	560.000	118.39	Didymos
224A16	258	483.000	102.11	Polyboulos s. Parmenion
225a9–10	259–250	483.000	102.11	
287A26, 137–38	250	435.406	102.11	Kallisthenes s. Diakritos
287A162–63	249 pro	473.000	100.00	Arkhedamas s. Ktesikles
290.19	246	473.000	100.00	Menekrates and Arkhedamas, heirs of Arkhedamas
353A7–8	219	201.000	42.49	Melesippos
354.36	218	201.000	42.49	Melesippos
356*bis*B34	210 pro	311.000	65.75	Elpines
362A17	209	311.000	65.75	—— ines
368.30	206	311.000	65.75	—— ines?
372A15	200	311.000	65.75	heirs (of —— ines?)
374Ab7	200 pro	225.000	47.57	Lampron s. Nikandros
399A80	192	225.000	47.57	Lampron
442A148–49	179	332.000	70.19	Demostratos s. Diogenes
456A14–15	174	332.000	70.19	Demostratos

IG XI 2.144A14: the renter is a suggestion by Tréheux, *EAC* 5 (1976): 93, in place of *IG*'s Φί?]λαρ̣χος. Cf. *SEG* 26.857.

IG XI 2.223A34: read and supplemented by Kent, *BCH* 63 (1939): 237.

IG XI 2.287A26, 137–38, D27–28: The renter for 259–250, Polyboulos, failed to renew his guarantors for 250 and defaulted, and Kallisthenes rented the estate. Payments by Hermon and Polyboulos himself are recorded at A26–27 and D27–28. Corrected readings at A26 and D29 by Kent, *BCH* 63 (1939): 239.

ID 356*bis*B34: text by Roussel *apud* Lacroix, *BCH* 56 (1932): 381–82. Kent, *BCH* 63 (1939): 241 n. 3, corrects the rent from 310 dr 1 ob to 311 dr.

ID 456A14–15: for the date, see Tréheux, *BCH* 109 (1985): 493 n. 29.

ESTATES ON MYKONOS

21. KHERSONESOS-DORION

Source	*Date*	*Rent*	*Renter*
366A100, 101–2	207	331.250	Aristopappos s. Tellis
452.25–30 + 467	177	[310]	Melesippos s. Xenos
456A + 440B23	174	310	Antigonos s. Menyllos
461Bb54–57	169	210	Xenon s. Xenon

ID 452 + 467: see G. Reger, *Hesperia* 63 (1994): 105–10.

ID 456A + 440B: rerental after failure of Melesippos son of Xenos (?) to renew guarantors. For the rent figure, see Kent, *BCH* 63 (1939): 244.

ID 461Bb54–57: rerental after failure of Antigonos to renew his guarantors.

22. THALEON

Source	*Date*	*Rent*	*Renter*
366A100, 101	207	381.000	Thymias s. Ekhekratides

COMMERCIAL AND RESIDENTIAL BUILDINGS: THE "HOLY HOUSES"

The basic works are Dieter Hennig, "Die 'heiligen Häuser' von Delos," *Chiron* 13 (1983): 411–95, abbreviated below as "Hennig" (cf. *Chiron* 15 [1985]: 165–86, on the houses under Athenian domination), Philip A. Davis, "On the Upkeep of 'Sacred Houses' on Delos," *BCH* 59 (1935): 77–91, and Sylvain Molinier, *Les 'Maisons sacrées' de Délos au temps de l'indépendance de l'île, 315–166/5 av. J.-C.* (Paris, 1914), abbreviated below as "Molinier." In compiling my catalogue I have generally followed Hennig, 420–41, supplemented by Molinier, 19–34, for the identification of the buildings.

The index year for the houses is either 269 or 268 B.C. (*IG* XI 2.203 or 204). Too few rents were preserved for 250 B.C. to use that year. Only one-half of the rents is recorded in *ID* 353.

1. HOUSE THAT FORMERLY BELONGED TO THE CHILDREN OF ARISTOBOULOS

Source	*Date*	*Rent*		*Renter*
		Raw	*Indexed*	
156A1	288–283	[22.500]		Diakritos
158A23	282	22.500	28.9	Diakritos
161A18–19	279	39.750	51.1	Autosthenes
162A18	278	39.416	50.7	Autosthenes
199A10	274	39.750	51.1	Kharmos
203A27	269	77.416	100.0	Aristoboulos
204.33–34	268	77.750	100.0	Aristoboulos
224A20–21	258	66.000	84.9	Aristoboulos
226A14	257	[66.000]		Aristoboulos
287A36–37	250	122.167?	157.1	Aristoboulos
290.23	246	132.000	169.8	Aristoboulos
316.59	231	89.000	114.5	Menestratos
317.21	230	[89.000]	114.5	[Menestratos]
353A18	219	65.847	169.4	Kallistratos
353A25–26	219	17.000	—	Empedokles
354.31	218	135.750	174.6	Kallistratos
366A98	207	106.000	136.3	Gorgos
399AB4	192	52.500	67.5	Pyrros
400.7–8	192	120.000	154.3	Pyrros
404.20	188	[120.000]	154.3	Pyrros
442A140–41	179	85.333	109.8	Sonikos

Repairs and improvements: *IG* XI 2.287A94.

IG XI 2.156A1: both renter and rent are restored.

IG XI 2.203A27: the rent figure is corrected from 79 dr $\frac{1}{2}$ ob by Lacroix, *BCH* 48 (1924): 407.

IG XI 2.204.33: building restored.

IG XI 2.226A14: building, renter, and rent restored.

IG XI 2.287A36–37: no building is named, but the entry reads παρ' Ἀριστοβούλου τοῦ Λυσιξένου τὰ τρία μέρη τοῦ ἐνοικίου 𐅄ΔΔΔΔ⊢ΙΙΙ Ϲ̣Τ. If this passage means that Aristoboulos paid three-quarters of the rent, then the full figure was 122 dr 1 ob, as restored above.

ID 317.21: I restore the rent from *ID* 316.59. No doubt the renter was the same, too.

ID 400.7–8: rented to one Pyrros πορφυροβά[φος]; on the production of porphyry dye on Delos, see Philippe Bruneau, *BCH* 102 (1978): 110–14.

ID 404.20: rent restored, Lacroix, *REG* 43 (1930): 379.

Hennig, 421–23, no. 2a + b; Molinier, 21–22.

Use: commercial, Molinier, 34.

2. HOUSE THAT USED TO BELONG TO ARKEON

Source	Date	Rent		Renter
		Raw	Indexed	
158A16–17	282	25.000	75.8	Arkeon
161A23	279	25.000	75.8	Arkeon
162A17	278	25.000	75.8	Arkeon
199B94	274	30.000	90.9	Arkeon s. Sotades or Sotas
203C6–12	269	33.000	100.0	?
204.28	268			Boulon
226A21	257	45.000	136.4	Panteles s. Stratonikos
287A38	250	42.000	127.3	Dionysodoros
290.27	246	58.000	175.8	Ktesias
2.289.2?	249/240	[58.000]	175.8	Ktesias
366A97	207	35.000	106.1	Episthenes
368.34	206	35.000	106.1	Episthenes
399A105–6	192	10.000+	—	
400.23–24	192	50.000	151.5	Telesarkhides
442A141–42	179	50.000	151.5	Dexithes

Repairs and improvements: *ID* 442B251–53.

Further references without rent: *IG* XI 2.157A9, 230.7, *ID* 356.6, 356*bis*A17, 399A84.

IG XI 2.199B94: despite the rent difference, this is very likely the same property, rented out at a slightly higher price to the same tenant. For the patronym, see *IG* XI 2.199B94 and *ID Index*, s.v. Ἀρκέων.

IG XI 2.203C6–12: the current renter, Pyrros, had defaulted—no doubt by failure to provide guarantors—and the building had been rerented. The passage is very mutilated and probably in part misread; Durrbach's text is τῆς Ἀρκέοντος Πυρρ...εγγ...αμ..ας [Ἀ]μεινίου? Φίλλακος ε...των .. τοῦ μισθώματος τῆς οἰκίας [Δ]ΔΔ⊢⊢⊢.

IG XI 2.204.28: the rent is missing.

IG XI 2.289.2: figure and building restored by Lacroix, *REG* 35 (1922): 421, but the renter is preserved.

ID 399A105–6: default, the full figure is missing.

Hennig, 423–24, no. 3; Molinier, 22–23.

Use: warehouse (*Lagerhaus*), Hennig, 424; dwelling, Molinier, 34.

3. THE HOUSE WHERE EPHESOS HAS HIS SHOP (τὰ οἰκήματα ἐν οἷς Ἔφεσος καπηλεύει)

Source	Date	Rent		Renter
		Raw	*Indexed*	
157A14	287–283	55.000	78.6	Aristolokhos
158A21	282	55.000	78.6	Aristolokhos
161A16	279	51.000	72.9	Ephesos
162A13–14	278	51.000	72.9	Empedos
203A25–26	269	147.000	210.0?	Eteokleides
204.27	268	70.000	100.0	Siges
353A18–19	219	60.000	171.4	Dionysios
354.31	218	120.000	171.4	Dionysios
356*bis*A16	210	60.000	85.7	Boulagoras
366A96	207	100.000	142.9	Lysixenos
368.34–35	206	100.000	142.9	
372A23	200	[50.000]	142.9?	Theodoros
400.8–9	192	116.000	165.7	Xenokleides
442A141	179	110.000	157.1	Hippon

Repairs and improvements: *ID* 338A75, 402.17, 444B99–100.

Further references without rent: *ID* 340.18

IG XI 2.157A14: restoration of houses and higher rent as opposed to *IG*'s 15 dr were first suggested by Molinier, 49 n. 1; Lacroix, *BCH* 48 (1924): 403, confirms the figure.

ID 356*bis*A16: Hennig, 429–30, suggests a possible rental of only part of the property because of the low rent in comparison with the years before and after and the use of the expression ἐκ τῶν [Ἐφ]έσου.

ID 368.34–35: Theodoros and Autonymos are listed each as paying "his share"; they were clearly guarantors, and the renter, Boulagoras in *ID* 356*bis*A16, has defaulted.

ID 372A23: rent actually paid by Pherekleides, who may be paying half the rent as a guarantor (hence the uncertain indexed rent).

ID 445.24–28: house rerented because Euphranor's heirs failed to provide guarantors.

Use: commercial, Molinier, 34.

Hennig, 427–30, no. 6a + b; Molinier, 24–25.

4. HOUSES OF EPISTHENES

The series that comprises the several units the temple obtained from Episthenes (see Hennig, 432, Kent, 257–58, Tréheux, "Dernières Années," 1016 n. 2) presents a complicated and puzzling picture. At least three, and probably four, different buildings are involved. For discussion of the problems, see Hennig, 430–33. I am interested only in two houses, which are described at *IG* IX 2.158A15–16 as τῆς οἰκίας ἣ ἦν Ἐπισθένους ἧι γείτων ἡ Σίμου οἰκία and as τῆς οἰκίας ἣ ἦν Ἐπισθένους ἧι γείτων ἡ Πιστοξένου οἰκία. Thereafter they appear with the designations τῆς Ἐπισθένους and τῆς ἑξῆς τῆς Ἐπισθένους. *ID* 442A140 and 144–45 prove that the designations are consistent and not simply an artifact of the order the houses are recorded in each time, because there the house called τῆς ἑξῆς Ἐπισθένους comes first (A140), but with the same rent and renter as in *ID* 400.4–5, where the house is listed second and immediately after τῆς Ἐπισθένους. I identify them below as (1) and (2).

Source	*Date*	*Rent* *Raw*	*Rent* *Indexed*	*Renter*
158A15 (1)	282	55.000	61.1	Episthenes
161A22 (1)	279	51.000	56.7	Apemantos s. Leophon
161D69–72 (1)	279	25.500		Apemantos
162A17–18 (1)	278	51.000	56.7	Apemantos
203A26 (1)	269	90.000	100.0	—— kos
224A19 (1)	258	50.000	55.5	Demetrios s. Nikon
287A38 (1)	250	60.000	66.7	Poseidikos
290.22 (1)	246	108.667+		Aiskhrion
353A16 (1)	219	25.500	56.7	Xenokritos
356*bis*A14 (1)	210	70.083	77.9	Kyknos
366A94–95 (1)	207	78.000	86.7	Parmenon s. Kyknos
369A37 (1)	206	69.000	76.7	Parmenon
399A83–84 (1)	192	46.000	51.1	Glaukos
400.2–3 (1)	192	105.000	116.7	Xenomedes
442A144–45 (1)	179	43.000	74.6	Euphranor
442D2–11 (1)	179	24.111	—	Euphranor
445.24–28 (1)	178	67.097	74.6	Khresimos
158A16 (2)	282	25.000	50.0	Nikon

Source	Date	*Rent*		Renter
		Raw	*Indexed*	
161A24 (2)	279	60.000	120.0	Tolmides s. Leophon
162A20 (2)	278	60.000	120.0	Tolmides of Paros
199B94 (2)	274	[60.000]	[120.0]	See note
203A27 (2)	269	60.000	120.0	Apollodoros
204.29–31 (2)	268	50.000	100.0	Apollodoros
226A22 (2)	257	70.000	140.0	Praximenes s. Menandros
287A38 (2)	250	67.000	134.0	Kallisthenes
353A16–17 (2)	219	25.000	100.0	Patroklos
356*bis*A14 (2)	210	65+?	130.0	Eutykhos
366A95 (2)	207	105.000	210.0	Eutykhos
368.36 (2)	206	[105.000]	210.0	Eutykhos
399A83–84 (2)	192	45.000	90.0	Aristo[lokhos?]
400.4–5 (2)	192	60.000	120.0	Telemnestos
442A140 (2)	179	80.000	160.0	Telemnestos
456A25 (?)	174	10.000		

Repairs and improvements: *IG* X 2.219A10, *ID* 462.13–14.

Further references without rent: *IG* XI 2.268.13, *ID* 316.58, 340.16.

IG XI 2.161A22: this was a rerental because of the failure of the (unfortunately unnamed) previous renter to pay. At ll. 22–23 we read "from Protole[on] the guarantor with respect to the half 25 dr 3 ob". Tolmides, who is also tardy (see below), is probably renting the other house.

IG XI 2.161A24: the guarantors paid the rent on Tolmides's behalf.

IG XI 2.161D69–72: Apemantos paid only one-half of his rent.

IG XI 2.162A17–18: one half of the rent was collected from each of the two guarantors, whose patronymics were Orthokles and Autosthenes.

IG XI 2.162A20: the figure of 60 dr is a restoration for a payment by the named guarantor.

IG XI 2.199B94: in the rubric dealing with defaulting renters (cf. B93), Durrbach read τῆς Ἐπειθένους (*sic*) Πόρος καὶ ἔγ(γ)υος Προκλείδης 𐅄 [- -]. The renter Poros is otherwise unknown, although the name occurs on Delos for a laborer, a metic, and possibly a slave (*IG* XI 2.163Ba12, 199A36; 105.11; 203A60). In view, however, of Tolmides the Parian, I would prefer to restore τῆς Ἐπειθένους (*sic*) Πά̣ρ[ι]ος καὶ ἔγ(γ)υος Προκλείδης 𐅄 [Δ], "(the) Parian (i.e., Tolmides) and his

(*continued*)

guarantor Prokleides." The figure is not complete, but it is not possible to tell how much might be missing; perhaps a Δ should be restored, in line with the rents that bracket it.

IG XI 2.203A26: Gustave Glotz, *REG* 26 (1913); 37, thought that Epistheneia must be wrong here because he accepted only two houses called Epistheneia during this period; contra, see Hennig, 431 with n. 48. Rent partly restored.

IG XI 2.204.29–31: payment by guarantors of a total of 60 dr; 50 dr is restored. The building was rerented, implying default.

IG XI 2.224A19–20: one house went for 50 dr; the other was rented to one Theron, but the rent is lost.

IG XI 2.226A22: building restored. This is a lease year (cf. A11).

ID 290.22: there is space at the end of the figure for two more digits, but they could not amount to more than 1½ ob. The other house is lost in the lacuna.

ID 356*bis*A14: renter's name read correctly by Lacroix, *BCH* 56 (1932): 379; building restored.

ID 366A94–95: the same house rents for 69 dr in *ID* 369.37. The variation is unexplained; although 77 dr ½ ob would be 110 percent of the 70 dr ½ ob of the previous period, house rents are not subject to the 10 percent rule (Molinier, 142), and my examination of the stone in July 1990 confirmed the reading: cf. Lacroix, *BCH* 56 (1932): 385.

ID 368.36: rent restored.

ID 369A37: cf. *ID* 366A94–95.

ID 442D2–11: rent not paid by Euphranor; this and the amount paid at 442A144–145 are combined to yield the indexed rent.

ID 456A25: there is no way to know which house is meant.

5. HOUSE THAT USED TO BELONG TO ORTHOKLES

		Rent		
Source	*Date*	*Raw*	*Indexed*	*Renter*
158A22	282	10+		——inis
161A20	279	41.000	82.0	Geryllos s. Python
162A16–17	278	41.000	82.0	Geryllos s. Python
199A10	274	45.379	90.8	Boulekrates
203A26–27	269	50.000	100.0	Boethos
204.27–28	268	50.000	100.0	Boethos
290.21–22	246	80.000	160.0	——os
353A19–20	219	20.000	80.0	Kallistratos
356*bis*A15	210	50.667	101.3	Phillis
366A94	207	95.000	190.0	Nikokles
366B29–31	207	26.000	52.0	Phillis
399A87	192	37.000	74.0	Euelthon
442A144	179	109.000	218.0	Antigonos

Repairs and improvements: *IG* XI 2.203A56, 204.83 (details lost); *ID* 402.3–6.

Further references without rent: *IG* XI 2.277.12.

IG XI 2.158A22: the range for possible rents runs from 10 dr 2 ob to 30 dr (two missing digits).

IG XI 2.161A20: the figure, against 40 dr 1 ob, comes from a revision of the stone by Lacroix, *BCH* 48 (1924): 404.

IG XI 2.204.27–28: house partly, renter fully restored.

ID 353A19–20: three figures are missing for the rent, so that my total is too low; 90 dr would be the maximum, 41 dr the minimum.

ID 366B29–31: addition to the list of those not paying rent at A130. Phillis evidently owed part of this year's rent (figures at A94 refer to the next rental period).

Use: not determined, Hennig, 433; commercial, Molinier, 34.

Hennig, 433, no. 8; Molinier, 28–29.

6. HOUSE OF PYTHAS

Source	Date	Rent: Raw	Rent: Indexed	Renter
199A9	274	40.000	200.0	Dionysios s. Autokles?
203A26	269	20.000	100.0	Dionysios
204.33	268	20.000	100.0	Dionysios
224A21	258	38.000	190.0	Dionysios
226A20	257	33.000	165.0	
290.22–23	246	61.000	305.0	
316.61?	231	60.000	300.0	Sosthenes
353A22–23	219	15.000	150.0	Sosthenes
366A94	207	51.000	255.0	Herakleides
369A38	206	51.000	255.0	Herakleides
400.6–7	192	70.000	350.0	Phillis
442A142	179	68.000	340.0	Doros
459.36	172 or 170	92.000	460.0	

Repairs and improvements: *ID* 290.124–25, 403.15.

IG XI 2.199A9: from restorations and new readings (including the rent) by Lacroix, *REG* 33 (1916): 207 n. 1, and *BCH* 48 (1924): 405.

IG XI 2.203A26: renter mostly restored.

IG XI 2.226A20: building restored.

ID 316.61: building restored, not surc.

ID 369A38: last digit restored.

Use: not determined, Hennig, 434; commercial, Molinier, 34.

Hennig, 433–34; Molinier, 29–30.

The buildings used to belong to Kleokritos (cf. *IG* XI 2.161A19–20); they may have come to the temple as a dedication (see Hennig, 435 n. 58, with Kent, 329, no. 135). For the view that the *sidereion* was a forge or smithy, and not a mine, see Marie-Christine Hellmann, *ZPE* 80 (1990): 65–66. The numbers involved vary; I have indicated entries referring to a plural number with (p), singular with (s).

		Rent		
Source	*Date*	*Raw*	*Indexed*	*Renter*
161A19–20 (p)	279	42.000	105.0	Protomakhos
162A19 (p)	278	40.000	100.0	Elpinos
199A9 (p)	274	[40.000]		
199B94 (p)	274	15.000		
203A26 (p)	269	40.000	100.0	Demeas
224A21?	258	40.000	100.0	Demeas s. Eumedes
287A37 (p)	250	54.000	135.0	Demeas
353A26–27 (s)	219	21.000	105.0	Antikrates
354.26 (s)	218	200.167		Antikrates s. Timagenes
354.34 (s)	218	42.000	105.0	Antikrates
366A97–98 (s)	207	44.000	110.0	Xenomedes
366A130 (s)	207	37.514	—	Aristodikos
369A38 (s)	206	44.000	110.0	Xenomedes
400.24–26 (s)	192	50.000	125.0	Demeas
442A144 (s)	179	59.500	148.8	Aristoboulos

Repairs and improvements: *ID* 290.129; 370.24–25; 402.14–15; 443Bb150–51.

Further references without rent: *IG* XI 2.156A3, 201A13, 226A19–20 (?), *ID* 399A87.

IG XI 2.161A19–20: for evidence of iron mining on Delos, see Hennig, 435 n. 57.

IG XI 2.199A9: the first two digits are restored. I am very dubious about this entry in view of that at B94, which implies that 25 dr was paid. I see however no way to restore an appropriate figure.

IG XI 2.224A21: the entry reads, – – Δ]ημέας Εὐμήδους· ΔΔΔΔ. The name and figure practically assure the restoration [τῶν οἰκημάτων πρὸς τῶι σιδηρείωι Δ]ημέας Εὐμήδους· ΔΔΔΔ (cf. Hennig, 436 n. 59).

ID 354.26: this appears to be a late payment and therefore may not represent the full rent.

ID 366A130: the renter's heirs are in default; for the figure, read now ΔΔΔΠ ⊢⊢[ΙΙΙ].

ID 369A38: rent restored by Lacroix, *REG* 39 (1926): 461.

ID 400.24–26: rented originally by Demeas, who however could find no guarantor; rerented to Epiktemon son of Melikos.

Use: industrial, Hennig, 435, and Molinier, 34.

Hennig, 434–36; Molinier, 30.

8. SOSILEIA HOUSE

Source	Date	Rent		Renter
		Raw	*Indexed*	
199A8	274	60.667	95.4	Telesarkhides
199B94	274	76.667		Telesarkhides
203A25	269	144.000	100.0	Androlas
204.26–27	268	144.000	100.0	Androlas
287A35–36	250	51.000	35.4	Aristoboulos
353A20	219	30.000	41.7	Arkileus
353B46–48	219	40.000		Empedokles
354.32	218	[60.000]		Arkileus
366A98	207	124.171	86.2	Diogenes
372A20–21	200	78.000	54.2	—— des
399A86	192	91.000	63.2	Ostakos
400.10–11	192	133.000	92.4	Ostakos
442A141	179	163.000	113.2	Ktesikles

Repairs and improvements: *IG* XI 2.156A29, 156A33, A55, 159A56, 199A68–69, *ID* 296A30, 354.64.

Further references without rent: *IG* XI 2.201A10 (?), 224A21 (?), 268.12, 277.14.

IG IX 2.199A8: Glotz provided the restoration of the name and the renter; the figure, as against *IG*'s 110 dr 4 ob, was suggested by Molinier, 83–84, and confirmed by Lacroix, *BCH* 48 (1924): 405.

IG XI 2.224A21: building fully restored, not sure.

ID 353B46–48: rent owed by renter and guarantors.

ID 354.32: rent and building restored.

ID 372A20–21: building fully restored, not sure.

Use: commercial, Molinier, 34.

Hennig, 436–38; Molinier, 31–32.

9. THE *XYLONES*

There are two buildings, which I have distinguished as (1) and (2).

Source	*Date*	*Rent* *Raw*	*Rent* *Indexed*	*Renter*
203A28 (1)	269	25.000	100.0	Dexikrates
287A36 (1)	250	15.000	60.0	Amphias
290.24 (1)	246	48.500	194.0	Akhaios
353A21–22 (1)	219	13.500	108.0	Eirenaios
354.32 (1)	218	27.000	108.0	Eirenaios
356.9–10? (1)	216–212	[27.000]	108.0	[Eirenaios?]
366A96 (1)	207	39.597	158.4	Lysixenos
366A106–7 (1)?	207	39.597	158.4	Noumedes s. Noumedes
369A36 (1)?	206	33.000	132.0	Noumedes s. Noumedes
203A28 (2)	269	25.000	100.0	Aristodemos
287A36 (2)	250	20.000	80.0	Philon
290.24 (2)	246	20.000+?		Nikias
353A21–22 (2)	219	13.000	104.0	Melesippos
354.32 (2)	218	[26.000]	104.0	Melesippos
366A96 (2)	207	15.000	60.0	Pistoxenos
226A17 (1), (2)?	257	27.000	108.0	Aresimbrotos s. Philoxenos
400.18–19	192	61.000	244.0	Apollodoros

Further references without rent: *IG* XI 2.223A46, *ID* 356*bis*A16–17, 399A85–86.

IG XI 2.226A17: probably (1) because a separate house immediately precedes the entry.

ID 290.24: rent for the second xylon, Δ̣[Δ – –].

ID 354.32: second rent restored but sure.

ID 356.9–10: fully restored, not sure.

ID 366A96, 106–7: Lysixenos had failed to find guarantors and Noumedes took over the rent, with Lysixenos himself as guarantor; cf. Hennig, 439–41.

Use: warehouse, Hennig, 439; commercial, Molinier, 34.

Hennig, 439–41; Molinier, 27–28.

Ancient and Premodern Weights and Measures, with Modern Equivalents

Modern equivalents are approximate. Abbreviations used for certain measures are given below in parentheses.

MEASURES OF CAPACITY

1 *keramion* = 8 *khoes* = 25 l
1 *khous* (*kh*) = 3.12 l
1 *kophinos* = 36 *kotylai* = 3 *kh* = 9.4 l
1 *medimnos* (Attic) (*med*) = 48 *khoinikes* = 52.176 l
1 *metretes* = 12 *kh* = 37.4 l

MEASURES OF SURFACE AREA

1 *plethron* = 10,000 ft^2 = .09 hectares (ha)
1 *iugerum* = .25 ha

MEASURES OF WEIGHT AND MONETARY UNITS

1 talent = 6,000 drachmas (dr)
1 dr = 6 obols (ob)

PREMODERN TURKISH MEASURES

1 *binek* (volume) = 38 l
1 *binek* (area) = 1000 m^2

Works Cited

Adams, Catherine F. *Nutritive Value of American Foods in Common Units.* USDA Handbook 456. Washington, D.C., 1975.

Afriat, S. N. *The Price Index.* Cambridge, 1972.

Akroyd, W. K., and J. Doughty. *Wheat in Human Nutrition.* Rome, 1970.

Alcock, Susan. *Graecia Capta: The Landscapes of Roman Greece.* Cambridge, 1993.

Allbaugh, Leland G. *Crete: A Case Study of an Underdeveloped Area.* Princeton, 1953.

Allen, R. E. *The Attalid Kingdom: A Constitutional History.* Oxford, 1983.

Amouretti, Marie-Claire. "Oléiculture et viticulture dans la Grèce antique." In *Agriculture in Ancient Greece: Proceedings of the Seventh International Symposium at the Swedish Institute at Athens, 16–17 May, 1990,* ed. Berit Wells, 77–86. Skrifter Utgivna av Svenska Institutet i Athen, 4°, 42. Stockholm, 1992.

———. *Le Pain et l'huile dans la Grèce antique.* Centre de Recherche d'histoire ancienne, vol. 67. Paris, 1986.

———. "La Transformation des céréales dans les villes, un indicateur méconnu de la personnalité urbaine: L'Exemple d'Athènes à l'époque classique." In *L'Origine des richesses dépensées dans la ville antique,* 133–46. Aix-en-Provence, 1985.

Ampolo, Carmine. "A proposito di M. I. Finley, *Ancient History: Evidence and Models.* Le 'statistiche' ateniesi: Una verifica." *Opus* 5 (1986): 139–42.

———. "Il Pane quotidiano delle città antiche fra economia e antropologia." *Opus* 5 (1986):143–51.

———. "Premessa a K. J. Beloch, *Die Landwirtschaft Athens.* 1." *Opus* 4 (1985):7–8.

Andel, Tjeerd H. van, and Curtis Runnels. *Beyond the Acropolis. A Rural Greek Past.* Stanford, 1987.

Andel, Tjeerd H. van, Curtis N. Runnels, and Kevin O. Pope. "Five Thousand Years of Land Use and Abuse in the Southern Argolid, Greece." *Hesperia* 55 (1986):103–28.

André, Jacques. "La Résine et la poix dans l'antiquité: Technique et terminologie." *Antiquité classique* 33 (1964):86–97.

Arnon, I. *Crop Production in Dry Regions.* 2 vols. London, 1972.

Aschenbrenner, Stanley. "A Contemporary Community." In *The Minnesota Messenia Expedition: Reconstructing a Bronze Age Environment,* ed. W. A. McDonald and G. R. Rapp, 47–63. Minneapolis, 1972.

Astin, Alan E. *Cato the Censor.* Oxford, 1978.

Austin, M. M., and P. Vidal-Naquet. *Economic and Social History of Ancient Greece: An Introduction.* Tr. and rev. M. M. Austin. Berkeley, 1977.

Badian, Ernst. "History from Square Brackets." *ZPE* 79 (1989):59–70.

Bagnall, Roger S. *The Administration of Ptolemaic Possessions outside Egypt.* Columbia Studies in the Classical Tradition, 4. Leiden, 1976.

———. *Currency and Inflation in Fourth-Century Egypt. BASP* suppl. 5. Atlanta, 1985.

———. "The Origins of Ptolemaic Cleruchs." *BASP* 21 (1984):7–20.

Baker, Patrick. *Cos et Calymna, 205–200 a. c.: Esprit civique et défense nationale.* Québec, 1991.

Barber, R. N. L. *The Cyclades in the Bronze Age.* Iowa City, 1987.

Baslez, M.-F. "Une Association isiaque: Les Mélanéphores." *Chronique d'Egypte* 50 (1975):297–303.

———. "Déliens et étrangers domiciliés à Délos (166–155)." *REG* 89 (1976):343–60.

———. *L'Etranger dans la Grèce antique.* Paris, 1984.

———. "Les Etrangers à Délos: Formes et évolution de la vie de relation dans un sanctuaire panhellénique." Diss., Université de Paris IV, 1982.

———. "Le Rôle et la place des Phéniciens dans la vie économique des ports de l'Egée." *Studia Phoenicia* 5 (1987):267–85.

Baslez, M.-F., and Claude Vial. "La Diplomatie de Délos dans le premier tiers du IIe siècle." *BCH* 111 (1987):281–312.

Bauslaugh, Robert. "The Posthumous Alexander Coinage of Chios." *ANS Museum Notes* 24 (1979):1–45.

Beloch, K. J. *Griechische Geschichte.* IV[2] 2. Berlin and Leipzig, 1927.

———. "Die Landwirtschaft Athens 1." *Opus* 4 (1985):9–28.

Bennet, J., and S. Voutsaki. "A Synopsis and Analysis of Travelers' Accounts of Keos (to 1821)." In *Landscape Archaeology,* 365–82.

Bengtson, Hermann. *Die Strategie in der hellenistichen Zeit: Ein Beitrag zum antiken Staatsrecht*[2]. 2 vols. Münchener Beiträge zur Papyrusforschung und antiken Rechtsgeschichte, 32 and 36. Munich, 1964–67.

Bernard, Paul. "Nouvelle contribution de l'épigraphie cunéiforme à l'histoire hellénistique: A propos d'un ouvrage de A. J. Sachs et H. Hunger,

Astronomical Diaries and Related Texts from Babylonia, Vol. I (1988)." *CRAI* 1989: 294–307.

———. "Nouvelle contribution de l'épigraphie cunéiforme à l'histoire hellénistique." *BCH* 114 (1990):513–41.

Berthiaume, Guy. *Les Rôles du mágeiros: Etude sur la boucherie, la cuisine et le sacrifice dans la Grèce ancienne. Mnemosyne* suppl. 70. Leiden, 1982.

Berthold, Richard M. *Rhodes in the Hellenistic Age.* Ithaca, N.Y., 1984.

Bettalli, Marco. "Case, botteghe, *ergasteria:* Note sui luoghi di produzione e di vendite nell'Atene classica." *Opus* 4 (1985):29–42.

Bickerman, E. J. *Chronology of the Ancient World*[2]. Ithaca, N.Y., 1980.

Billows, Richard A. *Antigonos the One-Eyed and the Creation of the Hellenistic State.* Berkeley, 1990.

Bingen, Jean. "Le Règlement samothracéen sur le fonds d'achat de blé." *Antiquité classique* 50 (1981):38–44.

Bintliff, John. *Natural Environment and Human Settlement in Prehistoric Greece.* British Archaeological Reports, suppl. ser., 28. Oxford, 1977.

Blinkenberg, Christian. *Lindos: Fouilles de l'Acropole, 1902–1914,* vol. 2, *Inscriptions.* Berlin, 1941.

Blondé, Francine, Arthur Muller, and Dominique Mulliez. "Le Comblement d'un puits public à Thasos: 5. Le Matériel amphorique." *BCH* 115 (1991):213–42.

Boehringer, Christian. *Zur Chronologie mittelhellenistischer Münzserien 220–160 v. Chr.* Berlin, 1972.

Bogaert, R. *Banques et banquiers dans les cités greques.* Leiden, 1966.

Bonneau, Danielle. *Le Fisc et le Nil: Incidences des irrégularités de la crue de Nil sur la fiscalité foncière dans l'Egypte grecque et romaine.* Paris 1971.

Boscherini, Silvano. *Lingua e scienza greca nel "De agri cultura" di Catone.* Rome, 1970.

Bosworth, A. B. *Conquest and Empire: The Reign of Alexander the Great.* Cambridge, 1988.

Boussac, M.-F., and G. Rougemont, "Observations sur le territoire des cités d'Amorgos." In *Les Cyclades: Matériaux pour une étude de géographie historique. Table ronde réunie à l'Université de Dijon les 11, 12 et 13 mars 1982,* 113–120, 235. Paris, 1983.

Braudel, Fernand. *The Structures of Everyday Life: The Limits of the Possible.* Vol. 1. Tr. Siân Reynolds. New York, 1981.

Braunert, Horst. *Das Mittelmeer in Politik und Wirtschaft der hellenistischen Zeit.* Veröffentlichungen der Schleswig-holsteinischen Universitätsgesellschaft, n.s., 49. Kiel, 1967.

Bresson, Alain. "Rhodes: Une famille camiréenne de commerçants en blé." *Index* 9 (1980):144–49.

Briggs, D. E. *Barley.* London, 1978.

Briscoe, John. *A Commentary on Livy Books XXXI–XXXIII.* Oxford, 1973.

———. *A Commentary on Livy Books XXXIV–XXXVII.* Oxford, 1981.

Brulé, Pierre. *La Piraterie crétoise hellénistique.* Centre de recherches d'histoire ancienne, vol. 27. Paris, 1978.

Brun, Patrice. "Les Lagides à Lesbos: Essai de chronologie." *ZPE* 85 (1991) 99–113.

Bruneau, Philippe. "Contribution à l'histoire urbaine de Délos à l'époque hellénistique et à l'époque impériale." *BCH* 92 (1968): 633–709.

———. "Deliaca (III): Textes littéraires. 30. Encore la pourpre: Δήλιος κυρτεύς (Hérondas, III, 51) et Δήλιος κολυμβητής (Diogène Laërce, II 22 et IX, 12)." *BCH* 103 (1979): 83–88.

———. "Deliaca (IV): Topographie et architecture. 35. 'Le vrai temple d'Apollon.'" *BCH* 105 (1981): 79–106.

———. "Deliaca (VII): 52. Deux 'allusions obscures' de Ciceron.—Le 'digamma' d'Atticus." *BCH* 112 (1988): 569–73.

———. "Deliaca (VIII): 65. Religion et politique." *BCH* 114 (1990): 583–91.

———. "Documents sur l'industrie délienne de la pourpre." *BCH* 93 (1969): 759–91.

———. "La Fabrication de la pourpre à Délos." *BCH* 102 (1978): 110–14.

———. "Les Jardins urbains de Délos." *BCH* 103 (1979): 89–99.

———. "Peparethia." *BCH* 111 (1987): 471–94.

———. "Le Quartier de l'Inopos à Délos et la fondation du Sarapieion A dans un 'lieu plein d'ordure.'" In *Etudes déliennes, publiées à l'occasion du centième anniversaire du début des fouilles de l'Ecole française d'Athènes à Délos,* 111–36. *BCH* suppl. 1. Paris, 1973.

———. *Recherches sur les cultes de Délos à l'époque hellénistique et à l'époque impériale. BEFAR* 217. Paris, 1970.

Bruneau, Philippe, and Jean Ducat. *Guide de Délos*[3]. Paris, 1983.

Bruneau, Philippe, and Philippe Fraisse. "Un Pressor à vin à Délos." *BCH* 105 (1981): 127–53.

———. "Pressoirs déliens." *BCH* 108 (1984): 713–30.

Bruneau, Philippe, et al. *L'Ilot de la Maison des comédiens. EAD* 27. Paris, 1970.

Brunet, Michèle. "Campagnes de la Grèce antique: Les Dangers du prisme athénien." Τόποι 2 (1992): 33–51.

———. "Chôrai grecques antiques," pt. 2, "Le Territoire délien." Thèse de doctorat inédite, Université de Rennes II, 1988.

———. "Contribution à l'histoire rurale de Délos aux époques classique et hellénistique." *BCH* 114 (1990): 669–82.

———. "Ferme aux jambages de granit." *BCH* 111 (1987): 644–46.

———. "Ferme aux jambages de granit." *BCH* 113 (1989): 754–61.

———. "Ferme aux jambages de granit." *BCH* 114 (1990): 906.

———. "Fouille de la ferme aux jambages de granit et exploration du territoire." *BCH* 112 (1988): 787–91.

Bulard, M. *La Religion domestique dans la colonie italienne de Délos d'après les peintures murales et les autels historiés. BEFAR* 131. Paris, 1926.

Buraselis, Kostas. *Das hellenistische Makedonien und die Ägäis: Forschungen zur Politik des Kassandros und der drei ersten Antigoniden (Antigonos Monophthalmos, Demetrios Poliorketes und Antigonos Gonatas) im Ägäischen Meer und in Westkleinasien.* Münchener Beiträge zur Papyrusforschung und Antiken Rechtsgeschichte, 73. Munich, 1982.

———. "Παρατήρησεις στὶς συνθήκες τοῦ Βασιλία Ἀντιγόνου μὲ τὴν Ἐλεύθερνα καὶ τὴν Ἱεράπυτνα." *AE* 1981: 114–25.

———. "Zu BCH 1975, 52–53." *AE* 1982 [1984]: 136–60.

Burford, Alison. *The Greek Temple Builders at Epidauros.* Toronto, 1969.

———. *Land and Labor in the Greek World.* Baltimore, 1993.

Burke, Edmund M. "Athens after the Peloponnesian War: Restoration Efforts and the Role of Maritime Commerce." *Classical Antiquity* 9 (1990): 1–13.

———. "The Economy of Athens in the Classical Era: Some Adjustments to the Primitivist Model." *TAPA* 122 (1992): 199–226.

———. "Eubulus, Olynthus, and Euboea." *TAPA* 114 (1984): 111–20.

Burkert, Walter. *Greek Religion.* Tr. John Raffan. Cambridge, Mass., 1985.

Bury, J. B. *A History of Greece to the Death of Alexander the Great*[3]. London, 1951.

Carandini, Andrea. "Columella's Vineyard and the Rationality of the Roman Economy." *Opus* 2 (1983): 177–204.

Cargill, Jack. *The Second Athenian League: Empire or Free Alliance?* Berkeley, 1981.

Carmichael, W. J., and John B. Rice. "Variations in Farrow, with Special Reference to the Birth Weight of Pigs." *University of Illinois Agricultural Experiment Station Bulletin* no. 226: 67–95. Urbana, 1920.

Cartledge, Paul. "'Trade and Politics' Revisited: Archaic Greece." In *Trade in the Ancient Economy,* ed. Peter Garnsey, Keith Hopkins, and C. R. Whittaker, 1–15. Berkeley, 1983.

Cartledge, Paul, and Antony Spawforth. *Hellenistic and Roman Sparta: A Tale of Two Cities.* London, 1989.

Casson, Lionel. "The Grain Trade of the Hellenistic World." In *Ancient Trade and Society,* 70–95. Detroit, 1984.

———. *Ships and Seamanship in the Ancient World.* Princeton, 1986.

Cavagnola, Bruno. "Aspetti economici dell'allevamento a Delo e Reneia in età ellenistica." *Istituto lombardo, rendiconti, Class. di lett. e sc. mor. e stor.* 107 (1973): 511–45.

———. "I locatari delle proprietà fondiare del dio Apollo a Delo." *Istituto lombardo, rendiconti, Class. di. lett. e sc. mor. e stor.* 106 (1972): 51–115.

Cayeux, L. *Description physique de l'île de Délos. EAD* 4. Paris, 1911.

Chamonard, Joseph. *Le Quartier du théatre: Etude sur l'habitation délienne à l'époque hellénistique. EAD* 8. Paris, 1922–24.

Champlin, Edward. "The Testament of the Piglet." *Phoenix* 41 (1987): 174–83.

Charre, Roger. Marie-Thérèse Le Dinahet, and Vassiliki Yannouli. "Vestiges antiques à Rhénée." In *Recherches dans les Cyclades,* 123–42. Lyon, 1993.

Cherry, John F., and Jack L. Davis. "The Ptolemaic Base at Koressos on Keos." *BSA* 86 (1991): 9–28.

Cherry, John F., Jack L. Davis, and E. Mantzourani, eds. *Landscape Archaeology as Long-term History: Northern Keos in the Cycladic Islands from Earliest Settlement until Modern Times.* Monumenta Archaeologica, 16. Los Angeles, 1991.

Cherry, John F., Jack L. Davis, and E. Mantzourani. "Greek and Roman Settlement and Land Use." In *Landscape Archaeology,* 327–47.

———. "*Miltos* and Metallurgical Extraction." In *Landscape Archaeology,* 299–303.

Clarysse, W., and E. Lanciers. "Currency and the Dating of Demotic and Greek Papyri from the Ptolemaic Period." *Ancient Society* 20 (1989): 117–32.

Clinton, Kevin. "Inscriptions from Eleusis." *Arch. Eph.* 1971: 81–136.

Coale, Ansley J., Paul Demeny, and Barbara Vaughan. *Regional Model Life Tables and Stable Populations.* 2d. ed. New York, 1983.

Cohen, Edward E. *Athenian Economy and Society: A Banking Perspective.* Princeton, 1992.

Cohen, Getzel M. *The Seleucid Colonies: Studies in Founding, Administration and Organization. Historia* Einzelschrift 30. Wiesbaden, 1978.

Comptes et inventoires dans les cités grecques: Actes du colloque de Neuchâtel en l'honneur de Jacques Tréheux. Ed. Denis Knoepfler. Neuchâtel and Geneva, 1988.

Connell, Christopher. *In the Bee-Loud Glade.* Nafplion, 1980.

Cook, J. M. "Cities in and around the Troad." *BSA* 83 (1988): 7–19.

Couilloud, Marie-Thérèse. *Les Monuments funéraires de Rhénée. EAD* 30 Paris, 1974.

Coupry, Jacques. "Inscriptions de Délos: Actes administratifs du temps de l'Amphictyonie attico-délienne (V[e]–IVe s.)." In *Atti del terzio congresso internazionale di epigrafia greca e latina,* 55–69. Rome, 1959.

Crampa, Jonas. *Labraunda: Swedish Excavations and Researches,* vol. 3, part 1, *The Greek Inscriptions. Part I: 1–12: (Period of Olympichos).* Lund, 1969.

Les Cyclades: Matériaux pour une étude de géographie historique. Table ronde réunie à l'Université de Dijon les 11, 12 et 13 mars 1982. Paris, 1983.

Daux, Georges. "Inscriptions de Delphes." *BCH* 83 (1959):466–95.

Davidson, Donald, and Catriona Tasker. "Geomorphological Evolution during the Late Holocene." In *An Island Polity: The Archaeology of Exploitation in Melos.* Ed. Colin Renfrew and Malcolm Wagstaff, 82–94. Cambridge, 1982.

Davies, J. K. *Athenian Propertied Families, 600–300 B.C.* Oxford, 1971.

Davis, Philip H. "On the Upkeep of 'Sacred Houses' on Delos." *BCH* 59 (1935):77–91.

Delamarre, J. "Amorgos et les pirates." *Rev. Phil.* 27 (1903):111–21.

———. "L'Influence macédonienne dans les Cyclades au IIIe siècle avant J.-C." *Rev. Phil.* 26 (1902):301–25.

Déonna, Waldemar. *La Vie privée des Déliens.* Ecole française d'Athènes Travaux et Mémoires 7. Paris, 1948.

Le Dinahet, M.-T. "Fortunes hellénistiques et grand commerce d'après les documents épigraphiques." In *L'Origine des richesses dépensées dans la ville antique,* 39–45. Aix-en-Provence, 1985.

———. "Identification des domains d'Apollon à Rhenée." In *Les Cyclades,* 135–40.

Dörmer, W. *De Graecorum sacrificulis qui* ἱεροποιοί *dicuntur.* Dissertationes philologicae Argentoratenses selectae, 8. Strassburg, 1885.

Doulgéra-Intzessiloglou, Argyroula, and Yvon Garlan. "Vin et amphores de Péparéthos et d'Ikos." *BCH* 114 (1990):361–89.

Drexhage, Hans-Joachim. *Preise, Mieten/Pachten, Kosten und Löhne im römischen Ägypten bis zum Regierungsantritt Diokletians: Vorarbeiten zu einer Wirtschaftsgeschichte des römischen Ägypten.* Vol. 1. St. Katharinen, 1991.

Ducrey, Pierre. "Nouvelles remarques sur deux traités Attalides avec des cités crétoises." *BCH* 94 (1970):637–59.

Dunant, Chr., and J. Thomopoulos, "Inscriptions de Céos." *BCH* 78 (1954):316–48.

Duncan-Jones, Richard. *The Economy of the Roman Empire: Quantitative Studies*[2]. Cambridge, 1982.

Dunst, G. "Ein neues chiisches Dekret aus Kos." *Klio* 37 (1959):63–68.

Durrbach, Felix. *Choix d'inscriptions de Délos avec traduction et commentaire.* Paris, 1921–22. Reprint, 1977.

———. "Fouilles de Délos." *BCH* 29 (1905):417–573.

———. "Fouilles de Délos." *BCH* 35 (1911):1–86, 243–87.

———. "La ἱερὰ συγγραφή de Délos." *REG* 32 (1919):167–78.

Edwards, G. R. "Panathenaics of Hellenistic and Roman Times." *Hesperia* 26 (1957):320–49.

Effenterre, Henri van. *La Crète et le monde grec. BEFAR* 163. Reprint. Paris, 1968.

Empereur, J.-Y. "Les Anses d'amphores timbrées et les amphores: Aspects quantitatifs." *BCH* 106 (1982): 219–33.

Empereur, J.-Y., and N. Tuna. "Hiérotélès, potier Rhodien de la Pérée." *BCH* 113 (1989): 277–99.

Empereur, J.-Y., and Maurice Picon. "Des ateliers d'amphores à Paros et à Naxos" and "Note complémentaire." *BCH* 110 (1986): 495–511, 647–53.

Errington, R. M. "Diodorus Siculus and the Chronology of the Early Diadochoi, 320–311 B.C." *Hermes* 105 (1977): 478–504.

Etienne, Roland. "Le Capital immobilier dans les Cyclades à l'époque hellénistique." In *L'Origine des richesses dépensées dans la ville antique.* Ed. Philippe Leveau, 55–67. Aix-en-Provence and Marseille, 1985.

———. "Les Etrangers et la politique: Le Rôle de Rhodes dans les Cyclades dans le premier tiers du IIe siècle." In *L'Etranger dans le monde grec: Actes du colloque organisé par l'Institut d'études anciennes,* ed. Raoul Lonis, 159–67. Nancy, 1988.

———. "Le *koinon* des Hellènes à Platées et Glaucon, fils d'Etéoclès." In *La Béotie antique,* 259–63. Paris, 1985.

———. "Les Rations alimentaires de la 'familia rustica' d'après Caton." *Index* 10 (1981): 66–77.

———. *Ténos II: Ténos et les Cyclades du milieu du IVe siècle avant J.-C. au milieu du IIIe siècle après J.-C. BEFAR* 263*bis.* Paris, 1990.

Etienne, Roland, and Jean-Pierre Braun. *Ténos I: Le Sanctuaire de Poseidon et d'Amphitrite. BEFAR* 263. Paris, 1986.

Etienne, Roland, and Denis Knoepfler. *Hyettos de Béotie et la chronologie des archontes fédéraux entre 250 et 171 avant J.-C. BCH* suppl. 3. Paris, 1976.

Etienne, Roland, and Marcel Piérart. "Un Décret du Koinon des Hellènes à Platées en l'honneur de Glaucon, fils d'Etéoclès, d'Athènes." *BCH* 99 (1975): 51–75.

Evans, John K. "*Plebs rustica:* The Peasantry of Classical Italy." *AJAH* 5 (1980): 19–47, 134–73.

Fabrer, H. Camps, ed. *L'Huile d'olive en Méditerranée: Histoire, anthropologie, économie de l'antiquité à nos jours.* Aix-en-Provence, 1985.

Fantasia, Ugo. "Mercanti e 'sitonai' nelle città greche: In margine a tre documenti epigraphici della prima età ellenistica." *Civiltà classica e cristiana* 5 (1984): 283–311.

FAO/WHO. *Energy and Protein Requirements: Report of a Joint FAO/WHO Ad Hoc Expert Committee.* Rome, 1973.

Ferguson, William Scott. "Egypt's Loss of Sea Power." *JHS* 30 (1910): 189–208.

———. *Hellenistic Athens: An Historical Essay.* London, 1911.

Feyel, Michel. *Contribution à l'épigraphie béotienne.* Publications de la Faculté des lettres de l'Université de Strasbourg, 95. Le Puy, 1942.

Figueira, T. "*Sitopolai* and *sitophylakes* in Lysias' 'Against the Graindealers': Governmental Intervention in the Athenian Economy." *Phoenix* 40 (1986):149–71.

Fine, J. V. A. "The Background of the Social War of 220–217 B.C." *AJP* 61 (1940):129–65.

Finley, M. I. *The Ancient Economy*[2]. Berkeley, 1985.

———. *Ancient History: Evidence and Models.* New York, 1985.

———. *Studies in Land and Credit in Ancient Athens, 500–200 B.C.* New Brunswick, N.J., 1951.

Flacelière, Robert. *Les Aitoliens à Delphes: Contribution à l'histoire de la Grèce centrale au IIIe siècle av. J.-C. BEFAR* 143. Paris, 1937.

———. "Les Rapports d'Athènes et de l'Aitolie au IIIe siècle." In *Athenian Studies Presented to William Scott Ferguson*, 471–81. *Harvard Studies in Classical Philology* suppl. 1. Cambridge, Mass. 1940.

Forbes, Hamish. "The Ethnoarchaeological Approach to Ancient Greek Agriculture: Olive Cultivation as a Case Study." In *Agriculture in Ancient Greece: Proceedings of the Seventh International Symposium at the Swedish Institute at Athens, 16–17 May, 1990*, ed. Berit Wells, 87–101. Skrifter Utgivna av Svenska Institutet i Athen, 4°, 42. Stockholm, 1992.

———. "Of Grandfathers and Grand Theories: The Hierarchised Ordering of Responses to Hazard in a Greek Rural Community." In *Bad Year Economics: Cultural Responses to Risk and Uncertainty.* Ed. Paul Halstead and John O'Shea, 87–98. Cambridge, 1989.

Fourastié, Jacqueline. *Essai sur la mesure des quantités économiques.* Ecole practique des hautes etudes VIe et Laboratoire d'econométrie du Conservatoire national des arts et métiers, Etudes et mémoires, 68. Paris, 1972.

Foxhall, Lin. "Greece Ancient and Modern: Subsistence and Survival." *History Today* 36 (July 1986):35–43.

Foxhall, Lin, and H. A. Forbes. "Σιτομετρεία: The Role of Grain as a Staple Food in Classical Antiquity." *Chiron* 12 (1982):41–90.

Fraisse, Philippe, and Tony Koželj. "Une Carrière de marbre au sud-est du Cynthe." *BCH* 115 (1991):283–96.

Fraser, P. M. "*Alexandria ad Aegyptum* Again." *JRS* 39 (1949):56.

———. *Ptolemaic Alexandria.* 3 vols. Oxford, 1972.

Fraser, P. M., and G. E. Bean. *The Rhodian Peraea and Islands.* Oxford, 1954.

Fraser, P. M., and E. Matthews, eds. *A Lexicon of Greek Personal Names*, vol. 1, *The Aegean Islands, Cyprus, Cyrenaica.* Oxford, 1987.

Fraser, P. M., and C. H. Roberts. "A New Letter of Apollonius." *Chronique d'Egypte* 47 (1949):289–94.

French, A. *The Growth of the Athenian Economy.* New York, 1964.

Gabbert, Janice J. "The Anarchic Dating of the Chremonidean War." *CJ* 82 (1986/87):230–35.

Gajdukevič, V. F. *Das bosporanische Reich.* Berlin and Amsterdam, 1971.

Gallant, Thomas W. "Crisis and Response: Risk-Buffering Behavior in Hellenistic Greek Communities." *Journal of Interdisciplinary History* 19 (1989):393–413.

———. *Risk and Survival in Ancient Greece: Reconstructing the Rural Domestic Economy.* Stanford, 1991.

———. Review of *Beyond the Acropolis: A Rural Greek Past,* by Tjeerd von Andel and Curtis Runnels. *CJ* 86 (1990–91):184–86.

Gallo, Luigi. "Alimentazione e classi sociali: Una nota su orzo e frumento in Grecia." *Opus* 2 (1983):449–72.

———. *Alimentazione e demografia della Grecia antica.* Salerno, 1984.

Garlan, Yvon. "Elisavetovskoe: Un *emporion* grec sur le Bas-Don." *DHA* 8 (1982):145–52.

———. "Greek Amphorae and Trade." In *Trade in the Ancient Economy.* Eds. Peter Garnsey, Keith Hopkins, and C. R. Whittaker, 27–35. Berkeley, 1983.

———. "Remarques sur les timbres amphoriques de Sinope." *CRAI* 1990: 490–507.

Garland, Robert. *The Piraeus from the Fifth to the First Century* B.C. Ithaca, N.Y., 1987.

Garnsey, Peter. *Famine and Food Supply in the Graeco-Roman World: Responses to Risk and Crisis.* Cambridge, 1988.

———. "Grain for Athens." In *Crux: Essays in Greek History Presented to G. E. M. de Ste. Croix.* Ed. P. A. Cartledge and F. D. Harvey, 62–75. London, 1985.

———. "Yield of the Land." In *Agriculture in Ancient Greece: Proceedings of the Seventh International Symposium at the Swedish Institute at Athens, 16–17 May, 1990,* ed. Berit Wells, 147–53. Skrifter Utgivna av Svenska Institutet i Athen, 4°, 42. Stockholm, 1992.

Garnsey, Peter, Tom Gallant, and Dominic Rathbone. "Thessaly and the Grain Supply of Rome during the Second Century B.C." *JRS* 74 (1984): 30–44.

Garnsey, Peter, Keith Hopkins, and C. R. Whittaker, eds. *Trade in the Ancient Economy.* Berkeley, 1983.

Garnsey, Peter, and Ian Morris. "Risk and the *Polis:* The Evolution of Institutionalised Responses to Food Supply Problems in the Ancient Greek State." In *Bad Year Economics: Cultural Responses to Risk and Uncertainty,* eds. Paul Halstead and John O'Shea, 98–105. Cambridge, 1989.

Garnsey, Peter, and C. R. Whittaker, eds. *Trade and Famine in Classical Antiquity.* Cambridge Philological Society suppl. 8. Cambridge, 1983.

Gauthier, Philippe. *Les Cités grecques et leur bienfacteurs. BCH* suppl. 12. Paris, 1985.

———. "De Lysias à Aristote (*Ath. pol.,* 51, 4): Le Commerce du grain à Athènes et les fonctions des sitophylaques." *Revue historique de droit français et étranger* 59 (1981):5–28.

———. "Etudes sur des inscriptions d'Amorgos." *BCH* 104 (1980): 197–220.

———. "L'Inscription d'Iasos relative à l'*ekklesiastikon* (*I. Iasos* 20)." *BCH* 114 (1990): 417–43.

———. "Sur le don de grain numide à Délos: Un Pseudo-Rhodien dans les comptes des hiéropes." In *CICG,* 61–69.

———. *Symbola: Les Etrangers et la justice dans les cités grecques.* Annales de l'Est, mémoire 42. Nancy, 1972.

———. "Les Ventes publiques de bois et de charbon: A propos d'une inscription de Délos." *BCH* 101 (1977): 203–8.

———. "Les Villes athéniennes et un décret pour un commerçant (*IG,* II^2, 903)." *REG* 95 (1982): 275–90.

Geagan, Daniel J. "Inscriptions from Nemea." *Hesperia* 37 (1968): 381–85.

Gelder, H. van. *Geschichte der alten Rhodier.* The Hague, 1900.

Genike Statistike Hyperesiates Hellados. Στατιστικὴ Ἐπετηρὶς τῆς Ἑλλάδος. Athens, 1937, 1938, 1939.

Ghiron-Bistagne, Paulette. *Recherches sur les acteurs dans la Grèce antique.* Paris, 1976.

Gill, David W. J. "Pots and Trade: Spacefillers or Objets d'Art?" *JHS* 111 (1991): 29–47.

Giovannini, Adalberto. *Rome et la circulation monétaire en Grèce au IIe siècle avant J.-C.* Schweizerische Beiträge zur Altertumswissenschaft, 15. Basel, 1978.

Glotz, Gustave. "L'Histoire de Délos d'après les prix d'une denrée." *REG* 29 (1916): 281–325.

———. "Note sur les archontes déliens de 314 à 302." *BCH* 44 (1920): 362–66.

———. "Notes sur les comptes de Délos." *REG* 26 (1913): 26–39.

———. "Les Prix des denrées à Délos," *Journal des Savants* 11 (1913): 16–29.

———. Review of *Wirtschaftliche Schwankungen der Zeit von Alexander bis Augustus,* by Fritz Heichelheim, *REG* 45 (1932): 241–49.

———. "Les Salaires à Délos." *Journal des Savants* 11 (1913): 206–15, 251–60.

———. "Un Transport de marbre pour le théâtre de Délos." *REG* 32 (1919): 240–50.

Gould, Stephen Jay. *The Mismeasure of Man.* New York, 1981.

Grace, Virginia R. "The Middle Stoa Dated by Amphora Stamps." *Hesperia* 54 (1985): 1–54.

———. "Revisions in Early Hellenistic Chronology." *Ath. Mitt.* 89 (1974): 193–200.

———. "Stamped Amphora Handles Found in 1931–1932." *Hesperia* 3 (1934): 197–310.

———. "Standard Pottery Containers of the Ancient World." In *Com-*

memorative Studies in Honor of Theodore Leslie Shear, 175–89. *Hesperia* suppl. 8. Athens, 1949.

———. "Timbres amphoriques trouvés à Délos." *BCH* 76 (1952): 514–40.

Grace, Virginia R., and Maria Savvatianou-Pétropoulako. "Les Timbres amphoriques grecs." In Philippe Bruneau et al., *L'Ilot de la Maison des comédiens, EAD* 27, 287–386. Paris, 1970.

Grainger, John. *The Cities of Seleukid Syria.* Oxford, 1990.

Graßl, Herbert. "Zur Geschichte des Viehhandels im klassischen Griechenland." *MBAH* 4.2 (1985): 77–88.

Grigson, Caroline. "Porridge and Pannage: Pig Husbandry in Neolithic England." In *Archaeological Aspects of Woodland Ecology.* Ed. Martin Bell and Susan Limbrey, 279–315. BAR International Series, 146. London, 1982.

Groningen, B. A. van. *Aristotele: Le Second Livre de l'Economique.* Leiden, 1933.

Gruen, Erich S. *The Hellenistic World and the Coming of Rome.* 2 vols. Berkeley, 1984.

———. "Material Rewards and the Drive for Empire." In *The Imperialism of Mid-Republican Rome.* Ed. William V. Harris, 59–82. Papers and Monographs of the American Academy in Rome, 39. Rome, 1984.

Habermann, Wolfgang. "Statistische Datenanalyse an den Zolldokumenten des Arsinoites aus römischer Zeit II." *MBAH* 9.1 (1990) 50–94.

Habicht, Christian. "Athens and the Ptolemies." *Classical Antiquity* 11 (1992): 68–90.

———. *Gottmenschentum und griechische Städte*². Zemata, 14. Munich, 1970.

———. "Der rhodische Eponym Autokrates (I.G. XII 5, 824)." *Chiron* 19 (1989): 273–77.

———. *Studien zur Geschichte Athens in hellenistischer Zeit.* Hypomnemata, 73. Göttingen, 1982.

———. *Untersuchungen zur politischen Geschichte Athens im 3. Jahrhundert v. Chr.* Vestigia, 30. Munich, 1979.

———. "Eine Urkunde des Akarnanischen Bundes." *Hermes* 85 (1957): 86–122.

Hackens, Tony. "Les Monnaies." In Philippe Bruneau et al., *L'Ilot de la Maison des comédiens,* 387–419. *EAD* 27. Paris, 1970.

Hadjisavvas, Sophocles. *Olive Oil Processing in Cyprus from the Bronze Age to the Byzantine Period.* Studies in Mediterranean Archaeology, 99. Nicosia, 1992.

Halstead, Paul. "The Economy Has a Normal Surplus: Economic Stability and Social Changes among Early Farming Communities of Thessaly, Greece." In *Bad Year Economics: Cultural Responses to Risk and Uncertainty.* Ed. Paul Halstead and John O'Shea, 68–80. Cambridge, 1989.

Halstead, Paul, and Glynis Jones. "Agrarian Ecology in the Greek Islands: Time Stress, Scale and Risk." *JHS* 109 (1989): 41–55.

Halstead, Paul, and John O'Shea, eds. *Bad Year Economics: Cultural Responses to Risk and Uncertainty.* Cambridge, 1989.

Hammond, N. G. L., and F. W. Walbank, *A History of Macedonia, vol. 3, 336–167 B.C.* Oxford, 1988.

Hanson, Victor D. "Practical Aspects of Grape-Growing and the Ideology of Greek Viticulture." In *Agriculture in Ancient Greece: Proceedings of the Seventh International Symposium at the Swedish Institute at Athens, 16–17 May, 1990,* ed. Berit Wells, 161–66. Skrifter Utgivna av Svenska Institutet i Athen, 4°, 42. Stockholm, 1992.

———. *Warfare and Agriculture in Classical Greece.* Biblioteca di studi antichi, 40. Pisa, 1983.

Harvey, Paul. "New Harvests Reappear: The Impact of War on Agriculture." *Athenaeum* 64 (1986) 205–18.

Hasebroek, Johannes. *Trade and Politics in Ancient Greece.* Tr. L. M. Fraser and D. C. MacGregor. London, 1933.

Hauben, Hans. "Philokles, King of the Sidonians and General of the Ptolemies." In *Studia Phoenicia V: Phoenicia and the East Mediterranean in the First Millennium* B.C., 413–28. Orientalia Lovaniensia Analecta, 22. Leuven, 1987.

Head, B. V. *A Catalogue of Greek Coins in the British Museum.* Vol. 18. *Caria and the Islands.* London 1897.

Heckel, W. "A Grandson of Antipatros at Delos." *ZPE* 70 (1987): 161–62.

Heichelheim, Fritz M. "On Ancient Price Trends from the Early First Millennium B.C. to Heraclius I." *Finanz Archiv* 15 (1954–55): 498–511.

———. "Sitos." *RE* suppl. 6 (1935).

———. *Wirtschaftliche Schwankungen der Zeit von Alexander bis Augustus.* Beiträge zur Erforschung der wirtschaftlichen Wechsellagen Aufschwung, Krise, Stockung, 3. Jena, 1930.

———. *Wirtschaftsgeschichte des Altertums vom Paläolithikum bis zur Völkerwanderung der Germanen, Slaven und Araber.* 2 vols. Leiden, 1938.

———. "Zu Pap. Michigan III 173 und Hesperia V (1936) 419 ff. Nr. 15." *Aegyptus* 17 (1937): 61–64.

Heinen, Heinz. *Untersuchungen zur hellenistischen Geschichte des 3. Jahrhunderts v. Chr. Historia* Einzelschrift 20. Wiesbaden, 1972.

Hellmann, Marie-Christine. "A propos de certains termes techniques dans les inscriptions de Délos." *ZPE* 80 (1990): 65–71.

Helzer, M., and D. Eitan, eds. *Olive Oil in Antiquity.* Haifa, 1987.

Hennig, Dieter. "Die 'heiligen Häuser' von Delos." *Chiron* 13 (1983): 411–95 and 15 (1985): 165–86.

Hill, H. *The Roman Middle Class in the Republican Period.* Oxford, 1952.

Hiller von Gaertringen, F. "Inschriften aus Rhodos." *JÖAI* 4 (1901): 159–66.

Hoefner, Wolfram, et al. *Haus und Stadt im klassischen Griechenland.* Munich, 1986.

Holleaux, Maurice. *Etudes d'épigraphie et d'histoire grecques.* Ed. Louis Robert. 4 vols. Paris, 1938–52.

Homolle, Theophile. *Les Archives de l'intendance sacrée à Délos (315–166 av. J.-C.).* BEFAR 49. Paris, 1887.

———. "Comptes & inventaires des temples déliens en l'année 279." *BCH* 14 (1890): 389–511.

———. "Comptes & inventaires des temples déliens en l'année 279. Deuxième article. II. Inventaires des temples." *BCH* 15 (1891): 113–68.

Hopkins, Keith. *Conquerors and Slaves: Sociological Studies in Roman History.* Vol. 1. Cambridge, 1978.

Huss, Werner. *Untersuchungen zur Aussenpolitik Ptolemaios' IV.* Münchener Beiträge zur Papyrusforschung und Antiken Rechtsgeschichte, 69. Munich, 1976.

Isager, Signe, and Mogens Herman Hansen. *Aspects of Athenian Society in the Fourth Century.* Odense University Classical Studies, 5. Odense, 1975.

Isager, Signe, and Jens Erik Skydsgaard. *Ancient Greek Agriculture: An Introduction.* London and New York, 1992.

Jacobsen, Thomas W., and Peter M. Smith. "Two Kimolian Dikast Decrees from Geraistos in Euboia." *Hesperia* 37 (1968): 184–99.

Jameson, Michael H. "Agricultural Labor in Ancient Greece." In *Agriculture in Ancient Greece: Proceedings of the Seventh International Symposium at the Swedish Institute at Athens, 16–17 May, 1990,* ed. Berit Wells, 135–46. Skrifter Utgivna av Svenska Institutet i Athen, 4°, 42. Stockholm, 1992.

———. "Agriculture and Slavery in Classical Athens." *CJ* 74 (1977–78): 122–45.

———. "Sacrifice and Animal Husbandry in Classical Greece." In *Pastoral Economies in Classical Antiquity.* Ed. C. R. Whittaker, 87–119. Cambridge Philological Society suppl. 14. Cambridge, 1988.

Jardé, Auguste. *Les Céréales dans l'antiquité grecque: La production.* Paris, 1925. Reprint. 1979.

Jasny, N. "Competition among Grains in Classical Antiquity." *AHR* 47 (1941–42): 747–64.

Jones, J. R. "Some Numismatic Problems in the Delian Inscriptions." *ANS Museum Notes* 17 (1971): 127–36.

Kent, John Harvey. "Notes on the Delian Farm Accounts." *BCH* 63 (1939): 232–45.

———. "Stamped Amphora Handles from the Delian Temple Estates." In *Studies Presented to David Moore Robinson,* 2: 127–34. St. Louis, 1953.

———. "The Temple Estates of Delos, Rheneia, and Mykonos." *Hesperia* 17 (1948): 243—338.

Klinkenborg, Verlyn. *Making Hay.* New York, 1986.

Knoepfler, Denis. "Carystos et les Artémisia d'Amarynthos." *BCH* 96 (1972):283–301.

———. "Contributions à l'épigraphie de Chalcis." *BCH* 114 (1990): 473–98.

Koehler, Carolyn G., and Malcolm B. Wallace. "Appendix. The Transport Amphoras: Description and Capacities." *AJA* 91 (1987):49–57.

Kohler, Heinz. *Statistics for Business and Economics.* Glenview, Ill., 1985.

Kolodny, Emile Y. *La Population des îles de la Grèce: Essai de géographie insulaire en Méditerranée orientale.* 2 vols. Aix-en-Provence, 1974.

Kreissig, Heinz. *Wirtschaft und Gesellschaft im Seleukidenreich.* Schriften zur Geschichte und Kultur der Antike, 16. Berlin, 1978.

Krider, J. L., J. H. Conrad, and W. E. Carroll. *Swine Production*^{5}. New York, 1982.

Kruit, Nico. "The Meaning of Various Words Related to Wine: Some New Interpretations." *ZPE* 90 (1992):265–76.

Lacroix, Maurice. "Les Architectes et entrepreneurs à Délos de 314 à 240." *Rev. Phil.* 38 (1914):303–30.

———. "Les Étrangers à Délos pendant la période de l'indépendance." In *Mélanges Gustave Glotz,* 2: 501–25. Paris, 1932.

———. "Une Famille de Délos." *REG* 33 (1916):188–237.

———. "Notes sur diverses inscriptions de Délos." *BCH* 48 (1924): 399–410.

———. "Notes sur les comptes des hiéropes déliens." *BCH* 56 (1932): 372–87.

———. "Notes sur les inscriptions déliennes (*I.G.,* XI, II et IV)." *REG* 35 (1922):415–25.

———. "Nouvelles notes sur les inscriptions déliennes." *REG* 39 (1926): 448–61.

———. "Nouvelles notes sur les inscriptions déliennes." *REG* 43 (1930): 372–83.

Lacroix, Maurice, and Gustave Glotz. "Suite aux notes sur les comptes de Délos." *REG* 27 (1914):138–43.

Laet, Siegfried J. de. *Portorium: Etude sur l'organisation douanière chez les Romains, surtout à l'époque du Haut-Empire.* Bruges, 1949.

Laidlaw, W. A. *A History of Delos.* Oxford, 1933.

Larsen, J. A. O. "Phocis in the Social War." *Phoenix* 19 (1965):116–28.

———. "The Price of Tiles at Delos from 210 to 180 B.C." *CP* 36 (1941): 156–66.

———. "Roman Greece." In *An Economic Survey of Ancient Rome,* vol. 4, ed. Tenney Frank, 334–414. Baltimore, 1938.

Launey, Marcel. *Recherches sur les armées hellénistiques. BEFAR* 169. 2 vols. Paris, 1949–50. Reprint, with additions and corrections, 1987.

Lehmann, G. A. "Der 'Lamische Krieg' und die 'Freiheit der Hellenen': Überlegungen zur hieronymischen Tradition." *ZPE* 73 (1988):121–49.

Leonardos, V. I. "Ἀμφιαρείου ἐπιγραφαί." *AE* 1892: 33–56.

Lewis, D. M. Review of *IK* 30 Keramos. *CR* 38 (1988): 124–25.

Lewthwaite, J. G. "Acorns for the Ancestors: The Prehistoric Exploitation of Woodland in the West Mediterranean." In *Archaeological Aspects of Woodland Ecology,* eds. Martin Bell and Susan Limbrey, 217–30. BAR International Series, 146. London, 1982.

Ligt, L. de. "Demand, Supply, Distribution: The Roman Peasantry between Town and Countryside: Rural Monetization and Peasant Demand." *MBAH* 9.2 (1990): 24–56.

———. "II. Supply, Distribution and a Comparative Perspective." *MBAH* 10.1 (1991): 33–77.

Lohmann, Hans. "Agriculture and Country Life in Classical Attica." In *Agriculture in Ancient Greece: Proceedings of the Seventh International Symposium at the Swedish Institute at Athens, 16–17 May, 1990,* ed. Berit Wells, 29–57. Skrifter Utgivna av Svenska Institutet i Athen, 4°, 42. Stockholm, 1992.

Lousset, Raymond, and Gérard Brousse. *L'Olivier.* Techniques agricoles et productions méditerranéennes, 1. Paris, 1978.

MacDowell, Douglas M. *The Law in Classical Athens.* Ithaca, N.Y., 1978.

Macve, Richard H. "Some Glosses on Ste. Croix's 'Greek and Roman Accounting.'" In *Crux: Essays in Greek History Presented to G. E. M. de Ste. Croix,* ed. P. A. Cartledge and F. D. Harvey, 233–64. London, 1985.

Magie, David. *Roman Rule in Asia Minor.* Princeton, 1950.

Marangou, Lila. "Découvertes récentes à Amorgos." In *Les Cyclades,* 121–29, 236.

Marasco, Gabriele. *Economia, commerci e politica nel Mediterraneo fra il III e il II secolo a.c.* Università degli studi di Firenze, dipartimento di storia, studi, 1. Florence, 1988.

———. "Interessi commerciale e fattori politici nella condotta romana in Illiria." *Studi classici ed orientali* 36 (1986): 35–112.

———. "Roma, Rodi e il grano di Sicilia." *Prometheus* 11 (1985): 137–50.

———. "L'ultima spedizione di Demetrio Poliorcete in Asia." *Res publica litterarum* 8 (1985): 148–63.

Marek, Christian. "Handel und Proxenie." *MBAH* 4.1 (1985): 67–78.

———. *Die Proxenie.* Frankfurt am Main, 1984.

Matson, F. R. "Power and Fuel Resources in the Ancient Near East." *Advancement of Science* 23 (1966): 146–53.

Mattingly, D. J. "Olea mediterranea?" *J. of Roman Arch.* 1 (1988): 153–61.

May, J. M. F. *Ainos: Its History and Coinage.* London, 1950.

McDonald, A. H. and F. W. Walbank. "The Origins of the Second Macedonian War." *JRS* 27 (1937): 180–207.

McDonald, W. A., and G. R. Rapp, eds. *The Minnesota Messenia Expedition: Reconstructing a Bronze Age Environment.* Minneapolis, 1972.

McShane, Roger B. *The Foreign Policy of the Attalids of Pergamum.* Illinois Studies in the Social Sciences, 53. Urbana, 1964.

Meadows, Dennis L. *Dynamics of Commodity Production Cycles.* Cambridge, Mass., 1970.

Meiggs, Russell. *The Athenian Empire.* Oxford, 1972.

———. *Trees and Timber in the Ancient Mediterranean World.* Oxford, 1982.

Meiggs, Russell, and David Lewis, eds. *A Selection of Greek Historical Inscriptions to the End of the Fifth Century* B.C. Oxford, 1969.

Melville-Jones, John R. "Greek Coin Names in *-phoros.*" *University of London Institute of Classical Studies Bulletin* 21 (1974): 55–74.

Mendoni, Lina G. "Ἀρχαιολογικὲς ἔρευνες στὴν Κέα: Ἀρχαῖα Καρθαῖα." *Arkhaiognosia* 4 (1985–86): 149–84.

Meritt, Benjamin D. "Athenian Archons 347/6–48/7 B.C." *Historia* 26 (1977): 161–91.

———. "Greek Inscriptions." *Hesperia* 5 (1936): 355–441.

———. "Greek Inscriptions." *Hesperia* 30 (1960): 1–77.

———. "Three Attic Inscriptions." *AJP* 66 (1945): 234–42.

Merker, Irwin L. "The Ptolemaic Officials and the League of the Islanders." *Historia* 19 (1970): 141–60.

Meyer, P. M. *Das Heerwesen der Ptolemäer und Römer in Aegypten.* Leipzig, 1900.

Michell, H. "The Impact of Sudden Accessions of Treasure upon Prices and Real Wages." *Canadian Journal of Economics and Political Science* 12 (1946): 1–17.

Migeotte, Léopold. *L'Emprunt public dans les cités grecques.* Québec and Paris, 1984.

Molinier, Sylvain. *Les 'Maisons sacrées' de Délos au temps de l'indépendance de l'île, 315–166/5 av. J.-C.* Paris, 1914.

Morelli, Donato. "Gli stranieri in Rodi." *Studi classici ed orientali* 5 (1956): 126–90.

Moretti, Luigi. "Chio e la lupa capitolina." *Rivista di filologia e di istruzione classica* 108 (1980): 33–54.

———. "Il problema del grano e del denaro." In *Storia e civiltà dei Greci,* vol. 4, *La società ellenistica,* pt. 8, *Economia, diritto, religione,* eds. Luigi Moretti et al., 354–74. Milan, 1977.

Moritz, L. A. *Grain Mills and Flour in Classical Antiquity.* Oxford, 1958.

Mossé, Claude. *La Fin de la démocratie athénienne.* Paris, 1962.

———. "The 'World of the *Emporium*' in the Private Speeches." In *Trade in the Ancient Economy,* eds. Peter Garnsey, Keith Hopkins, and C. R. Whittaker, 53–63. Berkeley, 1983.

Mulliez, Dominique. "Notes sur le transport du bois." *BCH* 106 (1982): 107–18.

Murray, Oswyn, and Simon Price, eds. *The Greek City from Homer to Alexander.* Oxford, 1990.

Musti, Domenico. *L'Economia in Grecia.* Rome and Bari, 1981.

Neesen, Lutz. "Die griechische Polis—nur ein Import- und Konsumzentrum?" *MBAH* 4.1 (1985): 49–66.

Neeve, P. W. de. "The Price of Agricultural Land in Roman Italy and the Problem of Economic Rationalism." *Opus* 4 (1985): 77–110.

Niese, B. *Geschichte der griechischen und makedonischen Staaten seit der Schlacht bei Chaeronea.* 3 vols. Gotha, 1893–1903.

Nigdelis, P. M. *Πολίτευμα και κοινωνία των πόλεων των Κυκλάδων κατά την ελληνιστική και αυτοκρατορική επόχη.* Thessaloniki, 1990.

Nikolaou, Nicos. "Le Cochon d'Edesse." *REG* 98 (1985): 147–52.

Nixon, Lucia, and Simon Price. "The Size and Resources of Greek Cities." In *The Greek City,* 137–70. Oxford, 1990.

Ober, Josiah. *Fortress Attica: Defense of the Athenian Land Frontier. Mnemosyne* suppl. 84. Leiden, 1985.

Olshausen, Eckart. *Prosopographie der hellenistischen Königsgesandten. Teil I: von Triparadeisos bis Pydna.* Studia Hellenistica, 19. Louvain, 1974.

Ormerod, H. A. *Piracy in the Ancient World.* Liverpool, 1924.

Orth, Wolfgang. *Königlicher Machtanspruch und städtische Freiheit.* Münchener Beiträge zur Papyrusforschung und Antiken Rechtsgeschichte, 71. Munich, 1977.

Osborne, Michael J. "Kallias, Phaidros and the Revolt of Athens in 287 B.C." *ZPE* 35 (1979): 181–94.

Osborne, Robin. "Buildings and Residence on the Land in Classical and Hellenistic Greece: the Contribution of Epigraphy." *BSA* 80 (1985): 119–28.

———. *Classical Landscape with Figures.* London, 1987.

———. "'Is It a Farm?' The Definition of Agricultural Sites and Settlements in Ancient Greece." In *Agriculture in Ancient Greece: Proceedings of the Seventh International Symposium at the Swedish Institute at Athens, 16–17 May, 1990,* ed. Berit Wells, 21–25. Skrifter Utgivna av Svenska Institutet i Athen, 4°, 42. Stockholm, 1992.

———. "Land Use and Settlement in Classical and Hellenistic Keos: The Epigraphic Evidence." In *Landscape Archaeology as Long-term History: Northern Keos in the Cycladic Islands,* ed. J. F. Cherry, J. L. Davis, and E. Mantzourani, 319–25. Los Angeles, 1991.

———. "Social and Economic Implications of the Leasing of Land and Property in Classical and Hellenistic Greece." *Chiron* 18 (1988): 279–323.

Panessa, Giangiacomo. "L'*Endeia sitou* di Entella e le carestie nel mondo greco." *ASNP* 12 (1982): 905–15.

Papageorgiou-Venetas, Alexandre. *Délos: Recherches urbaines sur une ville antique.* Munich and Berlin, 1981.

Papalas, Anthony J. *Ancient Icaria.* Wauconda, Ill., 1992.

———. "Pramnian Wine and the Wine of Icaria." *Platon* 35–36 (1982–83):49–54.

Pares, Richard. *Yankees and Creoles: Trade between North America and the West Indies before the American Revolution.* Cambridge, Mass., 1956.

Paris, J. "Contributions à l'étude des ports antiques du monde grec: II. Les Etablissements maritimes de Délos." *BCH* 40 (1916):5–73.

Parker, Robert. *Miasma: Pollution and Purification in Early Greek Religion.* Oxford, 1983.

Parkin, Tim G. *Demography and Roman Society.* Baltimore, 1992.

Parsons, James J. "The Acorn-Hog Economy of the Oak Woodlands of Southwestern Spain." *Geographical Review* 52 (1962):211–35.

Paton, W. R. and E. L. Hicks. *The Inscriptions of Cos.* Oxford, 1891.

Pečírka, Jan. "Homestead Farms in Classical and Hellenistic Greece." In *Problèmes de la terre en Grèce ancienne,* ed. M. I. Finley, 113–47. Paris, 1973.

Peek, Werner. "Griechische Inschriften." *Ath. Mitt.* 59 (1934):35–80.

———. *Inschriften aus dem Asklepieion von Epidauros.* Abhandlungen der Leipzig Akademie, 60.2. Berlin, 1969.

Perlin, John. *A Forest Journey: The Role of Wood in the Development of Civilization.* New York, 1989.

Petropoulou, Angeliki. *Beiträge zur Wirtschafts- und Gesellschaftsgeschichte Kretas in hellenistischer Zeit.* Europäische Hochschulschriften, 3d ser., vol. 240. Frankfurt am Main, 1985.

Picard, Olivier. *Chalcis et la confédération eubéenne: Etude de numismatique et d'histoire (IVe–Ier siècle). BEFAR* 234. Paris, 1979.

Plassart, André. "Fouilles de Délos." *BCH* 40 (1916):145–256, 353–56, 359–60.

———. "Inscriptions de Delphes: La Liste des théorodoques." *BCH* 45 (1921):1–85.

Pleket, Henri Willy. *Epigraphica.* Vol. 1, *Texts on the Economic History of the Greek World.* Textes Minores 31. Leiden, 1964.

———. "Urban Elites and the Economy in the Greek Cities of the Roman Empire." *MBAH* 3.1 (1984):3–36.

Polanyi, Karl. *The Livelihood of Man.* Ed. Harry W. Pearson. New York, 1977.

Préaux, Claire. *Le Monde hellénistique: La Grèce et l'Orient de la mort d'Alexandre à la conquête romaine de la Grèce (323–146 av. J.-C.).* 2 vols. Paris, 1978.

Price, M. J. "The Larissa, 1968 Hoard (*IGCH* 237)." In *Kraay-Mørkholm Essays: Numismatic Studies in Memory of C. M. Kraay and O. Mørkholm,* 233–43. Louvain-la-Neuve, 1989.

Pritchett, W. Kendrick. "The Attic Stelai." *Hesperia* 22 (1953):225–99, 25 (1956) 178–328.

Pritchett, W. Kendrick, and B. D. Meritt. *The Chronology of Hellenistic Athens.* Cambridge, Mass. 1940.

Pulak, Çemal, and Rhys F. Townsend. "The Hellenistic Shipwreck at Serçe Limani, Turkey: Preliminary Report." *AJA* 91 (1987): 31–49.

Rackham, Oliver. "Ancient Landscapes." In *Greek City,* 85–111.

———. "Land-Use and the Native Vegetation of Greece." In *Archaeological Aspects of Woodland Ecology,* eds. Martin Bell and Susan Limbrey, 177–97. BAR International Series, 146. London, 1982.

Rackham, Oliver, and Jennifer A. Moody. "Terraces." In *Agriculture in Ancient Greece. Proceedings of the Seventh International Symposium at the Swedish Institute at Athens, 16–17 May, 1990,* ed. Berit Wells, 123–30. Skrifter Utgivna av Svenska Institutet i Athen, 4°, 42. Stockholm, 1992.

Rathbone, Dominic W. *Economic Rationalism and Rural Society in Third-Century* A.D. *Egypt: The Heroninos Archive and the Appianus Estate.* Cambridge, 1991.

———. "The Grain Trade and Grain Shortages in the Hellenistic World." In *Trade and Famine in Classical Antiquity,* eds. Peter Garnsey and C. R. Whittaker, 45–55. Cambridge Philological Society, suppl. vol. 8. Cambridge, 1983.

———. "The Grain Trade in the Hellenistic East." In *Eighth International Economic History Congress, Budapest, 1982, ser. B12: Trade in Staples in Antiquity (Greece and Rome),* org. P. Garnsey and C. R. Whittaker, 44–51. Budapest, 1982.

Reekmans, Tony. "The Ptolemaic Copper Inflation." *Studia Hellenistica* 7 (1951): 61–118.

Reger, Gary. "Apollodorus of Cyzicus and His Delian Garden." *GRBS* 32 (1991): 229–37.

———. "Athens and Tenos in the Early Hellenistic Age." *CQ* 42 (1992): 365–83.

———. The Date and Historical Significance of *IG* XII 5.714 of Andros." *Hesperia,* forthcoming.

———. "The Date of the Battle of Kos." *AJAH* 10 (1985 [1993]): 155–77.

———. "The Delian ΧΩΜΑ." *ZPE* 74 (1988): 29–30.

———. "The Family of Balakros son of Nikanor, the Makedonian, on Delos." *ZPE* 89 (1991): 151–54.

———. "The Public Purchase of Grain on Independent Delos (314–167 B.C.)." *Classical Antiquity* 12 (1993): 300–34.

———. "The Political History of the Kyklades: 260–200 B.C.," *Historia* 43 (1994): 32–69.

———. "Private Property and Private Loans on Independent Delos (314–167 B.C.)." *Phoenix* 46 (1992): 322–41.

———. "Some Boiotians in the Hellenistic Kyklades." In *Proceedings of the VII*[th] *International Conference on Boiotian Studies.* Amsterdam, forthcoming.

———. "Two Estates of Delian Apollo on Mykonos: I.D. 452 + 467." *Hesperia* 63 (1994): 105–10.

Reger, Gary, and Martha Risser. "Coinage and Federation on Hellenistic Keos." In *Landscape Archaeology as Long-term History: Northern Keos in the Cycladic Islands,* eds. J. F. Cherry, J. L. Davis, and E. Mantzourani, 305–17. Monumenta Archaeologica, 16. Los Angeles, 1991.

Renfrew, Colin. "Polity and Power: Interaction, Intensification and Exploitation." In *Island Polity,* 264–90.

Renfrew, Colin, and Malcolm Wagstaff, eds. *An Island Polity: The Archaeology of Exploitation in Melos.* Cambridge, 1982.

Rey-Coquais, Jean-Paul. "Une Prétendue 'Dynastie' syrienne dans la Délos hellénistique." *Mélanges Beyrouth* 37 (1960–61): 249–54.

Richter, G. M. A. "Silk in Greece." *AJA* 33 (1929): 27–33.

Rigsby, K. J. "Bacchon the Nesiarch on Delos." *AJP* 101 (1980): 194–96.

Robert, Louis. *Collection Froehner: I. Inscriptions grecques.* Paris, 1936.

———. "Documents d'Asie Mineure: XI. Une fête de Cyzique et un oracle de Delphes à Délos et à Delphes." *BCH* 102 (1978): 460–77. =*Documents d'Asie Mineure,* 156–73. *BEFAR* 239*bis.* Paris, 1987.

———. *Etudes de numismatique grecque.* Paris, 1951.

———. "Inscriptions d'Athènes et de la Grèce Centrale." *AE* 1969 [1970]: 1–58.

———. *Noms indigènes dans l'Asie-Mineure gréco-romaine.* Bibliothèque archéologique et historique de l'Institut français d'archéologie d'Istanbul, 12. Paris, 1963.

———. *Opera minora selecta: Epigraphie et antiquités grecques,* vols. 1, 6, and 7. Amsterdam, 1969, 1989, 1990.

———. "Sur un décret des Korésiens au Musée de Smyrne." *Hellenica* 11–12 (1960): 132–76.

Robert, Louis, and Jean Robert. *Claros I: Décrets hellénistiques.* Paris, 1989.

Roebuck, Carl. "A Note on Messenian Economy and Population." *CP* 40 (1945): 149–65.

Roesch, Paul. "Notes d'épigraphie béotienne." *Rev. Phil.* 39 (1965): 252–65.

———. *Thespies et la confédération béotienne.* Paris, 1965.

Rostovtzeff, Michael. "Alexandrien und Rhodos." *Klio* 30 (1937): 1–7.

———. "The Hellenistic World and Its Economic Development." *AHR* 41 (1935–36): 231–52.

———. "Rhodes, Delos, and Hellenistic Commerce." In *Cambridge Ancient History*[1], vol. 8, *Rome and the Mediterranean,* eds. S. A. Cook, F. E. Adcock, and M. P. Charlesworth, 619–67. Cambridge, 1930.

———. *The Social and Economic History of the Hellenistic World.* 3 vols. Oxford, 1941.

Rougement, Georges. "Amorgos colonie de Samos?" In *Les Cyclades,* 131–34, 236–39. Paris, 1983.

Roussel, Pierre. *Délos colonie athénienne. BEFAR* 111. Paris, 1916. Reprint, with new material, 1987.

———. "La Population de Délos à la fin du IIe siècle avant J.-C." *BCH* 55 (1931):438–49.

———. Review of *Choix d'inscriptions de Délos,* by F. Durrbach. *Journal des Savants* 22 (1924):103–16.

Royal Statistical Society. *Food Supplies and Population Growth.* London, 1963.

Runnels, Curtis N., and Tjeerd H. van Andel. "The Evolution of Settlement in the Southern Argolid: An Economic Explanation." *Hesperia* 56 (1987):303–34.

Ruppel, Walter. "Zur Verfassung und Verwaltung der amorgischen Städte." *Klio* 21 (1927):313–39.

Ruschenbusch, Eberhard. "Getreideerträge in Griechenland in der Zeit von 1921 bis 1938 n. Chr. als Maßstab für die Antike." *ZPE* 72 (1988): 141–53.

———. "I.G. XII 5 609: Eine Bürgerliste von Iulis und Koresia auf Keos." *ZPE* 48 (1982):175–88.

———. "Modell Amorgos." In *Aux origines de l'Hellénisme: La Crète et la Grèce. Hommage à Henri van Effenterre,* 265–69. Paris, 1984.

———. "Die Zahl der griechischen Staaten und Arealgrösse und Bürgerzahl der 'Normalpolis.'" *ZPE* 59 (1985):253–63.

———. "Zur Wirtschafts- und Sozialstruktur der Normalpolis." *ASNP* 13 (1983):171–94.

Sacco, Guilia. "Su alcuni etnici di stranieri in Rodi." *Rendiconti Lincei* 35 (1980): 517–28.

Ste. Croix, G. E. M. de. "Greek and Roman Accounting." In *Studies in the History of Accounting,* eds. A. C. Littleton and B. S. Yamey, 14–74. London, 1956.

Sallares, Robert. *The Ecology of the Ancient Greek World.* Ithaca, N.Y., 1991.

Saloni, M. Ἱστορία τῆς Τήνου. Athens, 1888.

Samuel, Alan. *Greek and Roman Chronology: Calendars and Years in Classical Antiquity.* Handbuch der Altertumswissenschaft, section 1, pt. 7. Munich, 1972.

Sanders, Guy D. R. "Reassessing Ancient Populations." *BSA* 79 (1984): 251–62.

Sandy, D. Brent. *The Production and Use of Vegetable Oils in Ptolemaic Egypt. BASP* suppl. 6. Atlanta, 1989.

Sarikakis, Th. Ch. "Commercial Relations between Chios and other Greek Cities in Antiquity." In *Chios: A Conference at the Homereion in Chios,*

1984, eds. John Boardman and C. E. Vaphopoulou-Richardson, 121–31. Oxford, 1986.

———. Χιακὴ Προσωπογραφία. Athens 1989.

Sarpaki, Anaya. "The Palaeoethnobotanical Approach: The Mediterranean Triad, or Is It a Quartet?" In *Agriculture in Ancient Greece: Proceedings of the Seventh International Symposium at the Swedish Institute at Athens, 16–17 May, 1990*, ed. Berit Wells, 61–75. Skrifter Utgivna av Svenska Institutet i Athen, 4°, 42. Stockholm, 1992.

Sauciuc, Theophil. *Andros: Untersuchungen zur Geschichte und Topographie der Insel.* Sonderschriften der Österreichischen Archäologischen Instituts in Wien, 8. Vienna, 1914.

Schaps, David. "When Is a Piglet Not a Piglet?" *JHS* 111 (1991): 208–09.

Schmitt, Hatto H. *Die Verträge der griechisch-römischen Welt von 338 bis 200 v. Chr.* Vol. 3 of *Die Staatsverträge des Altertums.* Munich, 1969.

Schulhof, Emile. "Fouilles de Délos éxécutées aux frais de M. le Duc de Loubat: Inscriptions financières (1904 et 1905)." *BCH* 32 (1908): 5–132.

Seager, Robin. "Lysias against the Corndealers." *Historia* 15 (1966): 172–84.

Shear, T. Leslie, Jr. *Kallias of Sphettos and the Revolt of Athens in 286 B.C. Hesperia* suppl. 17. Princeton, 1978.

Sherwin-White, A. N. *Roman Foreign Policy in the East, 168 B.C. to A.D. 1.* Norman, Okla., 1983.

Sherwin-White, Susan. *Ancient Cos: An Historical Study from the Dorian Settlement to the Imperial Period.* Hypomnemata, 51. Göttingen, 1978.

Sherwin-White, Susan, and Amélie Kuhrt. *From Samarkhand to Sardis: A New Approach to the Seleucid Empire.* Hellenistic Culture and Society, 13. Berkeley, 1993.

Shimron, Benjamin. *Late Sparta: The Spartan Revolution, 243–146 B.C. Arethusa* monograph 3. Buffalo, N.Y., 1972.

Shipley, Graham. *A History of Samos, 800–188 B.C.* Oxford, 1987.

Sifakis, Gregory M. "Notes on Delian Inscriptions." *BCH* 92 (1968): 486–92.

Simonson, Gustave. *A Greek Grammar: Syntax.* London, 1911.

Sippel, Donald V. "The Meeting Place of the Rhodian Nesiotic League." *Ancient World* 13 (1986): 35–40.

———. "A Reward for Athens, a Punishment for Rhodes?" *Ancient World* 12 (1985): 97–104.

Slot, B. J. *Archipelagus turbatus: Les Cyclades entre colonisation latine et occupation ottomane, c. 1500–1718.* Uitgaven van het Nederlands historisch-archaeologisch Instituut te Istanbul. 2 vols. Istanbul, 1982.

Smith, D. R. "The Function and Origins of Hieropoioi." Diss., University of Pennsylvania, 1968.

Snider, G. L. "Hesiod's Sailing Season (*W & D* 663–665)." *AJAH* 3 (1978): 129–33.

Snodgrass, Anthony. *An Archaeology of Greece: The Present State and*

Future Scope of a Discipline. Sather Classical Lectures, 53. Berkeley, 1987.

———. "Survey Archaeology and the Rural Landscape of the Greek City." In *The Greek City,* 113–36.

Stanley, Phillip V. "*Agoranomoi* and *Metronomoi:* Athenian Market Officials and Regulations." *Ancient World* 2 (1979): 13–19.

Stefan, Alexandra. "Die Getreidekrisen in den Städten an den westlichen und nördlichen Küsten des Pontos Euxeinos in der hellenistischen Zeit." In *Hellenische Poleis: Krise, Wandlung, Wirkung,* ed. Elisabeth Charlotte Welskopf, II.648–63. Berlin, 1974.

Strauss, Barry S. *Athens after the Peloponnesian War: Class, Faction and Policy, 403–386 B.C.* Ithaca, N.Y., 1986.

Strubbe, J. H. M. "The Sitonia in the Cities of Asia Minor under the Principate (II)." *EA* 13 (1989): 99–122.

Sutton, S. B. "Population, Economy, and Settlement in Post-Revolutionary Keos: A Cultural Anthropological Study." In *Landscape Archaeology,* 383–402.

Svoronos, J. N. Τὰ νομίσματα τοῦ κρατοῦς τῶν Πτολεμαίκων. Athens, 1904.

Tarn, W. W. *Antigonos Gonatas.* Oxford, 1913.

———. "The Social Question in the Third Century." In *The Hellenistic Age: Aspects of Hellenistic Civilization,* ed. J. B. Bury, 119–26. London, 1923.

Tournefort, J. Pitton de. *A Voyage into the Levant.* 3 vols. London, 1741.

Tozer, Henry Fanshawe. *The Islands of the Aegean.* Oxford, 1890.

Transier, Werner. *Samiaka: Epigraphische Studien zur Geschichte von Samos in hellenistischer und römischer Zeit.* Mannheim, 1985.

Tréheux, Jacques. "Les Dernières Années de Délos sous le protectorat des amphictions." In *Mélanges d'archéologie et d'histoire offerts à Charles Picard,* 1008–1032. *Rev. Arch.* 31/32 (1948).

———. "Un Document Nouveau sur le *Néôrion* et le *Thesmophorion* à Délos." *REG* 99 (1986): 293–317.

———. "Etudes critiques sur les inventaires de l'independance délienne." Diss., Paris, 1959.

———. "Etudes d'épigraphie délienne: II. Le Sens de l'expression ΤΟ ʾΕΠΑΝΑΒΛΗΘΕΝ dans les comptes déliens et la date de la Hiéra Syggraphe." *BCH* 68–69 (1944–45): 284–95.

———. "L'*Hiéropoion* et les *oikoi* du sanctuaire à Délos." In *Stemmata: Mélanges de philologie, d'histoire et d'archéologie grecques offerts à Jules Labarbe,* eds. Jean Servais, Tony Hackens, and Brigitte Servais-Soyez, 377–90. Liège and Louvain-la-Neuve, 1987.

———. "Les Hiéropes déliens de 171 avant J.-C." *BCH* 109 (1985): 483–97.

———. *Inscriptions de Délos: Index,* vol. 1, *Les Etrangers, à l'exclusion des Athéniens de la clérouchie et des Romains.* Paris, 1992.

———. "Koinon." *REA* 89 (1987):39–46.

———. "Notes de lecture." *BCH* 110 (1986):425–32.

———. "Une Nouvelle Lecture des inventaires d'Apollon à Délos." In *CICG* 29–35.

———. "Observations sur l'Amphictyonie attico-délienne." *EAC* 5 (1976) 87–95.

———. "Le Règlement de Samothrace sur le fonds d'achat du blé." *BCH* 110 (1986):419–23.

———. "Sur la hiéra syngraphè de l'indépendance à Délos," *Mus. Hel.* 48 (1991): 248–51.

———. "Sur le *Néôrion* à Délos." *CRAI* 1987: 168–84.

Tzortopoulos, P. "Non-urban Consumption Patterns in Greece: An Analysis of the 1963–1964 Household Budgets." Ph.D. diss., London, 1969.

U.S. Department of Commerce. Environmental Science Services Administration. *World Weather Records, 1951–1960.* Vol. 2, *Europe.* Washington, D.C., 1966.

U.S. Department of Commerce. National Oceanic and Atmospheric Administration. *World Weather Records, 1951–1960.* Vol. 2, *Europe.* Washington, D.C., 1987.

———. *World Weather Records, 1961–1970.* Vol. 2, *Europe.* Washington, D.C., 1979.

———. *World Weather Records, 1971–1980.* Vol. 2, *Europe.* Washington, D.C., 1987.

U.S. Department of Labor. Bureau of Labor Statistics. *BLS Handbook of Methods.* Vol. 2, *The Consumer Price Index.* Bulletin 2134-2. Washington, D.C., 1984.

Urban, Ralf. *Wachstum und Krise des achäischen Bundes: Quellenstudien zur Entwicklung des Bundes von 280 bis 222 v. Chr. Historia* Einzelschrift 35. Wiesbaden, 1979.

Valavanis, Panos. "Les Amphores panathénaïques et le commerce athénien de l'huile." In *Recherches sur les amphores grecques, BCH* suppl. 13, 453–60. Paris, 1986.

Vallois, René. *L'Architecture hellénique et hellénistique à Délos jusqu'à l'éviction des Déliens (166 Av. J.-C.),* vol. 1, *Les Monuments,* vol. 2, *Grammaire historique de l'architecture délienne.* Paris, 1944, 1966–1978.

———. *Le Portique de Philippe. EAD* 7, pt. 1. Paris, 1923.

———. "Les Strophes mutilées du péan de Philodamos." *BCH* 55 (1931): 241–364.

Vial, Claude. *Délos indépendante (314–167 avant J.-C.): Etude d'une communauté civique et de ses institutions. BCH* suppl. 10. Paris, 1984.

———. "Les Sources de revenues des Déliens à l'époque hellénistique." In *L'Origine des richesses dépensées dans la ville antique,* ed. Philippe Leveau, 47–53. Aix-en-Provence and Marseille, 1985.

Vita-Finzi, Claudio. *The Mediterranean Valleys: Geological Changes in Historical Times.* Cambridge, 1969.

Wagstaff, Malcolm, and Siv Augustson. "Traditional Land Use." In *An Island Polity: The Archaeology of Exploitation in Melos,* eds. Colin Renfrew and Malcolm Wagstaff, 106–33. Cambridge, 1982.

Wagstaff, Malcolm, Siv Augustson, and Clive Gamble. "Alternative Subsistence Strategies." In *An Island Polity: The Archaeology of Exploitation in Melos,* eds. Colin Renfrew and Malcolm Wagstaff, 172–80. Cambridge, 1982.

Wagstaff, Malcolm, and John F. Cherry. "Settlement and Population Change." In *An Island Polity: The Archaeology of Exploitation in Melos,* eds. Colin Renfrew and Malcolm Wagstaff, 136–55. Cambridge, 1982.

———. "Settlement and Resources." In *An Island Polity: The Archaeology of Exploitation in Melos,* eds. Colin Renfrew and Malcolm Wagstaff, 246–63. Cambridge, 1982.

Wagstaff, Malcolm, and Clive Gamble. "Island Resources and Their Limitations." In *An Island Polity: The Archaeology of Exploitation in Melos,* eds. Colin Renfrew and Malcolm Wagstaff, 95–105. Cambridge, 1982.

Walbank, F. W. *Aratos of Sicyon.* Cambridge, 1933.

———. *A Historical Commentary on Polybius.* 3 vols. Oxford, 1957–79.

———. "Sea-power and the Antigonids." In *Philip II, Alexander the Great, and the Macedonian Heritage,* eds. W. Lindsay Adams and Eugene N. Borza, 213–36. Washington, D.C., 1982.

Welles, C. B. "New Texts from the Chancery of Philip V of Macedonia and the Problem of the 'Diagramma.'" *AJA* 42 (1938): 245–60.

———. *Royal Correspondence in the Hellenistic Period.* London, 1934.

Wells, Berit, ed. *Agriculture in Ancient Greece: Proceedings of the Seventh International Symposium at the Swedish Institute at Athens, 16–17 May, 1990.* Skrifter Utgivna av Svenska Institutet i Athen, 4°, 42. Stockholm, 1992.

Wersch, H. J., van. "The Agricultural Economy." In *The Minnesota Messenia Expedition: Reconstructing a Bronze Age Environment,* eds. W. A. McDonald and G. R. Rapp, 177–87. Minneapolis, 1972.

Whitelaw, T. M. "The Ethnoarchaeology of Recent Rural Settlement and Land Use in Northwest Keos." In *Landscape Archaeology,* 403–54. Los Angeles, 1991.

Whitelaw, T. M., and J. L. Davis. "The *polis* Center of Koressos." In *Landscape Archaeology,* 265–81. Los Angeles, 1991.

Whittaker, C. R. "La Cliometria e lo storico." *Opus* 5 (1986): 127–32.

Wilhelm, Adolf. *Attische Urkunden III.* Akademie der Wissenschaften in Wien, Phil.-hist. Kl., Sitzungsberichte, 202, pt. 5. Vienna and Leipzig, 1925.

Will, Edouard. *Histoire politique du monde hellénistique (323–30 av. J.-C.)*². Annales de L'Est, 30. 2 vols. Nancy, 1979, 1982.

———. *Le Dodekatheon. EAD* 22. Paris, 1955.

Will, Elizabeth Lyding. "Shipping Amphoras as Economic Indicators." *Rei cretorice romanae fautorum Acta* 26 (1987): 71–77.

Willetts, R. F. *Aristocratic Society in Ancient Crete.* London, 1955.

Wilski, P. *Klimatologische Beobachtungen aus Thera.* Vol. 4, *Thera: Untersuchungen, Vermessungen und Ausgrabungen in den Jahren 1895–1902,* ed. F. Hiller von Gaertringen. Berlin, 1902.

Wittenburg, Andreas. "Olivenanbau im Zenon-Archiv." In *Producción y comercio del aceite en la antigüedad,* 501–14. Madrid, 1983.

———. "Zur Qualität des Olivenöls in der Antike." *ZPE* 38 (1980): 185–89.

Wörrle, M. "Ägyptisches Getreide für Ephesos." *Chiron* 1 (1971): 325–40.

Zangger, Eberhard. "Prehistoric and Historic Soils in Greece: Assessing the Natural Resources for Agriculture." In *Agriculture in Ancient Greece: Proceedings of the Seventh International Symposium at the Swedish Institute at Athens, 16–17 May, 1990,* ed. Berit Wells, 13–18. Skrifter Utgivna av Svenska Institutet i Athen, 4°, 42. Stockholm, 1992.

Ziebarth, Erich. *Beiträge zur Geschichte des Seeraubs und Seehandels in alten Griechenland.* Abhandlungen aus dem Gebiet der Auslandkunde, 30, ser. A, Rechts- und Staatswissenschaft, 2. Hamburg, 1929.

———. "Delische Stiftungen." *Hermes* 32 (1917): 425–41.

———. "Die ἱερὰ συγγραφή von Delos." *Hermes* 61 (1926): 87–109.

———. "Zur Handelsgeschichte der Insel Rhodos." In *Mélanges Gustave Glotz,* 2: 909–24. Paris, 1932.

Zimmermann, Martin. "Die lykischen Häfen und die Handelswege im östlichen Mittelmeer: Bermerkungen zu PMich I 10." *ZPE* 92 (1992): 201–17.

Zolotas, Georgios. "Ἐπιγραφαὶ Χίου καὶ Ἐρύθρων ἀνέκδοτοι." *Athena* 20 (1908): 119–381.

General Index

Against Dionysodoros, (speech), 77–78, 264
Aitolians, as pirates, 44–46
Alexander the Great, colonizing activities, 157–58, 177
alphita: Delian production, 98–99; produced on estates of Apollo, 193–94; 197–201, 238
Amorgos: economy, 52; pirate raids against, 45; population estimates, 85
amphora handles as data, 163–64, 175, 266–67
Ancient Economy, The (Finley), 2–3, 5
Andros: economy, 52; grain production, 101; strategic position, 25–26
Antigonids: collect tribute in the Kyklades, 38; control Nesiotic League, 31–32, 37, 39, 253; establish garrisons in the Kyklades, 35; hegemony and operations in the Kyklades, 46, 53, 265
Antigonos Gonatas: hegemony and operations in the Kyklades, 18–19, 23–26, 29, 41, 66, 161–63; intervenes in Kykladian internal affairs, 40; rebellions against, 23–24
Antigonos Monophthalmos: dies, 32; hegemony and operations in the Kyklades, 16–17, 22, 25, 31–33, 39, 182, 192, 253, 265, 270; intervenes in Kykladian internal affairs, 39
Antiokhos III: hegemony and operations in the Kyklades, 27–28, 37, 66, 69, 182, 184–85
Apollo, traditional connection with Delos, 1
Apollodoros of Kyzikos, 65, 71
Apollo's estates. *See* estates of Apollo
Apollo's sanctuary on Delos. *See* Delian sanctuary
asylia arrangements, 43-44, 71, 121
Athens: collects tribute in the Kyklades, 37–38; controls Delos, 1, 3, 15, 59, 160–62, 165, 168, 250, 252–53; controls the Delian sanctuary and estates of Apollo, 160–61, 215–17, 238; dependence on trade, 159–60; exports olive oil, 159–62
Autosthenes (renter), 221–23

barley: Delian production, 96–99, 125; preponderant crop in the Kyklades, 87; price history, 11; staple Greek cereal crop, 52, 213
Black Sea, Delian trade relations with, 49, 52, 64, 67–69
Brunet, Michèle, on estates of Apollo, 201, 208, 214, 224

calendars, Greek, 13–14
Casson, Lionel, on cargo capacity of merchant ships, 140–41
charcoal. *See* firewood
commodities. *See alphita;* barley; firewood; grain; olive oil; pigs; wheat; wine
Coupry, Jacques, on Delian economy, 249
currencies and coinage, Greek, 12–13, 40, 267

Delian economy: ambiguity of economic data, 56–58, 131; in context of Kykladean regional economy, 3–4, 49–55, 58–60, 249, 261; decoupled from Kykladean regional economy, 270–71; in Hellenistic international trade network, 4, 46–47, 55; historical development during independence, 250–64; increase in personal wealth, 260; local markets, 51; local taxes imposed, 254–56; origins of participants, 58–63; and proxeny decrees, 64–65, 72–73, 258; relations with Black Sea, 49, 52, 64, 67–69; sanctuary's effect on, 52–53, 257, 271–73; small scale in Hellenistic economic context, 256–57; statistical analysis, 6–10
Delian population: caloric intake, 85–87, 92, 140; family patterns, 86; firewood consumption, 152; olive oil consumption, 138–41, 152, 164, 170–71; pork consumption, 151–52; social makeup, 86–87; trends, 83–84, 97
Delian sanctuary: accounting methods, 7–10, 12–13, 127; administration, 1, 7, 127; banking functions, 6, 9, 38, 60–61, 63, 111, 118, 160, 251, 254; effect on local economy, 52–53, 257, 271–73; effect on prices, 10–11, 56, 151–52; estates. *See* estates of Apollo; foreign contractors, 58–62; Hellenistic respect for, 57–58; international connections, 249; Kykladean contractors, 58–63, 251; military neutrality within, 28–29; ongoing building and repair program, 58–59; purchases commodities, 8–10, 56, 61–63, 69, 127–28; subsidizes public feasts, 129; wealth increased by rent defaults, 221, 225, 227, 239, 250
—non-agricultural buildings, 238–47; available rent data, 240–43; leasing methods, 239–41; rent trends, 244–47, 253, 258
Delos: arable land, 95; under Athenian control, 1, 3, 15, 59, 160–62, 165–68, 250, 252–53; calendar, 13–14; currency, 12–13; declared a free port, 267, 270; degree of self-sufficiency, 92, 184, 249, 272; foreign wine imports, 236–37, 259–60; foreigners living on, 58–63; government buys grain for public distribution, 111–113; grain consumption, 88–89, 93–95; grain cultivation methods, 95–96; grain production, 96, 99, 115, 119; grain trading center of the Kyklades, 53–54, 116–23, 126, 253–54, 258; impact of outside hegemony, 15; imports grain from Rheneia and Mykonos, 99–101; imports olive oil, 159–65, 170–71, 250; inadequate grain supply, 83; in Kykladic regional economic context, 3–4, 249; local political changes, 260–61; Naxian influence, 15; olive and olive oil production, 137–38, 144, 167–69; Phoenecian traders on, 56–57; population, 50–51; port activity, 253–54; prices on, 47, 55, 81–82; regulates importation of wood, 173–74, 245–46, 254–55, 258; relations with Egypt, 47; relations with Makedon, 47; retaliates against Athenian control, 161–62, 165, 217; Roman traders on, 55; strategic economic location, 49, 53;

traditional connection with Apollo, 1; transfer point for Ptolemaic grain trade, 116–17; water supply, 50; wine production, 235–37
Demetrios II of Makedon, war against Aitolians and Akhaians, 119–21, 126
Demetrios of Pharos, raids the Kyklades, 19, 27, 30, 44–45, 261, 263, 264
Demetrios Poliorketes: collects tribute in the Kyklades, 38; hegemony and operations in the Kyklades, 16–17, 22, 25–26, 29, 31–33, 36, 55, 162–63, 177–78, 182, 184, 192, 253, 266, 270
Dikaiarkhos, pirate raids in the Kyklades, 19, 24, 27, 44–45, 263, 266
Diodoros of Sicily: on eastern Aegean, 111; on Rhodian trade, 264
Diodorus of Sicily, on piracy, 44

economics, disjunction with politics in Hellenistic Greece, 269–70
economy. *See* Delian economy; Hellenistic economy; Kykladean regional economy
Egypt, grain production and prices, 124
epigraphic evidence: nature of, 7–8; statistical analysis, 6–10
estates, private, 50, 137; olive and olive oil production, 167; pig-raising on, 150–51, raise livestock, 167–68
estates of Apollo, 1, 6, 8, 50; *alphita* production, 193–94, 197–201; categorization by number of vines, 193–95, 200–3; competition between Athenians and Delians, 215–17, 250; crops produced, 193–97, 201; exploitation strategies, 189; lack firewood, 194, 206; lack of olive oil production, 127, 165, 169–70, 189, 196, 213; on Mykonos, 189; origins, 190; pig production, 197, 206–7; raise livestock, 167, 197; rental regulations. *See hiera syngraphe;* rental restricted to the aristocracy, 218–19, 229–30, 250–51; rented by foreigners, 59; on Rheneia, 189–90; wine production, 96, 193–94, 253, 259–60
—rents, 8–9, 51, 95–96, 128, 160, 175, 213–14; available data, 189–90; competitive bidding methods, 190–92, 215–20; correlation with *alphita* prices, 212–13, 238, 252; correlation with commodity prices, 195–97; correlation with livestock prices, 206–8; correlation with olive oil prices, 201–6, 213, 238, 252; correlation with wine prices, 194, 203, 209–12, 233–38; lack of correlation with firewood prices, 206; trends, 190–92, 196–97, 209–10, 212–15, 229–31, 234, 251–52, 260–61
Eumenes of Pergamon, 19–20, 37, 73

Finley, M. I., *The Ancient Economy,* 2–3, 5
firewood: limitations of data, 128–29; sources, 129–30, 143–44; storage and stockpiling, 143; tax income on sales, 174
—price history, 11, 56, 127–28, 206, 237, 244–46, 257–58; connected to pig prices, 176, 178, 181, 206; models and theories, 173–76; seasonal fluctuations, 141–44, 187–88; stable price trend, 145, 171–73, 251

Gallant, Thomas, on Hellenistic caloric intake, 86–87, 140
Glotz, Gustave, on Hellenistic trade, 47
goats. *See* livestock
grain: Delos as trading center in, 53–54, 116–23, 126, 253–54, 258; destroyed by war, 91; international market, 77–82; shortages, 90–91, 93, 98–99, 124–26; standard

grain, (*continued*). ration, 88–90, 139; storage and stockpiling, 92–93, 118. *See also alphita;* barley; wheat
—price history, 56, 78–80; correlation with olive oil prices, 205–6, 252
grain trade, importance in Hellenistic international trade network, 83
Greek cities, economic nature of, 4
Gyaros, 1

Heichelheim, Fritz, Hellenistic economic model, 47, 157–58, 177, 212, 250
Hellenic League, 30
Hellenistic economy: diverse nature, 2–3, 273, 275–76; modernizing vs. primitivizing view of, 2–3, 55–56, 166; as price-setting market, 2, 49, 53, 75–77, 79; Ptolemaic economic impact on, 267–69
Hellenistic international trade network, 4, 49, 268–69; importance of grain trade, 83; protectionist policies, 46–47
hiera syngraphe: defaults and seizures under, 220–25, 228–29, 246, 250; and estate rent trends, 229–31; impact, 215, 220–21, 227–29; motivations and provisions, 220, 223, 226–27, 231, 233, 238, 250
hieropoioi: administer the Delian sanctuary and estates of Apollo, 7–13, 96, 127, 167, 205, 214, 218–19, 237, 241; decennial estate inventories, 96, 137, 189, 192–93; prosecute rent defaulters, 220–30; purchase commodities for the Delian sanctuary, 127–31, 138, 148, 167

Island League. *See* Nesiotic League

Kallias of Sphettos, 64
Kassandros of Makedon, 17, 22
Kent, John, on estates of Apollo, 190, 193, 201, 206, 209–12, 220, 224, 232, 234
Keos: economy, 52; independent political arrangements, 43; pirate raids against, 45; population estimates, 85
Khians, on Delos, 62
Khremonidean War, 18, 23, 26, 33, 35, 38, 40, 268; effect on population, 108
Kleokritos, (rent guarantor), 221–23
Kleomenes of Naukratis, establishes international grain market, 77–79
Kretan Wars, 19, 181, 264, 266
Kretans, as pirates, 44–46, 262, 264
Krete: contact with independent Kyklades, 43–44; strategic position, 21, 23
Kykladean regional economy: cash flow problems, 60; Delian economy decoupled from, 270–71; Delian economy in context of, 49–55, 58–60, 249, 261; diverse nature, 49–50, 273; effect of weather on, 54–55; small scale of, 79
Kyklades: absence of outside hegemony, 41–47, 120, 126, 261–63, 269; Antigonid hegemony and operations, 16–17, 22, 25–26, 29, 31, 41, 66, 161–63, 182, 184–85, 253, 265, 270; arable land, 104–7; become economic unit under Nesiotic League, 165–66, 252–53, 269; conflicting currencies, 12; crop failures, 90–91, 93, 98–99, 102–4; decline in natural resources, 20; foreign intervention in internal affairs, 39–42; foreign military garrisons, 34–36, 40, 45–46, 181, 244, 263, 268, 272; grain production, 87, 98–99, 101–2, 105–8; impact of outside hegemony, 15–20; import grain from eastern Aegean, 109–11; independent contact with Krete, 43–44; Makedonian operations, 19–20, 24–25, 27, 30, 35, 45, 186; military struggle for, 16–20; olive and olive oil production, 141, 165–66; Persian control, 15; piracy

reemerges, 42, 44–46; piracy suppressed, 29–31; pirate raids in, 19, 24, 27, 44–45, 262–63, 266, 271; population trends, 108–9, 275; Ptolemaic hegemony and operations, 17–19, 24, 26, 30, 41, 53–67, 76, 109, 184–85, 247, 253, 265–66, 270; rainfall, 102–4; regular military obligations, 36–37; relations among islands, 46–47; Rhodian hegemony and operations, 18–20, 25–26, 41, 67–68, 163–64, 244–45, 263–66; Roman hegemony and operations, 15, 19–20, 27–28, 169, 186; strategic military and trade importance, 20–29, 35, 117; treaties with pirate groups, 44–46; tribute and taxes, 37–40

Larsen, J. A. O., study of Delian economy, 2, 250
livestock: Delian production, 167–68, 197; price history, 206–8, 259–60
Livelihood of Man, The (Polanyi), 2, 76–78

Makedonian Wars, 19, 27–30, 40, 124–25, 182, 244–45, 263
Marek, Christian, on proxeny decrees, 64, 71, 74–75
Massinissa, donation to Delian *sitonia* fund, 112–13
Melos, grain production, 101
Mykonos, grain production, 100–1, 119

Naxos: economy, 52; grain production, 101; influence in Delos, 15; pirate raids against, 45
Nesiotic League, 17–18, 20, 22, 26, 65, 74, 166, 237, 250, 253, 269–70; administrative bureaucracy, 31–34; Antagonids control, 31–32, 37; collects taxes in the Kyklades, 38; disintegrates, 44, 46; intervenes in Kykladian internal affairs, 39; organizes the Kyklades into an economic unit, 165–66, 252–53, 269; Ptolemies control, 32–33, 37; Rhodians control, 34–35, 37, 245

Oikonomikos, 47, 77–78
olive oil: Delian demand, 138–41, 152, 164, 170–71; limitations of data, 129; not produced on Delian estates, 96, 252; produced on Delos, 137–38; production cycles, 134–38, 167; production squeezed out by other commodities, 167–68
—price history, 10, 56, 81, 128, 201–6, 244, 259; correlation with grain prices, 205–6, 252; declining trend, 135–36, 138, 155–59, 175, 251; fluctuations connected to sailing season, 159; models and theories, 157–71; seasonal fluctuations, 132–41, 187–88
olive presscake as fuel, 144

Paros: economy, 52; grain production, 101
Perseus of Makedon, operations in the Kyklades, 28–29, 47, 265
Persia, controls the Kyklades, 15
Philip V of Makedon, operations in the Kyklades, 19–20, 24–25, 27, 30, 35, 45, 186, 244, 264
Phoenician traders, on Delos, 56–57
Phytalia (estate), 206–8, 223–24
pigs: limitations of data, 130–31; methods of raising, 179–80, 206; price-elastic demand fluctuations, 149–52, 187–88; production cycles, 148–49; prone to diseases, 145–48; raised on private estates, 150–51; special requirements for sacrifice, 148
—price history, 9–10, 128, 237–38, 244–45, 251, 257–58; connected to firewood prices, 176, 178, 181, 206; fluctuations connected to sailing season, 145–46; models and theories, 178–81
piracy: economic benefits, 30–31, 261–63; reemerges in the

piracy, (*continued*). Kyklades, 42, 44–46; suppressed in the Kyklades, 29–31
Polanyi, Aristotle Karl, *The Livelihood of Man*, 2, 76–78
Polemaios, operations in the Kyklades, 17, 22, 31, 36
politics, disjunction with economics in Hellenistic Greece, 269–70
Polybios, on piracy, 44–46
prices: effect of Delian sanctuary on, 10–11; effects of military operations on, 178, 181–88, 251
prices, long-term: analytical methods, 152–53; history, 47, 55, 81–82, 127; trends, 152–55
proxeny decrees, 56–57, 59, 62–63, 100, 182; assumptions regarding, 64–65, 67; changes in privileges granted, 73–74; and Delian economy, 64–65, 72–73, 258; granting citizenship, 70–71, 75; honoring Byzantines, 68–70; honoring Khians, 69–72; honoring piracy, 262–63; honoring Rhodians, 67–70; honoring Romans, 65, 69, 72; Marek on, 64, 71, 74–75; nature of, 63–64; political motivation, 65–66, 68, 70–73; privileges granted, 72–75; purposes, 65–67; religious motivation, 67, 68–73
Ptolemaios I, operations in the Kyklades, 17, 23, 25, 35, 265–66
Ptolemaios II, military operations, 184–85
Ptolemies: collect tribute in the Kyklades, 38; control Nesiotic League, 32–33, 37; economic impact on Hellenistic economy, 267–69; establish garrisons in the Kyklades, 35, 45–46; hegemony and operations in the Kyklades, 17–19, 24, 26, 30, 41, 53, 67, 76, 109, 117, 184, 247, 253, 265, 270; intervene in Kykladian internal affairs, 39, 117; trade with Rhodos, 264–65
Publius Cornelius Scipio, 65, 69

Rheneia, grain production, 99–100, 119
Rhodos: collects tribute in the Kyklades, 38–39; controls Nesiotic League, 34–35, 37; exports olive oil, 162–65; grain trading center, 54, 124; hegemony and operations in the Kyklades, 18–20, 25–26, 41, 46, 67–68, 163–64, 244–45, 263–66; intervenes in Kykladian internal affairs, 40, 45; trade war with Byzantion, 45; trade with Egypt, 264–65
Roman traders, on Delos, 55
Rome: declares Delos a free port, 267, 270; hegemony and operations in the Kyklades, 15, 19–20, 27–28, 169, 186; Rhodos and Pergamon ally with, 19–20, 27, 264
Rostovtzeff, Michael, on Delian economy, 75–76, 250
Ruschenbusch, Eberhard, on Greek population trends, 85, 97–98, 108

Sallares, Robert, on Greek population trends, 83–84
Samos, independent colonization, 42
sheep. *See* livestock
ships, merchant, cargo capacity, 140–41
sitonia fund for grain purchases, 111–14, 119, 122, 171, 237, 258
Social War, 15, 159
Sosilos (renter), 223
Sostratos of Knidos, 65, 71
Syrian Wars, 18–19, 183–85, 264–65

Telemnestos, dominates Delian politics, 261, 266
Tenians, on Delos, 62
Tenos, strategic position, 35, 40
Thera: pirate raids against, 45–46; strategic position, 19, 23, 35, 40

Therans, on Delos, 62
Tréheux, Jacques, on estates of Apollo, 213–17, 224

wages, uncertainty of, 9
weather, effect on Kykladean regional economy, 54–55
wheat: Delian production, 97, 99; increased demand in the Kyklades, 87
wine: price history, 56, 125, 157, 193–94, 209–12, 231, 233–38, 259–60; produced on estates of Apollo, 96, 193–94, 203, 209, 231, 253; production methods, 231–33

Index of Sources

I. ANCIENT AUTHORS

Aelian
16.32: 63n55, 268n46
[Aiskhines]
Ep. 1.1: 21n12, 54n21
Ep. 5.2: 162n74
Alkiphron
1.8: 31n39, 262
Amphis
CAF 2, p. 236, fr. 38: 180n112
Andokides
1.133–134: 256n11
Appian
Mak.
4: 24
4.1: 25n23
11.1: 154n56
11.2: 21n12
18.4: 28
Syr.
1: 158–59n64
1.1: 158–59n64, 213
13: 27n28
20: 27n29
22: 28n31
57: 82n118
Ps.-Aristeas
180: 18n6
Aristotle
Ath. pol.
51.4: 117n97, 121–22n113
De plant.
1.7: 135n22
Hist. anim.
8.6: 148n44
8.6.2: 180nn110, 111
8.21: 148n40
8.21.4: 180n111
Oik.
2.3a (1346b20): 256n14
2.33a (1352a16–23): 78n111
2.2.15a–17 (1348b1–49a3): 93
2.33e (1352b14–20): 78, 123n117
2.7 (1347a32–b2): 181n116
2.8 (1347b3–16): 181n116
2.23c (1350b4–7): 181n116
2.23d (1359b7–15): 181n116
2.24a (1350b15–16): 181n116
2.25a (1350b33–51a12): 181n116
Arrian
4.3.1: 158n63
4.16.3: 158n63
4.22.5: 158n63
7.20.3: 129n9
7.20.5: 129n9
Asklepiades of Samos
Anth. Pal. 5.44: 31n39, 262n25
Athen.
25f–34e: 234n94
67a: 137n24, 162n74
226a–b: 173n100
375a: 149n45
375a–e: 149n46
396d: 149n47

Ausonius
3.1.27: 93n31
Cato the Elder
De agr. cult.
11.1: 232n86
Cicero
Att.
9.9.4: 96n38
105.1: 21n12
Columella
1 praef. 20: 237n103
5.3.1–8: 232
7.9: 180n110
7.9.6: 180n111
7.9.7: 180
Q. Curtius
7.6.25–27: 158n63
7.10.15: 158n63
7.11.29: 158n63
Demosthenes
22.134: 161n70
22.167: 145n39
33.23: 54n21
[Demosthenes]
34.37: 78n110
35.50: 78n110
42.7: 129n9
42.9: 129n9
54.39: 149n47
56.3: 77–78, 264n33
56.3–13: 162n73
56.7–8: 123n116
56.10: 78
Dio Cassius
48.26.3–4: 182n118
Diodoros
5.51.3: 91n27
5.53.2: 91n27
5.82.1: 110
5.82.2–4: 111, 111n73
8.7.2: 147n39
12.58.3–4: 110n69
18.7.1: 158n63
18.25.5: 158n64
19.37.1: 117
19.62.9: 16, 17n1, 31, 31n40
19.77.3: 17n2, 22
20.19.2: 22
20.27.3: 17n2, 22
20.37: 17n2, 23n16, 25
20.37.1: 35
20.45–46: 17n2
20.45.1: 22
20.46.6: 22, 264n33
20.81–88: 162n75
20.81.2: 163, 182n119
20.81.4: 162 and n73, 264n33
20.82.5: 29n35, 180n119
20.83.1: 29n35
20.83.3: 163, 182n119
20.83.3–4: 29n35
20.83.4: 163, 176n105
20.84.2: 108
20.84.5: 163, 182n110
20.91–100.4: 162n75
20.93.2–3: 163, 182n119
20.93.5: 163
20.95.4: 163n76
20.96.1: 163
20.96.3: 163
20.97: 29n35
20.97.5–6: 163
20.98.1: 163
20.98.2: 163n76
20.99.2: 163
20.99.3: 163n76
20.110.4: 22, 29n35, 55n22
20.111.3: 22, 55n22
28.1.1: 19, 27
28.5: 25n23
29.24: 37n57
31.45: 30n38, 262
Dioskourides
1.77: 70n83
Etymologicum magnum
129: 62n50
Eupolis
CAF 1, fr. 453: 151n48
Frontinus
Strat 3.2.11: 280n5
Galen
De simp. med. temp.
11.872K: 137n24
Peri troph. dyn.
3.2: 149n46

Geoponica
9.17.1: 135n21
10.77: 169–70n91
Heniokh. (Kostel-Austin)
fr. 2: 149n47
Herakleides of Lembos (Dilts)
fr. 41: 129n9, 137n24
fr. 55: 91n27
Herodotos
1.133.1: 151n50
2.48: 149n47
3.57.2: 20
4.151: 91n27
6.56: 151n50
8.137.2: 151n50
Hesiod
Op.
663–65: 54n21
Hippokrates (Littré)
vol. 2, p. 492–95: 149n46
Hippon. (Bergk)
fr. 40: 149n47
Homer
Od.
14.5–22: 180n112
14.24–26: 180n112
14.409–12: 180n112
14.524–33: 180n112
Homeric Hymn to Apollo
14–18: 52n12
Hypereides
fr. 13: 161n70
Isaios
3.80: 152n53
Josephus
AJ
12.147–53: 158n64
Livy
31.15: 20, 24, 35n50
31.45.2–8: 20
31.45.2–13: 27, 245n119
33.18.5: 27, 55n22, 245
33.30.11: 245n119
33.44.8: 30, 263
34.32.18: 30, 263
34.35.9: 30, 263
34.36.3: 30, 263
35.43.3–4, 6: 27
35.47.5–6: 27n28
36.20.7: 27
36.21.1: 27
36.42.8: 28n31
36.43.1: 28n31
36.43.11: 28n31
37.13.11: 67n76
37.13.11–14.2: 28, 29–30n35
37.14.1–2: 67n76
37.15.6: 67n76
37.28.1–11: 29–30n35
Per.
40.3.7: 120n108
42.12.3–4: 21n12
42.13.7: 154n56
42.40.6: 154n56
42.42.4: 154n56
44.20: 143, 169n90, 173
44.28.2: 28
44.28.16: 29
44.29.1: 21, 29
44.29.3–4: 29, 53n13, 121
45.10.1: 29, 121
45.10.2: 21
Longus
Daph.
3.3: 180n112
Lykourgos
Leo.
14–15: 162n73
18: 162n73
Memnon, *FGrHist* 434
F 10–11: 183n120
Menandros
Epitr.
749–51: 152n53
Oribasios,
Coll. Med. Reliquae VI.1.1
2.63: 63n55
Pausanias
1.1.1: 25n25
3.23.3: 55n24
3.23.3–5: 186n125
4.4.6: 145n39
Phereklides
CAF I, p. 145, fr. 186: 180n112
Phrynikhos
CAF I, fr. 43: 151n48

Plato
  Rep.
    373c: 149n46
    378a: 149n47
Pliny the Elder
  Nat. hist.
    4.22: 52n10
    15.3: 135n21
    15.4: 135n21
    27.120.145: 149n46
Plutarch
  Ara.
    12: 24n21
    12.2–3: 35n50
    12.3: 129n9
    17.2: 24n20
    18.1–2: 24n20
  Dem.
    8.4: 22, 38
    8–15: 17n2
    10.1: 38
    15.1: 22
    23.5: 178n107
    30.2: 178n107
    33.5: 182n119
    33.6: 181
    46.4: 22
  Nik. 3.7: 190n1
  Per. 17.2–3: 21n12
  Sol. 24.1: 159n65
  Mor.
    295f–296b: 81n116
    328e: 82n118
    669f: 149n46
Pollux
    4.169: 279
Polyainos
    4.6.18: 29n35
    4.16.6: 163
    5.18: 18n5, 26
Polybios
    2.15.2–3: 149n46, 180n112
    2.66.6: 121
    4.3.1–5.10: 45n79
    4.3.10: 182n118
    4.16.2–4: 45n79
    4.16.4–6: 27
    4.16.6–8: 19, 27, 44n78
    4.19.8: 27, 44n78, 45n80
    4.25.1–4: 45n79
    4.38.4–5: 67, 118n101
    4.47.1: 19, 45–46
    4.71.11: 121
    5.23.2: 121
    5.34.7: 280n6
    5.63.12: 43n75
    5.65.7: 43n75
    5.90.5: 19, 45–46
    13.8.2: 30, 263
    14.5–15: 25n23
    14.24: 25n23
    16.1–12: 25n23
    16.24.4–9: 25n23
    16.26: 24
    18.2.2–4: 25n23
    18.44.4: 25n23
    18.54.8: 19, 27
    21.12.1: 29–30n35
    21.13–15: 69n82
    21.13.3: 66n67
    21.14: 66n67
    21.15.12: 66n67
    22.8.10: 263n30
    23.10.9–11: 120n108
    25.2: 37n57
    25.4.8–10: 21n12
    27.7.5: 37n57
    28.23.1: 67
    30.31.10: 267n43
    30.31.12: 55n24, 256n12
Schol. Apollonios Rhodios
  2.498–527a: 91n27
Sidonius
  Carm.
    22.170: 93n31
Steph. Byz.
  Ankyra: 183n120
Strabo
    10.5.3 (C485): 1, 52n10
    10.5.4 (C486): 21n12, 55n24, 84n6
    10.5.6 (C486): 275
    12.3.11 (C545): 37n57
    14.1.7 (C635): 31n39

14.2.24 (C660): 182n118
14.5.2 (C668–9): 55n24, 262
Theophrastos
Char.
3.3: 252
23.5: 252
23.8: 252
De caus. plant.
1.20.4: 135nn21–22
1.21.7: 129–30n9
3.11–12: 232n89
5.5.4: 169–70n91
6.8.1: 135n21
6.8.5: 135n21
6.19.3: 135n21
10.3: 232n89
Hist. plant.
1.11.4: 135n21
2.2.2: 129n9
3.16.3: 180n111
4.13.5: 135
5.3.4: 129–30n9
5.9.6: 129–30n9
9.20.5: 149n46
Thucydides
1.13.6: 190n1
3.104.2: 190n1
3.104.6: 190n1
Trogus
Prol.
26: 24n20
28: 263n30
Varro
Rust.
2.4.6: 130n11, 151n49, 180n111
Xenophon
Anab.
1.7.3: 224n63
7.85: 149n47

II. INSCRIPTIONS

A. EMENDED OR REREAD

ID
291b+ 83: 299
316.92: 305
98: 305
317.21: 339
338Aa19: 299
Aa35: 306
354.58: 294
62: 294
72: 294, 299
80: 305
80–81: 299
362A15: 336
366A102–3: 333
368.29: 333
372A76: 299
A84: 294
A92: 305
A95: 299
373B15–16: 333
396A67: 299
A69: 294, 299
A70: 305
A71: 294
A72: 299
406B80: 316
440A17–18: 294
A18–19: 305
A19–20: 294
A23–24: 294
442A189: 294
452.9: 306
456B11: 305
B11–12: 294
456B18 + 440A4: 300
456B23 + 440A9: 300
456B25–26 + 440A11–12: 294
456B26 + 440A12: 300
459.44: 305
45–46: 294
46–47: 294
50: 294
460t53–63: 305
t56: 305
460v12: 305
IG XI 2
144A30: 298
145.5: 304
147A3: 298
148.62: 130n12
152A8: 226
A12: 226

IG XI 2, (continued)
159A10: 304
A53–54: 117
162A7: 323
199A71: 293
B94: 343–44
200.2–3: 323
201A8: 317
204.7: 323
45–46: 298
56–57: 304
74–75: 298
219Ab49: 293
Ab54: 293
224A14: 325
A29: 306
A31: 293
226A30: 325
228.4–5: 304
287A58: 299
A82: 299
IG XI 4
511.7: 73n92
534: 74, 74n99
842: 74, 74n99
REG
99 (1986), 293–301, A30: 293

B. DATED

ID
503: 220, 281–83
IG XI 2
142: 298
147: 281–82
152: 225–26
165: 304
274: 298–99
275: 299
SEG
1.366: 279–80n4

C. QUOTED AND/OR TRANSLATED

BCH
78 (1954), 338–44, no. 14 (*SEG* 14.544): 20n9
line 13: 40n65
Choix
13: *see IG* XI 4.1036
43: *see IG* XI 4.691
47: *see IG* XI 4.680
48: *see IG* XI 4.666
50: *see IG* XI 4.1055
63: *see IG* XI 4.752
67: *see IG* XI 4.751
72: *see IG* XI 4.1114
Holleaux
II.74–75, lines 13–14, 17–18: 91 with 92n28
III.27–37, lines 2–4: 39
ID
98A24–25: 280
104.1–7: 161n70
104–8A15: 228
104–11 (*IG* II[2] 1638), A18–19, A20: 224n60, 216–17n35
290.11–12: 299
79: 14n32
291b9–10: 131
b20–21: 131
d5: 131
d33: 227, 227n73
d35: 227, 227n73
316.76–80: 131, 131n15
87: 131, 131n15
101: 131, 131n15
354.67: 295
356*bis*A16: 341
372A77: 305
400.2: 239n108
4–5: 342
7–8: 339
406B80–83: 316
440A38–39: 305
442A140: 342
A198: 305
D2–11: 240n111
461*bis*13: 305
503.33–34: 231
34–36: 220, 220n47
46–48: 220, 220n47
509.1: 173
13–14: 254–55
IG II[2]
222: 161, 161n70
844 (*SIG*[3] 535): 262, 262n28
1638: *see ID* 104–11

IG V 2
515.13–14: 91, 91n26
IG XI 2
130: 37n57
135.22–23: 227
26–27: 228
142.5–6: 226n68
144A13: 336
A14: 337
A83: 128
B78–81: 336
145.27: 282
43: 282
146A77: 61
147A18–19: 281–82
148.75–76: 254n7
151.4: 227n71
6: 227
152A3: 226
A5–6: 226
A7: 226
A8: 226
A9: 226
A10: 226
A12: 226
A14–15: 226
A16: 226
153.6–7: 148n42
8–9: 148
11: 304
154A41: 151n48
156A14: 219, 219n43
B16–20: 222n51
157A4–5: 225n65
158A12–13: 225n65
A15–16: 342
A16–17: 260n21, 284
A21: 241
A71–72: 89
159A53–54: 116, 116n93
A58: 277
161A18–19: 220
A22–23: 343
A125–31: 327
162A18: 222
A39–40: 239–40
199A50: 130n12
203A49: 128
A50: 304
C6–12: 340
224A21: 347
226A30: 325
287A22: 138
A32: 316
A68–69: 304
A74: 61
A113–114: 62
A129–131: 224
A136: 224n63
A137: 224n63
A139: 325
IG XI 4
566. 15: 32
595.3–6: 64
596.3–6: 27
623.5–12: 72
666 (*Choix*, 48): 119
680.3–5 (*Choix*, 47): 120
691.4–6 (*Choix*, 43): 71
5–6: 123
745.23–27: 72
750: 27n28
751.12–13 (*Choix*, 67): 28
752.3–5 (*Choix*, 63): 28, 34
5–6: 28n33
759.6: 74n100
776.14–15: 57n30
15–17: 57
789.6–7: 74n100
1036.2 (*Choix*, 13): 31
44: 38
45–46: 32n42
1049.6–7: 118, 118n100
1055.9–14 (*Choix*, 50): 122
1114.4–5 (*Choix*, 72): 258
1248.3–4: 61
IG XII 5
7.2: 40
541.1–2 + *BCH* 78 (1954): 336–38, no. 13 (*SEG* 14.543): 40, 40n62
658.30–31: 114n86
830.12–13: 40
1004.2, 4–5: 36
1010.6: 116

IG XII 5, (*continued*)
    1065.2, 4, 5–12: 39
    1066.2–3, 4: 38
IG XII 7
    11.6: 114
    36: 45, 45n79
    40.9: 116
    84: 70n86
    386.13–15 (*SIG*³ 521): 45, 45n79
    387: 45n79
    506.13–15 (*SIG*³ 390): 39
        16: 38
        57–61: 38
IG XII suppl.
    168.7: 31n41
IK 34 Mylasa
    602.17–20 (*SIG*³ 768): 182, 182n118
ISE
    1.7: 31n41
IvMag
    61.18–19 (*OGIS* 233): 158–59n64
IvPerg
    246.41: 117n97
JRS
    14 (1924), 178–79, no. 5, lines 4–5: 91n27
OGIS
    56.17–18: 117
    233: *see IvMag* 61
    338.6: 117n97
Milet III
    147.7: 91, 91n26
SEG
    1.366.27–28: 279–80n4
    14.543: *see IG* XII 5.541 +
    14.544: *see BCH* 78 (1954): 338–44 no. 14
*SIG*³
    390: *see IG* XII 7.506
    495.176–179: 182
    521: *see IG* XII 7.386
    535: *see IG* II² 844
    768: *see IK* 34 Mylasa 602

Compositor: G&S Typesetters
Text: 10/13 Aldus
Display: Aldus
Printer: Thomson-Shore, Inc.
Binder: Thomson-Shore, Inc.